W9-BRC-825

Americans and the California Dream

1850–1915

AMERICANS *and the* CALIFORNIA DREAM

1850–1915

KEVIN STARR

OXFORD UNIVERSITY PRESS
New York Oxford

Oxford University Press

Oxford New York Toronto
Delhi Bombay Calcutta Madras Karachi
Petaling Jaya Singapore Hong Kong Tokyo
Nairobi Dar es Salaam Cape Town
Melbourne Auckland

and associated companies in
Beirut Berlin Ibadan Nicosia

First published in 1973 by Oxford University Press, Inc.,
198 Madison Avenue, New York, New York 10016
First issued as an Oxford University Press paperback, 1986

Library of Congress Cataloging-in-Publication Data

Starr, Kevin.
Americans and the California dream, 1850–1915.

Reprint. Originally published: New York : Oxford
University Press, 1973.
Bibliography: p.
Includes index.
1. California—Civilization. I. Title.
[F861.S82 1986] 979.4'04 86-18077
ISBN 0-19-501644-0
ISBN 0-19-504233-6 (pbk.)

8 9 7

Printed in the United States of America

For Sheila Gordon Starr

Preface

The unfolding of California as a regional culture in the nineteenth century is a rich and colorful chapter in American history. This book attempts to deal with the imaginative aspects of California's journey to identity. It is also an elegy to its struggle and hope. From the beginning, California promised much. While yet barely a name on the map, it entered American awareness as a symbol of renewal. It was a final frontier: of geography and of expectation. After seizing the territory from Mexico, Americans entered California and there, in a variety of ways, responded to its imperatives. This study is intended as a dramatization of the actual and symbolic relationships they achieved. I hope to recover something of the texture of that lost California, to chronicle the efforts of certain Californians as they sought to interpret and celebrate the Pacific commonwealth where they chose to pass their lives: a choice, indeed, on the part of most (born elsewhere) which was their highest form of testimony. Through representative moments, public and private, I will suggest what they accomplished—and what they left undone.

In that this book is preoccupied with the shaping work of the imagination, the approach is literary, in the broadest sense of the term. It seeks to integrate fact and imagination in the belief that the record of their interchange through symbolic statement is our most precious legacy from the past. I would like, in short to suggest the poetry and the moral drama of social experience.

The story of American California presents a startling richness of materials. I have of necessity restricted the topics and the scope of this study. *Americans and the California Dream, 1850–1915* is concerned with California's frontier and provincial days, the era between its admission into the Union in 1850 and the opening of the Panama-Pacific International Exposition at San Francisco in 1915, when, in its own eyes and in the eyes of the world, California came of age. It leaves California just as it enters its fully twentieth-century period. Because of its focus, the narrative tends to favor Northern California. Southern California (with some backtracking) dominates the next sequence of the story, where Central California also comes in for more ample consideration.

It was an adventure of imagination and spirit to return to California's early years. Reaching its maturity sometime in the decade before World War I, provincial California, its population a bare fraction of what it is today, possessed an intimacy now impossible. Artists and intellectuals knew one another and tended to share certain hopeful assumptions regarding the region where they lived and worked. They were hopeful because, although many opportunities had been squandered, all was not lost. California yet ached with promise. In this more complicated time, when hope is not so certain and the promise is unclear, the faith of those years must come to our aid. Although Californians of today inhabit a civilization and grapple with problems only dimly dreamed of in the nineteenth century, the struggle of previous generations, the emergence of provincial California, deserves scrutiny. It was, after all, the founding time, when, for good and for evil, what it meant to be a Californian was first probed and defined. That past act of definition is part of a present identity. That California continues, in part, to live. One blind to its beauty and moral significance, one dead to the drama of its yearning, has little chance of continuing its struggle: a struggle, it must be remembered, undertaken and carried on amidst corruptions and failures as distressing as those which assault the present. Obscurely, at a distance—then with rushes of clarity and delight—Americans glimpsed a California of beauty and justice, where on the land or in well-ordered cities they might enter into prosperity and peace.

Of course, the dream outran the reality, as it always does. California experienced more than its share of social problems because its development was so greedy and so unregulated. No evocation of imaginative aspiration can atone for the burdens of the California past, especially the violence and the brutality. Acknowledging the tragedy, however, Californians must also attune themselves to the hope. The struggle for corrective action in the face of history put earlier generations in touch with their best selves. What they attained, attained in the struggle and the dreaming, deserves our respect—and our most sincere celebration.

San Francisco and Eliot House K. S.
December 1972

Acknowledgments

Acknowledgment is made to the following publishers and holders of copyright: to the Administrator C.T.A. of the Estate of Stewart Edward White for permission to quote from *The Rules of the Game* and *The Cabin*, by Stewart Edward White; to Mrs. Isabel White Chase for permission to quote from *California Coast Trails*, by J. Smeaton Chase; to the editors of *The Philosophical Review* for permission to quote from "Words of Professor Royce at the Walton Holtel at Philadelphia, 29 December 1915"; to Charles Scribner's Sons for permission to quote from Ernest Peixotto's *Romantic California* and *The Letters of Henry James*, edited by Percy Lubbock; to Harper and Row, Publishers, Inc., for permission to quote from Gertrude Atherton's *California, An Intimate History*; to the University of Pennsylvania Press for permission to quote from *A Quaker Forty-Niner, The Adventures of Charles Edward Pancoast on the American Frontier*; to the Bobbs-Merrill Company, Inc., for permission to quote from Mary Austin's *Experiences Facing Death*, copyright, 1931, by the Bobbs-Merrill Co., Inc., R 1959; to Holt, Rinehart and Winston, Inc., for permission to quote "The Black Vulture" from the *Selected Poems* of George Sterling; to the Hougton Mifflin Company for permission to quote from *The Journal of Henry D. Thoreau*, *The Story of My Boyhood and Youth*, by John Muir, Muir's *My First Summer in the Sierras*, Luther Burbank's *The Harvest of the Years*, and Mary Austin's *Earth Horizon*; to the Liveright Publishing Corporation for permission to quote from *My Life*, by Isadora Duncan, Copyright Renewed (R) 1955 by Liveright Publishing Corp., New York, and *Adventures of a Novelist*, by Gertrude Atherton; to The Arthur H. Clark Company for permission to quote from *The Ashley-Smith Explorations,* by Clifford Dale; to Alfred A. Knopf, Inc., for permission to quote from *Son of the Wilderness,* by Linnie Marsh Wolfe, Copyright 1945 by Alfred A. Knopf, Inc.; to The Book Club of California for permission to quote from *Bayside Bohemia,* by Gelett Burgess; to E. P. Dutton & Co., Inc., for permission to quote from the book *Scenes and Portraits: Memories of Childhood and Youth,* by Van Wyck Brooks, Copyright, 1954, by Van Wyck Brooks, published by E. P. Dutton & Co., Inc.; and to Western Hemisphere, Inc., for permission to quote from *In Pursuit of the Golden Dream,* by Howard Gardiner, edited by Dale Morgan.

A number of Harvard and Radcliffe undergraduates generously joined me in a marathon of proofreading. My thanks to Kathy Agoos, Jane Asch, Michael Bettencourt, Seth Borgos, Karen S. Fogel, William E. Forbath, Sallie Gouverneur, Bruns Grayson, Sally Griffith, James W. Henderson, Jr., Helen M. Hershkoff, David Hoffman, Erica Horwitz, Parkman Howe, Jeff Judd, Don Keplinger, Jane M. Kramer, John Lundeen, Theodore Lyman, Jeffrey D. Melvoin, Richard Worthington Mixter, Eliot W. Nelson, Kirk Panneton, Glenn Schwetz, Deirdre Snyder, and Richard N. Weinberg.

This book was researched in the various libraries of Harvard University, the Library of the San Francisco Theological Seminary at San Anselmo, the Library of the California Historical Society in San Francisco, and the Bancroft Library in Berkeley. For their active collaboration, I am grateful to Theodore Alevizos, H. Gordon Bechanan, and Frank Nathaniel Bunker of Harvard Library; Maude K. Swigle, Peter Alston Evans, and Jay Williar of the Library of the California Historical Society; and John Barr Tompkins, Suzanne Gallup, William M. Roberts, and Peter E. Hanff of the Bancroft.

For reading and commenting upon various stages of my manuscript, I would like to thank Daniel Aaron, Brooks Byrd, Thomas Mark Caplan, the late Warren Coffey, Peter Davison, Raymond Dennehy, Terence Des Pres, Donald Fanger, Andrew Foley, Michael T. Gilmore, James M. Gordon, R. Brooke Hopkins, John Brinckerhoff Jackson, David Keyser, Robert J. Kiely, Earle Labor, Kenneth Lewes, Charles Maier, John Howard Mansfield, David Perkins, Joel M. Porte, R. John Powell, Francis Paul Prucha, Judith Rascoe, Forrest Robinson, Margaret Gordon Robinson, Martha B. Robinson, Philip C. Rule, Paul Sheats, Prudence Steiner, Gordon Taylor, Philip Weinstein, George Abbott White, and Maud Wilcox. James Raimes and Caroline Taylor of Oxford University Press provided me with constant encouragement and superb editorial guidance.

For other varieties of encouragement and assistance over the course of five years of research and composition, I am grateful to William Alfred, Mr. and Mrs. Donald Bacon, Professor and Mrs. Herschel Baker, Morton Bloomfield, Joanna Brent, Mr. and Mrs. James M. Brown, Robert Ignatius Burns, Max Byrd, Hugh Cecil, Phebe Chao, Gerrie Dennehy, the late Bruce Diaso, LaVal Todd Duncan, Ann England, Gwynne B. Evans, Howard Felperin, Desmond J. Fitzgerald, Professor and Mrs. Robert S. Fitzgerald, Terry Fortier, Mr. and Mrs. R. A. Fortier, Ann Escobosa Fracchia, Charles A. Fracchia, John B. and Elisabeth G. Gleason, Mary H. Gordon, George L. Harding, J. S. Holliday, Howard Mumford Jones, the late David M. Kirk, Ralph Lane, Jr., Ron Loewinsohn, Kenneth S. Lynn, Professor and Mrs. Frederick Merk, Lewis Mumford, Dolores Muscatine, Mr. and Mrs. Peter McClelland, Frank M. Oppenheim, Earl Pomeroy, Diana Powell, Mr. and Mrs. Robert Ralls, Mr. and Mrs. Christopher Reed, Mr. and Mrs. Thomas Riggio, John Paul Russo, Albert J. Smith, Henry Nash Smith, Edmond J. Smyth, Michael Soper, Mr. and Mrs. James V. Starr, Mr. and Mrs. John Charles Stein, Mr. and Mrs. Lawrence F. Stevens, Penny Weinstein, and Franklin Walker. I owe special thanks to Eugene R. Strain and Laurence V. Taylor.

James D. Hart, Walter Jackson Bate, Harry Levin, and Alan Heimert have my warmest and most explicit gratitude. Professor Hart, Director of the Bancroft Library, a scholar whose knowledge of California is unmatched and whose devotion to its best possibilities is inspiring, gave a draft of this book a very generous and very rigorous reading, pointing it in the direction of its final form. He advised me to work with a wide range of materials. From the example of this dedicated Californian, I tried to learn a certain tone of approach: to identify, as he has, with the best possibilities of the subject, and not to perceive California from the vantage point of contemporary cliché and stereotype. Professor Bate also encouraged me in my determination to present the Californians sympathetically in the context of their struggle: to respond without embarrassment (but with proper balance) to the poetry of their lives and somehow to attempt to suggest the present meaning of the past. Personal and professional attachments have over the years kept Professor Levin interested in the history and culture of California. The generous, knowledgeable response of such an accomplished internationalist toward what some others had initially dismissed as mere local materials was one of the great consolations of this project.

Over the course of five years, Professor Heimert made himself available for countless consultations. I am grateful to him for specific advice and for the example of his own broad, integrative approach to the study of the American past. As Master of Eliot House, Alan Heimert saw to it that I had the best circumstances possible in which to complete my work.

Those who know Sheila Gordon Starr will have some idea of what I owe her.

Contents

Illustrations

Grateful acknowledgment is made to the Bancroft Library for permission to use the following illustrations

Americans and the California Dream

1850–1915

1
Prophetic Patterns
1786–1850

The territory of Alta California, a network of scattered settlements on the lower edge of an empty American West, had a number of visitors during its Spanish and Mexican period. They came by sea from France and England, from the American Republic, and from Russian colonies in the Far North. In 1826 American trappers beat their way across the Southwest, opening California to overland travel. As they visited this northernmost outpost of Latin America, travelers knew they were witnessing a unique society and an incomparable natural setting. Returning to ships' cabins or to campfires, they wrote of what they saw. Their letters, reports, journals, diaries, and memoirs expressed patterns of experience which would in time be the founding elements of a new identity. Writing of Old California, they anticipated the New.

Taken in its full range, from hastily jotted notes to more considered reports, California travel literature rarely showed the artistry of Richard Henry Dana, Jr.'s *Two Years Before the Mast* (1840). Yet because Alta California was a simple society, clinging to the narrowest stretch of explored coast, visitors encountered a repetitive range of experiences. Guidance by previous reports gave interpretations a degree of standardization. In time, through a cumulative travel literature, a shared sense of California arose, a community of interpretation from which developed the later and larger myth of California.

Captain Jean François Galaup de Lapérouse of the Royal French Navy began this process on a September morning in 1786, when he brought the frigates *Boussole* and *Astrolabe* to anchor in Monterey Bay as whales spouted in the distance. On a round-the-world scientific expedition, Lapérouse remained at anchor but ten days, replenishing supplies for a voyage to the Philippines. He and his staff made as many scientific observations as time allowed. Before disappearing two years later in a South Seas typhoon, Lapérouse forwarded an account of his California stay to the French Ministry of Marine. A British expedition under George Vancouver visited California three times between 1792 and 1794. Safely back in England, Vancouver filed an account of his voyage with the Admiralty.

The accounts of Lapérouse and Vancouver, published in 1797 and 1798, respectively, became the founding classics of California travel literature, referred to again and again in the reports of later travelers. As first expressions of how California struck the foreign imagination, they went far to shape the expectations of those who came after. Lapérouse's visit to Mission San Carlos Borromeo, for instance, became the paradigm of European Enlightenment confronting a quasi-feudal civilization. In the opinion of Lapérouse, and of other visitors over the next fifty years, California needed intervention if it were to have a society worthy of its beauty. Vancouver's inspection of the feeble Spanish defenses at the entrance to San Francisco Bay provoked thoughts, in him and in three generations of naval men, of just how easy it would be for a maritime power to seize this commanding harbor of the Pacific. As the first non-Spanish penetrations into the interior since Sir Francis Drake landed in 1579, Lapérouse's ride from Monterey to Mission Carlos Borromeo, through an abrupt landscape of cliffs and canyons, and Vancouver's ride down the San Francisco peninsula from Mission Dolores to Mission Santa Clara, through an easy landscape of rolling hills and broad plains, assumed in subsequent travel literature the significance of long-remembered pilgrimages of recovery: prototypes for all those journeys of the next fifty years in which visitors took imaginative possession of the awaiting landscape.

In spite of its status as a possession of Spain and, after 1821, of an independent Mexico, California was coveted by foreign visitors. Lapérouse and Vancouver were the first to prepare for California's eventual seizure. Although Spain's occupation of Alta California was not yet twenty years old in 1786, Lapérouse castigated the Spanish Crown for placing California in the hands of the Franciscans, for permitting reactionary ecclesiastical control over a territory which French administration could make a model of Enlightenment. Vancouver declared himself scandalized that the rude adobe settlements overlooking the strategic harbors of San Diego, Monterey, and San Francisco should represent the European presence in

California. The slightest military force, he noted, might seize and occupy this magnificent land of wasted opportunity.

French, Russian, English, and American visitors during the next fifty years confessed themselves astonished at the frailty of the Spanish and Mexican hold: a society without schools, without manufactures, without defenses, administered by a quasi-feudal mission system and inhabited by a population that barely exceeded 1500. Travelers complained of difficulties in obtaining supplies, lack of transportation, an absence of skilled workmen, poor houses and furniture, sour wine, indifferent food, and persistent fleas. It was a society so backward that its plow and ox-cart were those of ancient times, so disorganized that in spite of the fact that countless cattle roamed its hills, it had to secure dairy products from the Russian colony at Fort Ross and have leather shoes shipped around the Horn from Boston. Visitors were appalled at the lack of agriculture in such an obviously fertile land, at the contrast between California's grand topography and local indifference to inland expansion. Presidial garrisons seemed like dress rehearsals for a comic opera. In 1816 the seventeenth-century cannon of the San Francisco Presidio was fired to welcome Governor Don Pablo Vincente de Sola. It exploded, injuring two cannoneers. In 1827 the same unintimidated garrison attempted to answer the seven-gun salute offered by the French ship *Le Héros* as it sailed into San Francisco Bay. This time two guns burst apart. In another incident, before replying to a visiting vessel's salute, the Presidio commander had to be rowed out to the ship to borrow the necessary gunpowder.

As the principal social institution, missions received continuous, usually hostile, scrutiny. Spain's method of colonization had roots in the ancient Roman practice of holding a frontier through presidial towns. It was a civil, military, and ecclesiastical campaign. Staffed by Franciscan friars under the jurisdiction of a Father-President, twenty-one missions stretched up the coast, a day's journey apart on *El Camino Real*, beginning in the south with Mission San Diego de Alcalá, founded in 1769 by Father José Altimira. Surrounded by vast herds of longhorn cattle; richly planted with wheat, barley, grapes, figs, dates, and citrus, these missions were sprawling, self-contained plantations, centered in a main complex of church, friary, dormitory, and workshop. The Fathers aimed at introducing the Indians to Christianity, agriculture, crafts and manual arts. In their "wild" state Indians were considered *gentiles*, or heathens. At the missions they became *neophytes*, or candidates for promotion to the *gente de razón*, the people of reason, which included all of white or mixed blood. In time, when enough Indians had become *gente de razón,* the missions were supposed to be disestablished, leaving a fully developed secular order.

Supporting and protecting the work of the friars were military garrisons at the presidios of San Diego, Santa Barbara, Monterey, and San Francisco. They were under the command of the governor of California, an army officer who was the military counterpart of the Father-President. Independent pueblos (municipalities) were located at Los Angeles, Branciforte (near present Santa Cruz), and San Jose. Smaller pueblos were attached to Missions San Luis Obispo, San Juan Capistrano, San Juan Bautista, and Sonoma. These pueblos, together with land-grant ranchos, rounded out the simple social structure of Old California.

Reaching their prosperity in the 1820's, the missions in general tended to become ends in themselves rather than transitional institutions. To Europeans, Indian neophytes seemed worse off than feudal serfs. Passive, squalid, syphilitic, dying in large numbers and giving birth infrequently, the Mission Indian hardly seemed to be on the road to civilized independence. Visitors chided the padres for forcing rote adherence to Spanish phrases expressing dimly understood dogmas of an alien religion, for whipping the Indians when they grew inattentive at prayer, and for encouraging a childish state of dependence. Only twice a year, when they were allowed to visit their homelands or to perform tribal dances, did Mission Indians throw off their torpor. Only when singing liturgical music, accompanying themselves on violins and cellos, did they demonstrate any positive response to European culture. Captain Duhaut-Cilly of the *Héros* claimed that during six weeks away from mission jurisdiction two Indian felons he was transporting from Monterey to San Diego in 1827 seemed to regain dignity and good behavior. One night they escaped overboard, to the delight of their negligent jailer. Whatever the assurances of mission life, noted Duhaut-Cilly, "the instinct of liberty is there crying to them to prefer to this quiet, though monotonous state, the poor and uncertain life of their woods and their marshes."[1] That same year, Captain Frederick William Beechey of H.M.S. *Blossom* watched a padre of Mission San Jose amuse himself after dinner tossing pancakes to Indian boys, who, like dogs, caught them in their teeth and devoured them rapidly.

However, when the padres lost their hold on California, that is, when missions were disestablished and plundered in 1834, visitors noted an immediate deterioration in social conditions. "The old monastic order is destroyed," wrote Abel du Petit-Thouars of his visit in 1837, "and nothing seems yet to have replaced it, except anarchy."[2] Visitors noted crumbling buildings, neglected vineyards and orchards, scattered herds, bewildered Indians, and dispirited padres. The decay of California, Sir George Simpson complained, had not even the charm of antiquity to recommend it; for, from establishment to secularization, the mission era had not exceeded the span of a human lifetime.

In the decade between the Revolution of 1836, in which young Juan Bautista Alvarado won autonomy from Mexico, and the raising of the American flag over Monterey in 1846, criticism of California reached the climax of a half-century of complaint. In part this criticism reflected a search for justification as awareness intensified that one or another maritime power must soon seize California. In part it reflected reality, for the final decade of California's Mexican era was a confusion of revolution, counterrevolution, graft, spoliation, and social disintegration as Northern and Southern factions struggled for power in a series of internecine clashes which only the most patient historian might unravel.

Exasperation fills the narrative of Abel du Petit-Thouars, captain of the French frigate *Venus*. Having forwarded an order for supplies two months previously from the Sandwich Islands, Du Petit-Thouars arrived in Monterey in October 1837 to find, not beef, grain, vegetables, wood, and water, but baffled glances and shrugged shoulders. He saw his plight as proof of the impossibility of leaving such important ports in Mexican hands, and he backed up his belief with a capsule political history of the territory during the preceding two decades, a hopeless tale, as he saw it, of retarding anarchy.

As might be expected, the Governor-General of Her Majesty's Hudson's Bay Territories, Sir George Simpson, detested the economic backwardness he saw everywhere. California in the year 1841 struck Sir George as a "fragment of the grandest of colonial empires," shabbily held by "perhaps the least promising colonists of a new country in the world." Life was too lush in California, Sir George asserted, nature too abundant, and the naturally indolent Mexicans had succumbed too readily to the spirit of *dolce far niente*. On sailing into San Francisco Bay, Sir George beheld thousands of cattle roaming unattended on the surrounding hills. "Here, on the very threshold of the country," he noted, "was California in a nutshell, Nature doing everything and man doing nothing—a text on which our whole sojourn proved to be little but a running commentary." In Sonoma, General Mariano Vallejo furnished his parlor with cane chairs from the Sandwich Islands. In the mind of the Hudson's Bay official, "this was California all over—the richest and most influential individual in a professedly civilized settlement obliged to borrow the means of sitting from savages, who had never seen a white man till two years after San Francisco was colonized by the Spaniards." California, concluded Sir George, was a splendid country, wasted "on men who do not avail themselves of their natural advantages to a much higher degree than the savages whom they have displaced, and who are likely to become less and less energetic from generation to generation and from year to year!"[3]

California, so tenuously held, invited national schemes, not so much schemes of chancelleries and foreign offices (although by the 1840's there were certainly these), as schemes engendered in the imaginations of travelers on the scene, overwhelmed by the rich possibilities of the territory and its present misuse.

Count Nikolai Petrovich Rezanov, plenipotentiary of the Russian American Fur Company, sailing the *Juno* into San Francisco Bay in April of 1806 in search of food for the famished Russian colony at Sitka, found that sunny land a total contrast to the Tsar's bleak possessions to the north. Had there not been a continuous arc of Russian expansion, Rezanov asked himself, since Vitus Bering pushed eastward to North America? And was not California the obvious object of that south-seeking Russian advance? California! from whose fields and herds the Russian North might be fed and from whose ports the Navy might screen Russia's Pacific flank. As he tarried in California, negotiating for seldom-granted trade rights, the Count became obsessed with his dream. He planned to return to St. Petersburg to have himself appointed Ambassador Extraordinary to Madrid, where he could work out more satisfactory commercial agreements with the Spanish Crown than was possible with officials in California. Ingratiatingly, the still-young widower courted fifteen-year-old Doña Concepción de Arguello, daughter of the San Francisco commandant, and won her hand on the promise that he secure a papal dispensation allowing her marriage to a non-Catholic. Having the full confidence of the Californians, to whom he was now bound by promised family ties, Rezanov sailed north on the first leg of his grand diplomatic journey which would in the next few years, he hoped, see him in St. Petersburg, Rome, Madrid, Mexico City, and then back in California for his marriage. Plunging recklessly overland, Rezanov succumbed to fever, exhaustion, and the Siberian winter, dying at Krasnoiarsk on 1 March 1807, symbol and victim of impetuous hopes for a Russian California.

The alliance of family, religion, and mutual interests which Rezanov sought through marriage, Frenchmen hoped existed naturally between themselves and another Latin culture. With the growth of French naval activity in the Pacific, visiting captains coveted San Francisco Bay as a port of refitting and resupply. They dreamed of bringing Gallic order to Californian confusion. Already, they suggested, Frenchmen on the scene had made an adjustment paradigmatic of a possible Franco-California, marrying into families whose culture was congenial to their own, planting vineyards reminiscent of the South of France.

Comparisons of California to the South of France occurred frequently. Frenchmen became excited with evidence provided by Jean Louis Vigne that California could grow good grapes. A native of Bordeaux who arrived in 1831 at age forty-eight, Vigne dedicated the remaining thirty years of his life to the improvement of his Los Angeles vineyards. He imported cuttings from France and patiently upgraded the vintage of his firm, Sainsevain and Company. Travel literature of the period is filled with near-ritualistic moments of sampling Don Luis' wines and finding them to be surprisingly good. In their genial Gallic host, with his knowledgeable love of vines and wine-making, French visitors saw the possibility of their race flourishing on California shores. Anchoring at Santa Barbara (the most Spanish of the California settlements), they were delighted to discover that the feel of Europe could survive in such a remote place. Frenchmen considered Santa Barbara evidence that a civilized administration might raise California into style and significance. Let France establish a protectorate over California, Louis Gasquet, Acting Consul in Monterey, urged the Minister of Foreign Affairs in October 1845. Let France show herself as "carrying afar her civilizing action and spreading her noble protection over all scattered members of the great Catholic family."[4]

These were not simply the dreams of minor sea captains and acting consuls. In 1839 the French Foreign Office commissioned an attaché at the Madrid embassy, Count Eugène Duflot de Mofras, an expert in Spanish history, to tour Mexico and her northern possessions, investigating opportunities for French settlement. Reaching California in mid-1841, De Mofras made a five-month tour. Scholars agree that his *Exploration du Territoire de l'Orégon, des Californies, et de la Mer Vermeille,* published in Paris in 1844, is the best account by a European of California before the American conquest: an encyclopedic travelogue, spiced with wit and detail, dominated by maritime ambition. San Francisco Bay moved De Mofras to ecstasy. Residents of Yerba Buena remembered long after how the Count, standing on the very edge of the shore, would fling his arms out theatrically towards the Marin hills and discourse to the residents of the sleepy Mexican village about the great potential of this magnificent harbor. De Mofras dreamed of establishing in California a revived New France, a promised land to which the scattered French populations of the New World might migrate, renewing the lost glories of Quebec and Louisiana, where men had served God and King. Representative of the Orleanist monarchy, scholar, and admirer of Spanish royalism, De Mofras documented with anger the decline that Mexican republicanism had brought to California, especially the cynical spoliation of the missions after their secularization in 1834. He bitterly resented the fact that Britain and the United States, who had already harvested the fruit of French effort in the New World, should now seem ready to divide between themselves the Pacific Coast. What a tragedy, he lamented, if this last chance for a Catholic power to gain a foothold in North America were lost!

In a secret appendix to his report De Mofras proposed a plan for a French take-over. Agents would purchase property commanding harbors and roads. French Canadians in the employ of the Hudson's Bay Company, drifting southward, would congregate at New Helvetia, where under Sutter (erroneously believed to be an ex-officer of French Guards) they would form a force of occupation. At an arranged time Sutter's Canadians would seize the interior, while, under the pretext of protecting the violated rights of French Californians, ships of war would sail into the Bays of San Francisco, Monterey, and San Diego. Like the seventeenth-century founders of New France, De Mofras planned boldly for God and King, but his were not to be the glorious enterprises of La Salle, Frontenac, or Laval. While others seized the California prize, De Mofras' scheme gathered dust in a Paris archive.

British aspirations were less dramatic but had a more venerable history. In the course of his epic circumnavigation of the globe, Sir Francis Drake beached the *Golden Hinde* in June 1579 for repairs somewhere in the vicinity of San Francisco Bay. He left a plate of brass, claiming California (which he called New Albion because its white cliffs reminded him of England) IN THE NAME OF HERR MAIESTY QVEEN ELIZABETH OF ENGLAND AND HERR SVCCESSORS FOREVER. Drake of course was acting out of bravado. There was no way England could hold the Pacific Coast of North America; indeed, the first Elizabethan attempt to settle the far more accessible Atlantic shore, Sir Walter Raleigh's doomed settlement at Roanoke, was itself six years in the future. Stepping ashore two centuries later, George

Vancouver in a sense revived ancient hopes for an Anglo-California. In the early nineteenth century British subjects filtered up from Valparaiso, Lima, and the Pacific ports of Mexico, settling down in California as merchants and rancheros. An Englishman, William Petty Hartnell, and two Scots, David Spence and Hugo Reid, appear again and again in visitors' reports as avatars of Anglo-Californian contentment. Arriving in California in 1834 after a Cambridge education and six years in Mexico, Hugo Reid of the Rancho Santa Anita in the San Gabriel Valley made a consciously aesthetic adjustment to the region: he married an Indian woman, raised her three children, and settled into harmony with the land, the sun, and the local rhythms of life.

A suggestion made by Vancouver about immigration to California from the British Isles grew desperately important in the famine-stricken 1830's. In 1835 Thomas Coulter told the Royal Geographical Society of London that California should not be overlooked as a haven for England's poor and dispossessed. An Irish priest, Eugene McNamara, petitioned the Mexican government in the spring of 1845 for land in California to settle 2000 Irish Catholic families as a barrier against invading "Methodist wolves" of the United States. McNamara's scheme, brought to naught by the American conquest, might have been a cover for a London company anxious to acquire land. Nevertheless, it expressed an idea which would in time flower in the minds of Irish-born Californians: here on Pacific shores was their promised land, where their long-suppressed culture and Catholicism, their long-starved hunger for land, and their hopes for social dignity and a voice in their own governance might be brought to fruition, safe from British—or Yankee—repression.

The grand design of De Mofras had a British analogue in the suggestions of Alexander Forbes, a Scots merchant in Tepic, Mexico, whose *History of Upper and Lower California*, published in London in 1839, was the first book in English to deal exclusively with the California question. Since Mexico owed British subjects over $50 million, argued Forbes, let her meet this debt in the form of shares in a California Company modeled on East India or Hudson's Bay. Charged with management of the territory, this British company might set about developing an agricultural and maritime colony: cutting a canal across the Isthmus of Panama in order to link California-based steamers in a four-way trade with the Orient, South America, the United States, and Europe. Such a scheme similarly quickened the imperial sensibilities of Sir George Simpson of Hudson's Bay. "English, in some sense or other of the word," he predicted, "the richest portions of California must become: either Great Britain will introduce her well regulated freedom of all classes and colours, or the people of the United States will inundate the country with their own peculiar mixture of helpless bondage and lawless insubordination."[5]

II

Even as Europeans contrived for the future they felt something inevitable about the American presence. Americans had been visiting California since the last years of the eighteenth century. Orient-bound, the *Columbia* and the *Lady Washington* skirted the California coast in the late 1780's. In October 1796 Captain Ebenezer Dorr brought the *Otter* of Boston into Monterey harbor for wood and water before continuing on to China. From the late 1790's onward American ships hunting and trading in sea otter were operating off the California coast. In March 1816 two American sailors, a black known as Bob and Thomas Doak of Boston, jumped ship. Doak was baptized as Felipe Santiago and Bob as Juan Cristóbal. They took out Spanish citizenship and married California women, living out their days as prosperous householders: California's first permanent American residents. In their near-anonymous struggle for a better life Bob and Doak were setting a pattern of California liberation; for Juan Cristóbal found release in the Californians' acceptance of color (so many themselves having black ancestry), and Felipe Santiago found being a respected, well-paid carpenter, son-in-law of Mariano Castro, preferable to the hardships of life before the mast. By the late 1820's Americans of a more sophisticated sort were taking up residence on the Pacific. They were merchants and representatives of Boston trading firms like Bryant and Sturgis, which began a hide and tallow trade with California in 1822: thrifty, hard-working Massachusetts men for the most part, not without affection for the cattle-covered land which supported them and to which they were bound by ties of money, marriage, and long residence.

In 1826 Jedediah Smith led a party of trappers overland, and during the 1830's mountain men joined the Yankee traders: men not from Massachusetts, but from Virginia, the Carolinas, Kentucky, Tennessee, and Missouri; men who dressed not in black Boston broadcloth but in sweat-stained buckskin; men whose hair fell shaggily about their shoulders and whose beards reached their waists, who laughed with a mixture of contempt, violence, and glee when they were mistaken for savages by their reluctant California hosts. They trapped beaver in the interior or they took to the sea in canoes, hunting the elusive sea otter with the deadly fire of their long rifles. They gathered about Kentucky-born Isaac Graham's distillery at Natividad near Santa Cruz, drinking raw whiskey, swapping stories, amusing themselves with horse races and shooting matches—leather-shirted vagabonds, a continual source of uneasiness in the minds of California officials. Governor Alvarado used them in 1836 to seize power, but they constituted a rowdy, potentially subversive Pretorian Guard. In 1840, during the so-called Graham Affair, he ordered a large number of them rounded up and deported, but it was too late. Merchants and mountain men, North and South, Americans were everywhere. With the arrival in 1841 of the Bidwell party, the first emigrants to arrive overland across the Sierras, a new sort of American, the settler and his family, began to fill up the lower Sacramento Valley. In April of 1846, a month and a half before the military conquest of California, Thomas Oliver Larkin, first and last American consul in California, noted that "a person traveling from San Diego to San Francisco or Bodega can stop at a foreigner's farm almost every few hours, and travel without any knowledge of the Spanish language."[6]

As they moved from tentative contacts to full occupation, what did Americans think of California? First of all, almost as an act of the will, Americans struggled to convince themselves of California's fertility. Cattle on a thousand hills, sea otter swarming along the coast, deer and elk which even a shipboard observer could see bounding on the sides of coastal mountains, flocks of geese and ducks which at times blackened the sky and filled the air with the clatter of their wings, grizzlies and redwood trees: certainly these assured them of California's capacity to support life. Americans envisioned rice paddies in the marshy Sacramento Delta, wheat fields in the San Joaquin, orchards and vineyards in the valleys of Napa, Santa Clara, and San Gabriel. The crudeness of local agriculture caused universal lament but reinforced a conviction of fertility; for even with such feeble scratchings of the soil the Californians were yet reaping a hundredfold.

But there was another side to this expectation. Fears of sterility undercut paeans to fertility. Much of Southern California was arid and the fertility of the interior was only a guess. "People generally look on it as the garden of the world," remarked John Bidwell, "or the most desolate place of Creation."[7] Lieutenant Henry Augustus Wise of the United States Navy was convinced of California's desolation. "Under no contingency," he wrote, "does the natural face of Upper California appear susceptible of supporting a very large population; the country is hilly and mountainous; great dryness prevails during the summers, and occasionally excessive droughts parch up the soil for periods of twelve or eighteen months."[8]

Visits to mission orchards and gardens calmed such fears. A common moment in American travel literature was that of reaching a mission after traversing a forbidding, uncultivated landscape: coming across the great desert of the Southwest, as did the traders of the Spanish Trail and the invading Army of the West, into the luxuriance of Mission San Gabriel; or coming, as did merchant Alfred Robinson up from San Diego along a barren coast, then suddenly seeing from atop a rocky hill the irrigated gardens of Mission San Luis Rey unfolding below; or like Edwin Bryant, beating one's way down the baked terrain between Santa Barbara and Mission San Fernando, feeling at dusk the contrast between the day's hot journey and the cool peace of the mission, where one strolled smoking a cigar in a twilight fragrant with lemon and roses. In such moments fears of infertility vanished and California seemed truly a Pacific Eden.

Americans preferred their luxuriance to be controlled and put to use, so they were delighted by the formality of the mission gardens. And they respected good engineering, so they were impressed by the aqueducts which watered the fields of Missions San Jose and San Luis Rey and the tree-lined alameda which linked the Pueblo of San Jose to Mission Santa Clara. Encountered in prosperity, mission agriculture afforded Americans symbols of what could be. Encountered in decline, neglected and overgrown vines spoke of lost civilization, and of history held in abeyance. The fact that gardens bore fruit even when untended confirmed American faith that "California, from one end to the other, is capable of being metamorphosed into a perfect orchard."[9] Like Lieutenant Joseph Warren Revere of the Navy (grandson of Paul Revere, and an officer who had done duty in the Mediterranean, Caribbean, and South Pacific), Americans were pleased by the exotic range of planting, temperate and tropical, which California supported. Apples, pears, melons, lemons, oranges, dates, olives, figs, and grapes flourished side by side with sugar cane, bamboo, and bananas.

Americans had American plans for this Mexican garden. Captain Sutter's baronial establishment at New Helvetia—fields, herds, and industries—made travelers from the American South think of establishing similar plantations in the fertile valleys of the Sacramento and the San Joaquin. San Francisco Bay always called to mind the inevitability of a great city on its shores. Lake Tahoe in the North and Agua Caliente in the

South, so visitors suggested, would someday be among the world's great resorts. The prophetic vision of Lansford W. Hastings, an Ohio-born lawyer, might serve as a composite of all that Americans dreamed of as they stood before the empty Pacific region. The time was not distant, wrote Hastings in *The Emigrants' Guide to Oregon and California* (1845), "when those wild forests, trackless plains, untrodden valleys, and the unbounded ocean, will present one grand scene of continuous improvements, universal enterprise, and unparalleled commerce: when those vast forests shall have disappeared before the hardy pioneer; those extensive plains shall abound with innumerable herds of domestic animals; those fertile valleys shall groan under the immense weight of their abundant products: those numerous rivers shall teem with countless steam-boats, steam-ships, barques and brigs; when the entire country will be everywhere intersected with turnpike roads, rail-roads, and canals; and when all the vastly numerous and rich resources of that now almost unknown region will be fully and advantageously developed."[10]

Openly and without shame, Americans coveted what they saw. They felt California's present possessors unworthy of the land. The first American report from California, William Shaler's in the *American Register* for 1808, together with the circumstances of Shaler's visit, dramatizes the acquisitive core of the American attitude. Shaler sailed the *Lelia Byrd* into San Diego harbor in March 1803, after a trading cruise up the coasts of South America and Mexico. Less than a month previously the commandant of San Diego had seized a contraband cargo of otter skins from the American ship *Alexander* and so was understandably cool toward the arrival of another American vessel. He allowed the *Lelia Byrd* to resupply itself but placed a guard aboard to prevent attempts to secure otter skins without payment of customs. Shaler nevertheless attempted some midnight pelt-collecting, and one of his boat crews was seized. Richard J. Cleveland, Shaler's supercargo, led a rescue party on the morning of 22 March, returning to the *Lelia Byrd* with the captured crew and a number of Spanish soldiers he had taken hostage. Setting sail, the Americans decided to risk running the Presidio guns. They tied their hostages to the rigging, hoping to dissuade the battery from firing upon the ship, but the corporal in charge of the gun crew gave the order anyway. Two broadsides were exchanged, the Spanish damaging the *Lelia Byrd*'s rigging and puncturing her hull. Putting ashore the three rather frightened but unhurt hostages (who with confused relief yelled from the shore, "*Vivan los Americanos!*"), Shaler headed to Baja California for repairs, then to the

Sandwich Islands, and from there to China. In his *American Register* report, the American captain leaned heavily upon Lapérouse and Vancouver. The aggressive center of his remarks, however, was strictly his own. Having tasted firsthand the ineffectiveness of the Spanish military, Shaler proposed an amphibious seizure of San Diego. Once landed, an invading American force could move northward, supporting itself off mission farms. "In a word," he remarked, "it would be as easy to keep California in spite of the Spaniards, as it would be to wrest it from them in the first instance."[11]

On a surface level of argument, Shaler and later Americans justified their lust for seizure on the basis of bad management, some suggesting that General Santa Ana could not find California on the map, others complaining that the practice of deporting Mexican felons to California was turning the territory into another Botany Bay. Putting aside Protestant and republican prejudice, they discovered a preference for Spanish royalist order over Mexican anarchy. The image of the ruined mission as a symbol of political neglect filled these American reports.

Deep hatred pervaded their remarks. It was that perennial American Protestant contempt for the Latin way of life, the origins of which went back to the Reformation. William Shaler said he wanted to liberate California from the "degrading shackles of ignorance and superstition," that is, from Catholic Spain. As anti-Catholic sentiment grew in the 1830's and 1840's, Americans liked to believe that California was under the control of debauched demons right out of a Jacobean drama: Machiavellian, wine-drinking, virgin-seducing priests. "If the one half be true that is told of the abomination of the priesthood in that garden spot of the globe," one American wrote of the Franciscans, "that order there must be a perfect embodiment of every wicked attribute that darkens the character of corrupt human nature."[12] The more intense grew the Americans' ambition, the more violent and racist grew their abuse of the Mexicans, a process which culminated in an orgy of invective in the immediate pre-conquest years. Isaac Graham said openly that he considered Californians "niggers." William Maxwell Wood, a naval surgeon obsessed by the mixed blood of the Californians, approvingly reported Graham's slur. In *The Emigrants' Guide* Lansford Hastings, who later served the Confederate government, indulged in ferocious racist abuse of Californians. Settlers guiding themselves overland with Hastings' book arrived inculcated with a racist mythology with which to justify hatred of the rightful owners of the lovely land they desired for their own.

Lieutenant George M. Colvocoresses of the United States Exploring Expedition, which arrived in California in 1841, summarized the American viewpoint. "Descended from the old Spaniards," he wrote of the Californians, "they are found to have all their vices and scarcely any of their virtues; they are cowardly, ignorant, lazy, and addicted to gambling and drinking; very few of them are able to read or write, and know nothing of science or literature, nothing of government but its brutal force, nothing of religion but ceremonies of the national ritual."[13] What one traveler called "the destructive prodigality of the Mexicans" especially annoyed Americans. They found it morally reprehensible that Californians lived so easily off their herds, slaughtering for hides and tallow, leaving thousands of half-used carcasses to decompose in the sun. Horned skulls, skeletons, and carrion littered countless fields; and for Americans such scenes of prodigal slaughter, where bleached bones rattled under horses' hooves and vultures circled overhead, provided the perfect imagery of a society doomed by the intemperate waste of its lavish resources.

The American response to the women of California combined sexual anxiety, contempt, and acquisitiveness. Mountain men and sailors—who rarely kept journals—took what sex came their way. Where journals of such men survive, mention of sex consists usually of unreflective registrations of achieved bliss. The middle class naval officer or commercial traveler, on the other hand—the sort of man most anxious to acquire California—did not find things so simple. After a period of sexual abstinence, he came into a society where women as a matter of culture were uninhibited in language and manner, and where all classes and types associated democratically within a sparse population. As a matter of class and race, American bourgeois travelers resented such mixing. Sexually anxious themselves, they resentfully called all California women whores. Significantly, they linked this alleged lack of virtue to bad politics. The California female, like California herself, was a tarnished prize, awaiting the saving embrace of American possession.

James Ohio Pattie's *Personal Narrative* (1831) and Thomas Jefferson Farnham's *Travels in California and Scenes in the Pacific Ocean* (1844) show how Americans prepared for conquest. In the fall of 1830, in Cincinnati, Pattie told an extraordinary tale of adventure to the Reverend Timothy Flint, editor of the *Western Monthly Review*. After four years of trapping in the Southwest, Pattie, his father, and their companions crossed the arid peninsula of Lower California to Mission Santa Catalina on the Pacific coast. By order of José María Echeandía, governor of both

Californias, the Pattie party was brought in chains to San Diego and imprisoned for being in Mexican territory without passports. The elder Pattie died in confinement. James Pattie, granted parole, remained in California for about a year before traveling to Mexico City in a futile attempt to claim reparations for furs lost during imprisonment. By August 1830 he was back in Cincinnati, broken in health and spirits, with nothing to show for six years on the frontier. Flint, to whom Pattie told his story, was a New England minister who had gone West as a propagandist of American Protestant expansion. In the tale of the haggard youth before him, Flint beheld the epic thrust of Protestant rectitude and enterprise into the infernal regions of the Southwest. Recasting Pattie's recollections for publication, the minister fashioned a Protestant psychomachy of wilderness travail: desert-crossings and desert-temptations, thirsts and self-scrutiny, all in the context of remorseless warfare against the demon-Indian, hundreds of whom fall writhing before the exterminating fire of the Patties' long rifles in an Armageddon that threatens to go on forever without meaning or goal.

Hatred of Mexicans is total—and totally in the service of American expansion. From Santa Fe to San Diego, the Mexican is depicted as a swarthy desperado, treacherous, cruel, cowardly. A theme of American liberty versus Mexican tyranny pervades the *Personal Narrative*, reinforcing Flint's suggestion that the Southwest and California must fall into American hands. In Santa Fe an extortionist governor seizes the Patties' furs on the ground that they had no license to trap. In San Diego the "miserable republican despot" Lieutenant Colonel Echeandía personifies Mexican tyranny at its worst. The Bancroft *History of California* tells us that Echeandía was soundly educated in letters and engineering. Far from being the gasconading coxcomb presented by Pattie—pretentious in uniform, feathers, and medals—Echeandía was refined, tall and slight, speaking in a soft Castilian accent. Under Mexican law, the Bancroft *History* asserts, he had legally arrested the Patties, and James Ohio ("a self-conceited and quick-tempered boy, with a freedom of speech often amounting to insolence") no doubt provoked whatever harsh treatment he received. If their treatment was as monstrous as Pattie claimed, why did some of the party elect to remain permanently in California? Pattie longs to have Echeandía in the sights of his long rifle; indeed, the fantasy of exterminating a cringing Mexican flits frequently through his brain, an obsession which Flint insists results from Pattie's American sense of outrage at Mexican infamy.

The parable of the *Personal Narrative* becomes explicit when Echeandía, grateful to Pattie for inoculating thousands during a smallpox epidemic, offers the young trapper a rancho on the condition that he become a Roman Catholic and a Mexican citizen. Certainly in the next two decades many an American would find such an offer the agreeable beginning of a new California life. Pattie, however, in a moment no doubt heightened by the Reverend Flint, spurns Echeandía's proposal with full Protestant American indignation. After crossing the desert, the Lord's people did not lie down with Canaanites! Conquest, not accommodation, would be the pattern of the Yankee presence in California!

The *Personal Narrative* ends with a dress rehearsal for such a take-over. Between November 1829 and August 1830 Joaquin Solis, a ranchero living outside Monterey, led a revolution against the government—the first of many such bloodless tumults, characterized by wrathful pronunciamentos and furious maneuvering of irregular cavalry, which would fill the next two decades. Pattie and other foreigners in Monterey formed a pro-Echeandía company because they feared that if Solis gained power, he would drive them from the country. The Bancroft *History* found Pattie's account of his military activities "absurd inaccuracies built on a substratum of truth," yet the paradigmatic intent of this incident as told by Flint is obvious. The balance of power in California, Flint suggests, belongs already to foreigners, most particularly to Americans. Ignoring the cosmopolitan composition of the Monterey company, Flint made it appear totally American. He claimed that after the capture of Solis the company rased the Stars and Stripes over Monterey. The Bancroft *History* might later dispute this as a point of fact, but in 1831 the image of Old Glory flying over Monterey was indeed prophetic.

Published two years before the conquest, Thomas Jefferson Farnham's *Travels in California and Scenes in the Pacific Ocean* brought a lurid racism to the service of Manifest Destiny. A Yankee lawyer practicing in Peoria, Illinois, Farnham left Independence, Missouri, in May 1839 as captain of the Oregon Dragoons, a group of nineteen young adventurers, upon whose ensign Mrs. Farnham had embroidered "Oregon or the Grave." In Farnham's case the motto was no boast. Describing himself as "a stranger, fleeing from my grave," and actually destined to die in 1848 at age forty-four, Farnham was crossing the plains in an attempt to regain his health through outdoor life. Reaching the Pacific, the young lawyer left Oregon for the Sandwich Islands and from there sailed on the *Don Quixote* for Monterey. He spent little more than two weeks in Monterey and Santa Barbara before continuing homeward via Mexico. His brief visit coincided with the arrest on 7 April 1840 of undesirable foreigners, an incident known to history as The Graham Affair after one of its chief protagonists, Isaac Graham, American owner of a grogshop and distillery. Governor Alvarado charged that Graham and his cronies, a miscellaneous crew of mountain men and deserting sailors, few of whom possessed passports, planned to take over the country—which he knew them capable of, having himself been put in power four years previously with their aid. Established foreigners—merchants, rancheros, and the like—were left unmolested; or, as in the case of William Heath Davis of Yerba Buena, they were held hospitably for a brief period and then released. About a hundred were arrested, and on 25 April 1840 about fifty of these, English and American, were shipped in irons to San Blas. The Bancroft *History* denies excessive cruelty, but Farnham, who acted as self-appointed legal counsel for the deported men, dramatized the Graham Affair as an atrocity.

Needing a hero for his melodrama of Manifest Destiny, Farnham naturally chose Isaac Graham, the enormous ex-Kentuckian. The Bancroft *History* describes Graham as a rather unsavory character. For Farnham, however, Graham was the personification of the noble frontier yeoman, "a stout, sturdy backwoodsman, of a stamp which exists only on the frontiers of the American States—men with the blood of the ancient Normans and Saxons in their veins—with hearts as large as their bodies can hold, beating nothing but kindness till injustice shows its fangs, and then, lion-like, striking for vengeance." In Oregon Farnham had sponsored a petition asking the United States to annex the territory. He now did his best to make the Graham Affair a pretext for the seizure of California. Putting expansionist speeches into the mouth of Isaac Graham, the wronged American yeoman, Farnham brought the frontier to the support of Manifest Destiny. Although arrest and deportation represented a temporary setback for Anglo-Saxons, Farnham asserted, "no one acquainted with the indolent, mixed race of California, will ever believe that they will populate, much less, for any length of time, govern the country. The law of Nature which curses the mulatto here with a constitution less robust than that of either race from which he sprang, lays a similar penalty upon the mingling of the Indian and white races in California and Mexico. They must fade away; while the mixing of different branches of the Caucasian family in the States will continue to produce a race of men, who will enlarge from period to period the field of their industry and civil domination, until not only the Northern States of Mexico, but the Californias also, will open their glebe to the pressure of its unconquered arm. The old Saxon blood must stride the continent, must command all its northern shores, must here press the grape and the olive, here eat the orange and fig, and in their own unaided might, erect the altar of civil and religious freedom on the plains of the Californias."[14]

Thus, by the last lingering days of Mexican rule, Americans had worked out for themselves a California expectation: a sense of mismanagement awaiting correction, of luxuriance awaiting a better pattern.

Racist contempt flawed the origins of American California in hatred, injustice, and bloodshed. Tragically, one California was destroyed so that another might take its place. At noon on Washington's Birthday, 1847, on a clear and lovely day, Edwin Bryant, who had ridden with the California Battalion of John Charles Frémont during the conquest, heard the saluting cannons of American war-vessels in San Francisco Bay. Their triumphant salvos, remembered Bryant, "bounded from hill to hill, and were echoed and re-echoed until the sound died away, apparently in the distant gorges of the Sierra Nevada. This was a voice from the soul of Washington, speaking in majestic and thunder-like tones to the green and flowery valleys, the gentle hills and lofty mountains of California, and consecrating them as the future abode of millions upon millions of the sons of liberty."[15] This liberty belonged only to California's American sons. Hearing the booming Yankee guns, Old California residents of Yerba Buena and the ranchos in the hills of Marin and Contra Costa might well have felt they were hearing the funeral cannonade of their race.

III

Was it all as harsh as this? Were there no patterns of accommodation between Old Californian and Yankee? Only disrespect and mistrust? Viewed thus far, the prestatehood experience offers no hope that something new and good might be achieved. American California begins as an act of conquest climaxing a history of contempt. This was not the total truth, although as American soldiers and sailors occupied the territory it seemed the dominant one. There had been some blending in the preceding decades, some moments of amalgamation and imaginative identity wherein Americans had glimpsed possibilities of an alternative California. Fragile forms of value and style, discarded now in the arrogance of seizure, they remained buried within the memory of those who had been there before dragoons and men-of-war. A later generation—after the conquest, after the Gold Rush, after the first flush times—would call upon these memories as they sought out for themselves what it meant to be a Californian.

Not every American came in contempt. Zenas Leonard was the chief clerk of the trapping party led by Joseph Reddeford Walker across the Sierras in 1833. In Leonard's *Narrative* (1839) the time spent by the Walker party in California is remembered as a pastoral interlude in a larger tale of suffering, a time free of murderous Indians and hostile terrain, a time of trapping in quiet rivers and of boisterous festivity in Monterey. Having been the first white men to cross the Sierras east to west, the Walker party felt they had earned a rest. Set so strategically against invasion, the Sierras, once crossed, reversed their significance. Now for Leonard these snowy peaks, this Range of Light, divided California from the dark animosity of the Great Desert of the interior, where mountain men suffered so bitterly.

An intensified awareness of the Pacific accompanied Leonard's sense of cismontane security. Leonard's was not the Pacific of the bored sea-voyager hundreds of days from home port, but the Pacific dreamt of at night by campfires after days of exhausting overland struggle. Skirting the eastern shores of San Pablo and San Francisco bays, the trappers bedded down on the night of 19 November 1833 in the Coast Range. In the distance they heard a rolling thunder. At first they feared an earthquake, but then they suspected they might be hearing the roar of the Pacific as it dashed against the coast. A strange thrill filled Leonard as he lay in his blankets, hearing the distant crash of the surf. This was the farthest one could go. "The idea of being within hearing of the *end* of the *Far West*," he remembered, "inspired the heart of every member of our company with a patriotic feeling for his country's honor, and all were eager to lose no time until they should behold what they had heard."[16] Breaking camp early the next day, the Walker party, striding eargerly across the remaining hills, burst like Xenophon's Greeks into full view of the sea. It was a moment of American joy, yet one, as Leonard realized, ancient in associations. As if by design, the symbolic aspect of their experience was completed two days later. Forty miles south of San Francisco the Walker party sighted the *Lagoda*, a Bryant and Sturgis ship from Boston. Captain John Bradshaw invited the trappers aboard for a day of feasting, drinking, sporting, and storytelling. The next day the sailors came ashore to continue the celebration in the camp of the mountain men. Amidst the hilarity, sailors and trappers felt the representative nature of their meeting. By sea and by land, California's American destiny stood assured.

Zenas Leonard felt no need to degrade the Californians. The hell-raising of the Walker party in Monterey became a local legend; but there was no violence, there were no imprisonments, there was no racial hatred. Governor José Figueroa, in fact, gave Walker permission to hunt and trade, and offered him a large land grant if he would lead fifty trained American artisans with their families into California. Seeing how valued were their skills and how welcoming the Mexicans, six of Walker's men decided to remain. The returning party left Monterey, recalled Leonard, delighted with California and well pleased with the charm and courtesy of her people.

Thus not every American saw the Californian as an inconsequential semi-barbarian. Certain characteristics struck the American imagination. The costume of the caballero (described by one visitor as "the old Castilian court dress modified by association with savage life") suggested values quite opposite those of American black broadcloth. The feel of the eighteenth century clung to the Californians' knee breeches, long stockings, buckled shoes, sashes, embroidered vests, and queued hair. The Californian seemed dropped out of time, possessed of an assured identity which belonged to an older order of experience. Elaborate, individualistic, defiantly antique—his costume expressed the Californian's respect of himself as lineal descendant of an ancient and revered race. Armed with willow lances, the horsemen who charged invading Americans at La Mesa and San Pasqual seemed to gallop out of the pages of a medieval Spanish romance.

The survival of European elegance on the California frontier provided surprise and delight. At Mission San Antonio de Padua in 1829 Alfred Robinson found Padre Pedro Cabot "a fine noble-looking man, whose manner and whole deportment would have led one to suppose he had been bred in the courts of Europe, rather than in the cloister."[17] "Next to the love of dress," wrote Richard Henry Dana of his visit in the mid-1830's, "I was most struck with the fineness of the voices and beauty of the intonations of both sexes. . . . A common bullock-driver, on horseback, delivering a message, seemed to speak like an ambassador at an audience." The rude simplicity of their life deprived Californians of everything "but their pride, their manners, and their voices."[18] Calling upon Governor Manuel Micheltorena in 1843 to apologize for his embarrassingly premature seizure of Monterey, Commodore Thomas Ap Catesby Jones was delighted to find not the "bombastic, gasconading, and very ridiculous personage" predicted by his staff surgeon, but an elegantly correct officer, capable of handling a delicate diplomatic situation. Santa Barbara, so self-consciously Spanish, always charmed Americans, and even Monterey, noted one visitor, "shows in spite of its primitiveness a certain aristocratic character which is especially recognizable at balls and other public affairs."[19]

At balls and festivals Californian showed American that work was not everything. From twilight, when guitars, violins, and castanets began to play, until dawn of the next day; kept going by the juice of jimsonweed or fired by draughts of brandy—the Californian danced. Shouting encouragement to those who moved rhythmically in the stately *contradanza,* the joyous *fandango,* the sensual *jota,* or the intricate *jarabe,* the Californian celebrated a wedding, a harvest, a national or religious holiday, or perhaps just life itself. To many Americans California life seemed a perpetual round of feasting, dancing, love-making, and visiting back and forth. They condemned such unproductive carnival, but there were also times of quiet envy.

French and English visitors never felt compelled to slander Californian women as a class. Even Americans were not totally disapproving. Yankee anxiety, suggested William Heath Davis, a longtime American resident, was as much political as sexual, for the women of California, feeling most intensely the threat to their Catholicism, actively resisted annexation. Yet envy and fear could not obscure moments of genuine appreciation. Americans like Alfred Robinson and William Heath Davis, married to local women, might naturally praise the talent and virtue of the California female, pointing out that other Americans erred grossly when, confused by the absence of caste, they lumped all women into the lower order. Permanent residents were not alone in their praises. Again and again American visitors described the California woman as possessed of simple dignity. The sexy wanton of ambivalent American longing also appeared in travel literature as devoted wife, chaste daughter, or maidservant going about household tasks with gentle grace. "There are no women in the world," noted Edwin Bryant, "for whose manners nature has done so much, and for whom art and education, in this respect, have done so little, as these Hispano-American females on the coast of the Pacific. In their deportment towards strangers they are queens, when, in costume, they are peasants. None of them, according to our tastes, can be called beautiful; but what they want in complexion and regularity of features, is fully supplied by their kindliness, the soul and sympathy which beam from their dark eyes, and their grace and warmth of manners and expression."[20] Admiration at this point has almost overcome racism. She is black—but beautiful!

Americans might condemn anti-intellectualism, but they loved the exuberant physicality of California life. Climate in itself called to health. "It was none of your commonplace Atlantic atmospheres," said a naval officer of an April day, "but laden with fragrance; soft and voluptuous, yet not enervating, but gently bracing." Americans bragged that they could sleep out of doors most of the year, and some exaggeratedly described the territory as disease-free. "I knew a man to have several chills," admitted John Bidwell, "but he had been intoxicated several days in succession." Dropped off in California in the mid-1830's by his ship's captain because of poor health, John Coulter, an English physician, threw himself into a six-month regime of outdoor life in the company of an American hunter. Coulter returned to Monterey restored to health. Navy men especially appreciated the chance to harden muscles and to forget the confinement of shipboard. *Los Gringos* (1849), by Lieutenant Henry Augustus Wise, is an idyll of outdoor life on horseback. "I am not aware of any higher and truer enjoyment of mere physical existence," said Revere concerning the Californians' habit of riding at breakneck speed. "Who cares for the artificial world across the continent, when he can thus enjoy wild and uncontrolled independence?"[21]

Physically, the Californian, like the grizzly bear and the redwood tree, showed size, strength, and longevity. Many observers insisted Californians were a race apart, their physiques (running frequently to six feet and two hundred pounds) in obvious contrast to the slighter build of the Mexican. In a society without physicians, health never seemed a problem. Depending upon his own private indisposition, the visitor envied the Californian for his teeth, his hair, his physique, or his potency. On horseback, where he spent most of his time, the Californian seemed a very centaur of animal well-being. Dancing, he emanated sensual joy. Astride his mount; riding at full gallop; flamboyant in spurs, poncho, and sombrero—the Californian unconsciously assumed oneness with the physical. To the American he bespoke the possibility of his own rejuvenation.

Americans residing permanently in California incorporated local values into their own lives. By the early 1840's the American community had achieved a blending of cultures, a lifestyle which pointed in the direction of a California sadly destined never fully to flourish, or at least doomed never to unfold naturally. Later generations would be haunted by its memory.

American adjustment proceeded on two fronts: there was a maritime elite, made up generally of New Englanders; and there were hunters and trappers, generally Southerners or men from Border States. The two communities interpenetrated but remained distinct. Most New Englanders came to California by sea as mariners or agents of commercial houses. Tending to cluster in the Santa Barbara area, their experience ran to pattern: citizenship (which implied nominal conversion to Catholicism), marriage into a prominent family, prosperity in trade, prominence in local affairs, a land grant. Don Abel Stearns (born in Lunenburg, Massachusetts, in 1798) had the most spectacular success. After a period at sea as a supercargo in the South American and China trade, Stearns acquired Mexican citizenship and settled in 1829 as a trader in Los Angeles. Within ten years he was the wealthiest man in Southern California. Married to the lovely Arcadia, daughter of Don Juan Bandini, settled comfortably at *El Palacio*, his spacious adobe manor, Stearns lived the life of a frontier merchant prince. In 1842 he purchased the sprawling *Rancho Los Alamitos*, where he lived until his death in 1871, lord of land and cattle.

Most hunters and trappers who arrived overland were Southern or Border State men who had been at least one generation on the frontier. They had less formal education than their maritime counterparts, and they were a lot tougher. Already a Catholic, a Mexican citizen, a trapper, hunter, and trader on the Santa Fe Trail, William Wolfskill (born in Boonesboro, Kentucky, in 1798) led an overland party to Los Angeles in 1831. Settled into a common-law marriage, Wolfskill worked as a carpenter, buying land with his earnings. In 1841 he acquired a legal—and socially prominent—Santa Barbara wife to grace his growing prosperity. Wolfskill died in 1866, master of extensive vineyards and citrus groves, the patriarch of Old Adobe, his vine-covered Los Angeles home.

For these men and for many others, California offered freedom and a second chance. They remained Yankees and Border men, but their values and lifestyles were modified. They went by Spanish names, used Spanish in daily conversation (even in private correspondence), dressed as Mexicans, and fathered Mexican families. Their children, felt William Heath Davis, were the eugenic beginnings of a new people, a Latin-Yankee California stock partaking of the best of both strains. Trained in youth as a carpenter, Thomas Oliver Larkin bore witness to the harmonious blending of cultures in the home he built at Monterey in 1835. Strictly as a practical consideration, Larkin combined the two-story wood-frame of New England with the adobe of California. Known to history as Monterey Colonial, this fusion of New England construction and California materials, so symbolic of a briefly achieved Yankee-Mexican culture, remained the dominant domestic style until the 1850's, when the straight white-frame replaced it, the architectural sign of a more restrictive sort of American sovereignty.

The *Pioneer Register and Index* attached to the Bancroft *History of California* tells the story of many an American who improved his lot by remaining in California. Joseph Chapman, who somehow in 1818 got involved with an invading squadron from the Republic of Buenos Aires, joined the two other Americans on the coast, the black man Bob (Juan Cristóbal) and Thomas Doak (Felipe Santiago). Captured by the Californians, Chapman made himself useful as a carpenter and mechanic. He obtained the King's amnesty for his part in the abortive invasion, was baptized as Jose-Juan, and married Guadalupe Ortega. A former apprentice in the Boston shipyards, Chapman built the second vessel ever launched in California. A vineyard of 4000 vines was attached to the Los Angeles home he built in 1824. Twelve years later he moved his family to a spacious rancho outside Santa Barbara. Not a bad end for an illiterate sailor who had begun his California career in the calaboose!

George Yount also rose beyond his station. In 1825 Yount left Missouri for the rigors of trail life after an embezzling partner had ruined his cattle business. Seeing the herds, orchards, gardens, and vineyards of Mission San Gabriel after beating his way across the Spanish Trail from Taos in 1831, Yount knew that he had reached his promised land. Granted the Caymus Rancho in Napa Valley, Yount flourished there for his remaining thirty years, loved and respected by his Californian neighbors; raising an adopted Indian daughter; and developing a ranch famous for cattle, orchards, strawberries, and honey.

Thomas Oliver Larkin arrived in 1832 with little formal education and a record of business failure. By 1842 he was worth $37,958—a fairly spectacular sum in currency-bereft California. No wonder Larkin and men like him felt they had a chance to bring California peaceably into the American Republic. Did they not themselves show the pattern of an integration that could lead to non-violent acquisition? As their numbers grew, was not California drifting closer and closer to the United States without violation of its rights and values, without abrupt distortion of its culture? In September 1845 Larkin accepted a confidential mission from Secretary of State James Buchanan to promote the peaceful annexation of California. Turning over his own business to an agent, Larkin devoted all his

Thomas Oliver Larkin (1802–1858)

Arriving in California with a record of business failure in the East, this self-educated Yankee rose to prosperity in the years before annexation. His Monterey home and his efforts as American Consul to bring California peaceably into the Union signified an evanescent détente between Mexican and Yankee in the possession of California. The Mexican War ended Larkin's hopes of a peaceful transition.

time to the enterprise. As war with Mexico grew certain, Larkin found himself in a race with time. He wrote to prominent Americans throughout the territory, sounding them out and urging them to promote American interests in their areas. On 20 April 1846, a little more than a month before the Bear Flag Rebellion, Larkin sent Buchanan a long memorandum in which he urged that the State Department make it worth the while of key California leaders to declare themselves a republic. Under Californian and Yankee-Californian leadership, this republic could then petition for statehood.

Taken as an act of imagination, Larkin's plan had a long history. So contemptuous in many ways of their neighbors to the South, Americans yet cherished a desire to coax Latin Americans into North American political institutions and alliances. Writing in *The Western Monthly Review* for September 1827, the Reverend Timothy Flint had predicted that by 1900 California would be an independent republic, Mexican in culture but with American political institutions. Erroneously thinking that Mexico and the United States were at war, Commodore Thomas Ap Catesby Jones sailed the Pacific Squadron into Monterey in 1842 and raised the American flag. Tired of Mexican misrule, went American reports of the incident, Californians secretly welcomed the Commodore's arrival. Jones himself was only officially apologetic. Privately he claimed that the better sort of Californian welcomed the hoisting of the Stars and Stripes.

Further assurance that Californians were prepared to accept an American destiny on their own volition came from General Mariano Guadalupe Vallejo, protector of the northern frontier and after 1836 the most powerful man in California. Intelligent, widely read, fundamentally secular—Vallejo was the Californian counterpart of the Hispanicized Yankee. The fact that this powerful hidalgo was said to favor annexation flattered Americans before and after the conquest. A visit to Vallejo's baronial Sonoma estate, flourishing and orderly, took on the significance of a prophecy: here was the model of the Californian as progressive American. A legend grew up that Vallejo argued brilliantly before the junta at Monterey in favor of joining the American Union—a legend which as wish-fulfillment sought to soften American guilt and offer some hope of reconciliation between conquered and conqueror, the hope Edwin Bryant was feeling when he assured an old Californian couple "that all was peaceable now; that there would be no more wars in California; that we were all Americans, all Californians,—*hermanos, hermanas, amigos.*"[22]

Walter Colton, a Congregationalist clergyman, left California believing that something very valuable would be lost if native Californians were not given a full place in the American order. Born in 1797 in Rutland, Vermont, a graduate of Yale and the Andover Theological Seminary, Colton arrived in California in 1846 as chaplain on the *Congress*. From 1846 to 1848 he served as alcalde of Monterey, where he also co-edited California's first newspaper. Re-assigned in early 1849 to the Philadelphia Navy Yard, Chaplain Colton wrote a classic of California travel literature, *Three Years in California* (1850), dedicated to General Vallejo. Spanning the interregnum period—conquest, Gold Rush, and constitutional convention; in touch with an Old California yet undestroyed by the American presence, Colton's *Three Years in California* contains within itself the full range of the pre-statehood experience.

If Larkin's 1835 home signified an evanescent *détente* between Mexican and Yankee in the possession of California, the whitewashed, severely classical town hall Colton had built for Monterey in 1847 prefigured uncompromising Yankee dominion. Minister, penal reformer, journalist, educator, administrator, naval officer, admiralty judge—Colton represented the best the Yankee could bring to his new mastership. Like the Greek Revival hall he kept convicts busy working upon (and which now bears his name), Colton's character was constructed upon balanced, clean lines. He was glad to be part of "the tide of Anglo-Saxon blood" which would bring "steady triumphs of commerce, art, civilization, and religion." His administration of Monterey was a model of Puritan efficiency. He built a school and a town hall, closed grogshops on the Sabbath, suppressed gambling, collected taxes, and punished lawbreakers with equitable severity. At the same time Colton did not remain an aloof administrator. He fell passionately in love with California—land and people. The Greek lines of Colton Hall expressed the rule of law, true, but they also bespoke an Hellenic quality of aesthetic repose. The Vermont Yankee and Puritan preacher discovered himself enthralled by the Mediterranean aspect of California: sun, sea, and sky; "the wild waving background of forest-feathered cliffs, the green slopes, and the glimmering walls of the white dwellings, and the dash of the billows on the sparkling sands of the bay;" and the vines of the South, "which send through California a wine that need not blush in the presence of any rival from the hills of France or the sunny slopes of Italy." In such a climate and in such abundance, felt Colton, where hunger was unknown, health taken for granted, the problem of shelter at a minimum, and ambition softened by voluptuous surroundings, American life could take on for the first time a repose, a classical simplicity which, as in the case of Greece, might prove the physical basis for the well-led life. That is why Colton hated the Gold Rush. The Forty-niners had a totally different California in mind. "The lust of gold will people the one," said Colton of the two Californias, "but all that is lovely in the human heart spreads its charm over the other."

As the Gold Rush filled California with Americans, Colton began to identify with the displaced Mexicans. His initial opinion had been critical, but not vicious. With good-humored bafflement, Colton had brought to Monterey a little Yankee efficiency. Very shortly, in the face of a chaotic American presence, he found himself more advocate than reformer. Values threatened by the Gold Rush, Colton realized, had belonged to Old Californians in the first place. He resented the American assumption of cultural superiority. On the contrary, California was filling up with the worst sort of American speculator, piker, and cardsharp. If he had to choose between the two cultures, Colton had "no hesitation in saying, give me the Californian." In contrast to Americans, who were physically and mentally and morally destroying themselves in pursuit of gold, Californians cherished life itself as their most precious asset. "There is hardly a shanty among them," he believed, "which does not contain more true contentment, more genuine gladness of the heart, than you will meet with in the most princely palace." Initially suspicious, Colton grew to see more than trivial meaning in the Californians' round of picnics, fandangos, holy days, and three-day wedding celebrations. He himself became a willing if somewhat self-conscious participant in such pleasures. The courtesy of Californians delighted him; the little ceremonies with which they adorned life, "trifles in themselves, but they refine social intercourse, and soften its alienations." Whereas Americans brought a destructive selfishness to California, its former owners always took care of one another. There had been no need for an orphan asylum in a culture which considered children wealth, no need for public charity among a people who freely shared what they possessed. "If I must be cast in sickness or destitution on the care of the stranger," Colton exclaimed, "let it be in California; but let it be before American avarice has hardened the heart and made a god of gold."

At first guilty of the usual Yankee ambivalence, Colton grew to approve of the frank vigor of the California woman. Her health and elastic physicality seemed in sharp contrast to the corseted, parlor-imprisoned females of his own people. "Look here to California," Colton urged American women; "among all these mothers and daughters, there is not

Walter Colton (1797–1851)

Appointed alcalde of Monterey in 1846, Colton, a naval chaplain, represented the best the United States could bring to its new mastership. The Vermont clergyman, whose administration was a model of Puritan efficiency, softened under California's sunny skies and grew to love its Spanish-speaking people. He detested what the Gold Rush brought to California.

one where the cankerworm of that disease [tuberculosis] is at work which has spread sorrow and dismay around your hearths. . . . It is in your in-door habits, hot parlors, prunellas, and twisting corsets, that clothe this generation with weeds, and bequeath to the next constitutions that fall like grass under the scythe of death." In her liberated, outdoor, and un-corseted condition, Colton admitted, the California woman could perhaps stray from virtue more easily than her American counterpart. Such lapses, however, did not proceed from innate unchastity, but were imprudent expressions of abundant charity. "She is often at the couch of disease," Colton claimed for the women of California, "unshrinkingly exposed to contagion, or in the hovel of destitution, administering to human necessity. She pities where others reproach, and succors where others forsake."

To these California imperatives of simple, gracious, and abundant living, Americans had come in disrespect and violence—Colton said this, although he himself wore a military uniform. The conquest had put an end to Larkin's dream, which was now also the Reverend Walter Colton's: that of an organic integration of California's people into the American commonwealth. "Its lightning has shivered the tree before the fruit was ripe," said Colton of the violence between Yankee and Californian, "and blasted a thousand buds that might have bloomed into fragrant beauty." Back in Philadelphia, knowing that an opportunity had been lost, Colton grew nostalgic. Almost in spite of himself, the Reverend Walter Colton, United States Navy, whose Greek Revival hall said so much about the new Yankee order, the Reverend Walter Colton, a Protestant from Vermont, had joined the ranks of those Americans in whom California had awakened a taste for an alternative way of living, a lifestyle in which Yankee stiffness softened under a warm sun and personality expanded into hitherto repressed ranges of value and emotion.

Like his dream, Colton was dying. He would not long outlive the publication of *Three Years in California*. Longingly, he took a last look at the friends with whom he had shared the joy of California days, naming them one by one. California-born, European, or Yankee emigrant; Catholic or Protestant—they had all shared the happiness of his Monterey years. They had made together a special California. Now, the roll call of their names had a distinct pathos; for the culture they represented, the delicate balance of the 1830's and 1840's, had become impossible. Yerba Buena—now the sprawling Gold Rush town of San Francisco—dominated the scene, leaving Monterey a near-deserted village, filled with those too old to go to the mines, filled with memories, filled with homes whose architecture bore witness to a time when a possible California had been given fleeting reality.[23]

IV

In August 1826 Jedediah Smith, twenty-seven, led a party of seventeen trappers southward from the Great Salt Lake in search of beaver. Guided by two runaway Mission Indians, the Smith party crossed the Mohave Desert, reaching Mission San Gabriel on 27 November 1826, having completed the first recorded journey from the Missouri River to California. From Mission San Gabriel Smith went south to San Diego, where he conducted lengthy negotiations with Governor Echeandía for permission to trap in California. On 20 May 1827 he and two companions left the party's base camp on the Stanislaus River in Northern California and in eight days made the first crossing of the Sierras by white men. Emerging near the present-day Ebbetts Pass, the three men crossed the Great Basin, and on 3 July 1827 they reached Bear Lake, Utah, for rendezvous with Smith's partners. Jedediah remained in camp ten days. Putting together a party of eighteen men supplied for two years, he led them down along the route of a year before. Ambushed by Mohave Indians as they crossed the Colorado River, the party lost ten of its eighteen men. The survivors struggled across the Mohave Desert and up through California to the base camp on the Stanislaus. On 30 December 1827 Smith and his combined parties (now numbering twenty) set out northward, driving before them 300 horses and mules, trapping slowly down the Trinity and Klamath rivers. Smith could not discover a route east across the Sierras, so he was forced to make a treacherous journey of six months into Oregon, his men being the first whites to penetrate the region overland from California. On the morning of 14 July 1828 on the Umpqua River, while Smith was out scouting, the Kelawatset Indians massacred the expedition. Smith and two other survivors eventually found their way to Fort Vancouver on the Oregon coast.

It was incredible: the double encirclement of the uncharted Far West! No wonder Smith seemed to his contemporaries already an epic figure: first among mountain men; a new Daniel Boone, possessed of the heroic, stoic energies of the early American Republic; a Yankee Adam passing through the wilderness, giving American names to things and places. Smith's father had been born in New Hampshire and his mother in Connecticut. They had moved West on the New England frontier—New York, western Pennsylvania, Ohio. Jedediah had pushed on to Missouri, where in 1822 he answered William Ashley's advertisement in the Saint Louis *Missouri Gazette and Public Advertiser* for 100 enterprising young men to join him in the fur trade. The fragments of Smith's journals which survive (they were not brought to light until 1934) reveal Methodist piety, terse intelligence, and subtle self-awareness. "My horses freezing, my men discouraged and our utmost exertion necessary to keep from freezing to death," Smith entered into his journal on the night of 20 April 1828, as his men rested uneasily after an exhausting day of picking their way through the tangled forests of Northern California. "I then thought of the vanity of riches and of all those objects that lead men in the perilous paths of adventure. It seems that in times like those men return to reason and make the true estimate of things. They throw by the gaudy baubles of ambition and embrace the solid comforts of domestic life. But a few days of rest makes the sailor forget the storm and embark again on the perilous Ocean and I suppose that like him I would soon become weary of rest."[24]

The phrase "weary of rest"—hastily jotted by an evening fire—provides the leitmotif for Smith's brief life. Aside from a frankly confessed love of gain and adventure, Smith envisioned himself embarked upon a great religious enterprise. "Men of good morals seldom enter into business of this kind," he wrote his parents in 1829. His contemporaries recognized Smith as a glaring exception. He neither smoked, swore, chewed tobacco, nor consorted with squaws. He shaved daily, kept himself as clean as possible, and read the Bible by the evening campfire. "The lone wilderness had been his place of meditation," noted Smith's eulogist, "and the mountain top his altar. He made religion an active, practical principle, from the duties of which nothing could seduce him. He affirmed it to be 'the one thing needful,' and his greatest happiness; yet was he modest, never obtrusive, charitable, 'without guile.' "[25] The letters Smith forwarded from remote sites in the Far West pulsate with Christian feeling. Smith suffered deeply his isolation from church fellowship, but he saw in the missionary journeys of Saint Paul a comforting analogue for his own many sufferings in the work of the Lord. Significantly, Harrison Rogers, Smith's chief clerk on the California expedition, was also a man of intelligence, Protestant piety, and possibly New England origins. Rogers did not survive the Umpqua River massacre, but Smith later retrieved his clerk's journals from the Indians. It is from Rogers' more full account, in fact, rather than from Smith's elliptical entries, that we piece together the party's California experience.

Smith's arrival posed a substantive and symbolic threat not lost on Governor Echeandía. California's continental barrier had been broken. In the Smith party Echeandía beheld, if not the detail, at any rate the inevitability of American overland migration, an awareness compounded three years later when the Pattie party arrived across Lower California; in 1830 and 1831 when Ewing Young and William Wolfskill led their men across the Southwest; and in 1833 when Joseph Walker's expedition crossed the Sierras. Smith surrendered passports and journals to Echeandía to prove good faith, and the American captains in San Diego harbor attested their belief in Smith's non-military intentions. But the Americans were not being honest. Smith came not without design. Intrigued by the plan of John Jacob Astor to ship furs from Pacific ports, he hoped to discover the mythical Buenaventura River, which generations thought flowed westward from Salt Lake to the Pacific. If the Buenaventura existed, Smith planned to establish a network for ferrying pelts down to California for shipment around the Horn.

Released by Echeandía on the promise that he would return the way he came, Smith violated his word, proceeding up through California, gathering in by April about 1500 pounds of illicit pelts. Arriving at Mission San Jose on 23 September 1827 during his second encirclement of the Far West, his equipment and supplies lost in the Mohave massacre, Smith was arrested and sent to Monterey for an interview by a now totally exasperated governor, who kept his unwanted guest waiting there until the middle of November. By the time of Smith's second departure northward, each side knew the intentions of the other. The pattern of their encounter—American illegality and evasion; official frustration at a growing American presence—held true for the ensuing twenty years.

In hospitable California, however, hostility had its limits. Mission San Gabriel Arcángel, where 1000 Indians were needed to tend to the harvest, was in its era of greatest prosperity. Harrison Rogers felt it the most desirable part of the world he had ever seen. "All peace and friendship"—he described each day of his San Gabriel sojourn. The pastor, Padre José Bernardo Sánchez, whom Rogers esteemed as "the greatest friend that I ever met with in all my travels," treated the Smith party with exuberant friendliness, "as gentlemen," says Rogers, "in every sense of the word." He treated the Americans to dinner, whiskey, wine, brandy, and cigars on the night of their arrival and many merry nights after. He invited them to a wedding festival, begging them not to be embarrassed about their travel-stained clothes. He provided them with supplies and materials of repair. As they waited for Smith to return from negotiating with Echeandía in San Diego, the trappers found themselves falling into the easy rhythms of California life: the lack of physical hardships, the plenitude of good company and food, the genial climate, the Indian women who "think it an honor to ask a white man to sleep with them."

As believing Protestants, Smith and Rogers were glad the padres said nothing about religion. Smith and his chief clerk attended services at the Mission, and Rogers' journal is devoid of the disparaging remarks Americans usually made on such occasions. Although he confessed himself a little scandalized at Padre Sánchez's propensity to play cards on the Sabbath, Rogers found the old priest a worthy Christian. Not until two weeks into Rogers' stay do any religious tensions appear in his journal—and this merely a polite debate between Rogers and Sánchez regarding the sacramental forgiveness of sin. Two weeks later, on New Year's Day 1827, Rogers delivered—or at least copied into his journal—a most extraordinary address to Padre Sánchez, manifesting a degree of awareness rarely encountered in journals kept by mountain men.

Briefly, Rogers related the history of the Apostolic Church. Did Rogers compose this? Its literary quality exceeds anything else in the journal. Yet evidence makes it appear that he did, although the circumstances of its delivery are uncertain. Stimulated by after-dinner discussions with the Padre, Rogers might very well have written out this address for delivery through an interpreter. Aside from asserting that a trapper could quote a Church Father, Rogers is subtly using the missionary journeys of the Apostolic Age as a type for the present errand of Protestant America into the Far Western wilderness. Did Jedediah Smith and his equally devout chief clerk reach agreement as to the religious significance of their overland probe? It is not unwarranted to think so. Rogers' address could very well have been intended as an indirect *apologia* for the work of Christian men in the Far West. Christian life is a trial, Rogers affirms, and most specifically, in light of its apostolic origins, it is a missionary labor. Providence and probation: as agents in a divine plan, missionaries are tested in hardship—in Nineveh, Macedonia, Corinth, the Great American Desert, California. Delivered from the sea, Jonah went to Nineveh; delivered from the desert, Jedediah Smith arrives in San Diego. Then death, says Rogers; remember those who have died this past year and remember that the apostles died martyrs in forgotten corners of the world. This from a mountain man, who knew death as a companion on the trail, who himself in a year and a half would meet a bloody end. Christ commissioned the

Richard Henry Dana, Jr. (1815–1882)

Sickness and the suffocating orthodoxies of Cambridge, Massachusetts, compelled the young Harvard undergraduate to ship before the mast to California. A complication of liberation and trauma, Dana's California sojourn proved the high point of a life characterized by anxiety and repressed longing. His was a California of escape, half-desired, half-feared.

apostles to spread the churches, to provide the gospel with social and historical unfolding. Was not California part of that "world to be converted"? At first the apostles remained at Jerusalem—like Americans sojourning on their side of the continent but ever aware of an inevitable missionary labor westward. The apostles spread out to the Gentiles. The Smith party, under the leadership of an American Paul, had come over to Macedonia. Simple, unlearned men brought the churches to Spain, France, Germany, Britain. They now brought them to the Far West. As in those days the gospel was being preached "in every part of the globe which was then known."

One of Rogers' last entries is a prayer scribbled into his battered journal as Smith's exhausted and harassed party picked its way into Oregon: "Oh! God, may it pleas thee, in thy divine providence, to still guide and protect us through this wilderness of doubt and fear, as thou hast done heretofore, and be with us in the hour of danger and difficulty, as all praise is due to thee and not to man, oh! do not forsake us Lord, but be with us and direct us through."[26] A few days later the body of Harrison Rogers lay butchered on the banks of the Umpqua.

Thus one pattern of Protestant consciousness: inner vision externalized into action, a wilderness encountered by religious men who had the comfort of great analogues. It was simple, heroic, and it had the feel of the seventeenth century. In the transcontinental migrations of the 1840's and 1850's, hundreds of diaries, journals, and memoirs attest to the power of scriptural analogue. Lost in the desert, besieged by Indians, hunger, thirst, confusion, and despair, Protestant pioneers found in the memory of earlier wilderness wanderings sources of sanity and hope.

There was another pattern of Protestant consciousness, a less integrated one, for which the California visit of Richard Henry Dana, Jr., of Cambridge, Massachusetts, provides a model. Of all Americans who came to California in the years before statehood, Dana's visit held the most significance for literature. *Two Years Before the Mast,* published in 1840, was an immediate best seller and has since held its own as a minor but enduring American classic. Forced to withdraw from Harvard College in his junior year with shattered nerves and with eyes severely weakened by measles, Dana shipped before the mast in an effort to regain his health. He left Boston at age nineteen in August 1834 on the *Pilgrim,* a Bryant and Sturgis brig bound for California in the hide and tallow trade. Rounding Cape Horn, Dana spent about sixteen months on the California coast before returning to Boston, age twenty-one, bronzed and healthy from life at sea. Resuming studies at Harvard, he graduated first in the Class of 1837, then studied for the bar. In January 1839, after a six months' stint of part-time writing, the young law student completed the now classic account of his voyage and California sojourn.

More than his eyes bothered Dana in 1834. He fled to California during a time of acute personal crisis. Leaving Cambridge confused as to identity and career, he returned determined to play his part. The losses and gains of Dana's California experience, like the encounters of Smith and Rogers, are of representative value.

Even at twenty-seven—newly married, his law practice beginning, his Cambridge life promising rich social rewards—Dana could not conceal his anger at the oppressive world of his childhood. Schooldays seemed a succession of floggings. One Cambridge schoolmaster had pulled Dana's ear so hard that he brought blood. Dana remembered with pride how unflinchingly and with what sense of caste he had stood up to such corporal punishment. Harvard's rigid rules and narrow curriculum had proved equally repressive. Rusticated for taking part in a student rebellion, Dana had spent six months in quiet rural study at Andover under a kindly clerical tutor. "When my six months were over," he recalled in his *Autobiographical Sketch*, "I would have given a great deal to have my sentence extended six months more; but it could not be, and I went back to college recitations, college rank, college gossip and college *esprit de corps*, as a slave whipped to his dungeon."[27]

Forced to withdraw a second time when measles weakened his eyes, Dana was driven to distraction during the nine months he idled about the family home in Cambridge. His father, Richard Henry Dana, Sr., a failed minor essayist who had long since given up the struggle for significant effort, content querulously to pass his life in literary puttering, and his uncle, Washington Allston, likewise squandering early promise as an artist in middle-aged dilettantism, seemed frightening examples of family failure. As he prowled restlessly about his home—unable to read, hearing the pad of slippers and dry coughing from his father's study, or the distant chitchat from his uncle's studio—Dana began to fear that, as if by some family curse, he too was winding down. All his life he equated physical vigor with good character, and at nineteen he dreaded that his weakened constitution signaled the onslaught of moral decline. Sexual temptation racked him and his sense of religion waned. Sick, confused, neurasthenic, he seemed hemmed in on all sides. And so—upon his own insistence and very much against the practice of his class—he shipped before the mast as a common sailor.

He thus achieved a number of liberations. Did Cambridge orthodoxy—social, cultural, religious—threaten to subdue his desire for more expansive experience? From the forecastle Dana defied genteelism. When they traveled for their health, New England gentlemen went as passengers with access to the captain's table. Working his way around the Horn as a common sailor was Dana's dramatic assertion of a bolder self. It was a voyage of personal discovery, a search for an almost impossible adjustment between Cambridge expectations and adolescent rebellion. Before the mast he regained health and self-confidence. "I kept myself from freezing," he wrote home to his father after rounding Cape Horn; "and I found that I—home-bred, gentleman-bred, and college-bred—could stand it as well as the roughest of them."[28] He learned to appreciate a "Well done!" from the mate more than a *bene* from his Harvard tutor. Had sexual desire tormented him in Cambridge? During months spent ashore at San Diego Dana consorted with Indian girls—rambling with them in spare hours through coastal hills; sitting with a favorite at sunset atop a rock overlooking the Pacific. Was he anxious about a career? Did aesthetic needs conflict with the financial necessity of legal drudgery? Dana (who learned Spanish while ashore) admired how Californians derived their sense of worth not from labor, but from innate conviction. He learned to respect the point of view that life was not solely a matter of career. For someone whom material pressures would force into an uncongenial occupation, for whom shoring up sagging family finances would become an arduous lifetime task, it was not a trivial lesson.

Nor did he learn it without ambivalence. Like most Americans, Dana—in his Yankee side—found the Californians unworthy of California. "In the hands of an enterprising people," he wrote in *Two Years Before the Mast*, "what a country this might be!" As author of the first best-selling book about California, Dana did much to bring on annexation.

Another side of him, nevertheless, sympathized with the people who held onto their doomed empire with a mixture of pride, pathos, and *dolce far niente*. "There's no danger of Catholicism spreading in New England," Dana noted; "Yankees can't afford the time to be Catholics." Juxtapositions of caballero and Yankee in *Two Years Before the Mast* often redound to the favor of the Californian. Dana unfairly maligned such beloved Yankee-Californians as Alfred Robinson, author of *Life in*

California Before the Conquest, one of the most sympathetic of all California accounts, and Henry Delano Fitch. He made Fitch, whom the Old Californians revered as Don Enrique, seem the worst sort of Yankee pedlar. Such juxtapositions of aristocratic Californians and scheming Americans worked against the annexationist thrust of *Two Years Before the Mast*, but they expressed Dana's deeper identification with the plight of the Californian, which so much resembled his own self-image of being a gentleman held in bondage to business.

Each aspect of Dana's California liberation made necessary an eventually more compelling repression. He escaped Cambridge caste, but that freedom held its terror. He could never let himself forget who he was and where he came from. Playing the democrat was rather difficult for the grandson of a Massachusetts Chief Justice and the son of an elitist essayist who once suggested that the United States needed an hereditary monarchy and House of Lords. Even in remote California the fact of being a Dana of Cambridge got him transferred to a ship returning earlier to the Atlantic coast. *Two Years Before the Mast* is shot through with the anxiety of caste. He promised a description of life at sea from the viewpoint of a common sailor and in matters of fact he succeeded marvelously. But his perspective was that of a sojourner from above, ever on the edge of condescension. "We must come down from our heights, and leave our straight paths," he wrote self-righteously of his decision to go before the mast, "if we would learn truths by strong contrasts; and in hovels, in forecastles, and among our own outcasts in foreign lands, see what has been wrought upon our fellow-creatures by accident, hardship, or vice." Dana secretly loved and was terrified by low life. As a boy he defiantly "played with boys whom I was warned against as vulgar" while simultaneously fearful that "a boy lost caste by being vulgar and profane." Falling deeper and deeper into the profanity and promiscuity of life as a sailor on the California coast, Dana fretted over loss of caste. Despite the fact that he was writing *Two Years Before the Mast* in retrospect, he could not sustain his initial pose of droll acceptance. When a fellow sailor is flogged, pity and terror break through Dana's dramatization of himself as a detached observer. The young law student, back in the security of Cambridge, remembered how, stripped of caste's ego-reinforcements, he had felt the trauma of isolation "on a coast almost solitary; in a country where there is neither law nor gospel, and where sailors are at their captain's mercy."[29]

Dana might be free from career in California, in a period of moratorium during which contradictory impulses could be sorted out, but what if his whole life became a California interval? Nausea, upset stomach, and nervousness flit in and out of the record of Dana's cruise. Afraid that a long period at sea would incapacitate him for professional life, he pictured Harvard classmates "walking off the stage with their sheep-skins in their hands; while, upon the very same day, their classmate was walking up and down a California beach with a hide upon his head." A warning parade of failures, drifters, deserters, and beach bums fills Dana's narrative, men for whom California had become the scene of degradation and obscurity. A loose-living Hawaiian stricken with venereal disease and a brilliant crewman condemned by weakness of character to a life of obscure toil before the mast are two especially intense projections of Dana's inner fears. When Dana feels attracted to the California coast, it is to topographical features associated with loneliness, isolation, and doomed hopes—like Dead Man's Island in San Pedro harbor, where a nameless Englishman lay buried. "The only thing in California from which I could ever extract anything like poetry," he wrote of this symbol for his own adolescent fears of lost career.[30]

Returning to Harvard from California, Dana attacked his studies with none of his former ambiguity. He won prizes for composition and elocution, joined a number of good clubs, and ran with a group of elegant young Southerners. At commencement in 1837 he graduated number one and had a spoken part. Then the law. That he wrote *Two Years Before the Mast* while a law student had significance: Dana editing, ordering, and subduing California memories in the face of a Boston future. It had to be a work of reconstruction, for he somehow managed to lose the journals he had kept during the voyage. It was also a work of suppression. Dana tried to reduce experience to statements of fact. Forced into the enameled constraints of hard prose, California and the sea are fixed at a distance; a possible subversive escape becomes an acceptable prologue to career. It was Dana's lesson to himself about the things that counted. Suppressing all sentiment, he said that he wrote the book to attract business in admiralty law.

Dana also married—and found religion. Before going to sea he had struggled with a depressing belief in his own moral depravity—the dark corollary of his desire for sexual freedom. Sailor-fashion, he found sex in California—at the price of increasing guilt. On returning to Boston, he learned that Sarah A. Woods, nineteen, had offered deathbed prayers for his safety and salvation. Dana had flirted somewhat cavalierly with Sarah before his voyage, overtures which this girl of loving and religious temperament responded to with credulous devotion. Stricken with remorse over his California promiscuity and his toying with the dead Sarah's affections, Dana underwent a religious conversion. He began to court another Sarah—Sarah Watson, a girl of sound Connecticut Calvinism who reminded Dana of his dead mother. Their courtship consisted of confessions of unworthiness by Dana to Sarah, who in turn devised plans for his improvement. In what he interpreted as Sarah's profound religion and morality, Dana found fulfillment.

Married and converted and admitted to the bar—he set to work. He wore his hair long, sailor-fashion, self-consciously exuding an atmosphere of Cape Horn in his Boston law office. He found the law "hard, dry, uninteresting, uncertain and slavish," yet he plugged away. Henry Adams remembered him as a "man of rather excessive refinement trying with success to work like a day-laborer, deliberately hardening his skin to the burden, as though he were still carrying hides at Monterey." "We must bend to the wind," Dana was fond of saying, "and live by rule."[31]

In spite of application, in spite of so many twelve-hour days, Dana never had the career he wanted. Men once talked of him in terms of the presidency. He could manage neither election to Congress nor confirmation as Ambassador to England. Like so many New Englanders of his caste and generation, he lost out in post-Civil War America and became ensconced in Brahmin disaffection. As Dana's dreams failed, as encasement progressed, he found certain releases. Working himself into nervous exhaustion, he would flee to the woods with hunters and trappers, miniature enactments of the great flight of 1834. His aesthetic nature, suppressed in the law, found expression in an ultra-High Church Episcopalianism which catered both to his love of the luxuriant and to his Tory sense of caste. He would have become a Roman Catholic, as did his sister and his cousin, except for Sarah's opposition and his own dislike of the Boston Irish. Sarah herself—she who had seemed the healer of his soul—soon proved a bitter disappointment: nagging, petty, sentimental, morbidly religious (she refused him sex during Lent), hypochondriacal, stout, and afflicted with a facial tic. He worked heroically to support her love of lavish display and to help her social ambitions, but she kept him constantly in debt. In time, he managed to be away from home as much as possible. As early as his first year of marriage, Richard Henry Dana, Jr., Brahmin lawyer, would don his old sailor's togs and cruise waterfront brothels and dives. Picking up a prostitute, he would accompany her to her lodgings and then, revealing himself as a religious gentleman, proceed to lecture the astonished lady against the evil of her ways. Going home, he would tell Sarah of his mission of mercy.

The travels of Richard Henry Dana and Jedediah Smith provide two distinct patterns. In both cases at the psychological core are moral and religious formulations characteristically Protestant. In Smith's case these energies flow outward into an externalized arena of heroic endeavor. Smith pushed across alien and impassable geography guided and empowered by inner vision seeking externalization. A pillar of fire led him through the wilderness. As fragmentary as his surviving journals are, they, and those of Harrison Rogers, outline an integrated encounter in which experience has stability and meaning. Where Dana—even in the pages of his memoir—remains unintegrated, ambiguous, Jedediah Smith moves toward epic stature. Arriving in California, he possesses the repose, the simple strength of Vergil's *pius Aeneas* on a religious mission to transplant the culture of Troy to Latian shores. Dana brings with him the full burden of divided consciousness. California remains a drama of the mind, a tangled complication of fact, fantasy, and repressed longing.

At the head of the Cimarron River in what is now southwestern Kansas, on 27 May 1831, Jedediah Smith met death at the age of thirty-three, in a moment of stark drama. A band of Comanches surrounded him as he searched for a water hole. They rode in an ever-decreasing circle. With cool courage Smith reined up before their chief and for fifteen agonizing minutes the two men took each other's measure. Smith's horse reared and he was fired upon. Leveling his rifle, he killed the chief. He was reaching for his pistols as the Comanches closed in with their lances.

"Dana lived his bit in two years," D. H. Lawrence tells us, "and knew, and drummed out the rest. Dreary lawyer's years, afterwards." Dana himself felt his California days a "parenthesis." In time this parenthesis seemed to mark off the only meaning. He returned to California in 1859 for a brief visit—motivated like the visit of 1835 by broken health and the pressure of events—and was delighted to find how much Californians revered him as one of the founding figures in the history of their state. "My life has been a failure compared with what I might and ought to have done," he admitted to his son in 1873. "My great success—my book—was a boy's work, done before I came to the Bar."[32] A few years later Dana and his wife moved to Paris, and then to Rome, a city which he especially loved. Like his father, Dana ended his days in literary puttering, ineffectually trying to put together a treatise on international law.

Long before, at age nineteen, he had feared that such might be his end. He died in Rome on 6 January 1882 after days of wild ravings during which he shouted snatches of sermons and legal arguments. In the final moments, Sarah had to hold Dana to his bed, for he was struggling to get up and to embark upon one last great journey.

V

What did all this hold for the future? What prophetic patterns emerge from travel literature before statehood? Certainly an ideal California—a California of the mind—underwent composite definition: the elusive possibility of a new American alternative; the belief, the suggestion (or perhaps only the hope), that here on Pacific shores Americans might search out for themselves new values and ways of living. In this sense—as a concept and as an imaginative goal—California showed the beginnings of becoming the cutting edge of the American Dream. Geographically and psychologically, it was the ultimate frontier. No wonder it gripped the American imagination from the first! Spacious, dramatic in contours and resources, its unessayed beauty brought wonder to the heart—and in the brain engendered utopian schemes. Military men intended strategic advantage: ports from which to command sea lanes, sources of recruitment and supply for conquest of the interior. Men of commerce dreamt of ship-filled harbors, inland routes of trade, flourishing enterprises of fishery, farm, mill, and quarry. Expansionists took fire at the prospect of reaching the Pacific, of achieving the long-desired Passage to India. They talked of America as a continental nation, of spheres of influence in the Orient, of Aryan migration toward the setting sun. Men of faith hoped for a renewed Christian commonwealth. Amidst frontier suffering, they found themselves pushed back to primary experience—stresses of body and spirit for which only a saving Scriptural faith could offer symbol and mediation. Sunlight, blue water, cypress and pine-lined coasts made many think of an American Mediterranean littoral, a place where there could be health, outdoor life, gracious community in cities, a balance of physicality and intelligence, perhaps even an escape from the Puritan past.

When not blinded by racist hatred, Americans beheld Spanish-speaking Californians already living such a life, and they associated as they were able with the values of Old California. In any event, the Hispanic past—as a matter of history or romance—would always be an essential premise in American California's struggle for regional identity. Debased initially in sentimental legend and later in dishonest architecture; enshrined reverently in the monumental scholarship of the Bancroft volumes; surviving mellifluously in a thousand Spanish place-names which dotted the land—a promise lay hidden in and behind California's Latin past, a promise somehow identified with the region's sunlight and call to passionate living.

Whether or not these aspirations had any integrity was not clear from their haphazard appearance in travel literature. Nor would there be systematic pursuit of them until the frontier had vanished. At its most compelling, California could be a moral premise, a prescription for what America could and should be. At its most trivial it was a cluster of shallow dreams, venial hankerings which mistook laziness for leisure, selfishness for individualism, laxity for liberation, evasion and cheap escape for redemption and a solid second chance. All of it—ideality and possible disaster—was set in motion in the early travel literature, because from the first it was fundamental to the experience, somehow part of the region's imperatives. Good or bad, California never came easy—or without divided meaning. The experience of Richard Henry Dana, Jr., asserted that California could not unequivocally reverse history or void the past. Having to develop from what was brought, California could only be as good as Americans were capable of making it, and the American capacity for certain forms of bad behavior was already notorious. Seized in an unjust war, California began in tension. Conquest and bloodshed prevented a gentle gathering of new and needed associations into American consciousness.

Other discouraging patterns were also present, some matters of nature and fate, some the result of bad decisions. Disputed land titles, squatterism, aridity, and gold fever worked against the predicted agricultural utopia. Crude indeed had been Mexican use of the land, but, as Henry George was pointing out by the early 1870's, Americans also had ways to hold the land in bondage. So much had been claimed about putting Americans in fruitful possession of the soil, but such a pitiably small number ever found their way to ownership. And once there, were they capable of living as spaciously, as joyously as their Spanish-speaking predecessors? Or did they strip the soil like hydraulic miners—crop after crop of bonanza wheat—squeezing out in a decade all the land had to offer? Did their huge ranches confer liberation, or intensify greed? What quality of life obtained in those lonely white-washed shacks and bunk-houses which for so long constituted much of California's rural civilization?

The treatment of the Indians by the padres had often been justly criticized, but Americans introduced an era of systematic extermination which hardly represented a step forward. The Gold Rush postponed certain sorts of growth and accelerated others. Lansford Hastings might dream of Greek temples in the Sierras, but what would be more visible in the next few decades were hills scarred by mining and rivers clogged with hydraulic waste. San Diego, Los Angeles, Monterey, and Yerba Buena were indeed as American travelers described them, scruffy adobe villages, yet what sort of aesthetic case could one make for the ramshackle, false-front towns that took their place?

All such aspirations and paradoxes took their beginnings in the era of travel, were intensified during the period of conquest, interregnum, and Gold Rush, and emerged in the post-frontier era as the issues around which Californians struggled to know what they were as a regional culture and what they wanted to be.

2
Beyond Eldorado

Aside from the facts, now virtually part of American folklore, what did the Gold Rush mean—for its protagonists and for California? As a matter of social history the legacy of the Gold Rush was obvious: thousands upon thousands who otherwise would never have thought of migrating to America's remote Pacific territory poured into California, which in 1848, when gold was first discovered, had a population of barely 18,000. California developed as much as a maritime colony as a frontier—that is to say, within twenty years it developed a type and style of civilization, especially in San Francisco and adjacent areas, resembling nothing else in the Far West: urban, cosmopolitan, reminiscent in a provincial sort of way of the Atlantic states and parts of Southern Europe. At this time, the late 1860's and early 1870's, the era of *The Overland Monthly*, Bret Harte fixed the Gold Rush into formula and made it serve as California's mythic history. Harte depicted the Gold Rush as quaint comedy and sentimental melodrama, already possessing the charm of antiquity. As pseudo-history, as an uproarious and Dickensian saga, Harte's Gold Rush gave Californians a stabilizing sense of time past. Harte softened and enriched the raw present of what was yet a frontier—which he would soon leave for England—filling in the empty and perpetual Sierras with comforting memories of finite human comedy and civilizing human sentiment. Bret Harte gave California charm. Because he cast so strong a spell, his formulation, his massive fiction-history, dominated the imaginations of historians, animating and coloring—as myth will—conclusions squeezed from ponderous documentation and scholarly judgment.

Historians of provincial California—the annalists of San Francisco, Franklin Tuthill, John S. Hittell, Theodore H. Hittell, Hubert Howe Bancroft—also assessed an effect of the Gold Rush on the California personality: a permanent internationalization of flush times, an attitude of recklessness and swagger and competitive democracy. Was not the Californian, they asked (ignoring census reports and their own statistics), the Forty-niner who stayed on? In the late 1870's, a time of intense promotional activity, the Forty-niner, so recently Bret Harte's red-shirted rowdy, was recast as the Pioneer, the entrepreneur of the Far West. In the corporative 1880's and imperial 1890's, the time of self-congratulatory volumes like Bancroft's *Chronicles of the Builders* (1891-1892), filled fat with portraits and biographies of those who had made good, the enterprising Pioneer became the assured Capitalist, the Darwinian man of brains and energy, a little flamboyant perhaps, but always purposeful, who had made the Gold Rush serve the constructive purposes of capital.

However useful to the eras which devised them, none of these identities caught the feel of the Gold Rush as preserved in contemporary records. Moments of self-conscious definition are rare in the primary documents. Anxious to strike it rich, having risked their lives to do so, miners wasted little time in asking who they were. They would have considered Bret Harte's Forty-niner a fool and Bancroft's Pioneer a premature idealist. The closest thing to formulation they indulged in was calling themselves Argonauts in search of the Golden Fleece, and this was just another one of those simplified mythological overlays with which Americans of the early nineteenth century liked to gloss experience. And yet, like Jason's adventure, the Gold Rush was a heroic exercise of wit and will, and reference to the dawn world of Greek myth was as good a way as any to suggest that there was something primal and immemorial going on, a repetition bordering upon the mythic of ancient struggles of heroes, cycles of empire, and migrations of men in ships.

Feeling the excitement and the temerity of what they were doing, knowing that this would be the one great adventure of their lives, men wrote about it. They wrote an extraordinary amount. No other phase of the American frontier witnessed such a pouring forth of prose, a literature which six score years has yet to catalogue completely, much less read and assess. One sort of Forty-niner, like the poet and essayist Bayard Taylor, author of the classic *Eldorado, or, Adventures in the Path of Empire* (1850), came out of literary ambition, seeking the experience because he wished to shape it. Most Americans, however, wielded a more instrumental pen. In a moment's privacy aboard a crowded ship, lying in a bunk in a San Francisco flophouse or under canvas in the Mother Lode, they wrote out of simple human needs: to speak to loved ones, to pass the hours, to store up in rudimentary form what might in time and retrospection be given a better measure of definition. Some found the opportunity to shape and polish the scattered fragments of their youthful adventure. Others died, early and late, in California and elsewhere, leaving it all just as it had been written down, a rush of half-comprehended event.

Taken compositely, Gold Rush literature has some claim to theme, direction, and even—at its best—epic sweep. No one writer brought together the full implications of the material, although Bayard Taylor came close. The Gold Rush left little time for the symbolic arrangement of experience. In the majority of documents, experience was written down as it was perceived, raw, untouched by historical imagination or dramatic art. Sheer repetition of event, the inevitable result when there is no selective intelligence, makes Gold Rush writing a chore to read. What holds the literature together, however, and enables it to be taken in retrospect as a unified expression, is its collective return to primary experience. For a few brief years, in far-off California, the bottom fell out of the nineteenth century. Americans—and not just Americans of the frontier—returned en masse to primitive and brutal conditions, to a Homeric world of journeys, shipwreck, labor, treasure, killing, and chieftainship. No James Fenimore Cooper or Francis Parkman appeared to give the material its needed preservation, but, inadequate as was their response when judged from the point of view of literature, the Forty-niners themselves were not unaware that they were being reduced to the elemental. Moments of stark experience, recorded without self-consciousness and yet shot through with mythic power, filled their narratives: there were murder, death, the falling out of friends, food by a fire, gestures of voice and action appropriate to the mining camps of California—and not out of place in an epic memorializing a lost world and ancient heroes.

The facts of mining itself underscored the Gold Rush's return to primary experience. At great expense and effort, miners lugged out to California elaborate machines bought in the East. Virtually all of them turned out to be worthless. Some never left the wharves of San Francisco. Others rusted in the Mother Lode. Beginning with pick and shovel, Americans discovered for themselves the art of mining. Through trial and error they worked their way up through the ages—and then, in fact, advanced the art.

II

As epic experience, the Gold Rush was both Iliad and Odyssey. It was an Odyssey in that it was a wandering away from home, a saga of resourcefulness, a poem of sea, earth, loyalty, and return. It was an Iliad in that it was a cruel foreign war, a saga of communal ambition and collective misbehavior, a poem of expatriation, hostile gods, and betrayal. At first impression, the years 1849-51 seem more burdened with suffering than victory, more Iliad than Odyssey. From the day sails were set for the voyage around the Horn or oxen goaded on the first step of the transcontinental trek, the hardships of the enterprise were overwhelming.

Of the more than 500 vessels that left Eastern ports for California in 1849, the majority sailed around the Horn. Americans traveling thus faced a voyage of 15,000 miles which took five months—and which could take as long as eight—in crowded ships hastily fitted out and most likely past their best sailing days. If the Forty-niner could afford to take a steamer from New York to Chagres, cross the Isthmus of Panama by dugout canoe up the Chagres River and by mule go over the mountains to Panama City, then sail by steamer to San Francisco, he could cut the time of the voyage by two-thirds, providing that he was willing to take his chances with the cholera, malaria, and dysentery of the Panama crossing. He might lie moaning in his bunk the first weeks out, spend terror-filled days and nights in the Straits of Magellan, or in later months limp with sore joints and swollen feet; yet seasickness, shipwreck, and scurvy seemed but obvious hardships compared to the psychological stresses of spending half a year in a floating tenement, squeezed into dark and fetid cabins, eating bad food, and never being alone. There were signs of psychic strain: ugly incidents, persecutions, assaults. Somewhere off the southeastern coast of South America burials at sea began, of those too weak to stand the mounting hardships. Further on, off the southwestern coast of South America, a ship could lie becalmed for weeks. Empty sky and horizon, waveless sea, unbearable heat, not even the solace of motion—the monotony escalated into torture. Men paced the decks in desperation, climbed the rigging, or lay prostrate in their bunks staring at the bulkhead. They began to gamble and to drink. Some went insane and had to be shackled in a storeroom for the remainder of the voyage, their California adventure, over before it started, reduced to years in the Stockton Asylum or a merciful death in San Francisco. Grudges which would have been insignificant on land grew into violent hatreds and were settled with fists and knives. Tainted meat, wormy biscuit, foul water, the conviction that every corner was being cut in the matter of provisions, set passengers against crew. Passengers on the *Osceola* accused one steward of making their duff with dirty bath water. Unused to the customs of the sea, passengers found the captain a tyrant, which he often was. Committees of grievances met with profanity and the threat of irons.

The journey overland was no better. "Any man who makes a trip by land to California," observed Alonzo Delano in October 1849, after having himself done so, "deserves to find a fortune."[1]

Rufus Porter, a scientific writer, proposed the feasibility of constructing steam-driven dirigibles to take passengers to California at 100 miles per hour, and he went so far as to float stock in an airship company. Emigrants in covered wagons, family people for the most part, farmers and mechanics, had to be content with twelve miles a day. A migration now celebrated in national myth as the westering trek of the American people, the crossing of the continent seemed to those who walked it to be a weary succession of prairies, deserts, mountains, painfully measured out in the plod of hooves and the creak of wheels. One could die in a variety of ways: from fever, poisoning, the accidental discharge of guns, gangrene. A wagon could roll backward down a mountain grade and crush those behind it. An oak tree camped under during a stormy night, struck by lightning, could fall and destroy a sleeping family. Men, even good men, under stress, might resort to gun and bowie knife—and be shot or skewered by someone more adept. If one were dying, and things were bad for the others, he could be left on the trailside to die alone. Children lost both parents. Women sat sobbing on the side of the trail as men trekked off to reach water or tried to repair an axle before the main caravan got too far ahead. Gravesites lined the overland trail ("may he rest peaceably in this savage unknown country"), becoming more and more frequent along the banks of the Humboldt River, where progress became most difficult. Animal carcasses littered the Humboldt Sink, together with broken wagons, abandoned furniture, trunks of clothes, cases of books. Men quarreled and made bad decisions, striking off on erroneous routes. One diarist felt that he had witnessed the nadir of human malice when he discovered signs left behind deliberately giving false information about cut-offs so that parties a day or two ahead might not be overtaken and forced to share grazing and water.

Descending the formidable Sierras just ahead of the winter snows, overland emigrants arrived in California tattered, weatherbeaten, emaciated. Many were too exhausted to take to the mines. Many died from the lingering effects of the journey. When it came down to it, what had they and those arriving by sea come to? Further hardship and squalor. For all their swaggering names and later aura of romance, mining camps were foul collections of tents and shacks, and mining was a back-breaking labor whose discomforts included heat prostration, pneumonia, rheumatism, and hernia.

Again, there were the usual frontier ways of dying from diseases carried by rats, fleas, and lice, and kept persistent by contaminated water: cholera, malaria, dysentery, typhoid. (William Stephen Hamilton, son of Alexander Hamilton, having crossed the plains and worked in the mines, died of cholera in Sacramento on 6 or 7 August 1850 and was buried in a trench alongside other victims.) Exhausted from work in the mines and from a just completed sea voyage or transcontinental journey, miners had little resistance once they became ill. If they were not as lucky as Edward Gould Buffum, who found some sprouting beans dropped along the trail, they could die of scurvy, after a painful illness. A more distinctly Californian end was met by those mauled to death by grizzly bears. As mining grew more complicated it grew more dangerous. There were landslides and cave-ins. "Indeed, it always seemed to me," noted one writer, "strange and unaccountable that men should die in California—they came there for so short a time, and for so different a purpose; unless it should be thought they had gone twenty thousand miles simply for that."[2]

But die they did, by the thousands. Before they could even get to the mines, they died in San Francisco. "Early this morning the body of a dead man was found near our tent," observed Enos Christman on the evening of 24 February 1849, camping out in the Happy Valley area south of the city—"no unusual occurrence."[3] An obituary in *The Pacific* for 8 October 1852 dramatized better than statistics the nightmare which could be Eldorado. "Died," it read, "on Wednesday morning, September 6th, a daughter of Mr. and Mrs. Wise, lately deceased, aged about three years. The family came to California some months ago from some part of South America. The marriage certificate of the parents, found among their papers, is dated in Clay, Onondaga County, New York. On arriving here they went to the mines. Being unfortunate, they returned to the vicinity of Sacramento and commenced preparations for cultivating some land. But they were soon taken sick and weak and exhausted; they returned to this city, where they arrived some three weeks ago. A kind friend, learning of their destitution and distress, secured their admission into the hospital. They had been there but a few days when they wrote a note to him saying that if they were left there they must certainly die of want. Upon seeing their condition, he immediately removed them to his own dwelling, where one child soon died. Shortly the father followed, and soon the mother also, and this poor little sick girl was brought to the [San Francisco Orphan] Asylum, too sick and exhausted to be able to speak. Medical attendance was immediately called, and everything was done that could be to restore her, but she was too weak. She survived only three days and fell asleep. Thus a whole family was cut down in the space of a few days, and now lie side by side in their last resting place."

Incidents of lonely deaths fill Gold Rush journals, men discovered dead in their tents after being missed for a week or so from the diggings, or dead in their bunks after a night in a Stockton or Marysville flophouse. "It is an everyday occurrence," wrote Garrett Low from Nevada City on 29 August 1851, "to see a coffin carried on the shoulders of two men, who are the only mourners and only witnesses of the burial of some stranger whose name they do not know."[4] Delirium tremens carried off more than its share of Argonauts. John Steele, age eighteen, spent a night of horrors in a flophouse in the Feather River area in 1851. Drunken curses from a number of bunks kept him awake all night. One man lay shrieking and writhing in delirium tremens. About dawn he died. "A well dressed young man was seen, very drunk, lying on the ground," ran an entry by J. D. B. Stillman in November 1850 at Sacramento, "and a couple of boys we have with us took him to a shelter and medical aid was rendered him, but he died and was buried."[5] Each squalid death—and there were thousands—turned California's golden fleece into a vomit-stained shroud.

As if such deaths were not enough, men killed each other. A truly Homeric number of homicides fills the literature of the Gold Rush, a catalogue of slit throats, gunshot wounds, and crushed skulls. Murder, especially from the latter part of 1850 through 1851, became a way of life. Howard C. Gardiner witnessed eight deliberate killings, so horrible that forty years later he could not bear to recollect them in detail. In the course of working his diggings near Downieville, John Steele uncovered the corpse of a young man shot through the head. Both the anonymous man's death and Steele's grisly discovery were not uncommon occurrences. In a saloon at Nevada City, listening with a hushed crowd to a tenor, accompanied by the violin, singing the plaintive notes of Robert Burns's "Highland Mary," Steele found himself dropping to the floor as shots rang out.

Seconds later three men lay dead. At another camp where Steele was working, a miner in a fit of drunken rage killed his wife. He was lynched almost at once, leaving a one-year-old child where yesterday there had been a family. To his horror Steele found the atmosphere of violence infectious. He quarreled with his partner, with whom he had crossed the plains, over a minor matter. Within seconds both had drawn weapons. Luckily they both came to their senses; upon most such occasions Americans began to blaze away. "Yesterday one American shot another in the street," Enos Christman noted from Sonora in 1850, "and the occurrence was not noticed as much as a dog fight at home."[6]

Sonora, in Tuolumne County, was among the most violent of mining camps. For the third week of June 1850 William Perkins listed four killings: two Massachusetts men were robbed and had their throats slit as they slept in their tent; a Chilean was shot to death in a gun fight; and a Frenchman stabbed a Mexican. Two weeks later, there were six murders within seven days. Coming home one evening, Perkins, who lived on the main street, tripped over the body of a man stabbed to death on his doorstep. The gambling hardly stopped, he noted one evening, when a man shot another dead at the bar of the saloon. "It is surprising," noted Perkins, "how indifferent people become to the sight of violence and bloodshed in this country."[7]

In reaction, lynch law could be equally capricious and violent. An innocent French sailor was kicked to death in San Francisco as a suspected arsonist. At Weber in 1849 William Kelly saw "one lad shorn of the rims of his ears, and seared deeply in the cheek with a red-hot iron, for the theft of a small coffee-tin."[8] Josiah Royce would later comment at length upon how the lynching habit brought out the most vicious side of the American character. Certainly one sees his point when reading accounts of mob justice. At Weaver's Creek Edward Gould Buffum mounted a stump and pleaded with a mob "in the name of God, humanity, and law" not to lynch three Spanish-speaking men who did not know enough English to understand what they were being charged with. Buffum was told to keep quiet or he would swing with them. Horrified, Buffum watched as the three pleading men were hoisted to their doom. No wonder diarists speculated that the Gold Rush might represent a communal relapse into barbarism on the part of Americans! "Whatever depravity there is in man's heart," observed J. D. B. Stillman, "now shows itself without fear and without restraint."[9]

Men who had come in hope now slid into depression and defeat. Realizing, as most did, that they would not strike it rich, they brooded over what they had become and what they had failed to do. A sense of aborted effort undercut the continual attempts at rollicking good humor in Gold Rush songs. Men grew tired of themselves, tired of the ambitions and petty hopes which had brought them to such desperate ends. "Suicides, caused by disappointment," wrote home an adventurer of 1849, "are as numerous as the deaths resulting from natural causes."[10]

Was it worth it? Forty-niners asked themselves, beholding broken dreams and dragging about broken bodies, seeing months of digging yield barely a living wage, seeing men killed and going mad and weeping like confused children. Was it worth it? Even as he landed in San Francisco, Enos Christman knew that "thousands will curse the day that brought them to this golden land."[11] Even as they ascended into the foothills of the Sierras, they beheld deserted clusters of shacks where mining had proven futile, or encountered emaciated men coming down the trails of the Mother Lode, warning them not to waste their time, to go back. Young men, they came with the hopes of youth. "This country is no doubt a great place to give a young man a fair start in the world," Jasper Hill wrote to his parents, "as he can make money quite fast by being industrious and economical."[12] Hill failed, as did George W. B. Evans, an attorney from Defiance, Ohio, who left family and practice to make the journey across the parched and bandit-infested Mexican route. Hill's journal, kept in the Mariposa mines, is a record of one misery after another. No mail reached him. He suffered from scurvy and rheumatism. He spent dreary days confined to a rude cabin. He found no gold. After a year, he went to Sacramento and died. "It was heart-rending," wrote John Hale of such disappointed miners, "to see stout-hearted men shedding tears over their horrible situation, not knowing what to do."[13]

Those who survived did what they could. They dug for wages, did day labor on the docks of San Francisco, Sacramento, and Stockton, hauled freight—anything to keep alive and perhaps earn the price of a ticket home. In diaries and journals and letters they admitted that it all had not amount to much. "A residence here at present," Franklin Langworthy felt of his California sojourn, "is a pilgrimage in a strange land, a banishment from good society, a living death, and a punishment of the worst kind, and the time spent here ought to be considered as a blank period in existence, and accordingly struck from the record of one's days."[14] Alonzo Delano felt very bitter toward promotional writers and propagandists and all their exaggerated claims for the territory. "I think when the sufferings of the emigrants both on the plains and after their arrival is known at home," he wrote, "our people will begin to see California stripped of her gaudy robes, her paint and outward adornments, which have been so liberally heaped upon her by thoughtless letter-writers and culpable editors, and they will be content to stay at home and reap their own grain, and enjoy the comforts which they really possess, rather than come here to starve or pick up what would be thrown from their own tables at home to satisfy the cravings of hunger. The greatness of California! Faugh! Great for what and for whom? Great at present as an outlet to a portion of the surplus wheat, pork and clothes, blacklegs, prostitutes and vicious at home, and for the would-be politicians of the country and the ultras who quarrel over us in Washington."[15]

III

This was the Gold Rush as Iliad, as a disastrous expedition to foreign shores. Had Helen been worth it to Trojan or Greek? After the fall of Troy, Odysseus went home and there was a new poem, an Odyssey, soaked through with the consolations of sensation and consciousness which keep men alive and coping and, no matter what is suffered, able to affirm. The Gold Rush had its Odyssey, its times when experience invigorated and the gods were good.

Hope gave zest to the long sea voyage. "California, the El Dorado of our hopes," intoned the toastmaster during Fourth of July festivities aboard the *Henry Lee* as it sailed down the lower southeast coast of South America in the year 1849. "May we not be disappointed, but find stores of golden treasures to gladden our hearts, and make ample amends for the ills and trials of acquisition. May our families and friends be enabled to rejoice in our success, and all end well."[16] Pleasant hours were passed on deck overhauling gear, talking of gold and the second chance they thought they might be finding. Ships returning from California with gold aboard, which they encountered at sea or at anchor in the harbors of Rio de Janeiro or Valparaiso, intensified their expectancy to an exquisite pitch. Sailing at last through the Golden Gate, Americans drank in every detail of the Republic's new Pacific harbor, spectacular in its spaciousness, mountain-guarded and mediterranean. They were almost ready to swim ashore, to feel earth under foot, and to get moving to the mines.

The voyage had not been without its pleasures. The sea could be beautiful, clear and bracing days, nights radiant with the stars of the Southern

Hemisphere. Tropical sunsets delighted Americans with a range of color unknown in northern latitudes. Porpoises played about the prow. A sailfish leapt in the distance. An albatross soared overhead. Whales and sea turtles surfaced, then returned to unknown depths. Beauty, the sense of being in a world apart, the rhythmic rocking of the ship, prompted recollection. There was time for reading and for thought, for reflection upon past life and present purposes. Harold Gardiner of Sag Harbor, Long Island, trained himself to brave the maintop. Roped to mast and spar he would gaze by the hour at the sea and the sky, or read—three times—*The Three Musketeers*. He never again enjoyed a book so much. Gardiner and other young landsmen with time on their hands learned the craft of the sea. They helped the crew, hoping to pass the time and hasten the voyage. Standing the test of deck and rigging in storms off Cape Horn, they felt they were preparing for California. In one case, the captain proving incompetent, the crew elected a passenger to take command.

The monotony which drove men to madness could also be a challenge to ingenuity and cooperation. Men formed debating societies, musical ensembles, and dramatic groups. They attended lectures. "In the evening," wrote John Stone of Friday, 1 June 1849, aboard the *Robert Bowne*, "we had a lecture on Phrenology by Mr. Abbott, who examined several heads." Two weeks later Stone "went with a few others at the evening hour to hear Wm. Hamilton—the irrepressible dandy in tight boots and straps, wig and dyed whiskers both on sea and land—read some original sketches about London and its surroundings or suburbs."[17] Washington's Birthday, Thanksgiving, and the Fourth of July called for day-long celebrations, with sermons, speeches, military marching, and banquets followed by the grandiloquent toasts of the American nineteenth century. Men did not entirely lose their sense of humor. A group of young passengers secretly lowered a boat one night from the *James W. Paige* and simulated a piratical boarding. Another night on the same ship an excellent mimic walked out on the deck attired like the captain and in the captain's voice gave a string of contradictory orders to a baffled crew. Sharing laughter at such capers, talking together of the future, men felt a solidarity with their fellows. "We are fast becoming a united family," wrote one diarist. "It is easily seen that our common interests are causing us to become necessary to one another, and when the time comes to disband it, it will be with many regrets that we are forced to separate."[18]

The disruption of daily life for overland travelers was less dramatic than for those who sailed. Caravans of prairie schooners kept the organization and rhythms of village life. There were courtings, marriages, births, and there was more to do. At night men sat talking around campfires, planning for the next day, and women saw to the care of the household. Pleasures were less contrived than those aboard ship, more part of frontier life. "Sunday we had preaching by the Rev. Mr. Donleavy," Charles F. Putnam wrote home to his parents, as his wagon train rested twenty-five miles outside of Independence, Missouri; "our tent was crowded with young ladies. We set our table and spread a table cloth and they eat and drank as much milk as any ladies I ever saw set down to a table. We are now on a Prairie it is the most beautiful sight I ever saw they are filled with beautiful flowers and they cover over a space as far as the eye can reach."[19]

As they did against the sea, young men tested themselves against the continent. Lorenzo Sawyer, a lawyer from Wisconsin, felt that crossing the plains had expanded his imagination and strengthened his grip on life. Whether he found gold or not, remained in California or not, it had been worth it. "I have crossed the broad continent of America from shore to shore," Sawyer exulted, "have seen its magnificent lakes and rivers, have traversed its almost illimitable plains, have stood upon the Rocky, and other mountains, where the eye could take in a circle of perhaps three hundred miles diameter. I have been upon the desert and again upon the Sierra Nevada, have seen human nature under a great variety of circumstances, and in every stage of development from the most degraded specimens of the American savage to the intellectual and polished European race. I feel that I have a more enlarged, a more comprehensive view of the works of nature, a more accurate conception, and a nicer appreciation of their beauty and grandeur. I am sensible that I have obtained a more thorough knowledge of mankind, of their character, their energies and capabilities, of the motives and springs that govern human actions. In short, I feel that I am better acquainted with the world, my fellow man and myself, and I am thus far satisfied with my enterprise, though, in some respects it may not turn out as favorable as I could wish."[20]

Sawyer's sense of release, of excitement and high drama expanding his self-image and self-possession, was typical of an elation often felt during the Gold Rush. Tearing themselves free from routines of farm and city, from dull professions, stores, and clerkships, Americans threw themselves, indeed staked their lives upon, an unprecedented hope, a way, in striking it rich, of pushing instantaneously into the possession of human happiness. In time they learned better. The lesson broke some and deepened others. But for the moment it was liberating to be in pursuit of a golden dream, to be escaping the destiny of circumstance. Standing on the deck of a steamer as it sailed from New York in March 1849, Howard Gardiner, who had led an ordinary life, envisioned himself another Childe Harold, bound for adventure on a distant coast. "Adieu, Adieu," Gardiner quoted to himself,

My native shore
Fades o'er the waters blue;
The night winds sigh, the breakers roar,
And shrieks the wild sea mew.
Yon sun that sets upon the sea,
We follow in his flight;
Farewell awhile to him and thee,
My Native Land–Good Night!

Would Gardiner ever again have a chance to feel such a Byronic glow?

There was a gaudy freedom to California. "The very air," wrote Bayard Taylor of San Francisco in the year 1849, "is pregnant with the magnetism of bold, spirited, unwearied action, and he who but ventures into the outer circle of the whirlpool, is spinning ere he has time for thought, in its dizzy vortex."[21] At the Parker House or the El Dorado women dealt the cards, a brass band or banjo music played, and gold nuggets were piled high on the tables. One could take a brandy-smash at the bar, then stroll the crowded streets rakish in hussar boots, corduroy pants, sash, red flannel shirt, and sombrero. Costume was posturing and romantic. Daguerreotypists did a good business in portraits of young men in miner's dress. J. Douglas Borthwick, an English artist sensitive to social distinctions, noted that it was the gentlemen who insisted on posing in the most picturesque attire.

If there were quarrels, there was also a new intensity to companionship as men took each other's measure under difficult conditions. "There is more intelligence and generous good feeling than in any country I ever saw," believed J. D. B. Stillman. "Men are valued for what they are."[22] William Perkins met a former dandy, who on the East Coast had resorted to padded clothing, hair dye, makeup, and a dental device for filling out the cheeks. In California he discarded all of this, delighted to find himself a gray-haired, hale and hearty man of middle age. "Thanks to California," he told Perkins, "I have broken my chains. I am fifty-two this year and I don't care who knows it!"[23]

Under stress, men came to moral insight as well as to violence. Indians stole Charles Pancoast's supplies, upon which he depended for his life. "A few days after this," Pancoast wrote in his journal, "as I was walking up the shady path beside the River, I discerned three Indians sitting in the bushes on the opposite side. I raised my Rifle to shoot at them, when the thought came to me that I should be taking the life of a Human Being without necessity or adding to my own security, and I should perhaps regret the Murder. I dropped my aim, and I have ever since rejoiced that I did not pull the trigger of my Rifle that day."[24] It was true that Americans indulged in an orgy of self-seeking. It was also true that there were times of pity. "Right below me, upon a root of our wide-spreading oak, is seated an old man of three-score and ten years," Daniel B. Woods entered into his journal at Weaver's Creek on 21 August 1849. "He left a wife and seven children at home, whose memory he cherishes with a kind of devotion unheard of before. He says when he is home-sick he can not cry, but it makes him sick at his stomach. He is an industrious old man, but has not made enough to buy his provisions, and we have given him a helping hand."[25]

There were other experiences, ones which kept the Gold Rush on a human scale, kept it bearable. Letters came from home. ("So if you should not be among the fortunate," Ellen Apple wrote her fiancé Enos Christman, "be not discouraged but return to those who devoutly love you in good old West Chester and let well enough alone."[26]) There were Sundays when one sat before his cabin mending clothes, writing letters, smoking a pipe, or turning the pages of a Bible. Were later diversions ever as satisfying to Luther Melancthon Schaeffer as the evenings spent after work in Grass Valley with other miners singing to banjo, violin, and harmonica? Or the nights at Swett's Bar when the boys would gather together for a reading aloud from Shakespeare or Dickens? Did any other food ever taste so good to Howard Gardiner as the salmon he caught in the American River near Horse Shoe Bar and broiled over a fire at his campsite? Or the tinned turkey, sweet potatoes, bread, butter, doughnuts, coffee, and Bass Ale with which he celebrated in his Sierra cabin the Christmas of 1851? "The appetite one acquires in California is something remarkable," believed Bayard Taylor. "For two months after my arrival, my sensations were like those of a famished wolf."[27] Miners found time to note beauties of landscape, to marvel at valleys and foothills in the spring, "this now most fairy-like country, everything so smiling and beautiful, flowers of the smaller varieties by thousands."[28]

When they began to see signs that the Gold Rush was the prologue to lasting settlement, Forty-niners solaced themselves that they had been pioneers. Borthwick, an Englishman, claimed that the Gold Rush gave Americans their first opportunity to develop a territory as a colony in the English manner, as opposed to a frontier. The Gold Rush, Borthwick pointed out, brought to California not just wild people, but the cultivated populations of the Atlantic states. California blended frontier and civilization, laying foundations for a regional culture which from its inception combined qualities of the East, the South, and the Far West. As colonists, Borthwick believed, Americans in California had held to a civilized center and not degenerated, although in the early years of the Gold Rush social chaos posed a real threat. Even rugged frontier types seemed to improve in civility after a period of California residence.

Even without the comfort of seeing himself as a pioneer, a miner could admit that, although he had not made his fortune, he had at times enjoyed himself, had found something to affirm amid so much that was wasted and inconsequential. "I have enjoyed myself," wrote Franklin Buck after three years in California, "and lived most of the time just as I wanted to."[29]

IV

"Five years," wrote Prentice Mulford, "was the longest period any one expected to stay. Five years at most was to be given to rifling California of her treasures, and then that country was to be thrown aside like a used-up newspaper and the rich adventurers would spend the remainder of their days in wealth, peace, and prosperity at their Eastern homes."[30] Leonard Kip of Albany, New York (brother of the first Protestant Episcopal missionary bishop to California), and John Hale of North Bloomfield, New York, rushed home after a year to write discouraging reports. M. T. McClellan of Jackson County, Missouri, made his opinion known in no uncertain terms: "I do not like this country—I do not like the climate, and more than all I abhor and detest the society; I never expect to sow a seed or plant a grain in this country."[31] Others found themselves and their future in California, although the West was not to be the scene of their fulfillment. Having seen the elephant (as the expression went), they returned to Eastern careers. Lucius Fairchild, a seventeen-year-old clerk in a dry goods store, left Madison, Wisconsin, in 1849 to cross the plains. "I don't see how I could be satisfied to work for 12 or 15 dollars per Month when I can make that here in two days," Fairchild wrote home from

California.[32] He stayed six years, a miner, a cattleman in Siskiyou, and a businessman. He considered those years a time of emancipation and preparation, a way of making sure that he would never have to step back behind the dry goods counter. When he returned to Madison—in high boots, spurs, a wide-brimmed hat, a money belt strapped around his waist—it was to play a man's part. Fairchild studied for the bar, won promotion to brigadier in the Civil War, served three terms as governor of Wisconsin, represented the United States at the Court of Saint James's, and had his portrait painted by John Singer Sargent.

For Fairchild, and for others, California became a time and a place possessed in memory, an era when "life was robust, and the relaxing pleasures intense. Intellect was at high tide, and passion at a white heat."[33] Finishing his Gold Rush memoirs in 1896, just before his death, Howard Gardiner of Sag Harbor said farewell for a generation. "Four decades have passed since then," reminisced Gardiner, "and the writer who was at that period in the first flush of manhood, looks back to his last six years in California as the happiest in the whole course of his experience. No one can tell how dear the memory of that wild life is to him who has enjoyed it. How often his thoughts recur to it in the commonplace of civilized surroundings! Its freedom from anxiety, its dangers, its risks, its sense of animal health, its constant series of adventures; the exciting gallop over hill and plain, the thrilling explorations amid mountain gorges, all come back to me as I write this, and I lay aside my pen with a sigh as I bid my reader farewell and close my narrative."[34] Forgotten now are the eight horrible murders, the suffering, the failure to find the Golden Fleece. Like an aged Odysseus on a Long Island Ithaca, Gardiner, on the edge of death, has looked back upon experience and found it good, found it best, in fact, in those California years when it was most intense and most surprising.

"If a man comes to California and stays two years," claimed James Carson in 1852, "he will never want to leave it."[35] To their surprise, the Gunn family of Philadelphia found this to be the case. In 1849 Lewis Gunn came out from Philadelphia, where he had not been doing too well, and did even worse in California. "We made about half a dollar in the morning," he entered into his journal for 4 September 1849, discussing a typical day of mining, "and then we separated to try and find some better place for a day or two. I tried a place by myself but with no success, and this made me thoroughly heartsick. I thought of home, of wife and children, how they used to hang about my neck, and sit on my knees, and laugh and enjoy themselves, and how I used to enjoy myself, and I became homesick. Every effort I have made to obtain a support for my family since 1845 has failed, and even the bright prospects of the mines have proved a disappointment. I threw myself on the ground under a tree in the woods and cried." Gunn gave up mining. He settled in Sonora, making some headway as a druggist and a newspaper editor, and put together enough money for his wife and children to make the half-year voyage around the Horn. "I don't intend to call California 'home,'" said Mrs. Gunn shortly after her arrival in 1851. She died in San Diego at the home of her daughter in 1906, when she was ninety-five. In the midst of violence-torn Sonora of the early 1850's the Gunns made a home. When there was a hanging, which was frequent, Mrs. Gunn kept the children indoors. Lewis Gunn insisted the children keep up their Latin. Now and then the more prevalent life of Sonora intruded. "You never saw such actions as they have here," Mrs. Gunn wrote home to Philadelphia. "One man said Sonora is a perfect hell, and so it is. Today is election for mayor; I sent the boys to get me some matches, and they went by a house where a well-dressed woman was lying dead drunk on the floor, and lots of men there—the doors wide open so every one could see. In the gambling saloons are pictures of naked women, and women half dressed, dancing on the tables. I never saw a place where there was so much need of teaching and preaching and living as we ought to live." Amid drunkenness, brothels, and shoot-outs, the Gunns lived as they thought people ought. Amid the Gold Rush, they anticipated the next California. "Our free outdoor play," remembered a Gunn daughter, "our pets, the books father chose for us, the many simple celebrations mother planned, the love and spirit of co-operation which they put into our home life, gave us a very normal childhood."[36]

The legacies of the Gold Rush were good, bad, and ambiguous. In the experience of the Gunn family was a hopeful pattern. California, sought for treasure, became a home; or, as Josiah Royce later put it, a frontier became a province. Values of care and preservation, however, did not overwhelm the habits of exploitation. Leaving the mountains of the Mother Lode gashed and scarred like a deserted battlefield, Californians sought easy strikes elsewhere. Most noticeably in the areas of hydraulic mining, logging, the destruction of wildlife, and the depletion of the soil, Americans continued to rifle California all through the nineteenth century.

The state remained, after all, a land of adventuring strangers, a land characterized by an essential selfishness and an underlying instability, a fixation upon the quick acquisition of wealth, an impatience with the more subtle premises of human happiness. These were American traits, to be sure, but the Gold Rush intensified and consolidated them as part of a regional experience. Missionary ministers and educators did their best to counter it, but American California arose out of an enormous materialism. Its founding stresses were unalleviated by conscious ideals, although, as Josiah Royce observed, there was a pragmatic intelligence at the core of events, committed to sane goals and finer American purposes. Because of the Gold Rush this sanity would always be under suspicion; the outcome of California would always be in doubt. Ralph Waldo Emerson, exaggerating California's beginnings as "a rush and a scramble of needy adventurers, and, in the western country, a general jail delivery of all the rowdies of the rivers," could nevertheless see by 1851 a benevolent pattern of history being worked out. "But nature watches over all," observed Emerson, "and turns this malfeasance to good. California gets people and subdued, civilized in this immoral way, and on this fiction a real prosperity is rooted and grown."[37] Henry David Thoreau, on the other hand, considered the Gold Rush proof of the moral bankruptcy of American culture. "The hog that roots his own living, and so makes manure," Thoreau said of Americans in California, "would be ashamed of such company. If I could command the wealth of all the worlds by lifting my finger, I would not pay such a price for it. It makes God to be a moneyed gentleman who scatters a handful of pennies in order to see mankind scramble for them. Going to California. It is only three thousand miles nearer to hell."[38] Emerson's view or Thoreau's view—the vindication of America or the final proof of American aberrancy—the Gold Rush left California capable of being interpreted either way.

It also brought to the region a great number of Europeans who after an initial period of hostility and exclusion began to affect Americans in matters of value and lifestyle. Because the situation was so undefined, the American presence itself so recent, foreigners became more co-colonists than alien immigrants. With no industrial economy, developed as in the East and already in American hands, California made available a middle ground where foreigners and Americans interacted to their mutual transformation. The perception of California as a Mediterranean coast, developed in the travel literature of pre-Gold Rush years, was reinforced by an influx of Southern Europeans who added their presence to that of Chileans and Mexicans and began to order the landscape with villas and vineyards and launch red-sailed feluccas in San Francisco Bay.

Tragically and ironically, the Gold Rush further suppressed the Old

Californians, who in the first place had inspired the Southern European analogue. Between the conquest and the Gold Rush—that is, between 1846 and 1849—Old California lingered on. The American military, administering the territory as a conquered province, did not tamper with what they found. They enforced Mexican law and used the Mexican administrative and judicial system. American officers held key alcaldeships, but Old Californians were not without a voice in their own affairs. This interregnum period, in other words, formalized pre-conquest patterns. Annexation by the United States disrupted but did not destroy the integrity of Old California. How long this situation might have lasted is uncertain, but as long as it held there was the possibility that the old Yankee-California might reassert itself. Mexican and American might yet come together in the making of a new California. The massive influx of Americans during the Gold Rush made this impossible. With the approval, indeed the initiative, of the military, a constitution was drafted and California won statehood—all by 1850. There had been no time for Old Californians to consolidate themselves. Their participation in the new American regime grew more and more minimal. In Southern California, where there was no gold and where up to the late 1870's the American presence was light, they held on with something of their old style during the era of cattle on a thousand hills—but in the long run they were a doomed race.

The energy of the Gold Rush, the thirst for excitement, and the habit of speculation remained part of the Californian temperament. Americans seemed caught in a frenzy of schemes. Money-making became a fixed mania, justifying at times even Thoreau's bitter condemnation. In San Francisco, where the management of money was centered, the pressures of speculation, together with habits of fast living which had taken root in times of sexual maladjustment, put many a Californian into an early grave. The rates of alcoholism and suicide remained high and by the early 1870's were discernible social problems.

For all its lovely landscape, there was a harshness to life in California, an ethos of survival of the fittest which began in the Gold Rush and continued throughout the century. Exploitation characterized urban and rural life alike. It called itself Progress, but in the case of land and railroad monopolies and the consequent politics of corruption it made life miserable for thousands. By the late 1870's California was on the brink of violent social upheaval. A new constitution was drafted in 1879. A counterrevolution occurred, however, and California remained under the control of a land and railroad oligarchy, the various elements of its population pitted viciously against each other. Economically, politically, socially, the Gold Rush put California up for grabs.

It also witnessed an accrual of psychological associations. Whatever else California was, good or bad, it was charged with human hope. It was linked imaginatively with the most compelling of American myths, the pursuit of happiness. When that intensity of expectation was thwarted or only partially fulfilled, as in the nature of things was bound to happen, it could backfire into restlessness and bitterness. It could surface in a thousand forms of indulgence and eccentricity with which Americans tried to recapture and to vindicate lost hopes. California would never lose this symbolic connection with an intensified pursuit of human happiness. As a hope in defiance of facts, as a longing which could ennoble and encourage but which could also turn and devour itself, the symbolic value of California endured—a legacy of the Gold Rush.

3
City on a Hill

Ministers on the Atlantic Coast did not like what was happening on the Pacific Coast. A threat to religion and order, the Gold Rush emptied congregations of young men, tempting them halfway around the world to the corruptions of a profligate shore. Preaching against the Gold Rush, pastors turned to Old Testament analogues of Egyptian and Babylonian bondage. They pleaded with young men not to sell themselves for a mess of California pottage, not to abandon family and callings in an enterprise which imperiled immortal souls. Like Jacob, they asked, was not the East sending her sons to a captivity beyond ransom or redemption? Even if you returned a wealthy man, Elisha Cleaveland asked the young men of the Third Congregational Church in New Haven, could you ever settle down? "Will you not bring back with you a restless, morbid desire for change, excitement and wild adventure?"[1]

Many listened. Many did not, and so sermons of departure succeeded the sermons of condemnation, sermons in which embarking companies were exhorted to keep the faith and preserve their heritage. When parishers died in far-off California, the sermons of departure were succeeded by sermons of lament. He did not want to hear of sudden wealth, said William Thayer of Ashland, Massachusetts, mourning the California death of a nineteen-year-old. "Tell me, rather, of disappointed affections, of blasted hopes, of severed ties, of suffering, want, starvation, vice, death and endless ruin, and declare over this aggregate of woe whether gold is not purchased at too dear a price!"[2]

Not content to exhort at a distance, men of the cloth joined the exodus, determined to coax California into right paths. Old Testament jeremiads were succeeded by New Testament calls to missionary labor. California's ministers considered themselves protagonists in an era of apostolic challenge. No missionary to a pagan land, they felt, ever faced a more difficult call: to bring religion to the most profligate society America had yet produced, to cry forth Christ in a moral wilderness. Like the miners to whom they preached, these missionaries were young, for only young men could withstand the rigors of such a ministry. Despite the strength of youth, many broke under the strain, physically, psychologically, and—causing greatest stress—spiritually. To struggle against vice and violence seemed hopeless. Pitiably few, isolated, possessed of visions at odds with the scene of their labor, they saw themselves a brotherhood unbothered by divisions of doctrine or denomination.

The fact that so many died in California intensified religious awareness but gave to it also a certain morbidity. A grim parade of funerals—up to four or five a week in 1849—winds through the recollections of ministers. Obituary columns intoned a litany of broken hopes, parables of warning against Eldorado. Ministers lost their own children. In one ghastly week Doctor Jean Leonhard Ver Mehr of Grace Church San Francisco dug graves for four of his five daughters, dead from diphtheria.

Amidst such suffering, and amidst routine frontier discomforts, ministers went about their work, the record of their days surviving now in forgotten sermons, reports, memoirs, and collections of personal papers. They tell of days—for those with settled parishes—of morning study and sermon writing, afternoon marriages (Albert Williams of First Presbyterian San Francisco performed 150 weddings in three years), funerals, visits to the sick and dying, evening lectures. They tell of days—for rural parsons—of riding from camp to camp, arriving for supper with a faithful remnant, ministering to them, then trudging over to saloon or hotel parlor where men sat around a stove drinking whiskey, hoping to persuade a few to listen to a brief sermon. James Wood of First Presbyterian Stockton twice conducted impromptu funeral services in a brothel. Reports filed with sponsoring agencies in the East abound with the tragedy and pathos of daily life during the Gold Rush: murders, lynchings, men dying in bitterness, their heads turned to the wall, families separated, intemperance, insanity, adultery.

They were ordinary men for the most part, bent upon an extraordinary work. Some brought superior talents—Samuel Hopkins Willey of Howard Street Presbyterian in San Francisco, William Taylor of Seamen's Bethel, and William Anderson Scott of Calvary Presbyterian; Joseph Augustine Benton of First Church Sacramento and Bishop William Ingraham Kip of the Episcopal Diocese of California—talents which the frontier intensified and put to immediate use. One, a latecomer, Thomas Starr King of Boston, played a role of lasting significance to the emerging commonwealth. Great and small, in white-frame country churches or stately San Francisco Gothic, they all sought to lay foundations of religion and good order for the turbulent land to which circumstances and the Spirit had led them and which faith assured them might one day redeem their dream.

Detractors accused them of preaching to the converted, of exaggerating wickedness in order to assert their own importance. No one who knew the work of William Taylor in the San Francisco City Hospital or among the tents and shanties of the poor would agree. The church cared for abandoned children, protected the troubled and insane, relieved the destitute, and sponsored social agencies. In the mines, where social organization was tenuous, churches doubled as hospitals, schools, lending libraries, community centers, lyceums, and debating societies. Church-sponsored newspapers fought a continual battle for social reform. William Speer, former Presbyterian missionary in Canton, came to San Francisco in 1852 expressly to work among the Chinese. As editor of *The Oriental,* Speer broke his health campaigning against oppression of the Chinese.

The primary ministerial forum was the pulpit. Whatever else they were doing, in season and out, the California ministers preached. A number of sermons from the 1850's found their way into print. California ministers tended to avoid speculative questions in favor of pragmatic attempts to shape society. Opposed to the frenzied materialism at the base of California life, they sought to slacken the pace and to redirect energies. Reprimand, however, was not the only note. The California sermon affirmed the hope and challenge of the Pacific Coast. Joseph Augustine Benton of First Church Sacramento, for instance, preached a California transformed and redeemed. Descendant of John Eliot, the Puritan missionary, a graduate of Yale College and Divinity, Benton turned down a pastorate in Massachusetts to sail on the *Edward Everett* in 1849 as chaplain to the Boston and California Joint Stock Mining and Trading Company. When the company disbanded (as most did in California) Benton began preaching in a blacksmith's shop and in a general store. Upon the gathering of the First Church of Christ Sacramento, the young licentiate was ordained in March 1851, the first such ceremony on the Pacific Slope. From his arrival to his death in 1892, Benton was a leading California clergyman:

pastor, editor, professor (Yale awarded him a doctorate in 1870), hymnologist, and preacher.

As a preacher Benton fused theological and promotional expectations. His Sermon *California As She Was: As She Is: As She Is to Be*, delivered on Thanksgiving 1850, construed events in the light of a special providential plan. There was present confusion, Benton admitted, but the Gold Rush brought to California a Protestant order to finish the work of the padres. Serving God's plan, the Gold Rush had within itself the seeds of its own correction. "For the Lord your God is bringing you into a good land," Benton read to his congregation from Deuteronomy 8:7-10, "a land of brooks of water, of fountains and springs, flowing forth in valleys and hills, a land of wheat and barley, of vines and fig trees and pomegranates, a land of olive trees and honey, a land in which you will eat bread without scarcity, in which you will lack nothing, a land whose stones are iron, and out of whose hills you can dig copper."

It was this precious gift of California, Benton urged, this providential promise of sanctified abundance, which gave hope, which enabled men to look beyond present grubbing. Not for nothing had God held this Pacific land hidden from men's eyes until a worthy people might possess it. Not for nothing had He allowed the discovery of gold to speed its growth. Here, shining on the edge of the Pacific, facing the pagan darkness of the Far East, was surely destined to be America's City on a Hill, by whose example the Orient would be brought to Christ. Such was California's hidden destiny, her secret promise. "In some way the Providence of God will bring it to pass," Benton exhorted, "that California shall fully compensate for every mischief she has done—that there shall be an antidote for her poison—that for all the avarice, covetousness and cold-hearted miserliness of which she has been the occasion, she shall make ample returns of good; of good, in driving away superstition, breaking down the walls of prejudice and dissipating the darkness that has so long veiled and confused the minds of men uninstructed and half-civilized."[3]

In *The California Pilgrim* (1853), lectures written in imitation of Bunyan's *Pilgrim's Progress*, Benton expressed hope in the effect of a saving remnant of the faithful. Accompanied by Mr. Keep Faith and Mr. Antiquary—religion and history—Pilgrim tours Bustledom, inventorying evils and assessing spiritual needs. He encounters the usual unsavory cast of California characters committing the usual unsavory catalogue of California sins, but he also discerns the beginnings of a Christian counter-culture, men and women of good will, hidden away, working for social redemption.

Because Bustledom offered so many temptations, they had passed through the Valley of the Shadow to tested virtue. Pilgrim's hope that the saved might make a difference underscored the theme of many sermons. Even the most condemnatory Eastern preachers left some hope that a saving elite might turn the tide. Middle-of-the-road righteousness was not enough, exhorted California ministers. Given the conditions, churchfolk had to give good example in a bold, public way.

In Eastern departure ceremonies, missionaries were charged to sustain their ideals, not to become themselves castaways. Edward Ely claimed that the only minister he saw in California was setting up pins in a bowling alley. This said more about the circles to which Ely restricted himself than about actual conditions, but the figure of the renegade minister—salt having lost its savor—recurs in California sermons, a projection of inner fears that the struggle for righteousness stood a good chance of going down in defeat.

Despite disappointments, a feeling surfaced by the late 1850's that the moral crisis of California had passed. A note of hope, in fact, runs through all the decade: self-fulfilling prophecies of arriving order like Albert Williams' possibly premature remark, upon resigning the pulpit of First Presbyterian San Francisco in 1854, that "beneath all the ruffled agitations of society, and the strifes and excitements of the times, there has been a deep, steady undercurrent of morality and religion."[4] *The Annals of San Francisco* (1855) depicted a city of flourishing churches and philanthropic institutions. "Happily," wrote one annalist, "the long record of vice and immorality (the black pages of our diary) has a bright and noble counterpart, like the gold-dust among the muddy atoms of our own river-beds, that redeems our character from wholesale condemnation."[5] After 1855 the American Home Missionary Society (AHMS) found it unnecessary to send new missionaries to California, but continued to support those in the field. "Mr. President," Timothy Dwight Hunt addressed the 1857 AHMS General Convention, "I have come from the frontier, and were I asked, 'Watchman, what of the night?' I would at once reply: 'The morning cometh.' "[6] A religious revival swept California in 1858.

What a struggle it had all been! Samuel Hopkins Willey told his congregation at Howard Street Presbyterian San Francisco in 1859. Eloquently he recalled early feeble gatherings of believers, the moments of discouragement when churches burned to the ground or members fell away. Now, although the struggle for California had not been won, at least a plateau of hope had been secured, a plateau from which the California Pilgrim might look down behind and see stony trails conquered, cliffs scaled, and chasms skirted. 1859 was a time to celebrate achievement and to urge renewal. The crisis of the 1850's was past, but there would be others. "So let us go forth then anew," Willey urged his congregation, "in the name of our divine Master. Though few, we are entrusted with the establishment and defence of the gospel in one of the most important parts of the world. We are central."[7]

Material achievement, now that it began to express itself in terms of urban culture, to raise stately churches and to talk of colleges, became more trustworthy, more amenable to ministerial interpretation. Providence and Progress conjoined, William C. Anderson told First Presbyterian San Francisco toward the end of the decade, had brought about in California the prophetic beginnings of a modern utopia, a possibility of simultaneous secular and sacred well-being. Such a balance was always delicate, William Anderson Scott of Calvary Presbyterian warned Californians, but not impossible; California's rich resources, in fact, would seem to make accommodation between godliness and abundance absolutely necessary. Here would be no Sinai wanderings, Scott assured, but holy repose amidst the goodness of Canaan. Born in a Tennessee log cabin, a circuit rider in his youth and an Army chaplain during the Black Hawk War, Scott had been educated at Cumberland College, Kentucky, and Princeton Theological Seminary. Before coming to California he had served as Andrew Jackson's pastor at the Hermitage. A former pastor of the prestigious First Presbyterian of New Orleans and a former Moderator of the Old School Presbyterian General Assembly; an eloquent preacher, possessed of massive reading and prodigious memory; a published Biblical scholar, traveled in Europe, North Africa, and the Holy Land—Scott in and of himself symbolized the frontier arrived at religion, learning, and urban elegance. His acceptance in 1854 of a San Francisco pastorate authenticated to Californians an impending maturity, a coming of age. Like the impressive Roman Corinthian building on Bush Street which housed his flock, Scott (who kept a carriage and who lived with other wealthy Southerners in the antebellum dignity of South Park) brought to his congregation prominence, culture, and prosperity. His pilgrimage from frontier to civilization, they hoped, was also their own. On the lecture platform Scott celebrated the age of progressive urbanism he saw dawning in San Francisco, an Athenian age of trade and letters. He warned lest this age not also include a sense of responsible stewardship. Remember Achan in the Book of Joshua, Scott pointed out in one lecture series. At the fall of Jericho Achan seized gold and silver in excess of the booty allowed by the Lord. Only the execution of Achan, his family, and his retainers could remove Yahweh's curse. "Gold in its place is indeed a precious thing. It was made for man, and not man for it. The golden wedge must not therefore be converted into a golden calf to be worshipped."[8]

Let San Francisco become another Antioch, mother-city of churches, Flavel S. Mines urged at the dedication in 1852 of Trinity Church on Pine Street. Architecturally at least, San Francisco, city of spires, took the advice. By the 1860's an elegant ecclesiastical culture prevailed where a decade previously organization had been rudimentary and architecture a minor consideration. Young unknown missionaries had come out in 1849 to undertake an obscure labor. In the 1860's prominent preachers were lured at fine salaries from Eastern pulpits: Thomas Starr King from Hollis Street Unitarian in Boston, Andrew Leete Stone from Park Street Congregational in Boston, Horatio Stebbins of All Souls in New York, Charles Wadsworth of Arch Street Presbyterian in Philadelphia—accomplished men with advanced degrees, who wrote scriptural commentaries, revised sermons for publication, and made tours of the Holy Land. John Shertzer Hittell, an aggressive non-believer, claimed in 1863 that 86 per cent of all Californians were indifferent to religion, but the sermons published in *The Pacific Coast Pulpit* asserted that the believing minority at least sustained an erudite and eloquent clergy.

Called to Calvary Presbyterian in 1862, Charles Wadsworth of Philadelphia is typical of those later ministers who came not so much to a frontier as to a province. A doctor of divinity, a lucid preacher, handsome, forceful—beloved in passionate secrecy by Emily Dickinson—Wadsworth was a worthy successor to William Anderson Scott, in European exile because of Confederate sympathies. Whereas in the 1850's Scott sought to direct emerging energies, Wadsworth in 1868 could thank God for a city "not yet twenty years old, with a population as large and an architecture surpassing all that Paris could show after a thousand years of progress, and all around, spreading away in matchless loveliness, these valleys, where our merchant-princes even now delight to plant gardens like Eden and to build palaces to embosom a new social life and enshrine coming types of art fairer than the Greek."[9]

II

Thus certain citizens of California's Christian City on a Hill clothed themselves in garments of purple and gold, piled high marble temples, and appointed an Aaronic priesthood. It was a long way from the blacksmith shops and workbench pulpits of 1849. What, if anything, had been lost in between? Did this rush to elaboration signify the inevitability of two Californias, mutually exclusive definitions based upon class, the prosaic reality of those worshipping in white-frame and the aestheticizing ideality of those meeting behind façades of English Gothic? Or does religious history show one California available to all? One land of hope and promise?

The black church had no choice but to be locked in fundamental struggle. California offered blacks a measure of prosperity (their assets were listed in 1855 as near three million dollars) but no cessation of persecution. Southerners could bring in slaves, but the Constitutional Convention of 1849 almost forbade the entrance of free blacks from the North. They were prevented from voting, forbidden to testify in court, huddled into segregated schools, and threatened by a Fugitive Slave Bill passed in 1852. Church structures spun off self-protective associations like a Franchise League and a Convention meeting yearly in Sacramento. Hope and anger fill black utterances of the 1850's. Black leaders, so many of whom were churchmen, preached solidarity, enterprise, diplomacy, and—in moments when all seemed hopeless—defiance. "In one thick, mighty phalanx come," Peter Cole told the black Convention of 1855, assembled in the African Methodist Episcopal Church of Sacramento; "for we are here, a terrible host, ready, willing, eager to do battle, such as ne'er was seen, 'gainst the oppressor. We must teach him that the battle is not always to the strong. *The Rights of the Negro, or War!* We must, we will have it! Not another century shall catch us slumbering. Say ye not so, 'Where there's a will there's a way.' Here, in this Western World, let the work begin. Here let the tyrant tremble, fall and bite his mother, Earth, with fear! In the East, in the West, in the North, in the South—wherever he be—upon this sunny Indian soil, robbed from its rightful owners by his unjust hand,—tilled by the reeking sweat of Ethiopia's wronged children. Let him beware, for our DESTINY IS WITH US! The blood, the wrongs, the rights of our sires, all cry for revenge."[10] Charged with Biblical energy, Cole's call to militancy takes California as a premise. It is here, he suggests of California, that the work of black liberation was destined to begin. From pulpit and newspaper black leaders like Darius Stokes, Jeremiah B. Sanderson, Mifflin W. Gibbs, and Phillip A. Bell forwarded the struggle for civil rights. The Afro-American press in San Francisco, begun in 1855 when Gibbs founded *The Mirror of the Times*, was especially vigorous. In 1862, under the editorship of Phillip A. Bell, the paper changed its name to *The Pacific Appeal*, with the motto: "He who would be free, himself must strike the blow." Called by black historian I. Garland Penn "the Napoleon of the Afro-American press," Bell had come to San Francisco after a distinguished twenty-year career on the East Coast. A man of powerful mind and vital prose, Bell, as editor of *The Pacific Appeal* and after 1865 as editor of *The Elevator*, challenged both black and white to redeem the promise implicit in California.

Methodism, North and South (together comprising California's largest denomination), showed a similar sense of immediacy. Methodists were by nature a frontier people; their system of supervised itinerant preaching adapted itself easily to frontier conditions. In California a host of lay preachers and licensed exhorters aided the ordained ministry. They were hard-working, unpretentious men, these preaching farmers and mechanics, most of whom arrived overland by covered wagon and settled in rural areas. Their faith was Biblical and vernacular; their expectation close to daily life and simple things. There was a tang to Methodist personality, an individualism and a humor fitting right in with the flavor of the Gold Rush. They were common people whose burning belief raised them above the commonplace. Born in 1808 in what later became West Virginia, a country teacher and a missionary to the Shawnees, Lorenzo Waugh brought his family overland to California by ox-drawn prairie schooner as did thousands of others—except that God personally called him there. Lying sick from exhaustion and malaria in Missouri in the fall of 1851, Waugh prayed to God and was answered with a vision. "I had a clear and most satisfactory presentiment to my mind," he tells us, "that God would help me in an attempt to reach the Pacific Coast, there to seek for the restoration of my health, and for a new home; and I can say in truth, that there was not a thought of the gathering of gold in the New El Dorado connected with it. But the singularity of this presentiment to my mind, as I lay on my sick bed, was the seemingly clear view of the lovely Pacific Coast, a beautiful valley and plain, a lovely grove, and outside scattering big trees—all beautiful to behold."[11] Camping overnight in the Petaluma area on the way south to join fellow Methodists at San Jose, Waugh awoke to find himself in the exact valley and plain of his vision. He settled there, a rancher-preacher, an Old Testament patriarch of land and sons and cattle, convinced that he had been brought overland by the Lord to till the soil and to harvest souls.

Methodist scholars came also—but even here the feel was not of lamplight and library, but of battered books read by firelight in a log cabin. Scholarly, self-taught Isaac Owen ("costumed in buckskin, fed on pounded cake"), who as a boy on the Indiana frontier taught himself enough Greek to read the New Testament, had his books shipped by sea when he and his family set out overland. In San Francisco he helped William Taylor establish the Methodist Book Depository. As a pastor in San Jose, Owen was key to the founding of Methodist-sponsored California Wesleyan College. Chartered in 1851, housed in a simple brick building in Santa Clara, this humble institution (later known as the University of the Pacific) helped keep the idea of higher education alive throughout the heedless 1850's. While erudite Congregational and New School Presbyterian ministers, talking grandly of a Pacific Harvard and a Pacific Yale, met with indifference from their congregations, the Methodist people of California got to work and founded a college which graduated its first class years before the College of California in Oakland, sponsored by Congregationalists and Presbyterians, opened its doors.

In no one was the Methodist ministry of service more vital than in William Taylor of San Francisco. Born in Virginia in 1821 to hill-dwelling Scots-Irish parents, opposed to slavery; standing six feet and weighing near 200 pounds, Taylor was dispatched to California by the Methodist General Conference in September 1848 because of his courage, strength, and abilities as an evangelist. Aboard the *Andalusia* Taylor packed his expectant wife Anne ("my sweet singer in Israel, the partner of my youth"), their children, hymnals, books, and a 24-by-36-foot prefabricated chapel. "The voice of one crying in the wilderness," Taylor preached upon reaching San Francisco, "Prepare ye the way of the Lord, make straight his paths." For seven years Taylor, like John the Baptist whom he praised in his opening sermon, carried on a ministry of proclamation. He was a street preacher, a pastor, a hospital chaplain—and "Father" Taylor, friend of the destitute, comforter of those broken by Eldorado. Condemning no one, Taylor preached Christ's healing love to miners, prostitutes, drunkards, and devout alike. "What St. Peter saw *in vision* on the house-top of Simon the tanner," he said of his ministry, "is exhibited *in fact* in California, and none of them common or unclean, nor excluded from the covenant of mercy, but all are subjects of redeeming love and living objects of the Savior's sympathy and intercessions." Taylor had a special sympathy for the sailors of San Francisco, for whom he built a Seamen's Bethel, where he preached with the pungent vigor of Father Mapple in Herman Melville's *Moby Dick*. Because he was "a Methodist preacher of the old school" with a "mania for self-support," he refused to have a collection taken up when he preached in public, although his audience often numbered in the thousands. An excellent writer (the best, in fact, of all ministers working in California during the 1850's), he supported himself as a journalist. In lumber-scarce San Francisco Father Taylor built his home out of planks and shingles he himself logged and fashioned, taking the opportunity afforded by lunch-breaks to preach a short sermon to lumberjacks working in the Marin hills.

With true Methodist love of the circuit, Taylor itinerated about the state. "Ministers of the Gospel, in California's worst days," he tells us, "were permitted to preach in bar-rooms, gambling saloons, public thoroughfares, or wherever they wished without hindrance or disturbance. For example, I went into the city of Sonora at nine o'clock one Saturday night, not knowing a man in the place; and finding the streets crowded with miners, who had gathered in from all parts of the surrounding mountains, I felt a desire to tell them about Jesus and preach the Gospel to them; so I asked a brother whom I chanced to meet to roll a dry-goods box into the street nearly in front of a large crowded gambling house; and taking my stand I threw out upon the gentle zephyrs of that mild April night one of Zion's sweetest songs, which echoed among the hills and settled down on the astonished multitudes like the charms of Orpheus. My congregation packed the street from side to side. Profound attention prevailed while the truth, in the most uncompromising terms, was being proclaimed. At the close of the exercise many, strangers to me, who had heard me preach in the streets of San Francisco, gave me a hearty greeting, among them a notorious gambler, who shook my hand and welcomed me to the mountains."[12]

There was some deep strength in Taylor, a depth of religious faith and an empathy with California life, which enabled him to mount a dry-goods box in front of a gambling house with full confidence that he would at least get a fair hearing. Perhaps Californians were only returning some of Taylor's own compassion. "Of Christians," said a San Francisco rabbi, "the Unitarians have the best heads and the Methodists have the best hearts." The very day his steamer landed Taylor visited the sick. He was a daily visitor to the San Francisco City Hospital, a chamber of horrors where men, virtually unattended, waited for death. The groans and the stench were so oppressive his first day there that Taylor had to force himself to remain—to write letters for the sick and dying, to wash them, to turn them over in bed and dress their sores, and—finally—to bring some

William Taylor (1821–1902)

Heroic of heart and lungs, this Methodist street-preacher was the John the Baptist of the Gold Rush. At a time of greed and neglect, he stood for democratic responsibility and service of the spirit. He knew firsthand the dark side of California life, its desperation and defeat and lonely dying. He preferred to preach on San Francisco's Long Wharf so that the first thing disembarking passengers heard in California would be the gospel truth.

consolation to their final hours, as they died alone and far from home.

Like Methodists of the eighteenth century, he made his greatest impact as an outdoor preacher. His audiences on the Long Wharf, where he preached every Sabbath, frequently ran to 1000, and once at least, in Portsmouth Plaza, he preached to ten times that number. Intending "to throw Gospel hot shot right through the masses of every saloon," Taylor marched down to the Plaza, center of the city's casino life, for the first time one Sunday afternoon in December 1849, accompanied by Mrs. Taylor, who carried an umbrella as protection against brickbats. Mounting a bench in front of the El Dorado, the Plaza's largest gambling house, Taylor sang out in his rich baritone one of the fine old Methodist hymns. Above the brass bands blaring from within the casinos, above the raucous laughter of saloon and street, the passing of horses, the murmur of a Sunday afternoon in a crowded city of strangers, was heard Taylor's hymn:

> Hear the royal proclamation,
> The glad tidings of salvation,
> Publishing to every creature,
> To the ruined sons of nature—
>   Jesus reigns, He reigns victorious,
>   Over heaven and earth most glorious,
>   Jesus reigns!

Quiet fell over the crowd. Over 1000 men gathered silently before Taylor—and he preached to them: "For what is a man profited, if he shall gain the whole world, and lose his own soul?" It was a magnificent moment. Mrs. Taylor had no need of her umbrella. In a city where a murdered corpse or two was the morning's expectation, seeing before them a preacher whose courage and manhood they could not help but respect, men fell silent, remembering, perhaps, the Sabbath stillness of boyhood afternoons, feeling again the quickening of sentiments left abandoned on the Atlantic Coast. In the next seven years Taylor gave 600 or so such outdoor sermons, preferring the Long Wharf so that the first thing disembarking passengers heard in California was the gospel truth.

He brought to perfection the California sermon. Because faith made him assent to the holiness of human life, because in the profane facts of Gold Rush California he saw the sacred drama of the struggle for salvation, because he stayed close to experience, because he spoke from the heart, Taylor connected in a way unmatched by fellow ministers. Through the prism of his simple language, the Bible, Christ, and California lost their disparity and dissolved together into the light of Methodist vision.

His sense of timing and occasion was perfect; his love of the California context steady and sure. Six times he preached amid the charred ruins when the city burned. He preached over yet-warm corpses when gamblers had shot it out in saloons. He was a master at turning interruptions into jokes against the heckler. He preached a temperance sermon from atop a full whiskey barrel. He preached at the funerals of children (once it was his daughter Oceania, born at sea, dead in California), of a young mother not yet out of her teens, of a bitter miner who had turned his face to the wall. Young couples considered it an honor to be married by him. And he brought about through prior introductions many of the weddings he performed.

Taylor loved California, the spiritual heights of mountains through which he rode on circuit, the lonely repose of valleys he made echo with the old Methodist hymns, the miners who saw to it that he got a chance to speak. "Men here deal in realities," a missionary wrote in 1851; they want religion to be made a *great reality* to them, or they have nothing to do with it."[13] Father Taylor tried for such realism, and Californians were grateful. He neither condemned nor glorified. He took the Gold Rush as he found it and he tried in his way and according to his lights to leave men and women not so much changed as better off. He avoided promotional rhetoric because he knew too well the other side of California life, its desperation and defeat and lonely dying. And yet he sympathized with the enterprise, believing that a fine society might emerge on the Pacific Slope. He had moments when he saw himself preaching in vain. He had moments when he knew how desperately city and state needed his compassion. At a time of materialism and neglect he stood for democratic service and the life of the spirit. After 1856 the Methodist Church had many assignments for this indefatigable apostle: the Atlantic Seaboard, Canada, England, Europe, Australia, New Zealand, India, South America. In 1884, at age sixty-three, he was elected missionary bishop of Africa. But California was the scene of his first great labor. "It was a weak and delicate plant in Zion," he said of it, "but we watered and cultivated it, and it lived and grew, and is now quite a tree, bearing fruit to the glory of God."[14]

Taylor's sort of identification with the frontier differed from that of most members of the Protestant Episcopal Church. For a variety of reasons, the response of educated churchmen to the remoteness and harshness of California life being chief among them, the Protestant Episcopal Church in California was very autonomous and very orthodox. Neither in the name of, nor with the authority of, the General Convention, Episcopalians organized the Church of California in 1850 and talked of sending Doctor Ver Mehr of Grace Church San Francisco up to Sitka to seek episcopal consecration from a Russian bishop. They wanted a church which would be a product of California and the heir to apostolic tradition.

Ignoring California's assertion of autonomy but encouraging the tendency toward orthodoxy, the General Convention in 1853 sent out as missionary bishop to California William Ingraham Kip, a Yale-trained historian and scripture scholar, urbanely High Church in the Tory manner of New York. Eight bishops attended Kip's consecration at New York's Trinity Church. A surpliced choir sang, and as Kip rose to give his blessing the clouds outside cleared and sunlight poured through the stained glass windows. To observers it seemed to symbolize that Kip was coming to help Californians preserve in the raw Far West the religious and aesthetic values of High Church Episcopalianism. That he might find his mission trying became obvious as early as Cruces, Panama, where at an overnight hostel the drinking, oath-taking, cat-calls, fiddling, and ribaldry of California-bound passengers "was enough to convince one of the doctrine of total depravity." Encouragement came in San Francisco, where he found the congregation of Grace Church "comprising as much intellect and cultivation as I ever saw gathered in a similar assemblage." Kip learned to love the city, and San Franciscans in turn were proud of their gracious prelate.

Kip's ripe Anglo-Catholic aestheticism, his experienced eye, and his trained historical sense enabled him to see in California a rich legacy. He liked the feel of Southern Europe—the dazzling sunlight, the interplay of mountain, sea, and sky. Scholar and connoisseur of things Catholic and Mediterranean, he was charmed by what remained of Old California, and he befriended Spanish families in San Diego, Santa Barbara, and Monterey. In debating whom to send to California, the House of Bishops had felt that Kip was perhaps too scholarly, too genteel, for such a charge; and there were those who later thought him not fully up to the demands of administering a frontier diocese. Yet Kip brought a valuable gift. In an era of disregard he had time for the beauties of landscape, worship, and language. In an era obsessed with the fortunes of the present, in a commonwealth feeling itself so new that it put on its state seal the goddess Minerva, sprung full-grown from the brain of Jove, Kip coaxed Californians toward possession of their heritage. Amidst all their raw newness he made them feel that they were children of the ages. Besides—much of the

William Ingraham Kip (1811–1893)

As the first Protestant Episcopal Bishop of California, Kip brought the Tory manner and Anglo-Catholic assumptions of New York. An urbane scholar, Yale-trained, he encouraged Californians to look to the ages, while filling out their days in present labor. He considered the struggle for California a work of faith and time and patience.

criticism was unwarranted. Anyone who followed Kip as, perched atop an Army ambulance, he visited the still dangerous southern part of the state, sleeping by night in rolled blankets, preaching and confirming and appointing lay readers at scattered cavalry outposts; as he headed by stagecoach into the Mother Lode, road dust streaking his black frock coat and purple vest; or as, sweltering under the heat of the interior, he rode from town to town bent upon an annual visitation of parishes—such a person knew that Kip could well play the part of frontier bishop.

Above all, he brought his love of the Church. He envisioned her as an interpenetration of time and eternity. He fought to keep her austerely above the fray and committed to the long course of history. Filling out his days in present labor, Kip was content to await the fulfillment of the future, to let Californians discover for themselves the pearl of great price. For the Church, apostolic and immemorial, the struggle for California had to be a "work of faith, and time, and patience."

Each relationship to environment and experience—the black Church, Methodist, and Protestant Episcopal—showed significant patterns. Methodism and the black Church sustained a California charged with present meaning, in which personal salvation and social struggle were one. Episcopalianism maintained a denser cluster of interpretive symbols. It sought to soften frontier harshness through the mediating agency of a rich ecclesiastical culture; through an act of imagination and will, it sought to historicize the California wilderness into its potential garden. The Episcopalian sense of the Church, taken to extreme, was capable of being transformed into an ecclesiastical ultima Thule, offering not dialectic with the frontier, but a rubric of escape. Father Taylor perfected the possibilities of the Methodist relationship; Bishop Kip, those of the Protestant Episcopal. Experiential, commiserative, unquestioning in faith, uncluttered in intellect, Taylor fought for a California of democratic decency, a California saved in the existential present. Kip's was a vision of California redeemed in futurity through the recovery of history and the aesthetic elaboration of the present, a California of religion, learning, and art. Nourished in faith, borne witness to in personal action, neither vision was trivial.

III

New Englanders (Congregationalists and New School Presbyterians) wanted to bring to Pacific shores a Puritan commonwealth. One hundred and twenty-one of the 275 vessels anchoring at San Francisco in 1849 came from New England ports. Many contained cooperative companies, exhorted upon departure to keep to the ways of their fathers, to build up in California a second New England. Staffed by an aggressive, educated ministry, the New England churches, together with the New England Societies, sustained a sense of New Englanders as being destined to be the founding race of California. It was a messianic conception that went right to the heart of New England identity. Ever since the early nineteenth century, New England had sought to revitalize itself through religious and cultural conquest of the West, to authenticate values feared on the wane through vindicating them on the frontier. Founded at Boston in 1826 and by 1835 supporting over 700 missionaries in the field, the American Home Missionary Society spearheaded New England's evangelical effort. With its rapid growth California provided an especially exciting challenge. "A nation that is born in a day," said *The Home Missionary*, "cannot wait half a century to be enlightened and saved."[15]

Was this not a Pilgrim experience, New England ministers asked congregations, a righteous people's seaborne colonization of a wilderness? The Pilgrim analogue dominated New Englanders for a decade. "Sons and daughters of New England!" Timothy Dwight Hunt told the New England Society of San Francisco on 22 December 1852, anniversary of the landing at Plymouth Rock. "You are the representatives of a land which is the model for every other. You belong to a family whose dead are the pride of the living. Preserve your birth-right. . . . Here is our Colony. No higher ambition could urge us to noble deeds than, on the basis of the colony of Plymouth, TO MAKE CALIFORNIA THE MASSACHUSETTS OF THE PACIFIC."[16] This was no superficial hope, orated Hunt, but the logical end of a process of settlement and Christianization begun two centuries earlier when the Pilgrims landed. Like their seventeenth-century forebears, New Englanders in California should attempt a society founded upon religion and self-rule. While others took but temporary interest, let New England "lay foundations for ages to come."

The most ardent beheld an actual Christian State on the Western Sea. They entered the political arena on its behalf, fighting slavery, gambling, prostitution, lenient divorce laws, and—with the most symbolic intensity—the absence of laws protecting the Sabbath. "Ship a good old-fashioned New England Sabbath with you," ministers advised departing companies. Aboard the *Henry Lee* the injunction was obeyed. "The cleanliness of the ship," noted a passenger of a shipboard Sabbath in April 1849, "the neatness of the men, and the reverence paid to the day, speak well for Connecticut. Bibles, religious tracts, and good moral works in every corner and amidships, meet the eye. New England's sons, with all of her nobleness and dignity, are with us, and never will they forget the precepts and examples of their fathers."[17] In California, however, Forty-niners preferred such Sabbath rites as shooting matches, bear-and-bull fights, horse races, and balloon ascensions. Fletcher Haight, an attorney and a Presbyterian elder, argued that the offended Protestant majority (and here he begged the question) had the right to put such abuses under legal restraint. After a near decade of New England agitation, the Legislature passed a Blue Law in 1858. The California Supreme Court, dominated by men from the Southern states, promptly declared it illegal. A subsequent law, passed in 1861, had too many loopholes. By this time New England's campaign for direct civic control had spent itself.

Efforts in education met with more success. School accompanied Church in the New England program of settlement. Many ministers taught during the week, and New England laymen accounted in the main for the establishment of California's common-school system. Hearing of the discovery of gold, John Pelton, principal of Phillips Free School at Andover, Massachusetts, packed aboard the steamer *New Jersey* books, maps, school furniture, his young bride, and a shiny new school bell. On 26 December 1849 at First Baptist San Francisco, Pelton opened California's first free common school, promising a course of study as "taught in the public schools of New England." Within three months he had 130 pupils. Thomas J. Nevins, a New Hampshire-born lawyer arriving in San Francisco in 1850 as agent of the American Tract Society, drafted the city's organizing public school law and served as founding Superintendent. The Board of Education in San Francisco for 1853-54 was made up exclusively of New Englanders, all of whom, in the words of John Swett, "held faithfully to old-time precedents." In Sacramento John G. Marvin, a Harvard man, served as first State Superintendent of Public Instruction. The Boston Plan was made mandatory for San Francisco public schools in 1857: fifty pupils to a room, a room and a teacher to a class, a non-teaching principal, a curriculum including art, music, hygiene, dancing, and gymnastics. By 1860 visitors were favorably comparing the San Francisco school system to anything in the East.

Called in his lifetime "the Horace Mann of the Pacific," John Swett of New Hampshire incarnated New England's best effort in education. A schoolteacher with a common-school and academy education, Swett came to the Coast in 1853 hoping to build up his health before returning to study medicine at Harvard. Five months in the mines restored his strength but left him broke. At San Francisco he obtained a teacher's certificate, embarking at twenty-three upon one of the great careers of nineteenth-century California. From his election in 1862 as State Superintendent to his death in 1913, Swett—founding editor of *The California Teacher*, poet, essayist, schoolmaster, and administrator of the highest sort, who as the years drew on became a beloved public figure—vigorously advanced a New England philosophy of education: an education which, while based upon religion, patriotism, and moral precept, sought to remain sunny and open; which practiced both drill and embellishment; which above all insisted upon public support, open admissions, and (here Swett was fought) nondiscrimination. He thought of himself as, like California, a blend of old and new. No one maintained more stringent standards of reading, writing, and arithmetic; yet no one had more faith than this disciple of Emerson in lessons learned from experience. Swett was instrumental in the introduction of physical education and the performing arts into the classroom. He practiced what he called Situational Teaching, instruction in real life contexts: botany walks in the Potrero, lessons in marine biology at North Beach. He insisted that free adult education be available, himself devoting extra hours to tutoring a clerk in business arithmetic or teaching an Irish teamster how to read. The May Day Festivals Swett organized in San Francisco during the 1850's became celebrations of civic maturity. As they beheld their children congregate at Russ' Garden to recite poetry, to declaim, to dance, to sing, to put on plays, to spell each other down, San Franciscans felt the promise of the future. In gratitude they revered their Yankee teacher. As with the vines he tended on his Martinez ranch in years of retirement, John Swett cherished the children of California.

Higher education also concerned New Englanders—although it took a decade before the College of California accepted its first class. They could never make the College financially secure, and in 1868 it was deeded to the state as the basis for a land-grant university. In the 1850's ministerial scholarship constituted California's higher learning. "To bury one's self in books and studies, while human passions surge, and the storms of life beat, is often wholesome," remarked Joseph Benton, a Yale graduate who on the voyage out, while others prepared mining gear, completed a commentary on the Epistle of St. James. "Study," ran frequent diary entries of William C. Anderson, former president of Miami University in Ohio.

Before beginning the business of the day, Samuel Hopkins Willey, a graduate of Dartmouth and Union Theological, shut himself away with his books, bolting his door from the inside. Time so devoted to learning stood as a counter-definition to California's obsession with mining and commerce.

New England ministers repeatedly called for the founding of a California Harvard or a California Yale. Appeals echoed Harvard's founding statement, *New England's First Fruits* (1643). Like their forefathers, ministers urged, let California Puritans seek "to advance learning and perpetuate it to posterity, dreading to leave an illiterate ministry to the churches when our present ministers shall lie in the dust." Horace Bushnell of Hartford—on the Pacific Coast for his health—toured the State in 1856-57 in search of a university site, eventually settling upon a hilly grove and gentle canyon watered by Strawberry Creek in the East Bay. Until they came together in the creation of a university, Bushnell berated the Californians, they would "never become a people in the proper and organic sense of that term." The value of one out of every twenty cigars smoked in the State, he estimated, would finance the enterprise. Californians seemed to prefer that twentieth cigar, for the humble College of California which opened its door in 1860 at temporary quarters in Oakland was no Harvard or Yale—unless one was referring to the seventeenth century. As then, a handful of clerical professors instructed a handful of rustic youths in a centuries-old curriculum of classics, natural philosophy, and divinity. Morning chapel and Sunday worship were compulsory, and the mood was that of New England earnestness bent upon Pacific purpose.

In significance, span, and variety of endeavor, the life of Samuel Hopkins Willey, executive vice president of the college, might stand as a parable of the best aspects of New England in California. The AHMS asked Willey to go to California just as he was getting established in a pastorate in Medford, Massachusetts. He slept little the night he received their letter. The next day—a bracing but clear November New England day—Willey climbed a near-by hill. From there, like Bunyan's Pilgrim or Milton's Christ, he saw the world and all its glories spread before him: the distant chimneys and spires of Boston, dominated by Bulfinch's golden dome; Cambridge alongside the Charles, seat of an already ancient university; Andover, center of theological study; in the middle distance, including Medford below, the steeples and roofs of country villages, linked by late autumnal woods and just harvested fields. Perhaps because he loved it all so much, he made an offering of it. Perhaps because it all was so complete, he knew that California needed him more. Within a month he sailed from New York.

Young and romantic, he saw himself an apostle out of Acts, crossing a Greek sea to bring the Galilean news, preaching in an agora before a monument to the Unknown God. At New Orleans the dignity of the Bible gave way to gross melodrama. Word of the discovery of gold had just reached the Atlantic states. Hundreds clamored for passage aboard the steamer, the sort of people, Willey noted, who could afford to leave in a hurry. Heading into the Caribbean, Willey's apostolic ark had transformed itself into a Ship of Fools, packed stem to stern with adventurers who regarded him with amusement. Had he known that a Gold Rush should throw such obstacles in his way, he wrote home while yet at sea, he might not have come. "But if I can do a work toward good order and religion, in a new and soon to be powerful state, I am satisfied to go."[18] At Cruces, Panama, his party was struck with cholera; many died and Willey himself was confined by the disease to a hammock in a dark hut. The young minister grew to a more realistic sense of what his California mission involved. Not romance, but faith tested in fear and suffering, came to his aid. In the darkness, not knowing whether he would live till morning, Willey repeated and repeated to himself Psalm 121: "I will lift up mine eyes unto the hills, from whence cometh my help. My help cometh from the Lord, which made heaven and earth." By dawn he knew that he would live. Experience had deepened him. He would not whine because others shared not his vision. He would work. He would harbor within himself a counter-Gold Rush, a counter-California whose realization would be the labor of his life.

Anchored off Monterey on Saturday 24 February 1849, Willey saw the very hills of his Cruces prayer, California hills, fresh from the winter rains. "There was inspiration in the air," he remembered of that day of offshore expectation, "in the landscape, in the occasion, in the theme, in everything." Tomorrow was the Sabbath. Finding a quiet corner on the deck he set up a camp stool and wrote his first California sermon. He took his text from I Corinthians, which he hoped might signal his purpose in being there: "But we preach Christ crucified, unto the Jews a stumbling-block, and unto the Greeks foolishness; but unto them which are called, both Jews and Greeks, Christ the power of God, and the wisdom of God." Because he heard Hunt was already preaching in San Francisco, Willey decided to stay in Monterey. Living at Colton Hall, he taught school in

Samuel Hopkins Willey (1821–1914)

In scope and variety of endeavor, Willey's career as pastor and educator epitomized the struggle of New Englanders to civilize frontier California. As tough and flinty as the New Hampshire hills of his youth, Willey struggled to make California a Christian commonwealth. Because of men like him, the serious side of nineteenth-century California had the stamp of New England ways.

the mornings (simultaneously learning the Spanish of his students!), read what he could about California in the afternoon, and in the evenings walked and talked with Alcalde Walter Colton. He found Colton's love of this new Pacific empire inspiring. It restored some of the romance burned away by Panama fever.

Willey served as chaplain to the Monterey garrison and to the Constitutional Convention which met there through September and October 1849 to frame a state government. He founded California's first public library. He had been sent out from the East to be a pastor, and so it was no surprise that in May 1850 San Francisco drew him. "I fell into the spirit of the place at once," he remembered; "I felt the stimulus of its intense life; its breezes were bracing to my nerves and its excitement was welcome to my youthful energy." In a carpenter's shop at Second and Minna, in a district called Happy Valley, he gathered together a dozen adults and a few children. It grew into Howard Street Presbyterian, a congregation of Maine men who built a handsome New England church out of lumber shipped round the Horn from Down East. "They were people who came to California to live and make it their home," Willey said of them, "and to do their utmost, with all of like purpose, to make it a Christian state." Willey made Howard Street Presbyterian stand for something, the survival of New England values on the suburban edge of a wild frontier town.

When Willey resigned his pulpit in 1862 the city had expanded outward to Howard Street. The years had been full. From 1849 to 1855 he served as agent for the AHMS, promoting the interdenominational New England front. Among the founding editors of *The Pacific* in 1851, he penned many a crusading article. Two thugs, hired by parties angered at an anti-lottery campaign, invaded the offices of *The Pacific* and beat Willey up. Needless to say, he supported the Vigilance Committees of 1851 and 1856. In September 1851 Willey organized a parade down Montgomery Street of 100 of San Francisco's more than 300 children, to demonstrate that something had better be done about public education. San Francisco passed a free-school ordinance by the end of the month. Bushnell brought needed national prestige to the cause, but it was Willey who campaigned ceaselessly throughout the decade for the College of California and who, upon leaving Howard Street Presbyterian, served as its executive head until a permanent president could be found. Scholar-preacher who prepared more than 1200 hand-written sermons between 1850 and 1862, Willey had high hopes for learning in California. He organized college graduates into an Associated Alumni of the Pacific Coast, gathering them each June at commencement in Oakland for literary fellowship and a New England bean supper. His own publications in local history were numerous. Incredibly, when the University which grew out of the College of California celebrated its fiftieth year in 1910, Willey, age ninety, was there to receive an honorary doctorate. "Your life is a bond between our beginning and our present, between your dreams and its embodiment, between your prayer and its answer," President Benjamin Ide Wheeler told Willey, handing him his degree. As tough and flinty as the New Hampshire hills of his youth, Willey lived on until 1914—sixty-five years after he had first seen the rain-washed hills of Monterey.

To those honoring him in 1910, Willey symbolized New England resonances in California culture. He did not represent that more total New Englandism envisioned by the AHMS. Even in the 1850's there were signs that it would never come about.

For one thing, the Roman Catholic presence was too strong. Anti-Catholicism was an integral part of New England's mission to the West. In *Plea for the West* (1835) Lyman Beecher put the entire Protestant domestic missionary effort in terms of saving the frontier from Catholic immigration and Jesuit proselytism. Once administered by Franciscans, California would seem to offer the perfect paradigm of a frontier rescued from Romanism—except that by the 1850's Catholicism was flourishing more than ever. Irish immigration swelled the Catholic population. Irish diocesan priests and Irish nuns came out to supplement the local clergy. Italian Jesuits opened colleges at Santa Clara and San Francisco. Catholic grammar schools, an orphanage, a hospital, and a girls' academy were established. Two Spanish-born prelates, Archbishop Joseph Sadoc Alemany, a Dominican, and Bishop Thaddeus Amat, a Vincentian, presided ably over the episcopal sees of San Francisco and Monterey–Los Angeles. Accomplished, ascetical, schooled in theology and in the rich spiritualities of their respective orders, Alemany and Amat brought a high European style to the administration of their dioceses.

The Pacific and *The Home Missionary*, in tune with the larger Know-Nothing mood of the nation, accused Catholics of political plots. California's Jesuits became an obsession. While New England ministers struggled futilely to found a college, the Jesuits of Santa Clara in June 1857 awarded California's first bachelor's degree. Protestant families began to send their sons to the Jesuits at Santa Clara and Saint Ignatius College in San Francisco and their daughters to the Notre Dame Sisters at San Jose. The Society of Jesus planned a take-over of California, Timothy Dwight Hunt warned the AHMS, although Jesuit intentions could be thwarted if Protestant Zion were half aware of the danger. Protestant agitation led to the repeal in 1855 of a law, passed in 1853, that granted state assistance to parochial schools. Against the wishes of Catholics, San Francisco's New England-controlled Board of Education enforced daily reading of the Bible in public schools and the teaching of a Protestant-flavored morality. Since such lessons were useful toward "the harmonizing of our heterogeneous population into one people," it was claimed they did not violate separation of Church and State.

Anti-Catholic and anti-Irish feeling seethed through the Vigilance committees of 1851 and 1856. Irish immigrants from Australia and New York were branded wholesale as a criminal class. Yankees and Southerners put aside their quarrels, including the slavery issue, to unite behind the Know-Nothing party and the Vigilance Committee of 1856 (an organization redolent of Masonry) in the fight against growing Irish political power. A Know-Nothing Citizens' Reform Ticket defeated the Irish machine in the San Francisco election of 1854, even to the point of getting one mayoralty candidate dropped from the ballot because he was Roman Catholic. Know-Nothing candidates took control of Stockton, Marysville, and Sacramento. In 1855 there was a Know-Nothing sweep of statewide offices, including the governorship.

Anti-foreign reformism on the part of outraged businessmen accounted for both Know-Nothing and Vigilance movements. New England ministers fanned the flames of what they considered a Cromwellian cleansing of the body politic. Ambiguity, if not outright hypocrisy, characterized efforts to justify the mob action of 1851. "Not while I stand in the sacred desk will I advocate mob-law," Timothy Dwight Hunt protested, and all the while he did his best to upgrade with supportive sacred and profane theory the lynching in Portsmouth Plaza of a petty thief by a drunken mob. "The respectability of the names," he said of those authorizing the hanging, "relieved the community of all fear of rash and mob-like procedure."[19] Frustrated in their efforts to usher in the Christian polity of their dreams, New England ministers had a fatally uncritical attraction to direct civil action. The highly organized, quasi-military San Francisco Committee of 1856, with its ruling directorate and drilled armed patrols, gave vent to fantasies of a Cromwellian Revolution of the Saints. Ministers rushed to the Committee's aid with the solace of theological theory.

When James P. Casey, an Irish politician incensed at having his Sing

Sing past brought to light, assassinated the journalist-reformer, James King of William, on the streets of San Francisco, the revolution found its martyr. In funeral eulogies across the state ministers shifted the pattern of King of William's California career—a progress from failed banker to crusading editor—from possible bitterness at having gone bankrupt to a conversion from the pursuit of wealth to the struggle for righteousness. A vague member of the First Unitarian parish, King of William, after martyrdom, seemed in New England eyes a Puritan pamphleteer born anew, dying a death right out of Foxe's *Book of Martyrs.* Beware lest your Puritan Commonwealth become a Jacobin Reign of Terror, Horace Bushnell, essentially an outsider, told the Congregational parish of San Francisco during the height of Vigilance Committee power. But warnings like Bushnell's and that of Joseph Augustine Benton in Sacramento ran counter to the general *Walpurgisnacht* of pulpit wrath. "The pulpit and the press," Timothy Dwight Hunt reported to the AHMS, "with scarcely an exception advocate the cleansing now in process and bid the Committee godspeed; and the *people,* from the snows to the sea, say every day in thunder tones, Amen!"[20]

Amen was soon said to the entire movement. The San Francisco Committee disbanded itself in August 1856 after a parade of its 6000-man New Model Army. Similar disestablishments occurred throughout the state. A businessmen's insurrection had intrinsic limits of scope and ambition, and Know-Nothingism could not long remain a power in a commonwealth filled with Catholics and foreign-born. In the elections of 1857 it went down in defeat. Political reform and a religious revival followed the upheavals, but what in the spring and summer of 1856 appeared as the dawn of the Commonwealth of the Saints turned out to be the sunset of a dying hope. Taken as a concerted program, the New England effort fell apart. Its broad front collapsed and denominational ecclesiasticism replaced the interdenominational attempt to gain control of an emerging society. By 1860 the New School Presbyterian Synod and the Congregationalist General Association were beginning to drift apart. In 1863 Presbyterians withdrew support from *The Pacific* and in 1868 the College of California was turned over to the state. Timothy Dwight Hunt, first practicing Protestant clergyman in California, returned to the East in January 1857, dispirited by the instability and materialism he had failed to subdue. On the same steamer was Horace Bushnell. When, upon his return to the East, Bushnell wrote of California, it was not to call for a Christian Commonwealth, but to describe a province of many peoples where churchfolk might find, not dominance, but a chance for private fulfillment. In California a fine ecclesiastical culture obtained, but it was not the Puritan City on a Hill.

New England's conquest of California had been made in other terms—in terms of lives whose works and days had been crucial to the making of California. A significant part of the developing Californian identity would, because of them, always belong to New England. In the next generation, a Californian of New England ancestry, John W. Buckham, a minister and a professor of divinity, claimed much for the Puritan legacy. "Here are men and women," he wrote of the generation ministered to by Benton and Willey, "who in the midst of a people in the main sordid and self-seeking cherished an ideal of the true California, men of vision and high purpose, who were here not to exploit but to appreciate, not to dig but to build, not to get but to give, not to carry something away but to leave something behind. They alone saw the highest values of California,—not money values, but social values, happiness values, religious values. The future belongs to them. California moves toward their ideals, slowly but surely. Not to furnish gold to such as rifle her hills and are gone, not to yield gain to such as would extract the virtues of her rich soil and then abandon it, not even to restore health to such as would bask in her sunshine for a few months and then depart; but to sustain a great, happy, healthful, beauty-loving, educated, brotherly, reverent people,—this is the true aim and end of California. A great motive and impulse are bequeathed to us. In this smiling, sumptuous, splendid domain of God's favor, with such deeds and such memories back of us, we may go forward, conscious that we are in true succession of Pilgrim and Puritan,—behind us a great consecration, before us a great opportunity."[21]

Buckham was overstating the case. In those frontier years others also had visions of what California should be, non-New Englanders like Kip and Taylor and a host of the unremembered upright. Old Californians, the French, the Irish, the Italian Jesuits might look with irony, if not hostility, at American Protestant insistence that it had been exclusively responsible for the making of California. They too felt—and in feeling, enriched—California imperatives. They too wanted a California of enduring value. Protestant presumptions to exclusive virtue were often accompanied by arrogant acts of exclusion, as the minorities of California well knew. Yet despite all this there was a certain validity to Buckham's claim. Perhaps to no one more than to these New England ministers mattered the shaping of reality by vision, the subsumption of the City of Man by the City of

God. Charging California with the energy of their quest, the inaccessibility of their ideal, they gave it a symbolic value it would never lose. Here on Pacific shores might be realized that ideal polity described by Governor John Winthrop of Massachusetts Bay, that City on a Hill, ever haunting the American imagination: so New Englanders on the California frontier dreamed and struggled. Having once been endowed with such hopes, having once been the arena of such a salvation history, California could never lose its promise, never fully succumb to the prosaic. No wonder that, as two generations later Buckham looked back, he found himself still stirred by that early expectation.

IV

New England—and the pulpit in general—achieved a measure of victory in the popularity and influence of a fiery young Unitarian preacher from Boston, Thomas Starr King. King died in 1864 at the age of thirty-nine from diphtheria and pneumonia, after four short years on the Coast, yet in his California career were fulfilled the aspirations of a ministerial generation.

The First Unitarian Church of San Francisco, to which King came in 1860, offered the only Unitarian pulpit west of St. Louis. It was a distinguished but ill-fated post. A succession of learned New Englanders (three out of five holding Harvard degrees) were called in the 1850's, but no one seemed able to take hold. Two pastors died of illnesses compounded by frontier hardships. Two others could not adjust to San Francisco. Knowing that only a preacher of talent, stamina, and reputation could vitalize their Society—indeed could pay off their debt—the Unitarians of San Francisco extended a call to the dynamic young pastor of the Hollis Street Church in Boston.

He could not accept, King wrote back. He was neither heroic nor talented enough as a preacher to face such a task. He could not sacrifice the security he had worked so hard to attain. Prevented from attending Harvard when the death of his father, a Universalist minister, forced him into a clerkship at the Charlestown Navy Yard to support five younger brothers and sisters, King had educated himself, making a university of Boston in the 1840's. He read voraciously in borrowed books. He tutored himself in Latin, Greek, French, Spanish, Italian, and German. He listened to the best preachers of the day, attended lectures at the Lowell Institute, and sought out private tutoring in divinity. By twenty-one King was accomplished enough to be elected to his father's Charlestown pulpit. The Hollis Street Church called him in 1848. By 1850 his reputation was such that he was invited to preach at Harvard and was awarded an honorary Master of Arts. King worked hard for his success and he enjoyed it. Fond of society, he cultivated the prominent, and in one sense they accepted him. But only so far. Describing himself with defensive irony as "a graduate of the Charlestown Navy Yard," King knew the limits of his acceptance. Emerson might have him to tea and spend a morning in close talk, but a New York parish offered to call King only on the condition that he attend Harvard for a year—which he indignantly refused. "Any attempt of his to assume the position of a leader of public opinion in Boston," a friend of King's tells us, "would have been crushed by the mere superciliousness of the educated and fashionable classes. All that would be necessary to teach him his subordinate position would have been a few blandly ironical sneers, a little lifting of the eyebrows, a slight shrugging of the shoulders, and, in the clubs, an expression of apathetic wonder as to who was the Unitarian parson who talked in such 'tall' language."[22]

By his early thirties, King had risen about as far as he could go. And so, despite the risks of California, despite objections raised in earlier letters of refusal, despite the comforts of his fixed but acceptable status as a self-educated preacher and lecturer, he accepted the San Francisco call. He could, he thought, count for more on the Pacific Coast.

King was right. On the voyage out he was besieged by passengers claiming letters of introduction. More than twenty women at one time or another applied to be seated next to him at the captain's table. With a droll detachment which would have scandalized some of his parishioners he wittily described to Randolph Ryers, a New York importer and a lifelong friend, the success he was having on the Coast. His sermons and lectures were thronged. His congregation presented him with a silver tea service and jewelry for Mrs. King. Businessmen guided his investments in Washoe silver, making him financially secure for the first time in his life. The Frémonts entertained him at their home, where he met young Bret Harte and Herman Melville (who had a letter of introduction to King) and where Mrs. Frémont began a move to put King in the United States Senate.

Although King took a boyish delight in doing well, he was more than a Charlestown clerk on the make. He indulged in playful irony as a means of self-defense, but he took seriously his role as a Unitarian clergyman of Boston, an advocate of Liberal Christianity and highmindedness. King's profession was the one safe anchorage of his life, the means by which he harmonized and made effective his contradictory impulses of insecurity and ambition, triviality and depth, skepticism and faith, ironic detachment and desire for social service. As Thomas Starr King of Boston's Hollis Street Church he found an identity and an objectivity of valued effort. Now California challenged that consolidation. Was it sound? Or was it only a hothouse plant in the solarium of literary Boston? "I do think we are unfaithful in huddling so closely around the cosy stove of civilization in this blessed Boston," King argued with himself, "and I, for one, am ready to go out into the cold and see if I am good for anything." He put his resignation before his Hollis Street congregation in terms of his duty to help lay moral foundations for the California experiment, where "civilization is weaving out of the most various and in many respects the best threads of the American character."[23] His great ambition, he wrote Ryers, was to do something for California.

Duty—and ambition—brought King to California, but he pined for New England. Even at the height of his California fame he intended eventually to return to Boston after study in Germany, to write a treatise in support of Liberal Christianity. Confessions of homesickness fill his letters from California. He found it hard to adjust to San Francisco. Its compromised atmosphere of elegance and frontier ramshackle, its winds and stinging sands, its wet fogs and capricious chilliness irritated him and depressed his wife. Mrs. King—Julia Wiggin of East Boston—spent the voyage out in sick-bed seclusion. She was frail and ill-tempered, "an ardent hater of this city, coast, state and slope." In contrast to Mrs. Jessie Benton Frémont ("a superb woman"), King rarely mentioned his wife in his letters, except to say that she was prostrate with this or that ailment. Ascending the pulpit on 29 April 1860, his first day in San Francisco, King was encouraged by the packed and expectant congregation, but he felt heartsick at the thought of what he had left behind in the East. "People are very kind," he wrote Ryers. "But it isn't New England. I wonder why I came."[24]

King came to work and work he did, with an expense of energy which weakened his system. He preached to thronged congregations in San Francisco and across the state. He prepared a catechism for Sunday schools. He visited hospitals and founded a Shakespeare club. He lectured up and down the Pacific Coast—as far north as British Columbia. He threw himself into a variety of social causes. California's freedom from caste enabled King to become a personage of the first rank, and he rewarded the state with a flatteringly high level of public discourse. He soon came to stand in the minds of Californians as the very symbol of religion, culture, and the greater scene beyond the Far West. San Franciscans were proud of King's eloquence, his ties with literary Boston, his line of ministerial descent in the church of Emerson, Edward Everett, William Ellery Channing, and Theodore Parker. The very fact that King seemed to be thriving in California was a comforting sign of provincial maturity. That he was self-educated, that he has risen in the learned Unitarian ministry without benefit of an earned degree, reinforced the assumption that talent, not birth or background, was what counted. In four short years King became California's man for all seasons, a hero and prophet of the Pacific commonwealth.

Seeing King off in New York, Horace Greeley, himself just returned from the Pacific Slope, told him that whatever disappointments were in store, the beauty of California would never disappoint. As the steamer delivering him to his new destiny sailed through the Golden Gate, King rejoiced in the warmth of the April day, the white-capped blue of the Bay, and, crowding the shore, the hills of Marin banked in wildflowers. Arriving at their lodgings, the Kings were greeted with baskets of strawberries and roses. A lover of gardens, King was delighted by the garden of California. In his letters he mentioned the jasmine and honeysuckle that covered the trellises of San Francisco cottages; the fuchsias that swayed in the breeze as he walked at twilight with Mrs. Frémont through a garden of roses and rhododendrons. Geraniums greeted his sight as, putting down his pen, he gazed out his study window; strawberries, peaches, pears, and grapes graced his table; and he could not get over the giant vegetables piled high in such nonchalant abundance on the open stalls of the marketplace. Sensitive to grandeur, to the sublime, he was thrilled by the wild scenery of northern California through which he traveled by stagecoach in the course of lecturing—forests of pine and Sequoia lifting themselves to a height in itself on the verge of religious metaphor. Addressing the San Joaquin Valley Agricultural Society, he invoked Scripture and Vergil's *Georgics*. He talked of California as a sun-drenched Canaan to be cultivated by the godly, as a landscape of Italian promise to be given the cherishment of history.

He wanted to interpret the Sierras—especially the Yosemite—in a book similar to the one he had written about the White Hills of New Hampshire. King's conception of nature as a direct expression of the Divine Mind was part and parcel of that Puritan New England passion to sanctify the hostile wilderness by discovering in it the living God. The deepest understanding of nature, wrote King, comes from spiritual insight. "Nature is hieroglyphic. Each prominent fact in it is like a type: its final use is to set up one letter of the infinite alphabet, and help us, by its connections, to read some statement or statute applicable to the conscious world."[25] What a magnificent revelation, then, awaited construal of the Sierras! What communion with the Creator! He spoke movingly of that day in spring 1860 when, sailing up the Sacramento River on a steamer, he first beheld the Sierras in the eastern distance. It was, he reported, "like a vision from another world, like the street and wall of the New Jerusalem." In July 1860 he made the rugged inland journey to Yosemite Valley. He was overwhelmed. Entering the valley floor, he felt "that which the Israelites felt amid the passes of Sinai when the Divine glory was on the mount." As a direct expression of the Divine Mind—direct because each cliff and fall was the present result of an on-going act of creation—the Yosemite seemed to King a revelation as compelling as Holy Writ. It was California's scripture of stone, calling to spiritual greatness. "So many of us there are who have no majestic landscapes for the heart—no grandeurs in the inner life. We live on the flats. We live in a moral country, which is dry, droughty, barren. We look up to no heights whence shadow falls and streams flow singing. We have no great hopes. We have no sense of Infinite guard and care. We have no sacred and cleansing fears. We have no consciousness of Divine, All-enfolding Love. We may make an outward visit to the Sierras, but there are no Yosemites in the soul."[26]

Yosemites in the soul! King himself seemed to speak with the majesty of California's mountains and rivers. As they listened to his deep voice, so unexplained by his five feet and one hundred twenty pounds, as they watched the play of emotion across his face, Californians felt in the presence of a natural force.

It had not always been so. He had been a different sort of preacher in Boston, a giver of prepared sermons, dictated to a secretary, eloquent in a diffuse sort of way, but lacking fire. King had admired Daniel Webster from boyhood, hearing him often. He believed in William Ellery Channing's assertion that the pulpit should be used for large social ends. He had learning, range of reference, and a thirst for general principle inspired by Victor Cousin. He loved the opera and the stage and studied carefully the techniques of preachers and lecturers of the day. But somehow Boston intimidated him; somehow he could not consolidate his talent and ambition into extempore preaching. He knew that San Franciscans expected a dramatic preacher, and he almost refused the call on that basis. If only he

Thomas Starr King (1824–1864)

Duty and ambition brought him to California, where his popularity as a preacher and a lecturer soon made him moral tutor to the commonwealth. To Californians, the very fact that King was among them indicated a new maturity. He challenged them to highmindedness, to seek, as he put it, Yosemites of the soul. During the Civil War he stumped the state, preaching with fiery eloquence the Union, one and indivisible. Exhausted by the effort, he died asking Californians to keep his memory green. They did.

were a Lyman Beecher—"or even Beecher divided by 75!"—King wrote in his shipboard journal, when he recognized what little appeal he had for steerage passengers. During his first year on the Coast he drew mainly upon his stock of prepared sermons. California's full approval and the press of events soon weaned King from his manuscript. He discovered within himself what he had always hoped for: a capacity for extemporaneous speech, an ability to sway varieties of men, to meet the challenge of events with living language.

The Civil War brought this all about. The legend grew up that King saved California for the Union. It was only a legend, but like all such things it contained an element of symbolic truth. King did not so much save California for the Union as he invoked and pushed to symbolic level —in an atmosphere electrified by Civil War—California's authentication of itself as part of the American Union. Alternative identities had been proposed from the pulpit. In the course of a Fourth of July address in 1857 at Sacramento's Congregational Church, Charles Edward Pickett, foreseeing the eventual break-up of the Union, excoriated California's colonial relationship to the East and called for a Pacific Republic, to be governed by an oligarchy of classical republicans. William Anderson Scott of Calvary Presbyterian fought the secular ambitions of the New England churches at every turn. Scott argued for tolerance and pluralism, for California as a haven for both Northerners and Southerners. He opposed the Vigilance Committee of 1856 and the enforced reading of the Bible in public schools. In 1861, having the temerity to offer prayers for both American presidents, he was hanged in effigy and run out of the state.

Pro-Union sentiment ran high and King's eloquence was its cutting edge. He campaigned for Lincoln in 1860 and for Leland Stanford and the Union party in 1861. There was talk of putting him in the Senate. From his flag-draped pulpit in San Francisco, from lecture platforms decorated in red, white and blue bunting, up and down the state, from saloon porches and tree-stumps in Deadwood, Rough and Ready, Scott's Bar, Horsetown, Mugginsville, Piety Hill, Modesty Gulch, and Mad Mule—King showed himself capable of enjoying a good fight. "In Stockton a dozen Southerners or less hissed," he wrote Ryers on 10 March 1861. "What a time we had! I gave them cracks on the raw. The house cheered and applauded like a thunder cloud. It was a great time." Inspired by King's oratory, California led the nation in contributions to the Sanitary Commission. On his first day in California he had preached of the Pacific Slope as an arena of sectional reconciliation: "And they shall come from the east and the west, and from the north and from the south, and shall sit down in the kingdom of God." Now, in the face of the Atlantic conflict and local Southern talk of a Pacific Republic, King preached the Union: one, indivisible, ordained by God. In the charged context of Civil War he brought to the peak of intensity the themes of a decade's New England preaching. He said that the Republic came from God, that its destined unity was expressed in its very geography. Like the keel of a vessel or the spine of a vital being, the Mississippi ran through the center of the nation. Look to the interior, King urged Californians, an isolated, self-regarding people, bound by Sierra and Pacific, thousands of miles ahead of the real frontier. Look inward to the mystic heart of the continent. There lay a promise for which California and the Atlantic States were protective prophecies. The Pacific Slope must no longer see itself as a colonial thrust of Atlantic civilization, but as full partner with the Atlantic Seaboard in the guardianship of an American future in the interior, a future now under threat by Southern secession. King sought not to evoke New England, but to bring Californians to the recognition that they, on their own terms and in their own way, held full sonship in the Kingdom.

It was an exhausting crusade. King knew the pace he was keeping would destroy a constitution already weak. In January 1864 he officiated at the dedication of a magnificent new English Gothic church on Geary Street. Seating 1500, it symbolized the strength he had brought to Pacific Unitarianism. On 26 February he complained that his bones ached, that he had a sore throat and felt like a sponge squeezed dry. He took to his bed, and on the evening of 4 March 1864 he died of pneumonia and diphtheria. He was thirty-nine years old. He died peacefully, knowing that it was the end, saying goodbye to family and friends, reciting the Twenty-third Psalm: "The Lord is my shepherd; I shall not want." The next day San Francisco shut down all public buildings. The legislature adjourned for three days. Flags were flown at half-mast. Crowds poured through the new Unitarian church to see King lying in a flag-draped coffin, holding a sprig of violets sent by Jessie Benton Frémont. On the day of burial canons were fired in tribute and 20,000 mourners lined the funeral route. John Greenleaf Whittier and Bret Harte wrote poems.

"Keep my memory green," King whispered before dying. Californians did more than that. They enshrined him in legend. They made him the primary symbol of more than a decade's struggle for order and lasting value. Preserver of loyalty to the Union, interpreter of their landscape, moral tutor to their commonwealth, apostle of culture—King's place in

California history was secure. His name was given to a sequoia, a mountain in the Yosemite, a clipper ship. His brief career became the touchstone, the standard of ministerial effort. In 1931, when the legislature selected statues of Junípero Serra and Thomas Starr King to represent California in the National Hall of Fame, it showed how green the memory of King had remained. Serra stood for Spanish Catholic beginnings; King stood for the best possibilities of the American Protestant succession.

V

What legacy was there in all this? What elements of enduring significance had the ministry funded into California? Is the record of ministerial effort the chronicling of a peripheral enterprise, a culling of fugitive themes best left in denominational archives? The seven-volume *History of California* compiled under the direction of Hubert Howe Bancroft in the 1880's virtually ignored the ecclesiastical side of the American era, feeling the story of mines and land titles and popular tribunals and railroad building more central to a conception of what had brought California about. Although many ministers wrote autobiographies, no *Magnalia Christi Californiana* appeared, no epic record of the churches' founding time, bulky with biography, anecdote, and annals. Not until Josiah Royce's work in the early 1880's was there a systematic attempt to assess the moral history of California. Royce, in fact, was probably the first secular historian to take seriously the broader resonances of California's religious history. With the exception of Royce, historians of California had a singleminded passion for demonstrable, indeed inflatable, expressions of progress on the Pacific Slope, for statistical and political verifications of Anglo-Saxon enterprise. Evaluation of effects so unsure and of such elusive extension as those arising from religious experience never came up as an issue, the long-term results of ministerial effort being not a matter of cause and effect, of aspirations given local habitation and a name, but of modalities of consciousness, alternative ways of seeing things which made available to the frontier era a rich store of social and psychological symbols. In some cases, say the College of California and certain social agencies, there were concrete results; but in so many cases—even in Thomas Starr King's crusade for the Union—the primary vitality was symbolic. What was important was a drama of consciousness, an interplay of California fact and shaping analogues of religion.

Strictly as such—as symbolic debate, as an unstable force-field of gesture and desire—there were failures. Blinded by prejudice to the possibility of at least imaginative empathy with Old Californians (although here one does not speak of all, and especially not of Bishop Kip) ministers forced Mexicans to play Canaanites in an American Protestant Israel. They ignored the fact of their continuing dispossession and the extermination of the Indian. They showed little concern for the foreign-born flooding into California. As a matter of imagination and moral feeling—and as a matter of fact—Protestant possession could be restrictive, narrow, harsh; in direct contradiction to the liberating imperatives which pervaded the general sense of Pacific future; in willful defiance of the inevitable cosmopolitanism of the Californian people, manifest from the start in the international maritime city of San Francisco.

This narrowness of sympathy found expression in naïve efforts to control the civic side of things. As if such an explosion of energy, driving hundreds of thousands to the gold fields from every corner of the world, throwing up cities and settlements within weeks in the remotest regions of the Far West, could be channeled into the forms and procedures of a village parish! If there were to be tempering and direction of these energies on the part of church people, then there first had to be an empathetic discernment of their best possibilities, the sort of capacious acceptance shown by William Taylor, and then, proceeding from such consent, a willingness, again like Taylor's, to struggle with half-comprehended forces. Instead there too often occurred little more than a begrudging acknowledgment of an opportunity, or outright hostility to the secular basis of California culture. The general ministerial response to Vigilance Committees in 1851 and 1856 showed how self-indulgent, confused, and self-defeating constant condemnation could become. The pulpit allowed itself to be used because for the time being and for its own purposes the mercantile establishment seemed to be fulfilling clerical fantasies of cleansing regeneration. Ministers never straightforwardly attacked establishment complicity in social conditions. They blessed more times than they protested the lynching of petty criminals. Benton, Willey, Bushnell, and Scott came off clean in this regard, but the ingratiating advocacy of illegal and often capricious violence by many ministers points out a larger failure to make the pulpit an autonomous forum for uncompromising social comment.

Finally, when affirmation of secular energies came, it was perhaps too facile, too ready to equate each event with the Lord's purposes. Mistrust transformed itself into an uncritical identification of Progress with Providence and again there was lost an independent basis for understanding, the sort of consciousness and moral stance appropriate to religious witness: in and of the world, yet secretly and strangely free. California as Babylon, as hopelessly flawed, and California as Eden of the West, as continual recipient of special grace—this polarity, this disjunction, began and endured partly because of the lack of the stabilizing, integrating vision which religion held forth but to which ministers could never completely adhere.

No matter what their failures, ministers managed to found schools, libraries, and philanthropic agencies. They put into public discourse great questions which might otherwise have gone unasked, questions of history and moral choice, social responsibility and cultural growth. Who else during those distracted days was asking such things, or asking them with a like degree of force and intelligence? Who else, aside from a few lawyers and newspaper editors, cared as much? The mere presence of the church in frontier California anticipated stability. The gathering of parishes invoked remembered order; the twice-weekly meetings of congregations reestablished in the midst of flux and confusion comforting rituals of communal encounter. San Francisco became a city of spires because from the first the church was one of her few vital institutions, and to this day in the far mountain forests of the Mother Lode, in the oddly Atlantic towns of the north coast and the river villages of the interior valley, white-frame meeting houses, soundly constructed and adjacent to the simple stonework of pioneer graveyards, testify to times of taking and giving of the Spirit amid the pressing uncertainties of the frontier.

They, the ministers, as public figures, each in his own way yet grouped as a brotherhood, brought to California models of American personality, resonances of regional character which were then blending into the new California identity. Because as clergymen they had a representative role and were accepted at large as a high American type, they intensified and accelerated the process of amalgamation. Isaac Owens and Lorenzo Waugh bespoke the border, the frontier of the Old Southwest. They could cut it—and yet be possessed of belief; they knew the taste of parched corn —and of a Greek verb. Parsons in buckskins, they stood for the notion that the frontier did not of necessity lead to ruffianism and disregard. Oscar P. Fitzgerald, William Taylor, and William Anderson Scott were in various ways men of the South, although none were of the fire-eating variety. Scott signified the Southerner as classical republican of sound learning and civic virtue, a toga-draped figure of *pietas* and Roman repose. Fitzgerald knew the backtrail cabins of Georgia and Alabama, the slave, the poor white. Taylor came from hill people, the Southerner as mountain man, independent in the way of his kind, giving each his due and expecting the same. The Southern presence in California was small but vocal, especially in politics, which they dominated throughout the 1850's. Southern ministers like Fitzgerald, Scott, and Taylor pushed this presence to its best possible level. Freed from the corrupting burden of slavery, California, they hoped, might nourish a purified and transformed Southernism, a preservation of the best aspects of their identity: a love of sun and genial skies and flourishing estates, a sense of responsibility for the *res publica,* manners, the code, and physical courage. Bishop Kip brought along the differing conservatism of New York, more British than Roman, more Tory than classical republican. It imparted elegance, urbanity, and affability. It effected a balance of luxuriance and restraint. The New England presence of Benton, Willey, Bushnell, and the missionaries of the AHMS was the most self-conscious and in many ways the most dynamic. California never became as Hunt wanted it, the Massachusetts of the Pacific, but New Englandism remained a key element of regional identity, continuing as a confessed motivation through the founding of Stanford University and through the public utterance of its first president, David Starr Jordan, coloring regional efforts in art and life style at the turn of the century.

California's utopian connotations were by no means the result of religion. Oregon to the North and the Mormon commonwealth beyond the Sierras had strong and explicit religious foundations. Yet the California clergyman had a richer field for his imagination than either his Oregon or Utah counterpart. Challenged by an awesome topography and by a suggestive set of historical origins, challenged by the very ferment of a pluralistic society, the California clergyman planned and dreamed on a bold scale. Black churchmen dreamed of liberation. They spoke out with an anger made doubly bold by the realization that not even a continent's distance from legal bondage, not even a measure of wealth and social stability, could protect them from the curse of injustice and discrimination. They helped effect a tradition of militancy that is alive to his day. Taylor's Methodist-inspired democracy foreshadowed what would later receive more specific formulation in the writings of Henry George: the expectation of a good life for the many which California held forth—and then took away. Both promise and failure would contribute to tensions of self-awareness in years to come. The scope and temper of Bishop Kip's involvement suggested the turn-of-the-century search on the part of certain Californians for a ceremonially appropriate way of living, for an art and an architecture and a historical self-consciousness which would evoke and authenticate their sense of themselves as a people of mellow tradition and colorful futurity.

Theologizing the Passage to India added weight to an already fundamental California myth, one at the core of Manifest Destiny: that the United States was destined by God to exercise Pacific influence. Christianization of the Orient was the only possible good that certain ministers in the East allowed the entire California phenomenon. Locally it endured as a pious justification, a way to give spiritual significance to flush times. Over the years belief in California as springboard and agent of American influence in the Far East was secularized and amplified, but always kept on the forward edge of regional identity. The plans of Providence to send missionaries to the Orient became, in the rhetoric of new preachers like Jack London, Frank Norris, and David Starr Jordan, an irreversible Anglo-Saxon march of conquest. The use of San Francisco as a base of operations for the invasion of the Philippines; American intervention in the Boxer Rebellion; the joining of Atlantic and Pacific by the Panama Canal—all held special significance for Californians, corroborating a persistent element in their public understanding of themselves. From the earliest, Orientals in California might well have had doubts as to the sincerity of conversion rhetoric. Their treatment in California was more truly prophetic of things to come, domestically and internationally. A lonely champion like William Speer could not offset the tale of exploitation, exclusion, disenfranchisement, and murder which characterized the Chinese experience in California.

Ministers contributed much—and through the figure of Thomas Starr King they were remembered. As a protagonist, King subsumed every theme of a decade's preaching and incorporated every line of ministerial endeavor. Because he operated on many levels he achieved in action that synthesis of aspirations other clergymen often found baffling. Frankly ambitious, he had no ambivalence regarding the dream of betterment as the core of the California experience. For him secularity and religion existed neither in disjunction nor in a continuum, but were brought together by spiritual insight. Then through the world one leapt to faith. He transcendentalized California and at the same time came to terms with its specifics. Ambition and faith intensified and upgraded each other in the crusade for the Union. Here, at its most mystical and fiery level, King preached the imminent emergence of a California transformed, redeemed, and full of future promise.

4
A Rapid, Monstrous Maturity

From the start, Californians cherished their history. The Society of California Pioneers was founded in August 1850 "to collect and preserve information connected with the early settlement and conquest of the country, and to perpetuate the memory of those whose sagacity, enterprise, and love of independence induced them to settle in the wilderness, and become the germ of a new State." The new state had not yet been admitted to the Union, but that did not bother the Pioneers. History was as much a matter of anticipation as accomplishment. Since the Gold Rush, a certain speed-up had characterized events. "California," said *The Annals of San Francisco* in 1855, "was a hot-bed that brought humanity to a rapid, monstrous maturity, like the mammoth vegetables for which it is so celebrated."[1] Structuring this monstrous maturity became the task of the historian. Californians demanded that design be given their startling experience; hence, the writing of history began incongruously soon. The initial efforts were promotional. They sought primarily to get out information and to propagandize. As society grew more sophisticated, historiography became more subtle; the structure and interpretation of events more a matter of art and aspiration than promotion. Through their historians, Californians were to seek out a usable past and to construct a present self-image, which, they hoped, would also be the pattern for the state's future. If that self-image were a matter of dishonesty and deceit, of false history, then the pattern for California's development as a regional culture would be flawed. If it were the result of an honest facing of the lessons and burdens of the past, then perhaps foundations would have been laid for a true and viable regional society, one whose dreams could be the fulfillment, not the denial, of its history. In the process of sorting and structuring its past, California took an important step on the road to regional culture.

Not surprisingly, the first histories were chaotic. They aimed to capitalize upon the excitement of the Gold Rush, not to structure its experience. John Frost's *History of California* emerged in 1850 from the author's history-writing factory in Philadelphia, where over 300 such items were eventually written. Concerned primarily with details of the Gold Rush, Frost did little more than quote wholesale from the reports of Colonel Richard B. Mason and Thomas Butler King from the gold fields. He also provided descriptions of routes to the mining regions, compiled from previously published travel narratives. The whole affair had little claim to being called a history. Yet even this hack promotional effort included a few chapters on the Spanish and Mexican eras—cursory, insignificant chapters, to be sure, but nevertheless expressive of a historical pattern. Even in its most unaware beginnings, California history was never written just from the American period. Behind the raw American surface of things lay a past which Americans had taken over just as surely as they had seized the land. The problem of how to graft that past onto the American present would always prove troublesome.

While Frost managed a corps of history-writing assistants in Philadelphia, many historians were the protagonists of their own histories. Elisha Smith Capron came to California for a few months in 1853 as the agent for several New York firms. Returning home, the New York attorney wrote a *History of California,* which he divided into four parts: a history of the state, a description of San Francisco, a guide to the mines, and a narrative of his experiences in California. The book was a compromise between history and travel literature, and the blending of the two genres expressed Capron's stance as an historian. On the one hand, California in 1853 was a society so new that one's very presence in it had historical overtones; everyone had a chance to make history. On the other hand, California already contained a rich accumulation of human experience. Capron saw this history evident in the settled portions of the landscape, where, "although the country has been thus occupied but four years, it looks, in all respects, as old as Massachusetts or Connecticut," and in San Francisco, where "many parts of the city have the appearance of an old town; and, in passing through them, one often forgets that he is not in New York or Boston!"[2] Because he could sense a past, Capron felt a responsibility to include an objective, third-person history along with the report of his own travels. Gold mining accounted for only a fourth of Capron's pages, reflecting the growing complexity of California society. Whereas Frost's *History* merely described the gold fields, Capron felt the necessity of sociological discussion. The conceptual control Capron exercised over his materials stood in marked contrast to Frost's careless redaction of information. Still a promotional effort, Capron's *History of California* nevertheless pointed in the direction of an emerging California historiography.

The Annals of San Francisco, which appeared in 1855, gave that historiography its first epic statement. Written by three San Francisco journalists, the *Annals* reflected the composite, unresolved nature of California life. A narrative history up to the conquest opened the *Annals*, followed by a month-by-month history of San Francisco from 1846 to 1854. The whole was interspersed with essays on specific aspects of San Francisco life and concluded with a topical survey of the city and biographies of its prominent citizens. Running to more than 800 pages, *The Annals of San Francisco* was a protean, *sui generis* sort of a book, part history, part epic, part fantasy, part promotional journalism. Its lack of resolution, its extravagance, was to be the glory and the curse of future historians. Frank Soulé, John Gihon, and James Nisbet assembled the *Annals* on a commission from D. Appleton and Company. Hubert Howe Bancroft was quite correct when he described the *Annals* as a book intended to sell. Its lurid descriptions no doubt appealed to Eastern readers.

Sensationalism, however, was but one part of this complex and contradictory book, just as the whore houses and street fights it described were but one part of San Francisco. A sustained, if not always sophisticated, historical impulse motivated the authors of the *Annals*. Their attention to sources had no parallel in previous historical writing by Californians. Besides using extensive newspaper files, the authors dug into the already sizable collection of Californiana assembled by the Society of California Pioneers, of which both Soulé and Gihon were members. They consulted public records and interviewed old residents. Seven years previously, San Francisco had been a village with a population of forty. Now it had reached the point when even journalists concerned with its colorful surface must respond to the history behind the present—and had a range of research materials suitable for the task. The more purely promotional and journalistic ambitions of the *Annals*, its descriptions of crowds in Portsmouth Square, raging fires, Steamer Day, and public amusements, obscured its historical impulse, but that in itself was appropriate to a city concerned so much with the dramatic present. Nevertheless, the historical impulse was there, and a sense of history pervaded even the most uproarious of the *Annals'* passages. The book formulated for San Francisco a self-image that would last over a century: fun-loving, somewhat sinful and shortsighted, but ever mindful of its past.

San Francisco was not alone in this concern. Even remote and sparsely settled Trinity County found historical expression, testifying to the necessity for self-definition through history that characterized California from the first. Isaac Cox's *Annals of Trinity County* (1858) was the first of over 150 county histories written between 1860 and 1900. The fact that Cox, a trader and hotel-keeper of some education, felt compelled to dig out the already obscure events in the history of a county which had but one town, Weaverville, the rest of the settlements being mining camps inhabited by transients, demonstrated the vitality of the historical impulse in the pioneer era. Cox himself said that he at first thought the task was hopeless. As source materials, he had only the scanty files of *The Weekly Trinity Journal.* In his preface he frankly confessed that "parts of chapters and whole chapters bear the intrinsic marks of refuge to tales, where history, undoubted and indisputable, ought to be."[3] Trinity County's magnificent alpine landscape dominated the dwarfish events Cox could scrape together, so he let topography unify the narrative. Following the Trinity River and tributaries downstream, Cox gave, as far as he could, the history of each bankside settlement—ironically amused at the bearded Lilliputians who dug for gold amid the mighty landscape. And yet each motley collection of miners' shacks already had its memory of strikes, murders, and hilarious incident. Cox felt the irony of landscape and event, but he also knew that from now on this landscape would nourish an American future. Beginnings might be trivial, but for the sake of that future they must be chronicled.

Early histories had only a partial intention and point of view, reflecting the unresolved nature of the California experience. Not until 1866 did a balanced, comprehensive history appear, Franklin Tuthill's *History of California*—evidence, it later seemed to Josiah Royce, that California was moving into a more resolved stage of culture. Aware of itself as a society, California could produce a mature work of history. For Hubert Howe Bancroft, Tuthill's publisher, the work was "the first History of California deserving the title," a sentiment echoed repeatedly by successive historians.[4] A New York physician who turned to journalism, Tuthill wrote his history in hours spared from editing the San Francisco *Bulletin,* which he owned. Traveling in Europe for his health, he was the first California historian to consult European libraries. No doubt Bancroft, who commissioned the history, allowed Tuthill to consult his own collection. In any event, Tuthill did not find sources a problem. In his preface he cited the wealth of archival material, memoirs, travel narratives, newspaper files, government documents, oral evidence, and previous histories at his disposal. More than this, Tuthill was convinced that California was ready for historical evaluation. "The sixteen years that have elapsed since the American occupation," he noted, "embrace such physical and social changes as oftener require a full century for their development." Within the span of these sixteen years, Tuthill saw a search for law and institutions as the sustained process beneath California's surface confusion. He arranged his *History* around this theme. Coherence, order, meaning—for the first time history reflected these values as part of the California experience. Tuthill did not ignore the Gold Rush, but he paid more attention to the first constitutional convention. He wrote of gambling casinos, but also of schools and law courts. Tuthill's lengthy analysis of the Mexican *alcalde* system as the basis of American administration further fused the histories of the two California orders.

His superb chapter on the debates in Congress over the admission of California to the Union was written with a constant sense of its importance for the Civil War, putting remote California into the context of that conflict, which raged as Tuthill wrote. Both in his emphasis upon institutions and in his desire to see California in national perspective, Tuthill anticipated the work of Josiah Royce by twenty years. As the author of California's first mature work of history, Tuthill set high standards. "No doubt a better history can be written," he admitted, "when the country is older, and time has more thoroughly tested some social experiments that seem already successful."[5] As a historian, Tuthill had paid detailed attention to the social side of the California experiment. Isolating constructive aspects of the California story, his *History* acted as both paradigm and imperative. Tuthill stood between frontier and provincial eras, formulating a heritage and exhorting to development along lines already discernible. On his deathbed, he called for proofs of his *History* and, feebly, worked for a while correcting them. Franklin Tuthill knew the importance of the usable past he had given California.

Thus, between 1850 and 1866, the foundations of California historiography had been laid. No one history before Tuthill's had expressed the full range of concerns, yet the spectrum had been developed in a variety of books, coalescing in Tuthill's synthesis. A number of central issues faced historians of the last third of the nineteenth century. What had been the nature of the dispossessed Hispanic society? What, if any, were the vital links, as a matter of fact or aspiration, between that lost era and the present American one? Had American character and institutions been modified significantly by translation to California? In the light of California's frontier past, what would be, or should be, the pattern for provincial development? Would the California past turn out to be a burden for the new era, or an inspirational memory of achievement?

In the year 1856 these issues seemed very important to a young San Francisco book-seller. Hubert Howe Bancroft had been in California four years and, at age twenty-four, was already on the way to a fortune. After the turmoil of the Vigilance Committee of 1856 had subsided, Bancroft later recalled, a period of stocktaking seemed to seize San Franciscans, including himself. Looking at the bustling, money-making city about him, Bancroft suddenly had the intuition that California's real destiny, after this era of economic consolidation had passed, would be with the intellectual life. Although deeply involved in business himself, and as yet uncertain what his role would be, Bancroft resolved to play a part in that creative destiny.

Throughout his long life (he died in 1918), Bancroft liked to consider himself a son of the Puritans. His parents, Vermont- and Massachusetts-born, emigrated to Granville, Ohio, where Bancroft was born in 1832 "into an atmosphere of pungent and invigorating puritanism."[6] A strong strain of resentment, however, ran through Bancroft's memories of his Ohio boyhood. He remembered himself as an overly disciplined, narrowly educated, repressed child. "Puritan Granville was a good place to be reared in," Bancroft said of his move as a teenager to Buffalo, New York, "but it was a better place to emigrate from." In Buffalo, where he went to work in the bookstore of his brother-in-law, the young clerk plunged into a period of dissipation, including (if one judges from veiled hints) sexual debauchery. Luckily, his brother-in-law found it necessary to send Bancroft to California on business. "No sooner had I departed from Buffalo on my way to California," Bancroft remembered, "than all desire left me to commit these foolish boyish excesses. There was then no one to hoodwink, no watchful eye to circumvent; it ceased to be amusing when I was my own master; so when thrown into the pandemonium at San Francisco I had not the slightest inclination to make a beast or a villain of myself."

Instead of squandering his energies, Bancroft went to work. Whatever the condition of his sex life, his business life prospered. Returning to Buffalo for a visit in 1856, he decided to settle permanently in California. "There was that in California which harmonized with my aspirations and drew forth energies which elsewhere would remain dormant." In 1856, the year in which he decided to become a Californian and the year in which he said he first envisioned the state's intellectual destiny, he opened H. H. Bancroft and Company on the corner of Montgomery and Merchant Streets in San Francisco—in a short time the largest bookseller's and stationer's west of Chicago. "Get money," Bancroft later expressed as his motto, "but get it only in order that you may ransom mind, for it is mind and not money that makes the man."

How he would ransom mind was not clear. California seemed to offer but one model for a career: money-making. "Of what is called the culture of letters," he later complained, "there was none during my working days in California." With no definite plans for their use, he began to collect materials pertaining to the discovery and settlement of the Pacific Coast. By 1866 he was wealthy enough to spend a year in Europe, adding to his collection. By 1869 some 16,000 books, manuscripts, pamphlets, maps, files of newspapers and journals ranged the shelves of the fifth floor of the Bancroft Building on Market Street. Bancroft hired a librarian, Dartmouth-educated Henry Lebbeus Oak, who began a catalogue and an index. The question of the library's use haunted Bancroft. For a while plans were underway for an encyclopedia of the Pacific Coast, then dropped.

In 1869 Bancroft's wife died, and with her death he lost the little that was left of his religious faith. He felt dissatisfied with success in the narrow business sense of the term. The years following the death of his wife have the feel of a Victorian faith-doubt crisis, with overtones of a mild nervous breakdown. The complete psychological side of this 1869-71 crisis in Bancroft's life can never be fully known. But it was resolved in the choice of a career in history, and Bancroft's conception of the nature of the historian's task offers a clue. Although his own writing never attained such olympian remoteness, Bancroft saw history as an exercise in controlling intelligence. The primary act of the historian was control: control of a society through the ordered knowledge of its past and present. History was a new kind of power, more satisfying than business, but conceived—administratively and functionally—along the same lines. The Big Four built railroads. Bancroft built history. As an historian, Bancroft could satisfy that mixture of idealism and vanity which had led him to thirst for the role of visible intellectual. History as a science, the science of progress, offered a satisfying substitute for abjured religious categories. Hiring a corps of researchers and writers, Bancroft manufactured his histories according to an industrial system, then marketed them throughout the West through teams of salesmen. History conceived thus as a business enterprise kept him in the mainstream of California's economic life. He turned down the Republican nomination to Congress in 1875, having found a better role.

Throughout the 1870's, the method of production and the design took shape. Its scope would be the entire West, from Alaska to Central America, an area which Bancroft grouped under the title "the Pacific States." "It was my ambition to do for this last western earth's end," he said of the enterprise, "what Homer did for Greece, with these differences: Homer dealt in myths, I should deal in facts; Homer's were the writings of poetical genius, mine of plodding prose." Between 1881 and 1890 the prose of *The History of the Pacific States* plodded on for thirty-nine volumes. A five-volume survey of Indian cultures, *The Native Races of the Pacific States of North America,* appeared in 1875. California itself received an eleven-volume treatment within this larger framework, about 8800 pages, totaling 4,500,000 words. There was a seven-volume *History of California* (1884-90), a two-volume study of the Vigilante era, *Popular Tribunals* (1887), a survey of Spanish and Mexican days, *California Pastoral* (1888) and one of the Gold Rush, *California Inter Pocula* (1888).

Bancroft wanted his histories to be complete annals. "My conception of the province of history," he was later to say, "is a clear and concise statement of facts bearing upon the welfare of the human race in regard to men and events, leaving the reader to make his own deductions and form his own opinions."[7] The perspective implied in "the welfare of the human race" was in itself a judgment. Bancroft wanted to chronicle progress, and in that sense his histories were in the California promotional tradition. In the *History of California,* however, he came close to providing pure annals. The very completeness of Bancroft, although it made difficult a sustained reading, ensured that nothing useful to future interpreters would be lost. No other portion of the country, except New England, had such an aid to regional culture, such a systematized memory of the past. "I am firm in the belief that the record is worth preserving," said Bancroft of his heroic efforts as a collector, "and for its completeness I expect in time the appreciation and approbation of all true Californians."[8]

The importance of the Bancroft collection transcended its use in the Bancroft histories. Bancroft's library and the books which issued from

Hubert Howe Bancroft (1832–1918)

As far as this San Francisco bookseller was concerned, California represented the cutting edge of the American experience. He determined that its history must be written. Assemblying a marvelous library and a massive array of documents, he put to work a corps of researchers, publishing their volumes under his own name. However dubious his methods, Bancroft ensured that California would have a well-developed sense of the past.

there, aside from being an immediate accomplishment, were a gesture in the direction of California's historiographical future. As a historian, Bancroft was often ludicrous and sometimes dishonest. His failure to acknowledge the work of assistants compromised his reputation. Bancroft fought a fight for California in a very Californian way, although many Californians despised him for it. He himself said that he had dared to write the history of the West (more correctly, have it written) in the same way that the Big Four had dared to build a trans-Sierran railroad. He was not a professional historian and they were not railroad men. Was this not the meaning of California, that ordinary men could do great things? "Mine was a great work," he said of his histories, "that could be performed by a small man."

It could be performed because California encouraged small men to reach beyond themselves. The whole theme of Bancroft's autobiography, *Literary Industries*, often such a distressingly self-congratulatory book, is the notion that California liberated energies and ambitions. For all his sham and commercialism, Bancroft honestly saw himself playing a representative role. He had gone East in 1874 with copies of *Native Races* in his luggage as both a shrewd stager of reviews and as an example that an intellectual career was possible in California. It had not been pleasant, standing hat in hand before James Russell Lowell, John Greenleaf Whittier, Francis Parkman, Ralph Waldo Emerson, William Dean Howells, and George Bancroft, asking them to take a look at an example of Californian scholarship. Many Eastern luminaries had been kind enough. So many others had not been home when he called that he "began to suspect that most Boston people had two houses, a city and a country habitation, and lived in neither." He remembered the whole trip as "one of the most disagreeable tasks of my life." It put him in bed for two weeks from nervous exhaustion. All his life, he remained bitter at the price he had to pay for those first reviews. "I had been entirely successful," he admitted; "but success here was not won as in San Francisco, by years of tender devotion to an ennobling cause, but by what I could not but feel to be an humiliating course. I sought men whom I did not wish to see and talked with them of things about which of all others it was most distasteful to me to converse."[9] His pilgrimage might have seemed vulgar to the Eastern establishment, but would they have reviewed his books otherwise? Californians might justly condemn some of Bancroft's business practices, but he had fixed the history of his state in permanent form, and he had made the nation take notice.

II

Throughout this era of historical and promotional writing a fable was being put together, a means by which Californians sought to know—and sometimes to delude—themselves. This fable was both a history of the past and a taxonomy of present and future hopes. It was the complimentary, hopeful side of their self-image.

In dealing with the history of the conquest, the fable conferred upon California honorable beginnings. The story included an English plot to seize California and a Mexican plot to exterminate American settlers in the Sacramento Valley. The embarrassing problem arising from the fact that Captain Frémont had illegally made war against a nation with whom the United States was officially at peace was covered over by the assertion that secret orders must have been given in Washington. No mere captain of topographical engineers, not even the son-in-law of Thomas Hart Benton, would have dared act otherwise. "There can not now be a doubt," said Edmund Randolph in 1860 of Frémont's actions, "that it was prompted, as it was approved, by the Government of the United States; and that Captain Frémont obeyed his orders no less than than his own feelings."[10] The half-droll, half-drunken events of the Bear Flag revolt could not remain in memory as the unsure actions of some two dozen Sacramento settlers. From the start, Bear Flag leader William B. Ide feared that his men would appear to the world as "a band of Mountain thieves and robbers." "We are robbers, or we must be conquerors!" Ide exhorted fellow Bear Flaggers, fearful over the consequences of their seizure of Vallejo's Sonoma estate.[11] Not surprisingly, the Bear Flaggers decided to be conquerors. They declared an independent nation, running up an appropriate pennant. In later years, the ambiguous events of June 1846, in which Vallejo's brandy seems to have caused the most significant casualties, emerged as a full-blown heroic myth, a California version of the Texas Republic.

The mining era, thanks in part to Bret Harte, also offered a comforting fable. Historians, with the exception of Josiah Royce, accepted Harte's stereotype of the miner as rough and racy but with a heart of gold. Bancroft, for instance, while admitting in *California Pastoral* that "the age of gold was the age of avarice, the age of brutal murders, of wild rudeness and insane revellings," glorified the era shamelessly in *California Inter Pocula*. The notion of the miners' reverence for women and children, mainstay of so many Bret Harte stories, held an especial appeal for California historians. Somehow it mitigated the overwhelming violence and sexual repression of the era. "They could cut each other with knives—these miners," wrote Bancroft in his florid fashion, "riddle enemy or friend with bullets and smile at it; they could strangle a sluice-box thief, snap the neck of a Chinaman by a twist of his pigtail, whet their appetite for breakfast by the butchery of a rancheria of natives, but injure a child, ill-treat an old man, or do violence to a woman, they could not."[12] With its awareness of the concrete facts of Gold Rush violence, Bancroft's statement is a perfect example of the process by which Californians covered over traumatic aspects of their past with sentimentality.

Miners' law provides another example. Here the fable had to justify extra-legal and sometimes erroneous hangings. As Josiah Royce pointed out, the resort to lynch law was in itself an expression of pervading lawlessness, not its correction. But it was Charles Howard Shinn's *Mining Camps, A Study in American Frontier Government*, published in 1885, and not Royce's *California*, published in 1886, which formulated what turn-of-the-century Californians believed about the mining era. A California journalist who at the age of twenty-eight entered Johns Hopkins as an undergraduate, Shinn came under the influence of William Stubbs's *The Constitutional History of England* (1874). Guided by Stubbs's Germanic theories, Shinn set about casting the mining era into an Anglo-Saxon mould. The miners' efforts at self-government, he asserted, constituted "a stanza in the political epic of the Germanic race to which we belong." Shinn considered miners' courts as "the folk-moot of our Germanic ancestors," evidence of "that political instinct, deep rooted in Lex Saxonum." "It was this miners' court," wrote Shinn, "that our Norse and Saxon ancestors, could they have risen from burial mounds like Beowulf's . . . would have undoubtedly recognized as akin to those folk-moots held of old in primeval German and Scandinavian forests." Shinn replaced the Bret Harte stereotype with a more Anglo-Saxon figure: plain-spoken, cooperative, heroic. "From Klamath to Colusa, from Siskiyou to Fresno, from Lake Bowman to Trinity Peak," he asserted, "manhood and honesty ruled the camps of the miners." For Shinn the mining era taught the lessons of social cooperation and human fellowship. "The men and women whose childhood was passed in these camps," he wrote, "are beginning to control the State. Each community, once welded together in camp-life, possesses a unity of feeling that bids fair to be permanent." Let each Californian, then, see mining days "as a classical and heroic background for modern life," a model for building the California commonwealth of the 1880's along lines of amity and cooperation.[13]

The fable provided the commonwealth with heroes, especially from the Civil War period. California's connection with that great conflict had been minor. Five hundred or so volunteers served with the Second Massachusetts Cavalry, a few columns did patrol duty in the Southwest, and 16,000 locally raised troops manned garrisons at home. Symbolically, however, participation had been intense. The war forced Californians, after a decade and a half of isolation and ambiguous relationship, to assert their loyalty to the Union, despite the thousands of uncivilized miles between itself and the Atlantic states. Thomas Starr King led that assertion of loyalty, that symbolic drama, and in California he was second only to Lincoln in the regard of the people as a martyr to the Union cause. Two others who died, David C. Broderick and Edward Dickinson Baker, both United States Senators, were linked with King as heroes of local patriotism. An Irishman and a Roman Catholic, trained as a stonemason in his youth, Broderick rose in the tough world of New York and California politics without forsaking a finer strain in himself, an empathy for the downtrodden which flashed forth quixotically in the course of the ruthless game he usually played. Despite odds of birth and education, Broderick secured election to the Senate in 1857, where in his maiden speech he said that he was proud to represent California in the very building which his Irish-born father had once worked on as a stonemason. Blunt and unafraid, Broderick, although a Democrat, fought the proslavery Kansas policies of the Buchanan administration. Back in California in 1859, David S. Terry, a State Supreme Court judge and a fiery Southerner, stung to fury by Broderick's campaign to smash the Chivalry in California, challenged him to a duel and at dawn, on the fog-shrouded banks of Lake Merced outside San Francisco, mortally wounded the young Senator. "They have killed me," Broderick was supposed to have said in his last moments, "because I was opposed to a corrupt administration and the extension of slavery."

Born in London, Edward Dickinson Baker was brought to the United States at age four, grew up in Philadelphia, and in 1825 moved with his family to Indiana. Opening a law practice in Springfield, Illinois, Baker was elected to Congress but resigned to fight in the Mexican War. In 1852 he removed to California, where he gained a reputation as a lawyer and an orator. In 1859 he moved to Oregon, which sent him to the United States Senate. With the outbreak of the Civil War Baker served as Lincoln's advisor on Pacific Coast affairs. He was killed at Ball's Bluff on

22 October 1861, leading a regiment of Pennsylvanian, Californian, and Oregonian volunteers he himself had raised.

When Broderick died, Baker gave the eulogy. King preached at services for Baker. When King died, Californians conjoined the three as representative of their best participation in the national struggle. Self-educated and ambitious, each man had risen to prominence in the West. Each had preached—Baker and King with extraordinary forensic power—a doctrine of progress and prosperity upgraded by justice, generosity, and finer feeling. Baker resonated with the sensibility of the frontier Whig: mercantile, knowing rural America, preaching sectional balance and internal improvements. Broderick bespoke the immigrant working class: urban, torn by a complicated network of loyalties, learning to handle a new sort of politics. King, by profession and by affiliation, if not by caste, knew the America of Boston and Brattle Street and Concord. All three had made a Californian consolidation of their talents and ambitions. All three had given themselves to something more important than the scramble for wealth, diversely in each case yet the same, and lost their lives in doing so. For the 1860's and 1870's they stood for what California, in the optimistic side of its identity, thought that it could bring to the Union.

For Californians were becoming more and more conscious of the fact that they were developing what they hoped could pass for a civilization. They claimed that the violence in their temperament had subsided. In 1863 John S. Hittell described Californians as "ready to avenge an insult, accustomed to carry pistols and knives, quick to use them in a quarrel."[14] By 1876 Walter Fisher felt that California's "rudest and ruggedest days must be past, or nearly past."[15] B. E. Lloyd, that same year, used statistics to prove that San Francisco had one of the lowest crime rates in the nation. In contrast to the 1850's and 1860's, remarked Lloyd, "the ordinary citizen does not see a street fight once a year."[16]

Walter Fisher, an Anglo-Irishman of Tory tastes, loved the "simmering or sub-excitement" he found in Californians, the sense of heroic expansiveness "to be found among these hearty sunburnt men exalted with corn and wine." "These are people that Fielding would have understood."[17] John S. Hittell agreed. Californians were "a race marked by large size, healthy bodies, industrious habits, and clear complexion." In San Francisco, each class had "better houses, better furniture, better tables, better clothes than the same class in American cities on the Atlantic slope." As a result of California's exuberant, erratic economic history, Hittell stated, democracy came easily. "The sand-shoveler and the millionaire may change places tomorrow, and they know it; so the former does not usually cringe nor the other strut when they meet. They measure each other fairly; each has had his ups and downs; each pays the respect due to the character rather than the money of the other."[18] If there were any aristocrats in California, B. E. Lloyd asserted, they were not the Silver Kings, but the Pioneers. "To be a Pioneer," Lloyd believed, "is to assert a claim to aristocracy, as absolute as attaches to a descendant of the Knickerbockers in New York, or to a resident of Boston who traces his ancestry in the passenger list of the *Mayflower.*"[19]

Exuberant, expansive, democratic—Californians also cherished an image of themselves as cosmopolitan. *The Annals of San Francisco* abandoned its xenophobic stance to praise the pleasure principle that foreigners had introduced into staid Yankee life, "particularly the light-hearted, theatre-loving French, the musical Germans, and laughter-loving, idle, dancing Hispano-Americans."[20] Josiah Royce denied any fundamental change in American personality as it developed in California, but he was in the minority among historians. Much was made about San Francisco's cosmopolitan style. An international port, stressed John S. Hittell, San Francisco reproduced intact cultures of its polyglot population without the American modifications an inland city would have effected. If anything, Hittell wrote, the Americans of San Francisco had taken on the style and attitudes of foreigners, especially the French. San Franciscans thought of their city as the Paris of America. This pretense to a Parisian style was more than a matter of the numerous French restaurants throughout the city—dining tables on the first floor, private rooms on the second, ambiguous arrangements on the third—although these establishments certainly expressed a Parisian spirit. Nor was it only the gaiety of the San Francisco Sunday, with its bands, dances, picnics and promenades, although that too represented a departure from Yankee tradition. There was a public quality to life in San Francisco that seemed to commentators different from the normal American style of city living. "Home is less and the street more for the San Franciscans," said Hittell, "than for the citizens of New York or Charleston." Few built private homes in early San Francisco, Hittell pointed out. A vigorous hotel and restaurant economy developed. "This excellence is still maintained," Hittell remarked regarding San Francisco's eating places, "and many of the influences potent against housekeeping twenty years ago continue nearly as powerful as ever."[21] For B. E. Lloyd the two architectural symbols of San Francisco's personality in the mid-

1870's were not government buildings, but the Palace Hotel and Wade's Opera House. Both piles expressed an aspiration as much as a reality. It would be some years before the 850 luxurious rooms of the Palace Hotel would ever be filled, and even San Franciscans questioned the wisdom of building the third largest opera house in the United States "in a city scarce thirty years old, and remote from the great centres of art." Both buildings celebrated public life, however, reinforcing San Francisco's self-image as a place where public pleasure predominated.

Such was one aspect of what Californians considered the immediate result of their history. But what was the significance of the entire movement from Gold Rush frontier to resolved provincial society? Other than the qualified critique of Josiah Royce, most historians of California, from compilers of county "mugbooks" to men like the Hittell brothers and Bancroft, believed the California story to be one uninterrupted tale of progress, especially the version of progress advanced by Herbert Spencer, Aaron of serious thinkers in late-nineteenth-century California. Bancroft's essay "Savagism and Civilization," in the second volume of *Native Races*, expressed the underlying assumption of California historiography. Bancroft saw a "progressional impulse" in human history, "one and universal, though of varying rapidity and extent." Its basis was in physical evolution, although science did not yet understand the precise relationship between natural and social orders. "In this ceaseless coming and going," Bancroft asserted, "there is somewhere a mysterious agency at work, making men better, wiser, nobler, whether they will or not." Bancroft discerned a finality in events. "Not only does evil decrease," he stated optimistically, "but the tendency is ever towards its disappearance. Gradually the confines of civilization broaden; the central principle of human progress attains greater intensity, and the mind assumes more and more its lordly power over matter."[22] As historian of the West, Bancroft considered himself poet and prophet of progress, chronicler of California's development "from a wilderness into a garden of latter-day civilization." He had been driven to write the history of the West in the first place, he remembered, because he had become convinced that "there was here on this coast the ringing-up of universal intelligence for a final display of what man can do at his best, with all the powers of the past united, and surrounded by conditions such as had never before fallen to the lot of man to enjoy."[23] California, newest arena in the newest of nations, stood at the forefront of human history, and Bancroft stood at the forefront of historians.

III

At the turn of the century, thus stood the fable of California history: pastoral past, progressive and colorful present, imperial future—a proud and optimistic fable, one that conferred a sense of importance and glamour upon a remote, underdeveloped region, unsure of its status in the eyes of the Atlantic Seaboard and torn by pressing internal problems. The fable comforted Californians upon public occasions, lending itself to expansion on Admission Day.

But the fable did not contain the entire truth. The California experience had its nether side, a burden of violence and frustration and failure. A sort of counter-fable ran through California historiography—which took its design from the expectations of the primary fable. Surveying their brief history, Californians detected a terrible burden as well as a glory.

The tragedy of the Donner party provided California with its most compelling counter-fable. Caught by early snows, the Donner party, the last wagon-train in the migrations of 1846, made winter camp on 4 November 1846 near Truckee Lake in the Sierras. Between November and their rescue in April 1847, the men, women, and children of the party endured a catalogue of horrors which Walter Colton, writing in *The Californian* at Monterey on 24 April 1847, could only compare to the sufferings of the Jews during Titus' siege of Jerusalem, as described by Josephus. Only forty-five of the seventy-nine survived. What shocked Californians about the Donner ordeal was its intensity of misery and its force as a dystopian symbol. Taken collectively, the Donner party was Everyman in a morality play of frontier disintegration. As a group, acting democratically, representative of the varieties of settlers coming into California, amateurs on the frontier, filled with hopes for a better life, the Donner party showed itself capable of bad behavior and bad decisions—which the wilderness compounded into disaster. They took an erroneous short cut, eating up necessary energy and travel time. They quarreled among themselves. On 5 October one man killed another. On 8 October an old man was left on the trail to die. There were few enough men as it was, and their leadership disintegrated. Families refused to look after the children of others—then refused water to children not their own. By the time the snow caught up with them in the Sierras, forcing an encampment, the Donner party, having squandered its resources, having fatally enervated itself, had established the conditions of a cruel winter tragedy.

When they were rescued in the spring, Californians forgot their heroism and remembered only that they had eaten one another's flesh. That the American as overland pioneer should come to this! That there should be such collective bad behavior! In cases like this a scapegoat is necessary, and one was found in Lewis Keseberg. An immigrant from Westphalia, Germany, only two years in the country, handsome, in his early thirties, married and the father of two children, Keseberg, who joined the party with two well-turned-out wagons, spoke and wrote four languages and was easily the best educated man in the group. He was also something of an outsider and a troublemaker. Like the rest he suffered horribly, losing his wife and children. Keseberg was discovered by the fourth relief, a group of men led by William Fallon, all of whom had volunteered for the rescue mission in the hope of finding and claiming as reward valuables and the $10,000 in cash known to be in the Donners' possession. They came, in other words, as scavengers. Convinced that Keseberg knew where the money was, Fallon used physical force against him, beating him and accusing him of having killed Mrs. Donner and hidden the money. Keseberg protested his innocence. It was in Fallon's diary-journal of the relief expedition, published in *The California Star* on 5 June 1847, that the accusations which ruined Keseberg's life were made. Fallon described the German as loving the taste of human flesh, as a repulsive ghoul surrounded by half-eaten remains which he preferred to the food they offered him. He suggested that Keseberg murdered Mrs. Donner. He told how he had forced Keseberg to follow the relief back at a distance, unfit, as he was, for human company.

Keseberg sued for slander at Sutter's Fort about a year later, won the verdict—and was awarded a dollar's damages. For by this time he had become the Cain of California, with every man's hand turned against him. "I have been born under an evil Star!" he later said of himself. "Fate, misfortune, bad luck, compelled me to remain at Donner Lake. If God should decree that I should again pass through such an ordeal, I could not do otherwise than I did. My conscience is free from reproach. Yet that camp has been the one burden of my life. Wherever I have gone, people have cried 'Stone him! stone him!' Even the little children in the streets have mocked me and thrown stones at me as I passed. Only a man conscious of his innocence, and clear in the sight of God, would not have succumbed to the terrible things which have been said of me—would not have committed suicide! Mortification, disgrace, disaster, and unheard-of misfortune have followed and overwhelmed me. I often think that the Almighty has singled me out, among all the men on the face of the earth, in order to see how much hardship, suffering, and misery a human being can bear!"[24] Keseberg managed to marry again, but both his daughters were born imbeciles. Interviewed in 1879, he was living in a shack behind a brewery in Sacramento, his two children so violent they had to be locked up during the day when he was at work. Brought by historian C. F. McGlashan face to face with Eliza Donner, who as a child of three had gone through the ordeal of 1846-47 and whose mother Keseberg had been accused of killing, Keseberg fell to his knees and protested his innocence. Instinctively, Eliza Donner believed him.

In 1895, after fifty accursed years, Keseberg died in Sacramento—peacefully, saying nothing, asking nothing of anyone, like those who have long lived beyond the reach of human sympathy. History had demanded that he play a symbolic role. General Kearny's dragoons, on the way East after the conquest of California, buried the mangled remains of the Donner party and set to the torch their squalid huts. The survivors resumed normal life, the youngest member of the party, an infant, not dying until 1935. In time they became respected for what they had undergone. But because atonement was necessary for their communal failure, Keseberg was made the guilty one. It was the communal failure which frightened most profoundly, and cannibalism was but its exponent. The Donner party had crossed the outer frontier of California as dystopia. The earthly eden could turn—for ordinary men and women and children—into an eating of one another's flesh. In that each wagon train was a society and California was a sum total of wagon trains, the implications of the Donner experience terrified. It provided an anti-type to the whole myth of the West, California in particular. Keseberg ate flesh, but so did others. He bore the collective guilt so that they might be free. Through circumstances, but also through design, he was forced to go through life as a warning that California's history might have locked within it some unutterable horror.

The fable felt a bracing excitement in the California air. The counter-fable wondered whether that excitement was not the sign of inner anxiety. An entry in Frederic Hall's *History of San Jose*, describing the Fourth of July of 1863, dramatized the duality. "This day was celebrated with a great deal of enthusiasm," Hall noted. "Edward Berri committed suicide by cutting his throat from ear to ear."[25] Had California grown up too closely concerned with economic values, asked the counter-fable? Were there spiritual foundations, or was California a competitive nightmare? Capron was struck by the degree of alienation and anonymity in early San Francisco, a city composed of "individuals, strangers to each other, speaking different languages, unlike in all the elements of social and political life, generally poor."[26] *The Annals of San Francisco*, in the midst of glorifying the city, expressed its underlying social instability through evocative descriptions of trashy streets, oozing with mud, huge rats darting across rubbish piles never cleared away, and a sickening stench pervading every quarter, carrying with it the dreaded suggestion of cholera. Here might be romance, but here also could be the city of dreadful night.

Twenty years later San Francisco's mud would be cleared away, but the possibility of alienation remained. "San Francisco is full of social wrecks," observed Walter Fisher, "—wrecks more complete and miserable than any possible in calmer seas. There is said to be a greater proportion of suicides here than anywhere else in the civilized world. No wonder. A society so new that its members are bound to each by few and slight ties —a society that has in general lost all old faith and found no new faith either in God or man—it foams on like a battle, like a riot towards its ends. Quarter is neither given nor expected. Victory! victory or nothing! . . . That ghastly eternal slaughter, that grim war-game of the fates, called Selection-of-the-Fittest, goes on here like a frontier war, without convention, without checks, without mercy; not with circumstances of deliberate cruelty, but worse—amid panic."[27] J. W. Boddam-Whetham, an English naval officer in San Francisco in the early 1870's, witnessed a San Franciscan who had lost money in a mining speculation put a gun to his head on a public thoroughfare and pull the trigger. "This darling and sunny child of our young Republic," said Stephen Powers, "is already old as Europe in suicide."[28]

At the root of such complaints was the sense that life in California had never transcended the search for wealth which had filled it in the first place. "With the Americans, in the cities where they are in the majority," said Frost's *History* in 1850, "business is the uppermost consideration upon all occasions, and profit and loss, and chances of obtaining a competency, the constant subject of thought." Naturally San Francisco breathed the spirit of Mammon, wrote Capron in 1854. "When or where else did ever legitimate commerce, or religious faith, or the principles of universal freedom, congregate so many natives of every nation on a barren shore and rear so large a city in so short a time?" "Most men in California," complained John S. Hittell, "do not live here to enjoy life, but to make money so that they may enjoy life in some other country." Rather than see the state continue on its present course, Hittell half-seriously suggested it might be necessary to declare gold mining a felony, so that Californians would turn to farming and industry. "We must have a political war," urged Hittell; "the permanent Californians must conquer the rovers, and compel them to settle down or leave." "The dollar jingles, the bill rustles with every movement of the tongue," said Walter Fisher of conversation in San Francisco. San Francisco Society, raising its garish monuments atop Nob Hill, seemed a vulgar and shoddy affair, indicative of the fact that in California "the capacity for appreciating finer distinctions than a money one, is confined to a secluded and impuissant few." "Nowhere else will such bad manners be found in families possessing so much wealth," said John S. Hittell of the Silver and Railroad kings. "Refinement is the growth of time." But time, according to the fable of California history, had already produced a local variety of aristocrat, the Pioneer, compared by B. E. Lloyd to Knickerbockers of New York or descendants of the *Mayflower*. In Walter Fisher's opinion, a greedy and uncouth past had made Pioneers not Knickerbockers, but comic louts. Their buffoonish celebrations in San Francisco's Pioneer Hall displayed the true nature of the greedy and vulgar frontier Californian. There was no aristocracy in California, felt Fisher, nor any reverence—except for a "tendency to cringe, from weakness at the knees, when a coin jingles."[29]

The Pioneer himself, in fact, by the late 1860's and early 1870's began to show a tragic side. "And where are they now?" Mark Twain asked of all the brave young men who twenty years ago had come to California. "Scattered to the ends of the earth—or prematurely aged and decrepit—or shot or stabbed in street affrays—or dead of disappointed hopes and broken hearts—all gone, or nearly all—victims devoted upon the altar of the golden calf—the noblest holocaust that ever wafted its sacrificial incense heavenward. It is pitiful to think upon."[30] John Augustus Sutter and James Wilson Marshall, who had brought about the Gold Rush, seemed especially emblematic of the pioneer past tapering off into a tale of poverty, depression and defeat. Sutter once ruled the vast estates of New Helvetia like a medieval baron. With the Gold Rush, his workers deserted him, squatters seized his property, and by the time the Supreme Court confirmed his titles he was too bankrupt to do anything about it. He quit California in the early 1870's, pathetically imploring Congress for compensation, which never came, and died in a Washington, D.C., hotel room.

In partnership with Sutter in building a sawmill on the south fork of the American River, James Wilson Marshall, a wheelwright and a carpenter, picked up a few nuggets of gold on 24 January 1848 from a gravelly river bed—and lived miserably ever after. He had already lost a ranch in Butte County when he had been discharged with no pay from Frémont's California Battalion; now, having brought on the Gold Rush, Marshall was once again ignored for services rendered. Never stable, he grew morose and misanthropic, drinking heavily, feeling himself under a curse. He should have become a public hero; instead he was an embarrassment. "The history of California has not yet been written in detail," pleaded George Frederic Parsons in 1870, "but when it is we trust the historian will not have to record that James Marshall, the discoverer of gold, the Founder of the State's prosperity, was permitted to sink into a pauper's grave by the people to whom he gave all that they possess."[31] Briefly during the 1870's Marshall held a state pension, which the legislature failed to renew in 1878 because of Marshall's public drunkenness. He died in brooding obscurity in 1885 at Coloma in Eldorado County, near the site of his famous discovery.

Unambiguous disasters, redolent of the sense of defeat which permeated the 1870's, the lives of Sutter and Marshall directly served the counter-fable of the California past. Another broken pioneer, Joshua Norton, made a more indirect and ambiguous contribution to the counter-fable. In one sense Norton was not a negative figure at all. San Franciscans were delighted by and humored their beloved eccentric, Norton I, Emperor of the United States and Protector of Mexico, without realizing what an ironic commentary His Imperial Majesty offered them on themselves. Like Sutter and Marshall, Emperor Norton possessed a paradigmatic sadness. Of English Jewish descent, Joshua Norton came to San Francisco in 1849, where he flourished as a wholesale grocer. In 1853 he lost everything—a quarter of a million dollars—in an attempt to corner the rice market. After a few attempts to recover from bankruptcy, Norton, around the summer of 1857, dropped out of sight—and emerged two years later as Norton I, Emperor of the United States. For the next twenty years, until his death in 1880, Norton carried on his mock sovereignty, dressed in imperial attire, issuing proclamations, which the newspapers published, and scrip, which merchants honored. Aside from the fact that he added color and personality to San Francisco, Norton was tolerated because he was intensely likable and not without a certain shrewd intelligence. His scrip never exceeded manageable sums and his edicts always contained a good deal of sound advice. As a parodic anti-type, furthermore, Emperor Norton advanced a complex statement. Speculation had driven him mad and so he stood as a warning against it, yet the identity arising out of his insanity had kept Norton from a suicide's grave or a madman's cell, and so it was from another point of view an affirmative way of coping. Simultaneously, Norton—like California—was the victim of the very delusions in and through which he survived. Ironically, he escaped the competition which had destroyed him. While his former colleagues continued to drop from overwork, oblivious of their own happiness and the betterment of the commonweal, Norton I lived imperially above the fray. He dined at public expense and devoted himself full time to the improvement of society. In madness he had found a bizarre sort of freedom and a not unappreciated sense of public purpose.

Joshua Norton thus tenuously held himself together, but most of California in the decade of the 1870's seemed to be falling apart. On 26 August 1875 the Bank of California failed and a depression set in. The Central Pacific and its subsidiaries tightened their hold on state and local governments, transportation rates, land titles, and water rights. Unemployed workingmen flooded into San Francisco, angrily hanging about street-corners and sand-lots. In July 1877 they rioted and a Committee of Public Safety was formed against them, headed by William T. Coleman, leader of the Vigilance Committee of 1856. A Workingmen's party arose, dominated temporarily by a demagogic Irish teamster, Dennis Kearney, who fanned hatred of the Chinese and talked loosely of a bloody revolution. Discontent fortunately took more peaceful forms. A convention met at Sacramento to draft a reformed state constitution, which the voters ratified on 17 May 1879. From start to finish, north and south, the 1870's had been an unmitigated disaster of drought, crop failure, urban rioting, squatter wars, harassment and murder of the Chinese, cynical manipulation of politics by the railroad, depression, price fixing, bank failure, and stock swindles.

No wonder Jannett Blakeslee Frost felt compelled to issue a jeremiad regarding the whole California experiment. Although *California's Greatest Curse* (1879) took as its central metaphor the state's drinking problem, Jannett Frost addressed herself to the failure of California on a variety of fronts. Alcoholism symbolized a larger and more total squandering of energies. It symbolized exuberance run to seed. J. D. Borthwick had considered the drinking of Californians as part of their habit of living life to the full: "They make the voyage through life under a full head of steam all the time; they live more in a given time than other people, and naturally have recourse to constant stimulants to make up for the want of intervals of abandon and repose."[32] By the late 1870's when Frost wrote, drinking no longer assuaged a thirst for life—if it ever really had—but betokened social decay. With statistics and detail, Frost gave an anatomy of San Francisco's alcoholism: the wretched deaths, suicides, and murders, the men and women in prison cells or lying on the streets in their vomit, the magistrate's court where was unfolded the miseries of families. Evoking the struggle of the pioneers in their migration of thirty years previously, surveying the miserable California present, Jannett Frost asked in the year 1879: was this what it had all come to?

She was especially distressed by the degeneration of California's youth. A wave of juvenile delinquency and street crime swept San Francisco in the 1870's, where a new word—hoodlum—was coined to describe the hordes of idle, vicious young men who loitered about on corners or ran in marauding gangs. They were especially cruel to the Chinese and in one horrible case tortured an Oriental to death. Restless, randomly violent, going nowhere and doing nothing, the hoodlum was the very opposite of what had been hoped for. Here, then, in the counter-fable, were the children of California.

The California dream seemed to have spent itself, and, not surprisingly, the state began to lose some of its most talented literary men. One by one they deserted: Mark Twain, Clarence King, Bret Harte, Ambrose Bierce, Prentice Mulford, Charles Warren Stoddard, Joaquin Miller, Henry George. Death claimed J. Ross Browne, Alonzo Delano, and Benjamin Parke Avery. In 1875 *The Overland Monthly* folded (it would be revived in 1883) and the literary vein in such surviving journals as *The Golden Era* ran very, very thin. Some who left—Bierce, Stoddard, Miller—would someday return, but to an impoverished literary California which had never recovered from the mass exodus of talent. New writers—only children in the 1870's—Jack London, Frank Norris, and Mary Austin, among others, would restore California's lost literary luster; but in the meanwhile that miraculous time when San Francisco was the literary capital of the nation, that brilliant bohemian time preserved so charmingly in Franklin Walker's *San Francisco's Literary Frontier* (1939), vanished like a decade's dream. The Civil War had partly accounted for the congregating of talent in a remote frontier city. Mark Twain and many others had been content to wait out the conflict. Now an East once again at peace—and marvelous Europe—called them away from their Pacific bohemia. To be frank, there was little to stay for, and they knew it. The basis of San Francisco's literary culture had been a temporary expatriation. During the 1860's outsiders with other places and other commitments on their minds culled the state's romance as a miner dug for gold. For writers, California's gifts were not serious thought or high art, but the evanescent gifts of sentiment, charm, and humor. Now, in the 1870's, California had become a very grim place indeed. Even at its best, in the 1860's, there had been times when the vein of romance threatened to run thin before facts of violence, mismanagement, and seedy defeat. The affirming humor of Harte, Twain, and Mulford always operated on the edge of perjury. There was so much that even they could not make funny, and by the 1870's they were tired of trying. Their charming sketches and stories were part of California's fable. Now their departure became part of the counter-fable.

IV

Commentators and historians advanced fable and counter-fable alike. As historians and cultural critics, Californians rarely indulged in pure jeremiads. The promotional impulse natural to a new region ran too strong. Henry George, a San Francisco journalist, came to intellectual maturity during this era of promotional writing, first a time of hope and then, by the mid-1870's, a time of bitter disillusionment. The shattering of George's hopes resulted in no mere qualification of official fable, but in a searching scrutiny into the socio-economic processes that had fenced off the garden of California. If, in the 1860's, Thomas Starr King had been California's Moses, pointing the way to the Promised Land, then George, in the 1870's, played Jeremiah, rebuking Californians for the havoc they had wrought in the land of milk and honey God had given them. Like King, George was self-taught, religious, and filled with love for California. In 1868 he expressed his fears and enthusiasms in an essay in *The Overland Monthly* entitled "What the Railroad Will Bring Us." Many were asking that same question. A sense that California stood on the threshold of a new era pervaded the state as two bands of track crept closer to their Utah connection.

George opened his essay with a contribution to the California fable. The state, he said, had a charm difficult to analyze. Life in California possessed "a certain cosmopolitanism, a certain freedom and breadth of common thought and feeling, natural to a community made up from so many different sources . . . a feeling of personal independence and equality, a certain hopefulness and self-reliance, and a certain large-heartedness and open-handedness." Equality, enthusiasm, and hope—that had been the message of California's frontier. George feared the frontier's passing when the railroad brought an industrial order. "There was something in the great possibilities of the country," he wrote, using the past tense as if those possibilities had already slipped away, "in the feeling that it was one of immense latent wealth; which furnished a background of which a better filled and more thoroughly developed country is destitute, and which contributed not a little to the active, generous, independent social tone." Industrialism, George warned, might turn out more curse than blessing. Already he saw signs of dangerous land speculation, speculators consolidating huge holdings in an effort to push up prices for the wave of immigrants expected to arrive on the railroad. Let Californians beware the dangers of the coming era. "A great State is forming; let us see to it that its foundations are laid firm and true."[33]

The fact was, California's foundations were already fatally shaky in the area George specified: land ownership. On 3 March 1851 Congress passed "An Act to Ascertain and Settle the Private Land Claims in the State of California," introduced by California's Senator William Gwin. Articles VIII and IX of the Treaty of Guadalupe Hidalgo had guaranteed property rights of Mexicans who lived in territory acquired by the United States. But Gwin's bill made it mandatory that every holder of a Mexican title appear before a Land Commission and prove the validity of his claim. In other words, the burden of proof—and the cost of proceedings—rested with native Californians. Appealed up the judicial ladder, the average case remained in litigation for about seventeen years, an eighth of them reaching the Supreme Court. By the early 1860's it was clear to John S. Hittell that the instability of land titles in California was retarding the growth of a sound social order. Immigrants refused to come to the state, at least the thrifty, hard-working sort of immigrant who would want to make certain that the land he sweated over really belonged to him. A million citizens, Hittell believed, should have been on the California land by 1863, conferring "all those blessings of inestimable value which come only with numerous fixed and happy homes, and the best regulated social order." As it was, "fifty years of peace and justice cannot place California where she now would have been had justice and sound policy been adopted twelve years ago."[34]

In place of Hittell's vision of American yeomen on the California soil, a plantation-like pattern developed, huge acreages worked by gangs of paid laborers. Many landowners were of Southern birth or sympathies, and the baronial style of California ranch life, supported by crews of Chinese or

Mexican employees, had antebellum overtones. By the early 1870's, one five-hundredth of the California population held half of California's land, or, as Professor E. S. Carr of the University of California dramatically put it, 516 Californians owned 8,685,439 acres, an area nearly twice the size of Massachusetts. Another twelve million or so acres were tied up in grants to railroads. California had been carved into a series of feudal domains.

American settlers refused to become contented peasants. Throughout the 1850's, 1860's, and 1870's, squatter violence was commonplace. The era opened in 1850 with squatter riots in Sacramento and closed in 1880 with the famous shoot-out at Mussel Slough depicted in Frank Norris' *The Octopus* (1901). Surely, the immigrants' promised land had an ironic reality. The dream of owning land came true for few Californians. San Francisco filled up with unemployed migrant workers, poverty-stricken and disaffected. "The rule is that success attends merit," said Bancroft in 1890 of the California experience; "the unsuccesful is pretty sure to be faulty. No one has a right to be poor in California. Unaccompanied by ill health or other misfortunes, poverty is a sin."[35] Henry George knew that poverty in California was no sin, but an unavoidable condition. In 1864, broke, out of work in one of San Francisco's seasonal depressions, he had begged on the city streets in order to feed his wife and child. His experiences as a working man had made him fear the coming of an industrial economy to California. "She will have more people," he wrote of the railroad era; "but among those people will there be so large a proportion of full, true men? She will have more wealth; but will it be so evenly distributed? She will have more luxury and refinement and culture; but will she have such general comfort, so little squalor and misery; so little of the grinding, hopeless poverty that chills and cramps the souls of men, and converts them into brutes?"[36]

The question was not rhetorical, but prophetic. Conditions grew worse with the arrival of the railroad. Riding in the Oakland foothills on New Year's Day 1870, George realized with the clarity of a revelation that land monopoly was the cause of California's polarization into tight sectors of poverty and wealth. The long-range effect of George's insight was publication of *Progress and Poverty* in 1879. More immediately, George diagnosed California's dilemma in a brilliant pamphlet, *Our Land and Land Policy, National and State*, published in San Francisco in 1871. In terms of the counter-fable of California, the pamphlet provided one of the most eloquent expressions of the reverse side of the California myth. California

Henry George (1839–1897)

King played Moses, pointing the way to the Promised Land; George played Jeremiah, rebuking Californians for the havoc they had wrought in Canaan. Riding in the Oakland foothills on New Year's Day 1870, George realized with the force of a religious revelation that land monopoly was the cause of California's polarization into sectors of poverty and wealth. A specifically Californian anger was at the core of his Progress and Poverty.

had begun with so many possibilities, George lamented, especially the opportunity of ensuring a good life on the land for greater numbers of people than possible anywhere else in the nation. Had the United States honored the Mexican land grants as it was morally obliged to do, the government could have easily bought up the land and placed it in the public domain. As it was, California's history began with a fatal curse, a legacy of "greed, of perjury, of corruption, of spoliation and high-handed robbery, for which it will be difficult to find a parallel." An alien way of life, supposedly destroyed in the Civil War, reigned supreme in the valleys of California, a plantation economy supported by coolie labor. "What the barbarians enslaved by foreign wars were to the great land lords of Ancient Italy," George believed, "what the blacks of the African coast were to the great land lords of the Southern States, the Chinese coolies may be, in fact are already beginning to be, to the great land lords of our Pacific slope." The beauty and the richness of the California landscape, he lamented, mocked the rotten foundations of California society. Instead of a humanized landscape, dotted with farms and farmhouses, showing the care of resident families, California yawned open with empty wheat fields, dotted by occasional shacks—"unpainted frame shanties, without garden or flower or tree"—housing hirelings who worked for a landlord living luxuriously in San Francisco. Larger than Great Britain, Holland, Belgium, Denmark, and Greece combined, California, George complained, "does not contain the population of a third-class modern city." Such was "the blight that has fallen upon California, stunting her growth and mocking her golden promise."

The state's one significant urban opportunity had been mismanaged. When San Francisco obtained title to its public land, it had "an opportunity to build up a great city, in which tenement houses and blind alleys would be unknown; in which there would be less poverty, suffering, crime, and social and political corruption than in any city of our time, of equal numbers." Instead of building this Western City or a Hill, instead of realizing a paradigm of urban possibilities flung dramatically on the edge of the continent, San Francisco had sold the bulk of its public lands to speculators, who, in turn, subdivided them into dreary gridiron patterns—patterns of maximum profit and minimum social responsibility. Mocking the grandeur of the Golden Gate, stood just another ugly American city. Roaming its streets, just another urban proletariat. The most pernicious effect of all this hopelessness was upon the character of Californians, "the gradual decadence of that independent personal habit both of thought and action which gave to California life its greatest charm." Instead of sturdy farmers and mechanics, depressions and landlessness had reduced California's population to a debased condition "more shiftless, perhaps, than that of any State in the Union where slavery has not reigned."[37]

Progress and Poverty, which appeared in the last year of George's residence in California, reached beyond the limits of the state, examining the premises of the entire industrial order. Yet the processes George unraveled on an international scale were first observed on the immediate stage of California during his career as a journeyman and a journalist, processes exceptionally discernible because they had been compressed into a brief thirty years of history. The roots of *Progress and Poverty* in George's California experience were evident in the examples he used and the allusions he made. But it was more than as a stock of images that California figured in *Progress and Poverty.* A specifically Californian anger that the land had been denied the people stood at the psychological core of the book. The image of empty California landscape, so present in *Our Land and Land Policy,* still haunted George. "And on uncultivated tracts of land in the new State of California," he noted, "may be seen the blackened chimneys of homes from which settlers have been driven by force of laws which ignore natural right, and great stretches of land which might be populous are desolate, because the recognition of exclusive ownership has put it in the power of one human creature to forbid his fellows from using it." George's pivotal assertion, that "the ownership of land is the great fundamental fact which ultimately determines the social, the political, and consequently the intellectual and moral condition of a people," can easily be construed as a California cry. For had not George seen the vigor of Californians drained away as land conditions destroyed the social fabric?

There was for George an opposing analogue in California's own past. In the Gold Rush, for the first time in Anglo-Saxon history George believed, land had been held in common. The government owned all mining claims. Each miner had right to title as long as he worked his claim. Abandoned, a claim reverted to common ownership until assigned to another miner willing to make use of the property. In no case could land be held by non-occupants for purposes of speculation. California provided a model of free use of the land, just as it provided a model of the disastrous effects of land monopoly: in the image of the miner, the pattern of hope; in California's empty wheat fields, the fearsome image of "the final goal towards which the whole civilized world is hastening." George's approximation of frontier—and frontier virtues—with free land anticipated Frederick Jackson Turner's thesis by more than a decade. "To see human beings in the most abject, the most helpless and hopeless condition," George wrote, "you must go, not to the unfenced prairies and the log cabins of new clearings in the backwoods, where man single-handed is commencing the struggle with nature, and land is yet worth nothing, but to the great cities, where the ownership of a little patch of ground is a fortune."[38] The nostalgia and the ideality of this statement, like many of Turner's, betrayed a very Western viewpoint.

For if California brought George to the brink of despair, it also provided the wellsprings of hope. "The promised land flies before us like the mirage," he lamented in *Progress and Poverty*. True, as any Californian caught in the turmoil of the 1870's would admit. But even a mirage can offer hope. California was the measure of failure because it had promised so much. Surveying the state's history three years after the publication of *Progress and Poverty*, Alfred Wheeler would not be completely deluded when he described the "dominant idea" of California history as "a revelation of the possibilities of man released from despair and stimulated by hope."[39] George himself believed that such could still be, and a message of hope pervaded *Progress and Poverty*. Like another product of California's frontier, Josiah Royce, George felt the significance of the truism that "civilization is co-operation." George's notion of progress, as something to be fought for anew with each generation, had also a Roycean ring. "Men tend to progress just as they come closer together," believed George, "and by cooperation with each other increase the mental power that may be devoted to improvement. . . ."[40] With this mental power men could free themselves from history, restructure and reform their societies, slough off the mistakes of the past: such was the hope of George in *Progress and Poverty* and would be the hope, six years later, of Royce in *California*. There was nothing exclusively Californian in these beliefs, except that each man had felt the hope for a better life, the chance for a new start, that was part of the heritage of his state. Forget for a moment, implied George, that the dream seemed to be an elusive mirage. It was also a call to action. Redeem the dream—"substitute for the tenement house, surrounded by gardens"—but do not deny both dream and garden because of their present elusiveness.

Thus George struggled to realize the ideality implicit in California. In mental power, imagination, vision, and moral fervor, he stood like a giant above the other California commentators. Only a young instructor on the

University of California faculty, Josiah Royce, in rebellion against his native state because of its hostility to philosophy, would ever rise to similar heights. With varying degrees of power, historians, social commentators, and promotional writers had detected a pattern of hope in the California experience. It was, to be sure, a dual design, a divided fable, because California's experience had been a rhythm of expectation and disappointment, ideality and harsh fact. Certain related issues loomed paramount throughout the entire effort. What had been California's past, in both ideality and reality? What patterns of the present did that past illuminate and what imperatives were there for the future? The authors of *The Annals of San Francisco,* for all their prejudices, had asked such questions, and so had Franklin Tuthill, John S. Hittell, and Hubert Howe Bancroft.

A final answer never came to them, nor would it come at the turn of the century. California would always have an atmosphere of lingering promise, even when its inhabitants were most sure that they had captured its dream, fully lived out its fable. There would be a variety of efforts in the next quarter-century to give expression to a specifically Californian sense of things: in education, literature, art, architecture, and city planning, in individual lives. No one attempt ever fully expressed the regional culture of the state, but each demonstrated the vitality of California as a regional ideal.

5

"Because I am a Californian": The Loyalties of Josiah Royce

In 1883 the editors of Houghton, Mifflin, looking for someone to do the California volume for their *American Commonwealth* series, turned to a young instructor in the Department of Philosophy at Harvard, Josiah Royce. A native of California, Royce had left the University of California at Berkeley the previous year to fill in for William James, then on sabbatical, and was to remain for a distinguished career during Harvard's golden age of philosophy. He agreed to take on the assignment "as a thing for leisure hours," but it turned into an engrossing three-year project. Royce researched his book at Harvard, at government archives in Washington, and, most importantly, at the library of Hubert Howe Bancroft in San Francisco. Henry Lebbeus Oak, Bancroft's chief writer for the *History of California,* then in progress, guided Royce through the library's treasures and refined Royce's command of the sources. Back in Cambridge the young philosopher put his *California, From the Conquest in 1846 to the Second Vigilance Committee in San Francisco, a Study of American Character* into shape for publication in 1886. In one sense Royce's study was a commentary upon the Bancroft *History.* It avoided formal narrative in favor of reflections upon the first decade of the American presence in California. In that period, Royce felt, could be detected the burden and the promise of the California experience.

Who was this young Californian who set about to interpret the meaning of the California past? What had been the pattern of his own experience there that he now felt himself capable of construing the meaning of his native state for the rest of the nation? A certain ambiguity clung to Royce's exegesis of California events from the safety of Harvard. He had, after all, chosen to expatriate himself rather than to remain on the scene as a faculty member at Berkeley, and he now made the first task of his Harvard years an interpretive portrait of the commonwealth he had left behind. But if all this seemed strange, it was even more strange for a Californian to be teaching philosophy at Harvard in the first place. The tension could be creative as well as ambiguous. Royce's own life, the development of his intelligence from California to Germany to Harvard, was the underlying analogue and metaphor, the initiating pattern, for all that he would say about California.

Josiah Royce had been born in Grass Valley, California, a mining town in the foothills of the Sierras, in 1855. His parents, English-born but brought to America as children, moved to Iowa in 1848 after their marriage in Rochester, New York. In April 1849 they began a six-month overland trek to California, traveling by ox-drawn prairie schooner. They settled in Grass Valley after a variety of moves around the state. Royce remembered his boyhood as family-centered. His mother taught the school he attended, which met in his own home. Not until the age of ten did he have another teacher. His older sisters provided him with his only companionship. Since Josiah Royce Senior, a man destined never to find much success in California, left home quite often on business trips, and since Mrs. Royce excluded other children from the Royce household as not good enough to play with her own, Royce spent the first ten years of his life in a feminine environment, dominated by his mother.

The daughter of a Rochester merchandiser, educated as a girl at an academy, Mrs. Royce found California raw and threatening. She saw her home as a haven from the rudeness of a mining frontier. Her memoir of frontier life, drawn up for her son during his research for *California*, shows a strong sense of domestic management as a means of preserving civilized values on the frontier. Tales of rampant vice in early California might be true, Mrs. Royce told her son, "but just beside them, within the walls of neighboring dwellings, sometimes under the same roof, might have been drawn pictures, as true, of social circles in which refinement, morality, and religion were as fondly cherished, and as faithfully illustrated in domestic life, as in homes on the Atlantic shore."[1] A photograph of young Josiah, taken in Grass Valley in the early 1860's, shows a brushed and combed boy in a frogged jacket who would have done any Eastern mother proud. In view of the rawness of Grass Valley and the Royces' humble circumstances, the elegance of young Josiah said much about his mother's struggle for refinement and self-respect.

At the core of the Royce household was religion. A Baptist, Sarah Royce read the Bible two hours every day. In Rochester she had broken off her first engagement because her fiancé would not accept the necessity of total immersion. On the trek across the plains, the Royce wagon often had to travel alone because Mrs. Royce refused to travel on Sundays, delays which almost lost them their lives in a Sierra snowstorm. Royce's father, a Disciple of Christ, could quote freely from Scripture and spurned demon rum. Just as she forced her left-handed son to write with his right hand, Sarah Royce administered liberal doses of religion to a resisting Josiah. Forced to attend church on Sunday, the young boy would sneak away to pass the Sabbath morning with old-timers who sat sunning themselves. Even as a student at the University of California, Royce was spirited off on Sunday morning by his mother to the First Congregational Church in Oakland. (Understandably, he could never bring himself to attend formal worship services until a few years before his death, and he married a woman devoid of interest in traditional religion.) The stress which resulted from such an early forced feeding must have been intense; but the persistence of religious problems after rejection of formal religion drove Royce to philosophy. The boy who fled Grass Valley sermons was to spend a lifetime in search of an alternative formulation.

In the case of religion as a cultural and psychological expression, Royce never had the problem of rejection. He respected the fact that religion had operated as an organization of experience for his mother. It had sustained her, and so many like her, on the westward journey. Sarah Royce envisioned the whole trek in scriptural terms. She kept a "Pilgrim's Diary" in which she described herself as having a continuing "consciousness of an unseen Presence" Who guided the Royces in the desert like Israelites of old. Depressed by hardships, she remembered Hagar, an outcast, wandering and forsaken. The sight of burning tumbleweed, like the vision of Moses, refreshed her. "For a few moments I stood with bowed head," she recalled, "worshipping the God of Horeb, and I was strengthened thereby."[2] It was this spiritual aspect of the westward journey which impressed Royce and which he described at length in *California*. He portrayed it as a moral and imaginative preparation for life in California: "one element more of religious steadfastness for the struggle that was yet to come, in early California, between every conservative tendency and the forces of disorder."[3]

That overland migration also taught the value of community. Royce saw the struggle for community as the key factor in California history. As much of California memory as German Idealism went into the forging of his later theories of loyalty and community. California made Germany psychologically possible. Instances of community abound in his mother's memoir. Gear was lent the Royces when their own, infected with cholera, had to be destroyed on the trail. A relief team was able to rescue them from certain death in the Sierras only because passing parties secured aid. When they were flooded out of their Sacramento home, Samuel Hopkins Willey lodged them with his own family. "Any newcomer into San Francisco in those days," Mrs. Royce noted, "had but to seek, in the right way, for good people, and he could find them."[4]

In 1853 the Royces settled on a small ranch a mile outside Grass Valley in a two-story white frame house, porched on three sides, overlooking the Sierran countryside. There Royce spent his first ten years. To the end of his life, he insisted upon the rich experiences of community of his Grass Valley boyhood. This sense of community was linked up with a sense of the past. "A child born in one of our far western settlements," Royce once said, "grows up amid a community that is a few years older than himself, and not as old as his eldest brother. Yet he shall look upon all these rickety, wooden houses, and half-graded streets, full of rubbish, as the outcome of an immense past; he shall hear of the settlement of the town as he hears of ancient history, and he shall reverence the oldest deserted, weather-beaten rotting log-cabin of the place, with its mud chimney crumbling to dust, quite as much as a modern Athenian child may reverence the ruins of the Parthenon."[5] As a boy Royce was very much aware of the burden of the past. In the simple context of a mining town, he took his first intellectual steps. "My earliest recollections include a very frequent wonder as to what my elders meant when they said that this was a new community," he said of his first analytical efforts. "I frequently looked at the vestiges left by the former diggings of miners, saw that many pine logs were rotten, and that a miner's grave was to be found in a lonely place not far from my own house. Plainly men had lived and died thereabouts. I dimly reflected that this sort of life had apparently been going on ever since men dwelt thereabouts. The logs and the grave looked old. The sunsets were beautiful. The wide prospects when one looked across the Sacramento Valley were impressive, and had long interested the people of whose love for my country I heard much. But what was there then in this place that ought to be called new, or for that

Josiah Royce (1855–1916)

Pictured here as an undergraduate at the newly founded University of California at Berkeley, Royce left California for a distinguished career at Harvard during its Golden Age of Philosophy. Yet he never ceased to think of himself as a Californian. In the struggle of his native state to achieve a regional identity, Royce wanted his thought to give direction—like that pillar of light which his mother claimed had in 1849 guided the Royce family across the trackless desert.

matter, crude? I wondered, and gradually came to feel that part of my life's business was to find out what all this wonder meant."[6]

Royce's wonder began in California; so did his education. Although his native state could not sustain a mature philosopher, it made that maturity possible. Remembrance of intellectual opportunities available through the bachelor's degree, taken from the infant University of California in 1875, helped account for his adult hopes for viable provincial societies in America. In 1866 the Royce family moved to San Francisco precisely so that Josiah could attend the free public schools. He attended Lincoln Grammar School from 1866 to 1869, then Boy's High School from 1869 to 1871. Although Royce's father peddled fruits and vegetables from a cart, although his home at 1032 Folsom, on the outskirts of the city, was shabby and his clothes were seedy and countrified, the boy had first-rate educational opportunities. At the Lincoln School on Fifth and Market Streets, Royce had the advantage of a 900 volume library, an excellent student-teacher ratio, and one of the most progressively designed school buildings in the United States. Psychologically and intellectually, Royce developed. "Redheaded, freckled, countrified, quaint, and unable to play boy's games"—so he later described himself—he had some trouble adjusting to the urban rough and tumble of the schoolyard, but he later considered the experience one of the most significant steps he took toward understanding the majesty of community. A student essay, "Is The Assassination of Tyrants Ever Justifiable?" written at age fourteen and published in the school newspaper, had an anticipatory ring. Royce concluded that assassination was never justifiable because of its bad effects upon society as a whole. It was a superficial means of social reform, just like lynching in the mines, "which everyone believes to be wrong."[7] Promoted to Boy's High School in 1869, Royce excelled in mathematics. In the fall of 1871, two months short of his sixteenth birthday, Royce and eighty others entered the University of California, then in Oakland and in its third year as a state university.

He spent two years at the Oakland campus, site of the parent College of California, before the university moved to its Berkeley location in the fall of 1873. The campus, hastily completed, consisted of two four-story buildings perched atop bare hills, one building of brick, the other of wood, and both of monumental ugliness. When it rained, the unplanted campus became a sea of mud. As a township, Berkeley hardly existed, a restaurant and a small hotel comprising the downtown area. There were neither sidewalks nor a practicing physician. Students and faculty continued to live in

Oakland, commuting by horse-drawn trolley until homes and boarding-houses could be built. Yet in this remote provincial university, as raw and ungainly as the state whose name it bore, a philosopher—one of America's few—spent undergraduate years as rich in memory as if he had strolled across the venerable turf of Harvard Yard. "Narrow, indeed, were the material conditions of our work," Royce said of his undergraduate years. "But great and beautiful was the world of learning to which we were privileged, even by means of these defective material conditions, and by the aid of the teachers who guided us, to win our first introduction." He began his studies with the vague idea of becoming a mining engineer, but he eventually chose to do classics under Professor Martin Kellogg. He read heroically, filling countless copybooks with notes. There were barely 12,000 volumes in the ill-lighted, almost uncatalogued library, Royce later recalled, but California's faculty encouraged students to pursue independent reading and research. "Under the influence of my teacher's counsel," he said of hours spent on the top floor of Brayton Hall, "I sought for these books, I found them, and I found in them what I shall never forget while I have any power to study left in me."[8] Just as a rude mining town offered a full range of community experiences, so the ill-equipped state university offered a stimulating introduction to higher learning. In both cases, it was not external rawness that retarded, but inner life that sustained.

Royce's freshman compositions were characterized by reverie, loneliness, and perplexity. Over the years, this self-absorbed mistiness gives way to an assured intellectual voice. In his senior year Royce sat on the board of editors of *The Berkeleyan*, a college journal. The gap between his *Berkeleyan* pieces and his freshman compositions testifies to the growth of his undergraduate years. His lifelong assertion that a sense of culture in its most far-reaching aspects had always been possible to him as a Californian is borne out by the range, variety, and allusiveness of his mature undergraduate writing.

Motifs of community and work for the Ideal are everywhere apparent. In one essay Royce warned against rivalries between undergraduate factions. The stage was trivial, but Royce saw great issues at play. "He who feels how small a part he and his fellow atoms make of the great living, moving whole, Humanity," wrote the young undergraduate, "will appreciate how minute are all the distinctions of position in College when compared with the truly great ends of life, the bettering of the whole race, a task in which each individual is but as a drop of water, but the aggregate is the vast tidal wave of progress."[9] In another essay he probed the way ideals shaped history. Environments give rise to specific ideal possibilities, Royce speculated, which in turn reshape events and environments. This is never a fully conscious process in a culture, rather a subliminal awareness of what ideals are both possible and necessary. Royce failed to provide an ontology for these ideals, but the direction his thought was taking in the matter of the Community and the Ideal was apparent.[10] An essay on Tennyson's *Idylls of the King* which Royce wrote just before he departed for graduate study in Germany serves as a summary of his intellectual self at age nineteen, on the verge of leaving California for the first time. He praised Tennyson for portraying the ideal of a transformed society and for conveying the reality of idealism and religious sentiment as concrete motivational factors. Religious motivation, Royce lamented, was becoming next to impossible for art to depict convincingly: an unfortunate turn of events for the historical function of art. For it was Spirit, in the long run, which shaped events. "We are to sympathize with every exhibition of that spirit, whatever it is, whether we choose to call it fanaticism or inspiration, with that spirit which has never allowed human nature to rest content with the existing realities of life, but has ever urged it on to seek to realize ideal conceptions of beauty."[11]

It is difficult to see why some critics say that Royce brought Idealism back from Germany as an exotic hothouse plant which he unsuccessfully tried to make bloom in America. Idealism, as imaginative response and conceptual reference, had already bloomed in California, before Royce set foot in Germany. German philosophy coaxed that disposition onto a higher level of awareness and expression, but its roots held firm near the Pacific. It is not impossible to see the relationship between Royce's lyrical Tennyson essay and some of the most magnificent portions of *The Problem of Christianity* (1913), Royce's undoubted masterpiece, although thirty-eight years lie between statements. In a quiet provincial university, in a remote and sparsely populated state, Royce had glimpsed the Ideal. He would always be grateful for the romance of that youthful encounter. It became the love and the work of his life.

In June of 1875, financed by a group of San Francisco businessmen, Royce left for a year's study at Göttingen and Leipzig. The next year Daniel Coit Gilman invited him to be among the first twenty fellows of Johns Hopkins, where he took his Ph.D. in 1878 at the age of twenty-three. Unable to find a post as an instructor of philosophy, Royce returned to the University of California, where he served as an instructor in rhetoric and logic until 1882. It was one thing for Royce the boy from the provinces to prosper in a provincial university. It was another thing for Doctor Royce, who had seen the great world and who had high intellectual ambitions, to content himself with the irksome task of pounding principles of composition into freshmen. It was a bad time to be at the University of California. The Constitution of 1879, expressing the resentment felt by so many in the 1870's against the supposedly aristocratic state university, had drastically cut back the state's educational system, especially public high schools. With no steady supply of secondary graduates, enrollment dropped, reaching a low of 224 in 1882, the year Royce left for Harvard.

Royce's personal situation participated in the general malaise. He had been hired to teach English when his real ambitions were for philosophy. "My work is not, so far, very uncongenial," he wrote President Gilman at the start of his first semester; "but it is for all that not exactly what I should choose as other than a preparation for more special tasks. . . . I doubt if philosophy is destined to succeed well in California, or Literary Criticism either. If I want to continue my worship at these two altars, I must make a pilgrimage again someday."[12] Writing to another Baltimore patron, Royce was more candid. "Here in the University I am after all much alone. It is not what it used to be when I was a student." Berkeley may well claim to be the Athens of the Pacific, Royce observed ironically. "The Athens, however, lacks so far its Pericles, its Socrates, its Phidias, in fact all its list of great names from Solon on. It also lacks wit and wisdom in the ranks of the common people. . . . We Californians make but poor figures in our daily walk and conversation. Foundations for higher growth we sadly lack. Ideals we have none. Philistines we are in soul most thoroughly. And when we talk, our topics of discussions are so insufferably finite."[13] Royce complained that many of the faculty resented his turning freshman composition into a logic course. When he felt himself liked, it was by those who still regarded him as a bright undergraduate.

Throughout these same years, in spite of isolation and lack of colleagues, Royce sustained and purified his philosophical ambitions. The "Thought Diary" he kept reveals the drama of a solitary mind in invigorating confrontation with first principles. There are few references to other thinkers. The aridity of the California philosophical landscape must have functioned for Royce in the same way that another desert crossing had functioned for his mother in 1849: the austerity of the ordeal drove one back to a dependence upon fundamentals. Dissipation and elaboration through scholarship become impossible, distracting satisfactions fade from experience, and one faces in the desert glowing tenets, bituminous pillars of negation and assent. After the rich diet of Germany and Baltimore, California's ascetic table gave Royce time, first for digestion, and then for the inducement of that state of near-hunger that always precedes great vision. In "Meditation Before the Gate"—written into the "Thought Diary" in 1879—Royce saw California as both garden and desert of philosophy. "With these problems," vowed Royce, regarding the great issues of mind and nature, "I shall seek to busy myself earnestly, because that is each one's duty; independently, because I am a Californian, as little bound to follow mere tradition as I am liable to find an audience by preaching in this wilderness; reverently, because I am thinking and writing face to face with a mighty and lovely Nature, by the side of whose greatness I am but a worm."[14] The paradox of Royce's Californianism stood apparent in these lines penned as he looked across the San Francisco Bay toward the Golden Gate. California's beauty inspired. Its newness encouraged independence and innovation. Yet how far he felt from the real centers of inquiry!

Fear gnawed at him, the fear of unrealized ambition. Sometimes that fear said that his excursions into original thought were naïve, doomed. In an untitled poem copied into the "Thought Diary," he lamented his seemingly futile attempts at philosophical growth:

> Like the waves
> That beat against grey water-sculptured rocks,
> And thundering at the base of frowning hills
> In foam and laughter die, so do thy thoughts
> Glistening, but breaking on the shore at last,
> Insult, yet conquer not eternal truth.

Sometimes this fear made him see in some of his colleagues the very image of ambition doomed by California. His mentor at Berkeley, Edward Rowland Sill, knew that Royce must not stay too long in the wilderness. "A certain period of isolation in the Desert," Sill believed, "and of being tempted by the Devil is probably good for any of the sons of men, but not too long."[15] Royce knew that Sill spoke from experience. Arriving in California in the early 1860's after graduation from Yale, Sill vowed that he "could not live here long—no culture, no thought, no art." After twenty years, he still considered California a "Cimmerian darkness," but he remained until 1883. What had kept him there? Even his Berkeley friends agreed that there had been a certain truncation to Sill's career, a truncation directly tied up with the obscurity and meanness of California.

An Eastern institution like Harvard or Yale, they agreed, would have encouraged his talents more than had the University of California. Sill willingly assumed the role of missionary. He at once wanted and did not want the failure such a role implied for his career as a poet. Of long ministerial descent, Sill could never justify himself to himself as a poet alone. He also wanted to play out a rather sad part as the Matthew Arnold of California. In time, he resigned himself to winning neither the battle for poetry nor the battle for culture. Psychologically, he half-desired both defeats.

If a New Englander like Sill had difficulty becoming a poet in California, Royce could surmise, how much more impossible for a native son to become a philosopher! Did he see this same career of fatally mixed aims in store for himself? Royce discouraged the poet from casting pearls before swine. "Ah, Royce," Sill answered, "you never know in this world whether you were really casting pearls at all until you feel the tusks." One could grow to love the tusks; their stabs conferred a sense of mission, assured one of his worth. "What most strikes me about him at this moment," Royce remembered on the occasion of Sill's death, "is the fact that he was, I might say, slain solely by his zeal for his ideals."[16] Subtle temptation for the would-be philosopher! Renounce philosophy as a Californian because California was not ready for philosophy; then strike out on a pseudo-career as a preacher of the necessity of philosophy for California. No! Better to leave, better to pursue the vocation straightforwardly and without messianic delusions. Let him devote himself to doing the thing itself, not to calling for it to be done. Get out of California—Royce knew that he had to.

William James of Harvard helped Royce make good his escape. Royce had made a pilgrimage to James's Cambridge home in the summer of 1877, asking advice regarding possibilities for a philosophical career in the United States. Others had discouraged Royce, saying that too few positions were available in American universities. But James encouraged the young graduate student and promised to be on the alert for an appointment. James even tried to secure Royce an instructorship at Harvard, an effort which intensified as Royce's dissatisfaction with Berkeley grew. He advised Royce to be patient. At twenty-four, he had a full career ahead of him. Royce complained to James of his isolation in California: "There is no philosophy in California—from Siskiyou to Ft. Yuma, and from the Golden Gate to the summit of the Sierras." And in another letter: "Nobody really studies philosophy here. Metaphysically I am lonely."[17] "You are, after all, not so very much isolated in California," James soothed

Royce. "We are all isolated. . . . Books are our companions more than men. But I wish nevertheless, and firmly expect, that somehow or other, you will get a call East, and within my humble sphere of power I will do what I can to further that end."[18]

Royce assuaged his loneliness by marrying Miss Katharine Head on 20 October 1880. Sill had introduced Royce into the Head family, transplanted New Englanders of California's upper middle class. Judge E. F. Head, Royce's father-in-law, a graduate of the Harvard Law School, sat as a superior court judge in San Mateo. The contrast between the successful and respected Judge Head and Royce's father could not have been more marked. In California terms, at least, young Royce had arrived. But Katharine Royce wanted more out of life than playing faculty wife in a forgotten corner of the world. A tall, good-looking brunette, poet, pianist, translator of German and Italian, she hungered for a more expansive stage. On 23 April 1882 James offered Royce an appointment of one year as his replacement, with the hope of a longer contract. Royce packed himself, wife, and child off that summer for Cambridge. He was twenty-seven. His California years were over.

II

Royce brought to the writing of *California* a theory of human progress as well as the supportive pattern of his life history as a Californian. First of all, unlike most historians of California, Royce did not believe that progress was inevitable and that the story of California best demonstrated that inevitability. Teleology in the physical world, Royce argued, in no way proved inevitable progress in human affairs. In fact, he doubted whether a teleological march toward perfection could be safely asserted regarding nature itself. As an Idealist, Royce admitted there might be design in nature, but that design was an expression of Transcendent Will, not the working out of an inherent teleology. Progress in history came as the result of conscious, voluntary acts. "All cases of voluntary progress are also cases of evolution," he admitted, but not of an evolution dependent upon the natural world. Physical evolution tended toward diversity of form, localized adjustment. Progress among men, Voluntary Progress, tended toward simplification and unification of forms, especially forms of social organization. Men, in other words, made their own history, and the record of that history was to be found in their response to the challenges of social experience.[19]

No moral imperatives, especially no historical imperatives, could be gleaned from analogies to the physical world. "The facts of evolution stand there," Royce believed, "mere dead realities, wholly without value as moral guides, until the individual assumes his own moral principle, namely, his ideal determination to do nothing that a person considering the order of the world as a whole and desiring universal happiness would condemn, from the point of view of the general tendencies of acts." Did an act, in other words, favor Voluntary Progress? Royce described this principle as "the moral insight"—the belief that individual acts had to be paradigms of social cooperation. "The moral insight, insisting upon the need of the harmony of all human wills, shows us that, whatever the human good may be, we can only attain it together, for it involves harmony. . . . Therefore the sense of community, the power to work together, with clear insight into our reasons for so working, is the *first* need of humanity."[20]

How men served their community was from the first Royce's primary norm of moral judgment. But what about the community-in-time? Did it have a pattern of movement, a teleology? Royce's idealistic metaphysics ("all reality must be present to the Unity of the Infinite Thought") implied an understanding of the historical process as "the progressive realization by men of the eternal life of an Infinite Spirit." This realization occurred in time but was not a necessity of time. Each generation and each man re-manifested that Spirit in his own life, passing on the fruits of his witness in the form of the social structures of an improved community. Royce rejected the notion that each age inevitably got better. All that each age could do was to fund its wisdom into its institutions, its thought, and its art. In this way, there could be incremental development in the direction of the good, as each age amplified its heritage. Since pain and evil were inherent in nature itself, no generation escaped struggle. "The conflicts of morality are and must be eternal," Royce believed. To be good was not to conquer evil, but to oppose evil. Goodness and evil stood united in the moral act, the one subduing the other. "There at the one moment are good and evil, warring, implacable, yet united in the present momentary triumph of the good will." Whether or not this process was eternal, whether time would end, Royce believed philosophy incapable of asserting. Yet men had no choice but to build in time, even if deprived of teleological comfort. Faced with the continual necessary of social recreation, men turned to history for models, for types. "Faithfulness to history," Royce believed, "is the beginning of creative wisdom."[21]

Such reflections had implications for Royce's analysis of the first decade of California history, although he sometimes found the gap between philosophy and historical research frustrating. "If California history were only philosophy!" he lamented to Henry Oak during the composition of *California*. "For the Infinite as philosophy deals with him, never talks back, leaves no documents on record, and always stands still to be counted."[22] Yet Royce saw in California history a process more related to the expression of the Infinite than his humor indicated. "The greatest foe to voluntary progress everywhere," he had written, "and especially in politics and morals, is the selfishness of individuals."[23] In *California* Royce related how men overcame such selfishness only after it nearly destroyed their community, how they learned the lesson of social cooperation, and how in the process of doing all this they took the first hesitant steps of a new commonwealth in the direction of Spirit.

Most immediately, Royce intended his study for Californians. But because he felt the American community in California's first decade represented "the average national culture and character," he hoped that its history would interest the nation at large. In one brief decade California had replayed on a representative scale the entire course of American history, from discovery to crisis to social cohesion. The nation of 1886 had much to learn from the experience of the 1846-56 California frontier. California proved that if an American community neglected to organize society along just and careful lines, it soon reaped the whirlwind. "Every piece of neglected social work they had to do over again, with many times the toil. Every slighted duty avenged itself relentlessly on the community that had despised it." The burden of the California past asserted a notion that in time would develop into theories of loyalty and community. Bear Flaggers, Forty-niners, Vigilantes, all the seemingly disparate data of California's violent adolescence, meant one thing—for Californians, for Americans, for society at large: "It is the State, the Social Order, that is divine. We are but dust, save as this social order gives us life . . . if we turn again and serve the social order, and not merely ourselves, we soon find that what we are serving is simply our own highest spiritual destiny in bodily form."[24]

Royce despised romanticizers of the California past. The philosopher who believed that "the good act has its existence and life in the transcending of experienced present evil" was also the historian who wanted neither the good nor the evil of California history distorted. Both were organic to a usable historical fable. As a researcher, he distrusted pioneer memoirs. He found most marred by nostalgic romanticism. Pioneers tended to remember gunfights, gamblers, and ladies of the night, and to forget farmers, storekeepers, wives, and children. Bret Harte, who gave the myth of colorful California its fixed literary expression, especially irritated Royce. He assailed Harte's "perverse romanticism," leveling the charge first made by Mark Twain, that Harte was a dude whose stories of mining life "were not the result of any personal experience of really primitive conditions." Royce hated Harte's sentimentalizing of the miners' brutal habit of lynching, which he felt displayed "barbarous fury," not rollicking good humor. He lamented that Harte had set a literary trend which still dominated *The Overland Monthly*. Having grown up in a mining community, Royce said, he knew for a fact that Harte's tales had nothing to do with reality, no more than pastoral shepherds and shepherdesses had anything to do with frontier sheepherders. The problem was not whether or not Harte's fiction made pleasurable reading, but whether it corrupted California's sense of itself. A good dose of Harte's perverse romanticism had entered into California's self-image. Californians would have to correct that self-image by correcting their historiography. Let historians seek out the unwritten history of California, Royce urged. Let them drop their fascination with the colorful and grotesque and take up instead the story of the struggle for society. For what they salvaged from the past determined the values of California's future.

Historians had always acknowledged, for instance, that the imbalance between sexes during the early years had made prostitution a major social institution and put conventional family life under great stress. They compensated for any ugliness with the exaggerated myth that all decent women and even their fallen sisters were treated with chivalric reverence. Royce rejected the myth of romantic respect but admitted strain upon the family. "The family grows best in a garden with its kind," he noted, and California as yet was barren soil. Historians told but half the truth. Present from the start of the American period was the family, fighting to survive its transplantation to a hostile environment. Overland immigrants came to farm as well as to pan for gold. They were family people, and like the Royce family they had kept together. Perhaps facts of domestic persistence were not as engrossing as details of San Francisco's courtesan culture, but they were more essential to the long-range struggle for order and civilization. If the California of the late 1880's were truly to become the land of homes and families as her promoters promised, Royce urged, historians would have to make available this forgotten story of family survival.

Royce felt that Frederic Hall's *History of San Jose and Surroundings* (1871) was a good example of history-writing as a culture--building enterprise. Hall, a Santa Clara County attorney, began writing in the mid-1860's, when California was moving into a settled era. The San Jose lawyer structured his history around the theme of the movement from disorder to order, from early settlement, a time of gunfights and lynching mobs, to the present epoch of schools, churches, gardens, and San Jose's new courthouse. He said that he chronicled the lawlessness of the 1850's not for the sake of romantic color, but "to illustrate the moral condition of the general community, at a time when the social laws and regulations were more than usually at variance with the settled state of affairs in the older parts of our nation." Details of violence were not ends in themselves, but points of reference from which the community of San Jose could measure its hard-won struggle for civilization. If San Jose after its frontier era seemed lacking in color, then well and good. Hall refused to heroicize. He would tell the epic of settlement, of anonymous sustained achievement that went into the building of a community, "those facts which encompass the attractive spots which the inhabitants of this Valley call their HOMES,—spots ever dear to the human race."[25]

If Hall's *History of San Jose* seemed mature, *The Annals of San Francisco* (1855) seemed monstrous. For Royce, the *Annals* stood as matrix and model of false emphasis. Not that the *Annals* neglected the struggle for order. Its discussions of fire and burial associations, churches, schools, libraries, and architecture measured up to what Royce considered useful history. The authors did deplore San Francisco's lack of public spirit, and they stressed service to the community in the string of biographies concluding the volume. They praised the "rays of refinement . . . shooting through the sordid mass, and gradually turning it towards a feeling that there was something higher, happier, and better than mere money gathering."[26] What, then, were Royce's objections? He resented what he considered the *Annals*' falsifying romanticism. The authors, Royce argued, feared the "rays of refinement" that had begun to spread, dreading that something essential to California's excitement—vigor, style, color—would be lost with the departure of flush times. Thus they mythologized events of but five years past as if they were "romantic and almost forgotten ancient history." The fact that the *Annals* could simultaneously celebrate California's religion and irreligion showed its confusion. "San Francisco was to them a mere rubbish-heap of broken facts, and they had no conception of the sense of it," Royce complained. "One can remember as these men tell us, all sorts of confused emotions, but, as we judge from their wild and whirling words, one can remember nothing rational." Royce condemned the claim to universal debauchery. "We are, after all," Royce argued, "a persistently serious people in the manner of social amusements. And in San Francisco we had a great deal of business to do; and we did it. It took up nearly all of our time."[27] It was simply not true that everyone in early San Francisco was as the *Annals* described, a drinker, gambler, and whoremonger. How could the *Annals* in one breath condemn dueling and in the next delight that the introduction of swords by Frenchmen had added éclat to affairs of honor? How could it rue the effects of California upon family life pages away from an exuberant description of San Francisco's plush houses of joy? An innocent man had almost been hanged by the Vigilance Committee of 1851. Royce saw the affair as traumatic. The *Annals* wrote up this near-tragedy as a gargantuan Western joke, to be smoothed over in a round of drinks. Standing, as it did, as a source and type of California historiography, *The Annals of San Francisco*, Royce contended, had helped to introduce a retarding tendency—in both California history and life—a confusion of unruliness with vigor, recklessness with style, and bravado with self-confidence.

Royce's treatment of John C. Frémont illustrated his determination to set California history aright. He devoted an inordinate amount of his book to an investigation of Frémont's activities during the Bear Flag revolt. "I was only overconscientious," he wrote Milicent Shinn of *The Overland Monthly*, "and hence prolix."[28] Royce was nearer obsession than conscientiousness. He claimed that he began his research possessed of "a very high opinion of the work of the gallant Captain Frémont in the acquisition of California," but that examination of the record had disillusioned him. His naïveté was assumed. As a Californian, he must have been aware of the murky aspects of Frémont's reputation. During interviews with the General and Mrs. Frémont, Royce played with them like a cat with mice, leading the pair into equivocation and contradiction. With a thunderous rattling of evidence, he destroyed Frémont's version of the conquest: the story of how a captain of topographical engineers, leading a scientific expedition across the Rockies, with peaceful intent yet with secret instructions in case of war, came to the aid of oppressed American settlers in the Sacramento Valley, after himself being harassed by the California government. Frémont had no instructions, official or otherwise, countered Royce, to act against California. The only official effort had been Consul Thomas Oliver Larkin's attempt to persuade California peacefully to enter the Union. At their dramatic meeting on the shores of Klamath Lake on 9 May 1846, Lieutenant Archibald Gillespie of the Marine Corps brought Frémont no secret instructions from Washington, only dubious promptings from Frémont's father-in-law, Senator Thomas Hart Benton, who was anxious for the seizure of Mexican territory. Coming to the aid of the Bear Flaggers, Frémont violated orders. His status as an army captain gave an aura of legitimacy to disgraceful filibustering.

What, in all of this, were the sources of Royce's anger? Why should he think of the whole affair as "Frémont's League with the Devil"? Frémont and the Bear Flaggers, Royce felt, committed the original sin of California's history. The intention of the United States government had been to bring California into the Union without violence—to bring for the first time a Spanish-speaking society into full dignity of statehood. What a chance for redemption from the American burden of bloody and cynical conquest! What a chance to enrich the cultural complexity of the American Union! Instead, Royce bitterly observed, Frémont "brought war into a peaceful Department; his operations began an estrangement, insured a memory of blood-shed, excited a furious bitterness of feeling between the two peoples that were henceforth to dwell in California." When two generations later, the generation of Royce's maturity, Californians began to look with interest upon their lost Latin heritage, it was too late. The Spanish-speaking had been reduced to a defeated and degraded minority. Minute scrutiny of Old California by historians, wrote Royce, expressed "not only the private ambitions of authors, but the late and now fruitless repentance of the American as he remembers the little world of life his cruel progress in California has destroyed."[29] Histories, revivals of Mission architecture, pastoral myths of Old California, fantasies of a Mediterranean civilization on the Pacific were poor and sometimes pernicious substitutes for California's lost opportunity for Yankee-Latin accommodation. With the cynical destruction of Mexican culture, Americans in California had rejected certain traits sorely needed in the American character—a love of leisure, a taste for the pageantry of life, and an inability to be brutal with any degree of efficiency. Royce never denied the romantic appeal of the Frémont legend or the personal charm of the Conqueror of California. But the gallant captain had baptized California in blood and Royce wanted historians of the state to face honestly that horrible burden.

He at least granted Frémont credit for charm. He unequivocally despised Bear Flaggers. Californians should face facts, Royce argued: the Americans who drifted overland in the decade before the conquest were hardly all noble Anglo-Saxons. Many were uncouth and vicious, and the Mexicans immediately knew them for what they were, low caste gringos: "a fact which these vagabonds themselves were not slow to realize, and one which inspired them individually with the most violent hatred and disgust towards the rightful dwellers in the land." The Bear Flag revolt, which history saw so glorious, was in fact "unspeakably ridiculous, as well as a little tragical, and for the country disastrous." Its leaders, Semple and Ide, were perfect examples, near parodies in fact, of the liquor-inflamed frontier orator and the nasal Yankee crank. Official paintings might depict lean-jawed Bear Flaggers rallying around a banner raised aloft by Frémont, but Royce felt the early morning scene of unshaven Bear Flaggers sleeping off the effects of General Vallejo's confiscated liquor more representative.

The war of conquest conducted by the United States Army and Navy seemed hardly above the mock heroics of the Bear Flag. The whole affair, from Commodore Stockton's choleric abuse of native Californians to Ide's lecturing of bewildered Sonomans on the benefits of liberty before throwing them into the calaboose, was the very prototype of American relations with Latin neighbors: imperialism disguised as missionary zeal. Let Californians, and Americans, he warned, take note of the capacity for self-delusion demonstrated by the Bear Flag revolt, "so that when our nation is another time about to serve the devil, it will do so with more frankness, and will deceive itself less by half-unconscious cant. For the rest, our mission in the cause of liberty is to be accomplished through a steadfast devotion to the cultivation of our own inner life, and not by going abroad as missionaries, as conquerors, or as marauders, among weaker peoples."[30]

Nor was the ensuing Gold Rush devoid of lessons once the truth were faced. Royce qualified the claim of Anglo-Saxon order. Stability did not come naturally to the mines; it had to be struggled for, and that pattern of struggle would prove more useful as a social paradigm than notions of folk-moots in the Mother Lode. Perhaps the early days of the Gold Rush had seen some of the comradeship and good humor beloved in song and story. By 1851, however, murder and theft pervaded almost every mining community. Lynch law, far from representing the struggle for order, was but one symptom of an inner social disease. It was claimed that miners bypassed legal government because it had failed. Royce said that government failed because miners did not support it. Research into local newspapers convinced Royce that miners were anxious about their extra-legal activities, continually feeling the necessity to upgrade and justify mob vengeance. The concept of an autonomous miners' law never occurred to on-the-scene apologists. They knew they were acting outside the law, but justified it to themselves on the basis of necessity. Historians had praised public good humor. Royce countered that public good humor alternated with brutal mob action. Let California acknowledge this ugliness and violence, Royce urged, and then proceed to show how the community began to overcome these evils in 1851, "the year of clearer self-consciousness, of lost illusions, of bitter struggles, of tried heroism, of great crimes and blunders indeed, and of great calamities, but also of the salvation of the new State."[31] The road back from anarchy demonstrated what Royce felt the very essence of the moral act: the transcending of present evil. Was this not a more usable past than Bret Harte's static fable?

The same held true for California's political life. Royce agreed with the majority of historians that the Constitutional Convention of 1849 demonstrated "that ancient proceeding of compromise in place of adherence to abstract principle which has been all along so characteristic of the Anglo-Saxon in his political life." But it would take more than instinct to put California upon a sound political basis. It would take "voluntary and loyal devotion to society," a virtue warred against by the very ease with which California began its statehood. A good structure had been created, but then Californians neglected duties of citizenship as they went about the business of getting rich. San Francisco dramatized the underlying selfishness. Fires leveled the city six times before 1851 because no one would take the time to organize a fire department. Municipal politics sank deeper and deeper into corruption. Violence and murder became commonplace. San Francisco might have appeared colorful to another generation, but to inhabitants of 1851 the city was a hell-hole. The reform efforts of the Vigilance Committee of 1851 had no follow-up in sustained community loyalty, but the Vigilance Committee of 1856 showed "the conversion of honest men to a sensible and devout local patriotism." Commitment followed reform. "What it teaches to us now, both in California and elsewhere," wrote Royce of San Francisco's attempt to transcend its social evils in the years after 1856, "is the sacredness of a true public spirit, and the great law that the people who forget the divine order of things have to learn thereof anew some day, in anxiety and pain."[32] In the pattern of San Francisco's struggle Royce found a better lesson for California's present and future than in unexamined assertions of Anglo-Saxon political expertise.

Like most historians, Royce deplored the burden disputed land titles had put upon the state, discouraging settlement, encouraging squatter wars. What happened had been a tragedy, but what might have happened would have caused even more harm. Suppose, asked Royce, the principle of squatterism had prevailed? Suppose that instead of the admittedly weak Land Act of 1851 there had been a total repudiation of Mexican titles? Such an act would have represented a rejection of the very basis of society on the part of the infant commonwealth, a rejection of the responsibility of a community to sustain just laws. Royce considered a half-way measure like the Land Act better than outright piracy. Under the leadership of Dr. Charles Robinson, later Free-Soil governor of Kansas, Sacramento squatters in 1850 demanded that they be granted land that belonged to Sutter, not because they disputed Sutter's title, but because they disputed all titles. As Americans, California belonged to them under a higher law. Royce deplored the precedent implicit in such an abstract rejection of law: "The divine ideal is partly and haltingly realized in just these erring social laws,—for instance, in the land laws of California—and we have to struggle in and for the actual social order, and cannot hope to reach the divine by sulking in the bush, or by crying in the streets about our private and personal Higher Law, nor by worshipping any mere abstraction." Fortunately for California, the community opposed the Sacramento squatters. "Had they been successful," Royce speculated, "a period of anarchy as to land property would probably have followed far worse in its consequences than that lamentable legalized anarchy that actually did for years darken the land interests of our State, under the Land-Law of 1851."[33] California had not succumbed to radicalism. Instead, it had chosen what Royce considered commitment to history, the upholding of land laws, even if in a flawed way. That thrust toward legality, however compromised by greed and injustice, represented a long-range movement toward social maturity.

Regarding the racist heritage of California, Royce saw no pattern of good overcoming evil. One feels him sigh in relief that the Chinese question did not become important in the 1846-56 period under discussion in *California*. The spectacle of miners passing a Sunday afternoon exterminating an Indian village like a hornets' nest had no place in the theory of history Royce was trying to advance. As a Californian he felt the bitter burden of his state's racist past. "All this tale is one of disgrace to our people," he noted with a brevity that revealed the depth of his horror. In the hanging of a Mexican woman at Downieville on 5 July 1851, Royce gave a case study in California racism. In the Downieville incident a modern historian—and to a lesser extent Royce—might see an almost ritualistic expression of racist and sexual hostility. Two thousand sexually starved American miners, in an elaborately staged pageant of hate and envy, hanged a very beautiful and spirited Mexican woman, most likely pregnant, for killing an American miner. She had lived openly, and with every sign of sexual felicity, with a Mexican in the midst of a community where sexual tensions ran high. What revenge was possible when she killed an American miner! Even Hubert Howe Bancroft, grand perpetrator of the miner-with-a-heart-of-gold myth, confessed his bafflement at the hanging. "Never have I met an instance," Bancroft wrote, "where so many men, or a tenth of them, were so thoroughly ravenous in their revenge. It was wholly unlike them."[34] For his part, Royce could only narrate the incident at length as a representative example of racist feeling in early California. Writing in 1885, he could as yet detect no pattern of solution, no transcending good, in the story of California's racism.

He hoped that his analyses of Frémont, the Bear Flag revolt, and the struggle for order in the first decade had provided a usable pattern of good overcoming evil. He knew that his book was controversial. Californians could simply resent evils disclosed, ignoring Royce's insistence upon the process of struggle and transcendence. "My book is full of kindling that I split and of matches that I collected to heat the water for myself," he wrote the editor of *The Overland Monthly*. "Let the water boil—I ask one thing only, that if my reviewers need replying to, you will give me a proper place for reply."[35] The hostile review Royce half-expected from the California establishment came in *The Overland Monthly* for August 1886. It was unsigned and violently condemnatory. The reviewer took Royce to task for being flippant, pedantic, and immature, for daring, at the age of thirty, to offer such a "sermonizing reproof of Americans." How dare a young philosophy instructor bring Frémont to the bar of historical justice "as a judge on the bench might deal with a crooked witness in charging a jury"! How dare he assert that the Spanish and the Mexicans were anything but more cruel than their American successors! Ignoring the philosophical intent of the book, the reviewer criticized Royce for organizing his material topically instead of turning out a chronological history. He attributed this to the fact that the book was "a piece of contract work, done under pressure, at short notice." His dismissal was curt and cruel: "both as literature and as history, it is, on the whole, a failure."[36]

At first Royce thought Theodore Hittell had taken revenge for Royce's mixed review in the *Nation* of the first two volumes of Hittell's *History of*

California, but Milicent Shinn said no. Royce had to face the more painful fact that the review most likely came from the California intellectuals he had most wanted to reach, probably, in fact, from a former colleague on the Berkeley faculty. Why were Berkeley people so bitter, Royce asked Milicent Shinn? The question must have been resignedly rhetorical. *California* made Royce, a native of the state, seem in the eyes of Pacific Coast intellectuals just another sneering, condemnatory outsider. Royce's book appeared not so much a contribution to California culture as a repudiation of it by a Californian turned Harvard professor. On the whole, the literary establishment of California ignored Royce's study. Henry Oak wrote a favorable review, but it afforded Royce little satisfaction to have preached to the converted. Marveling in 1890 at the wondrous persistence of the Bear Flag myth among Californians, Milicent Shinn wondered why no one ever attempted to dispute Royce on a point by point basis, but rejected *California* out of hand as if an explanation were unnecessary. Californians, Royce learned, preferred their history uncorrected.

He turned to fiction. Royce had a life-long interest in the novel as a vehicle for moral and social reform. George Eliot, with her provincial settings and ethical interests, especially delighted him. His own novel of California life, *The Feud of Oakfield Creek* (1887), showed Royce's love of Eliot's themes, if not exactly her literary skill. As an example of the novelist's art, *The Feud of Oakfield Creek* was at best tolerable, and frequently not even that. "It never had many readers," Royce later told a newspaper reporter, "but I had a lot of fun in writing it, and I don't grudge the time I spent in this diversion." He was putting a brave face on his disappointment. The failure of the novel hurt him deeply, helping to precipitate his nervous breakdown of 1888. He fashioned the novel as a parable of California life, and he wanted Californians to listen.

The Feud of Oakfield Creek takes place in 1882, the year Royce left California, and concerns the events that lead up to violence between the law and the squatters' association of Oakfield Creek, a valley community in the Contra Costa hills. Two aging California pioneers represent the divided stream of the California experience. Alonzo Eldon, a millionaire, is the Californian as empire-builder, hero of material progress on the Pacific Slope. Alf Escott is an idealist whose outspokenness has lost him a professorship, forcing him into an impoverished old age. Significantly for Royce's cultural fable, Eldon and Escott share many traits. Eldon the millionaire feels that he should have been a professor of ethics, and Escott the moral philosopher has a fatal passion for dabbling in mining shares.

They both love and despise each other—the successful man of affairs made uneasy by material success, the intellectual made bitter by material failure. Each sees in the other corresponding traits developed to the full but somehow lacking harmony. Each remains ambiguous about what California has meant in his life.

The crucial issue of *The Feud of Oakfield Creek* is the burden of the California past. Somehow Eldon's and Escott's California experience is not working itself out properly. They see this failure symbolized in their sons. Escott, who fought for intellect in California all his life, has an amiable, non-intellectual son. Eldon, powerful man of affairs, has produced Tom, a weak-willed habitué of San Francisco clubdom. However disappointed in his son, Eldon still has hope that the pioneer past, as represented in his wealth, might come to some fruition. Ironically, this California oligarch has come under the influence of Henry George's *Progress and Poverty*. He decides to devote his fortune to the endowment of a research institution in San Francisco, modeled upon the British Museum, for the investigation of George's theories. Eldon dreams of the day not far off when a $25-million complex will cover the foot of Twin Peaks, "an example of public spirit, and a memorial to the devotion of the California pioneers." The museum will house a variety of educational and research programs dedicated to "the welfare of this great and growing community . . . the cause of civilization on this coast, and the betterment of the lives of the youth of the future."

The flaw in Eldon's benevolence is his ruthless determination to drive off squatters from his Oakfield Creek holdings. This determination has estranged him from his old friend and *alter ego* Alf Escott, who sides with the squatters. In his better nature, Eldon would like to sign over his rights to the Oakfield Creek land. He does not need the money, and the prospect of dislodging women and children from their homes does not fit in with his philanthropic self-image. But the habits of a lifetime of business, the ruthless business of the pioneer era which formed him, make such a gesture impossible. Caught in the paradox of the California history he has helped to shape, Eldon forces affairs to bloody confrontation. Symbolically, the sons of Eldon and Escott, figures of disaffection and disappointment, goad squatters and lawmen into gunplay. Escott's son kills Eldon's son. Caught between squatters and posse in an effort to make peace, Alf Escott is shot dead in the crossfire. In the feud at Oakfield Creek, history has taken bitter revenge on Eldon, who loses his son and his delusion of sweeping atonement.

Royce's parable for California was clear: no one gesture can redeem a society from the history of its mistakes. Reform and cultural growth come from confrontation with, and transcendence of, recognized evil in the context of on-going life. Within Eldon had been the Ideal—expressed in his muted ambition to be a philosopher and in his hopes for the Eldon Museum—but not the willingness to work for the Ideal along patient and unselfish lines. Had he honestly grappled with the burden of his own past and made atonement at Oakfield Creek, Eldon might have taken steps in the direction of bringing his California career to fruition. Instead, his hopes for California and for himself end on the bloody ground of social strife.

III

Royce must have felt the failure of both novel and history among Californians as a keen disappointment. He had expressed in both books, especially the history, his intense awareness of himself as a Californian. The pattern of California history had been the pattern of his own development, a struggle for order and for significant achievement. He had become a philosopher because of—as well as in spite of—California, and the movement of his thought toward questions of religion, community, and social ethics, the grand probes of his philosophical maturity, had taken direction and texture from the raw material of his California years.

In the Harvard years that followed, he did not forget his native state. As he probed with more and more profundity the nature of human community, the memory of his earlier experiences in California rose to consciousness, entering into the composition of his theory of Provincialism. Although he never returned to California as a permanent resident, he did return in sentiment and theory. For the sake of American philosophy, that was not too bad an accommodation.

Paradoxically for one who had striven so hard to remove himself physically from California, Royce never denied the psychological aspects of his Californianism. His was the stance of the exile, still half in love with the rejected homeland. He dressed down outrageously, with true Western contempt for the dude, a cigar clamped between his teeth. He loved to see the effect his "slip-shod Western manners" had upon certain of his Proper Bostonian colleagues. References to California life filled his lectures. He described himself as "a native Californian . . . who neither can nor would outgrow his healthy local traits."[37] He promised Milicent Shinn that *California* represented only the beginning of his intended contributions to the literature of his home state.

Yet he never wanted to return permanently. He turned down professorships at California and Stanford. There might have been some bitterness, and certainly sadness, in his refusal of the Mills Professorship of Intellectual and Moral Philosophy and Civil Polity at Berkeley. President Eliot almost rejected Royce's appointment to Harvard because of Berkeley's refusal to appoint Royce to the Mills chair when it was first established. Eliot felt this reluctance cast discredit upon Royce's abilities. California had wanted an established Eastern figure. Now, Royce was that established Eastern figure, wooed by Berkeley, but it all seemed a little too late.

Royce's theory of Provincialism was a social corollary of his larger philosophical Idealism, especially his notion that Loyalty provided a fixed ethical formula. He was especially interested in loyalty to the province. Royce defined the province as "any one part of a national domain, which is, geographically and socially, sufficiently unified to have a true consciousness of its own unity, to feel a pride in its own ideals and customs, and to posses a sense of its distinction from other parts of the country."[38] The spirit of Provincialism sought to idealize the province—its history, landscape, and climate, the personality of its people—not to escape realities, but to summon forth full possibilities, which, once conceptualized, would in turn shape future development. All this in no way implied a renewal of harmful pre-Civil War sectionalism, which had excluded outside influences and subverted national unity. What Royce called "the Higher Provincialism" absorbed and transformed a variety of influences, employing local loyalties not against the nation, but as a mediation between local life and remote national government.

Provincialism, in fact, would correct tendencies enervating national life. Did great masses of unassimilated immigrants crowd American cities? Then an intensification of local identities, as long as it avoided exclusiveness, would combat the anomie of uprootedness by providing newcomers strong polarities around which they could immediately organize. Was American industrial society standardizing a once variegated quality of life? Did Americans, in Royce's words, tend "to read the same daily news, to share the same general ideas, to submit to the same overmastering social forces, to live in the same external fashions, to discourage individuality, and to approach a dead level of harassed mediocrity?" Then let the people of Maine, of Louisiana, of California conceive of new and unique possibilities of value and lifestyle, new aesthetic modes to express a sense of individuation and a sense of harmony with local history. On a deeper level, Royce asked, was not the American national spirit becoming estranged from itself? Did not America's new imperial era show all the signs of an immense, impersonal order, of far-flung empire ruled abstractly from an unfeeling capital? The province offered a human scale of political reference, where both control and coloration could be local. "Freedom," Royce believed, ". . . dwells now in the small social group, and has its securest home in the provincial life. The nation by itself, apart from the influence of the province, is in danger of becoming an incomprehensible monster, in whose presence, the individual loses his right, his self-consciousness, and his dignity. The province must save the individual." Without such a mediating provincial life, Royce feared, the American empire would run a Roman course toward a helotry controlled by a cynical central power. Already he thought he saw signs of this process: a growth of class hatred, a manipulation of people by mass communications, especially yellow journalism, an impatience with orderly political process—this last, above all, so dangerous, the old California taste for lynch law on a national scale. "Keep the province awake," Royce urged, "that the nation may be saved from the disastrous hypnotic slumber so characteristic of excited masses of mankind."[39]

Provincialism represented a philosophical ideal. It was also a fact of the California experience. "The 'winning of the West,'" Royce wrote, "has been a spiritual much more than a merely physical conquest. And the spiritual history of the West has been the history of the formation of local institutions,—the tale of the rise of local traditions and of local loyalty." He felt that he had witnessed in his boyhood the emergence of provincial consciousness in California. In 1855 he had been born without province or history, not because elements of both were not present in Grass Valley, but because the community had not yet brought to consciousness and structured its provincial materials. "And so, in childhood," Royce remembered, "I unconsciously learned what it was *not* to be provincial. For as yet I had no province. I had my home. But home meant my father and mother and sisters." One of the aspects of Bret Harte's falsity, in Royce's mind, came from the fact that Harte portrayed resolved provincial types and personalities as flourishing long before California had reached the coherence necessary to sustain such local individuation. Far different from the sub-culture depicted by Harte, Royce asserted, society in early California, with no controlling ideals or self-image, spun toward centrifugal disorder, toward a cultural autism characterized by alienation and selfishness.

Sometime in his boyhood Californians began to face "the problem of creating a province, of converting a frontier into a rational social order." In place of exploitation, they began to think in terms of permanent settlement. "They were building homes," Royce recalled, "and thinking of orchards and of gardens and of vineyards, and not merely of gold nor yet of further wandering."[40] Californians began to reflect upon their past, brief as it had been, and to honor community pioneers. Becoming conscious of climate and landscape, they began to isolate a distinct aesthetic. Through the growth of schools, churches, and libraries, provincial awareness sustained and refracted an awareness of the larger culture. "I was in California," Royce once told a British audience, "a child of the civilization of the fathers, as the like thing is true of any of you."[41]

As a young college graduate, he had grown sick and tired of California's provincial spirit, "already too set, as I thought, in the tradition of the pioneers, too unwilling to listen to what the world beyond the mountains was saying, too sure of itself, too disposed to thank God that it had no blizzards in winter, and needed no new ideas but its own at any season of its year's gracious climate." Researching into California history, the Harvard instructor discovered just how important had been that sense of regional identity. It prompted Californians to purge destructive tendencies and it made them anxious for civilization. "Now I know that California needs to be and to become, not less, but more, provincial," wrote Royce, "to have more customs of its own, even as it constantly acquires, as time flies, more ancestors to remember, more legends of the pioneer days to glory in, and more results of civil devotion to cherish and to revere. By provincialism California must conquer its new enemies, as it learned to conquer its old."[42]

How strange that the exile from his own province should so often turn to repudiated California for examples of provincial fulfillment! "Men who have no province," Royce once lamented, "wanderers without a community, sojourners with a dwelling place, but with no home, citizens of the world, who have no local attachments,—in these days . . . we all know of the existence of far too many such beings."[43] He might have had himself in mind. His connection with New England, with Cambridge, although lasting thirty-five years, was always that of a guest, a sojourner. He drew strength from being an outsider, but it also caused him sorrow. In a way, his stance as a half-member reflected something deep within his make-up, something which had helped forge his philosophy of community in the fires of reverse compensation. "So much of the spirit that opposes the community," he confessed on his sixtieth birthday, "I have and have always had in me, simply, elementally, deeply. Over against this natural ineffectiveness in serving the community, and over against this rebellion, there has always stood the interest which has taught me what I nowadays try to express by teaching that we are saved through the community."[44] Certainly a man who had deprecated himself for being "impractical, always socially ineffective as regards genuine 'team play,' ignorant of politics, an ineffective member of committees, and a poor helper of concrete social enterprises"—such a man might not have resented, were he alive to read it, a younger Harvard colleague's description of himself as "a lonely and imperfectly adapted man, singing the praise of a perfect society," although the remark, in spite of Royce's imagined acquiescence, would still have hurt deeply.[45]

Compensation must also have been a factor in his theory of Provincialism. Certainly, amidst songs of praise for provincial possibilities, Royce must have remembered the pain and frustration of his California years. His Harvard colleagues always had the impression that his boyhood had been a time of desperate poverty and isolation. His father had failed miserably in the West, and his mother had gone through life with a sense of reduced circumstances. One sister died in her forties, worn out by struggle with poverty. Not surprisingly, some saw Royce's Idealism, his hopes for Provincialism, as a romantic escape into a philosophical *outremer* far from the grim realities of his boyhood. There was some truth in this, but only some. For whatever their psychological origins, whatever their ambiguity in the context of his own life, Royce was a man of ideas. That was both his release and his burden. His personal California might have been fatally flawed; but through the prism of his experience Royce had glimpsed possibilities more real than his own fractured reality. The tardiness of his realization seemed symptomatic of the whole Western experience. "It is not that they pursued the ideas as they entered upon their wanderings," he had admitted of the pioneers, "but that great ideas were so fleet of foot to follow them,—this it is at which we wonder as we read their story." The ideal of California only caught up with Royce after he fled East. As a young man, he felt himself up against an inert, hostile environment. As a mature philosopher, he came to believe that "the great West is a region where ideas—ideas crude, multitudinous, conflicting, unformed, but still ideas,—have a potency such as no one who looks at the merely material side of our newer civilization could imagine to be possible."[46] Royce detected the pattern of those ideas. He wanted Californians to be aware of their implications as they built their regional society. To all their efforts to construct for themselves a distinctly Californian way, Royce wanted his thought to give direction—like that pillar of light which in 1849 guided his father and mother across the trackless desert.

6

Sport, Mountaineering, and Life on the Land

From the start, Californians were challenged by the landscape that surrounded them. It was not a subtle drama, but a bold confrontation of flatland, mountain, and valley. Topographically, California had few secrets. Two major mountain systems, the Sierra Nevada and the Coast Range, ran longtitudinally down eastern and western extremes. From these, secondary chains jutted out at various angles into the interior. On the central and southern coast, networks such as the Santa Lucia, the Santa Ynez, the San Rafael, the San Gabriel, the San Bernardino, the Santa Monica, the Santa Ana, and the Sierra Madre—names recalling the faith of the Spanish colonists who first saw these hills—amplified or intersected the general thrust of the Coast Range. In the northern counties, the southern spur of the Cascades, the Siskiyou Mountains, and the Trinity Alps knotted themselves into a Swiss-like cluster of jagged peaks. To the south, below the Tehachapis where the great American Southwest had its left edge, seethed a stormy inland sea of rugged back country—arroyos and foothills, mesas and desert. Valleys, great and small, fell away from the mountains of California. An enormous flatland, the valleys of the Sacramento and the San Joaquin dominated the interior. Smaller valley systems encircled the Bay Area—Sonoma, Napa, Livermore, Santa Clara; crowded the central and southern coast—Salinas, Santa Ynez, San Gabriel; banked the eastern slope of the Sierras—Owens, Eureka, Saline; or like Imperial and Death valleys were part of the finality of the southeastern desert.

There was a schematic quality to all this, reinforced by the similar convergence of California's two great rivers, the Sacramento and the San

Joaquin, and the dramatic certitude of 1200 miles of seacoast fronting an open Pacific. And yet, paradoxically, the region offered great variety. In Mount Whitney it had the highest point in the nation and in Death Valley the lowest. It was rich in distinct climates and ecologies. To the south, in fact, contradictions of seashore and desert broke on one another like opposing waves. Whatever the variety, California did not confuse. Varieties confronted one another as opposites, not as interpenetrations. Three-quarters of the region was mountainous; the rest, flatlands and valley: landscape structured an underlying drama which Josiah Royce claimed had psychological side-effects. "You get a sense of power from these wide views," wrote Royce of California, "a habit of personal independence from the contemplation of a world that the eye seems to own. Especially in country life the individual Californian consequently tends towards a certain kind of independence which I find in a strange and subtle contrast to the sort of independence that, for instance, the New England farmer cultivates." Accustomed to an obvious environment, the Californian tended to take men and events in the same way: on face value and along broad lines. "In California," Royce noted, "unless you are afraid of the rain, nature welcomes you at almost any time. The union of the man and the visible universe is free, is entirely unchecked by any hostility on the part of nature, and is such as easily fills one's mind with a wealth of warm experience."[1] Topographically spacious, California allowed for an expansion of personality as the self grew outward to fill in the large vistas which the eye always possessed. Rural life, Royce pointed out three years before the appearance of Frank Norris' *The Octopus*, had an especially generous cast. In the case of ranch life, history reinforced landscape; for open spaces allowed California's latent Southernism to surface, a taste for expansive living funded into the California personality by the many Southerners who had settled in the State.

Although in later years the American might lift up his eyes to the hills as he made the valleys bloom, during the Gold Rush he came to the mountains of California as a destroyer. Mining, especially in its more complex phases, devastated the foothills and stripped them of timber. By 1859 much of the Mother Lode had been left a wasteland of caved-in hillsides, heaped debris, and tree stumps. Hydraulic mining, the washing down of mountainsides by high-pressure hoses, poured thousands of tons of mud and silt into the Yuba, Feather, American, Merced, and Sacramento rivers, which ran reddish-yellow with waste. Hindering navigation and increasing the likelihood of floods as it accumulated, hydraulic sediment in its progress downstream destroyed lowland farms and ruined rich riverbanks. In certain rivers, where pollution was high, salmon no longer leaped upstream to spawn. "Nature here reminds one," wrote Bayard Taylor regarding the mining regions, "of a princess, fallen into the hands of robbers, who cut off her fingers for the sake of the jewels she wears."[2]

In the case of California's giant trees, the Sequoia, the maiming reached demonic proportions. Centuries-old, these trees were among the natural wonders of the world. For ages they had gathered strength from the sunlight and moist earth, some of them being already 1000 years old at the dawn of the Christian era. No other living things had sojourned so long on the planet or had reached such size. Clustered in mountainous groves, lighted by shafts of sunlight which slanted downward from a vaulting of branches meshed at soaring heights, the big trees of California were cathedrals of nature: cool, silent, the products of a profound historicity. In them Americans might possess a symbol defiant of communal newness, a near-religious metaphor for the ancient goodness of life. In 1853, at the Calaveras grove, five Americans spent twenty-five days cutting down a 3000-year-old Sequoia, 302 feet high and 96 feet in circumference. They polished the stump into a dance floor and hollowed out the fallen trunk into a bowling alley. Another tree, called the Mother of the Forest, had its bark stripped off to the height of 116 feet for exhibit in the East and Europe. The tree died as a result, its epitaph carved into its flayed sides in the form of numerous initials, dates, graffiti and intwined hearts. In the destruction of these trees Henry David Thoreau saw at work a primal human hatred of whatever reminded men of their own insignificance. "The trees were so grand and venerable," he said of the destruction in California, "that they could not afford to let them grow a hair's breadth bigger, or live a moment longer to reproach themselves."[3]

Contemplating the exfoliated foothills, the polluted rivers, the fallen trees, and the obscenity of a Sequoia destroyed to make a dance floor and a bowling alley, an outside observer, even one less generally hostile than Thoreau, might have little hope regarding the quality of relationship between the Californian and his environment. American frontiers had always been hard on regional ecologies and California was no exception—except that there was more to destroy. The slaughter of the animals underway since before the Gold Rush drove the sea otter from offshore and the grizzly and the elk from the Coast Range, thinned out the deer, and emptied the sky of condor and eagles. For sport, Americans walked up to sea lions basking in the sun and put a bullet between their eyes, leaving the carcasses to rot on the beach. Hunters bagged more game than they could use, and venison was often a glut on the San Francisco market. In the matter of landscape, flora and fauna, it seemed that Americans in California really did not care, that the destruction would go on until it exhausted either itself or the region.

In the late 1850's a certain sort of tourist began to argue against this ecological indifference, indeed, vehemently to upbraid it. They related in a new manner to California, in enjoyment, not exploitation or the throes of finding a living, and they brought a high degree of imagination and critical intelligence along with their delight. The literary tourism of writers like Bayard Taylor, Horace Greeley, Charles Loring Brace, Charles Nordhoff, Benjamin Taylor, and Sara Lippincott was an act of observation, selection, and judgment in which they described what California was and should be. Universally they agreed that it should mean the authentication and liberation of man through nature, since nature in California was such an overwhelming fact; hence indifference to and abuse of landscape and wildlife took on for them the significance of an especially distressing problem. Was there something in the American character, they speculated along paths already trod by Thoreau, that of itself resisted a redemptive relationship to nature, that destroyed beauty out of an uncouth rage or a maniacal urge to profit?

Over a period of time and through a variety of visits, they decided that Calvinist fears of total damnation were incorrect and even self-indulgent. Their own tourism, in fact, was part of the solution, for they came in the van of an expatriate colony which by the 1880's ensured that there resided in California at any given season a population of educated, financially secure Americans who came and stayed precisely because they liked the climate and the scenery. Helping to offset the work ethic of Gold Rush and early frontier, tourists sought out and shaped what there was to enjoy. Up and down the state, they visited geysers, hot springs, rivers, lakes, underground caverns, big trees, mountains, and beaches. Hotels and resorts sprang up, crude at first, but by the 1880's such elaborate affairs as the Del Monte in Monterey, the Raymond in Pasadena, and the Coronado in San Diego, all models of Atlantic elegance. This transition began sometime in the early 1870's, although there were traces of it a half-decade before. California did not abruptly soften, but it ceased being a uniformly harsh frontier.

A sense of sport arose. A San Francisco journalist and *bon vivant*, Albert S. Evans, caught the new mood in a series of jauntily written sketches, *À La California* (1873). Evans' descriptions of hiking, camping, hunting, and angling in the mountains of the Coast Range are soaked through with genial good feeling, a sense—vaguely bohemian—that life in California was now settled enough to be savored, not just compulsively gotten through. Charles Frederick Holder, the state's leading sportsman-writer, spent a career devoted to the practice and aesthetics of sport in California. Born in Massachusetts in 1851 and already a well-known naturalist before he emigrated, Holder came to Southern California in 1884 expecting to die from weak lungs. He plunged himself into one last desperate round of outdoor life in an effort to regain his health and survived for another thirty years: a bearded, robust figure, looking like an English squire in cap, hunting jacket, and plus fours. Holder rode after hare through the sand dunes near the sea and after lynx in the hills of the Sierra Madre. He hunted quail and water fowl near his home in Pasadena and went on long treks into the back country after wolf and wild goat. He fished off Santa Catalina for tuna and hiked into the hills after trout. But whatever the game, Holder acted with a style and a restraint which he hoped might characterize the emerging California sportsman. The chase, he felt, should be as much an act of sightseeing, botanizing, and geologizing as hunting *per se*. Let the sportsmen of California, Holder urged, be ever aware of a larger play of forces: the colors of the season, the air, the knowledge of oneself as also a natural creature, in kinship and respect with one's prey. Holder hated the game-hog. He considered conservation as part of the paradox of the hunt and worked to promote sane practices. Charles Frederick Holder pointed, in short, to a California where restraint and a civilized conception of the chase were possible, where men did not have to pile carcasses at their feet in assertion of manhood and mastery over creation. His California was a restricted one, but its metaphorical implications were obvious.

A hopeful sign of a creative relationship to the outdoors came in camping. The late 1860's saw the development of the *paseár*, holiday migrations by upper middle class San Franciscans south into the Coast Range or northward into the Russian River Valley. They went in groups, taking along their wives and children and setting up encampments which combined rusticity and elegance. From these, the men and often the women—for this was California—would make more rugged expeditions into the mountains or down towards the seacoast. Others set up encampments on the peninsula and commuted daily by train to San Francisco during the summer season. "Better one month of camp life in the California mountains," wrote Albert S. Evans, "than years on years of life at the fashionable 'watering-places' and 'summer resorts' of the East and Europe."[4] The style of these outdoor sojourns of the late 1860's and 1870's was a charming blend of frontier and *belle tournure*. One roughed it by day and returned at evening to society and civilized surroundings. In the 1880's camping became somewhat democratized, that is, enjoyed by less fashionable levels of the middle class. Mrs. Jessie Benton Frémont had been among the first in the state to have herself fitted out with a carriage-sleeper. Coaching as a subdivision of camping grew from this initially exclusive arrangement. Coaching extended the range of areas visited and simplified the style of outdoor living. "California is the campers' state," Stewart Edward White could write by 1910, describing the various horse-drawn rigs which after the rainy season took to the road. "For all alike the country-side is golden, the sun warm, the sky blue, the birds joyous, and the spring young in the land. The climate is positively guaranteed. It will not rain; it will shine; the stars will watch. Feed for the horses everywhere borders the roads. One can idle along the highways and the byways and the noways-at-all, utterly carefree, surrounded by wild and beautiful scenery. No wonder half the state turns nomadic in the spring."[5]

Of all attempts to connect imaginatively with the environment, mountaineering had the highest degree of self-consciousness. From the start it was more a matter of science and art than necessity. Now and then, degrees of aesthetic awareness or moral meaning flash through the journals of mountain men and overland emigrants, but, confronting the Sierras, most Americans of the first phases of settlement just wanted to get across. In 1860 a book appeared in San Francisco written by a young lawyer, later one of the State's great historians: *The Adventures of James Caspen Adams, Mountaineer and Grizzly Bear Hunter of California* by Theodore Henry Hittell, which pointed toward a transitional atttiude. Hittell put into shape the reminiscences of a Massachusetts Yankee who, after coming across the plains in 1849 and working as a miner, farmer, and businessman, decided that what he most wanted out of California was a free life in the mountains. Adams' conscious choice and the degree of self-awareness attributed to him by Hittell made him more than an uncouth mountain man, although it was true that his ability to befriend grizzlies and his near-legendary adventures belonged to the world of Far Western folklore. By no means a modern mountaineer, Grizzly Adams nevertheless sustained an imaginative relationship to the heights he roamed. "The mountain air was in my nostrils," he said of his life in the Sierras, "the evergreens above, and the eternal rocks around; and I seemed to be a part of the vast landscape, a kind of demigod in the glorious and magnificent creation."[6]

Others in the 1850's felt the challenge of the mountains of California. Presumably because it was so utterly there, rising out of a dark forest in Siskiyou County like an ancient volcanic god, thirty-five men and five women climbed Mount Shasta between 1854 and 1856, scattering its summit with plaques, American flags, and, prophetically, the litter of picnics. In so many places where Americans settled, local peaks tempted the climber. Its snowy summit visible for 200 miles, Shasta was among the more obvious challenges. Glacial ages had seared and sculptured this old volcano and driven from it living things. Forest sounds ceased as one ascended, and only the wind warded off the prehistoric silence. "The Alps are grand in their beauty," noted one climber; "Mount Shasta is sublime in its desolation."[7] In Tulare County, in south-central California, where the Kings and Kern rivers had headwaters in the high country, Mount Whitney, at 14,496 feet the highest peak in the United States, inaccessible, treacherous, remained unconquered until 1871. Less formidable heights, known since Spanish times, skirted San Francisco Bay. Monte del Diablo in Contra Costa County, like Shasta rising solitarily from a plain, was chosen in 1851 as the base point for all surveys. Indians worshipped this mountain as a god and Spanish legend held Diablo to be the abode of the devil, but in reality it offered a pleasant climb through carpets of wildflowers and forests of juniper, oak, sycamore, and pine. Although it was only 3890 feet high, many considered the view from Diablo the finest in North America. Encompassing an arc of thousands of square miles, it put one in visual possession of the North Coast, the Bay Region, the Central Valley and the Sierras. Mount Saint Helena looked down upon the farmlands and newly planted vineyards of Napa and Sonoma counties, where General Vallejo once guarded the northern frontier, and the leagues of rolling hills stretching westward to the Coast Range, where cattle and vaqueros roamed in the days of Spanish possession. Further romance was added by the fact that in 1841 Princess Helena de Gagarin, wife of the governor-general of the Russian colonies on the North Pacific, had climbed the mountain and named it in honor of the patron saint of herself and the Empress of Russia. "To the stranger," Evans wrote of the view from Saint Helena, "there is enchantment in the scene; to the old Californian, history, romance, suggestive memories."[8]

To its credit, California put the investigation of its topography on a systematic basis with the creation in 1860 of a Geological Survey. Support from the legislature, however, was minimal and intermittent. During the active existence of the Survey, from 1861 to 1874, Josiah Dwight Whitney, Director and State Geologist, never had adequate funds. Politicians wanted the Survey to seek out new mining regions, Whitney wanted a disinterested measurement and mapping of the entire state, and so the life of this group of superb field-scientists was ill-supported and brief. It did not dissolve, however, before coming to near completion of its heroic task.

William Henry Brewer, field director of the Survey, spent four years in the open, up and down California, supervising the work. A graduate of the Sheffield Scientific School at Yale, Brewer came to California in 1860 after two years of climbing and study in Europe. His wife and child had both just died, and in the wilds of California, measuring its heights, Brewer sought assuagement of his grief. By 1864 no man knew California better, especially the mountains. Remaining unpublished until 1930, Brewer's letters and journals must nevertheless be considered the founding statement of California mountaineering. Detailed, spacious, they put on record the exact extent of California's alpine heritage. The mountains of California offered Brewer an unambiguous challenge to stamina and intellect, and he responded with clarity of scientific purpose, bravery, and lack of pretension. Brewer made an imaginative connection with the mountains as an arena of objective endeavor. Their conquest was an act of will and intelligence in the service of science—and from that act came subjective gifts of beauty, spiritual drama, and escape from sorrow.

Brewer's younger colleague on the Survey, Clarence King, pursued a more self-regarding mode of mountaineering. Like Brewer, a graduate of the Sheffield School, King had come West to avoid the Civil War. He joined the Survey in 1863 and remained until 1866, when, at the absurdly young age of twenty-four, he was commissioned by Congress to direct the Fortieth Parallel Survey, a charge which would have been welcomed by many an unemployed major general. King, whom Henry Adams considered the outstanding young man of his generation, wrote up his California experiences for *The Atlantic Monthly* in a series of sketches later published as *Mountaineering in the Sierra Nevada* (1872). Like Dana's *Two Years Before the Mast*, this was the work of a young man who, although he could not know it, was having the finest moment in his life.

A trained geologist, King despised those who rhapsodized over the sublimity of the Sierras without restraint or scientific imagination. The Yosemite, he claimed, had been especially abused by transcendental rhetoric. At the same time King was himself not without an imaginative response to the facts of geological history, albeit his appreciation was a very instructed one. To the young Rhode Islander the Sierras were yet charged with the titanic energies of their ancient formation. Seas, convulsions, lava, and glaciers had left their record in monuments of stone which seemed to the imagination imminent of release, as if once again there could be a time of seething birth. King's continual awareness of the geological catastrophes at the core of Sierran history, his passion for what might be called the cataclysmic sublime, conferred a quality of heroic drama upon his mountaineering. It was as if King were testing himself against those archaic cataclysms which had sundered the earth, or even—in some mysterious act of the imagination—appropriating them as his own prehistory. In Clarence King, mountaineer, the American in California made symbolic contact with the lost life of the continent itself: and from that union there came new wonder and new power of soul.

There also came beauty and moral feeling. King had decided to become a geologist after hearing Louis Agassiz lecture at the Lawrence Scientific School at Harvard. Agassiz convinced King that geology represented a fusion of religious, aesthetic, moral, and scientific approaches. King had a lifelong aversion to science pursued to the exclusion of other modes of inquiry. The reading of John Ruskin intensified his interdisciplinary point of view. With Ruskin as a model, King trained himself to harmonize a variety of perceptions and to express them with precision and allusiveness. Brewer claimed that King brought to California as much Ruskin as Yale geology. "What would Ruskin have said, if he had seen this!" King was supposed to have exclaimed upon first seeing the Sierras in 1863. What Ruskin might have said, King said for him in *The Atlantic Monthly*. To the Sierras King brought the shaping associations of past art. Analogies to the Gothic, for instance, suggested an organic interchange between nature and art which had happened in medieval Europe and might happen again in California. By bringing to bear a complexity of comparisons, King subdued the Sierras to a very subtle aesthetic intention: he brought them to the verge of becoming a correlative and a challenge to art in California. Here, suggested King, in the absence of a complex civilization, was California's one adequate reference for aesthetic endeavor. King's continual attempts to associate the Sierras with the high art of Europe—as opposed to Europe's high mountains—drove home the point. His was the preliminary connection, from the Sierras to past art.

The next step, from the Sierras to future art, belonged to California.

Yosemite Valley, described by King with such force, was destined to become one of the primary symbols of California, a fixed factor of identity for all those who sought a specifically Californian aesthetic. Members of the Mariposa Battalion, a unit of mounted volunteers, discovered the Valley on 25 March 1851. Yosemite scenery did inspire, as Clarence King pointed out, much lavish language, but a man of sound intelligence and imagination like Thomas Starr King was capable of putting the Valley to disciplined, effective use as a communal symbol in a theological context. And that provided a model for future appropriations. Visually so stupendous, Yosemite inspired the visual arts. Albert Bierstadt and other painters of the Hudson River School rushed West to capture its grandeur in a series of grandiloquent canvases which even today, despite the stylization of idiom, convey the nineteenth century's first gasp of wonder. The infant art of photography felt itself especially challenged. Eadweard Muybridge, a San Francisco photographer who later did work crucial to the development of motion pictures, produced an extraordinary set of Yosemite plates between 1867 and 1872. Excluding human scale or reference, Muybridge concentrated upon the natural features of the Valley. He avoided, however, unrelieved documentation, demonstrating the impressionistic capabilities of photography in his use of weather. A drama of sunlight and shadow, shifting cloud formations, moonlight, mists, and rainbows plays across Yosemite's proscenium of granite cliffs, an evanescent dance of the hours before the Valley's eternal impassivity.

Celebrated in art, Yosemite was reverenced in life as the high shrine of California pilgrimage. Journalist, hotel-keeper, self-appointed guardian of the Valley, James Mason Hutchings, an Englishman who came during the Gold Rush, dedicated a lifetime to promoting the Yosemite in the consciousness of Californians. *Hutchings' Illustrated California Magazine*, which he founded in 1856, edited, and wrote much of singlehandedly, must take the most credit for helping to reverse the frontier relationship of Californians to their landscape. Through superb illustrations and marvelously detailed essays, *Hutchings' Magazine* encouraged Americans in California to take notice of their natural heritage and to relate to it in pleasure and informed appreciation. The Yosemite, of course, dominated Hutchings' imagination, and he settled there permanently in 1859 as a tourist-guide and hotel-keeper. His *Scenes of Wonder and Curiosity in California* (1860) provided detailed directions for an eight-day visit to the Valley.

A group of Californians and temporary Californians led by Frederick Law Olmsted, the noted traveler and landscape architect, lobbied through Congress a bill, which President Lincoln signed on 25 June 1864, setting aside under the protection of the State of California a huge tract of Sierran land which included the Yosemite Valley and the Mariposa Big Trees. The bill closed the area forever to commercial development. Nothing on such a scale and for such unselfish purposes had ever been passed by Congress, and one suspects that the distractions of the Civil War had much to do with the success of the measure. Olmstead had a comprehensive plan for the management of the preserve, but he returned to New York City in 1865 to finish the laying out of Central Park before he could put his ideas into action. It would be decades before intelligent arrangements for the supervision of Yosemite would be legislated and put into effect—but a startling fact was clear: the Yosemite had been saved. Considering the usual pattern of American behavior in such matters, considering the ravages already wrought upon the California environment by the 1860's, few could have predicted the success of this major act of preservation.

Throughout the 1860's and 1870's, in ever-increasing numbers, the tourists came to Yosemite, by train and stagecoach across the San Joaquin, by wagon into the foothills, and by horseback onto the Valley floor. They stayed at Hutchings' Hotel, where they found their host's love of the Yosemite inspiring and his abilities as a hotel-keeper abominable (although a visitor in 1868 noted that Hutchings served "a delicious breakfast of fresh trout, venison, and great pans of garden strawberries"). So standard became descriptions of the Valley in tourist literature that one writer excused himself from writing about his visit on the ground that he could not possibly say anything new. As his wagon ascended into the Sierras in May 1871, Ralph Waldo Emerson for some reason or another found himself very depressed over the thorny problem of the immortality of the soul. So refreshing did the Concord Sage find the Sierras that, throwing off his metaphysical gloom, he increased his allowance of cigars to two a day. At Mariposa Grove Emerson named a Sequoia after Samoset, a seventeenth-century Indian chief. "These trees," he observed, "have a monstrous talent for being tall." At Yosemite itself, the aging transcendentalist found corroboration for everything he had said about the spiritual effects of great scenery in a lifetime of writing—and for everything which in turn had been said about the Yosemite. "This valley," he observed one evening on the porch of Hutchings' Hotel, "is the only place that comes up to the brag about it, and exceeds it."[9]

Cumulatively, from literary accounts, from paintings and photographs, from reports of all sorts, Yosemite began to assume a primary significance in the minds of Californians. Here was the one adequate symbol for all that California promised: beauty, grandeur, expansiveness, a sense of power, and a sense—this in the geological history—of titanic preparation for an assured and magnificent future. As scenery, as a physiography that was deeply symbolic, Yosemite offered Californians an objective correlative for their ideal sense of themselves: a people animated by heroic imperatives. Its configuration of mountain and valley was a grand paradigm of California's geography as a whole. From the Valley floor, standing on the banks of the Merced River and looking up to the great cliffs, one was in full possession of limits, and yet these limits were of a grandeur and an inaccessibility beyond even the suggestion of intimacy. Like the land of California itself, all was comprehensible, but beyond reach. There was no mystery to Yosemite's walls, only direct and unambiguous power. These soaring cliffs seemed to hold safe from violation the fabled Garden of the West so that it might be there when Californians needed a reminder of what the land offered them, of what it had been preparing for them in the ages before their arrival. In 1864 Americans set the Yosemite aside because it was so unutterably beautiful and because it expressed their own best hopes.

II

That same year John Muir was trekking through the wilds of Canada in quest of who he was and what he should do. In a sense Yosemite was being set aside for the young Scot, or at least the Valley would have to await Muir's arrival before it received its best expression and most effective conservation.

Born in Scotland in 1838 of Highland stock long enamored of the wilds but reduced to living in the Lowlands, Muir was brought as a boy to the Wisconsin frontier, where in a "sudden plash into pure wildness—baptism in Nature's warm heart" he repossessed his outdoor Highland heritage: "Young hearts, young leaves, flowers, animals, the winds and the streams and the sparkling lake, all wildly, gladly rejoicing together!"[10] Muir's father combined rigid Calvinism with a distaste for the bourgeoisie; indeed, he brought his family to America precisely out of a desire to keep the faith and to escape the restraints of middle class Scottish life, a motivation blending dissent and orthodoxy. He forbade his sons contemporary novels and poetry but saw to it that they soaked themselves in Greek, Latin, and the Bible. The Calvinism of John Muir's boyhood can only be described as grim in the classic Scots manner. "I was first put to burning brush in clearing land for the plough," Muir tells us of his early Wisconsin days. "Those magnificent brush fires with great white hearts and red flames, the first big, wild outdoor fires I had ever seen, were wonderful sights for young eyes. Again and again, when they were burning fiercest so that we could hardly approach near enough to throw on another branch, father put them to awfully practical use as warning lessons, comparing their heat with that of hell, and the branches with bad boys. 'Now, John,' he would say,—'now, John, just think what an awful thing it would be to be thrown into that fire:—and then think of hellfire, that is so many times hotter. Into that fire all bad boys, with sinners of every sort who disobey God, will be cast as we are casting branches into this brush fire, and although suffering so much, their sufferings will never never end, because neither the fire nor the sinners can die.' "[11]

As an adult Muir claimed that such treatment did not traumatize him, that "those terrible fire lessons quickly faded away in the blithe wilderness air; for no fire can be hotter than the heavenly fire of faith and hope that burns in every healthy boy's heart."[12] The actual process of recovery must have been more painful and mysterious, although its broad outlines are clear. A Calvinist pattern of guilt and redemption characterizes Muir's adolescence. As a boy he hunted and killed forest animals with the abandon of a young savage while at the same time being nearly worked to death himself by his father, who put John to the plow as a frail young boy, stunting his growth as a result, and who once forced him to sink a ninety-foot well, at the bottom of which Muir almost died of poisonous fumes. In late adolescence Muir experienced a conversion to a religious reverence for nature and living things. He felt disgust at his own hunting and the way so-called godly people like his father worked their farm animals to death. The identification of such cruelty with his father's victimization of himself underlay Muir's conversion. He escaped his killing father—and the avenging God behind him—by projecting onto nature his deepest longings for love and psychic survival. Muir grew a beard and let his hair fall about his shoulders. In 1860, escaping the misery and monotony of farm life, he enrolled as a special student in the University of Wisconsin.

In retrospect, Muir's adolescence helps to explain the adult naturalist. Profoundly part of the assertive act by which he struggled to psychic survival, Muir's relationship to nature could never be trivial. It filled the void left by an abandoned Calvinism and cured some of its scars. It also kept some of Calvinism's characteristics: a deep longing for communion as a pledge of redemption and a continual searching of the literal for symbols of salvation, an asceticism of means and ends in the pursuit of holiness, a capacity for prophecy and stewardship, and—most importantly—a sense of power, sacred and awful, at the core of creation. Schooled in classics and the Scriptures, Muir had language. Toughened by farm labor, he had endurance and a sinewy ability to get by on very little. It took California to consolidate Muir's aspirations and to give them expression and purpose, but they had their origins on a farm in the Wisconsin frontier.

At the University of Wisconsin Muir studied science. As with Brewer and King, it is important to emphasize Muir's love of science and competence as a naturalist. He had, moreover, a taste for practical mechanics, inventing a number of laborsaving devices so ingenious that they were put on exhibit at the Wisconsin State Fair. At college, Muir tells us, he would lie awake at night, his mind reeling with new possibilities of combining gears, levers, flywheels, and shuttles. The very eccentricity of Muir's mechanical talents and the idiosyncratic way he insisted upon pursuing science betokened the fact that his deepest energies were not involved. He refused to volunteer for the Civil War on moral grounds, but seeing the returned wounded, both Confederate and Union, at a military hospital near Madison, he decided to become a doctor.

He was not, however, happy with so conventional a choice and, just about the time the Yosemite was being saved in Congress, Muir plunged himself into the Canadian wilderness, living on bread and tea, pushing himself on long marches and hoping to find out what he should be. He did not find out—and in 1867 we find him in Indianapolis, Indiana, working in a factory among the machines which so paradoxically expressed the other side of his nature. Bending over one day to adjust the belt on a whirring piece of machinery, Muir dropped the file he held in his hand. A spinning lever flung it back into his right eye. It went blind and so did the left eye in sympathy. Muir's sight returned, but not before he spent a month of blindness, bedridden in a lonely room. There, realizing what he might lose, his sight "in all the gardens of God," Muir made up his mind that if he regained his vision he would dedicate it to seeing God's beauty. When he recovered he was twenty-nine. He shouldered a pack and set out on a thousand-mile tramp to the Gulf of Mexico, keeping a journal which he inscribed "John Muir, Earth-planet, Universe." From

Florida he sailed for New York and from New York he sailed for San Francisco, arriving there on 28 March 1868. Three days later he set forth on foot for the Yosemite. "It was the bloom-time of the year over the lowlands and coast ranges," Muir tells us of that spring walk through California; "the landscapes of the Santa Clara Valley were fairly drenched with sunshine, all the air was quivering with the songs of the meadow-larks, and the hills were so covered with flowers that they seemed to be painted. Slow indeed was my progress through these glorious gardens, the first of the California flora I had seen. Cattle and cultivation were making few scars as yet, and I wandered enchanted in long wavering curves, knowing by my pocket map that Yosemite Valley lay to the east and that I should surely find it."[13]

Muir found the Yosemite and with it a consecration. "Born again!" he entered into his journal in language which dramatized the suppressed religious longings which were now at long last to find fulfillment. "As long as I live, I'll hear waterfalls and birds and winds sing. I'll interpret the rocks, learn the language of flood, storm, and the avalanche. I'll acquaint myself with the glaciers and wild gardens, and get as near the heart of the world as I can. Hunger and cold, getting a living, hard work, poverty, loneliness, need of remuneration, giving up all thought of being known, getting married . . . make no difference."[14] For the next half-century John Muir remained faithful to this vow, although he did eventually become famous and, at forty-two, quite happily married. Once he was known in person and through his writings, Muir became for Californians an avatar and prophet of all that the Sierras promised: simplicity, strength, joy, and affirmation. Through the moral force and imaginative depth of his own response, in which sensation had great concreteness and great spirituality, Muir upgraded the entire Californian relationship to the mountains. As a public figure he set a standard of what Californians should be: challenged to beauty and to new passion for life by the magnificent land in which they found themselves.

He might perhaps have done this had he not written a word. His life was myth and parable enough. But the fact is, he wrote and published an extraordinary amount for one so active as a mountaineer. At his death in 1914 there remained over sixty volumes of Muir's journals which had not yet found their way into print. In the spring, summer, and fall, Muir roamed the Sierras. In the winter he traveled down to the Bay Area, where he wrote; magazine articles mostly, many for *The Overland Monthly*, for he lived by his pen and needed a quick return. He would be fifty-six before his first book appeared, *The Mountains of California* (1894), an American classic. In the professional sense of the term, Muir was a better naturalist than either Henry David Thoreau or John Burroughs, his two peers in the field of nature writing. Muir wrote concretely, close to his subject, and the reason some of his more grandiloquent adjectives bother us is that they dissipate this mood of accuracy. On the whole Muir favored dense description, structured and kept in motion by narrative, as opposed to Thoreau's rhythm of observation and aphorism, or Burroughs' interplay of fact and lyrical flight. Muir was capable, however, of such a startling Thoreau-like reversal as: "The muskrat is one of the most notable and widely distributed of American animals, and millions of the gentle, industrious, beaver-like creatures are shot and trapped and speared every season for their skins, worth a dime or so,—like shooting boys and girls for their garments."[15]

In Clarence King the mountaineer defied nature, pitting himself against rocks and gorges in a test of courage conceived of as an abstraction and reveled in psychologically. Muir despised King's elaborate self-consciousness, his risk-taking as a form of existential encounter. The mountaineer should not defy a mountain in order to vanquish it, Muir believed; rather he should put himself in harmony with it, learn its spirit and secrets, and that invariably took one safely to the summit. "We are now in the mountains," he once wrote, "and they are in us, kindling enthusiasm, making every nerve quiver, filling every pore and cell of us. Our flesh-and-bone tabernacle seems transparent as glass to the beauty about us, as if truly an inseparable part of it, thrilling with the air and trees, streams and rocks, in the waves of the sun,—a part of all nature, neither old nor young, sick nor well, but immortal."[16] At times like this, and most especially in times of danger and decision, Muir felt himself in contact with an Other Self, a spiritual projection of his ego in mystical harmony with the mountains, telling Muir at moments of mountaineering crisis what moves were necessary and when they should be made. Near the top of Mount Ritter (which Clarence King had unsuccessfully tried to climb), Muir found himself caught on the edge of a precipice, seeing no further holds, baffled at what to do next. Suddenly his Other Self came to his rescue. "My eyes became preternaturally clear," Muir tells us, "and every rift, flaw, niche, and tablet in the cliff ahead, were seen as through a microscope. At any rate the danger was safely passed, I scarce know how, and shortly after noon I leaped with wild freedom, into the sunlight upon the highest crag of the summit. Had I been borne aloft upon wings, my de-

John Muir (1838–1914)

He was born in Scotland, where he learned to love the wilds. He came to California and there he found a consecration. To him, mountaineering was a form of religious witness, a worshipping of that sacred and awful power which pulsated at the core of creation. As a prophet of conservation, he warned Californians not to squander what the ages had prepared. He became an avatar of all that the Sierras promised: simplicity, strength, joy, and affirmation. He wanted that legacy preserved.

liverance could not have been more complete."[17] Similar incidents occurred atop Mount Shasta and Mount Whitney, which Muir scaled, as usual, without equipment, wearing low-quarter shoes and living off bread and tea. Upon the heights, Clarence King conceived of himself as poised above chaos, as having defied chasms without and chasms within. On the same and even more lofty peaks Muir saw himself as soaring over a singing creation, hearing the music which the ages had prepared.

The preservation of that song so that future generations might hear it became the work of Muir's major years. His articles in *Century Magazine* were instrumental in getting a Yosemite National Park Bill through Congress in 1890. In May 1903 Muir and President Theodore Roosevelt camped out together in the Yosemite for four days—in the Mariposa Grove one night, atop Glacier Point the next, and then for two nights in Bridalveil Meadow on the Valley floor. It was one of the happiest times in Roosevelt's life, and he left the Yosemite won over to Muir's conservationist program. In 1905 California ceded the Yosemite to the federal government as part of the Department of the Interior's National Park Service. Throughout the years of struggle, as dedicated Californians sought to put conservation of their environment on an intelligent and systematic basis, John Muir led the way, prophet and warrior-priest. In this prophetic role Muir resembled Henry George (whom he used to meet at John Swett's house on Taylor Street when he spent the winters in San Francisco) and Josiah Royce. All three men responded to a deep California hope: that a regional heritage could be defined and preserved. All three men believed that the final significance of California was in the realm of moral meaning and liberation of spirit. For expressions of this hope, George looked to rural life, Royce to provincial communities, and Muir to communion with the mountains, yet in each case the context of aspiration was a reverence for environment, a highly developed sense of special place. George brought to the Californian's understanding of place an awareness of the socio-economic forces which either fulfilled or baffled its imperatives, Royce gave place a philosophy of history—and Muir made place a premise for great flights of imagination and spirit in which men made their landscape the geography of the soul's journey.

On 4 June 1892, in the office of a San Francisco attorney, a group of Californians drew up and signed articles incorporating the Sierra Club, with John Muir as president. The Sierra Club gave formal expression to that distinctly Californian relationship to the outdoors which had been developing since the 1860's and which Muir best represented. The 162 charter members of the Club were in the main university-educated professional men, together with a large representation from the faculties at Palo Alto and Berkeley. Five professors, in fact, including David Starr Jordan, president of Stanford, sat on the founding board of directors. The Sierra Club represented the flowering of ecological stewardship on the part of California's upper middle class. The very wealthy were noticeably absent from the Club's charter ranks. Railroad kings, real estate developers, timber barons, and the like, profiting from unregulated exploitation, were naturally hostile to the conservationist core of the Sierra Club ideology. The Club gathered together those who by the 1890's were feeling themselves in the van of the California dream, people who had time, means, and taste enough to profit from what was available. They lived in beautiful homes (developing, indeed, a regional architectural style), worked just hard enough at their careers to sustain a rich and varied life, read widely, and loved the outdoors. It was they who brought to California university culture, staffing its institutions as faculty or just living in their proximity and sharing their spirit. In time, under the banner of Progressivism, they would set about the political reform of California, for they were tired of seeing their ideals mocked by corrupt corporate and union power. Meanwhile, in 1892, they rallied around unequivocal symbols of what was important about California and what they were looking for by living there. In the Sierras and John Muir and the Sierra Club they found a California already brought to redemption.

The preservation of the Yosemite was one of their greatest achievements, although in 1913 they would lose the battle for Hetch Hetchy, seeing that incomparable Sierra valley dammed up to make a reservoir for San Francisco. With the publication of *The Yosemite* in 1912, John Muir, writing the book Thomas Starr King had dreamed of writing in 1860, gave the Valley its highest celebration in language. Here, for future generations, was preserved the ideal Yosemite in its unspoiled state. Someday the Valley would have a smog problem, but because Muir described it so well, because he preserved its freshness in prose, Americans might always have some idea of what impact California's grand Sierra garden had upon the imagination of nineteenth-century Americans. At the turn of the century Americans in California needed John Muir as a prophet and propagandist, and after his death they continued to need him as a reminder of what sort of relationship to the Sierras had once been possible. John Muir achieved a California which would always challenge. "When I was a boy in Scotland," Muir once wrote, "I was fond of everything that was wild, and all my life I've been growing fonder and fonder of wild places and wild creatures."[18] It was this love of their land, wild and lyrical, that Californians learned from John Muir. It was the renewal of a Sierra morning which he continually asked them to regain. It was Muir's reverence for life and his joy in living that Californians found they most desperately needed when, in later years, California threatened to die before their very eyes.

III

Muir, it must be remembered, was a successful fruit-rancher near Martinez for a portion of his California career. Agriculture, not sport or tourism or mountaineering, constituted the most primary and workaday relationship of the Californian to the land. Long before the Gold Rush, letters home from Americans in the Sacramento Valley describing the region's fertility stimulated migration. Such reports had motivated the coming of the Donner party, and after the horror of their crossing it was to agriculture that the survivors turned themselves. "No healthier place can be found—no fever, no ague, no sickness," wrote home one Donner party member from Napa Valley on 2 July 1847. "The days are pretty hot, with cool nights. It is a fine location for fruit—apples, peaches, and grapes."[19]

In the opinion of Hugh Quigley, a priest of the Archdiocese of San Francisco writing in the late 1870's, California as an agricultural state had proved to be the second Holy Land of the Irish. As opposed to the Atlantic states, where they huddled in urban ghettos, the Irish had found land in California and a triumph for what Quigley called the Celtico-Roman spirit. "The Irish-American farmers and settlers in the southern tier of counties," the priest noted, "have had little or no difficulty in making settlements, from the fact that the Spanish always treated them with great hospitality and kindness on account of religion and ancient national affinities of the two races."[20] In the Murphy family of Santa Clara County, Father Quigley beheld the comforting vision of a landed Irish-Californian aristocracy, men of baronial holdings whose broad acres contrasted so sharply with the landless impoverishment of the Irish in their homeland. Born in County Wexford in 1785, Martin Murphy migrated to Quebec and then in 1842 took his family to Missouri. Dedicated to Roman Catholicism (two of his wife's brothers became bishops) Murphy removed his clan to California in 1844 with the express purpose of residing in a Catholic country. In the Santa Clara Valley Murphy purchased the Rancho Ojo de Agua de la Coche, south of San Jose, where he settled with his wife and three children. Through the years both the family and its holdings grew. Three generations of Murphys dominated the San Jose area like ancient Irish kings—much to the satisfaction of Father Quigley, whom the British had banished from his native soil.

"On the success or failure of our agricultural pursuits," wrote J. H. Carson in 1852, "depends the future wealth or poverty of California."[21] Throughout the 1850's and 1860's, promotional writers conjured up an imminent agricultural utopia in a never-never land of wheat, grapevines, oranges, and olives where might be finally realized the Jeffersonian dream of a life on the land for the greatest possible number of Americans. Despite the promises and the statistics, the dream failed to come true. Land monopoly and confusion of land titles caused the most retardation, but there were also natural difficulties: drought, unrelieved by systematic irrigation, and flood, brought on by California's torrential rains. The heat of the interior valley, felt one observer, was so great that no rural civilization could possibly flourish there. The absence of trees on the flatlands made shade a luxury and kept domestic building to the level of rude hovels. From May to November great clouds of alkaline dust burned the eyes and clogged the nostrils. During the rainy season it all became impassable mud. Mosquitoes and fleas drove men and beasts to madness, ground squirrels and jackrabbits devoured crops, and in the southern part of the state there were so many rattlesnakes that farmers were forced to wrap the hooves of their animals in burlap.

More discouraging than any such evils of nature was the fact that a significant part of California's rural population—called Pikes or Pikers, after Pike County, Missouri, where most of them were supposed to have originated—seemed degenerate. "He is the Anglo-Saxon relapsed into semi-barbarism," said Bayard Taylor of the California Pike. "He is long, lathy, and sallow; he expectorates vehemently; he takes naturally to whiskey; he has the 'shakes' his life long at home, though he generally manages to get rid of them in California; he has little respect for the rights of others; he distrusts men in 'store clothes,' but venerates the memory of Andrew Jackson; finally, he has an implacable dislike to trees."[22] The American yeoman, in other words, the noble son of the frontier whom Thomas Jefferson Farnham had predicted in 1844 would one day raise up a mighty race on Pacific shores, seemed by the late 1850's to have arrived on the scene as poor white trash. For Clarence King the Piker represented the degenerating effect of the whole frontier experience, its "conspicuous retrograde." He once camped near a Pike family, the Newtys, who had brought their swine into the Sierras for pasturage. Aside from a half-admitted sexual attraction to Susan Newty, the hog-calling daughter of the clan whose good-humored energy and buxom charm run counter to everything King says, the Newport geologist found the Newtys a sorry lot indeed. "Cursed with a permanent discontent," in a series of settlings which had seen children born and dying in prodigious numbers, farms half-cleared then abandoned, and life sordidly carried on in a succession of log cabins, tents, lean-tos, and wagons—the Newtys had drifted from Pike County, Missouri, to Oregon and from there to California, from which they were contemplating migration to Montana. As a family the Newtys, originally from New England, had been on the frontier but two generations. Susan's grandfather had been a judge in Arkansas. His son kept pigs in California.

"If, as I suppose," asked King, "we may all sooner or later give in our adhesion to the Darwinian view of development, does not the same law which permits such splendid scope for the better open up to us also possible gulfs of degeneration, and are not these chronic emigrants whose broken-down wagons and weary faces greet you along the dusty highways of the far West melancholy examples of beings who have forever lost the conservatism of home and the power of improvement?"[23] The absence of conserving civilization in rural California deeply bothered Horace Greeley. Farms were too large, noted the New York editor. There were no villages, churches, or schools, nor would there be "so long as ranches of five hundred to many thousand acres each, stand in place of small, neat, well-cultivated farms."[24] Lack of social intercourse would in time barbarize California's rural population, Greeley claimed, just as unstable land titles tended to make ranch life insecure and violent.

A decade later, walking through the California countryside, Stephen Powers found that Greeley's predictions had come true: an isolation and a sort of sordid barbarism seemed to have taken hold. With the exception of the Santa Clara Valley south of San Francisco, and Napa and Sonoma counties north of the Bay, rural life impressed Powers as resembling—for the lowest strata of society—the conditions of a peasantry after a long, cruel war: "mean huts of cottonwood logs, barely high enough for a man to stand erect therein; a can of wild honey, inside; a half-eaten carcass of venison hanging from a mighty oak, outside; a gaunt and sallow woman, with some almost naked children—that is the picture."[25] The class above this, the miners turned bonanza wheat farmers, impressed Powers (who had walked from Virginia to California via the southern route) as "the most shiftless, thriftless men of the class that can be found in the Union, except, perhaps, in Texas." Living alone or in casual concubinage in unpainted and shadeless shacks furnished with a cot and a stove, wallpapered with newspapers; caring nothing for the land but sowing it with crop after crop of wheat in an effort to get rich quick and move to San Francisco; gambling, drinking, whoring, and fighting on weekends in local Mexican villages—the California wheat rancher, lamented Powers, hardly represented the ideal American agriculturalist. What Powers feared most was a dangerous social pattern of limited ownership and migrant work, which gave rural California a feeling of cruel caste "deplorably un-American." "It is not unlikely," he concluded, "that within two centuries California will have a division of population something like that of ancient Greece, to wit: merchants, artisans, and many great lords of the soil, in the cities; and in the country a kind of peasantry of goatherds, shepherds, tough, little, black-haired, lazy farmers, and the like, to whom the cities will be unwelcome resorts."[26]

Novelists of ranch life in California were both celebratory and corrective. Horace Annesley Vachell, an Englishman who had ranched in Southern California for over a decade, made the most balanced critique. A graduate of Harrow and Sandhurst, Vachell turned down an Army commission in order to take up ranching in California, where he married and eventually, with his father-in-law, went into the real estate business, headquartered at San Luis Obispo. When Vachell's wife died in childbirth and his real estate office failed, he took his two children to England, determined to start a new career as a writer. Two novels published in 1899, *A Drama in Sunshine* and *The Procession of Life,* put on record what Vachell considered the strengths and challenges of California ranch life.

An avid sportsman, Vachell had loved life in the outdoors. "We worked and played, a happy combination," he wrote of his ranching years in the 1880's, "although I must admit—not at all regretfully—that play came first in this sportsman's paradise, still a land of *mañana*."[27] Southern California had a large British colony, many of whom were ranchers. Vachell felt that they provided their American counterparts a valuable service through their civilizing example. The English colony, Vachell asserted, pointedly refused to fall in with the American habit of overwork. They lived in a more diversified way, managing their ranches, but also making time for sport and society. He himself introduced polo into Southern California, playing it first with the vaqueros on his ranch and in 1887, upon the occasion of Queen Victoria's Golden Jubilee, organizing a British-American match, the first official polo to be played west of the Rocky Mountains. Soon thereafter the Southern California Polo Club was formed, and by 1897 *The Anglo-Californian*, the London-based journal of the English colony in California, was reporting on matches held in Riverside which attracted crowds into the thousands. For Vachell, born as he was into country gentry, polo—as well as hunting, fishing, camping, and tennis—was part of the British colonial style, a way of relating to the non-English environment through sport and thus preserving one's feeling of caste. He also felt that he and other Britishers were warning Americans in California not to pass by the chance for a healthy life on the land.

Vachell had, however, a realistic notion of what that life entailed. He knew from experience the dark side of ranch life: the boorishness and sordidness, the boredom, the constant debt. "When I came to California a year ago," says one of Vachell's characters, "the faces of the men and women—ay, and the children—shocked me. The sun seemed to have sucked from them the good red blood as it sucks the sap from the grass. I traveled about between Monterey and San Diego, but, leaving out the Spanish, I saw few smiles and heard little laughter."[28] Vachell's ranch novels concerned the decision to remain on the land and struggle for California's agricultural future. In *A Drama in Sunshine* William Chillingworth, a real estate speculator, under the corrective influence of his California-born wife, turns from cynical subdivision to the promoting of model agricultural colonies. In *The Procession of Life* ("a faithful presentment of my experiences as a rancher in California") two brothers-in-law, an Englishman and an American, turn to ranching in the region northeast of Santa Barbara. Blunted in sensibility by a ten-year struggle to survive as a rancher, Jeff Barber, an American forced to sacrifice any hope for personal culture when he took up life on the land, once that struggle is won has to fight his way back from harsh resentment and a desire to take his hard-won money and flee to the cultivated leisure of San Francisco. Instead Barber decides to make his own experience socially productive. He sets up an experimental station to show incoming immigrants the proper methods of agriculture in Southern California. "We love California because we are the sowers . . . ," Barber says, "and our love is the greater, I think, because, no matter how hard we may work, the harvest must be reaped when we are dead." Barber's English brother-in-law, Guy Warrender, an Eton graduate in California strictly for speculation and adventure, also comes to a sense of social mission. "At the quiet, easy gait set by London fashion," attired nattily in white duck breeches and polo boots, Warrender dabbles in ranching while putting his main energies into real estate schemes. He prefers the social life of Santa Barbara to the company of his wife and the companionship of his fellow ranchers. Vachell's plot is taken up with the conversion of his elegant English hero to a productive life on the land. "This was the lotos-land, so called," Warrender convinces himself. "What message had it for him? A message of peace? Yes, but not of rest. From the tiny blade of grass pushing upwards to light and sunshine to the stupendous ebb and flow of the ocean, was not the eternal energy made manifest? And was he created to stand aloof, an idle spectator, a mere time-killer? Not so."[29]

Vachell's own ranching career of course formed the basis for his assessment. Between 1882 and 1899, as a rancher and a real estate developer, he had witnessed and taken part in the transition of Southern California from a ranching to a farm economy. Although he had made many mistakes and although drought eventually forced him to abandon his holdings, Vachell never lost faith "that life in the open air, beneath the genial skies of the Pacific Slope, upon a rich and generous soil, ought to be a life worth living."[30] Defeated in his own attempt at such a life, having lost the California wife who encouraged him in its pursuit, Vachell never repudiated the hope of his young ranching days in the land he called Arcadia, where "good times were almost too good to be true." Vachell's own California dream had failed, but he kept his fictional heroes busy in its pursuit, animated by the promise "of better and happier days, when life on the Pacific Slope will be purged of what is mean and sordid." Says one of Vachell's characters: "Look at those foothills. What a glorious heritage for the strong!"

According to Frank Norris, heroic figures had already come into possession. He celebrated their epic relationship to the land in *The Octopus* (1901), the best by far of the many ranch novels which appeared at the turn of the century, and the only one to achieve any literary reputation. Norris fashioned *The Octopus* out of the facts of California ranching as transformed by his own passion for the heroic. Certainly something larger than life, justifying Norris' conception, had developed on the great ranches of California, especially those holdings under the ownership and personal management of pioneers of energy and purpose like Don Benito Wilson, Don Abel Stearns, and Martin Murphy. Diversified in their industries, employing scores of men bound together into an economic and social hierarchy, the great ranches of California resembled feudal baronies, having as their underlife very ancient modes of loyalty, dependence, and service. Over a hundred men, for instance, employed in such subdivisions as wheat, vines, fruit, sheep, cannery, apiary, sawmill, nursery, poultry, and the like, staffed the 26,000-acre Rancho Del Arroyo Chico in the Sacramento Valley, owned by John Bidwell, who in 1841 had led the first wagon train into California. Bidwell's wheat, the main product of the Rancho, won the gold medal at the Paris International Exposition of 1878 for being judged the finest grain in the world. So extensive were Bidwell's operations that he maintained his own steamboat on the Sacramento River. In his fine home, an elegant mansion surrounded by extensive gardens and a deer park, Bidwell entertained with a hospitality that, like himself, was generous, strong, and unpretentious. In 1863 Governor Leland Stanford made the Chico rancher a brigadier general of militia. From 1864 to 1867 Bidwell served in the United States House of Representatives, and in 1875 he ran unsuccessfully for governor. Hubert Howe Bancroft considered him California's foremost citizen-farmer, a Cincinnatus in Roman repose on the land.

A complexity of psychological and imaginative needs led Frank Norris in the last year of the nineteenth century to decide that he would celebrate the heroic possibilities of ranch life in California. From adolescence Norris had had a fixation upon heroic strength which some have seen in clinical terms as a means of defense against an over-protective mother, an arty would-be actress who appears as the heroine of Norris' last novel, and a philistine father, a successful businessman, whom Frank's mother eventually divorced, and who always wanted Frank to give up his artistic ambitions and join him in the wholesale jewelry business. Norris yearned for the strength which would enable him to defy his father and to dominate his domineering mother. (In Norris' youthful novel *Moran of the Lady Letty*, Ross Wilbur, a shanghaied San Francisco socialite, must defeat the heroine Moran Sternerson in hand-to-hand combat before he can win her respect and love.) Raised as a rich boy in Chicago and San Francisco, Norris identified with the primitive and the brutal. Although he broke his leg trying to turn himself into a player, Norris loved what he considered the bullying Anglo-Saxon spirit of American football. A dandy who, as a student at Berkeley, affected Parisian elegance and who once showed up to gym class in chic black leotards, Norris filled his early fiction with football players and the great big white men of Richard Harding Davis.

As an art student in San Francisco and Paris, Norris loved the medieval. He virtually memorized Froissart's *Chronicles* and learned enough Old

French to read *The Song of Roland* in the original. He haunted museums, sketching the armor and weapons of the Middle Ages. He had a gigantic canvas set up in his Paris apartment upon which he planned to execute a massive Battle of Crécy. He wrote a metrical romance with a medieval setting, *Yvernelle, A Tale of Feudal France,* which his mother had printed when he returned to the United States in 1892. For Norris, as for Henry Adams and many American aesthetes in the turn of the century period, the Middle Ages held forth the possibilities of both vigor and order. Norris felt a boldness in medieval literature, a oneness with experience sadly lacking in so much writing of the *fin de siècle.* Emile Zola also fascinated the young Norris. In Zola's sprawling fictions Norris found the strength and naturalism of medieval chronicles combined with the modernity of sociological vision. Zola alerted Norris to the diagnostic function of fiction, its possibilities as an instrument of social reportage in which massive forces could be seen at work in individual lives.

Three essays written by Norris in the year or so between the publication of *The Octopus* and his tragically premature death in 1902—"The Literature of the West," "The Frontier Gone At Last," and "A Neglected Epic" –provide a retrospective gloss of the theory of frontier history behind Norris' novel of Central California ranchers. The frontier, Norris claimed, had not so much passed as it had reached a point of transformation and return. The Anglo-Saxon trek toward the setting sun, geographically fulfilled in the possession of California, would continue on in other terms and in the reverse direction. The West would now move toward the East. Norris had once described that Anglo-Saxon advance as an unheeding plunder, a migration of reckless pillage. By his early thirties, free of parental domination, secure in his career as a novelist, married to the exquisite Jeannette Black, Norris no longer had need of such adolescent fantasies of self-asserting violence. He now began to conceive of the frontier in terms of a victory for law and community and brotherhood. In the wheat of the ranches of California, pouring forth to feed the hungry of the world, Norris found a transcendental symbol for the back-flowing of the frontier. He conceived of a trilogy called the Epic of the Wheat, "an idea as big as all outdoors," which would include novels of California production, Chicago distribution (*The Pit,* published posthumously in 1903) and European and Asiatic consumption, *The Wolf,* which he never lived to write. Feeding a famine-stricken world, the California of Norris' scenario returned to older cultures their own gifts of life and civilization.

Consider what ambitions and energies Norris brought to bear upon his novel of ranch life: his love of scale and sweep, first of all, nourished by Zola and the medieval, and totally appropriate to the vast baronies of Central California. Norris' Zolaesque conception of rural society as an arena of clashing social forces, his attempt to imitate Zola's techniques for suggesting sociological sweep and sprawling vitality, upgraded the California ranch novel from its previous naïveté. No California writer before Norris, except perhaps Charles Clement Post in *Driven From Sea to Sea* (1888)—a novel which, like *The Octopus*, climaxed with the 1880 shoot-out at Mussel Slough between ranchers and railroad men—had ever made such a massive attempt to depict the history and sociology of ranch life. In a bold and sometimes crude way, Norris made imaginative connection with subeval processes the immediate manifestations of which were conflicts of men and money but whose more ultimate life was the force of destiny itself. "The larger view always and through all shams, all wickedness," Norris tells us at the conclusion of *The Octopus*, "discovers the truth that will, in the end, prevail, and all things surely, inevitably, resistlessly work together for good." The fact that, at the last, Norris—a young man only then in the first possession of his powers—could not resolve the meta-historical conflicts he had conjured, the fact that he asked his readers to make with him a perhaps gratuitous leap of faith, represented a failure of intelligence and imagination. He had not earned such an assertion. But he had seen it at work in California.

Norris knew the feel of ranch life, the way it offered an arena for the expansion of certain American traits. He knew and depicted its violence and barbaric good humor, its male fellowship, and the loneliness of the women, their deferred hopes for graciousness and respect. Its authority figures, whatever the complexities of their personal lives, had by design simple public personalities, near-heroic conceptions of the self as instruments of will and action in elemental struggle with the land. No economist, Norris yet felt something symbolic in the conflict of railroad and ranch, as if two Americas, frontier and corporation, were at war, and behind this was something very significant for the American future.

Critics have pointed out many weaknesses in *The Octopus*—its melodrama, for instance, its overinvestment in the wheat as a symbol, its ambiguity as social protest. Just how fine a book Frank Norris wrote, however, becomes evident in a historical way when one compares it to similar novels of California ranch life. There is no comparison. This is to say that Norris came the closest to success in a generation's attempt to put the ranch era into significant fiction. In so doing he helped Californians in their quest for an imaginative relationship to the land, for ranch life—and Norris' novel—had its quintessence in the outdoor struggle with the soil. Norris set *The Octopus* in a representative California landscape which he made even more representative for the sake of the novel, to the point of bringing over a mission from the other side of the Coast Range. With few exceptions, the characters of *The Octopus* are not psychologically complex but are put and kept in motion by their setting. Central California, in this sense, is Norris' chief protagonist. Endless fields across which fifty plows move in echelon, vast and empty skies, mountains in the distance, wheat, and flowers—they all call to an imaginative relationship. It is part of the ambiguity of Norris' ranchers that they are unable to respond, that they ruthlessly exploit their acres as they in turn are exploited by the railroad. Annixter, Presley, and Vanamee, the three central characters of *The Octopus*, escape this indifference, each being brought into a significant relationship with the natural setting. Each—rancher, poet, and mystic—is healed by submission to the natural process. Each beholds a special California beauty. No California fictionist had ever so successfully integrated personality and setting as did Norris in his portraits of these men. Their response to region offsets the callow exploitations of the larger ranch world.

IV

Fortunately, there were counter-patterns to the vast ranches which even Norris could not celebrate without qualification. In 1851 a group of 300 Mormons from southern Utah purchased a 35,509-acre tract in the San Bernardino Valley, laid out a town, planted trees, and built fine homes which they smothered in rose bushes and clinging plants. In a cooperative venture which became the model for all such efforts in the semi-arid Far West, they brought 4000 acres under irrigation. In 1857 a group of German immigrants gathered in San Francisco and incorporated themselves as the Los Angeles Vineyard Society. Purchasing a tract in Southern California which had once been part of the Rancho San Juan Cajón de Santa Ana, the Germans founded the colony of Anaheim, irrigating the soil and planting the vines of California and the Moselle. "We drove through the clean and well-kept avenues or streets, scenting Rhineland on every side," wrote a visitor in the 1870's, "and, indeed, this Anaheim itself is nothing but a bit of Germany dropped down on the Pacific Coast."[31] At Pasadena he might have scented Indiana and high-seriousness of the American

Protestant variety. The excessively severe winter of 1873-74 convinced a number of middle class residents of Indianapolis, many of whom suffered from chronic ailments, that they had better emigrate to Southern California as agriculturalists. Incorporating themselves as the San Gabriel Orange Grove Association, they purchased and subdivided part of the Rancho San Pascual at the western head of the San Gabriel Valley: a superb spot, sheltered by the Sierra Madre and Verdugo Mountains, sunny, fertile, and conveniently near Los Angeles. Cottages were built and vines and fruit trees planted. In 1875, when the community acquired a post office, it called itself Pasadena.

Mormon, German, Indianan—San Bernardino, Anaheim, and Pasadena—each avoided the discouraging patterns of rural life in California: the isolation, the system of hireling labor, the shabby incivility. As early as 1855 the contrast between San Bernardino, with its watered fields and village of 1400 where flourished the life of church and school, and nearby Los Angeles, a wild cowtown, was not lost on travelers. Here and in Anaheim and Pasadena Californians lived both on the land and in community. Agriculturally, with their irrigation, diversity of crops, and cooperative marketing, these colonies surpassed the primitive economy of the bonanza ranches. Psychologically, as a place to live, a way of life, there could be no comparison. At Anaheim and Pasadena colonists made a vigorous effort to preserve the values of bourgeois life through churches, schools, libraries, and associations for music and debate. Whether the role-model was the Kingdom of the Saints, a Rhineland village, or the Indiana memory of Puritan New England, these communities, in the midst of a surrounding shabbiness and instability, showed what a good life might be lived on the California land.

Hope for a good life glowed white-hot in the 1880's, when thousands upon thousands of "Pullman emigrants" poured into the State in the most dramatic population growth since the Gold Rush. In 1884 Benjamin Cummings Truman, one of California's chief publicists, put out the call for a million "well-disposed, industrious people, who desire to better their conditions in life, to come to California and help to settle her vast territory and make for themselves comfortable and happy homes—to dwell under their own vines and fig trees—not only in the land of promise, but in the land of real fruition."[32] Truman's suggestion of a California life under one's own fruit trees caught the theme which dominated promotional pamphleteering at the turn of the century: that California would witness a return of the middle class to the land. The urban bondage of educated men and women, went the argument, had run its course. Intensive farming had made a new way of life possible, one possessing the benefits of country life and at the same time preserving values of diversity, leisure, and family living. With the subdivision of its large holdings underway, California offered the middle class a way out of the increasingly burdensome work loads of business and the professions. They could return to the land as scientific farmers. Photographs of snug ranches played up the new style of rural life. Flower and vegetable gardens surrounded well-designed bungalows. Walnut and almond trees or prize dairy herds filled out the middle distance, while on the horizon rolled row upon row of vines and blossoming fruit trees. It was both garden and industry, a way of making a living and a way of life in total contrast to what had characterized the previous agricultural frontier.

Central to this emerging rural lifestyle was the raising of fruit. As an agricultural pursuit, orchards bespoke stability, patience, a high yield per acre, a reasonable work load—and beautiful surroundings. By the late 1860's the Santa Clara Valley, flowering in the spring with apricot, plum, apple, and pear, stood prophetic of what could be brought about in the rest of the state. Writers praised the elegant homesteads of Santa Clara Valley fruit farms, their atmosphere of gracious living and measured prosperity. In the 1870's the growth of the citrus industry in Southern California gave new resonances to the ideality first glimpsed in the coastal valleys of the north. Of themselves, orange, lemon, and lime trees had poetic associations with Spain, North Africa, and the Levant. Under the Mediterranean skies of Southern California, they also flourished, their green leaves, dazzling blossoms, and bright fruit taking further color from the intense sun. Fruit ranching took time. One planted and then waited some years for a return. Hence orchardists tended to look for a long-range capital investment rather than a scheme to get rich quick. "They can sit on the verandas of their pretty cottages," wrote one observer in the late 1870's of the citrus farmers of Riverside, "—the refined essences of abstract existences—inhaling the pure air of the equal climate, reading novels or abstruse works of philosophy, according to their mental activity, from day to day, and waiting from year to year for their oranges to grow."[33] Overstated, this assessment yet pointed to the idyllic overtones of fruit ranching, as idealized in promotion and as sometimes lived. By 1891 Charles Howard Shinn could make the case that a new sort of American-on-the-land had made his appearance in California, the bourgeois horticulturist, "in some respects akin to the middle class of suburban dwellers near Boston and New York, with this very important difference, that he actually and constantly makes his living from the soil he owns."[34]

This concept of the Californian making his living from a small acreage dominated agricultural thought through World War I. In the case of the reclamation movement, the redemption of the Far West as farms for the common people became a near religion. Its most active and articulate proponent, William E. Smythe, a Californian who in 1900 published *The Conquest of Arid America*, brought an entire theory of history to bear upon the irrigation and subdivision of arid land. Smythe turned the middle class ideal of an exurban civilization in California into something sweepingly democratic in its implications, bound up with the very destiny of America itself. America's mission, Smythe warned in the year the marines landed in Peking, did not lie in Asiatic adventures, but in securing a good life for the common people. If reclaimed through irrigation, the Far West might provide a decent life on the land for millions. This, not foreign investments, represented the true challenge facing American private enterprise. The cooperation necessary for large-scale ventures of reclamation would, Smythe hoped, result in the moral reinvigoration of capital, labor, and government. The selfish and self-defeating factionalism of nineteenth-century enterprise would give way to new modes of association between worker and manager, and a sense of social mission and democratic service would animate the American soul. At the end of his dream Smythe saw millions of Americans, native and foreign-born, living on small holdings which provided a comfortable income. Through a variety of irrigation, investment, and marketing associations they managed their own affairs, having under their control the tools of both capital and labor. Because they lived and worked in proximity, they had the benefits of urban life, but on a manageable scale. Rapid transit systems would shuttle them into more densely populated areas where they might enjoy the pleasures of city life.

Taken as an imaginative construct, Smythe's vision answered a generation's fears concerning the quality of life in the rural Far West. It also, in its less desirable implications, prophesied suburban sprawl. Small holdings, intended in the imagination as self-sufficient farms, degenerated into infinitely repeated front lawns and back yards, pathetic in their fussy pastoralism; and transit systems intended to make available the delights of community became landscape-destroying freeways which flung men farther and farther from the *polis* until the quality of life in outlying districts repeated the patterns of loneliness and embittering restriction of an earlier rural frontier. California, especially Southern California, had done much to advance the exurban dream in the first place, and California would suffer the most when the dream went awry.

No matter what was envisioned, furthermore, certain realities could not be banished. Of the million and a half people living in California in 1906, over a third lived within a seventy-five-mile radius of San Francisco. Subtract also those who lived in the population clusters of Southern California, and it became clear just how empty was the countryside and how isolated remained rural life. The twentieth century, on the whole, was destined to witness the monopolies and consolidations of agri-business—and not the decentralization and diversification promised in promotional writing. Agriculture in California remained as tough and exploitative as ever and migrant labor just as disenfranchised. Evocations of rural idylls for the bourgeoisie had little to do with the persistent facts of California agriculture: the dreariness of much of the interior and its inhuman heat, the malaria carried by the hordes of mosquitoes which bred in the stagnant water of irrigation ditches, the sudden frosts, the collapse of markets, the disregard of the rights of labor, and the oppressions of capital upon the farmer, driving him to further exploitation. When John Steinbeck came to write about it, there would be more than salvific returns to the land to talk about.

Yet some relationship to the outdoors, to nature, had been fixed as part of the Californian identity. Self-consciousness regarding health, part of the American experience in California from the Gold Rush, played a dominant part after the coming of the railroad in the settlement of Southern California. Responding to exaggerated claims concerning the curing powers of the climate, thousands of invalids flocked there in the hope of restoring diseased lungs. Many were cured, but thousands died. Sunshine and oranges could not banish death. A restless hypochondria, a penchant for self-diagnosis and miracle remedies, going hand in hand with a taste for spiritualism and faith-healing, clung to the eccentric edges of Southern California. A variety of cults arose promising redemption of spirit and flesh. There also came about a mature respect for the biological premises of human life. Californians became interested in questions of diet and exercise and the possibilities of integrating themselves into a natural way of living. Desert, mountains, and seacoast offered differing challenges in this matter, not to mention differing clusters of symbols by which Californians might express their hopes for a natural life.

George Wharton James looked to the desert and to the Indians who had brought themselves into harmony with its ecology. There, James felt, the white man might find health, sanity and hope. From bitter personal experience, James knew what he was talking about. His own struggle for health and peace, about which he understandably remained reticent, provided a secret paradigm for all that he preached. A Methodist minister, born and ordained in England, James migrated to the United States in 1881, serving various churches in Nevada and California. By 1889 he had worked his way up to a solid pastorate in Long Beach. Then disaster struck. Mrs. James, who was obviously unbalanced, accused her husband of an absolutely prodigious number of adulteries with ladies of the parish, including one heroic feat of bedding down, all together, a matron and her three daughters. In Nevada, Mrs. James charged, her husband had been a well-known visitor to houses of ill fame. At one of them, she went on, Reverend James had played the piano while the girls danced. Aside from lurid divorce proceedings ("the evidence is of such a filthy nature that it would be impossible to print it," reported the Los Angeles *Times* on 24 April 1889), James stood an ecclesiastical trial in which he was accused of real estate fraud, invalid ordination, faking an English education and membership in learned societies, advocating free love, having a collection of obscene photographs, and allowing his children to bathe together in the nude. Certain charges were true: James had neither the education nor the learned recognition to which he pretended. Other charges arose out of the clash between James's naturalism—his idiosyncratic brand of muscular Christianity, that is—and the straitlaced fundamentalism of Long Beach. Sexual misconduct on James's part remained a possibility, but nothing of the monstrous nature Mrs. James pathologically insisted upon and which the Los Angeles *Times* reported in order to sell newspapers. Mrs. James admitted that while her husband was in the United States, before she joined him, she committed adultery with James's brother and two other men. Brooding over this might have unbalanced her mind. To his credit, James tried to forgive her, but the stress of the ordeal drove him toward a breakdown.

Deprived of his pulpit, driven into a state of nervous exhaustion, his reputation shattered in the most sordid manner (the *Times* pilloried him as the Irreverend James), George Wharton James would not appear to be at the beginning of one of the most expansive public careers in turn-of-the-century California. Living down the scandal of 1889, James embarked upon a career of lecturing and journalism. His innumerable talks, the countless articles, pamphlets, and books cascading from his pen all pointed in one direction: California and the Southwest, what it was and what it offered in values of living. James was not a brilliant writer. Working in haste, he tended to belabor points and to depend too much upon quotation. Now and then, in his enthusiasm to convince, he faked his material; for something of the pitchman was integral to his personality. Yet he knew what was important about California and the Southwest, and most of the time he wrote with feeling, dignity, and a quite respectable level of knowledge. *In and Out of The Old Missions of California* (1905), *The Wonders of the Colorado Desert* (1906), *Through Ramona's Country* (1909), *Heroes of California* (1910), *California, Romantic and Beautiful* (1914)—James's work radiated a love of region. Somehow, as he put his shattered self together, a broad, affirming conception of California, intensely ecological, soaked in the romance of the past, had proven therapeutic. California providing the symbols, James, the unfrocked parson, reached out toward a faith that stood for everything opposite to that which in Long Beach had nearly destroyed his capacity for living. Against self-defeating narrowness, he tried for a banishment of fear, for "courage, deep pity, self-knowledge, generous trust" and the belief "that life consists in expression and not repression." A semi-invalid as a boy and further weakened by the events of 1889, James affirmed joy, energy, physicality, and an appetite for life. Nearly destroyed by the community, he preached self-possession tempered by trust, and the emergence of a natural, liberated California. He was by no means a systematic thinker, nor was he a very deep one; yet his defiant, hard-won optimism, together with his hopes for an energized California, gloriously physical and alive to the spirit, gave conviction to James's prose and won him acclaim as a lecturer. "I believe," testified James, "in the buoyancy, the happiness, the radiancy, the perfection of life."[35]

"Let us call it what we will," James wrote, "and attain it as how we may, the desirable thing in our national and individual life to-day is health,—health of the whole man, body, mind, soul."[36] He pointed to the Indians of the Southern Californian and Southwestern desert as type and proof of healthy environmental living. Their restraint in eating, their rapport with climate, their deep slow breathing and steady pulse-rate, the regular hours of their work and rest, their longevity when not ravaged by white diseases, all corroborated James's sense of the healthful naturalism life in Southern California should afford. He himself favored organic foods and outdoor living as a key element in the California style. He tried to do some manual labor every day, not just for exercise, but to accomplish a job that needed to be done, believing, as he did, that separation from real work caused spiritual coarsening. In matters of sex, James praised the Indians' lack of shame regarding the body, their natural dignity in mating, and their careful, but not morbidly protective, parenthood. He contrasted this to the sexual anxieties underlying so much of white culture, and the fatiguing emotionalism of white family relations. Above all, James envied the Indians' ability to harmonize the elements of living into a unified consciousness. Reality for the Indian, James asserted, was a conjunctive perception of matter and spirit; environment played its part as an element of inner life, and vice versa: a circularity of circumstance and symbol, an interchange, that is, of internal and external ecologies which had been tragically lost by the white race, and which George Wharton James sought to reclaim for Americans in California.

Stewart Edward White looked to mountain living as the source of similar values. Scion of a wealthy lumbering family, born in Michigan, educated in the East, but eventually settling in California where he had spent his adolescence on a ranch, White came to manhood at about the same time Frederick Jackson Turner pronounced the frontier to be over. Like many of his generation and social background, White, author of about forty books and one of the noted outdoorsmen of the era, spent a lifetime trying to recover something of the frontier experience. He dug for gold in the Black Hills of the Dakotas, crossed the plains on horseback, explored the Southwest, and went on safari in German East Africa. In these pursuits White resembled his good friend Theodore Roosevelt, who sustained a similar symbolic relationship to the frontier ideal, and Jack London, whom White got to know through the Bohemian Club. In his travels and explorations White sought the frontier horizontally, hoping to duplicate its variety of physical challenge, its act of will in the face of hostile terrain. Mountain living represented a vertical probe into the frontier as homesteading, with an emphasis upon intuition and pioneer patience.

The poetry of Sierra living, as White wrote of it, was a poetry of environmentalism and self-reliance, a return to simple things in a mood of unpretentious reflection about basic values. He had to get out of the Bay Area and build his Sierra cabin, White argued, as a way of reintegrating himself; for the division of labor necessary in an urban civilization made one lose all sense of the unity of experience. Each citizen played such an insignificant, uninterpreted part. Fragmented and sprawling, the modern metropolis did not comfort men as smaller, pre-industrial cities had once been able to do, allowing each man, however obliquely, to see his effort fit into the functioning of the whole; rather, the new American city, keeping its operations secret, expressing itself only as an overwhelming process, made each citizen sustain a crushing awareness of dispensability. Thwarted in their deepest instincts of workmanship, given no sense of the social extension of their effort, men in cities began to disintegrate psychologically. They moved from frontier self-reliance to various forms of urban dependence, bread and circuses and alcohol. Building a log cabin in the Sierras and learning to live there in harmony with the environment restored in White a feeling of unity which he felt an older America must have known. Things fit: logs and stones brought together into compositions of wall and fireplace which sheltered and warmed and assured the inhabitant that his labor could yet have visible effect. "Little by little," White wrote of cabin life, "the commonplace, rich philosophies come back to us—the value of small things; the stability of the object created, even though it be but a new broom handle; the importance of taking your advantage from routine work, since there is so much of it to be done; the desirability of fixing your enjoyment on means rather than ends, for means occupy the greater hours, and ends are but moments. These things from one point of view are tiresome; from another they, like all the simple philosophies of life, are vases whose beauties show only where they are filled with experience and dear-bought wisdom."[37]

Nature, finally, had been the great fact and theme of art in California, and it was invariably the landscape they inhabited that Californians referred to when they wanted to describe who they were. True, they committed obscene outrages against what in other moods they acknowledged as the objective correlative for their own best selves. Later celebrations in art could not restore the fallen Sequoia to its ancient height, resculpture the destroyed foothills, or give wing once again to the mighty condor. To be honest regarding the quality of production, no poem or painting or prose celebration ever came remotely near to making one forget the damage and betrayal of heritage. And yet all had not been lost. Beauties had been glimpsed, affinities of imagination and spirit felt. The nexus of these, the Californian's dialogue with California and with himself, had been borne witness to and preserved in art and social history. In the literary legacy of Clarence King and John Muir, Californians might glimpse an ideality, achievements of art arising out of honest experience which in turn beckoned them to seek out new relationships of their own. The founding of the Sierra Club attested to the fact that many Californians of a very fine sort were in dialogue with the environment and wanted the premises of their conversation shared with others and preserved for the future. California, which once seemed to Thoreau caught in the throes of a destructive frenzy, emerged in the vanguard of conservation. Americans there, many of them at least, came to recognize along with John Muir that in the wilderness was strength and sanity and healing. Learning this, incorporating wilderness values into their lives, they moved toward that liberating transformation of spirit for which the beauty of California was but an image and a shadow.

7

The Sonoma Finale of Jack London, Rancher

On 23 July 1909 Jack London came home to California after two years in the South Seas. His health, finances, and writing career were in deep trouble. London told San Francisco newspaper reporters that he was "unutterably weary" and had "come home for a good rest." Settled in his Sonoma County ranch, he began to rebuild himself and his career. "Of course, I may be going to pieces as you suggest," he wrote an anxious admirer, "but I'm living so damned happily that I don't mind if I do go to pieces."[1] Characteristically, London was fooling himself. He cared deeply about going to pieces, about the downhill slide to alcohol, fat, and an idle pencil. He threw himself into the therapy of ranching, a therapy that in time became an orgy, and finally a dance of death. Through construction of an identity as a great California rancher, London hoped to stave off chaos; instead, he invoked a nightmare. The Sonoma chapter of Jack London's life, his last chapter, dramatized a modality of California madness.

It began with rather simple aspirations, if one judges from the declaration of intent made in the first long fiction London turned out after returning from the *Snark* cruise. As a back-to-the-soil novel, *Burning Daylight* (1910) advocated a not-too-startling version of the good life: that blend of healthy outdoors and personal culture typical to many versions of the turn-of-the-century California style. In the novel, Elam Harnish, known in his Alaskan days as "Burning Daylight," abandons his martini-soaked life as a San Francisco business tycoon for the rural pleasures of Sonoma County ranching. As a novel, *Burning Daylight* is obsessed with questions of physical strength and health, reflecting London's inner anxieties. His image of himself as a he-man received a shock in the tropics. Ill-health forced the cancellation of a proposed seven-year voyage after two miserable years. The experience compounded a lifelong neurosis about physical condition. London hated violent exercise, refusing to walk any great distance, doing most of his work lying in bed or a hammock. His Korean valet Manyoungi dressed him in the morning, even to the point of bending to tie London's shoelaces. Indolence and a love of good dining made a weight problem inevitable. He smoked and drank heavily from his early teens. Not having brushed his teeth until nineteen, London suffered from continual toothache. After thirty, ailments increased geometrically: nervous itch, cramps, headaches, sties, dyspepsia, insomnia, dysentery, and pyorrhea.

Yet psychologically and ideologically London needed to think that he was a superman, one of Nietzsche's blond beasts or the Anglo-Saxon hero of Social Darwinist fantasy. He told an interveiwer in Boston in 1905 that if he had any religion it was physical culture. He had photographs made of himself in the seminude flexing his muscles, which he handed out to visitors. London bragged about his hard-headed materialism, but the breakdown of his health in the South Seas frightened him severely. It betokened the end, and he found himself hysterical at the thought of death. "My body is a strong body," he bragged in an effort to keep up his courage. "It has survived where weaklings died like flies."[2] He took great comfort from a study by an Army surgeon, Lieutenant Colonel Charles E. Woodruff, which explained his South Sea illnesses as an example of what all white men experienced in the tropics. He peopled his fiction with characters who regained their health in natural surroundings: tuberculars in the Southwest, sedentary club-men in the Yukon, and urban hysterics in the South Pacific.

Burning Daylight undergoes an ordeal of physical decay and regeneration. In Alaskan days Daylight had the magnificent physical strength of all London's alter egos—Wolf Larsen, Ernest Everhard, Martin Eden. To demonstrate possession of "an almost perfect brain and muscular coordination" and "a supreme organic excellence residing in the stuff of the muscles themselves," Daylight celebrates his thirtieth birthday with a variety of Yukon feats, including the lifting of a 900-pound sack of flour. After a few years as a San Francisco businessman, he discovers that "he was not the man of iron muscles who had come down out of the Arctic." A University of California athlete defeats him in arm-wrestling, precipitating a psychological crisis. Stripped before his mirror, Daylight realizes that his "lean stomach had become a paunch. The ridged muscles of chest and shoulders and abdomen had broken down into rolls of flesh." Remembering how a local newspaperman had turned himself from "a little, anaemic, alcoholic degenerate, with the spunk of a rabbit and about one per cent as much stamina" into a sturdy outdoorsman through life in Sonoma County, Daylight repudiates business for life on a small ranch in the Valley of the Moon. At the end of the novel, he meets the Berkeley athlete for a victorious re-match.

The alcoholic theme loomed large in *Burning Daylight* and other pieces of the post-*Snark* period. London's own drinking was becoming more and more uncontrollable. He feared his weakness, but like many alcoholics could never honestly face his problem. Even *John Barleycorn* (1913), his alcoholic memoirs, was an elaborate evasion. Throughout the book London insisted that he was a heavy drinker but not an alcoholic. He would still take a drink upon occasion, he insisted in *John Barleycorn's* conclusion. Between 1913 and his death in 1916, such occasions often turned into sprees, like one which lasted five days, London leaving the ranch in an automobile and returning days later hilariously atop a burro, having drunk himself around most of Sonoma County. Such escapades left him sick and depressed. He saw death at the bottom of the glass. Desperately, he filled his fiction with drunks who sober up, resolving in fantasy what he could not effect in reality. *Burning Daylight* was half such an effort and half an evasion. London insists that Daylight is not an alcoholic but a heavy drinker who is "systematic and disciplined" in confrontations with the bottle. Sonoma farm life moderates Daylight's consumption of alcohol but does not stop it altogether. Daylight has his drink now and then. Intervals between London's now and then grew more and more brief.

As a fantasy of recuperation, *Burning Daylight* expressed a deep aspect of London's Sonoma dream, the hope for health. Yet London's Valley of the Moon ranch was to be more than a spa. It was to redeem the California past. Riding through the Valley on his first visit, Daylight makes a pilgrimage into history, into California's truncated and unfulfilled past. All about he discovers relics of aborted effort in the Golden West—broken fences, overgrown roads, untended grapevines, crumbling abode barns, deserted mine shafts. He broods over the grave sites of two pioneer children, whose death in the 1850's symbolizes the nether side of the frontier era. Daylight wonders why Californians have abandoned lovely Sonoma Valley and fled to crowded cities, why the work of subduing the land has been left half-finished. He encounters a pioneer, a sort of attendant spirit, who chose to remain on the soil. At eighty-four, the old man is possessed of a physical well-being and psychological serenity in obvious contrast to Daylight's paunch and frazzled nerves. Immersed in business, Daylight still cannot shake from his mind the image of the old farmer milking his cows in the twilight. At the novel's conclusion, Daylight, former financier and Alaskan rough, is seen carrying a set of milk pails into the Sonoma sunset, redeeming himself and California's unfinished work.

The impetus for London's parable of a second chance on the land came from his own family history. His people had not done very well in California, never managing to escape a wearying round of foreclosed ranching and business efforts in San Francisco, San Mateo, Oakland, and Livermore. Jack's mother, Flora Wellman London, who came to California after a reasonably comfortable middle class girlhood in Marietta, Ohio, deeply resented slipping into the urban proletariat. She made sure that her son (born of a liaison with a San Francisco astrologer the year before she married John London) took pride in the fact that the Londons were of old American stock, superior to the immigrants with whom they shared working class status. Jack later discovered that he was illegitimate and—worse!—Irish. A blatant, schizoid Anglo-Saxonism compensated for the meanness of his own origins—his mother attempting suicide when she discovered she was pregnant—and the obscurity of his family in contemporary California—his foster-father a night-watchman. Hauled in for vagrancy in 1894 while hoboing around the United States as "Sailor Jack" and "the 'Frisco Kid," London protested to a Niagara Falls court that no old American whose ancestors had fought in the American Revolution should be treated this way. "Shut up!" said the judge, giving London thirty days in the Erie County Penitentiary. It was one of the most traumatic moments in his life. The record of his hobo career, *The Road* (1907), and of his visit to London's East End slums, *The People of the Abyss* (1903), two of Jack's most moving and honest books, both express London's horror of being mistaken for an impoverished nobody, of being snubbed by the people who in his fiction always went to Yale. By adulthood, he had convinced himself that he had an heroic ancestry. It was no longer a matter of a simple lie, but a buttress necessary for psychic survival. In a biographical report to Houghton, Mifflin, London characterized his foster-father as "Pennsylvania-born, a soldier, a scout, backwoodsman, trapper, and wanderer." He bragged about his "Yankee ancestry, dating beyond the French and Indian Wars."[3] His widow, concealing the fact of Jack's illegitimacy, provided a noble English ancestor, Sir William London, for the family tree. London heroes like Ernest Everhard in *The Iron Heel* (1908), Kit Bellew in *Smoke Bellew Tales* (1912), and Darrell Standing in *The Star Rover* (1915) all descend from pre-Revolutionary stock.

The Anglo-Saxon cast London gave his forebears represented his participation in a common turn-of-the-century myth, one especially popular in California. He derived his ideology from a variety of sources, but it was David Starr Jordan of Stanford who articulated Anglo-Saxonism in a way that most appealed to the young writer. London's turn-of-the-century Alaskan fiction is filled with heroes and theories of Anglo-Saxon race destiny, plus specific mentions of notions advanced by the Stanford president. Frona Welse, heroine of *A Daughter of the Snows* (1902), makes her Yale-educated, somewhat genteel fiancé realize that his "line goes back to the sea-kings who never slept under the smoky rafters of a roof or drained the ale-horn by inhabited hearth." The Alaskan frontier represented one more chapter in the long tale of Anglo-Saxon conquest.

Themes of Anglo-Saxonism, lost American status, and return to the soil converge in *The Valley of the Moon* (1913). London envisioned the book as his great California statement. "I am a Westerner, despite my English name," he told a Sacramento reporter late in 1910. "I realize that much of California's romance is passing away, and I intend to see to it that I, at least, shall preserve as much of that romance as is possible for me. I am making of *The Valley of the Moon* a purely Californian novel—it starts with Oakland and ends in Sonoma."[4] London began the novel about the same time that he undertook construction of his stone mansion Wolf House. Like it and like his ranch, *The Valley of the Moon* was intended as a California testimonial. He and Charmian drove all over California for three months in an open trap, gathering information and atmosphere. The "magnificent, heroic, detailed pilgrimage" made by Billy and Saxon in the novel retraced their own journey. One of his more monumental New York sprees, that of the 1911 Christmas season, interrupted work. Firmly convinced that he "was going to write some book here," London finished the manuscript while drying out on a round-the-Horn voyage on the *Dirigo*, a three-masted schooner.

The Valley of the Moon is London's parable of the good life in California. Saxon Brown, laundress, and Billy Roberts, teamster, meet, marry, and set up housekeeping in Oakland, California. Both are of old American stock, descendants of California pioneers, reduced to working class circumstances. Billy at first has faith in the ability of organized labor to better his lot. Involved in a teamsters' strike, he is arrested and sentenced to thirty days. Upon release from jail, his arms are broken by fellow teamsters who mistake him for a scab. Saxon suffers a miscarriage when strikers and police clash in front of her home near the railroad yards. She and Billy decide to repudiate their urban working class life and find the happiness that has somehow eluded them. "Just as the Jews found the promised land, and the Mormons Utah, and the Pioneers California," Saxon and Billy set out upon a pilgrimage through California in search of a place to settle as farmers. In effect, they re-enact the migration of their parents in search of the California dream, lost in their generation. For over a year, they wander in quest of an appropriate locale and lifestyle, London using the opportunity to depict with loving detail most of the state north of Carmel. Eventually, they purchase a small ranch in Sonoma's Valley of the Moon. There, on the land as scientific farmers, Saxon and Billy achieve the good life which California had promised their parents but which had been turned into proletarian misery.

The themes of *The Valley of the Moon*—escape from the working class, redemption of a pioneer past, search for a California version of the good life—were fundamental to London's own experience. Socialism had provided young London a means of organizing himself against the threat of his class background, conferring conceptual control over life and society upon a would-be intellectual of spotty education. London's socialism always had a streak of elitism in it, and a good deal of pose. He liked to play working class intellectual when it served his purposes. Invited to a prominent Piedmont house, he featured a flannel shirt, but, as someone there remarked, Jack's badge of solidarity with the working class "looked as if it had been specially laundered for the occasion."[5] Mark Twain saw straight through to the ambiguity of London's hopes for revolution. "It would serve this man London right to have the working class get control of things," said Twain. "He would have to call out the militia to collect his royalties."[6] By 1911, when he began *The Valley of the Moon*, London was more bored by the class struggle than he cared to admit. He became less and less associated with Socialist causes, resigning from the party itself in the last year of his life. Saxon Brown voiced London's attitude. "I don't want to dream," she tells her socialist brother—whose broken body "seemed to symbolize the futility of his social creed"—"I want things real. I want them now." So did London, and he acted out his desires within the private world of his ranch.

Without socialism, London's ranch-world needed some sort of myth. He created one, intimately associated with California. *The Valley of the Moon* constituted a probe in its direction. History had played a cruel hoax, the novel said, which this generation of Californians must correct. Saxon and Billy transcend their grim circumstances with the aid of historical nostalgia, the memory of the heroic California past of their parents. Saxon's mother had come across the plains and settled in San Jose. A poet, she published in the journals of California's literary golden era, pieces anthologized in Ella Sterling Cummins' famous *The Story of the Files* (1893), repository of pioneer verse. Saxon cherishes a scrapbook of her mother's poetry. The memory of San Jose in the fresh days of early California provides an imaginative escape from the girm details of life as an Oakland laundry girl. What had gone wrong, Saxon and Billy ask themselves? Why had they lost out? They decide to repeat their parents' migratory experience, but not their mistakes. They decided to redeem the past.

This redemption, personal and historical, was an essential aspect of London's ranch aesthetic. His foster-father had lost three farms since coming to California in the 1870's. In later years, London had an official explanation. "My father was the best man I have ever known," he said, "too intrinsically good to get ahead in the soulless scramble for a living that a man must cope with if he would survive in our anarchical capitalist system."[7] ("We's the white folks that failed," says a character in *The Valley of the Moon*, "too busy being good to be smart.") Even without the evidence provided by London's widow and daughter in their respective biographies, one could surmise what London's ranch meant to him in personal terms, the redemption of his foster-father's failure, which had kept Jack as a boy upon a succession of shabby spreads. Socialism gave historical perspective to London's escape from urban Oakland, but its industrial aesthetic had little to do with Sonoma ranch life. Socialism was urban and international. London was moving toward the rural and the local. His moral interpretation of California history, that its promise had been denied its rightful heirs, justified the conspicuous utopianism of his Valley of the Moon ranch just as socialism had justified his early anger at the establishment.

Yet as fact and as symbol, London's ranch, supposedly in the center of the California historical process, derived much of its identity from a sense of opposition. Saxon and Billy's sense of alienation and exclusion from contemporary California, although cast in specifically working class terms, expressed London's conviction of apartness. His identity as a Californian was by no means fixed or secure. An Eastern critic might greet him as "a figure impossible save in California in the opening decade of the twentieth century," but London himself, especially in his last years, felt estranged from his native state.[8] "My situation here in California is very unusual," he wrote in 1913. "I have practically no personal contacts with the people of California. Either I am away traveling over the wild places of the earth, or I am settled down here in my mountain ranch in Glen Ellen."[9] He avoided San Francisco, except for visits once a year to the Bohemian Club, preferring to do his urban hell-raising in New York or have friends out to the ranch, which he filled like a hotel. The polarities of his life, "the wild places of the earth" and "my mountain ranch in Glen Ellen," were also the polarities of his art. Other than his ranch novels, London wrote surprisingly little about California. The fiction he did set in the Bay Area made only routine explorations of locale. What use he does make of California is usually in the order of dream or vision. In the East End of London, Jack had remembered "my own spacious West," and in muddy Manchuria he recalled "fresh California days in the open." His Alaskan characters, caught in the frozen North, dream of "the sunnier pastures of the Southland," "a home among the orange groves and flowers," "the mythland of California," "a smiling country, streaming with sunshine, lazy with quietude." Such was the quality of London's own personal response. His was a California of private dream. Everyday California was another matter. He felt alienated from its civilization. "I am at sword's points with everybody in California," said London in 1914, "and am not afraid to let everybody in California know it."[10]

He called himself a prophet without honor in his own country, and, like Saxon and Billy, he retreated into a California of the imagination. Only in his mid-thirties, he began to call himself an old-timer. Hating skyscraper San Francisco, he waxed nostalgic over the pre-earthquake city. He corrected those who objected to the name " 'Frisco" as uncouth. "We love the western tang of it," London said, "we oldsters."[11] He abandoned the pressed flannels of socialist days and affected aggressively Western dress, insisting upon a wide-brimmed Baden-Powell hat and riding boots in even the most urban situation. Meeting David Graham Phillips in New York, London claimed that the sartorially elegant Phillips snubbed him because "I was dressed in my unconventional Western way, and he looked like a fashionplate."[12] At the age of twenty-nine, London had refused to donate $10 to Charles Fletcher Lummis' campaign to preserve art and relics of the Southwest, saying that the socialist revolution was more important. At the age of thirty-five, he began his own extensive collection of Indian relics, bartering with holograph manuscripts when cash ran short. He collected California writers and undertook a systematic study of California history. The last thing he read on the night of his death was an 1852 narrative of a voyage from Maine to California. He planned a historical novel of the West, parts of which he included in *The Star-Rover*. A note of compulsive anti-Easternism crept into his life and fiction, climaxed by what is probably the most improbable scene he ever wrote—that of Burning Daylight holding a six-gun on a swindling group of New York financiers, forcing them to return $11 million they had cozened from him.

The central expression of London's post-socialistic Californianism was his Valley of the Moon ranch, which, from 1909 to 1914, he attempted to fashion into an enactment of his inner dream. In *The Valley of the Moon* London gave the outlines of that vision. In the course of their year's wandering, Saxon and Billy undertake a series of explorations of California possibilities. In San Jose, from the widow of a university professor, they learn the value of scientific farming and direct marketing. A graduate of the University of California School of Agriculture who had traveled around the world in search of agricultural techniques appropriate to California intensifies their farm education. At Carmel, Saxon and Billy fall in with a group of bohemian artists, the Abalone Eaters, an idealized version of London's Piedmont-Carmel circle. The Abalone Eaters lead a life of creative work balanced by outdoor play and exercise, an aesthetic of sun, surf, and art. Here Saxon and Billy mend the spiritual and psychological deformations of urban working class life. They learn to play, build up their bodies, enjoy long hours under the sun, and become aware of the intellectual life. They have isolated the elements of the California good life—but where and how can they make their dream come true?

At this point, London enters his own novel to tie up for Saxon and Billy the California package of scientific farming, outdoor life, and cultured leisure. It was not the first time he appeared in *The Valley of the Moon*. London included a portrait of himself as young Jack, who takes Saxon on a sail around the Bay when she was awaiting Billy's release from prison. Jack starts Saxon's thoughts in the direction of escape, telling her (in one of London's infrequent understatements), "Oakland's just a place to start from, I guess." Having started Saxon and Billy upon their quest, London returns as Jack Hastings to bring the pair to their California fulfillment. On a Sacramento riverbank, where he has tied up his yacht *Roamer*, the

Robertses meet Hastings—writer, war correspondent, rancher—his wife Clara, and their ever-faithful Japanese manservant. Hastings listens to the story of the Robertses' quest, then tells of his own ranch life in Sonoma. He suggests that they will find their California ideal in the Valley of the Moon, where he has found a measure of peace. In time, the Robertses follow Hastings' advice, purchasing the Madrono Ranch with money Billy has earned as a teamster. Under Hastings' guidance, they prosper as ranchers.

An older couple, the Hales (based upon Charmian London's aunt and uncle), complete Billy and Saxon's induction into the good life. The Hales exude the spirit of true California culture. They live in a wood and stone bungalow, covered within with redwood paneling, the parlor lined with bookshelves. In the Hales, the Robertses behold the serenity and health of a life near the soil balanced with a variety of intellectual pursuits. Mrs. Hale, with her knowledge of California history and her love of California literature, reminds Saxon of her mother. In the older woman's friendship and tutelage, Saxon regains her lost California heritage. Both Saxon and Billy had worried about growing old. Working class life would have broken them before their time, but so might the bohemianism of the Abalone Eaters. The Hales dramatize the possibility of maturing with dignity, of moving along a rich and full life cycle.

Settling in Sonoma, Billy and Saxon redeem the lost California dream. Their conversion to scientific farming symbolizes their determination not to repeat the mistakes of the past. The previous generation of Californians, the old Americans now in reduced circumstances, had treated the land as they had in Eastern regions, impoverishing it through greedy, unscientific agriculture. Their frontier carelessness typified a nineteenth-century American pattern, as Mark Hall, a Carmel poet, points out to Saxon and Billy. "Whenever a man lost his stake, all he had to do was to chase the frontier west a few miles and get another." But in post-frontier California, "there's no place to pull on." In earlier years London argued that socialism provided the answer to the dilemmas of post-frontier California. Scientific farming replaced that panacea, offering a rural alternative. Moving back to the soil, Californians could recapture the frontier, repudiate their growing urban-industrial pattern of life. Scientific farming, like socialism, spoke the language of technology, making its gesture toward a modern California, but also making possible a saving ruralism, a repetition of the frontier experience upon the same soil where that era had spent and mismanaged its energies. Replacing the cowboy with the breeder and the sodbuster with the soil-scientist, London hoped to save the old West for the new.

The racism of *The Valley of the Moon* indicated that he expected no help from outsiders. London saw himself, in fact, leading the fight of old Americans to rescue California from the immigrant. The pathological racism of *The Mutiny of the Elsinore* (1913), started on the *Dirigo* voyage as London was finishing up *The Valley of the Moon,* records the intensity of his hate for "the ruck and spawn of the dark-pigmented breeds" during the last years of his life, his ranch years. Even as a younger man, he had rejected the brotherhood aspects of his supposed political creed. "What the devil!" London would say, "I am first of all a white man and only then a Socialist."[13] Outside of San Leandro, Billy and Saxon notice the neat, prosperous farms of the Portuguese. They resent it that such recent arrivals in California should be doing so well while old Americans lived in cities as wage-slaves. Billy feels that the government should provide them with free land "for what our father an' mothers done. I tell you, Saxon, when a woman walks across the plains like your mother done, an' a man an' wife gets massacred by the Indians like my grandfather done, the government does owe them something." Not that such a donation would represent socialism, qualifies Billy. "All our folks was a long time in America, an' I for one won't stand for a lot of fat Germans an' greasy Russian Jews tellin' me how to run my country when they can't speak English yet."

II

London's next Sonoma novel, *The Little Lady of the Big House* (1916), the last novel to appear in his lifetime, provides a sort of last will and testament to California possibilities. His ranch life had begun in earnest in 1909 as a moratorium against chaos. Its last literary expression stank of madness and decay.

Art and ranching converged in London's last effort, neither sustaining the other. Jack had always wanted the limelight, as super-writer and as super-rancher. In one of his short stories, "Told in the Drooling Ward," he made a cameo appearance as "the man who owns the ranch and writes books." In 1899, with but a few short stories in the *Overland* to his credit, London chillingly predicted the course of his career. "Lucrative mediocrity," he told a friend, "—I know, if I escape drink, that I shall surely be driven to it."[14] No matter how well received his work, London refused to make any final commitment to art, to define himself as a writer. He wrote for money and frankly admitted that fact. As early as 1900, while he was turning out his fine Alaskan stories, London confessed that "all the time I am writing, deep down, underneath the whole business, is that same commercial spirit."[15] The success that came with the sale of his fiction allowed him to act out a variety of fantasies—socialist revolutionary, war correspondent, sportsman, brawler, drinker, womanizer. He never played the artist. By 1909, upon his return from the South Seas, London had refined something of an apologia: "I prefer living to writing."[16] The form living took was ranching. As a rancher, London hoped to find that organization of experience that had eluded him in art, adventure, and politics. Paradoxically, ranching would involve writing at an even more feverish pace, for London did not intend his utopian experiment to be self-supporting for some time to come.

Ideologically and practically, ranching failed to confer the desired identity. Matters were especially disastrous for the super-rancher in 1913, the year he began writing *The Little Lady of the Big House*. "My face changed forever in that year 1913," London said. "It has never been the same since."[17] Although he was making over $70,000 a year, his bank balance dropped to $3.46. He had to negotiate a loan to complete Wolf House—and it burned to the ground the night before the Londons were to move in. Appendicitis, crop failure, and a grasshopper plague rounded out the year. Further disasters accompanied the composition of the novel through 1914. "It is sink or swim with me at the present time," London said in January 1915, "and at the present time I am floundering hard."[18] Pushed to the wall as a rancher and a writer, London's vision of Glen Ellen and his novel became part of one last desperate effort to salvage his dream. "I am building, constructing, and making the dead soil live again," he wrote his publisher, coaxing an advance. With pride, he described his terraces, silo, brood-barn, liquid manure tank, dam, and "piggery that will be the delight of all pig men in the United States."[19] He told his friends that the novel he was working upon was "the greatest story ever conceived by man," which made his friend George Sterling fear for Jack's mental health.[20] "As I go over this novel, I am almost led to believe that it is what I have been working towards all my writing life, and now I've got it in my two hands"—thus London tried to convince himself and his publishers. He might have been off his gait recently, "but here, with this novel, I am hot. It will be big stuff."[21] The messianic implications of his ranch came more and more to the forefront. "I see my farm in terms of the world," London admitted, "and the world in terms of my farm." "My work on this land, and my message to America, go hand in hand!" At night he had dreams of himself directing a great agricultural enterprise. In these dreams, London would envision himself instructing intelligent foremen in their duties. In the last days of his life, he was planning to settle from thirty to forty families on his ranch into a model agricultural colony, with himself as saving despot.[22]

Central symbol of London's baronial aspirations was Wolf House. In redwood and stone he laid bare his fantasies of messianic isolation, lavish Western splendor, heroic possibilities in the face of a mechanized twentieth century. As a boy, on the seedy family ranch in Livermore Valley, London had built a large model of the Alhambra, modeled upon Washington Irving's description. Wolf House expressed a similar inner need. He had been thinking of the California dream house as early as 1906, a house "honest in construction, material, and appearance," a house of clean lines, hardwood floors, "air and sunshine and laughter."[23] By 1910, when construction began, London's conception had grown more grandiose. It was no bungalow Jack wanted now, but the most magnificent house in the West. On a knoll overlooking the Valley of the Moon, with a redwood grove in the background, London and his San Francisco architect, Albert Farr, designed a stone fortress intended literally to last a thousand years. As a defense against earthquakes, a concrete foundation was poured capable of sustaining a forty-story skyscraper. Volcanic rock, blue slate, boulders, chocolate-maroon concrete, and 10,000-year-old redwood logs with the bark left on constituted basic construction materials. Since all elements came from the property, Wolf House seemed to rise from its knoll like some gigantic natural formation. The wings of the mansion enclosed a garden-patio with a 40-by-15-foot pool in the center, fed by a mountain spring and overlooked by covered balconies. The wings of Wolf House converged in a two-story, 18-by-50-foot living room, housing the most massive of seven fireplaces. Beneath this vast and medieval cavern was a stag-room, replete with billiard table, leather chairs, bar, hunting trophies, and other such masculine touches. A spiral staircase connected the library to a tower which housed London's working quarters. His own room perched atop Wolf House's most lofty tower. The atmosphere of the home was one of near-barbaric display and total entrenchment. So confident was London of its construction that he did not bother to take out fire insurance. On the night of 22 August 1913, Wolf House burned to the ground, fired by an arsonist's torch. London wept as it burned. He lay on his bed for four days, despondent, staring at the ceiling.

The loss of Wolf House left only his novel as a means of expression, his last chance to realize inner vision. Interestingly enough, he was making plans to appear as leading actor in motion picture versions of his own stories at the same time he was completing the novel. In *The Little Lady of the Big House* he appeared as Dick Forrest, Jack London writ large. "Cultured, modern, and at the same time profoundly primitive"—such was London's description of his super-Californians, Dick and Paula Forrest, who run a super-ranch in the Valley of the Moon.[24] At age forty, Dick Forrest, five feet ten inches, 180 pounds, has the perfection of physique which sagging Jack had long since lost. His gray eyes, brown hair, high cheekbones, strong jaw, square chin, and "mouth girlish and sweet" idealize London's own puffy, alcohol-ravaged face. From the opening scene, in which the Sonoma rancher awakens at 4:30 a.m., "instantly identifying himself in time and place and personality," Forrest is surrounded with emblems of conscious control. On his sleeping porch (Forrest has London's living habits), barometers, clocks, thermometers, and a communication switchboard connecting various departments of the ranch keep Forrest continually supplied with information. In his quarters he maintains the true simplicity of the California style. He sleeps under a robe of gray wolfskins, tails a-dangling, and covers his concrete floor with a rug of mountain goat. A Colt .44 hangs from a holster on the wall. These images play against symbols of technology, creating a mood of blended modernity and outdoor primitiveness. A woman's "rosy, filmy, lacy boudoir cap," left on the floor the night before by Paula suggests Forrest's sexuality.

Dick has had the career London wanted for himself. Successful owner and manager of 250,000 acres, Forrest stands for everything best in California agriculture. Like London, he had been on his own from the age of thirteen, although, heir to a great pioneer fortune, Forrest had started life with $20 million in his own name. Like London, the Sonoma rancher had taken to the road to learn "two-legged, two-fisted democracy." His life had been a calculated balance of business and heroic achievement. After taking a degree from Berkeley and doing a year's graduate work in agronomy, Forrest adventured in the Klondike, Mexico, Tahiti, the Philippines, and South America until his thirtieth year, when he began his ranching career. London portrays Forrest as a combination of Red Cloud, Forrest's nickname, taken from the legendary acorn planter of the California Nishinam, whose song Forrest frequently chants, and "the ultra-modern man, the last word of the two-legged, male human that finds Trojan adventures in sieges of statistics, and, armed with test tubes and hy-

Jack London (1876–1916)

He sought redemption through an outdoor life; indeed, through the scientific farming of his Sonoma acres, he sought to redeem California itself. His dream degenerated into a nightmarish race with death, which he lost. Nothing went right. His crops failed. Wolf House, intended to last a thousand years, burned to the ground in one night. Retreating into fantasy, he wrote about super-Sonomans doing great big California things. He once said that he would rather be ashes than dust. He got his wish.

podermics, engages in gladiatorial contests with weird micro-organisms." London's widow tells us that Jack, clumsy of hand, had trouble buttoning buttons, rigging fishing gear, or filling an ink pen. Dick Forrest manipulates his swichboard "with a practiced hand," looks at his watch "without pause or fumble of focus," and guides his horse "automatically, with slightest touch of rein against arched neck." Overweight, tortured by cramps, dropsy, and dyspepsia, London gave Forrest "blond beast muscles" and "blond beast organs." Unlike his creator, Forrest has had the best of the bottle. "You put the other fellows under the table," Paula tells him, "or into the hospital or the grave, and went your gorgeous way, a song on your lips, with tissues uncorroded, and without even the morning-after headache." London dreamed of re-creating the expansive style of Spanish rancheros. He saw himself as *padron*, riding about his ranch on payday in a wide-brimmed hat, paying his men with gold he kept in Klondike pouches draped across his saddle. Forrest manages things in the same way, combining old California style with modern managerial techniques. Like London, he loves to ride about his holdings theatrically attired in riding togs, spurs, and wide-brimmed hat, gesturing, not just with an ordinary quirt, but one "Indian-braided of raw-hide, with ten ounces of lead braided into the butt that hung from his waist on a loop of leather." London tried to learn how with little success, but Forrest easily rolls his cigarettes with one hand, cowboy-fashion.

In their Big House, modeled after the Hispano-Mooresque Hacienda Del Pozo de Verona of Mrs. Phoebe A. Hearst in Livermore, Dick and Paula live in the baronial manner Jack had envisioned for himself, a dream mocked by the charred ruins of Wolf House. Their two-story-high dining room is "a replica of the hacienda dining rooms of the Mexican land-kings of old California." On the walls hang animal skins and depictions of Mexican-Californian life. Paintings by California artists hang in most rooms. London's Sonoma neighbors may be somewhat skeptical about Jack's lavish manner of living, his aristocratic pretensions, but Dick and Paula are the focal point of Sonoma high-life. Neighboring land-barons, all descendants of pioneers, drop in frequently at the Big House, where a sort of perpetual party prevails: riding and sports in the afternoon, cocktails at five, dinner in the huge hall, followed by dancing, conversation, and parlor games. London used to love to entertain in this manner. A typical guest list might include Luther Burbank, Hyhar Dyall (an Indian revolutionary), a writer, a Stanford professor, a sailor, an ex-denizen of an Ottoman harem (now in vaudeville), three tramps, and a visionary who wanted to build a house that would extend from San Francisco to New York. London's drinking, however, his tendency to dominate conversation by shouting down all disagreement, his bullying of guests, in time drove away all but the most unabashed freeloaders. The night he died, Jack and Charmian dined alone. In *The Little Lady of the Big House*, the party continued: naïve, pretentious, a little vulgar, and more than a little pathetic. At poolside, the Forrests play a Japanese version of strip-poker. Paula loses, but has a swimming suit under her riding togs. Bay Area intellectuals drop in for nights of conversation, pleasantly interrupted for recitals by Paula upon her Steinway.

There had always been an authoritarian streak in London, and in his last years on the ranch it emerged full-blown. On the ranch, noted a friend, Jack became a sort of top-sergeant, putting himself eventually "beyond the reach of everyone who refused to function as a menial." The ranch had "the air of a little factory or possibly a barracks with everything and everyone regimented."[25] A frequent motif in London's fiction was that of reform through a blend of dictatorship and technology. London admired the spick-and-span orderliness the United States Army brought to Vera Cruz in 1914, lamenting that such control could not characterize domestic reform. Forrest runs his ranch with ruthless efficiency, employing a quasi-military system of command and staff. London, absent from the ranch about six months a year between 1910 and 1916, managed matters through notes he passed on to his sister Eliza. He liked the show of managerial power, but not grinding attention to detail. Forrest devotes one hour a day to staff meetings, in which he unerringly makes correct decisions. London's workers laughed at his efforts to play big-time rancher. Considering the operation a rich man's hobby, they loafed when they could. London's foreman at one point was getting a 20 per cent kickback from all Glen Ellen merchants, who merely added the cost of graft to the prices they charged Jack's ranch. Forrest's employees regard him with a feudal-like love and awe. Basque herders pull off their hats and bow when he rides by. Forrest in turn answers their show of reverence, lifting his right hand, "the quirt dangling from wrist, the straight forefinger touching the rim of his Baden-Powell in semi-military salute." Over forty domestics sit down in the Big House servants' dining hall. Jack failed miserably as a businessman. Of $50,000 he had out in loans, when pressed he could only call in $50. Ventures in motion pictures, real estate, and eucalyptus groves drove him into financial ruin. Forrest masterfully conducts an international cartel. Did London lose $10,000 in Mexican land deals? Forrest unerringly manages his Mexican interests, even to the extent of backing anti-revolutionary forces to prevent confiscation of his holdings.

Wish-fulfillment succeeded wish-fulfillment. Scientific agronomy represented a key aspect of London's program for California. He considered himself a knowledgeable agriculturist and breeder, refusing advice from his ranch hands. "And they try to teach me," London snorted, "who spend my nights with the books."[26] He made Forrest "to the domestic animal world what Burbank is to the domestic vegetable world." London planned a book upon the cultivation of mountain fields, which he never could find time to write. Forrest turns out *Corn in California, Silage Practice, Farm Organization, Farm Book-keeping, The Shire in America, Humus Destruction, Soilage, Alfalfa in California* and *Cover Crops For California.* Forrest breeds a champion Short-Horn bull, which takes first place three times at the California State Fair in Sacramento. London's bull broke its neck. Forrest maintains a "prize herd of Angora goats, each with a pedigree, each with a history." London's Angora herd died of disease. Forrest's pigs sweep all competitions. London's pigs died of pneumonia, developed on the stone floor of the piggery he himself designed. Forrest introduces the Shire mare into Sonoma. London found that the clay-like mud which clung to a Shire's hairy forelegs made it impossible to use them in winter. Besides, local farmers were turning to tractors. As London hoped to do, Forrest has settled a colony upon a portion of his land, financing an experiment in intensive farming. London could never get along with academic advice. He would invite professors from Davis to inspect his ranch, then ignore their suggestions. Forrest maintains his personal platoon of college-trained advisors. He buys talent and is capable of utilizing it in a way London never could.

Yet for all its Technicolored fantasy, *The Little Lady of the Big House,* finished the year before London's own dying, is a story about death, the last in a long line of apocalyptic fictions by London, in which life battles against death, desire against satiety, civilization against chaos. The sexual element in the novel possesses an odd, strangely arrested quality. Dick identifies himself with Mountain Lad, the ranch's prize stallion. At times, he stamps his feet and sings a mating song in the *persona* of the stud. Yet he often asks himself, in the midst of his super-Californian splendor, "Why? What for? What's it worth? What's it all about?" Childless herself, Paula Forrest is a master breeder of horses. She discusses the merits of various studs with a vaguely pornographic relish. She enters the novel dressed in a flesh-colored bathing suit astride Mountain Lad, whom she forces to plunge into the swimming pool at the risk of being crushed beneath his weight should the stallion slip on the tiled surface around it. Evan Graham, the Forrests' house-guest—"good stuff, old American stock, a Yale man"—exudes much male energy but is subduedly celibate. "It is all sex, from start to finish," London had promised *Cosmopolitan* about this novel, "—in which no sexual adventure is actually achieved or comes within a million miles of being achieved, and in which, nevertheless, is all the guts of sex, coupled with strength."[27] In love with both Evan and Dick, Paula leaves her husband's bed but does not begin an affair with their guest. She admittedly enjoys the suspended situation, so erotic in its possibilities, so remote from resolution. This murky imbalance of sexual energies, this half-desired relief from satiety, dramatizes a quality that pervades the novel: for all their trumpeting of heroic possibilities, for all their self-conscious consumption of food, sun, fun, and culture, the characters of London's last novel are dead in spirit and in appetites. London strained to depict them in huge and laughing enjoyment but only manages scenes of lifeless, loveless consumption. The quality of Dick and Paula's poolside frolics is near-hysterical; their conversation, an orgy of pretentious banality and name-dropping. London sought to evoke civilization through an itemizing of what he considered its trappings, but succeeded only in producing a sort of monstrous Sears Roebuck catalogue, name-brand succeeding name-brand in a near-mad effort to shore up a collapsing sense of cultural identity. By the end of the novel even London is tired. When Dick and Paula think in terms of action, when they stop posing, it is to prepare for death, not life. No one aspect of their super-ranch life offers consolation. Dick plans suicide. Paula commits it, attired, appropriately, in her riding costume.

III

The suicide of one of London's California heroines has a special resonance. For a supposedly "male" writer, London made much use of the heroine as an instrument of cultural statement. Paula, super-Californian, was London's first heroine to commit suicide.

The California heroine first appeared in London's early Alaskan stories. Her role was essentially that of mother of the race, reclaiming her man from dusky concubinage, fighting to prevent the scattering of Anglo-Saxon seed among the tepees. Indian women offer London's heroes a non-structured, acultural sexual fulfillment. John Fairfax—in a 1902 story, "In the

Forests of the North"—has lived with an Indian woman for five years. "It may be a beastly life," says Fairfax, "but at least it is easy to live. No philandering, no dallying. If a woman likes you, she'll not be backward in telling you so." Standing for honor and for civilization, London's Californian women usually get their men back from the North, but their conquest is that of mother, not mistress. In his first fictional outpourings, the neglected son of a neurotic, gnome-like creature under five feet in height, a woman forced to wear a wig to conceal baldness, of whom nothing was really known of the time between her sixteenth and thirty-first birthday, who drove her son in terror from the house when she shrieked Indian war whoops in the course of seances—the son of such a woman wrote of bold and sturdy Anglo-Saxon mothers. "To the daughters of the wolf," London dedicated his second book, "who have bred and suckled a race of men." He had just married Bessie Maddern of Oakland, described by a friend as "the eternal mother." "A man is always looking for his mother in every woman he meets," claimed Jack, "especially if he has been deprived of her, or, for some reason she has tried to put him out of her life."[28]

London's marriage proved unsatisfactory. The search for the lost mother became a flight from her smothering embrace. In the *Kempton-Wace Letters* (1903), London, as Herbert Wace, instructor in economics at Berkeley, argues for a marriage based upon comradeship as opposed to romantic love. Frona Welse, heroine of *A Daughter of the Snows* (1902), offers a shift in emphasis from the Alaskan-Californian women of London's first two books. Frona is the first in a long line of London's young, upper class, educated, no-nonsense girls, who reject bourgeois urban life for the outdoors and who initiate the man of their choice into liberating freedom. Daughter of an Alaskan trader and capitalist, Frona carries on the mother-of-the-race tradition but is also a comrade. She believes that it is her female role to carry on "a race of doers and fighters, of globe-encirclers and zone-conquerors." Seeing an exhausted man lying on the side of the trail, knowing "that she was speaking for the race," she tells him to go home if he cannot take the pace of the North. She herself is more than adequate on the trail. At one point, she flexes her arms "till the biceps knotted" and is praised by one sourdough for "yer prize-fighter's muscles an' yer philosopher's brains." She has contempt for middle class women, "the hot-house breeds—pretty, helpless, well-rounded, stall-fatted little things" who "are not natural or strong; nor can they mother the natural and the strong." Frona makes a man out of Vance Corliss, a Yale-trained mining engineer. She insists that he shed his priggishness and treat her in an open, frank, comradely way. More importantly, she brings Corliss back to the land. In her Yukon girlhood, Frona "had nursed at the breast of nature—in forfeit of a mother." Ten years in the South and a Vassar B.A. have not taken away her love of the outdoor life. She rejects the city, "where men had wandered away from the old truths and made themselves selfish dogmas and casuistries," in favor of "the faith of trail and hunting camp."

With few exceptions, the type of heroine represented by Frona Welse dominated London's fiction. She incorporated and expressed the twin drives of London's ambition—so representative of turn-of-the-century California—a desire for simultaneous possession of frontier vigor and genteel culture. Other aspects went into the construction of these heroines—London's latent homosexuality being the most important. It accounted partially for his worship of physical force, and his taste for mannish heroines. But there was strong cultural significance in the woman who expressed in fiction London's inner experience. Dede Mason of *Burning Daylight* and Paula Forrest of *The Little Lady of the Big House* are psychological symbols, but they also are explicit enactments of London's post-*Snark* version of California value and style. Behind both of them was London's second wife, Charmian Kittredge of Berkeley. In her, London felt he had met his great comrade, his "Wolf-Mate," his "Mate-Woman." Charmian played the Californian as New Woman. She made much of her emancipation, was a showy horsewoman, affected a vaguely masculine, outdoor atmosphere, cultivated connections with Berkeley and *Overland* intellectuals.

Into her thirties when London married her, Charmian had a knack for creating the illusion of aristocratic possibilities, of offering that blend of class and vigor which so enchanted Jack, who married her the day after his divorce from Bessie Maddern. London idealized their courtship in *Burning Daylight*. Dede Mason represents the California Woman in all perfection. Born on a ranch in Siskiyou County and raised there by her widowed father, she lives in Berkeley, running with the university set, commuting to San Francisco, where she works as Daylight's secretary. A bluestocking, she carries a copy of Browning to work (one of London's persistent indications of intellectualism) and helps Daylight straighten out his grammar (telling him to say "It is I" for "It's me"). On weekends, Dede likes "the simple and the out-of-doors, the horses and the hills, the sunlight and the flowers." "Manlike in her saddle," daringly attired in a fitted corduroy suit, Dede rides the Berkeley hills. Daylight joins her on these excursions, finding his equestrian secretary "so bravely man-like, yet so essentially and revealingly woman." Dede's Berkeley apartment, like the Hales' Sonoma Bungalow and Dick Forrest's sleeping porch, is dramatically Californian, a blend of severe line, outdoorishness, and finer things. Wolf and coyote skins cover carpetless hardwood floors. A mountain lion pelt hangs tapestry-like from one wall, highlighting a Steinway, atop which is a small crouched Venus. There are plenty of books and journals, fresh flowers, sunlight, but no clutter. Dede's personal manner is a mixture of self-sufficient chastity and self-respecting assertiveness. She expresses contempt for Daylight's money-grubbing and martini-swilling, winning him over to the conviction that only on the land will he find happiness. They consummate their marriage in a Sonoma farmhouse, under the watchful guardianship of Daylight's Alaskan wolf-dog.

Five years later, Dede and Daylight, Jack and Charmian, reappear as Paula and Dick Forrest. The stagy yet believable consummation of Dede and Daylight becomes cartoonish sexuality. Daylight's Sonoma farm becomes Dick's super-ranch. As a character, Dede was stylized, but she stood for palpable California possibilities. Over-drawn, unconsciously mock-heroic, Paula represents London's desperate attempt to suppress his consciousness of failing ranch-life, failing flesh, failing glamour, failing appetite for life itself. "Sometime, when you're out in California," Jack had bragged, to a critic in 1911, "run up and visit my wife and me on our ranch, and we'll show you what comradeship, mateship, and connubial happiness are."[29] He liked to think that he and Charmian had the marriage of the century. In time, he grew bitterly disappointed over her failure to provide him with a son, threatening to take a maidservant, Abraham-like, for the purpose.

Moving into her forties when Jack was still in his mid-thirties, Charmian grew petulant and demanding. In Paula Forrest, he recreated her as the California dream-woman. Among other things, Paula is a magnificent pianist, horsewoman, diver, swimmer, and singer, who regales guests with Hawaiian hulas, German love-songs, and operatic arias with a voice "haunted with richness of sex"—which is to say that Charmian rode horses, played the piano, knew how to swim, and submitted guests to her singing. Was Charmian in her mid-forties, looking every bit of it? Paula is thirty-eight (Charmian's acknowledged age), looking ten years younger. Did London find Charmian at five-thirty one morning atop a haystack with a young male guest, watching the sunrise? Paula is the soul of fidelity, even under severe temptation. Did London, vexed by Charmian's petulant demands, tell his sister Eliza, "She is our little child. We must always take care of her"?[30] Paula is Dick's soul-mate, his companion, his "boy-in-breeches" and "boy-girl" whose occasional childishness charms. Charmian ignored ranch guests. An embarrassed Jack once had personally to conduct female guests to the ladies' room. Paula is a perfect hostess. Charmian, bothered by insomnia, refused to allow work to start around the ranch house until nine in the morning, forcing laborers to sit idle for two hours at London's expense. Paula has her sleepless "white nights" but bothers no one. Did Charmian try to get Jack to purge the ranch of the colony of philosophical tramps he supported, to whom he played feudal baron to retainers? Paula encourages Dick's support of the Seven Sages of the Madrona Grove, to the extent of designing for them a monastery residence. Was Charmian snobbish, insecure, sometimes paranoid over imagined slights? Paula has "a way with her, compounded of sheerest democracy and equally sheer royalty." Servants and society love her.

If all this was London's wish-fulfillment, then so was Paula's suicide. From the point of view of plot: the perfect California woman does away with herself. From the point of view of fantasy: London does away with Charmian. Paula is cartoon-relief from hated reality, not the imaginative idealization of California possibilities. As a character she is grotesque. As a cultural figure, she functions as a semi-obscene mannequin whom London can dress up in various costumes and arrange in striking poses, hoping to convince himself and others that Paula is an exciting person and that she manifests achievement of the good life. In killing her off, London admitted the falsity and weariness of his dream.

IV

His deficient sense of culture—which could see in Paula Forrest such heraldic expression of social value—was the direct result of personal experience. Yet London's psychological development took place within a specific context, California at the turn of the century. Social and personal experiences were concurrent and reinforcing. In a sense, London's was a representative quest. His search for identity, for a place in the sun, was also contemporary California's. Like many Californians, he often pathetically misread signals, confusing consumption with culture, display with code, and aspiration with achievement. London bore within himself the burden of an ambiguous history, with its violent hates and tangled drives, and so did California.

At the age of nineteen as a freshman at the University of California, he had history stolen away: he learned of his illegitimacy. Confused and stunned, London crossed the Bay to read in the files of the San Francisco *Examiner* the disreputable events surrounding his birth, a sordid tale of ambiguous paternity, attempted suicide, and public scandal. His reputed father categorically denied fathering him. Thus London could not with full assurance appropriate even the *Examiner*'s ugly scenario. In psychic terms, his dilemma reflected the larger issues of California historiography: from traumatic and chaotic experience, what could be structured and made useful, what should be repressed as unbearable? Josiah Royce might argue for an honest facing of the past because he detected a pattern of good overcoming evil. Jack could see no such process. His foster-father, John London, had been a vague and shadowy presence, embarrassingly aromatic with the smell of failure. He hounded his son for money (so London said in 1898), pursuing Jack to the offices of the school journal at Oakland City High School to borrow fifty cents. If unsuccessful, he would shamelessly wheedle the money from his son's friends. In his mother—a strange, eccentric creature, harsh, compulsive—London could see only a burden of mutual shame, mother for son, son for mother, and rejection. "I do not ever remember ever receiving a caress from my mother when I was young," he recalled.[31] Whether he did or not, he wanted that to be the case. He accused his mother of forcing her husband to beat him, after which London Junior and Senior fell weeping into each other's arms. Charmian felt of the incident that Flora was unconsciously punishing Jack for his illegitimacy. Making Jack withdraw from school (so he claimed) and take a factory job, she symbolized to her son fatal entombment in the proletariat. He later brooded that he had inherited her suspected insanity. He never invited her to the ranch and she never came.

Through the pseudo-historical terms of an imagined impoverished childhood, London gave mythic structure to his inner trauma of repudiation and rejection, a mythic past onto which he later grafted his version of California history. All his life he whined of the poverty of his childhood, which was simply not the case. "I never had a boyhood," Jack said, "and I seem to be hunting for that lost boyhood." He meant that he had a boyhood he chose not to remember. He had put together his personal myth as early as 1898, complaining to his upper bourgeois girl friend Mabel Applegarth (appearing as Ruth Morse in *Martin Eden*) that as a boy he was so hungry for meat that he would steal from lunchbags at school. "Great God!" moaned London, "when those youngsters threw chunks of meat on the ground because of surfeit, I could have dragged it from the dirt and eaten it"—"This meat incident is an epitome of my whole life"—"Hungry! Hungry! Hungry! From the time I stole meat and knew no call above my belly, to now when the call is higher, it has been hunger, nothing but hunger."[32] The fact was, Flora London often served steak—but she insisted upon putting newspapers under the plates to prevent meat juice from spashing upon her tablecloth. In the newspapers, London could remember his mother's eccentricity, with more than faint overtones of hostility and resentment, and the seedy inconsequentiality, not grim poverty, of their social position. Psychological and social expectations fused, and the memory became one of no meat, not no love and no social position, as symbolized in newspaper place-mats. In later life London loved bloody rare steaks and half-cooked duck, which he devoured with juice-spilling abandon.

The first larger myth to be grafted onto this story of a deprived childhood was socialism, London's youthful systematization of experience. Socialism explained boyhood rejection in socio-economic terms. Laced with strong draughts of Darwin and Nietzsche, socialism offered a route of escape. Around 1905 or so, just after the publication of *The Sea Wolf*, London had what he called the Long Sickness, a sense of failure and self-loathing. His marriage to Charmian was part of his effort to come out of this depression. Although he continued to sign letters "Yours for the revolution," socialism ceded to Sonoma as London's most vital myth. Like socialism, Sonoma explained the facts of dispossession and recovery: how old Americans had lost out in the California scramble and how on the land they would reclaim their rightful place. Sonoma's revolution was agricultural, not industrial, but just as redeeming a myth. If London could not storm the barricades in pressed flannels, then he would lead a countermarch across scientifically terraced fields and orchards, astride a spirited stallion, dressed in boots, riding togs, and Baden-Powell.

Both socialism and Sonoma were more matters of fantasy than hardheaded diagnosis. London could not relate closely enough to any society to coax forward realistic, pragmatic imperatives. Psycho-sexuality had much to do with determining what forms of social expression appealed to him. London grew up dominated by women, first his mother, and then his sister Eliza, who supervised Jack when their parents left them alone on the ranch to scour the countryside for spiritualist meetings. (Eliza later managed the Sonoma ranch in Jack's absences.) Lonely and shy, young London read a lot, dreamed of becoming a poet or a composer. Schoolmates taunted him for being a sissy. His aesthetic boyhood tastes later embarrassed him. "Somewhat of an exquisite, I'm afraid," he later admitted, "if only from my excessive physical sensibilities—but I'm surely not a sissy!" He recreated himself as a Huck Finn of the Oakland waterfront, ignoring his withdrawn pre-adolescent years. Ideologically and psychologically he developed a he-man complex, playing the well-advertised womanizer, instructing his barber that he wanted his hair "not fancy, you know, but rough," filling his fiction with vanquishing males. He cultivated an interest in the literature of perversion and admitted a tolerance of homosexuality dating from his days before the mast, but insisted that he was "prosaically normal." "The alienist interested him intellectually," confessed Charmian, "but he was nicely avert to perversion of any stripe." She told how, as a young oyster pirate, Jack defended his honor with a fork against the onslaughts of an amorous Greek sailor. London's friendship with George Sterling—to whom in 1909 he sent from the Solomon Islands a dried clitoris—was romantically intense, characterized at one point by an exchange of confiding and confessional letters slipped wordlessly into each other's pockets. London called Sterling "Greek" and answered to Sterling's "Wolf." He had always been searching for "the great Man-Comrade," London told Charmian in a love-letter, and had first wished that she were a man. He dreamed at night in later life of a man "to whom he would eventually bend a vanquished intelligence." "Imperial, inexorable with destiny," this vanquisher would descend a staircase, at the base of which waited a psychically ravished Jack.[33] Humphrey Van Weyden's fixation upon Wolf Larsen has much of this man-vanquisher element: "His body," says Van Weyden, "thanks to his Scandinavian stock, was fair as the fairest woman's. I remember his putting his hand up to feel of the wound on his head, and my watching the biceps move like a living thing under its white sheath. It was the biceps that had nearly crushed out my life once . . . I could not take my eyes from him."

Ambivalently, London could play Larsen or Van Weyden, receiver or giver of pain. Tormented by toothache, he loved to pull other people's teeth, having a portable dental kit for the purpose. Obsessed with meat, he once barbecued a snake, laughing as some of his guests vomited when told what they had just eaten. He loved violent practical jokes, hitting from behind with a rubber mallet, booby-trapping books with explosives. One contemporary at least felt Jack's tastes for aggressive pranks "evidence of a serious mental condition." He loved to write of the cruel matings of wild animals. Higher up the evolutionary scale, a pre-human anthropoid in *Before Adam* (1907) says of his inamorata: "It was strange how this anger against her seemed to be part of my desire for her." Caressing his fiancée, the boxer-hero of *The Game* (1905) has a sudden urge "to make the embrace crushing till she should cry out with the hurt." Many of London's heroines are roughed up and love every minute of it. In *The Valley of the Moon* Saxon and Billy romp with bizarre violence. Billy taps Saxon on the chin until her brain "snapped with a white flash of light, while her whole body relaxed, numb and weak, and her vision reeled and blurred." He then pummels her solar plexus until "she experienced a simple paralysis, accompanied by a stoppage of breath." He presses his finger into the middle of her forearm until "she knew excruciating agony." ("That's one of the death touches of the Japs," he tells her.) He throws a half-Nelson on her until "she felt that her arm was a pipe-stem about to break," then pressuring his thumbs into her eyes until "she could feel the fore-running ache of a dull and terrible hurt." Only then are they ready to proceed to less violent means of expression. London loved to box with women. One of Charmian's wifely duties was to put on the gloves with her Mate-Man. Frequently hurt and mildly gory after these connubial set-to's, she praised Jack for not hitting below the belt.

The shaming of an upper class woman appears as a frequent motif in London's stories. His characters often express loathing for the facts of heterosexual sex. Humphrey Van Weyden listens with fascination to the pig-like squeals of drowning women in the San Francisco Bay; "women . . . of my own kind, like my mother and sisters," says Van Weyden, "with the fear of death upon them and unwilling to die." London was a lifelong habitué of houses of prostitution. As a younger man, he especially relished San Francisco's Chinese bordellos, with their contrived practices. After bloody rare steak and drinks on the Barbary Coast, Jack would head for one of San Francisco's many houses, where, as he described it, "my most savage natural instincts are unleashed. I can be cruel or kind, according to my whim and my pocketbook. What more, after being well fed, may a man want? There is mastery in it. A feeling of power, a satisfaction of the instinct that inclines us toward beauty."[34]

Aggression, distrust, ambivalent sexuality, hatred of women—such psychological facts conditioned London's capacity for social existence and for a theory of society. Like his mannish heroines, the ranch represented a male ideal—managed, paradoxically, by Jack's older sister. As a utopian enterprise, it was conceived in aggression against the California fact. The lineaments and contours of that dream-realm proceeded partially from a subliminal life common to both London and California. Through the

Sonoma myth London partook in the larger myth of California. There—like California—he sought to find a heroic past. There—like California—he sought to synthesize vigor and intellect. There—like California—out of private but not irrelevant compulsions he sought to manifest a sense of regional identity and to glory in regional possibilities. A confused inner life made fulfillment of this ideal impossible, distorting his relation to the land, alienating him from any form of community, driving him to self-destruction: over-eating, over-drinking, and—on his sleeping porch in the early hours of 22 November 1916—over-dosing himself with morphine and atropine sulphates. It was not suicide in the unambiguous sense of the word. Waking in the night with an attack of renal colic, London took what proved to be an overdose, complicated by the alcohol in his system, in an effort to stop the excruciating pain. But when one considers what had brought about London's uraemic condition—his drinking, his disregard of doctors' advice that he exercise his disintegrating body, the compulsive devouring twice a day of near-raw venison and wild duck—a pattern of self-destruction is quite clear.

London's psychic distress paralleled California's own internal social tensions. Latent homosexuality, anxieties about manhood, had an analogue in California's turn-of-the-century determination to identify with the titanic energies that had pulsated through society during the frontier period, energies which both attracted and repelled a genteel generation. His insecurity, his intimidation by an imagined hostile high culture, characterized California's ambivalent speculations about style and value. It was the reverse aspect of the determination to retain frontier vigor, an intimidation by the East of the fact and the East of the mind—an East sophisticated, impervious, assured of its history, assured of its caste. Like California, London was certain of none of these things and so he constructed a myth, not by himself, but in concert with fellow Californians. His flight into narcissism and fantasy, expressed mythically in the remembered story of his own life and in his version of California history, expressed spatially on the ranch, paralleled California's appropriation of a fabled Hispanic era and a mythically redemptive frontier. London's death in one—and by no means exclusive—sense came when his myth, his identity, broke down.

In 1909, after his return from the South Seas, he had been worried about going to pieces. After 1913 he was in rapid decline. His stories became filled with old and beaten men, dreaming "of matings accomplished, of feasts forgotten, of desires that were the ghosts of desires, flaring, flaming, burning, yet unrealized in achievement of easement and satisfaction." He experienced a revival of interest in the family tradition of spiritualism. He thought of beginning a serious study of Freud and Jung, hoping to escape his downhill slide through self-knowledge. On 22 October 1916, a month before London did away with himself, Neuadd Hillside, his Shire stallion, suffered a rupture. London loved the animal, putting him into *The Little Lady of the Big House* as Mountain Lad, symbol of eros, the life-force. Neuadd Hillside refused to lie down, shuddering in agony before the end came. London wept. Nothing since the burning of Wolf House had so profoundly shaken him. The Shire, which London had hoped to put to stud, had been a major investment, but more, it had come to stand in his mind for the ranch, for life itself. Now it was gone. "Why should we clutter the landscape and sweet-growing ground with our moldy memories?" London asked. "Besides, we have the testimony of all history that all such sad egoistic efforts have been failures. The best the Pharaohs could do with their pyramids was to preserve a few shriveled relics of themselves for our museums."[35] After London's death, a dude ranch operated on the property. The Valley of the Moon ranch is now a museum and a State Park.

8
Bohemian Shores

"California, more than any other part of the Union," wrote Lord Bryce in *The American Commonwealth*, "is a country by itself, and San Francisco a capital."[1] More correctly, Bryce might have described San Francisco as a city-state; for the life, various and self-absorbed, of what by 1860 was the fourteenth largest city in the Union often appeared but remotely related to frontier California. Out of its dramatic setting on the Pacific, so distant from any comparable civilization, out of its sense of itself as a city possessed of an identity intrinsically international, San Francisco called Americans to pleasure and to the enhancement of life through the enjoyment of art. An unimaginative layout, the systematic reduction of its hills, the natural evils of fog and stinging sand-laden winds could not negate the superb physicality of San Francisco's situation. In one of the most significant acts of its early years, San Francisco in 1870 set aside over 1000 acres to the west of the city to be developed into an enormous public park, a gesture which symbolized and gave further substance to an already developed taste for public recreation. San Franciscans tended to live publicly. The Gold Rush had made San Francisco a city of unattached transients, and even after the excitement had subsided San Franciscans continued in significant numbers to live in hotels and boarding houses and to eat in restaurants. The construction of family housing lagged far behind that of business offices, hostelries (including the extravagant Palace Hotel, finished in October 1875), theaters, opera houses, restaurants, and saloons. The scale of San Francisco was intimate, and this, together with the communal manner of domestic living and the outdoor climate, made possible a continuing interchange among the city's diverse populations. At the minimum, they were in daily contact, eating and drinking together, stopping on street corners or in hotel lobbies to chat with a frequency that made visitors, used to the more reserved ways of Eastern cities, take notice of San Francisco's almost Latin love of public conversation. On holidays they gathered at the same few pleasure spots, Russ' Gardens out on the Mission Road, Woodward's Gardens nearer in, the Cliff House on Ocean Beach.

Visitors never seemed able to make up their minds whether or not San Francisco was respectable. Stephen Powers discerned by the late 1860's "a kind of subtility or conservatism of culture" which he found remarkable, considering the rawness of the Far West. Literature, the pulpit, architecture, and some of the practicing arts flourished, while social life, spiced by the presence of adventurers from every part of the globe, sustained a brilliant, if somewhat reckless, edge. Reactions varied, but in general San Franciscans were praised for their impetuous love of theater and cuisine; and in Flora Haines Apponyi's *The Libraries of California* (1878) the San Franciscan emerged as the connoisseur of books. Apponyi's loving descriptions of tastefully furnished studies, warm with Persian rugs and calf bindings, together with her exhaustive listings of rare imprints secured at great personal sacrifice by local collectors, many of whom were men of middle income, suggested that behind the frenzy of the Mining Exchange and the parvenu vulgarity of Nob Hill was also gathering strength a tradition of scholarship and care for finer things.

Vice, on the other hand, prospered. Men shot one another down on the street; and San Franciscans seemed insecure in matters of taste. "It has been said," archly reported Mrs. Frank Leslie (the Baroness De Bazus) in 1877, "that in other cities the *demi-monde* imitates the fashions of the *beau-monde*, but that in San Francisco the case is reversed."[2] Mrs. Leslie singled out what by the 1870's and certainly by the 1880's bothered even the least snobbish visitor to San Francisco: what another observer, young Rudyard Kipling, fresh from India and the Far East, termed the city's "aggressive luxury." So many San Franciscans, it seemed, pursued pleasure with an intensity that was sometimes disreputable, and most certainly disruptive of civic stability. The serving girl dressed like the society matron, and both, as Mrs. Leslie and others suggested, wore too much finery. Men drank too much, the divorce rate was scandalous, and supposedly proper circles admitted too many of the compromised into their ranks. What was worse, continued the complaints, a significant number of San Franciscans took pride in the headlong ways of their city. From *The Annals of San Francisco* (1855) onward, they had defined themselves as a people liberated from the Puritan past, glorying in an exuberant lust for life. Samuel Bowles, editor of the Springfield, Massachusetts *Republican,* reported in 1865 that even church-going San Franciscans went to dances and picnics and on Sunday outings recklessly dashed their carriages through the surf along Ocean Beach below the Cliff House. Some of San Francisco's self-advertised colorfulness represented an unbroken legacy from the Gold Rush. Another aspect of it can be considered a frantic effort in rhetoric and behavior to keep alive an exciting sense of special promise when the challenge of the frontier gave way to the more prosaic needs of a province. In any event, whether as a habit of history or out of the necessities of the present, Americans in San Francisco seemed to be burning the candle at both ends.

Bohemia made its appearance. "Spain," wrote a local writer, "perpetual spring, the flare of adventure in the blood, the impulse of men who packed Virgil with their bean-bags on the overland journey, conspired . . . to make San Francisco a city of artists."[3] The bohemianism of the 1860's tended to be simple and not very self-conscious. Genial and unpretentious in its ways, it arose out of an easy milieu created by frontier journalists who sustained an interest in the arts and who gathered to talk. With the collapse of San Francisco's literary frontier in the early 1870's, it became necessary for those devotees of the arts who remained behind to strengthen their identity as a brotherhood yet appreciative of the creative life. Bohemia closed in upon itself. It lost the breeziness of the frontier, becoming explicitly aesthetic in lifestyle and prone to consider itself a separate community. Minor artists of European background drifted into town, men who knew the bohemianism of the Continent, and in their exile they recreated so far as possible what they had known in younger days. Studios opened, and in 1871 an Art Association was established under the directorship of Virgil Williams, who had studied in Rome and Paris, which offered instruction in painting to young Californians, preparing the better of them for study in Europe.

Gradually, throughout the 1870's, San Francisco acquired a colony of those pursuing the arts more or less full time, and certainly pursuing *la vie bohème* with enthusiasm. Arriving in San Francisco in 1879, Robert Louis Stevenson came upon this second stage of bohemia and was charmed. Climbing of an afternoon the two flights of stairs leading up to the studio of Jules Tavernier at 728 Montgomery Street, he would be admitted after giving the secret knock which prevented creditors from bursting in upon the almost always broke French painter. Stevenson would throw his reedy body on a sofa to talk and smoke by the hour, or just watch Tavernier at his easel under the skylight (which in 1882, in honor of a visit by Oscar Wilde, Tavernier decorated with rosebuds). Others would drop by, journalists, actors and actresses from shows in town, painters such as Julian Rix, who kept his own studio nearby, or a group of friends from the newly established Bohemian Club, of which Tavernier was a leading member. Sending out for wine or fresh crab to supplement Tavernier's steaming ragout, they remained long after the evening fog had enveloped the city, drinking and talking into the night *à la bohème*. Born in France and educated there in painting, Tavernier had seen frontier service with the cavalry in a campaign against the Sioux as a correspondent-illustrator for *Harper's Monthly Magazine*. One of the founding fathers of the new San Francisco bohemianism, Tavernier, who wore long hair and otherwise dressed the part, lived from hand to mouth, painting a series of otherworldly canvases whose surreality must have come in part from his proclivity for opium and other dream-inducing drugs.

Stevenson made friends with Charles Warren Stoddard: poet, essayist and, in a very gentle way, bohemian extraordinary, who like Tavernier helped to set the tone for the local pursuit of things aesthetic. Tavernier represented the assertive, expatriate side of San Francisco bohemia, its garlic and wine, its risqué life of garret and studio. Stoddard, on the other hand, an essentially local personality, adhered to the genteel: his was a bohemianism of Chopin at twilight, Oriental bric-a-brac, incense, lounging robes, and fragrant cigarettes. In 1855, as a boy of twelve, Stoddard had been brought to San Francisco from Rochester, New York. Thomas Starr King encouraged Stoddard when the shy, sensitive teenager began contributing poetry to San Francisco newspapers under the pseudonym Pip Pepperpod. In 1867 Stoddard's *Poems* appeared, elegantly printed by Edward Bosqui and Company and illustrated by William Keith. With the founding of *The Overland Monthly* in 1868, Stoddard joined Bret Harte and Ina Coolbrith in the editorial leadership of the *Overland* during its greatest era. There was a plaintiveness to Stoddard's verse, a sadness in a minor key suggestive of the personality of the poet himself. Although his slightly feminine good looks reminded contemporaries of Shelley, it was not so much that Stoddard fell upon the thorns of life as it was that he was forever pricking his fingers in the picking of rosebuds. He wore a look of gentle disappointment on his face, perhaps because instead of

Charles Warren Stoddard (1843–1909)

Brought to San Francisco as a boy of twelve, he grew up to become the city's poet laureate and bohemian extraordinary. There was a plaintiveness to Stoddard's verse, a sadness in a minor key suggestive of the personality of the poet himself. Perhaps it was because his yearning sensitivity was so much bigger than either his discipline or his talent. In any event, he was gentle and kind. His was a bohemianism of Chopin at twilight, Oriental bric-a-brac, incense, lounging robes, and fragrant cigarettes. He died at Monterey in the spring, sadly, like an ancient shepherd.

Shelley's bed of thorns Stoddard could only find a sofa to stretch himself across and drink tea. Women wanted to protect him and, chastely, he allowed himself to be taken care of.

All his life Stoddard tried to find a better world and gain a more assertive identity. A convert to Catholicism, he had a portrait painted of himself in the robes of a Franciscan, one hand resting gracefully on the leaves of an open Bible. In his mid-twenties he sailed for the South Seas and lived for a while as a beachcomber in Papeete. He traveled throughout Polynesia, Europe, Egypt, and the Holy Land, turning his experiences into delicately phrased essay-sketches, warm with Tintoretto colors and pervaded by juxtapositions of the charmingly primitive and the exquisitely civilized. In between journeys, and apart from a later period spent teaching at the Catholic University of America, Stoddard lived in San Francisco, which was where Stevenson met him, atop Telegraph Hill one afternoon. Stoddard saw the frail Scot sitting down to rest after the climb and invited him into his snug aerie overlooking the Bay, filled with the bric-a-brac and *objets d'art* of travel. It was Stoddard who first got Stevenson interested in the South Seas, and Stevenson in turn tried, with minimal success, to get the ever-procrastinating San Francisco poet to take a less haphazard attitude toward his work. Something symbolic clung to their friendship. Scot and San Franciscan shared the same bohemia, and then again they did not. San Francisco offered Stevenson an interlude on the way to art and some of art's occasions and materials. For Stoddard the city became an end in itself. Stoddard represented San Francisco finding in its newly unfolding consciousness rich moments of living which, while sometimes brought to expression, most often had to rest content as a savored experience that eluded the community's talent or ambition to memorialize. For Stoddard San Francisco was in itself an achieved symbol of its own best suggestions.

Robert Louis Stevenson came to California on a romantic quest: the wooing of a Californian divorcee whom he had met in France and whom he married in San Francisco (the ceremony being performed by William Anderson Scott, returned now from his Civil War exile). Stevenson brought to California an eye for local color and an empathy for charming, out-of-the-way places. He found himself intrigued by California's mixture of mellowness and immediacy. To the imaginative young Scot, so caught up in the pleasures and perils of his own emotional situation, the Monterey Peninsula and Napa Valley, where next to San Francisco he sojourned most extensively, invited at once to repose and to quickened expectations. The characters which fill Stevenson's California sketches either bustle about in an urgent American present or remain quiescent in a landscape dropped from time. Stevenson loved the suspended, idyllic side of this Californian duality, but not always unambiguously. The venerable charm of Monterey, for instance, or the feel of history Stevenson experienced attending mass at Mission San Carlos Borroméo, hearing the Indians intone the Gregorian chants taught them generations ago by the Franciscans, tended to persuade the Amateur Emigrant (so Stevenson dubbed himself) that, as opposed to the terrifyingly empty plains he had crossed by train, here in America's Pacific province there existed some remnant of a mediating past: resonances of lives lived to purpose, the cumulative meaning of which had some effect upon the present. At the same time, the abandoned adobes of Monterey signified that Old California had been but a minor effort of the Spanish Empire, and a doomed one. Dilapidated, an obvious backwater, however charming, Monterey lulled ambition and mocked the struggle for expression. As Stevenson describes them, the European habitués of Simoneau's Restaurant in Monterey are picturesque enough, but they represent modes of inactivity and defeat. In their exile they are in contact with Europe only through ancient newspapers, which they pore over with a diligence that hopes somehow to postpone the final shock of severance.

At Simoneau's in Monterey traditions are on the verge of giving out. In San Francisco Stevenson felt that they had taken new hold and were growing strong. Stoddard and the bohemian colony of San Francisco fascinated Stevenson because they were so vigorously trying to respond to the multiplicity of a quaint, out-of-the-way, albeit international city. They were sensitive to the Polynesian Pacific and to the Far East, whose mystery and teeming prodigality they saw reflected in their own Chinese quarter. With some naïveté, but also with a good deal of creative appreciation, they read translations of Oriental classics, collected its art, affected its cuisine, incorporated elements of its architecture and decoration into their domestic design. The more dissolute among them sampled its drugs in the privacy of Telegraph Hill or in the dens of Chinatown. Stevenson felt in San Francisco a blend of both Peking and Marseilles, although in the long run bohemia's Latin resonances were more powerful than its Oriental elements. At the heart of the Californian identity, after all, ebbed and flowed a Mediterranean metaphor. Whatever the indefinable nature of the city, Stevenson loved San Francisco. Its artists' colony, grateful for the mantle of romance he cast about their town, endowed his visit with the richness of legend. Stoddard, who had helped him get to know the city, became in time himself revered as the friend of Robert Louis Stevenson during those all-too-brief days when bohemian San Francisco had felt the courage and good humor of an artist whose frailties of body never prevented him from saying yes to life.

Local affirmations took many shapes, one of them being the founding of a Bohemian Club. In March 1872 a group of journalists who were accustomed to gather on Sundays for conversation drew up a charter formalizing their group as the Bohemian Club of San Francisco. Renting rooms recently vacated by a convivial association known as The Jolly Corks, in the Astor House on Sacramento Street, the Bohemians extended membership to those having a lively interest in the arts, including business and professional men and Army or Navy officers stationed in the vicinity. They adopted "Weaving spiders come not here" as their motto, and as their symbol the owl, bird of Athene, goddess of wisdom, symbolic, too, of the night work of the journalists who provided the Club with its core membership. The Bohemians gathered for evenings of conversation and conviviality, which they called High Jinks and for each of which an artist-member drew up a commemorative cartoon. Outdoor excursions into the lovely redwood forests north of San Francisco, beginning in the late 1870's, developed into prolonged summer encampments in a grove which the Club acquired at Duncan's Mills on the Russian River, annual occasions which the Bohemians called the Midsummer Jinks and which manifested that combination of outdoor life and elegant living so typical of the period. The vitality of the Bohemian Club as a gathering place for productive personalities continued through the turn of the century; indeed, the Club's roster might function as a Who's Who of local creativity. Mark Twain and Bret Harte, although no longer on the Coast, held honorary memberships. Henry George belonged, as did Edward Bosqui, San Francisco's finest printer; Arpad Haraszthy, the father of California viticulture; and Jules Tavernier, who did some startlingly fine cartoons for the High Jinks. Other artist-members included William Keith, Virgil Williams, and Julian Rix. Figures from San Francisco's literary frontier joined: Ambrose Bierce, Joaquin Miller, J. Ross Browne, Prentice Mulford, and Charles Warren Stoddard; but also men who made their mark after the first era: the poet Edward Rowland Sill, for instance; Joseph Le Conte, the Berkeley scientist-philosopher; and John Muir.

"Like the helianthus," Oscar Wilde told reporters in Boston on 5 March 1882 in the course of his American tour, "I shall wend my willing way

Daniel O'Connell (1849–1899)

Irish-born, he resigned a commission in the British Navy to settle in California as a journalist. He preferred, however, to savor life rather than pursue a career. He was a founding member of the Bohemian Club. He loved learning, of which he had a great store; he loved wit and fellowship; and, with a tender Irish sadness at their evanescence, he loved the pleasures of the senses, especially good cuisine. He boxed, wrestled, and fenced. He fished and hiked and was prized as a companion on the trail or before the campfire. He wrote love songs and passable poetry.

toward the Occidental uttermost of American civilization."[4] In California Wilde stepped off the train wearing a Spanish sombrero, velvet suit, puce cravat, yellow gloves, and buckled shoes. In the course of his Bay Area visit, Wilde was entertained at the Bohemian Club, where, surprisingly for one who so outrageously dramatized himself as an enervated aesthete, he drank his hosts under the table. Eventually as a matter of habit the Club took on the pleasant task of entertaining those prominent in arts or letters who happened to be visiting San Francisco: Edwin Booth, Sir Henry Irving, and Tommaso Salvini from the theater, men of letters like Anthony Trollope, James Bryce, James Anthony Froude, and a young and relatively unknown colonial journalist, Rudyard Kipling.

Daniel O'Connell (grand-nephew of the great Irish orator) demonstrates the style and values of the Bohemian Club's founding generation. Born in Ireland and educated there by the Jesuits in classics and philosophy, O'Connell served as a midshipman in the British Navy before resigning to settle in California. He taught Latin, Greek, and mathematics at the Jesuit Colleges of Santa Clara and Saint Ignatius in San Francisco, then shifted into journalism. He assisted Henry George in founding the *Evening Post* and was one of the charter members of the Bohemian Club. Career, however, remained incidental to Daniel O'Connell, and the living of life paramount. He loved learning, of which he had a great store; he loved wit and fellowship; and, with a tender Irish sadness at their evanescence, he loved the pleasures of sense. Of large and robust physique, O'Connell pursued boxing, wrestling, and fencing. He fished and hiked and was prized as a companion on the trail or before the campfire. Savoring life as a whole, he most favored good cuisine. His *The Inner Man, Good Things to Eat and Drink and Where to Get Them* (1891) offered a history and a tour of San Francisco dining, for O'Connell considered fine food an essential part of the San Francisco style. A potpourri of literary and culinary lore, *The Inner Man* bespoke O'Connell's love of a well-appointed table, candle-lit and surrounded by friends, the charm of the evening brief—like life itself, like the taste of wine and fine food on the palate. As a boy he lost his mother and sister when their carriage careened into a ditch, and a conviction of mutability, of *sunt rerum lacrimae,* remained with O'Connell all his life. His poetry was graced by an Irish sense of love and passing beauty and the way death ends all good things. Religious hope, however, offset this Celtic melancholy; for O'Connell, the classicist who so much delighted in the pagan play of the senses, never lost touch with the Ignatian spirituality of his youthful formation, with its conviction that at its heart the world was good and led upward. Fellow Bohemians dubbed him The King of Munster, but O'Connell was neither dissipated nor trivial. His large family, which somehow he managed to support, worshipped him, and his wife died of grief a year after he was laid to rest.

Although no mediocrity, O'Connell was not a great figure in the world's eyes; nor in its early years when there reigned an era of simplicity did the Bohemian Club worry much about the social prestige of its members. A number of wealthy philistines were blackballed when they applied for membership. Club quarters remained unpretentious and refreshments ran in the direction of beer and sandwiches. Founded, among other reasons, so that journalists might have a place to congregate away from saloons, the Bohemian Club did not foster hardcore dissipation; rather it kept alive into the 1870's the feel of frontier journalists—vests opened, feet up, pipes lit, and a companionable glass filled—talking far into the night after the morning edition had been put to bed. The Bohemian Club was not very bohemian in the Continental sense of the term, although many members, like Jules Tavernier and Julian Rix, belonged both to the Club and to more classically bohemian circles. It eventually fell away from its founding ideals, but taken at its best the Bohemian Club represented a significant response to the art-impulse of San Francisco. It celebrated the city as a place where lightheartedness was possible, and it tried to ensure that such would always be the case. True, the Club was somewhat provincial and more than a little self-centered, but so was San Francisco. Like the Sierra Club, founded twenty years later and remaining much closer to its original ideals, the Bohemian Club of San Francisco invoked an ideality of relationship. The Sierra Club envisioned the new Californian in creative dialogue with his environment. The Bohemian Club expressed the hope that even in remote San Francisco a similar interchange might be carried on with the rich traditions of art.

Just how deep this hope ran became clear in the career of James Duval Phelan, who, among many other things, served as president of the Bohemian Club from 1891 to 1892. The son of an Irish-born Forty-niner who had become a San Francisco millionaire, Phelan grew up in an atmosphere of Irish ascendancy peculiar to California. The entire oligarchy was *nouveau riche* and diversified, railroad money being Yankee Protestant, for instance, and Comstock silver being largely in the hands of Irish Catholics. Archbishop Alemany celebrated a Solemn High Mass upon the occasion of the marriage of Phelan's parents in Old Saint Mary's in 1859, and the couple began life in a fine home on the corner of Bush and Hyde, where James Duval was born in 1861. Coming herself from an educated background, Phelan's mother imbued her son with a love for the best of the Irish and Anglo-Irish tradition. In San Francisco, a city where the Irish had come into their own, the Irish heritage could be assimilated openly, without the bitterness and self-rejection which prejudice had made part of the Irish-American experience in the East. Throughout his life, Phelan affirmed the Irish tradition, which for him was not narrowly Catholic and Celtic, but included Anglo-Irish culture as well.

His father's prominence determined Phelan's conception of himself. With certainty he knew from boyhood that he would play a role in San Francisco. Out of civic pride and respect for the Catholic tradition, Phelan Senior chose to have his son educated locally by the Italian Jesuits. In 1881 James Duval took a degree in classics and philosophy from Saint Ignatius College, giving the commencement address. He then went to Europe for further education and a grand tour. In the course of two years' travel Phelan made a comparative study of European cities: their architecture and city plans, their politics, schools, and museums, as well as their police departments and sewage systems. He wanted San Francisco to learn from the great cities of the Continent, for to his way of thinking they, and not the cities of the American East, provided the appropriate models of development. The Roman Catholic side of his imagination made Phelan sensitive to the cities of Southern Europe, Rome most of all. An Italianate quality, sun-splashed and baroque, would ever cling to Phelan's vision of the ideal San Francisco.

Taking up the study of law and politics upon his return to San Francisco, Phelan made an imaginative connection with the American Republic which prevented his Mediterraneanism from developing (as was happening among the upper classes of Boston during the period) into a form of expatriation through an aesthetic identification which excluded American premises. A Democrat who had more Hamilton than Jefferson in his make-up, serving his party in the United States Senate between 1915 and 1921, Phelan adhered throughout his life to a classical republicanism which he considered the true legacy of the Founding Fathers, a belief that the gifted, the educated—and the wealthy—should lead the Republic in a spirit of service and reform. In an essay published in 1891 in *The Overland Monthly*, "The Old World Judged by the New," Phelan looked forward to an impending high American era, an ascendancy of art and good government, together with a full presence on the international scene.

James Duval Phelan (1861–1930)

Mrs. Atherton considered him California's most elegant, accomplished gentleman, which he probably was. As a patron, he used his fortune to promote California's coming of age—in the arts, in city planning, in political responsibility. He wanted San Francisco, where he was born and educated and which he served as mayor, to be a city of graciousness and good governance. Devoted to Mediterranean Europe, he dreamed that San Francisco might one day emerge as a city in the style of Rome: sun-splashed, spacious, and baroque.

Phelan favored imperial expansion, a strong Navy, and an Anglo-American alliance. Approving of the urbanization of the United States, he called for the reform of American city governments, which, he felt, had been allowed to grow up without the systematic foundations federal and state governments had from their constitutions. Phelan's temperamental Hamiltonianism sometimes led him down ambiguous paths—his advocacy of Oriental exclusion, for instance, his urban bias in the Hetch Hetchy crisis—it also accounted for his effective service to San Francisco and to California. At bottom, Hamiltonianism and Mediterraneanism intersected at a point of dynamic orderliness. Each signified the hope for values of art and life which assuaged the longing for a past and met present need. James Duval Phelan of San Francisco would be both reformer and patrician; the Californian as the newest of new Americans, and the Irish-Californian as having validated his claim to a wider historicity.

Above all, he loved the city which from his early twenties he served in a variety of public capacities, climaxed in 1897 by his election as mayor. Inheriting an administration mired in the corruptions of boss rule and the confusion resulting from its jerry-built charter, Mayor Phelan aligned himself with other young progressive men of wealth and pushed for reform. From 1897 to 1902, when he stepped down, Phelan fought the political hold of unions and railroads alike. He secured the passage of a revised charter which streamlined city government and established public ownership of transportation and utilities. He sought measures to improve San Francisco's water supply and its streets and parks, especially the Golden Gate Park, set aside nearly thirty years previously and, since the appointment in 1887 of a young Scots gardener, John McLaren, as superintendent, on the way to becoming one of the great parks of the world. The speeches of Phelan's mayoralty are filled with hope for a new San Francisco. The young mayor, it was true, pursued reform more out of an affronted *noblesse oblige* than belief in the people. He related to San Francisco in the manner of a Renaissance prince, erecting statues, making opera tickets available to the Italian poor. Yet whatever his motivation, he left the city far better off than he found her. As a public figure James Duval Phelan had that independence which arises from inherited wealth joined to a passion for public service, an independence enabling him to steer clear of special interests in pursuit of broadly based ideals.

Although not formally an artist, James Duval Phelan responded to the artistic side of San Francisco. He wrote verse. He distinguished himself as an orator, an essayist, and an amateur scholar. Very few American mayors of the period in any part of the country could command Phelan's taste and learning, or felt called upon to use political office in such an overt way to encourage letters and the practicing arts. As a young banker, and throughout his career, Phelan cultivated the creative personalities of San Francisco, many of whom he knew from the Bohemian Club. He spent a small fortune playing regional De Medici, supporting some efforts, it must be said, which were hopelessly provincial or second-rate. His mistakes as a patron arose, however, not so much out of a lack of discrimination as out of a headlong desire to see California and San Francisco come of age. City and state constituted Phelan's major art-form, a genre he worked in as banker, mayor, senator, city father, and patron of the arts. Like any artist, he saw the ideality implicit in the material. He dreamed of San Francisco as a city of art and sound governance, the Florence of the Pacific. He dreamed of California as a sunny land of artists, an American Italy in the surge of new creativity.

II

The fact was, Phelan's tenure as mayor coincided with a revival of arts and letters in the Bay Area. Not since the 1860's had there been such a gathering of talent, nor would San Francisco again be so graced until the middle of the twentieth century. The Bohemian Club took on new vitality. One might meet Frank Norris there, a young reporter on the San Francisco *Wave*, the onetime society journal ("for those in the swim") into which a circle of recent Stanford and Berkeley graduates were breathing new life. Will Irwin might be there, another *Wave* reporter, destined to develop into one of the finest journalists ever produced by California, distinguishing himself during World War I as part of the California team which staffed Herbert Hoover's Committee for the Relief of Belgium. Another Bohemian, Arnold Genthe, born in Prussia and fresh from having taken a doctorate in classics at Jena, was experimenting in photography. Figures from San Francisco's first literary era still dropped by, Joaquin Miller and Charles Stoddard, for instance, but also younger men like Porter Garnett, Ernest Peixotto, and Gelett Burgess, who worked in criticism, crafts, painting, and the visual arts; Jack London, already nationally prominent; and George Sterling, the poet laureate of San Francisco. Other artists included painters Maynard Dixon, Charles Rollo Peters, and Xavier Martinez, and sculptors Arthur Putnam, Robert Aitken, and Haig Patigan. For most of these young men, membership in the Club also included affiliation with the bohemian circles of Telegraph Hill, Piedmont across the Bay, and Carmel down the coast. These various groupings had their distinctions and core cadres, but in general the situation was fluid. The poet George Sterling, for instance, was a central figure in a variety of Bay Area coteries.

San Francisco's French and Italian restaurants made inexpensive dining available to the artists of the city and offered them a place to congregate. "One dined so well in San Francisco in those days," remembered Mary Austin of her first visit to Coppa's at 622 Montgomery Street, most favored den of bohemia. "Such heaping platefuls of fresh shrimps for appetizers! Such abalone chowder, such savory and melting sand-dabs, salads so crisp, vegetables in such profusion, and pies so deep and flaky. Such Dago red, fruity, sharp and warming! And all for thirty-five cents!"[5] A would-be painter himself, Giuseppe "Papa" Coppa, born in Turin and trained as a chef in Paris, had a soft spot for artists. He extended them liberal credit and reserved a center table for a group calling themselves the Coppans; for the notoriety they brought to Coppa's as a bohemian haunt helped business. George Sterling, Porter Garnett, and Xavier Martinez led the Coppans, whose official darling was the lovely Isabel Fraser, an *Examiner* feature writer who, during one memorable party in the Telegraph Hill studio of Maynard Dixon, mounted a ladder and was acclaimed Queen of Bohemia, and whose passion for the mystic eventually took her to Persia where she became a priestess in a Bahai temple. Also among the Coppans: Nora May French, a hauntingly beautiful journalist and poet, whose brooding eyes foretold her soon-to-be-accomplished suicide beneath the pines of Carmel. Many, in fact, would come to tragic ends, but now they enjoyed a brief gaiety, meeting at Coppa's to launch many an evening which did not end until dawn. Around their center table, they talked bravely of the future and what they would accomplish. One hilarious weekend they decorated Coppa's walls with an elaborate mural in which, rather precipitately, they intwined their names among the immortals.

To the Coppans and to other Bay Area artists, Xavier Timoteo Orozco Martinez ("Marty") seemed the model California bohemian. Born in Mexico and brought to San Francisco when his stepfather was appointed consul-general, Martinez was defiantly proud of his Aztec blood. He studied painting at the San Francisco Art Association, then spent the years 1895-1900 as a student in Paris, living in the Latin Quarter. In a bohemia ever unsure of its exact relationship to the great world, the fact that Martinez had known the famous painters of the day and that his work had won honorable mention in the Paris Exposition of 1900 conferred upon him—and hence upon the Coppans themselves by implication—an aura of authenticity. Martinez played his role with gusto, dressing in corduroy suits and flowing crimson cravat, letting his thick Indian hair grow so abundant that someone once said that Martinez resembled a huge black chrysanthemum. His San Francisco studio was the scene of so many parties that Marty had to move across the Bay to Piedmont to get any work done. His friends built him a hillside studio, mounted on eucalyptus stilts, where they trouped every Sunday for spaghetti, chili con carne, and red wine. "Hot arguments on any subject which came into our minds were the order of the day," remembered Arnold Genthe of those Sunday open-houses, "and I have a picture in my mind of Jack London sitting at one end of the table, intense and questioning, and Marty at the other, gesticulating with a chicken bone."[6] London put Martinez into some of his short stories, resplendent in cravat and sombrero, the complete Californian as bohemian-artist, affirming and exuberant. Martinez' temper now and then got the best of him, like the time a guest showed too much admiration for Elsie Martinez, his young wife, a girl who Genthe felt had the poetic beauty of Rossetti's Blessed Damozel. Marty rapidly sketched out a portrait of the offender, tacked it to a tree and began firing away at it with a pistol, telling the guests who fled out to the garden to see what was causing the noise: "I am going to keel that son of a beech!"

"I was always dodging the bullets," Elsie Martinez recalled. "Marty should have been married to some nice little Indian girl who would spend her time looking down at her feet. I liked to look around and be admired."[7] For all the bullets with which he assuaged an affronted *machismo*, Martinez was fundamentally a kindly person, devoted to Elsie, to his friends, and to his students at the College of Arts and Crafts. Through the example of his own landscape meditations, done in the manner of Whistler, under whom he had studied in Paris, and through the force of his teaching, Martinez played a notable role in California art. There was a simplicity, a restraint to Martinez' painting style which characterized the best of local arts and handicrafts during the period, from painting, to architecture and furniture design, to printing. Much of this urge to simplicity came from outside influences, especially that of William Morris, who had a number of avid disciples in the Bay Area. A good deal of it, however, arose out of a local tradition favoring the elegantly unlabored. Printing and the graphic arts showed this most dramatically. Edward Bosqui and Company, Town and Bacon, and Charles A. Murdock and

Xavier Martinez (1869–1943)

Mexican-born, defiantly proud of his Aztec blood, "Marty" dressed in Left Bank corduroy and flowing crimson cravat. He let his thick Indian hair grow so abundantly that he resembled a huge black chrysanthemum. A painter, his San Francisco studio was the scene of so many parties that he was forced to move to the Piedmont hills to get any work done. His friends built him a studio mounted on eucalyptus stilts, where they trouped every Sunday for spaghetti, chili con carne, and red wine. Martinez, who studied under Whistler in Paris, played a notable role in California art.

Company, all printing firms of San Francisco, had experimented with the pre-industrial Franklin Old Style type used in conjunction with engravings, generous spacing and margins, and an uncluttered layout. As a flourishing art form, printing in San Francisco achieved a style which combined assertive modernity with graceful nostalgia. Through Franklin Old Style it recalled the time when printing existed as a craft, not an industrial trade; and yet the graphic elegance evident in even the most routine job-printing done by these firms declared that the machine could be made to serve beauty.

Since this interest in fine printing already existed, it was not surprising that a local circle calling itself *Les Jeunes* should turn to typography in a way which underscored their own aesthetic aims and the vitality of the genre. *The Lark*, their publication, ran for twenty-four issues between May 1895 and May 1897, selling for five cents. It was printed on one side of the page, in unjustified type and on bamboo paper bought in Chinatown, dampened and pressed to lie flat. The shaggy-edged paper had such texture that bits of undigested bamboo would sometimes break the delicate, gracefully archaic lettering provided *The Lark* by Charles Murdock and Company. *Les Jeunes* all had an interest in the visual arts. Ernest Peixotto studied painting in Paris. Willis Polk was a budding architect; Gelett Burgess, a trained draftsman who also designed furniture. Bruce Porter and Porter Garnett dabbled in a variety of the decorative arts, including sketching, bookbinding, and flower arrangement.

In paper, illustrations, format and typography, not to mention content, *The Lark*, during its brief flight, advanced its delightfully idiosyncratic version of the medium is the message. *The Lark* put forward a paradox of blithe innovation and recherché insouciance, which, according to *Les Jeunes*, perfectly expressed the mood of young San Francisco in the Year of Our Lord, 1895. *Les Jeunes* insisted, moreover, that from *The Lark* emanated the spirit of the redwoods as well as that of San Francisco. From these immemorial trees, claimed Gelett Burgess, leader of *Les Jeunes*, the editors of *The Lark* had absorbed a feeling that life in California was excitingly fresh—and ancient in associations. "To understand this," recalled Burgess, "one must have spent long days and nights in the mountains of northern California beneath the giant trees that have covered the hills for centuries,—before the Argonauts ravished the canyons of gold, before the Spaniards built their missions, before the Russians fortified the shores, before the American Indians hunted in the forests, before the migrating Aztecs filtered through the land from some mysterious homeland, seeking

Frank Norris (1870–1902)

Although his hair turned gray, Norris never lost his boyish charm. A fraternity man, a dandy, and a bit of a snob, he yet was fascinated by the brutal, the coarse, the elemental. As a reporter on the Wave he interviewed society women, shopgirls, the football teams of Berkeley and Stanford. He knew ranch life, bohemia, and Polk Street. By the time of his tragic death at thirty-two he had written some of the best fiction to come out of California. In Blix he wrote charmingly of youth and love and San Francisco.

for the warm site of the southern nation that was to be. One must have forded the rushing rivers, and trodden the mountain trails at dawn, in the glory of 'sunful-eyed noon,' at twilight, and in the dark fragrance of midnight. We had a camp there which was an Arden in an Arcady. We were all young, happy and sane beneath those boughs, and there came to us there a revelation of simple living, and clean-minded pastimes. To the town, variegated in its colour, so shut off from many of the tyrannies of the world, we brought back some of the impulse of the hills, and with those primal emotions were mingled many subtler reactions which no civilized being can do without."[8] For all their preciousness, for all their participation in the trends of the *fin de siècle*, *Les Jeunes* of *The Lark* sought something—a mood, a style—specifically and freshly Californian.

So did Frank Norris of *The Wave*, a young Bohemian and man-about-town who fell in love with San Francisco and its art possibilities. Founded originally by the Southern Pacific to promote the Hotel Del Monte in Monterey among the smart set, *The Wave* underwent a transformation in the mid-1890's under the editorship of John O'Hara Cosgrave. Assembling a staff of bright young reporters freshly graduated from Stanford and Berkeley, Cosgrave put out a periodical which combined the high spirits of an undergraduate humor magazine with the chatty nonchalance of a town-and-topics review. Unlike *The Lark*, *The Wave* was not precious or recherché; rather it conveyed in an exuberant Western way young San Francisco's sense of itself as sophisticatedly in-the-know. Cosgrave inspired his staff—the Irwin brothers, Will and Wallace, and Charles K. Field, all three just out of Stanford, and Jimmy Hopper, like Norris from Berkeley, where Hopper had been a star athlete—to capture the feel of San Francisco and the Bay Area. *The Wave* ran superb interviews and feature articles, alert to the charm of the passing scene. Without straining itself or pretending to an undeserved maturity, *The Wave* chronicled San Francisco and California as being rich in personality and event, as a culture at a challenging point of density and variation.

Between 1891 and 1898 Frank Norris did over 120 pieces for *The Wave*. Not since Mark Twain served briefly on the *Daily Morning Call* in 1864 had San Francisco had a reporter with such potential. Twain, however, had been putting in time at an indecisive period of his life. Norris was serving a literary apprenticeship out of which developed his best work. Twain shook the dust of San Francisco from his feet. Thirty years later, Frank Norris used it for bricks. For two years, 1896 and 1897, Norris worked full time for *The Wave*. He interviewed society women, shopgirls, fraternity men, the football teams of California and Stanford, tamale vendors, firemen, artists, actors, actresses, the crews of visiting battleships. He covered bohemia, the stock market, hotels, hospitals, the waterfront, and the Japanese Tea Garden. Out of it all arose in Norris a feeling for the romance of San Francisco. Things happened in San Francisco which called for literature: "Kearny street, Montgomery street, Nob Hill, Telegraph Hill, of course Chinatown, Lone Mountain, the Poodle Dog, the Palace Hotel and the What Cheer House, the Barbary Coast, the Crow's Nest, the Mission, the Bay, the Bohemian Club, the Presidio, Spanish town, Fisherman's wharf. There is an indefinable air about all these places that is suggestive of stories at once. You fancy the names would look well on a book's page. The people who frequent them could walk right into a novel or short story and be at home."[9]

Norris took his subject matter from San Francisco and from California, but he did his best writing in the East under such non-Californian influences as Harvard and New York. San Francisco's isolation might give rise to a splendid originality, but it could also lead to narcissism and a self-justifying tolerance for the third-rate. Part of the problem seemed to be that life was too easy. The picturesqueness, the general comfort of San Francisco living could conspire to make serious work impossible. The soothing critical climate, as well as the sunshine, was in danger of filling up San Francisco with poseurs, unchallenged by circumstances or discernment. Bohemia often concealed a colossal idleness, as Charles Warren Stoddard suggested in his only novel, *For the Pleasure of His Company* (1903). In it Paul Clitheroe, a genial minor poet, is caught, like Stoddard himself, in a round of dinners at the Bohemian Club, late evenings at places of wine and music, late mornings in bed combing through invitations, and late afternoons spent, on foggy days, smoking Russian cigarettes before a cozy fire or, when it was clear, lounging in the sunlight which poured through the neo-Gothic bay window of his Telegraph Hill bungalow, making desultory attempts at composition. Novels of the period are filled with would-be artists, for whom the temptations of San Francisco, its easy ways of life and opinion, prove fatal. He no longer desires to be a great California painter, confesses Philip Stone one night at the Poodle Dog in Gertrude Atherton's *Ancestors* (1907). San Francisco has blunted ambition. "San Francisco breeds all sorts," Stone tells others at his table. "A few are born with a drop of iron in their souls. They resist the climate, and the enchantment of the easy luxurious semi-idle life you can command out here on next to nothing, and clear out, and work hard, and make little old California famous. Where they get the iron from God knows. It's all electricity with the rest of us. There are hundreds of my sort. You've seen them at the real Bohemian restaurants; young men mad with life and the sense of their own powers; all of them writing, painting, composing, editing—mostly talking. Then at other tables the old-young men who have shrugged their shoulders and simmered down like myself; lucky if they haven't taken to drink or drugs to drown regrets. Still other tables—the young-old men, quite happy, and generally drunk. Business men and some professional are the only ones that forge steadily ahead; with precious few exceptions. But you don't see them often in the cheap Bohemian restaurants, which have a glamour for the young, and are a financial necessity for the failures. Never was such a high percentage of brains in any one city. But they must get out. And if they don't go young they don't go at all. San Francisco is a disease."[10]

Throughout the turn of the century San Francisco lost its best talent to New York: Norris himself, the Irwins, Gelett Burgess, and Ernest Peixotto of *Les Jeunes,* women writers like Gertrude Atherton, Kathleen Norris, and Juliet Wilbor Tompkins. (Isadora Duncan left for Europe.) After the decline of the Carmel experiment, George Sterling gave New York a try. Jack London remained in California, but was obsessed by what New York thought of him—if anything. In the winter of 1894, down and out, London had panhandled on the streets of "that man-killer New York," and he never forgot the shame. New York obsessed Jack London as a symbol of indifference and rejection on the part of the establishment he hated and very much wanted to get into. "I think it is the cocksure feeling of superiority which the people of the metropolis feel over the rest of the country that makes me rage," he told an *Oakland Tribune* reporter, returning in late 1911 from a trip East. And yet London wanted desperately to impress the New York literary establishment. "I've had the goat of New York all the way from California for fourteen years," he bragged to his stepsister Eliza Shepard, "and I think I shall continue to keep my hand on the goat of New York." When he was in New York, more than the usual number of demons seemed to possess Jack London. He boozed and womanized frenetically. He played outrageous practical jokes, such as the mock hold-up of a downtown whore-house. He lived in the theatrical Tenderloin and one evening had to be extricated from a wrecked taxicab along with the three burlesque queens with whom he was enjoying a night on the town. With more than a little vulgarity, he bragged about all he owned in California, his ranch, his yacht, his horses. "I no longer say 'To hell with New York,' " he wrote to his wife during his last visit, months before his death. "I am here to master New York and to enjoy New York."[11] While understandable in personal terms, London's failure to exorcise New York's hold upon his imagination dramatized a larger California dilemma. London, after all, so uniquely a son of California, remained committed to regional living while the others fled East—and yet even he could not be at peace with his decision.

As fruitful as had been Frank Norris' experience on *The Wave*, and as lovingly as he wrote of San Francisco from his Washington Square exile, he had to be East to push his best work to completion. Norris' novel *Blix* (1899) was in one sense a lyrical love song to San Francisco of the sort he had called for in *The Wave*, full of the charm and promise of the Pacific city. Condy Rivers, a journalist and member of the Bohemian Club who very much resembled Frank Norris, and Travis Bessemer ("Blix"), a lovely young San Francisco girl very much resembling Norris' wife Jeannette Black, explore San Francisco in an idyll of youth and unfolding romance. They roam about Chinatown and the Latin Quarter. They stroll the beaches, picnic on the high grassy cliffs of the Presidio Reservation overlooking the Pacific. They rendezvous at restaurants like Luna's, where they have pleasurable adventures. Delicately and good-humoredly, they develop through those marvelous stages between comradeship and sexual love. All through Norris' tale of love and San Francisco runs a parable of work. Before going East, Norris went through a period when he suffered a writing block as far as serious work was concerned. As a skilled feature-writer, Condy Rivers finds it all too easy to fake material, to achieve a veneer of realism through the judicious use of a few details. Getting by as journalist, he has more time to idle about the city or to play poker at the Bohemian Club. With Blix's help and the help of a retired sea captain, whose adventures inspire Condy to tap a deeper vein of art within himself, Condy gets down to business, turning out *In Defiance of Authority*, a novel paralleling Norris' first work to gain Eastern attention, *Moran of the Lady Letty* (1898). San Francisco has been both near occasion of sin and the source of Condy's renewal as a writer, but the city cannot hold him—or Blix. Together they leave for the East, Blix to study medicine and Condy to work, as did Norris, for a major publisher and to continue his writing. *Blix* concludes with Condy and Travis standing at sunset on the Presidio cliffs, bidding farewell to their "gay, irresponsible, hour-to-hour life of the past three months." "Then, with one last look [at San Fran-

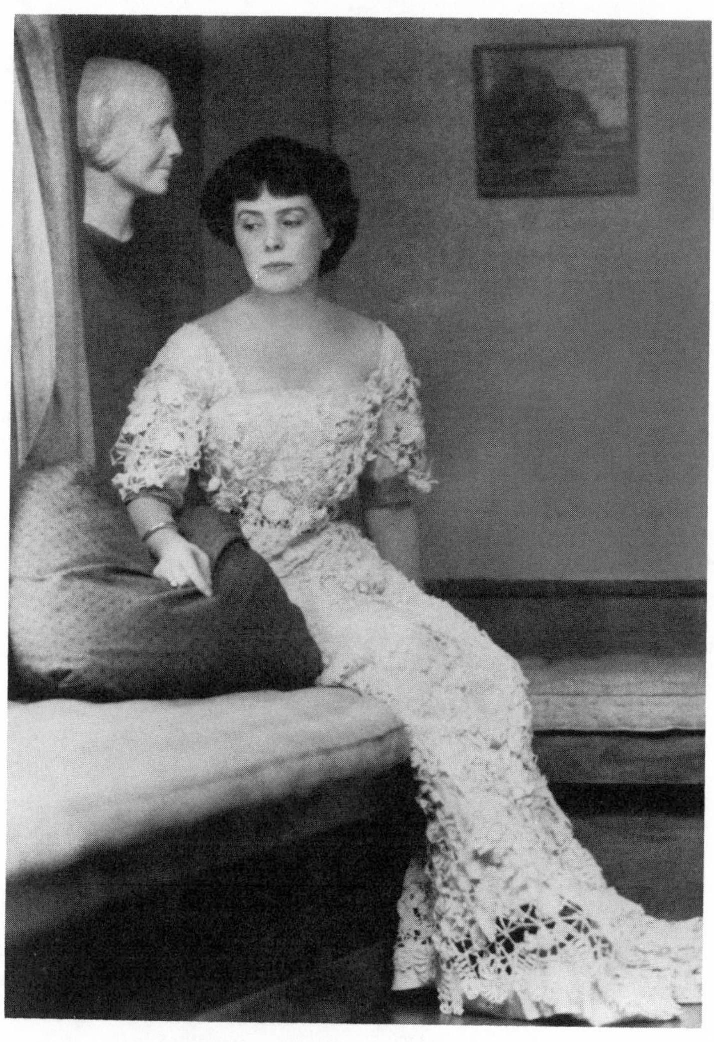

Jeannette Black (1878–1952)

She was the lovely daughter of an Irish-born Forty-niner. In the fall of 1896, when she was seventeen, she met Frank Norris at a sub-debutante party in San Francisco. He felt she embodied the vivacity and courage of the California girl. When he realized he loved her, he had to hike out to the Cliff House to calm himself down. After a San Francisco courtship, they were married in New York, where they lived near Washington Square. They planned a voyage around the world by tramp steamer.

cisco]," Norris tells us, "they turned about and set their faces from it to the new life, to the East, where lay the Nation."[12]

Like Saxon Brown's Oakland in London's *The Valley of the Moon*, San Francisco for Blix and Condy is just a place to start from. It becomes the scene of disastrous return in Norris' posthumously published *Vandover and the Brute* (1914), the central plot, as James D. Hart has shown, of a long San Francisco novel which Norris was working on during the 1890's and which he broke up into *Blix, McTeague*, and the unfinished *Vandover*. Vice and depravity of the worst sort had been synonymous with San Francisco since the Gold Rush, especially in Chinatown and an area of waterfront dives known as the Barbary Coast, where, as one visitor of the mid-1860's reported, "the brutality and bestiality of the Saxon and the Celt here comes suddenly to the surface, as if we were fiends incarnate."[13] Physicians testified before the Board of Supervisors in 1885 that San Francisco was suffering from an epidemic of venereal disease among its youngsters, some being infected by prostitutes at the ages of eight and ten. By 1890 the city had a saloon for every ninety-six citizens. Vice thrived in its most sordid and most elegant forms, from squalid opium dens and off-the-street brothels where the client was not permitted to remove his clothes, to the decorum and plush luxuriance of the so-called French restaurants. A stranglehold of graft and political corruption gripped the city from the mid-1880's onward, a system of kickbacks and payoffs which took its origins in the criminal underworld. No wonder, then, that Norris' sprawling San Francisco novel should have at its core a tale of moral ruin. Pre-earthquake San Francisco, as another novelist of the period put it, was "a black flower of sin."

Like Norris himself, Vandover is an upper-class young San Franciscan of artistic inclination and Harvard education. Condy Rivers leaves the city to write. Vandover returns from the East to paint. Gradually, however, he falls prey to the temptations of the demimonde, sinking into idleness. A girl whom he seduces commits suicide, throwing Vandover into depression. When his father dies, Vandover squanders his inheritance in a year-long debauch, at the end of which he realizes that he has forever destroyed whatever of the artist's soul he might have had. Disordered (syphilitic, Norris suggests), the victim of attacks of lycanthropy during which he prowls naked about his room on all fours, howling like a wolf, Vandover is reduced to working for a Harvard classmate as a handy man. San Francisco, while not the sole nor even the major cause of Vandover's degeneration, plays a part in the process. Its bars and restaurants, the company of its fast girls, the whole swirl of its compromised gaiety provide the setting and elements of Vandover's temptation. Norris knew this aspect of San Francisco from experience. Although himself a little on the fastidious, snobbish side, he had investigated the underlife of the city in the spirit of Zola, with the hope of turning it to fiction. He knew San Francisco as he described it in *Blix,* as bracing and as clean as its sea air, and as he described it in *McTeague,* close and pedestrian and even a little grim. Significantly enough, as a young artist-in-the-making Frank Norris built the central action of his projected San Francisco novel around a perception of the city as a place where idleness and easy ways lay in wait against the creative impulse. A self-devouring evil, Norris suggested, a willful degeneracy, seemed to fester near the heart of California's queen city.

Nor was he alone in this estimation. There could be no more glorious turn-of-the-century San Franciscan than Frank Gelett Burgess: poet, illustrator, designer of furniture, member of *Les Jeunes,* on the staffs of *The Wave* and *The Lark* and part of a brilliant circle at the Bohemian Club. "I was young and ardent," said Burgess of those San Francisco days. "I found Romance. I found Adventure. I found Bohemia."[14] In the novel *Heart Line* (1907), Burgess made a curiously ambivalent return to the San Francisco, destroyed now by the earthquake, where he had enjoyed such wonderful years. An atmosphere of obscure, menacing evil permeates Burgess' depiction of the old city. *Heart Line* concerns the conversion of Francis Granthope, palmist and chronic seducer of clients, from quackery to legitimate medicine. An avid reader of medical textbooks, interested in psychiatry, Granthope contents himself getting by as a socially fashionable palmist. Enmeshed in intrigues, he thinks of himself as a great adventurer, a Casanova of the Pacific Coast, but comes to realize the triviality of the gigolo role he plays among the ladies of Nob Hill and the Western Addition. A brooding malaise, a flavor of fakery and lingering evil, clings to virtually every scene in Burgess' story. Now and then Burgess tries to affirm the old San Francisco, but the general drift of the novel works in favor of a counter-mythic conviction of intrinsic dishonesty, decadent eroticism—and fake bohemia. Fancy Gray, bohemia's darling, whom Burgess modeled upon Isabel Fraser, a character having "that free, fearless gaiety, the almost abandoned good nature of San Francisco girls," throws herself off a ferry boat in despair. The city's artists leave for New York or Paris; the failures stay behind, dilettantes like Blanchard Cayley, who dabbles in "jade, Japanese poetry, Esperanto, higher space, Bahaism, and devil-worship."

III

Hopes for simplicity and harmony characterized the founding of the artists' colony on the seacoast of Carmel. Thirty years before Robert Louis Stevenson's famous sojourn, Bayard Taylor visited the Monterey Peninsula and found it the perfect place to loaf and invite one's soul. Bay Area artists maintained studios there from the 1870's. After Stevenson's visit Monterey grew in importance as an outpost of bohemia, for Stevenson had touched the region with the magic of romantic legend. David Starr Jordan, a young government scientist who was later to serve as the founding president of Stanford University, was given credit for first noting, in 1880, the beauty of the piny seacoast south of Cypress Point, especially one curve of beach near where the Carmel River flowed into the Pacific. Because of the area's associations with Mission San Carlos Borroméo, thought was given to developing Carmel as a Roman Catholic summer resort, but when the Carmel Development Company began subdividing in 1903 the intention had shifted toward the encouragement of an artists' colony, a direction which gained great momentum after the April 1906 earthquake, when San Francisco became an impossible place to work.

If setting were the sole criterion, then Carmel-by-the-Sea would surely witness a flowering of art; for its scenery was among the most magnificent in the state: a composition of surf, rocks, sand dunes, forest, and meadows, ablaze in Corsican color beneath the noonday sun or enveloped in morning sea fog, a region, for Mary Austin, of Greek mystery. "The dunes glistened white with violet shadows," she remembered, "and in warm hollows, between live oaks, the wine of light had mellowed undisturbed a thousand years."[15] A rough country road led overland from Monterey across the neck of the Peninsula. Descending through pines banked in lilac and thickets of buckthorn, over the sand dunes one caught sight of what Jack London called "the amazing peacock-blue" of Carmel Bay. To the south began the wild coast of Big Sur and the rugged Santa Lucia Mountains, their purple crests visible up through Carmel Valley from the ruined mission.

They took up residence in this lovely spot, the artists and near-artists and would-be artists of the Bay Area, building simple bungalows under the pines, without electricity, sparsely furnished, where, according to their best hopes, they would work and play in harmony with environment. In the morning they would write or paint, so went the idealized plan (and less frequently the practice); and in the afternoon they would drift together for swimming, long walks, dives for abalone down along the foamy rocks, or hunts for honeycomb in the bee-trees of the forest. At sundown there would be gatherings over a driftwood fire on the beach or, on rainy nights, in a kerosene-lit cabin, for broiled abalone (other Carmel specialties: tamales, enchiladas, fish chowder, stew), washed down with wine or beer or claret punch, and then hours before the fire for what Mary Austin remembered as talk, ambrosial talk. "It was the simplest occupations that gave the most pleasure," she said of Carmel, "and yielded the richest harvest of impressions, observations and feeling-response, which are the stuff of the artist life and the envy and hate-edged amazement of the outsider."[16]

In the decade of its greatest vitality (between 1904, say, and 1914) the Carmel colony did not support a stable cast of characters, nor was it organized as an utopian experiment or commune. It arose, rather, as an informal community of those responding to a similar cluster of California imperatives: simplicity, health, art. George Sterling settled there first, remaining for ten years as symbolic founder, master of the revels, and guru-in-chief. Arnold Genthe, the Prussian classicist-turned-photographer, came down next, from San Francisco, "building the kind of a bungalow I had always wanted to have. I drew up the plans myself. The sloping roof, following the lines of the distant hills, was shadowed by two great pine trees, the largest in Carmel, and was supported by four large redwood trunks, with the bark left on. A wide porch looked out on the sea. The spacious studio and living-room, thirty by sixty feet, with a high ceiling and two skylights, was built entirely of redwood, the rafters being, not box beams but solid redwood. My particular pride was the fireplace which was large enough to take four-foot logs."[17] In a darkroom built under his bungalow Genthe did pioneering work in color photography.

Mary Austin, the next arrival, who loved to dress in flowing Greek robes or in the beaded leather dress of an Indian princess, did her morning writing in a tree-house modeled upon the wickiups of the Paiute. Various Bay Area groups fed into the Carmel colony, but the Piedmont Crowd, which revolved around George Sterling, Jack London, and Xavier Martinez, and took Joaquin Miller as its grand old man, predominated. During the late 1890's and early 1900's the Piedmontese had already worked out for themselves that blend of outdoors and bohemia which Carmel took up and intensified. A loquacious socialism bound the Piedmont Crowd together, and their lively debates continued down the Coast. Ambrose Bierce, in fact, condemned the colony as a nest of radicals, visiting Carmel only reluctantly, at the insistence of George Sterling. James Duval Phelan motored down in a chauffeured white Mercedes; so the political climate could not have been too revolutionary. Further propriety came from the summer homes built by faculty members from Stanford and Berkeley, including David Starr Jordan, and the occasional presence of such revered figures as William Keith and John Muir. Lincoln Steffens and Ray Stannard Baker brought a note of political realism to the colony's posturing reformism; and its shallow socialism was challenged by the brief visit of Upton Sinclair, at Carmel for his health, living on organic foods and submitting himself to strenuous bouts of early morning sea bathing. Together with another Carmelite, Michael Williams, Sinclair wrote *Good Health and How We Won It* (1909), which put on record the urge toward physical renewal motivating many members of the colony. Jimmy Hopper, a superb athlete as well as a successful short-story writer, vindicated physical culturist hopes, being depicted in Jack London's *The Valley of the Moon* as the epitome of the Carmelite as muscleman-artist. Continuity with pre-earthquake bohemia came from the presence at one time or another of former Coppans and members of *Les Jeunes*, and an even more remote bohemia was recalled when Ina Coolbrith and Joaquin Miller took the train down from Oakland or Charles Warren Stoddard came over for the day from Monterey.

Devoid of program or ideology, Carmel had shrewd foundations in real estate. Its developers used artiness as their angle of promotion. "The purpose of the Carmel Development Company," declared an early pamphlet, "has been to develop a refined resort and to appeal to the aesthetic tendencies of those who can appreciate picturesque surroundings."[18] Prominent artists such as George Sterling received special rates of interest so as to get the colony heading in a direction that might attract a clientele in search of arty atmosphere. As a former real estate man himself, Sterling knew the value of the trade-off. He was not duped, but lent himself willingly, as did others. Harry Lafler, a poet and the literary editor of the *Argonaut*, started subdivision enterprises in Big Sur, building a magnificent home overlooking the Pacific in order to show the residential possibilities of the untouched coastline, soon to be celebrated for more significant reasons by a late-arriving Carmelite, Robinson Jeffers. Far from being a commune of impoverished bohemians, Carmel was an early example of the leisure community. Serious work could be carried on—and was, by Mary Austin most noticeably—but an atmosphere of pretension and trivial artiness continually threatened to dominate. In *The Valley of the Moon* Jack London depicted them all hard at work, but other sources document an infinite amount of escapades for every groat's worth of creation. "Hotbed of Soulful Culture, Vortex of Exotic Erudition," ran the headline over a Los Angeles *Times* article (22 May 1910) on Carmel by Willard Huntington Wright, who through satire and humor subverted any pretense to seriousness on the part of the Carmelite non-experiment. "The plumber of Carmel has subscribed to the Harvard Classics," Wright observed. "The butcher reads Browning, and the liveryman wears long hair." Upton Sinclair came to Carmel after fire had destroyed the Helicon Home Colony at Englewood, New Jersey, which had been a true writers' commune, based upon a sharing of domestic life and financial resources. Scandalized by the triviality and dissipation of Carmel, and letting his opinion be known in no uncertain terms, Sinclair left after three months. The Carmelites were glad to see him go.

It took time for the drama to play itself out, but something was wrong. Despondency lurked behind the laughter of the Carmelites. Many found their hoped-for period of creativity turning into an ordeal of apathy. "They gave themselves over to day-dreams," remembered Van Wyck Brooks, at Carmel for the summer of 1911, "while their minds ran down like clocks, as if they had lost the keys to wind them up with, and they turned into beachcombers, listlessly reading books they had read ten times before and searching the rocks for abalones. For this Arcadia lay, one felt, outside the world in which thought evolves and which came to seem insubstantial in the bland sunny air."[19] Jack London portrayed the Carmelites as struggling fitfully for states of child-like joy between bouts of manic depression and philosophical despair. Obscure melodramas of mental torment and compulsive need played themselves out in the charming cottages beneath the pines. Suicide was in the air, talked about constantly. "I have an idea that all sensible people will ultimately be damned," Nora May French remarked one day, lunching at Coppa's. Partly in humor, partly because he felt in Nora's remark a quality of chilling prediction, Porter Garnett inscribed it on one of Coppa's walls, the letters upside down and in reverse. At Carmel, where she stayed with Carrie and George Sterling, Nora May French continued to brood and to write her haunted, death-obsessed poetry, filled with suffering and defeated love. A hopeless entanglement with a married man occurred, and on 14 November 1907, in the early hours, she took cyanide of postassium. At the funeral services on Point Lobos, Jimmy Hopper, Harry Lafler, and George Sterling quarreled as to who should have the honor of scattering Nora's ashes to the winds. They began to grapple with each other, tussling on the ground, and, while they fought, another Carmelite cast Nora's earthly remains out over the sea. Nora's suicide served as a prophetic ritual. Both Sterlings eventually were to take cyanide, and Jack London brought on his own death. George Herman Scheffauer, another Carmelite, like Sterling a poet and a disciple of Bierce, murdered his mistress in Berlin after World War I, then took poison.

IV

When George Sterling's corpse was discovered in his room at the Bohemian Club in November of 1926, the golden age of San Francisco's bohemia had definitely come to a miserable end. The uncrowned King of Bohemia (so his friends called him), Sterling since the late 1890's had been at the center of every artistic circle in the Bay Area. Celebrated as the embodiment of the local artistic sense, though forgotten today, Sterling had in his lifetime been linked with the immortals, his name carved on the walls of the Panama-Pacific International Exposition next to the great poets of the past. At parties, or at the bar of the saloon-tent during midsummer encampments of the Bohemian Club, Californians often graced Sterling's handsome Dantesque head with laurel leaves, in parody of course, but also in hope and belief; for they so hungered for the assertion of local verse and for a laureate of their own that they made of Sterling a living symbol of regional art brought to maturity. And yet nothing in life or art seemed to work out for George Sterling. The laureate of California, the friend of the great, the admired of all, he destroyed himself in self-rejection and bitterness. Because his failures as man and poet were so inextricably bound up with California, because he willingly undertook a symbolic role, the tragedy of George Sterling—those things which failed him—had a pronounced regional significance.

First of all, Sterling inherited a restricted muse. If a tradition existed in California poetry, or at least if a trend was apparent, it was that of a defensive aestheticism which confined itself to highly formal verse patterns and minor ranges of thought and emotion. Throughout the nineteenth century, poetry in California tended to be escapist and amateur. No one talent capable of reversing its wistful, plaintive direction appeared, although the effort of Joaquin Miller to introduce historical themes and an epic sense, however much it resulted in more posturing declamation than solid verse, deserves credit as a sustained attempt to make the poet in California serve larger ends, to rise above the compulsive minor key. For all the bohemians' talk of California as a nursery of the arts, the local poet tended in the early years to define himself against circumstances. Amidst the undeveloped and the matter-of-fact, they wished to be genteel. Taken as a whole, and with the exclusion of isolated poems by the most competent practitioners (Charles Augustus Stoddard, Ina Coolbrith, John Rollin Ridge, Joaquin Miller, and Edward Rowland Sill), poetry in California had few high moments, few times when it engaged in any significant way the abundant nature which so manifestly challenged it or the ranges of thought and feeling which it had to attempt if it were to move beyond plaintive prettification. As he began to write verse in the early 1890's, George Sterling fell prey to this restriction of intent. A trivial time for American poetry in general, Sterling's weaknesses were not totally the fault of California, whose poetic narrowness only intensified the parochial spirit of the age. Sterling sought emotional solace in poetry, the magic of word-music and the elusive quest for Beauty, capitalized and Neoplatonic. As far as possible, he banished intellection and human reference, preferring to pursue—polysyllabically and in archaic verse forms—the cosmic, the exotic, the remote. Working as the private secretary to his uncle, an East Bay real estate mogul, and finding the routines of business very tedious, Sterling's need for personal escape dovetailed with the larger escape of the California poetic tradition. Accustomed to the sort of poetry he wrote, Californians rewarded Sterling for authenticating the enduring value of what they liked best.

In this process of restriction Ambrose Bierce played a major role. As later judgment had it, Bierce laid a hand of ice upon Sterling's warming talent. Bierce's impact upon the impressionable young poet, so lacking in formal literary culture, derived from the force of Bierce's personality and his enormous local reputation; for in matters literary Ambrose Bierce ruled the Bay Area like a capricious autocrat. Coming to San Francisco after distinguished service in the Union Army, which he left as a brevet-major, Bierce made himself notorious as a newspaper satirist. He was frequently threatened, and at least upon one occasion beaten up, for remarks he had made in print. There was an anger, a bitterness in Bierce, near-pathological, characterizing his private and public life. He made his wife's life hellish before they separated, and he crushed the individuality of his two sons. (One was shot to death in an amorous quarrel, and the other, repudiated by his father, died of pneumonia in lonely estrangement.) Although he

Ambrose Bierce (1842–1914?)

Although he got his start there as a writer, he despised California for being shallow and self-congratulatory. San Francisco ("the paradise of ignorance, anarchy and general yellowness") especially repelled him. Yet for all his posturing disdain Bierce remained in California out of deep need. He wanted to feel superior. Becoming increasingly bitter and apocalyptic, he alienated all but a few disciples, whom he ruined. He disappeared into Mexico, and rumor had it that he was put against a wall and shot.

had a lifelong habit of sexual intrigue, Bierce's love life had a stingy, begrudging quality to it, as if he hated the very flesh he indulged and the women who met his needs. He concealed his philandering behind a monumental prudery, a decorum in language and dress, together with a fastidiousness regarding bodily cleanliness and an exaggerated public chivalry. Between 1872 and 1876 Bierce lived in England, returning to California a convinced Anglophile. Having seen the great world (he was a personal friend of the exiled French Empress Eugénie), Bierce ridiculed provincial California's attempts to pull itself up by the bootstraps. "California, California, California," he mocked; "again California and California all the same. Her climate, her soil, her scenery, her literature, science, art! What is it in the conditions of this raw Western life that makes us all blockhead braggarts? Other communities are as backward in culture, none so forward in manners; others as low in intelligence, none so high in impudence. California has never produced a great scholar, a great writer, a great painter."[20] Bierce especially resented the pretensions of San Francisco, "the paradise of ignorance, anarchy and general yellowness." He defined the local bohemian as "a lazy, loaferish, gluttonous, crapulent and dishonest duffer, who, according to the bent of his incapacity—the nature of the talents that heaven has liberally denied—scandalizes society, disgraces literature, debauches art, and is an irreclaimable, inexpressible and incalculable nuisance."[21] Claiming that San Francisco was bad for his asthma, Bierce lived in mountain villages north and south of the city, from which he cast Olympian thunderbolts upon the foolish of the town.

As the years drew on, Bierce grew even more cynical and disaffected, his disgust with the human condition becoming obsessively morbid. He kept a skull on his desk, haunted moonlit graveyards and during the course of frequent visits to the morgue became a connoisseur of corpses. Much of this, of course, was a pose, appropriate to the author of some of the best tales of horror written in the United States since Edgar Allan Poe; then again, it was more than posturing. Brooding over the apocalyptic, Bierce genuinely yearned for the end. Meanwhile, he hated well. He hated democracy and he hated Walt Whitman. He hated ministers. If dogs harassed him as he pedaled his bicycle along country roads, he would dismount, draw his pistol and shoot the offending animal, sometimes before an astonished owner's eyes. (Needless to say, Ambrose Bierce hated dogs!) Anything vernacular or possessing the common touch, especially in literature, left him physically ill, as did any plea for social reform. ("I yearn for the strong-handed Dictator," he once wrote Sterling, apropos of the socialism at Carmel, "who will swat you all on the mouths. . . ."[22]) In 1887 young William Randolph Hearst hired Bierce as a columnist on the San Francisco *Examiner*. Bierce worked for the Hearst newspapers for the next twenty-five years, until he disappeared mysteriously into Mexico and no doubt—as he wanted it—was granted a violent end. In 1899 he transferred his base of operations to Washington, D.C. But not before he had brought George Sterling under his control.

In his messianism of reaction, Ambrose Bierce needed a few select disciples, just as in his pride and paranoia he needed eventually to cast them off and to stand in solitary defiance. Bierce brought Sterling under the mantle of a massive intimidation. Naïve in matters literary, flattered at being courted by the Bay Area's most powerful critic, Sterling believed that Bierce's rigid aesthetic represented the great tradition. Because he so hated human life, Bierce wanted it eliminated as much as possible from poetry, which he saw as a counter-definition to the human condition, an escape into aesthetic repose. He encouraged Sterling's taste for cosmic theme. "You shall be the poet of the skies, the prophet of the suns," he told him.[23] Bierce scrutinized Sterling's verse for the slightest deviations from his own austere standards of diction or departure from the most traditional of forms. "In view of the modern movement in poetry," Sterling later admitted, "he was not, perhaps, the best master I could have known, but I cannot look back to the days of my apprenticeship without feelings of gratitude."[24] Sterling might have been more frank in the matter of his resentment, for by the time he made this judgment, in the months before his suicide, he knew the full measure of his failure. Bierce repudiated Sterling in a vicious letter written just before his disappearance, but a desire to salvage something from the past, together with a fundamental loyalty, prevented Sterling from replying in kind after Bierce's death. In the face of what was beginning to happen to American poetry at the very time Sterling's discipleship ended, in the face, that is, of the return to American themes already underway in the work of Edwin Arlington Robinson and soon to flower in the poetry of Robert Frost and others, Sterling must have known that he had been tragically dispossessed. The absorption of European influences and techniques on the part of the next generation of poets compounded the disaster. In 1923, when he finally found an Eastern publisher, Sterling's *Selected Poems* (he called them his *Neglected Poems*) were cast up upon alien shores like timbers from an ancient shipwreck. He had his own lack of independence, the provinciality of California poetry—and Ambrose Bierce—to blame.

Sterling often regretted that he had not drawn more upon his New England background as a way of countering a totally Californian involvement. Born in 1869 in the former Yankee whaling town of Sag Harbor, Long Island, Sterling prided himself upon a distinguished New England heritage which went back to the seventeenth century. Coming to California when just out of his teens, he kept throughout his life a highly nasal Yankee way of speaking. The problem was, however, that Sterling, the uprooted, could never decide what was important about his New England heritage, beyond its snob appeal. With the exception of his maternal grandfather, Wickham Sayre Havens, a retired whaling captain who became the subject of one of Sterling's best poems, he seems to have made no deep connection with the New England past, although, as Mary Austin pointed out, some of his best work had a Sag Harbor setting. Sterling returned to the East at times of adult crisis, revisiting the scenes of his boyhood, browsing through the gravestones of his ancestors buried in Connecticut across the choppy waters of Long Island Sound. New England remained a haunting, ill-defined memory, confused by his family's alienating conversion to Roman Catholicism, unstructured by systematic education. Its best ideas and impulses, the cumulative drama of the New England conscience, had taken no deep roots in his soul. Once in a while a feeling surfaced in him that he should be doing better, that he should be carrying on some great New England labor in California through poetry as had been carried on in the past through religion; but he never knew what to do in response to these promptings and was left with only an aftertaste of discontent. Part of Sterling's attraction to Bierce arose out of the fact that he confused Bierce's purism and snobbery with high purpose in the New England manner. Sterling never managed to become the bringer of New England's gifts. Neither expatriate nor missionary, he fell victim to the sufferings of both conditions.

His Roman Catholic background further complicated matters—and represented another lost opportunity. Under the influence of the Oxford Movement, Sterling's father, a socially prominent Presbyterian physician, brought his entire family into the Roman Church. In reaction to the vigorously Protestant heritage it had to assert itself against, Catholicism in the Sterling household took on an Italian tone: lush, aesthetic, highly devotional. Sterling's brother became a priest and he himself studied at Saint Charles' Seminary near Baltimore, conducted by the Sulpician Fathers, a society of French priests dedicated to the training of the clergy. Parental pressure more than religious feeling put Sterling on the path to orders. He left the seminary and he left the Church, but not before he had the chance over a number of years of his education to come into contact with the austere piety and disciplined feel for tradition characteristic of the Sulpician spirit. Sterling was not a very profound man, and, as in the case of his New Englandism, he did not make as workable an imaginative connection with his Catholic background as he might have; but it was there all his life, a lingering influence, an unrealized promise. It showed up in his attempts to work in liturgical theater and in the theological imagery and baffled religious feeling which characterized his poetry. His deepest conception of the poet's role was akin to that of a priest; and despite renunciations of formal faith he kept a feel for Catholic California, attending mass at the Mission during his Carmel years, sharing with his patron James Duval Phelan the vision of California as the new Italy, sunny nursery of the arts. Looking back upon his days in the minor seminary, Sterling exaggerated his relationship to John Bannister Tabb, a poet-priest teaching on the Saint Charles faculty. A convert, like the Sterling family, of impressive Protestant lineage, an aristocratic Virginian who had borne arms for the Confederacy, a poet in the service of the Church, Tabb symbolized to Sterling that rich blend of traditions which had always eluded him, but which he felt his life should have borne forth. Claiming that he had been Father Tabb's protégé (and that Tabb had taught him to eat nasturtiums as the poet's best food), Sterling rescued some symbolic relationship to his Catholic past. It conferred upon Sterling a belief in the quality of his lineage, some useful continuity with the ravaged expectations of his adolescence.

George Sterling, the former seminarian, strayed far from the paths of righteousness. He arrived in California chaste and a non-drinker. "Handsome as a Roman faun," in Mary Austin's words, "shy, restless, slim and stooping," Sterling in 1896 married the sister of his uncle-employer's wife, Caroline Rand, a tall, elegant woman, praised by contemporaries for her Gibson Girl beauty. Together they made a startlingly handsome addition to the Piedmont Crowd. "Well, we were a pretty clean bunch all 'round," Jack London claimed of the East Bay bohemians, forgetting his own reputation as the Stallion of the Piedmont Hills.[25] Whether it was London who led Sterling into vice, as Carrie Sterling claimed, or whether George proved a willing learner on his own, he soon strayed into adultery and a perpetual novena to Our Lady of the Corn. From 1901 onward he maintained a studio in San Francisco's Montgomery Block for extramarital rendezvous. Around 1903 or so his drinking increased and he began to experiment with opium and hashish. Sterling's compulsive womanizing eventually drove Carrie to seek a divorce. (In 1918, dressed in a graceful gown, she put Chopin's Funeral March on the gramophone, arranged herself on her bed and took a lethal dose of cyanide.) In some moods Sterling tried to pass off his bacchic priapism as pagan joy. When he did not come as a medieval monk, he liked to attend masquerade parties (to which California bohemians seemed addicted) dressed as a pagan divinity, a Pan-figure in animal skins, with a garland of flowers on his head. At more serious moments he tried to take a philosophical attitude toward pleasure and pain, but his behavior proceeded more from temperament than consistent Epicureanism.

He loved his own very considerable beauty, which blended New England and the antique. Between bouts of dissipation, which got out of hand only toward the end, he took very good care of himself. At Carmel he displayed his lithe physique in a bathing suit so brief that it would have caused his arrest on a public beach. There is a strong possibility that he had portraits taken of himself in the nude or near-nude, striking classical stances. Over twenty photographs and sketches of himself adorned the walls of his Montgomery Block studio, where for twenty-five years the women and girls of San Francisco surrendered to their poet's voracious embrace. On the whole, he maintained discretion—until the last years—for he had a secure place among the proper and the established. Sterling's was not a scandalous amorality, but a covert indulgence in the Victorian manner, clothed in propriety and masking a thousand hells. Sterling never understood a woman in her psychic life, Mary Austin claimed, not even his wife; he used women sexually as an act of narcissism and as a stimulant to creativity. He wrote of Beauty, remote, ethereal, when all the while he served the sordid urgencies of his own insatiable flesh, angry if baffled, loathing itself when satisfied. To the degree he pursued pleasure, Sterling feared pain. On his person, as one carried keys or a pocket watch, he kept enough cyanide of potassium to destroy himself in case he were ever faced with an extended period of physical suffering. He eventually used it.

Meanwhile, for a generation of Californians, George Sterling embodied life lived for art. He was not a major figure in terms of local achievement if compared to, say, John Muir, Mary Austin, Frank Norris, and Jack London in literature; Arthur Putnam and Douglas Tilden in sculpture; Xavier Martinez, Charles Rollo Peters, Percy Gray, Francis McComas, and William Keith in painting; or the architects of the Bay Region style, Willis Polk and Bernard Maybeck especially. A case can be made that

George Sterling (1869–1926)

The discovery of his corpse, twisted in the agonies of suicide by poison, brought an official (and rather overdue) conclusion to California's turn-of-the-century era. Because this local poet so willingly assumed a symbolic role, his tragedy had all the elements of a regional paradigm. His failures were inextricably bound up with the failures of California. To a generation he embodied the life lived for art. He prided himself upon his resemblance to Dante. That was true, agreed Van Wyck Brooks in the summer of 1911: George Sterling looked like Dante in hell.

David Starr Jordan, who turned to verse only as recreation from his duties as president of Stanford, was in fact a better poet. Yet Sterling served as the archpriest of the whole revival. No gathering of Bay Area talent seemed complete without him. In the long run his poetry would turn out to be tragically passé, and in provincial gratitude Californians overrated it scandalously; but for a brief moment, in his own time, before the verdict of history was in, George Sterling held his own. Singlehandedly, he revived poetry in California, opening it up to new ranges of consideration. In terms of its plaintive aestheticism, its lack of symbolic intensity or engagement with reality, Sterling's verse belonged to the old provincial poetry. On the other hand it occasionally possessed a sub-philosophical relationship to local materials and a passion for transcendence which forecast the achievement of Robinson Jeffers. Sterling's sonnet "The Black Vulture" suggested a mode which one wishes had been more characteristic:

> Aloof within the day's enormous dome,
> He holds unshared the silence of the sky.
> Far down his bleak, relentless eyes descry
> The eagle's empire and the falcon's home—
> Far down, the galleons of sunset roam;
> His hazards on the sea of morning lie;
> Serene, he hears the broken tempest sigh
> Where cold sierras gleam like scattered foam.
>
> And least of all he holds the human swarm—
> Unwitting now that envious men prepare
> To make their dream and its fulfilment one,
> When, poised above the caldrons of the storm,
> Their hearts, contemptuous of death, shall dare
> His roads between the thunder and the sun.

A very old-fashioned exercise, "The Black Vulture" has all of Sterling's faults of archaic diction and poetic self-consciousness. In its attention and balance, however, in its ambitious use of Californian material, it was perhaps his best poem.

The harvest of Sterling's Carmel years, *Beyond the Breakers, and Other Poems* (1914), showed an environmentalism unknown in his previous work, a use of setting as the occasion of meditation and the source for the materials of symbolic response, pointing toward what Jeffers would be exploring in the next two decades. Sterling lived in Carmel more or less continuously between 1905 and 1914. He moved there, Sterling wrote

Ambrose Bierce, because he wanted to get away from the dissipations of San Francisco and live devoted to poetry and the simple life. He built a redwood bungalow at the end of a ravine lined by leaning bay trees and next to it he planted a vegetable garden. He fetched and chopped wood for his huge stone fireplace and made his own yogurt. He tested himself against the stinging Pacific surf and dove down along the rocks for abalone, or dared the rocky cliffs of Point Lobos. Carmel, however, did not prove to be the simple paradise for which Sterling had hoped. Exiled from a devastated San Francisco, bohemia migrated down the Coast, bringing its snares and temptations, its liquor and idleness and willing girls. He had sworn to Bierce that he would raise vegetables and honey bees, live on rice and water, and stay faithful to "just one girl"—which did not prove to be the case. An intra-Carmel entanglement had precipitated the suicide of Nora May French. Innocent of misdoing in Nora's case, Sterling was nevertheless shaken to the depths. Nora's torment of soul and body so much resembled the vipers' tangle of his own life. He began to offset fads of diet and exercise by frequent drinking bouts and destructive returns to San Francisco. Sterling's Carmel Diaries record a trivial existence, odds and ends of puttering days which never really amounted to much: days which seem imprisoned in a suspension which was neither rest nor creative leisure: days to no purpose: Carmel days under the sun and by the peacock-blue Pacific. Sterling prided himself upon his Dantesque profile; but to Van Wyck Brooks, in the summer of 1911, George Sterling of Carmel-by-the-Sea "had precisely the aspect of Dante in hell."

He took revenge against life in a ferocious slaughter of animals. The Carmel Diaries document the hundreds of rabbits, squirrels, and small birds which dropped before Sterling's rifle fire. With a blast of his shotgun he would bring down a half dozen birds at a time. He gathered abalone and mussels by the sackful, speared innumerable salmon, destroyed beehives and nests of gulls. Between 13 and 19 October 1910, Sterling killed, and meticulously recorded in his diary, twenty-six blackbirds, seven ducks, six killdeer, nine squirrels, two snipe, a mud hen, and, as a poetic gesture perhaps, a solitary lark. His total kill for October ran to eighty-seven small birds and animals, compulsively destroyed and just as compulsively accounted for. What did this mean, this slaughter? A murderous anger at the core of his soul? Something which paralleled the hunting of women, the cries of the wounded rabbit resembling the urgent pleas of another destruction? In any event, Carrie Sterling found herself down to her last act of forgiveness. On 24 November 1913 George Sterling made the final entry into his Carmel Diary: "Mild and mostly overcast. Rain after 7 p.m. —Carrie has left me, to sleep at Hopper's to-night and go to Berkeley on the morning auto-bus." Lonely, drinking heavily, Sterling moved into a nearby shack to get away from a bungalow haunted now by too much meaning. The Carmel experiment had come to an end, and in January of 1914 George Sterling left for the East.

New York did not welcome him with open arms. He was one among many minor poets. The Eastern literary establishment had always been indifferent to his work, Sterling not securing an Eastern publisher until 1923. Magazines like *The Atlantic Monthly* and *Harper's* continually rejected his poems, and only the insistence of Ambrose Bierce had persuaded the editors of *Cosmopolitan* to run "The Wine of Wizardy." He tried while in New York to write a poetry of social protest. He walked on picket lines and did some settlement work, but it was too late. Just as he worked for the revolution while living at The Lambs Club, he was pouring socialist sentiment into incongruously precious vials. Sterling's poetry was meant to bear an easier burden. Under the weight of protest it collapsed into an insincere, unearned shriek. With America's entry into the war, Sterling laid aside the international solidarity of the working class and threw himself into the jingoism gripping the nation. *The Binding of the Beast, and Other War Verse* (1917), an embarrassment poetically, gave the lie to previous claims to compassion. In his heart of hearts, Sterling did not care about Walt Whitman's America. Intellectually and aesthetically, moreover, New York put him out of his depth. A world of poetry was opening up in which he would play no part. As he sat in the bars and coffee houses of Greenwich Village, hearing the talk which had not quieted down since 1913, when the International Exhibition of painting and sculpture had electrified the city with a dramatization of avant-garde European trends; as he leafed through the pages of Harriet Monroe's *Poetry* magazine, seeing the new names and even stranger poetry of Carl Sandburg, Amy Lowell, Hilda Doolittle, Robert Frost, Vachel Lindsay, Ezra Pound, and T. S. Eliot—Sterling knew that it had passed him by. What light years separated his work from the Imagist doctrines of restraint, clarity of image, and simplicity of syntax! Uneasy in New York, uneasy in the new poetry, he meditated an ode on the Yosemite. James Duval Phelan sent him the money to come home.

Perhaps Carrie's suicide brought Sterling back for good, freeing him, as it did, from her reproach, yet riveting him to the scene of an unatoned sorrow. He had, in any event, no place else to go. San Francisco would always take him back, for the city needed Sterling to help it maintain a conviction of specialness. With its creative community dispersed throughout the world, with modern commercial buildings replacing the city's former ramshackle elegance, the new San Francisco found itself drenched in nostalgia for what had been lost. For the middle-aged who remembered and for the young who yearned for a link to the past, Sterling seemed a symbolic survivor from that better, more romantic era before the earthquake, when San Francisco held locked within itself a promise of life and art. Even in his disorderly decline, they cherished him for the memories he kept alive. After 1918 Sterling grew reluctant to leave the city which had conferred upon him his only lasting identity: poet laureate of "the cool, grey city of love." A new bohemian circle gathered about him, less brilliant perhaps than that of the days before 1906, but just as eager to feel themselves part of a place and a moment. Sterling helped them. At Bigin's Bologna something of Coppa's atmosphere was regained. Parties still went on atop Telegraph Hill, where amidst the drinks and love-making they talked of another Florence and the Renaissance which surely must come to San Francisco. And when, in the small morning hours after the party broke up, George Sterling made his exits into the fog, his overcoat draped like an opera cloak about his shoulders, then one felt the mood of the old bohemian city.

Rich men had always helped him along. Frank C. Havens, who was his uncle, his employer, and his brother-in-law, paid Sterling $100 a week to serve as his private secretary, taking him East to Sag Harbor on one occasion in a plush private railroad car. As Sterling moved into middle age, the Bohemian Club, where he had been a member since 1904, came to his rescue. From 1915 or so Barbour Lathrop, a Bohemian and a prominent businessman, anonymously paid for Sterling to have a room on the third floor of the Club. Needless to say, the Club had changed since its founding in 1872. The Club which had once discouraged owners of newspapers from applying and which had the temerity to refuse membership to William C. Ralston, president of the Bank of California and the most powerful man in San Francisco, over the years had become almost exclusively the preserve of rich men. Signs of this eventual shift were apparent as early as the late 1870's, as the Club moved to progressively more luxuriant quarters. Lunching at the Club in 1882, Oscar Wilde remarked that he had never seen "so many well-dressed, well-fed, business-like looking Bohemians" in his life. Rudyard Kipling, there for a visit in 1889, found himself "treading soft carpets and breathing the incense of superior cigars."[26]

The working journalists who had founded the Club in the first place defeated a measure in 1879 to introduce swallow-tailed evening wear at the High Jinks; by 1887, however, they were so hostile to the direction their once unpretentious society was taking that they broke off to form the San Francisco Press Club. The group of young Bohemians known as *Les Jeunes* founded *The Lark* in 1895 partly out of protest against the staid conventionality of the Club (where, incidentally, *The Lark* was not even displayed in the library, but tossed into the bottom drawer of an out-of-the-way desk). For all its charm of setting, after all, and for all its apparent romance, San Francisco was a businessman's town, from whose ever-higher office buildings was directed the economic life of the Far West. At the same time many of these businessmen felt the aesthetic imperatives of the city; men like Phelan, Templeton Crocker, Raphael Weill, and Edward Robeson Taylor (a physician, an attorney, a poet, and like Phelan a mayor of San Francisco), cultured men, patrons and collectors in the second generation of wealth, found in the Bohemian Club, especially in the elaborate theatricals of the Midsummer Jinks, an outlet for artistic interest, and, in some cases, for genuine talent. Sterling kept alive for these men the belief that, despite the abandonment of San Francisco by its artists, the Bohemian Club yet sustained the aesthetic ideal. He was a prisoner to their hope, but their aspirations served his needs as well.

In his last tragic years Sterling cast about for a way to go on living. Although in his fifties, he tried to keep up with the Jazz Age, humorously paying for bootleg liquor with inscribed editions of his poetry. A rather eccentric figure, dressed in a business suit, vest, and tennis shoes, he attended the parties and joined in the pranks, being arrested early one morning for wading in Strawberry Lake in Golden Gate Park, picking water lilies by moonlight in the company of a disrobed chorus girl. At the police station, he cheerfully identified himself to the desk sergeant by the poems in his overcoat pocket. He served a brief stint in Hollywood writing subtitles for *The Thief of Bagdad*, starring Douglas Fairbanks. Deep down, however, Sterling felt himself profoundly disaffected from the gin-ridden, automotive pace of the Jazz Age. On the surface at least, his had been a more leisurely and sentimental bohemia. Sterling hated motor cars and emancipated women. His splenetic and fractious "Rhymes and Reactions" column in *The Overland Monthly* betrayed a variety of alienations: most noticeably from modern poetry, about which he became near-hysterical. With an ire no doubt imitative of the wrathful tone of his friend H. L. Mencken, Sterling inveighed against the boobs filling up California, especially Southern California, destroying the repose and tone of the old provincial civilization. Nostalgia, in fact, for a lost California and for lost friends, began to grip him. So many of his fellow artists had by then passed on. Nora May French had been first. Sterling edited her poems, and every November on the anniversary of her death he traveled down to Point Lobos where her ashes had been scattered to the winds. Then Charles Warren Stoddard died at Monterey in 1909. He died in the spring like an ancient shepherd: the beloved sire of bohemia, winding down to a sad end, drinking, brooding in Franciscan robes over the slenderness of his achievement and the failure of all those lovely things which had made an idle career supportable, and even sweet. Sterling served as a pallbearer at the funeral. Then Joaquin Miller passed away in 1913, uproarious to the end, a womanizer into old age, and a fraud, but also in his own way a visionary, and a poet who dared the West in epic terms. Sterling had camped with Miller in the East Bay hills, and when the literary frontiersman had grown too feeble for such excursions he had drunk corn liquor with him from a jug which Joaquin kept under his bed. "To be a Gringo in Mexico," Ambrose Bierce had said before slipping across the border "—ah, that is euthanasia!" In that revolution-torn land, sometime in 1914, Bierce was most likely put against a wall and shot, an iron-gray old man in a dirty white suit, a hating look in his eye. Jack London died in 1916, another November death, like Nora May's and Sterling's own; then Carrie in 1918, committing suicide to Chopin.

Age and anxiety brought a thousand wrinkles to Sterling's once faun-like face, prompting the local witticism that his profile was that of a Greek coin run over by a Roman chariot. His flesh threatened continually to give out. Women kept him in money and liquor; but now the hangovers put him in the hospital and the dubious girls he brought back to his Montgomery Block studio infected him with VD. In April of 1924 he had to have seven decayed and abscessed teeth removed. He tried to escape the flesh through spiritualism or to restore it through diet fads and $65 treatments on Gaylord Wilshire's Ionaco Machine, an electronic device whose magnetic field was supposed to purify the blood. The publication of his *Selected Poems* in 1923 afforded little consolation. They seemed such a slender, inconsequential harvest; and critical reception was not exactly avid. To his credit, he generously acknowledged that Robinson Jeffers, who arrived at Carmel just as Sterling left, would do what he himself had failed to do: confer upon California the dignity of significant poetry. He wrote a glowing appreciation, *Robinson Jeffers, the Man and the Artist*

(1926), and in *Strange Waters* (1926), a poetic narrative of incest and suicide set on the rugged Mendocino Coast, Sterling paid Jeffers the compliment of such close imitation that Jeffers thought the poem a parody and was temporarily resentful. Completely dependent upon the opinion of the local establishment for his sense of worth, Sterling was crushed when he was passed over for the editorship of *The Overland Monthly* on grounds of instability. A similar rejection precipitated his suicide. He had been selected to serve as toastmaster at a Bohemian Club dinner in honor of H. L. Mencken, who admired his work. In anticipation of Mencken's arrival, Sterling gathered a supply of bootleg liquor, looking forward to an uproarious reunion. Mencken, however, enjoying himself in the South, delayed and delayed his arrival in San Francisco. Jealous and peevish, Sterling used his liquor supply to go on a self-destructive binge. By the time Mencken arrived, Sterling was suffering from such a debilitating hangover that Charles Norris, the brother of Frank Norris and a man whom Sterling loathed, was asked to serve as toastmaster in Sterling's place. Profoundly depressed by the effects of alcohol and by the slight he felt he had suffered at the hands of the Bohemian Club, Sterling lay on his bed, hearing, perhaps, the laughter from the Mencken banquet downstairs. He was fifty-seven. He got up and began to burn his papers. Sometime in late 16 or early 17 November 1926 he swallowed the cyanide he had carried about for years. Those who found his twisted corpse speculated that it must have been a horrible death.

A scrap of poetry was found in Sterling's room, charred from the burning of his papers but still legible:

> Deeper into the darkness can I peer
> Than most, yet find the darkness still beyond.

So many of Sterling's fellow bohemians, lost in a dark night, had wandered over a precipice that California stood mocked in general unhappiness. Philosophical pessimism compounded neuroses and they succumbed because everything failed them. In a way, their uncritical pessimism, so bewildering to Saxon in *The Valley of the Moon*, was a sign of provincialism and lack of major talent. They suffered, many of them, from bad ideas. At a time when avant-garde America, in Chicago, in New York, in European exile, was renewing itself through connection with the forward thrust of Continental aesthetics, Sterling was feeling the full weight of a played-out European despair, which allowed his personal disorders the dangerous justification of theory. Inflamed by philosophy, the flirtation with self-destruction which arose out of psychic distress became fixed in formula—and then irresistible. So often they considered themselves in the throes of intellectual torment when they were just hung-over. Had they known art, they might have avoided artiness. Had they loved the flesh, they would not have made it bear the full burden of their justification, for it was doomed to give way under the strain.

The record of so much devastation makes one wonder whether California was not to blame. As a provincial culture, eager to upgrade itself, it authenticated its artists too easily and they in turn fell into an exaggerated sense of their own importance, blunting their capacity for the intenser agonies of creation. As a place to live, California encouraged a subtle passivity which was more than the effect of the sunshine, although that—and all it stood for—soaked the Carmelites through with a delicious languor. As a region, California offered itself too easily as a self-justifying symbol of spacious identity. The artists of California were not the region they inhabited, nor were the grandeur and the promise emanating from California automatically characteristic of their art, although they were tempted to think so.

They looked back because they recognized their present personal instability and the transitional moment they possessed—on the horizon of Hollywood, Los Angeles, industry, the automobile, and a sociology of mass expectation. Each loved California for something preserved from the past. In the midst of confusion, each recovered an orthodoxy. As an act of will and imagination, and sometimes creation, they regained Indian prehistory and the mission past, with its values of myth, crafts, rhythmic living, and religious wonder. They regained the frontier, which as a symbol kept alive the possibilities of real work and direct experience. They sought to connect with the Orient, so estranged in local exploitation, and yet compelling as a mystery across the Pacific, telling them, especially the landscapists and the architects, of solutions in which philosophy and life and design came into repose. From topography, climate, historical associations, and the presence of Southern Europeans, they consolidated a Mediterranean metaphor, which softened and gave richness, linking them to something beyond harsh American concerns. Even the Bohemian Club, as it was first founded, represented a continuance, carrying into the 1870's the intimate and good-natured mood of the San Francisco literary frontier.

Many attained their best moments through love of California and relationship to its culture. Set in the context of their time, judged by their better aspirations, they take on significance. Their lives were explorations at a time of transition. Perhaps they were the last to feel the cumulative presence of provincial California and to try to take its values forward. Together they glimpsed an ideal which yet remains a challenge and which might become a tragic irony. They dreamed of a California of nature and art, lived with dignity and celebrated in creativity. They wanted a California of health, color, warmth, and heritage. They struggled for it, all of them, even the wounded ones. Their California dream could not dispel more serious sicknesses of soul, but it did soothe lesser failures, and for most of them times of consolation were very, very necessary.

9

The City Beautiful and the San Francisco Fair

In San Francisco's ugly and huddled lanes, critics had always beheld a symbol of lost California opportunities. Here on the empty edge of a nearly empty continental shelf should have been built the city beautiful, paradigm of the cultural order that time would bring to the Pacific Slope. The dystopian aspects of San Francisco played off against the innate utopian imperatives of California itself, imperatives being realized at the turn of the century in a rash of utopian communities. Mainly rural, these communities possessed ideological origins distinct from specific California considerations, but they reinforced the state's developing sense of place. Urban experiments were not lacking. The turn-of-the-century period saw a variety of planning ventures, ranging from civic drives for improvement to more fanciful enterprises like Joaquin Miller's development of his property in the Oakland Hills.

No matter how eccentrically, the "Hights" (the Poet of the Sierras believed in reformed spelling) represented a desire to celebrate a specifically Californian way of domestic living. In his overstated, idiosyncratic manner, Miller was planting the seed of a model city. We know of his intent from two novels, *The Destruction of Gotham* (1886) and *The Building of the City Beautiful* (1893). In the first, Miller anatomized the evils of New York's nightmare-world of poverty, filth, and vice. Amidst the squalor, a Miller-like figure, newspaperman John Walton, dreams of building a utopian city in the West, a community which resembles Edward Bellamy's Boston in political arrangements but has a Californian emphasis upon outdoors and physical health. In the finale, Gotham's oppressed

Joaquin Miller (1841?–1913)

His real name was Cincinnatus Heine. It was always difficult (especially for him) to separate the fact from the fiction of his life. He was a poet, a dramatist, a novelist, a squaw man, a bohemian, a devotee of corn liquor and fleshly sport, a visionary—and an outrageous fraud. He celebrated the Sierras in prose and poetry which was at best uneven. In the heights above Oakland he built a home and planted thousands of eucalyptus trees, dreaming that someday the hills surrounding the Bay would be covered with rhythmic sequences of landscaping and architecture.

proletariat put to the torch the hated tenements which caged them like beasts. In *The Building of the City Beautiful*, a similarly Miller-like hero, John Morton, sets out to realize the ideal of the first novel, a Western model-city. Single-handedly he begins to build and to terrace and to plant in the Oakland Hills overlooking the Golden Gate. In his mind is the memory of Toltec, a utopian community in the Mexican desert known to few outsiders but revealed to him by a mysterious female political leader. Through patient, Tolstoyan labor, Morton hopes to inspire the Bay Area to fill the hills that crowd the water's edge, not with commercially convenient lots, but with rhythmic sequences of landscaping and architecture.

Miller's imaginative aspirations had more down-to-earth counterparts. In 1896, Mrs. Phoebe Apperson Hearst, the grandame of California, proposed in a letter to the regents of the University of California that she sponsor an architectural competition in honor of her late husband, Senator George Hearst. Mrs. Hearst offered an award for the best campus plan for the university, surveyed by Frederick Law Olmsted in 1866 but still in the late 1890's relatively undeveloped. Architectural firms from all over the world submitted proposals for California's City of Learning, the sketches of M. Emile Bénard of Paris being chosen in 1900. The grand Beaux Arts buildings which began to appear on the Berkeley campus from 1903 onward under the supervision of John Galen Howard, the official university architect who revised Bénard's plans in light of Olmsted's previous suggestions, had little in common with Joaquin Miller's linked bungalows nestled among the eucalyptus, except for a common desire to bear witness through planning to California's assured future and gift-bearing past. Totally dissimilar, except for the fact that poet and patroness were both representative Californians, Miller and Mrs. Hearst wanted the factor of design introduced into California life, for immediate aesthetic benefits and as an anticipation of future history.

Across the Bay, the Association for the Improvement and Adornment of San Francisco was formed in 1904, under the presidency of James D. Phelan, "to promote in every practical way the beautifying of the streets, public buildings, parks, squares, and places of San Francisco; to bring to the attention of the officials and the people of the city the best methods for instituting artistic municipal betterments; to stimulate the sentiment of civic pride in the improvement and care of private property; to suggest quasi-public enterprises; and, in short, to make San Francisco a more agreeable city in which to live."[1] The men who belonged to Phelan's Association were businessmen of a new, progressive mould. The most conspicuous of them—Phelan himself; J. W. Byrne, president of the Pacific Union Club; Willis Davis, president of the San Francisco Art Association—were the Hamiltonian Californians of Gertrude Atherton's fondest wishes: wealthy, imperial, post-frontier in their style and culture, frontier in their vigor and capacity for bold action, men of business, patrons of art and learning, cosmopolitan, determined to make San Francisco a world city. In 1902 Phelan had approached Daniel Hudson Burnham, the famous architect and city planner, about the possibility of devising a plan for San Francisco similar to the one he, Olmsted, and Charles McKim had prepared in 1901 for Washington, D.C. In May of 1904 the Association for the Improvement and Adornment of San Francisco extended a formal invitation to Burnham, who was already familiar to San Franciscans through his design of the Chronicle Building, the Mills Building, and the Merchants' Exchange. From the vantage point of a Twin Peaks studio, working at no fee, Burnham devised a complete city plan for San Francisco, which on 27 September 1905 he formally presented to the Board of Supervisors.

Burham's imperial vision of San Francisco expressed a cluster of attitudes held in common with the business community which had brought him to the city. Burnham thought of himself as a man of affairs, dealing with counterparts. He wanted aesthetics grounded in sound commercialism. "Beauty in the public work of a city," he said in 1902, "has always paid. What would the prosperity of the inhabitants of Paris be if she were merely a convenient city, nothing more?"[2] Burnham felt certain that he could articulate San Francisco to itself, and in many ways he was correct. He was attuned to the historical and prophetic aspects of San Francisco's desire for a plan. "You would not have called me in," he remarked to James D. Phelan, "had it been to plan for the small expenditure of the present. The plan for your city must be framed in accord with your needs in the distant future—for all time."[3] A submerged historical parable, expressed in design and text, ran through the Burnham Report. Burnham had made his reputation as Director of Works for the Chicago World's Fair of 1893, and the mood and motifs of his plan for San Francisco were in the grand style made famous by the Great White City. Yet in California imperial motifs had special resonances, reinforcing a self-image continuing from the *Annals of San Francisco* through Bancroft. Burnham's San Francisco consolidated an epoch. As predicted from the 1850's, America's Pacific capital now assumed the marble mantle of empire. Like Standford University in Palo Alto and the Hearst-sponsored campus at

Berkeley, Burnham's San Francisco turned raw energy into fixed and splendid form.

Herbert Croly, the social critic, challenged San Francisco to follow through on what Burnham envisioned. Since life had so far taken place mainly in rural settings, Croly asserted, indifference to urban design had done California no permanent harm. With the twentieth century, however, California was destined to grow more urban. Adoption of Burnham's suggestions would take on substantive and symbolic significance: San Francisco would be rendered beautiful and California would have a metaphor for its urban future. The errors of the past had their explanation in the instability of Eldorado, but nothing could excuse San Francisco's failure to provide for the future, to make itself "the abiding-place of the men who will give form and direction to the intellectual life of that part of the country." Are San Franciscans ready for the new era of leadership, Croly asked? Beholding the Greater City from afar, will they accept or reject the vision?[4]

A subtle elitism pervaded Croly's remarks. San Francisco was to be refashioned by men who counted for the sake of men who counted. Such was not just Croly's attitude, but that of Burnham, his San Francisco sponsors, and the whole City Beautiful movement. An imperial city was designed for men of empire. Even the more democratic provisions of the Burnham Report took for granted an affable helotry, content in their part of the city, pacified by bread and circuses. A triumphant neo-baroque city, Burnham's San Francisco gloried in social and spiritual order, a sense of grandeur, obedience, and contained harmony. His plan flattered his sponsors' sense of San Francisco's importance, although they must have known it socially, politically, and economically impossible of realization. Atop Twin Peaks shimmered an acropolis: colonnaded shelters and temple-like edifices, courts and terraces where San Franciscans in oddly contrasting broadcloth might walk and talk in the sun. From a grand civic center at Van Ness and Market, nine boulevards radiated outward, intersected at intervals by concentric arteries which ringed the city, the largest skirting the waterfront and following the coast down the peninsula. Great parkways swept the city, making possible movement and magnificence, linking a number of open green areas: at Hunter's Point, Visitacion Valley, Buena Vista Heights, Lone Mountain, the Presidio, Twin Peaks, and Telegraph Hill. The park Burnham planned for Lake Merced was triple the size of Golden Gate Park. Throughout this dream-city of squares and boulevards, fountains splashed; and from reservoirs at staggered heights, water cascaded down open aqueducts into a system of inner-city lakes. Roadways moved in harmony with landscape, caressing hills, counterpointing contours. Geometric platting was abandoned and, where now stood checkerboards of uselessly small back yards, homes opened onto community gardens.

On 17 April 1906 the Burnham Report, fresh from the printer's, was deposited in City Hall prior to distribution. A little past five the next morning a mighty tremor struck the city. Within three days the interior portion of San Francisco lay in ruins. Telegraphed in France of the disaster, Burnham left at once for San Francisco, confident that his plan would provide the guidelines for rebuilding. "San Francisco of the future will be the most beautiful city of the continent, with the possible exception of Washington," he said upon arrival at the ruined metropolis.[5] He went to work lobbying among the business community, to whom he had always looked for support and who had commissioned the San Francisco plans in the first place. Matters looked hopeful. On 21 April 1906, while the city yet burned, the *Chronicle* headlined:

SAN FRANCISCO WILL RISE FROM THE ASHES
A GREATER AND MORE BEAUTIFUL CITY THAN EVER.[6]

Support for the implementation of the Burnham Plan grew among city leaders, spearheaded by James D. Phelan; Rudolph Spreckels; architects John Galen Howard and Willis Polk; Benjamin Ide Wheeler, president of the University of California; John McLaren, developer of Golden Gate Park. The Burnham Plan, like the proposed Panama-Pacific International Exposition, became a symbol of recovery. The *Call*, the *Examiner*, and the *Chronicle* all editorialized in favor of it. Had not the city risen from its ashes six times in the 1850's, asked Hubert Howe Bancroft? And had it not recovered from a number of stunning economic disasters in the last quarter-century? "Let us have the city beautiful by all means," Bancroft urged, "—it will pay."[7]

Beyond economic considerations, the rebuilding of San Francisco took on dimensions of atonement. Notorious for vice and corruption, the city, many said, had passed through an ordeal by fire. It had been purified, the slate wiped clean. Symbol of this redemption would be the shimmering city to rise on San Francisco's hills, expressing in outward beauty spiritual regeneration, just as ugliness had once expressed its sinfulness. Hubert Howe Bancroft was genuinely stirred by "the cleansing effect of fire." It rescued the city from sinful idleness, he asserted, giving back to San Franciscans the sense of mission and excitement known by pioneer forebears. San Franciscans seized upon this notion of a renewed frontier, this chance for quickening of purpose and regeneration of spirit. Even costuming reflected it, city clothes being abandoned for boots, jodhpurs, and Baden-Powells, representative attire of Stanford seniors and Jack London, redolent of heroic dash and California enterprise.

Purged by fire, rebuilt along lines of Burnham's City Beautiful, its population invigorated by a return to the frontier, San Francisco—so rhetoric went—would become America's new City on a Hill: "the new city by the western sea," said the *Bulletin* a week after the disaster, "the home of the strongest, bravest, and sturdiest people of their race." If indeed, backers of the Burnham Plan pointed out, a new Pacific civilization would be ushered in with the completion of the Panama Canal, then let San Francisco prepare herself for Pacific queenship. In that future day, wrote Bancroft, "when the shores of the Pacific are occupied as the shores of the Atlantic now are, when all around the vast arena formed by America, Asia, and Australia are great nations of wealth and culture, with hundreds of Bostons and Baltimores, of Londons and Liverpools, the great American republic would scarcely be satisfied with only a porter's lodge at her western gateway."[8]

Such was the dream of first days. Soon, less exalted voices were heard, sometimes from Burnham's backers speaking from the other side of their mouths. In late May opposition by the Downtown Business Men's Association to the Burnham Plan broke into the open. M. H. De Young, owner and publisher of the *Chronicle*, led the fight. "The crying need of San Francisco today," editorialized the *Chronicle*, "is not more parks and boulevards; it is business." "Are they here now, these new city-builders," Bancroft had asked, "or must San Francisco wait for another generation?" The decision was to wait for another generation and to rebuild San Francisco along the old lines as quickly as possible. Much of the blame lay with the Burnham Plan itself. Like other expressions of the City Beautiful movement, it was socially unrealistic, a paper renovation without context or muscle. The Committee of Forty appointed to oversee reconstruction was torn by faction, the progressive element, led by Phelan, opposing attempts by Abraham ("Boss") Ruef to roll out the pork barrel. A year later Ruef was brought before a grand jury. His sensational trial took attention away from the Burnham Plan once and for all. Within three and a half years downtown San Francisco was rebuilt along pre-earthquake lines. Within five years, recovery was total. Except for fireproof construction in commercial buildings, the new city reproduced the worst features of the old: gridiron streets crowded with flimsy wooden units packed side by side in treeless monotony.

Architectural critics took the rebuilt city to task. One chided San Franciscans for the impermanent air of its new homes, as if another holocaust were expected. Another complained of "dreary stretches of inharmonious architecture." "Its citizens like to talk about it as the Paris of America," scoffed a writer in *The Architectural Review,* "but French restaurants, electric lights and a prevailing atmosphere of gayety do not make a Paris. A metropolitan city must be tied together by a plan which provides for every essential economic and aesthetic need; and San Francisco still remains devoid of such a plan."[9] By 1914 German city planner Werner Hegeman, at work in the East Bay, found San Francisco a convenient source of examples of what not to do in planning a city. In eight years utopia had become dystopia, the premier California city an anti-Californian statement.

Not only were San Franciscans self-conscious regarding these criticisms, they themselves felt another loss, an awareness of changed mood and atmosphere between—in Jack London's terms—old 'Frisco and new San Francisco. Had the frontier been recovered in rebuilding the city, only to be lost again in the skyscrapers? Many were quick to assure themselves that fire and earthquake could do nothing to the inner spirit of the Pacific metropolis. Others were not so sure. Sitting at his typewriter at the New York *Sun* when news of the disaster began to come over the wires, Will Irwin, Stanford man, ex-San Francisco bohemian and journalist, stayed up all night to pound out a eulogy to the dying city. With moving nostalgia, Irwin recalled San Francisco's gay public life, its art, song, and spirited throngs. The town which now baked in its own fires, wrote Irwin, would never be the same. "It is as though a pretty, frivolous woman had passed through a great tragedy. She survives, but she is sobered and different. If it rises out of the ashes it must be a modern city, much like other cities and without its old atmosphere."[10]

Entering upon the design and construction of its international exposition, San Francisco was possessed of an ambivalent and somewhat contradictory self-image. As an imaginative ideal, the Burnham Plan offered a culmination, a fulfillment in urban terms of California history. As a post-earthquake program, it proved unacceptable. The ideal remained, giving rise to anxiety over failure to realize Burnham's projects, an anxiety compounded by awareness that the new city had neither the rascally charm of old San Francisco, nor the marmoreal grandeur of Burnham's vision. San Francisco seemed neither ramshackle frontier outpost nor baroque imperial city, but just another provincial business town. As a fantasy, the Panama-Pacific International Exposition offered a resolution to this identity problem. More malleable than Montgomery Street, it could be endowed with all the ideality absent in the new city, all the lost color, spaciousness, and gaiety. If gray, looming skyscrapers said something about one San Francisco, the Exposition might give utterance to the city of the mind which yet haunted Bay Area Californians. And it would pay.

In addition to functioning as a symbolic substitute for the disregarded Burnham Plan, the Exposition was also a serious effort in city planning. Since the Philadelphia Centennial Exposition of 1876, when Americans first glimpsed the possibility of large-scale arrangement of buildings, city planning and expositions had developed interdependently. Many fairs resulted in the salvaging of hitherto unusable areas. San Francisco proved no exception. The Exposition Company purchased and razed over 400 dwellings scattered across the marshy Harbor View area, filling in acre upon acre previously under twenty-five feet of water, pushing, as in the 1850's, San Francisco further into the Bay. Open to sea and sky, stretching panoramically beneath the hills of the Presidio, with an unobstructed view of the Marin hills across the Bay, the setting salvaged for the Exposition (known today as the Marina) was no doubt one of the most aesthetically exciting pieces of urban real estate in the United States. Upon this *tabula rasa,* as temptingly bare as inner San Francisco after the fire, architects and planners, under the leadership of Edward Bennett (who had assisted Burnham in Chicago in 1893 and in San Francisco in 1905) realized a City Beautiful, an interplay of boulevards, courts and monumental edifices, where fountains splashed and colors glowed in the sun. For ten months, from 20 February to 4 December 1915, San Francisco had its dream-city.

The link between the Exposition and the Burnham Plan was obvious, although there was an irony in the contrast between its California ideality, with gardens and marine esplanade all emphasizing outdoor living, and the huddled, indeterminate quality of rebuilt San Francisco. The Exposition itself became a metaphor for future California cities, dream engendering dreams. The integration of architecture, gardening, sculpture, and color seemed especially expressive of good regional design. Midway through the Exposition, an *ad hoc* committee urged the establishment of a commission in order to maintain city planning momentum and to preserve specific items of Exposition architecture, notably the California Building, magnificent in the Mission style, and the Palace of Fine Arts.

Desire to preserve Bernard R. Maybeck's Palace of Fine Arts was widespread. Together with San Francisco's Civic Center (initiated in conjunction with the Exposition and conceived as a permanent project), Maybeck's creation alone survived dismantlement. It did so primarily because of its overwhelming critical and popular success. Ironically, Maybeck had almost been excluded from participation in the Exposition on the ground that he had no large buildings to his credit. This threat represented another slight against the innovative architect by the Beaux Arts establishment, which was itself content to spread classical façades across the Californian landscape. Maybeck wanted a new, distinct California idiom, a blending of free form, wood and stone, an architecture that was organic, fond of color, open to sun, expressive of landscape. Whatever the commission might be, Maybeck, defying the conventional, bore witness to regionalism; the private residences he designed (central statements of what Lewis Mumford later dubbed the Bay Region Style), the faculty club and women's gymnasium at the University in Berkeley, the Christian Science Church of that city, Mrs. Phoebe Hearst's "Wyntoon," a summer retreat on the McCloud River—each product of Maybeck's drafting board was a success in itself and helped lay foundations for a new California architecture. Yet the California establishment refrained from offering Maybeck any large-scale commissions. Instead of hiring Maybeck, a university instructor and a Berkeley resident, they brought in traditionalist John Galen Howard from New York to supervise construction of Emile Bénard's master plan. Maybeck's dramatic, visually appropriate faculty club stood in marked contrast to the elephantine pedantry of imperial marble which rose under Howard's supervision. Willis Polk, a former student of Maybeck's, one of *Les Jeunes* and by the early 1900's a prominent San Francisco architect, was first given the commission for the Palace of Fine Arts. Seeing Maybeck's sketches, he persuaded the Architectural Commission to hand over responsibility to his former teacher. Maybeck designed the Palace while drawing draftsman's wages in Polk's office.

Remaining within the Beaux Arts idiom of the Exposition, Maybeck created a romantic orchestration of dome, column, colonnade, and lagoon. He avoided the showy eclectic ornamentation of the other buildings and kept to simple statement. The Palace, said Maybeck, was meant to suggest "an old Roman ruin, away from civilization, which two thousand years before was the center of action and full of life, and now is partly overrgown with bushes and trees." He noted that "physical forms reflect a mental condition." Nostalgic, time-drenched, evocative of a yearning for lost loveliness and glory, Maybeck's "California text" articulated the mood that pervaded post-earthquake San Francisco: a sense of vanished possibilities, lost romance, conquest by time. "This mighty work is to architecture," said one observer, "what tragedy is to drama."[11] The nemesis of this tragedy was San Francisco's obvious and affronting newness. Artificial travertine plaster covered Exposition buildings because, buff-colored and porous, it created the effect of age. John McLaren's huge hedge wall grew from the suggestion that something "moss-covered with age" should skirt the fairgrounds. In his color scheme, Jules Guerin explicitly sought to avoid the raw newness of Chicago's White City. Summarized in Maybeck's Palace of Fine Arts, the Exposition attempted a counter-statement to rebuilt San Francisco. Maybeck's Palace of Fine Arts had mythic dimensions. It expressed to San Franciscans something deep and fundamental about what they had lost in the destruction of their city, and they were loath to lose their symbol which magically regained for them the vanished past. California's City on a Hill, purged by fire, found expression not in downtown San Francisco, but in Maybeck's russet-hued evocation of time, tragedy, and romance.

II

The primary impulse behind the Exposition was promotional: California said to the world that it had come of age. So long accused of violence and barbarism, Californians now saw themselves preserving the arts of civilization while Europe sank into Armageddon. Camille Saint-Saëns composed a symphony to this effect, "Hail California!," scored for an orchestra of eighty, a military brass band of sixty (conducted by John Philip Sousa), an organ, and a 300-voice choir. "There is still much of the popular conception abroad," observed Eugen Neuhaus, "that the West has only very recently emerged from a state of semi-civilization inimical to the finer things of life, and to art in particular. But we may rest assured that the fortunate outsider who allows himself the luxury of travel will proclaim that the gospel of beauty has been preached most eloquently through the Panama-Pacific International Exposition."[12]

The most striking act of self-assertion on the part of California was the Exposition's color scheme. Architecturally speaking, there had always been a tension between the assumed colorfulness of life in California and the drab houses in which Californians lived. By the mid-1880's, Californians began to aspire toward a regional use of color in domestic architecture and decoration which they hoped would intensify a distinctly colorful quality of life. Villa Rose, a splendid mansion near Burlingame, won Porter Garnett's approval because of its daring use of rose-colored concrete. Charles Keeler, who paid a great deal of attention to the specifics of California living, advised bungalow builders to favor warm tones such as buff, brown, red, deep blue, and rich green. Psychologically, Keeler asserted, such colors acted as a reinforcement of the sort of consciously aesthetic life Californians should pursue. The California bungalow itself blended wood and stone exteriors with interior colors that were supposed to evoke the hues of the surrounding landscape, thus creating an interplay of coloration. The feeling that color was essential to California was manifest in criticisms directed against certain local painters, including such illustrious names as William Keith and Francis McComas, accusing them of using too low-keyed a color scheme in interpreting the California landscape. A passion for color played an important part in the Spanish-Colonial Revival. One authority on Spanish Revival decoration had to warn that, while blue-green, burnt-orange, vermilion, and ochre were acceptable, use of salmon pink and lavender was carrying matters a little too far.

In terms of color, San Francisco felt itself unfulfilled. *Picturesque California Homes* (1885) praised San Francisco's use of maroon, yellow, brown, and red in interior decoration, but from an exterior perspective San Francisco was a depressingly lead-colored city. Less than a month after the fire and earthquake, the *Call* urged San Franciscans not to use the old Quaker drab in rebuilding. Shall we, it asked, have the former "sack-cloth and penitential aspect, or will we blossom out in warm and cheerful tints?" With few exceptions, San Francisco was reclothed in banker's gray. The Exposition offered San Franciscans an opportunity to express their hunger for color, denied in the rebuilding of their city. Jules Guerin was selected to serve as Chief of Color. "I saw the vibrant tints of the native wild flowers," he said of Harbor View, "the soft browns of the surrounding hills, the gold of the orangeries, the blue of the sea; and I determined that, just as a musician builds his symphony around a motif or chord, so must I strike a chord of color and build my symphony on this."[13] Guerin's reputation resulted from his illustrations of Southern Europe and the Levant, work showing a fondness for a pastel treatment of Mediterranean settings. Guerin's inner vision thus articulated an important California fantasy. His Mediterranean dream was California's own.

"In coloring a vast city of this kind," Guerin said, "I treated it as I would a canvas for a picture." Because it absorbed light, blended into the landscape, and had Mediterranean associations, he chose an artificial travertine substance, made from gypsum and hemp fiber, as the basic tonal value. Upon this he spread his colors, "always," he noted, "having in mind the strong light of California, and keeping colors well toned down and mellow."[14] John McLaren made sure that flowering plants were in harmony with Guerin's scheme and had the sand used in pathways fired in a furnace until it reached an agreeable cinnamon. As Guerin intended, critics speculated what this chromatic spectacle signified. Guerin himself hoped that his scenic use of color would influence city planners and architects in California to depart from the staid coloration inappropriate to a region of sunlight. Agreement prevailed that, whatever else, something special had been said about California. Mary Austin, a member of the Pageantry Commission, saw in Exposition color evidence of much of what she hoped for from California. The Panama-Pacific International Exposition, she wrote, was California's first major communal expression. Californians, Austin asserted, had a Greek taste for pageantry, festival, and secular liturgy. It was part of the Mediterranean quality of California. Guerin's color scheme scenically expressed this pagan passion for sun and art and life. In these hues, she believed, "the West has satisfied the secret desire of its heart."[15]

The showing of the work of more than fifty California painters at the Palace of Fine Arts provided another opportunity for regional assessment. The tangible presence of sixty years of local art demanded interpretation. A symposium, published in 1916 as *Art in California*, gathered together the fruits of retrospect. First of all, although fifty painters had been on exhibit, California's critics did not yet see any cohesive California tradition. It was still a possibility, something to be achieved from present and past elements. Californians had produced art, Porter Garnett pointed out, but not an art, "that is to say, there is not yet an art that is characteristically Californian and at the same time universal." Most of the fifty painters on exhibit were either Europeans or Eastern-born and trained. California had liberated talent, but fragmentedly, without coherence or integration. There were no consistent regional traits. The work of Xavier Martinez pointed in the direction the emerging tradition might hopefully take: a note of freshness and a sense of wonder at new beginnings. Yet with sixty years of effort made visible in the showing, critics detected, if not a tradition, then at least patterns for future use. Indian art provided foundations next to nature itself, bringing the California artist to a realization that only in close, unconscious relationship to the land could he hope to interpret its mysteries. The more than 1000 canvases painted in the missions taught that true art sprang from a communal impulse and was grounded in the rhythms and myths of everyday life. Frontier artists such as Albert Bierstadt, Thomas Hill, Thomas Moran, and William Keith asserted the comforting fact that art had been present from the beginning of American California, running a faint but steady stream down the nineteenth century. The experience of the 1880's and 1890's provided a usable lesson, albeit a negative one; for during this era California developed a generation of artists only to lose them to New York, dramatizing the necessity of support.

Not only did California possess a usable art history, it possessed representative artists in Arthur Putnam and William Keith. Putnam demonstrated the vitality—and the inadequacy—of the California art experience. Former cowpuncher, lumberjack, and South-of-Market roustabout, Putnam devised animal sculptures of truly Western vigor. Yet Californians preferred Venuses, winged cupids, and dying gladiators in their foyers, finding Putnam's muscled honesty the antithesis of cultivation. Impoverished, Putnam was forced to live in a shack near the ocean, and he suffered a nervous breakdown in 1913, brought about in part by the failure of Californians to support his work. "The neglect of the presence of such an authentic original genius as Arthur Putnam here in California," said San Francisco *Examiner* critic Michael Williams, "does not do the state any credit. The City of San Francisco, which should be proud of his presence, and should exalt his art, disfigures its new Civic Center with cast-iron fountains and commonplace animal figures, while in the leaky little studio near the ocean beach there are models of truly monumental magnificence."[16] Putnam was represented at the Exposition by fourteen small bronze sculptures. William Keith was accorded an entire room. Putnam went hungry. Keith, bourgeois practitioner of muted Barbizon landscapes, attained an income of $60,000 a year.

The Putnam-Keith dichotomy fascinated critics because it seemed symptomatic of a divided sense within California as a whole: the perennial conflict between the desire for frontier vigor and genteel respectability. Keith's output, dating from 1859 to 1911, gave proof of sustained dedication. His Eastern origins with the Hudson River School, his self-tutelage, his response to Oriental influences, his rise to prosperity as a painter of California landscapes, the patronage and friendships accorded him by the establishment, all conspired to make his career a one-man epic, a story of regional justification and fulfillment. Strangely enough, however, critics withheld final laurels. The specter of Putnam haunted them. Keith's dreamy, muted landscapes lacked the vigor, boldness, and color felt appropriate to great California art. Keith the genteel might have been more rewarded—in his lifetime and at the Exposition—but Putnam's strength, honesty, and physicality held the critical imagination of 1915, on the lookout for a usable tradition.

Putnam's appeal lay in the democratic implications of his direct, uncomplicated sculptures, so opposed to the bourgeois self-indulgence of Keith's muted and melancholy landscapes. Exposition critics claimed they saw a democratic impulse central to the emerging California art tradition. They pointed to the high attendance at the California section of the Palace of Fine Arts. It was the people of California, noted Michael Williams, "more than the artists of the West who won the most notable victory. The extent, the depth, the seriousness of the public response to the art of the Exposition deeply impressed all competent observers. . . . California is experiencing what appears to be nothing less than the birth throes of a reawakened popular consciousness of art's place in human life."[17] All such hopes depended upon faith in California as an art environment. "We may kick against the pricks of environment out here in California," wrote Anthony Anderson, art critic for the Los Angeles *Times*; "we may bemoan our distance from the 'art centers,' but neither we nor our talents die of inanition. Nor do we know the suffocating feeling of being buried alive."[18] For if California was remote, asserted Bruce Porter, it was a special kind of remoteness, not that of a backward province, but that of a cosmopolitan colony, in intimate and vital relationship with Eastern and European trends, possessed of its own, non-derivative sense of life. Let this sense of life find its way into California's art, urged the critics of *Art in California*. Let California painting be vigorous, colorful, cosmopolitan, and democratic. In the California section of the Palace of Fine Arts was evidence of strong beginnings. "So far as we have gone," noted Bruce Porter, "our worth appears to lie, not so much in what we have *done*, as in what we are and promise to become."[19]

III

In one sense, the Panama-Pacific International Exposition was a text of California progressivism, a not-too-profound but large-scale expression of an important California attitude. The California progressive was of old American stock, neither unionist nor capitalist, and haunted by the lost simplicities of nineteenth-century America. He believed in individualism in the service of progress—the ideals, in short, advocated by David Starr Jordan. Within the manageable world of the Exposition, progressivist notions found extensive expression, although, like the Exposition genre itself, progressivism had somewhat passed its peak. Signaling the end of California's turn-of-the-century era, the San Francisco Exposition provided an opportunity for a last lingering look at the ideals of a generation.

For the final time, the rhetoric of the frontier flared up with assuring incandescence. Lotta Crabtree, who as a girl had sung for the miners, made an appearance in Festival Hall, flanked by survivors of the 1860's and 1870's. At the dedication of a statue to honor the Pioneer Mother of California, Mrs. Pattie Lewis Reed, the only surviving member of the Donner party, addressed the crowd on the horrors of the winter of 1846. The two most popular sculptures dealt with frontier subjects, James Earle Fraser's "The End of the Trail," depicting an exhausted Indian and his pony, and Solon Borglum's "The Pioneer," depicting an old frontiersman (many said Joaquin Miller) mounting his horse for a last ride. Both statues had overtones of finality, facts made much of by commentators. "Astride his ancient pony," said one writer of Borglum's equestrian, "hung with chance trappings . . . with axe and rifle with which he conquered the wilderness, he broods the past."[20] So too brooded California, for a final, and near impossible time. After 1915 the frontier was lost forever. During the Exposition year, for the last time in the California experience, it was felt as a faint, but palpable presence. The rebuilding of San Francisco had briefly revived frontier mythology just at the time when it was disappearing forever. The frontier provided an imaginative analogue for the task of creating a city *a novo*. United States Secretary of the Interior Franklin K. Lane, a Californian, told opening-day crowds that the Pioneer was the real hero of the Exposition, albeit a hero whose last days had arrived. "The long journey of this slight, modest figure that stands beside the oxen is at an end," said Lane, pointing to the sculpture "The American Pioneer." "But adventure is not to end. Here in his house will be taught the gospel of an advancing democracy—strong, valiant, confident, conquering—upborne and typified by the independent, venturesome spirit of that mythic materialist, the American pioneer."[21]

Lane's remarks underscored the Exposition's elaborate expression of the nineteenth-century historical fable which saw California as the grand exemplar of Social Darwinism. The spirit of Bancroft's *History of the Pacific States* informed architectural and sculptural motifs, themes described by one Director as "rough, brutal, Darwinian, evolutionary." Louis Christian Mullgardt's Court of Ages provided the central Darwinian text. Critics called it "the cathedral of the Exposition"—"the holy of holies"—"the place of prayer."If so, it was a temple to faith in the gospel of Progress. Like a medieval cathedral, Mullgardt's Court of Ages set forth the story of creation. Decorative motifs began with sea plants and crustacean life, ascending through the animal kingdom upward along the Tower of Ages until they reached Albert Weinert's sculptures of prehistoric man and woman, which surmounted the entrance to the Tower. Statues by Chester A. Beach and Robert Aitken carried the prehistoric couple through various stages of civilization until the apex of the Tower, where sat "the Present Age," a mother with her children. In the central courtyard, the Fountain of Psychology of Life and the Fountain of Earth depicted points of advance on the road to civilization. Lest the direction of all this evolutionary movement be forgotten, the Adventurous Bowman atop the Column of Progress loosed his arrow westward. Above the Arch of the Setting Sun were representations of the various racial stocks which peopled the trans-Mississippi. They guided a prairie schooner in which sat a young pioneer girl and two smaller boys. "A broad-shouldered, fine framed, brawny young woman," said one critic, just the type of courageous, no-nonsense person needed on the California frontier.[22]

Evolution, progress, the frontier—comforting notions to progressive Californians. But what of the overwhelming presence of industrial exhibits? The turn-of-the-century California dream had been anti-industrial and agrarian in its most fundamental nature, if not literally a return to the land, then at least the nature-worship of the Carmelites, the passion for the strenuous life of the Sierra Club, or the aesthetic proximity, the garden-consciousness, of the educated bourgeoisie. In their ideality, San Diego, Pasadena, Santa Barbara, and San Jose were consciously anti-industrial towns. But the fact of California's incipient industrialization was openly acknowledged at the Exposition; indeed, gloried in. In the Palace of Transportation, a Ford rolled off an assembly line every ten minutes. The diesel engine dominated the heavy machinery display. One visitor walked amidst the diesels in a spirit dramatically different from that of Henry Adams among the dynamos at Saint Louis. "Here, in truth, is the essence of this Exposition," wrote French Strother. "Ten years ago, men walked bewildered among the machines they had built, and even the strongest hearted feared that the race had delivered itself up to a soul-less Superman made of steam and steel and chemicals. To-day, men have conquered these servants and freed their own spirits."[23]

The Exposition declared the diesel an inevitable part of California's destiny. Well, then, answered the California progressive, let the age of the diesel be democratic. The administrative structure of the Exposition was supposed to demonstrate "according to the best Anglo-Saxon tradition . . . the organic principle of representation by delegated authority." President Charles Moore was the perfect example of a progressivist public official—"a democratic man and a vitalizing personality, honoring work, and doing loads of it himself every day." Designing the Fair had been a cooperative enterprise, "not designed for the greater glory of individual architects, but for the enjoyment and intellectual stimulus of the people." On opening day, 20 February 1915, elaborate ceremonies were shunned. Governor Hiram Johnson and San Francisco Mayor James Rolph led 150,000 people onto the grounds in democratic simplicity. Poet Edwin Markham thought the Panama-Pacific International Exposition presaged "what men can do when they unite in common service." "The artists have bent to one perfect expression," he noted, "like the strings and basses of an orchestra. Self was submerged in a composite achievement, not obliterating individuality but leaving it latitude to harmonize with others. . . . Here is an object lesson in the co-operative idea that will not be lost upon the world—the idea of a transcendent result obtained by a unity of noble efforts, a result that no massing of individual attempts could have achieved."[24]

The San Francisco Exposition carried turn-of-the-century aspirations into a new era. The destruction of San Francisco by earthquake and fire in 1906 provides a substantial and manifestly symbolic point of demarcation between nineteenth- and twentieth-century California. The Exposition, however, prolonged the transitional period and gave it spatial expression. Strolling down one of its grand boulevards on a bright California day, surveying the courts and palaces whose connection with the Chicago of 1893 was so obvious, a visitor could experience a mingled atmosphere of nineteenth and twentieth centuries, the naïve 1890's assertion of neo-imperial and the assured 1915 assertion of diesel. Moving from the mission romance of the California Building to the as-of-yet unassessed atmosphere of the Palace of Machinery, one might wonder where hovered the true consciousness of the host state. Frontier rhetoric and diesel fact resisted synthesis. Sentiment at the Panama-Pacific International Exposition pointed backward; facts pointed forward. Guerin's color scheme possessed different emotional resonances from the metallic gray of heavy machinery. Horses were being judged in the livestock sheds, but in the Palace of Transportation Fords rolled off the assembly line. The Exposition was San Francisco's dream-city, and it resembled its real prototype in that it was ready and anxious to do business. The Exposition simultaneously invoked a new California and bade farewell to an old dream. The dream was in the color, in the Mediterranean ideality of much of the architecture, in Maybeck's nostalgia-drenched Palace of Fine Arts. The invocation was in the myriads of industrial and technological exhibits. In the years that saw the planning and completion of the Exposition, progressives woke up to the fact that they wanted both realities, both Californias. Having experienced the breakup of their political coalition, they attempted to transfer old values into the new scheme, hoping to subdue the new California to their purposes. Sadly, they realized that their private, manageable California was no more. It had been lost somewhere between the pseudo-romance of the mission towers of the California Building and the skyscraper anonymity of downtown San Francisco. New myths, new formulations would be necessary for the upcoming urban-industrial phenomenon. Older, more naïve regional identities were breaking apart, although literature and architecture survived the hostility of the diesel age to go on to even grander assertions of locality.

Finally and most importantly, San Francisco's Panama-Pacific International Exposition bespoke the need for design, for the visual ordering of inner myths. If California had all the lush possibilities of Guerin's color scheme and McLaren's planting, then let a concern for line and form contain that luxuriance, domesticate it, make it accessible and significant. City, garden, home—let each express a concern for taste and harmony amidst almost overwhelming richness. Let California's cities structure the growth they would invoke. Let its architecture liberate romance, but also contain it. Let the land bloom, but let landscaping prevent a phantasmagoria of fecundity. Each point of Exposition rhetoric represented an inner nexus of past hopes and failures. San Francisco might dream of the ideal city, but opportunities for such achievement had been woefully squandered. But expositions were never under strong obligation to the reality principle, and the record of a dream always had value.

10

Life Among the Best and Truest:

David Starr Jordan and the Founding of Stanford University

Even before the death of his fifteen-year-old son in Florence in March 1884, Leland Stanford had been considering what to do with his wealth. Stanford provisionally intended to will the bulk of his fortune to his son, born in 1868 after eighteen years of childless marriage, but he also wanted to do something for California, where he had accumulated his millions. The death of his boy from fever left the Senator dazed and purposeless. His parental hopes and his half-formed notion of a California benefaction fused. Exhausted by his vigil at young Leland's deathbed, Senator Stanford fell into a restless half-sleep, half-stupor. "Live for humanity!" he heard his son say. When the Senator awoke, despair had given way to direction. "The children of California shall be our children," he vowed. The form of that adoption would be a university. Returning to the United States, Senator and Mrs. Stanford, neither of them college graduates, although the Senator did attend an upstate New York academy before reading for the bar, visited Yale, Harvard, the Massachusetts Institute of Technology, Cornell, Columbia, and Johns Hopkins in order to familiarize themselves with the forms and procedures of higher education. They tried to secure the services of the president of one of these institutions, but in each case the generous sums offered by Stanford could not lure such established captains of erudition from their Eastern posts. In the course of each negotiation, the Stanfords heard the name of David Starr Jordan, the dynamic young president of the University of Indiana. Stanford preferred a more established Eastern figure, but Jordan was willing to move to California. In 1891 Jordan left Bloomington for the Stanfords' Palo Alto farm south of San Francisco, the newly appointed president of Leland Stanford Junior University.

Expectation ran high. Everything conspired to surround the undertaking with an atmosphere of promise: the Stanford fortune; the tragic origins of the institution; the idea that California, barely emerged from the frontier, should be the site of a major institution of higher learning. After successive delays, opening day was set for the fall of 1891. Delay stimulated rhetoric on the part of those favorable to the new university and ridicule on the part of Senator Stanford's many enemies. Eastern papers flailed him for dividing California's higher educational effort. California needed more high schools, they claimed, not universities. The university rising in the wheat fields of the Palo Alto farm seemed to one New York paper about as useful as a summer hotel in Central Africa or a home for retired ship captains in Switzerland. "The professors for years," the New York *Mail and Express* felt certain, "will lecture in marble halls to empty benches." Many Californians feared that Stanford University would weaken the state institution at Berkeley. The *Overland Monthly* took another tack. Excited by the fact that the new university's $20 million endowment made it four times as well endowed as Harvard or Columbia, the *Overland* saw in the quadrangles rising in the Santa Clara Valley, forty miles south of San Francisco, evidence of California's cultural coming of age. At last, exulted the *Overland*, California fortunes were finding expression, not in garish Nob Hill mansions, but in great public benefactions.

As Jordan detrained at Menlo Park early in the summer of 1891, he was warmed by a similar optimism. The idea of Stanford's historical significance pervaded his inaugural address that October. In background and beliefs, David Starr Jordan fitted well into the California scheme. Within a few years after his arrival, he would become inseparably identified with the state's deepest cultural aspirations.

Jordan was that type of New Englander so prominent in the nineteenth-century struggle for higher education in California. Born in Gainesville, New York, in 1851, Jordan came of New England stock. His mother, Anne Waldo, enjoyed local prestige as the third or fourth cousin of Ralph Waldo Emerson. The *Atlantic Monthly*, symbolic of the family's cultural allegiances, lay on the table in the Jordan parlor. David's father, a farmer, nourished his leisure hours with a steady diet of New England transcendental and Unitarian writing. As a boy, David Jordan became so enamored with Thomas Starr King's *Christianity and Humanity*, with its Unitarian-Universalist call to service, that he assumed "Starr" as a middle name and, in later years, saw his own California career as being conducted in the pattern of the San Francisco minister's.

Unorthodox in religion, Jordan devised for himself a displaced Puritan ethic, with evolution for a metaphysic and physical fitness for an ascetical theology. Six feet two inches tall, Jordan pursued the strenuous life well into his sixties, as a field scientist, baseball player, hiker, camper, and mountain climber. He conquered the Matterhorn in 1881, one of the first Americans to do so. Californians appreciated the Stanford president's heartiness, with its evolutionary overtones. It reinforced their conception of themselves as a vigorous folk, on the spearhead of history. Trained as a physician, Jordan waged a lifelong campaign against alcohol, tobacco, and stimulants of any kind, even tea and coffee. His objections were philosophical as well as physiological. Indulgence destroyed health, and weak bodies meant weak perceptions of moral realities.

Jordan realized that "without the saving grace of humour," the Puritan mind could lead "into all extravagance, witch-burnings, Quaker-stoning, heresy trials, and intolerance of politics and religion." Yet he felt that the New England contribution lay at the base of American civilization, especially in the matter of what he praised as America's Puritan conscience, its final preference for moral standards above all others. As an amateur genealogist, he liked to point out that one-fifth of the American population was descended from Puritan stock, the one-fifth whose "influence and institutions predominate in the civic, educational, and religious life of the American community." The West itself, he told Californians, had been won by New England farmers, pushing out from rocky hills to better land. As immigration threatened to push that old American one-fifth to the wall, Jordan's fascination with Anglo-Saxon superiority grew. "Only the Saxon and the Goth know the meaning of freedom," he asserted, a statement read and cherished by young Jack London, hard at work in his Oakland home upon stories of Anglo-Saxon superiority in the Far North. "In these times," Jordan told the class of 1898 at Stanford (lines which Jack London copied out by hand), "it is well for us to remember that we come of hardy stock. The Anglo-Saxon race, with its strength and virtues, was born of hard times. It is not easily kept down; the victims of oppression must be of some other stock. We who live in America and who constitute the heart of this republic, are the sons and daughters of 'him that overcometh.' "[1]

Irish, Greeks, Italians, and Jews, Jordan believed, could never measure up to Anglo-Saxon standards. He kept a record of arrests in Santa Clara Valley and was gratified to see that immigrant names dominated the list. More biological elitist than bigot, he left open the possibility that other stocks might prosper in the United States, as long as they were represented by their best. How long would America thrive, he asked? "Just so long as the blood of the founders remains dominant in the blood of its people. Not necessarily the blood of the Puritans and the Virginians alone, the original creators of the land of free states. We must not read our history so narrowly as that. It is the blood of free-born men, be they Greek, Roman, Frank, Saxon, Norman, Dane, Scot, Goth or Samurai."[2]

The use of ancient designations instead of modern national names says much of Jordan's worship of unspoiled vigor. As a natural scientist and as a social thinker, he was fascinated by what Jack London called the Strength of the Strong. He believed that the major intellectual breakthrough of the twentieth century would be an explanation of the biological basis for social structures. His anti-war stand, in many ways atypical of an elitist position, was motivated by a belief that war kills off a nation's best human specimens. Jordan resisted immigration because too often, he felt, the eugenically inferior debarked at Ellis Island. Believing that "the survival of the unfittest is the primal cause of the downfall of nations," Jordan suggested that "at Castle Garden in New York, we should turn back . . . those whose descendants are likely through incompetence and vice to be a permanent burden on our social or political order."[3]

Within the California context, Jordan's notions had powerful overtones. His theory of history had been California's from the first. In a state undergoing severe demographic transformation, a state which, with fear and trembling—added to anticipated economic advantage—was positive that it would be the primary point of immigration once the Panama Canal was completed, Jordan trumpeted the Old American, the Yankee. Such had always constituted the elite of the state, in uneasy alliance with the wealthy Irish, and they were anxious to retain their position in the new era. As an educator, Jordan symbolically prepared the Protestant elite to control California's polyglot future. "The industry engendered by the pioneer life of the last generation is still in your veins," he assured California students. "Sons and daughters of the Western pioneers, yours is the best blood in the realm." In Jordan's mind, "the essential source of Californianism lies in heredity. The Californian of to-day is the type of his father of fifty years ago. The Argonauts of '49 were buoyant, self-reliant, adequate, reckless, thoroughly individualistic, capable of all adjustments, careless of conventions, eager to enjoy life and action. And we, their sons, with all admixture of other blood and of other temperament are still made in their image. It is blood which tells."[4] In the process of self-identification that characterized the turn of the century, Jordan played ideologue of an Anglo-Saxonism open to healthy outside influences. The basis of California, he suggested, might be New England Yankee, its best heritage Puritan, but new people, as long as they possessed vigor, could be fused into the California stock. Immigration need not upset social stability. The West allowed only the strong to survive, and upon the forge of that imperative would be beaten out new California steel.

"Never be betrayed into disparaging California," Jordan jotted into his notebook the year he was chosen to head Stanford. On the contrary, he became one of its major promoters and definers. California, in fact, initially disparaged Jordan. Many thought that Senator Stanford should have secured the services of a more prestigious president. Jordan eventually won the respect of the state, however, becoming a spokesman for both Stanford University and for California. When noted visitors came to the state, Jordan was at their side, the very model of the modern university president, explaining, defining, extolling. Jack London stood up at an Oakland meeting of the Stanford Extension and argued with Jordan's lecture on fish, in spite of the Stanford president's fame as an ichthyologist. It was London's form of compliment. Jack admired Jordan's theories on race and evolution, mentioning them explicitly in *A Daughter of the Snows*, his first novel. A collection of essays, *The Care and Culture of Men* (1896), consolidated Jordan's role as the new Thomas Starr King. "The people of California trust you," Benjamin Ide Wheeler, president of the University of California, told Jordan in 1912. "There is no one in the State whose word goes so far."

He would not attempt to conceal the fact, Jordan wrote in *California and the Californians* (1899), that "California is commercially asleep, that her industries are gambling ventures, that her local politics is in the hands of professional pickpockets, that her small towns are the shabbiest in Christendom, that her saloons control more constituents than her churches, that she is the slave of corporations, that she knows no such thing as public opinion, that she has not yet learned to distinguish enterprise from highway robbery, nor reform from blackmail."[5] These were inadequacies, grave ones, which Californians were setting about to correct. Countering its faults, California offered three distinct adjuncts to the good life: scenery, climate, and freedom.

Like Josiah Royce, Jordan believed that landscape held social and psychological imperatives. This belief took its origins in science, yet was informed by something quasi-transcendental. He once told a Sunday morning gathering of Stanford students that had he not been brought up a Christian, he would have chosen to be a Shintoist, worshipping nature. From nature—studied by science—came ethical direction. "The primal impulse as well as the final purpose of science is the conduct of life," Jordan held. "To believe that life is worth living" (so went his version of nature's code), "to trust to the reality of external things as reproduced in the realities of the human mind, to have red blood in one's arteries, to throw oneself with courage and enthusiasm into the affairs of the day, to be satisfied with the universe as it is, and to be happy to play a man's part in it."[6] Such was nature's code. Such was California's code, where nature was had in abundance.

In the course of his life, Jordan built up an extensive acquaintance with the Californian specifics of the natural code. In 1880 he had ranged up and down the state as part of a survey team for the United States Fish Commission. A few weeks after arriving in 1891, he plunged a team and surrey through the redwood forests of the Coast Range, breaking breathlessly onto the Pacific at Santa Cruz. He toured Southern California that same year, studying natural life, scenery, and the missions. These trips, with their swift, lyrical reconnoiterings of landscape, were gestures in the direction of his new Californian identity. He became a charter member of the Sierra Club, fighting for conservation and making rugged pack-trips into Sierran wilds. There, with sweat pouring down his face, straps biting into his shoulders, a long road ahead, Jordan acted out his moral vision of biological struggle and physical conquest. For milder moods, he maintained, as did many other Stanfordites, a stone home on the coast of Carmel, sharing beaches and cliffs and campfires with the region's growing artists' colony.

Jordan did not believe that nature in California—"a singular blending of richness, wildness, and warmth"—could automatically renew the race, pointing out that "California's scenery and climate did very little for the development of the Digger Indian and does even less for that of the hobo of to-day." Yet the troubled intellectual might find that "most of the philosophy of despair, the longing to know the meaning of the unattainable, vanishes with active out-of-door life and the consequent flow of good health." For the young, unless they should succumb to "cigarettes, late hours, or grosser forms of dissipation," California's "wholesome, sober, out-of-door life . . . invariably means a vigorous maturity." "Life in California is a little fresher, a little freer, a good deal richer, in its physical aspects," Jordan believed, "and for all these reasons more intensely and characteristically American."

Jordan wanted to believe that social structure in California remained the same as in the East; "for the same blood flows in the veins of those whose influence dominates it. Under all its deviations and variations lies the old Puritan conscience, which is still the backbone of the civilization of the republic." At the same time he exulted that "in California there is little which corresponds to the social atmosphere pervading the smug, white-painted, green-blinded New England villages." What Royce conceived as California's curse, Jordan saw as its glory—that is, its lack of community sanctions. People in California, he asserted, minded their own business, tolerating everything except untruth and hypocrisy. With plenty of elbowroom, traits of personality expanded in all directions, for good and for evil. "The development of the individual among her sons and daughters," wrote Jordan, moving in the opposite direction from Royce, "is the greatest contribution of California as a whole to American civilization. This is her work by virtue of being California, to give physical tone, heightened perceptions and a broader outlook on nature and life."[7]

Jordan despised the conception of California as a lotus-land. "The possibility of the unearned increment," he lamented, "is a great factor in the social evolution of California. Its influence has been widespread, persistent, and, in most regards, baneful. . . . Even now, far and wide, people think of California as a region where wealth is not dependent on thrift, where one can somehow 'strike it rich' without that tedious attention to details and expenses which wears out life in effete regions such as Europe and the Eastern states. In this feeling there is just enough of truth to keep the notion alive, but never enough to save from disaster those who make it a working hypothesis." *Dolce far niente* undermined strenuous individualism. To a certain extent, Jordan distrusted the California sunshine, symbol of soothing stasis and personal nonaggression. He deplored the influx of health-seekers into Southern California. "The invalid," he believed, "finds health in California only if he is strong enough to grasp it."[8]

California, he hoped, was in a process of transformation. "The forces that ally us to the East are growing stronger every year with the immigration of men with new ideas," Jordan noted. Key among these *émigrés* from the East were the university men of Berkeley and Palo Alto. For the first time, California had an intellectual elite. "Through their influence," wrote Jordan, "California will contribute a generous share to the social development of the East, and be a giver as well as a receiver." The academic man, California style, prophesied the Stanford president, would be no "dim-eyed monk" or "stoop-shouldered grammarian"—but "the leader of enterprise, the builder of states." After all, "life in the foothills makes a man, if need be, of the Harvard doctor of philosophy." University Man West would transform California. Professors of medicine would end the state's enslavement to quack healers. Law schools would end shysterism. The rise of business as an academic study would combat the enervating spirit of speculation, with its crushing cycles of flush times and depressions. Agronomists would make California's garden bloom. University-connected divinity schools would drive from California's pulpits fakers and the theologically illiterate. In short, system and science would come to California, housed in two great universities, Stanford and Berkeley. "Today," believed Jordan, "the pressure of higher education is greater to the square mile than anywhere else in our country. In no other state is the path from the farmhouse to the college so well trodden as here. It requires no prophet to forecast the educational pre-eminence of California, for the basis of intellectual development is already assured."[9]

II

In that rise to pre-eminence Leland Stanford Junior University would play a crucial role. Senator Stanford liked to think of himself as a promoter and civilizer. To his great profit, he had participated in each phase of California's development, and now, as university founder, he considered himself conducting California into its new era. "With the production of wealth," said the Senator, "comes the leisure to think, and no people is really great which is not a thinking people." Stanford liked to play the self-made man and wanted his university dedicated to the spirit of rugged individualism, the California spirit. Initially he had in mind not so much a university, as an elaborate trade school, "where," the San Francisco *Argonaut* reported in 1884, "practical education will be afforded in order to fit pupils for the scramble of life." The deed of trust read by Stanford in 1885 to a gathering in his San Francisco mansion proposed an institution in which agriculture, mechanical arts, livestock management, and trade skills would have equal place in the curriculum. Such was one side of Stanford's California pose: friend of the common man. But Stanford went

East, seeking models and personnel in the nation's prestigious, aristocratic universities. Such was another aspect of California aspiration: a naïve passion for first-cabin passage. Walking with President Eliot through Harvard Yard, Stanford asked what it would cost to duplicate Harvard in Palo Alto. Harvard consisted of much more than its buildings, Eliot replied, but he supposed $15 million would prove sufficient. Senator and Mrs. Stanford looked at each other with obvious satisfaction. "We can do it, Leland," said Mrs. Stanford. The Senator was perplexed and hurt by his failure to secure a famous educator as president, in spite of the outrageous salary he offered ($25,000, more than twice what Jordan received). "So far as I could see," Nicholas Murray Butler of Columbia remembered, "Governor Stanford's whole conception of university building was purely material. He thought money could buy anything and could do anything, and was both chagrined and surprised when he found sometimes that it could not."[10]

Jordan opposed the Senator in his belief that the university should have a library "such as a gentleman would have for his own use, to cost four or five thousand dollars." But in the main he sought to refine the Senator's notions, which, after all, were but a crude form of his own philosophy of democratic elitism. After Stanford's death in 1895, Jordan cherished and garnished the myth. In a poem, "On the North Fork," speaking through the yeoman voice of a tollgate keeper, he praised Stanford's honest, go-getting ways as a Gold Rush merchant in the Mother Lode. By the tenth anniversary of Stanford University, Jordan had fully elaborated a mythic founder: Californian of very Californians, the successful democratic individualist, the self-made man, simple, homey, dedicated to helping those who would help themselves, the very incarnation of pioneer enterprise, who had made the wealth of California's frontier era available for the fulfillment of turn-of-the-century youth.

If the life of the railroad-king founder had mythic overtones, so did the architecture of California's new university. Descriptions of Stanford from early years all stressed the success of its architectural statement. "Evening after evening," remembered Andrew D. White of his sojourn in 1892 as a visiting professor, "I walked through the cloisters of the great quadrangle, admiring the solidity, beauty, and admirable arrangement of the buildings, and enjoying their lovely surroundings and the whole charm of that California atmosphere." Only the University of Virginia, White felt, had architecture so expressive of locale. To freshman Ray Lyman Wilbur, catching his first glimpse of the campus at sunset in the fall of 1892, Stanford seemed "a dazzling dream come true." "The late afternoon sun deepened the sandstone arches into gold," remembered Stanford's third president, "and made the tiled roofs rosier against the blue California skies." Lecturing at Stanford in 1898, William James fell in love with the "atmosphere of opalescent fire, as if the hills that close us in were bathed in ether, milk and sunshine." James described how "the youths and maidens lounge together at Stanford in cloisters whose architecture is purer and more lovely than aught Italy can show." *Stanford Stories* (1900) showed a pervading awareness of the campus' architectural charm. A visitor from the East found "an indescribable air of peace, of spaciousness, of leisure, of freedom, an air of the farm and the frontier."[11]

Such effects had been planned from the beginning. Official credit went to Senator Stanford for suggesting to Frederick Law Olmsted that a combination of Mission and Romanesque would best express the aspirations of the new university, a sense of local tradition—Mission—informed by larger perspectives—Romanesque—"really creating for the first time," felt the Senator, "an architecture distinctly Californian in character." Mixed motifs of Mission and Romanesque blended elegance and economy, ornament and practicality, in just that manner Californians felt typical of California. It protected from sun, yet admitted light and health-giving warmth. Whatever the Senator's degree of responsibility, Frederick Law Olmsted formulated the over-all design. From August to October 1886 Olmsted surveyed the Palo Alto farm where the new university would be built. He had recommended a site in the foothills, overlooking the Santa Clara Valley, but was overruled by the Senator, who preferred to locate the campus on the flatlands where his son had loved to ride. Stanford accepted Olmsted's recommendation of a one-story quadrangle campus. Olmsted warned Stanford not to imitate the example of the British in India—that is, not to construct architecturally irrelevant buildings, trying to reproduce Oxford, Cambridge, Harvard, or Yale. The Victorian monstrosities at Berkeley offered a perfect example of what not to do. In Olmsted's opinion, "a great University in California ideals" should look to Syria, Greece, Italy, and Spain for architectural models, "an architecture of open, sun-drenched plains, like that of the Santa Clara Valley," an architecture practical but also expressive of the romance of California, precluding "hard materialism and 'Gradgrind practicality.' "[12]

The Boston firm of Shepley, Rutan, and Coolidge, successors to H. H. Richardson, drew up a plan of thirteen one-story buildings built around a quadrangle and connected by arcades. "Say it was the work of a young man," said architect Charles Allerton Coolidge of his designs, "who put his heart into it and who thought he had an inspiration." Coolidge's use of Mission Revival was the first such employment in educational buildings. Stanford's one-story construction, with its intimate grouping of rooms around a patio, its abundance of light and air, its unprepossessing scale, started a trend in school architecture away from stuffy, huddled classrooms. There was an obvious romanticism in the Stanford campus. Milicent Shinn felt that the architects, being Bostonians, might have overplayed romantic Mission motifs, pointing out that "the Mexican type of building has never been as well beloved by American settlers in California as Eastern artists think it should be; and this may be because the Eastern artists have an exaggerated idea of the heat and brilliancy of a 'semi-tropical' climate."[13] Whatever the degree of romanticism, the architecture of Stanford University did attempt to organize landscape, tradition, and aspiration into cohesive spatial statement. The most obvious sort of rhetoric was on the sculptured frieze of Memorial Arch, where alto-relievo figures depicted the triumph of progress in the Golden State. More subtle expression came through aesthetic overtones. Romanesque implied Mediterranean Europe. Like Mission, it had ecclesiastical resonances, suggesting also educational endeavor. Mission motifs, highly local in inspiration, suggested work for culture proceeding within an historical context. Richardsonian Romanesque conferred solidity and power upon the fragile romanticism inherent in Franciscan. Here there was the past, suggested Mission. Here there would also be grandeur, suggested Romanesque, permanence and a sense of large effort. Color and texture worked toward a single effect. Light yellow sandstone walls, edging toward buff, and red rooftiles played off against the blue California sky, the brown and green of the Coast Range, the grey Bay, and the golden wheat fields. At sunset a pastel haze filled the air. "The luminous atmosphere and brilliant coloring," wrote a Stanfordite in 1891, "give a certain stagey effect to the landscape and make you think you are in a play."[14] New Almaden sandstone, from nearby quarries, had been used in construction. Initially soft, it was easily cut and set in place, but quickly hardened and darkened from exposure. Its textured cut, like adobe, had an organic relation to environment, while its mellow, soon-weathered color conferred needed historicity.

The Stanford campus dramatized the Garden of the West. "Some day you will see Palo Alto blooming," Stanford planned, "with nearly all the flowers of earth, and the fruit and shade trees of every zone." To this end, he had 300 acres planted with 12,000 trees: Chinese palms, Japanese cedars, East and West Indian flowering plants, orange trees, indigenous oak and redwood. The arboretum symbolized California's capacities for leisure and outdoor recreation. Olmsted landscaped the entire campus, although he eventually resigned in disgust at having to haggle for funds. Before planting the mile-long arboretum which stretched between the entrance to the university grounds and the Quadrangle proper, he sent his partner, H. S. Codman, to Spain and North Africa to search out plants appropriate for Palo Alto. The very scene of Codman's horticultural quest bespoke the ideality of Olmsted's vision: a garden park essentially Mediterranean in mood, counterpointing Stanford's architecture in flora. Olmsted's integration of semi-tropical planting into courtyards, his reduction of turf areas in favor of stone-covered open space, and his rhythm of planted and undeveloped areas established a permanent California style of large-scale landscaping. A wealth of smaller gardens spun off from the main arboretum like clusters from a pinwheel. Clouds of roses smothered faculty houses along Alvarado, Salvatierra, and Lasuen Streets. The garden in front of Jordan's residence was a triumph. Here on a sun-drenched Santa Clara day, here in syntax of rose and palm, one felt the poetry of California.

Jordan's response to Spanish California demonstrates how much he quickened to the mythic aspects of Stanford's California setting. Jordan, the Unitarian Yankee, was by no means a lover of things Latin. He made an exception, however, in the matter of Old California. The larger myth of California overcame prejudice. Jordan dug into Old California lore, toured the missions, and met with survivors of the Mexican era. "It is fitting that the most varied, picturesque, and lovable of all the States," he told a Monterey audience in 1893 regarding California's Spanish place-names, "should be the one thus favored. We feel everywhere the charm of the Spanish language—Latin cut loose from scholastic bonds, with a dash of firmness from the Visigoth and a touch of warmth from the sun-loving Moor." He named the streets of the Stanford campus after figures from the Spanish and Mexican past. "The 'color of romance,'" he believed, "which must be something between the hue of a purple grape and the red haze of the Indian summer, hangs over everything Spanish."[15] In poems such as "Santa Clara Virgen y Martir" and "A Castle in Spain," Jordan celebrated Stanford as a Spanish dream-city. He hoped that something of the grace and simplicity of Old California, present in Stanford's architecture, would pervade the style of the new university community. Jordan's New England taste for plain living and sound learning found a

California setting. The Stanford style, as he developed it, combined line and color, morality and aesthetic warmth, the whole suffused with Western vigor.

The town of Palo Alto stood for this ideal of simplicity and intellect. In 1888 it consisted of empty wheat fields, but to Senator Stanford's mind it already had an identity. "I will want to regulate the style of the buildings," said the Senator of the new university town, "so that while they will be elegant they will never be extravagant. I want the standard of social life to be not according to wealth, but to depend upon manhood and womanhood."[16] An early promotional brochure elaborated Senator Stanford's hopes: "It requires no prophet's tongue," it said, "to foretell that in the future Palo Alto will be a center sun, whose rays shall clasp within their bright radii greater opportunities for culture and education, more forms of grace and beauty wrought from the willing elements at hand, and a community of higher intellectual development than can be found within the same extent anywhere else in the world." As a planned community, Palo Alto could escape the burden of California history. It would not have to go through the vulgar frontier stage, but could appear from the first a community of achieved maturity. The near-by town of Mayfield, with its false fronts, saloons, unpaved streets, and atmosphere of shiftlessness, violence, and shabbiness, provided a perfect example of what Palo Alto would transcend. Senator Stanford, especially, resented Mayfield's flourishing saloons and made sure that Palo Alto remained dry. One Palo Alto pilgrim of the 1890's remembered the community as "horribly Puritan." Under the supervision of the Palo Alto Improvement Association, established in 1892, the town was developed according to ideals of leisure, learning, and refinement. "Palo Alto has escaped most of the unpleasant features of the usual California small town," read an 1896 guidebook. "Building lots have been kept of fair, even generous size; dwellings are comfortable, even attractive; white paint and whitewash are conspicuously absent; streets are broad, and oaks abundant. There are no saloons, and the temperance sentiment is fortified by a clause in every deed, forever prohibiting the manufacture and sale of intoxicating liquors. . . . The growth of Palo Alto into an attractive, progressive modern town is assured."[17]

As president of Stanford University, David Starr Jordan had a high place in the scheme of things. As the prime ideologue for the assumptions behind the Palo Alto–Stanford style, he believed that the educated middle class formed the backbone of America: "the real Americans," he

David Starr Jordan (1851–1931)

As president of the newly established Leland Stanford Junior University at Palo Alto, Jordan also wished to shape California toward noble and generous ends. In landscaping, architecture, and commitment to upward mobility, Stanford University expressed the California dream. Jordan urged its undergraduates to achieve for themselves a blend of Eastern culture and vigorous frontier individualism. Herbert Hoover of the Class of '95 learned this lesson very well.

described them, "trying to live their lives in their own way, saving a little of their earnings and turning the rest into education and enjoyment." "The progress of civilization," Jordan asserted, "had been largely that of building up a middle class between master and slaves." Coupled with the assertion that "an aristocracy of brains is the final purpose of democracy," Jordan's thought expressed the Palo Alto ideal, a blending of elitist talent with a middle class democracy. He looked forward to "the new California of the coming century, no longer the California of the gold-seeker and the adventurer, but the abode of high-minded men and women, trained in the wisdom of the ages, and imbued with the love of nature, the love of man, and the love of God."[18] Looking about themselves, Palo Altoans imagined they beheld the first light of California's dawning age.

As university president, Jordan encouraged an unpretentious California style in academic life. His powers as president were strong, at least in early years. He could veto any measure passed by the faculty, and he had sole authority to hire and fire professors. With no deans or departments, Jordan in Stanford's first decade ran the university directly, a virtual and, in the main, benevolent dictator, responsible only to the founders. Although he often spoke of his role in terms of modern presidents like Eliot of Harvard, White of Cornell, and Gilman of Johns Hopkins, Jordan more often took as his model the pre-Civil War college president, part executive, part chaplain, and, usually, professor of ethics. He felt personally responsible for the character formation of students, giving weekly talks in Encina Hall, the men's residence, on "the conduct of life." His course on evolutionary theory become a pulpit for disquisitions on God, man, and society. Each departing class received a homily, "containing," in Jordan's words, "some lessons, moral, social, or political." Van Wyck Brooks, an English instructor at Stanford and the president's private secretary, felt that Jordan was too kind a man to make an effective executive. "I remember the puzzled look," wrote Brooks, "with which he said of Veblen, 'What can you do with such a man?' For Veblen had had a way of asking his girl students to spend weekends with him in a cabin in the woods." "There was nothing of the tough executive about him," recalled librarian Sydney B. Mitchell; "this was just not in his make-up. His informality and dislike of high pressure was reflected in the pleasant atmosphere of his office." "Jordan himself we grew to love," remembered bacteriologist Hans Zinsser. "He was actually far from a tyrant; rather a dreamer, bullied by a turbulent and largely radical faculty. While at academic meetings, he gazed through the windows at the blue California skies, lost in reveries of the future glories of free education for the boys and girls of the ranches of paradise, the faculty outvoted—often fortunately for his dreams—his dearest projects." Jordan entertained informally at his home, wearing slippers. He tended his flock like an Old Testament patriarch—"a sort of educational Moses," one colleague described him, "part poet, part legislator"—joining faculty or students for chats in the Sunday morning sun, leading yells at football rallies, seeing Stanford boys off to the Spanish-American War, and officiating at funeral services like that in 1899 for Wilbur Wilson Thoburn, a young Methodist minister and professor of bionomics (Jordan became so choked with emotion that he could not continue his eulogy). He was especially anxious to be close to the students, inviting them for evenings in his home, where he sermonized around the fire, joining science clubs for overnight excursions, ambling down the Stanford cloister arm-in-arm with a freshman, playing baseball, his favorite game, dining frequently in student residences. He would walk conspicuously about the campus at certain hours, open for consultation. One night, encountering a weeping co-ed who had been locked out of Roble Hall, the women's residence, he boosted the girl through an open window so that she would not be put on report for returning after curfew. "Ah, what a friend for a young fellow—" wrote Charles K. Field of Stanford's first four-year class, "pure gold in the pan of the pioneer! Educator, scientist, poet, and prophet of peace, a big man physically and mentally, with a heart to match body and brain."[19]

The 1890's were Stanford's Age of Innocence, recalled Vernon Lyman Kellogg, professor of entomology, a time when "president and faculty and students, all living together in the middle of a great ranch of seven thousand acres of grain fields, horse paddocks, and hills where jack rabbits roamed and coyotes howled, were thrown together into one great family, whose members depended almost entirely on one another for social life. Life was simple and direct and democratic. Real things counted first and most; there was little sophistication. Work was the order of the day; recreations were wholesome." The average age of the faculty members selected by Jordan in 1891 was thirty. "The newcomer at Stanford almost at once falls under the spell of romance, the illusion of eternal youth," an early guidebook not too surprisingly rhapsodized. With the exception of chemist John Maxson Stillman, none were native Californians. Nine of the original twenty had Cornell associations. He had deliberately chosen Western men, Jordan said—by which he meant men from Cornell, Wisconsin, Michigan, and Indiana—because such men "would fit themselves more readily to the pioneer life of a new institution." He did not mention his failure to recruit established Easterners, but there was no doubt as to the young faculty's adjustment. Stanford proved a liberation, a chance at direct effort in a new environment without the exhausting climb of an Eastern career. Hopes ran high. "Once there," remembered English professor Melville Best Anderson of early expectations, "we were no longer to be ridden by the night-hag of material care. Our children should grow up in the sunshine, strong, beautiful, and wise, while we, unimpeded by precedent, unhampered by prejudice, should remake history." Coming to Stanford in 1893 to teach economics, Edward Alsworth Ross was delighted to discover that "California was everything I dreamed—and more!" Initially, Ross recalled, "the 'Golden West' spirit of openhanded spending and frank joy in living was not ours. The temper of the faculty was tight-laced, Hoosier or Yankee rather than Californian. But how these winter-pinched, frost-bitten ultramontanes relaxed in the sunshine and mild air!"[20]

A passion for the outdoors seized the new Californians. "It was so easy at weekends or in vacations, whether short or long," recollected classicist Henry Rushton Fairclough, "to go off camping or fishing or hunting in the mountains near by, and these pleasures involved a minimum of expense."[21] Outdoor life was partly the substance and partly the symbol of the new faculty lifestyle. Something physical, individualistic, simple, and aesthetic characterized outdoor enterprise, metaphor of that elusive, yet felt, California imperative. Edward Howard Griggs, Ethics, and Earl Barnes, History, used to cover up to thirty miles a day in Coast Range rambles. Van Wyck Brooks, English, and Hans Zinsser, Bacteriology, preferred more leisurely excursions, interrupted by wine and sandwiches. So many Stanfordites roamed the High Sierras during summers that a special rendezvous, Fallen Leaf Lake Lodge, was opened in the early 1900's. The Sierra Club received much of its early support from the Stanford community. Even Thorstein Veblen, renegade in so many ways, and eventually dismissed because of sexual escapades, conformed to the outdoor aspect of the Stanford aesthetic. Veblen purchased a chicken coop and had it hauled into the Coast Range between the Santa Clara Valley and the Pacific. There, under the redwoods, he and occasional female company lived the simple life.

With many students in their mid-twenties and many faculty in their early thirties, student-faculty relationships were noticeably close. "The mutual attitude between student and professor at Stanford," said the

University of California *Occident* in 1892, "is one which we long to see here. The spirit which seems to influence the Stanford faculty, almost without exception, is one very much akin to comradeship." The fact that most books for course work, beyond the level of textbooks, had to be secured from professors' private collections reinforced intimacy. Stanford's major-professor system accounted for a great deal of association. Jordan devised the system, using for a model his experience in the 1870's at Louis Agassiz' Penikese Summer School. He abolished departments. Each professor formed a unit of organization. Upon entrance, each Stanford student was assigned a major professor, who designed for him a four-year curriculum tailored to individual needs, basic composition being the sole required course. Thus Jordan hoped to combine the best elements of the elective system and a fixed curriculum. As befitting a democratic institution, education could be both equal and diversified. No grades were given. Plus or minus signs were handed into the Registrar's office, or such individualized evaluations as "pass," "fail," "excellent," "good," "fair," "average," "poor," "unprepared," "indifferent," or "lazy." An early Stanford pamphlet promised that the major-professor system made possible "to an unusual degree, that simplicity, that ideal freedom of the scholar and teacher, that wholesome comradery of instructor and student, which is the crown of academic life."

Stanford prided itself upon its simplicity. Until 1906, no academic dress was worn at commencements. Faculty and students gathered in street clothes for a brief ceremony. "We of the West need no such follies to mark us in our University career," sermonized the *Daily Palo Alto* in 1896, when a few students dared suggest that cap and gowns be worn at graduation. In Jordan's mind, Stanford's severe ceremonials expressed deeper realities. "It is just what it pretends to be," he wrote of the university. "It has no pompous ceremonies to conceal idle action." At Berkeley life was conducted in the grand manner. Homes were lavish (many professors had private incomes) and there was a lot of travel, good dining, and social appearances in San Francisco. A number of Berkeley professors belonged to the Bohemian Club. At Stanford, the opposite was true. Faculty, including Jordan, bicycled to work and sat at noon munching sandwiches in the sun near the Administration Building, Jordan paring apples with a huge jackknife and trying to look tolerantly at the wine bottles peeping from his colleagues' lunch baskets. Social life revolved around a series of rotating "At Homes," to which students were invited. Nothing was served except serious conversation, and everyone liked to think of these evenings as being in the New England manner. "Among us simplicity ruled," recalled economist Edward Alsworth Ross; "less than the typical 'native son of the Golden West' we sought the pleasures of the palate, but the quiet joys of family bulked large in our scheme of life. None of us thought of 'keeping up with the Joneses.' We rated people by what they *are,* not by their apparel or style of living." It was considered bad taste at Stanford to lock one's doors. "Life is absolutely simple," wrote William James, a visiting professor in 1906, "no one being rich, servants almost unattainable (most of the house-work being done by students who come in at odd hours, many of them Japanese), and the professors' wives, I fear, having in great measure to do their own cooking. No social excesses or complications therefore. In fact, nothing but essentials, and *all* the essentials." "Eastern institutions," noted James a few months later, "look dark and huddled and confused in comparison with this purity and serenity."[22]

"The students," wrote the Harvard philosopher in the same letter, "though rustic, are very earnest and wholesome." Had he been alive, Senator Stanford would have been pleased by James's observation. He wanted his university to offer education to the disadvantaged. For most of the turn-of-the-century period, Stanford University did not charge tuition. Expenses were met from the endowment. Senator Stanford made sure that costs remained low, squelching his brother-in-law's plans to raise the board in Encina Hall. Mrs. Stanford reiterated her dead husband's wishes. "The University has been endowed with a view of offering instruction free or nearly free," she told the board of trustees in 1902, "that it may resist the tendency to the stratification of society, by keeping open an avenue whereby the deserving and exceptional may rise through their own efforts from the lowest to the highest stations in life. A spirit of equality must accordingly be maintained within the University."[23] The typical Stanford student of the 1890's and early 1900's was Western and upwardly mobile. Few came from families of established background. A survey revealed that most had been attracted to Stanford by the chance to be self-supporting while working for a university degree. Two-thirds of the 559 students who registered in October 1891 came from California, and the remaining third mainly from the Far West and Midwest. Of Californians, most were from the southern and central part of the state, and most had small-town or ranch backgrounds.

With Jordan's approval, the notion of the self-supporting student reached the intensity of a cult. As a Cornell undergraduate, Jordan had belonged to an association of self-supporting students calling themselves "The Struggle for Existence." The memory of hours spent lathing houses, digging potatoes, husking corn, waiting upon tables, and sweeping campus buildings seemed justified by his adult success. "The cards are stacked against the rich man's son," Jordan would say (although he was also fond of pointing out that eight scions of the Hawaii Doles had done marvelously at Stanford). "Of the many college men who have risen to prominence in my day, very few did not lack for money in college." The Stanfords, both from obscure backgrounds, agreed. "A student will be better fitted to battle with the trials and tribulations of life," Mrs. Stanford told the trustees in 1897, "if he (or she) has been taught the worth of money, the necessity of saving and of overcoming a desire to imitate those who are better off in the world's goods."[24] In other words, the Stanford student was expected to be a sincere go-getter, aware of his place, but hoping, through hard work, to rise in the world. It was claimed that no social disgrace attached itself to self-support. Working students, such as young Herbert Hoover, seemed the very paradigm of the possibilities for upward mobility at Stanford University. In one *President's Report* Jordan praised Stanford's 350 working students as representing "many of the ablest men and women in the university." Her flourishing colony of self-supporting students, ran one student-written article, ensured a no-nonsense attitude on the part of the student body, Stanford being "no detaining school for the sons of rich men to sport out their cubhood days until ready to be shoved into the stream of things with men of the world."

A cluster of whitewashed wooden shacks, used as barracks during construction of the Quadrangle, became the symbolic domicile of self-reliance. When the workmen moved out, students unable to afford Encina Hall moved in. Construction-gang cook Mock Chong stayed on, opening an eating place in one shack, where meals could be had for twenty cents. Students paid $3.00 a month rent. Its buildings called "The Camp" and its denizens "Barbs" (short for "Barbarians"), the barracks remained open for more than a decade, a self-managed democratic co-operative, free of hazing and other forms of collegiate hi-jinks, filled with serious, hard-working students. Mrs. Stanford took the boys of The Camp under her special protection, allowing the co-operative to stay alive long after its temporary buildings should have been torn down. Its presence seemed an expression of her husband's desire to assist the struggling collegians of California.

Another aspect of this cult of rugged individualism and upward mobility could be seen in the large number of special students registered at Stanford in its early years. Senator Stanford had insisted upon the admission of "specials." The poor state of secondary education in California, he pointed out, and the difficulty for rural youths to attend school regularly, might preclude talented youngsters from university work. Many special students preferred not to bother with a full degree but studied one area intensely, usually a technical skill such as engineering. Most were self-supporting and in their mid to late twenties. One hundred and forty-seven specials registered at Stanford in 1891, out of a student body of 559, as opposed to Berkeley's ratio of 76 out of 520. Mrs. Stanford, again following her husband's wishes, kept the category open in Palo Alto long after it had been closed in Berkeley. She also insisted upon reduced admission standards for applicants from rural areas. Specials exuded an atmosphere of railroad, ranch, and sea, their older, often rugged and weatherbeaten faces in marked contrast to the smooth cheeks of youngsters from San Francisco and Los Angeles academies. Joseph Jarnick, one of the outstanding students of classics in the 1890's, began his college education at thirty-three after a life of struggle and adventure. Edward Howard Griggs, teaching ethics in the 1890's to men often older than himself, felt that the presence of specials at Stanford introduced a note of realism and a respect for experience into the theoretical work of the classroom.

The presence of so much virile manhood on the Stanford campus reinforced Jordan's belief that "even yet California is essentially a man's state." Yet the women of Stanford also acted out a variety of California expectations. Arriving from the East or Midwest, faculty wives envisioned a distinctly new feminine style suitable for "the western edge of the world, where progress crested in foamy iridescence." "Perhaps it is the fabled spirit of the West," wrote home the wife of the registrar in 1891, "perhaps it is the tonic breath of the Pacific coming in to us over the mountains—whatever it may be, some enchantment has blinded us to the crudities, the drawbacks, the limitations of our state."[25] Under the aegis of the Stanford Dress Reform Club, faculty wives abandoned cumbersome Victorian dress in favor of simpler garb. They enrolled in gym courses and began part-time academic work, one taking a Ph.D. Housework was streamlined. One woman tied a pedometer to her maid's leg in an effort to improve efficiency. Another fed her family uncooked food in an effort to save time for finer things; another served popcorn and spring water. For a few years the faculty wives ran a central kitchen, freeing themselves from the drudgery of cooking. A co-operative progressive school opened for faculty children.

From its opening, the university was co-educational, although Senator Stanford's initial notions of female education consisted in a desire to have girls taught crafts like weaving and woodworking. So well did women perform in admission examinations that Mrs. Stanford set a limit of 500 upon women students lest Stanford become an all-girl institution. Jordan defended coeducation, which he thought especially appropriate to the West, with its egalitarian attitude toward women. In his mind, however, higher education prepared for the home: at Stanford were maturing the wives of the West's elite. Within limits, an effort was made at equality. The Stanford girl, a variety of the California girl, was supposed to be independent, vigorous, and athletic. Sports were encouraged to suppress any tendency toward frivolity, and women's athletics were experimentally granted varsity status. In 1896 Stella McCray, captain of the women's basketball team, received a block sweater on the same basis as a male varsity athlete. She was reprimanded, however, when she attended class in her symbol of equality: it revealed too much of her athletic form. This blend of Western freedom and Victorian restraint characterized co-educational life in Stanford's early years. Women participated freely in student activities, rising to editorships and presidencies of societies and clubs. Yet men avoided jogging past Roble Hall during track season so as not to offend the girls with their hellenic attire. Mixed dancing was forbidden. Men danced with men in Encina, and women with women in Roble. When women students gave a dance in which half the girls came attired as men, even the pre-Freudian mind balked, and restrictions against mixed dancing were lifted.

III

Such—in its democratic aspirations and myth of success, in its simple and liberated lifestyle, in its landscaping and architecture—was the Stanford ideal: a dramatic enactment of the larger turn-of-the-century California dream. California reality, however, was often less than ideal. Stanford University had its problems, some extrinsic to, but some directly resulting from the institution's California circumstances.

The Stanfords made the university possible. They stood as success figures from California's pioneer past, transforming the gains and experience of that era into turn-of-the-century uses. Having done his work as

Founder, Senator Stanford conveniently passed to his reward in 1893. Mrs. Stanford insisted upon remaining in vigorous supervision for another twelve years. Under the university's charter, she functioned as sole active trustee. Jordan had extraordinary powers, but he exercised them at the discretion of the Surviving Founder, who regarded the university as her exclusive bailiwick. President Eliot of Harvard felt that Senator Stanford had founded the Palo Alto institution primarily to give his wife something to live for after the death of her son. After the Senator's death, Mrs. Stanford consciously played out the role of California's Queen Victoria (whom she felt she physically resembled as well)—a stricken widow carrying on her husband's projects. An intense and somewhat spiritualistic religiosity grew with the years, causing no end of embarrassment to Jordan's Unitarian sense of propriety. "It is my direction," she informed the Board of Trustees in 1897, "that this vital and most important fact be not lost sight of: that the students be taught that everyone born on earth has a soul germ, and that on its development depends much in life here and everything in the Life Eternal." Encountering personal opposition, Mrs. Stanford had the habit of stepping to one side, cocking her head to the ceiling, and asking, "God, did you hear that?" The art department had to cancel its life class after she discovered undergraduates sketching a nude model. She stalked noisily out of an undergraduate musical because co-eds in Arabian bloomers displayed the lower part of their legs. She banned automobiles from campus and refused to allow the construction of a much-needed hospital lest people get the impression that Stanford was an unhealthy place.

After the Senator's death, Mrs. Stanford depended upon Jordan for moral support. Jordan on his part played the gallant champion. He knelt to kiss Mrs. Stanford's hand in 1893 when she refused to close the university in spite of a government suit against its endowment. He refused an offer in 1896 to head the Smithsonian Institution, saying that he would not abandon Mrs. Stanford while the university was still under assault. They both shed tears in 1900 when Jordan brought Mrs. Stanford the first copy of *Stanford Stories*. Jordan rushed to Honolulu in February 1905 to investigate rumors that Mrs. Stanford had been poisoned (she had not) and to escort her body home. There was sincerity in Jordan's public respect for the Surviving Founder, as well as diplomacy. Yet Mrs. Stanford's meddlesome interference proved a constant burden.

Her insistence that Jordan fire Edward Alsworth Ross from a professorship in economics and sociology was a case in point. Ross had been a close friend of Jordan's. Coming to Stanford in the early 1890's, the twenty-five-year-old Ph.D. epitomized the type of rising young man Jordan wanted on the faculty. A serious scholar with a growing list of publications, Ross cultivated an off-beat, irreverent style. He salted his lectures with current slang and delighted in playing the debunker. Students flocked to his courses and he was in wide demand as an outside speaker. Public pronouncements by Ross against the gold standard and in favor of municipal control of city transit systems outraged Mrs. Stanford. When he gave a speech in Oakland against Japanese immigration, she sniffed the odor of radicalism in one of her "employees" and demanded that Jordan fire him. Jordan defended her decision publicly, but privately he felt disgraced. A number of faculty resigned in protest. Mrs. Stanford forbade him to publish a report on the matter because she felt that in it Jordan had placed the burden of responsibility for firing Ross too squarely upon herself. A committee of the American Economic Association, meeting in Detroit in December 1900, exonerated Ross of any misconduct in the affair. Stanford's reputation, especially in the East, plummeted, its faculty and president considered timeservers. Ironic remarks were made regarding the motto Jordan had chosen for Stanford, *Die Luft der Freiheit weht* ("The winds of freedom are blowing"). As late as 1909, Hans Zinsser was warned against going to Stanford. "Jordan," he remembered, "was regarded by the academic world as having horns and a tail."

More painful than the Ross affair was Mrs. Stanford's notion of priorities. When the Supreme Court ruled in favor of Mrs. Stanford in the government suit against her husband's estate, she turned over the freed $11 million to the Board of Trustees, herself the only active member. Jordan had a scheme of development that began with the recruitment of a major faculty. Mrs. Stanford wanted to build buildings—garish, useless, self-congratulatory memorials to her son, her husband, and herself. Between 1899 and 1905, she spent about a half a million a year upon construction, roughly twice the budget she allowed Jordan. Wearily, Jordan made a case for what he called Stanford's Stone Age, justifying it as a necessary prelude for faculty expansion. Into a large and totally inappropriate university museum, Mrs. Stanford carted mementos of the Stanford family—2500 items in the Leland Stanford Junior Room alone. In the Memorial Room, she exhibited over 2200 pieces, including ceramics, family dishes, records of the Stanford and Lathrop families, mementos of her husband, personal costumes, and jewelry. In itself the exhibit was vulgar and naïve. From the point of view of a serious university museum, it must have driven Jordan to despair, although, as before, he defended Mrs. Stanford, saying—weakly—that her costumes had historical value. Nor did the art which Mrs. Stanford exhibited from her private collection help matters, consisting as it did of indifferent landscapes and conventional reproductions of Old Masters purchased by the Stanfords during European buying sprees. Memorial Church represented a similar obsession. "While my heart is in the University," Mrs. Stanford was fond of saying, "my soul is in the Church." She commissioned San Francisco architect Clinton Day to draw up plans, modeled upon Richardson's Trinity Church in Boston, for an elaborate Moorish-Romanesque edifice, which was begun in 1899 and completed in 1902. Memorial Arch completed the scheme. Facing it was a bronze group of the three Stanfords in noble attitudes. On the morning of 18 April 1906, a little over a year after her death, an earthquake reduced most of Mrs. Stanford's efforts to rubble.

Her lust for construction mocked Jordan's desire to turn Stanford into a great research institution. He could barely meet the expenses of running an undergraduate college. He believed that "the crowning function of a university is that of original research," but up to the time of his retirement from the presidency in 1913 he could not lead in such a direction. Upon Mrs. Stanford's death, the Board of Trustees opposed his plans, keeping faculty salaries and research grants on a low priority. Senator Stanford had promised salaries magnificent enough to attract internationally famous academics to the wheat fields of Palo Alto, and the New York *Commercial Advertiser* had upbraided him for reneging upon his promise, paying only enough to secure "comparatively unknown men from Indiana." Jordan tried desperately to recruit in the East, offering full professorships to men like Josiah Royce of Harvard. "In the Back Bay where I am now," he wrote discouragedly home from Boston during one of his hiring trips, "are men whom nothing would induce to go west of Springfield, and men the regret of whose lives is that they were born outside Boston." His second alternative, the one he followed, was to secure promising young men and develop a faculty at Stanford. But having secured young scholars, Jordan could not provide the means of growth. Tie-up of the endowment in litigation from 1893 to 1899, followed by Mrs. Stanford's building plan, enforced a harsh and brutal economy. Surveying the rubble outside his office after the 1906 earthquake, Jordan wrote Andrew D. White that he could not lament the destruction of buildings which had almost killed "the living organism of the University."

Teaching loads throughout the Stone Age were extraordinarily heavy.

Mathematics professor Joseph Swain, later president of Swarthmore, volunteered to head the student janitor service in an effort to keep expenses down. By the end of the Stone Age poverty had ceased to be picturesquely pioneer. A Stanford professor complained in 1904 that his colleagues were low-paid, over-worked, haggard, and in some cases literally not getting enough to eat. "It is too bad that the men can't feed their families buff sandstone," he said, bitterly surveying campus construction; "it seems to be the one plentiful thing." Jordan was forced to admit the hunger charge before the Trustees in 1905. "They haven't enough to eat," he said of Stanford's junior faculty, "to say nothing of travel and study." Even Mrs. Stanford began to worry, although not to the detriment of her building plan. "To know this institution is on such a low plane," she wrote Jordan in 1902, "has actually made me sick." "At present we are only a college of the Middle Western type," she complained to the Board of Trustees in 1904. "With few exceptions, no original investigation work is being done."

Visiting Professor William James felt deeply the possibilities of "this extraordinary little University." "It is really a miracle," he wrote his brother Henry; "and so simple the life and so benign the elements, that for a young ambitious professor who wishes to leave his mark on Pacific civilization while it is most plastic, or for *any one* who wants to teach and work under the most perfect conditions for eight or nine month, and *who is able to get to the East, or Europe, for the remaining three,* I can't imagine anything finer." James soon discovered the restricted circumstances of the permanent Stanford faculty. His own stipend of $5000 for a semester course meeting three days a week was hardly typical. "Unfortunately the authorities of the University seem not to be gifted with imagination enough to see its proper role," he wrote a friend. "Its geographical environment and material basis being unique, they ought to aim at unique quality all through, and get *somnites* to come here to work and teach by offering large stipends. They might, I think, thus easily build up something very distinguished. Instead of which, they pay small sums to young men who chafe at not being able to travel, and whose wives get worn out with domestic drudgery. The whole thing *might* be Utopian; it is only half-Utopian. A characteristic American affair!" James elaborated his ideas publicly in a Founders' Day address, "Stanford's Ideal Destiny." His words must have fallen with cruel irony upon Jordan's ears. James called upon Stanford to become a Johns Hopkins of the West, a research institution, hosting scholars from across the world, especially from the Pacific basin. "Let her claim her place," James urged, "let her espouse her destiny"—"not vast, but intense; less a place for teaching youths and maidens than for training scholars; devoted to truth; radiating influence; setting standards; shedding abroad the fruits of learning; mediating between America and Asia, and helping the more intellectual men of both continents to understand each other better." How futile must Jordan's long hopes have seemed as he listened to James, he who knew the secret life of the institution! And how painful to read the letter James wrote upon his return to Boston! Discontent pervaded the Stanford faculty, James warned Jordan. "What Stanford most needs now is the hearty, cheery sense that all the powers are absolutely at one and pulling together in a sympathetic collective life. Queer as it may sound, I think that reform and advance in pay is the shortest possible art to this situation."[26]

Other aspects of the Stanford ideality betrayed flaws: the cult of the self-supporting student, for instance, expression of California's upward mobility. At the going rate for student labor in 1892, a self-supporting Stanfordite would have to work forty-five hours a week to earn the $28 necessary for room and board at Encina Hall. Poor students lived in tents and converted piano-boxes. Many Barbs subsisted upon one of Mock Chong's meals per day. Two brothers went barefoot and subsisted upon nuts and raw vegetables. When The Camp closed, housing became intolerable. "Expecting in the Halls and in the fraternity and sorority houses," noted the *President's Report* for 1908-9, "lodgings on the Campus are dear, over-crowded, ill-supported with toilet and heating arrangements"—a far cry from Senator Stanford's promise of support for worthy sons of the working class. A later survey showed that self-supporting students did the poorest academic work. Robert Duffus, before he landed a sinecure in Thorstein Veblen's household, remembered with bitterness the lot of the self-supporting student at Stanford: "no time for companionship and not enough sleep, going from classroom to job and from job to classroom endlessly." *Stanford Stories*, a collection of tales of the late 1890's, revealed the exclusion of the self-supporting student from campus life. The Stanford Man of these stories is a blazered, mandolin-strumming, briar-puffing, fraternity good-fellow, who calls his friends "Old Boy" and "Old Sport" and regards working students with amused indifference. In one story, a student-waiter sadly realizes how the real Stanford has eluded him because of his job. "He went from the work at his room to his work at the Inn, and he saw this Other Thing expressed in the elevens straining against each other under the eyes of the College gathered on the bleachers; he found the echoes of it while he scrubbed and swept fraternity living rooms which Friday night had filled with foothill greens and the laughter of girls; the mysterious something called to him on soft evenings when the laboratory windows were open and fellows went singing down the arcades."[27]

For all the democratic rhetoric that surrounded Stanford's founding, caste lines formed immediately. Eight fraternities were chartered in the first year. They dined as groups in Encina Hall and moved to separate living quarters as soon as they could. By 1908 sixteen fraternities and six sororities dominated student body life. The social alienation between "rough-necks" and "queeners" ran deep. In 1899 the San Francisco *Chronicle* blamed Stanford's string of football defeats upon the fact that queeners had taken over the student body. Not one protagonist of the *Stanford Stories* fitted Jordan's depiction of the Stanford undergraduate as a democratic, hard-working man of action and responsibility. Students, moreover, had little interest in the elaborate shops the Senator had fitted out to teach manual skill and its corollary, self-reliance. This indifference extended to more formal academic pursuits. Coming from the University of Toronto, Henry Rushton Fairclough, a professor of classics, was shocked at the low level of student skill and ambition. Thorstein Veblen, known for his vigorous standards, lectured to virtually empty classrooms.

Jordan fought these trends. His severity with slackers was notorious, but he could not fire the entire student body. Senior class dress—corduroy pants, boots, flannel shirt, and Baden-Powell hat—expressed the rugged Western image Jordan advanced. Yet independence and virility could also account for behavior Jordan deplored. Throughout his presidency he fought a pitched battle with rowdyism. Frontier boys tended to riot, smash furniture, and play violent practical jokes. In 1904 student disorders so plagued the campus that one group complained to the Board of Trustees that Jordan had lost control of the university. It became necessary for an armed guard to patrol Encina Hall at night to prevent destruction of property. Violent hazing characterized student life at both Palo Alto and Berkeley. Frank Norris' defense of student roughhousing showed how such activities had an ideological significance. "If the boys in our universities want to fight," wrote Norris in the *Wave*, "let them fight, and consider it a thing to be thankful for. They are only true to the instincts of their race."[28] Let Jordan complain how he might against "the rowdy, the mucker, the hair-cutting, gate-lifting, cane-rushing imbecile," Norris had hoisted the Stanford president upon his own Anglo-Saxon petard! Hazing could be defended as that synthesis of barbaric vigor and modern civilization Jordan pretended to admire. Could the Stanford Man be both Anglo-Saxon and genteel? That seemed to be the way Jordan wanted him.

Drinking presented a problem. As a physician and as a social philosopher, Jordan hated alcohol. It destroyed the strenuous life and tempted chastity. "From the 'beer-bust' of college," he warned, "to the red-light district of the town, the way is short and straight." Stanford students seemed bent upon taking that primrose path: from the Cafe Anzini in Mayfield, where they drank beer from steins and carved their initials in great oak tables, or from the more elaborate setting of the bar of San Francisco's Palace Hotel, where they admired Maxfield Parrish's portrait of Maude Adams before winding up the evening at a Pacific Avenue sporting-house which featured a special undergraduate rate of two dollars. Student drinking caused a series of crises in the academic year 1907-8. In October the Menlo Park Board of Supervisors protested that drunken Stanford students made the streets unsafe. The California-Stanford Big Game in November was followed by, in Jordan's words, "a series of student celebrations and parades, in which the misuse or over-use of beer was without precedent in the history of the institution." Faculty families organized into a Campus Civic Federation to force Jordan to do something about drunken students. "As it stands now," read the Federation's complaint, "many of the residents of the Campus feel that they are unwise to bring up their children in such a community." In February an intoxicated student wandered into the wrong home and was shot dead as a burglar. When the Board of Trustees banned liquor from campus as a result of the incident, a mob of students, to the sound of a brass band and firearms, paraded through campus buildings in protest, hectoring the wife of the head of the faculty Committee on Student Affairs on her front porch. After anti-administration harangues, they burned a copy of the liquor ban at the base of the Founders statute in Memorial Court.

For Jordan, these problems—the increasing difficulties of self-supporting students, the class divisions created by the powerful fraternity and sorority element, the apparent frivolity of many students, the riots and drunkenness—all constituted affronts to his vision of the ideal Stanford. That each of these areas of concern, even the fraternity world's defensive snobbery, proceeded from the California situation which had given rise to Stanford's ideality in the first place was an irony not lost on Jordan. The strenuous, individualistic life, he discovered, could also mean rowdiness; a democratic style could become resistance to authority; and high spirits might take the form of boozy noise. Self-support could mean embittering poverty and personal alienation as well as ennobling struggle. Stanford's hope for a California elite could nourish a colony of snobs as well as worthy lads bent upon career.

Take, for instance, the matter of football. Physical fitness was part of the Stanford style from the first, and certainly it was a key point in Jordan's plan for the conduct of life. Stanford offered credit for gymnastics on an equal basis with academic courses. Football had been a minor sport on the Pacific Coast, but with the first "Big Game"—played between Stanford and California on 19 March 1892 at the Haight Street Park in San Francisco—it became a mania. Eight thousand spectators watched Stanford defeat California, 14 to 10. Victory on the gridiron gave perfect expression to the aspirations of the new university. Californians now took Stanford seriously. During the 1890's, the Big Game, held on Thanksgiving Day, in San Francisco, became the social high-point of the Stanford year. A special train, decked with cardinal-red bunting, left Palo Alto in the morning, filled, as *Stanford Stories* put it, with everyone "from Professor Grind and his wife to the Jap who cleans house Saturdays." Jordan himself, with a red ribbon on his coat, led the yells.

Jordan conducted the cheers because he felt football's combination of physicality and cooperation fit in with the spirit he wanted to see thrive at Stanford. Football players offered an immediate and conspicuous paradigm of the Stanford Man as California gentleman: competent, self-reliant, possessed of a style and code having overtones of the Ivy League. The same sort of youths must walk the paths of New Haven and Cambridge, Stanfordites thought, as they beheld their own football heroes strolling in distinct block-S sweaters, forbidden to other varsity athletes. Chroniclers of California manhood such as Jack London and Frank Norris found in football players the great big white man of their inner fantasies. Norris wrote football stories as an undergraduate, and he later covered games for the *Wave*. With typical flair, he and his fraternity brothers watched the first California-Stanford game from atop a hired stagecoach, pulled up to the side lines. Norris' *Wave* pieces extolled football as the embodiment of the fighting Anglo-Saxon spirit. Jordan put his approval less violently than Norris, emphasizing the educational value of football's code of sportsmanship, but in the main, during the 1890's, he and Norris agreed upon the value of the sport.

Football defined a relationship with the East. The impulse behind the first California-Stanford game was to imitate the Harvard-Yale rivalry.

"That a man may play a strenuous game, the fiercest ever seen on the gridiron," said Jordan, "and yet keep the speech and the manners of a gentleman, is one of the lessons Harvard may teach us, and we of the West cannot listen to any better lesson in college spirit." Walter Camp of Yale, the Father of American Football, came to California from New Haven to train the Stanford eleven. The first Stanford team had coached itself from Camp's manual. Receiving Stanford's request to recommend a coach, Camp replied that he himself would come out at no charge. He coached the 1892, 1894, and 1895 seasons. Yale greats Tom McClung and William W. Heffelfinger coached at Berkeley. "At each college," said a 1900 review of California-Stanford football history, the Yale emissaries "found players of fine, rugged Western physiques, comparing equally in this respect with the men of the trans-Mississippi universities; but from their stand-point football knowledge was indeed in its infant stage. There was little regard for cleverness in detail; practically none for team play."[29] Football offered an example of California's larger condition: fragmented vigor in need of cohesion. Walter Camp made Stanford men play the game with teamwork and observance of rules. He imparted a style of clean play which his Western pupils consciously adopted as being in the best Eastern tradition.

But across the United States football's emphasis upon Anglo-Saxon aggressiveness overcame its sense of sportsmanship. Eighteen players died in 1905, and 159 suffered serious injuries. President Roosevelt, who had extolled the football hero in *The Rough Riders* as one of the great American types, threatened to end the game by executive edict if something were not done about its brutality. The California-Stanford game of 13 November 1904 dramatized Roosevelt's complaint. The lines pounded each other with maniacal fury, ganging up on individuals of the opposing team. California's captain, an object of Stanford vengeance, was battered into semiconsciousness and had to be carried off the field weeping hysterically. Jordan deplored such brutality. This was not his interpretation of Anglo-Saxon vigor, of Western manliness! He hated the growing professionalism of the game, with its athletic scholarships and cigar-smoking coaches in derby hats. Football strangled other forms of sport. Two hundred students would show up to sit and watch the team scrimmage, but only a small percentage of Stanford men took part themselves in organized athletics. The university physician complained that football season left players physical and psychological wrecks. In the 1890's the Big Game brought about needed patriotic feeling (in 1892 Elsa Lovina, a pretty young art instructor, rode the train up to San Francisco swathed in scarlet bunting) but by the 1900's the California-Stanford clash most often brought about beery post-game riots. So severe were disorders following the 1905 Big Game that San Francisco authorities barred further events from the city. In 1906 Jordan banned American football from Stanford, a sport he had ushered in with full ideological approval fifteen years before. The supposedly Harvard-like gentleman had proven rather unmanageable. Not until 1919 would he be allowed back on the playing fields of Stanford.

IV

Football proved a disappointment. An even more important aspect of Jordan's hopes, however—success as an expression of evolutionary election—did not fail him. Stanford men did well in business. The highest possible confirmation of Jordan's educational theories came in the career of one of his students, a career that eventually led to the occupation of the White House for the first time by a President born west of the Mississippi. It was Jordan's dream of opportunity, of mobility, of pioneer virtues translated into modern action. It was the dream of the Stanford Man, the Californian, on the national and international scene, part Horatio Alger hero, part Richard Harding Davis' soldier of fortune, part philanthropist. Jordan regretted how some Stanford boys turned out. But he never complained about Herbert Hoover.

The college graduate, in Jordan's mind, was not a theorist, but a doer. American universities must leaven society with bold, courageous, "right-thinking" men, the basis of whose action was specialized knowledge. "Specialization implies thoroughness," Jordan wrote, "and I believe that thorough knowledge of something is the backbone of culture." At Stanford he discouraged any sort of general studies program. In the early years, students declared specialization in the freshman year. Law, structured as an undergraduate program, accounted for a large number of undergraduates, as did engineering in various forms. "The American University of to-day seeks neither culture nor erudition as its final end," said Jordan, having Stanford in mind. "It looks forward to work in life."[30]

In the summer of 1891, with scaffolding still clinging to some campus buildings, a young man from Portland, Oregon, nineteen years old and eager to prepare for work in life, presented himself to Jordan. Professor Joseph Swain, who recruited in the Northwest, had suggested that the

Quaker youth come down to Palo Alto for a summer of brushing up before registration in October. The student, Herbert Clark Hoover, had turned down a scholarship at Earlham College in Indiana, preferred by his Quaker relatives, because of Stanford's promise of sound, practical training. Graduating as a mining engineer in 1895 with Stanford's first four-year class, Hoover had become, even as an undergraduate, the perfect Stanford Man. Son of the frontier, self-supporting, outdoorsman by inclination and profession, individualist bent upon success and service, Hoover acted out Jordan's Stanford ideal, a pattern realized in the president's own varied career as scientist, administrator, governmental advisor, amateur athlete, and worker for world peace. The years shaped and polished Hoover's reputation, but even in its raw early form it had the stuff of California parable.

Senator Stanford had seen in the self-supporting student the model of frontier self-reliance. Hoover, an orphan raised by relatives, came to Stanford with a few dollars in his pocket, worked his way through the university, and left with a bachelor's degree, owing no money and $40 in the clear. He worked in the registrar's office, set up a newspaper and laundry service, acted as impresario for lectures, concerts, and theatrical performances, promoted sporting events. He led the fight against fraternity control of undergraduate affairs. "With others who lived in dormitories and diggings," Hoover remembered, "we resented the snobbery that accompanied the fraternity system and we suspected favoritism in handling student enterprises and their loose methods of accounting for money. We declared war for reform." Hoover and other Barbarians engineered a victory in the Spring 1894 student elections. "I wonder if I'm presiding over a young Tammany Hall," Jordan said, but he was pleased by the political resurgence of working undergraduates.[31]

Hoover left Stanford a mining engineer—possessed, as Jordan believed every Stanford Man should be, of a capacity for direct work in the world. The profession of mining engineer had a distinct glamour in California. Even Josiah Royce entered the University of California in 1871 with the idea of preparing for a mining career. Mining engineers incorporated in themselves old and new California, the era of gold and the new technology. It was a vigorous outdoor life, yet demanded scientific training. Less remote and more commercial than pure geology, it was justified as an intellectual and a business enterprise. A good deal of California's sound intelligence was concentrated in the profession, which in this respect was second only to the bar. California's mining methods were famous throughout the world. Thus it was not accidental that Stanford developed a strong program in the field and that an ambitious young man like Hoover would elect this specialization. Under the watchful eye of John Casper Branner, his major-professor, Hoover developed geological and technical skills, spending his summers on field trips in Arkansas, the Southwest, and the Sierras. Hoover's reputation as a devoted field man fit in well with the Stanford mystique. A passion for Sierran landscape, in fact, mitigated his otherwise dry and practical imagination.

The Stanford Man needed a Stanford Girl. After all, Jordan had said that such matings were the primary justification of higher education for women. Hoover's wife, a geology student from Monterey whom he met in his senior year and whom he married in a civil ceremony at the Carmel Mission while he was dashing from Australia to China, epitomized the ideal Stanford woman. From her ambiguous name, Lou Henry, to her desire to study geology, Hoover's future wife represented emancipated Western womanhood. "An athletic, out-of-doors girl," one contemporary remembered her, "who rode her bronco like a centaur." Another recalled that she "walked easily, as gracefully unconscious of her body as an animal." At Stanford, Lou Henry enrolled in the study of geology and became one of the few women to take degrees in that male-dominated subject. Ray Lyman Wilbur remembered her frank, comradely way of associating with men, devoid of tittering and flirtation. "She was in those days," said Will Irwin, "as slim and supple as a reed. Her face had and has a beautiful bony structure, regular and delicate yet firm; and her wealth of brown hair she coiled about her forehead fillet-fashion. Though she brought no horse to Stanford, she used often to rent a hack from a livery stable at Palo Alto—riding, as was then required of a lady, sidesaddle with much drapery of long skirts. I first noticed her for her horsemanship as much as for her beauty." Legend developed Lou Henry into Hoover's "self-respecting, clear-eyed, dauntless sort of comrade."[32] She was at his side: loading pistols in China during the Boxer Rebellion; pouring tea for fellow entrepreneurs in London, New York, and San Francisco; researching in libraries across the world for their joint translation of a Renaissance mining text; catching steamers with her globe-trotting husband for ports-of-call with magic, aromatic names. They were Californians as Gibson Man and Gibson Girl, characters from the pages of Richard Harding Davis, mates of Jordan's eugenic dreams.

Born in 1874 on an Iowa farm, Hoover shared with many of his Stanford classmates the memory of the frontier at the passing stage. After his father's death he spent time on an Oklahoma Indian reservation with his uncle, a government agent among the Osage. He passed his teenage years in the Quaker colony of Newberg, Oregon, on the Willamette River, a frontier settlement typical in everything save the absence of violence and saloons. The Stanford ethic, as patterned and articulated by Jordan, helped Hoover structure his own past, providing a conceptual framework for his rise from office boy to international entrepreneur. Hoover's brand of go-getting frontier individualism, conceived as the best form of democratic expression, had been a constant theme of Jordan's sermonizing. Because of Jordan and his own experiences as an undergraduate, Stanford became Hoover's city of the mind, the institutional expression of his ideals and the metaphor for his past.

What Jordan created at Stanford was a mood, an atmosphere. "Despite the beautiful comradeship linking professors and students," Edward Alsworth Ross recalled, "there was an influence at Stanford I mistrusted. In Dr. Jordan's 'Evolution' course, which every Stanford student took, the world of life was presented as the adaptations brought about by a 'survival of the fittest' continued through eons. Terms were used which seemed to link up the repulsive dog-eat-dog practices of current business and politics with that 'struggle for existence' which evoked the higher forms of life. It seemed to me that in the mind of the callow listener an *aura* was thrown about brazen pushfulness and hard aggressiveness."[33] Hoover's success in the strenuous field of mining dramatized Jordan's vision of the fittest doing the best surviving, and Jordan referred to Hoover often in his lectures, elaborating the legend to incoming generations of Stanford students. "A certain Stanford mining engineer," Jordan proudly told a group of San Francisco businessmen, "six years out of college now commands a salary greater than that of all the self-taught mining engineers in California put together."[34]

As an educator, Jordan had great regard for the professions, for in them learning and action reinforced each other. He fostered the movement to bring professional education under the aegis of the university. "A Stanford man," he urged, "should be one who knows something thoroughly and can carry his knowledge into action." Jordan had a special regard for engineers, who would, he felt, be the most important weavers of thought into action in the twentieth century. Hoover, tempted at one point in his undergraduate career to concentrate upon pure geology, was encouraged by both Jordan and Professor Branner to pursue the more managerial role of engineer. Jordan demanded that the man of action, the professional, have an awareness of the structure and implications of his profession, internally as a discipline and externally as a social force. Hoover, who always surrounded himself with university men, demanded the same. He cultivated the theory and the scholarship of mining, devoting five years to a translation of Agricola's *De Re Metallica* (1556), a mining treatise in crabbed and knotty Latin. In 1909 he lectured at Columbia and Stanford. These lectures were mainly technical, but Hoover did not ignore the social aspect of his profession. He described engineers as "the officers in the great industrial army," their task being to create "from the dry bones of scientific fact the living body of industry." In the case of the mining engineer, social responsibility was compounded. Most mines lay in remote areas, many in undeveloped countries; thus the mining engineer was an agent of civilization, a bearer of the white man's burden.[35] Such a sense of service had been a key point in Jordan's philosophy. Like so much of his thought, it was an ambiguously democratic ideal. "The few live for the many," believed Jordan. "The clean and strong enrich the life of all with their wisdom, with their conquests."[36] Such was the scenario for Hoover's progress-serving engineer, exponent of system, science, and social improvement: the Stanford Man.

Jordan, himself a tireless worker for world peace, wanted that service to take place on the international scene, and so it was no accident that Hoover's mining engineer was found far from home. Stanford's concept of itself as "red-and-buff arches at the western edge of our white man's civilization" participated in the larger California consciousness of facing Asia across the Pacific. Jordan encouraged an internationalist mood in the infant university. The History Department offered a variety of courses in Pacific-area studies and the library began special collections in these fields. "We sensed the stir of the world all about us," recalled Ray Lyman Wilbur of the provincial university set in the midst of a wheat field in the sleepy Santa Clara Valley. In one of the *Stanford Stories*, alumni meeting in San Francisco toast their internationally far-flung brethren, "a good many for so new a college."

Jordan was delighted by the figure Hoover cut on the international scene. Hoover's visit to London in 1897 to discuss with Bewick, Moreing and Company their Western Australian mines was his first time east of the Mississippi. The company wanted Hoover to bring California mining methods to Australia, which he did, along with a colony of Stanford-trained engineers. Hoover surrounded himself with Stanford associates throughout his conspicuous career, in Australia, the Far East, Europe, and the White House. In the years before World War I he maintained homes at London and Palo Alto, polarities of his pursuits as Californian and as internationalist. In 1913 the Panama-Pacific International Exposition, considering Hoover the most prominent Californian with world-wide contacts, appointed him European commissioner. He persuaded the British House of Commons to reverse its decision not to attend the San Francisco Exposition. The outbreak of war ended Hoover's Panama-Pacific efforts. In 1914 he began what was probably the high point of his entire career, the feeding of Belgium throughout the conflict. As director of the Committee for the Relief of Belgium, virtually a state within a state, with its own fleet, flag, and diplomatic corps, Hoover again gave prominence to Stanford associates. Professor Vernon Kellogg represented the CRB at German High Headquarters. Professor Frank Angell served as a staff-administrator, along with such other Stanford friends as Will Irwin, journalist, and Caspar Whitney, author, explorer, and big game hunter. "The whimsies of life," wrote Will Irwin of Hoover's Barb campaign of 1894, "have permitted some of us to follow him since in affairs and struggles whose actors were kings, principalities and powers, dynasties and armies, violences of which the nineteenth century never dreamed, incredible human sacrifices, God-like benevolences. But the game was the same."[37]

"Some fifty thousand boys are to-day at play on the fields of California," Jordan told an early Stanford class, echoing the Duke of Wellington's remark about the Battle of Waterloo and the playing fields of Eton. "Which of these shall be the great, the good of California's next century? Which of these shall redeem our State from its vassalage to the saloon and the spoilsman? Which of these shall be a center of sweetness and light; so that the world shall say, 'It is good to have lived in California.' Good not alone for the climate, the mountains, the forest, and the sea, the thousand beauties of nature which make our State so lovable; but good because life in California is life among the best and truest of men and women. This record California has yet to make; and there are some among you, I trust, who will live to help make it."[38] Such was Jordan's vision of Stanford's role in the new California: a university hovering between two ages of gold, that past age which had provided for its existence and that future age it hoped to shape. The ambiguities and obverse aspects of Jordan's thought were obvious. His eugenic concerns had pernicious implications in an America filling up with Europe's sick, tired, and poor. His exultation of the strength of the strong said little concerning the rights of the weak. His American meritocracy, taken as an ideal, had little to distinguish itself from a very inadequate status quo. Thorstein Veblen no doubt regarded Jordan as the very model of what the American university president had become, a timeserver to business interests.

And yet Jordan's hopes for California had great significance. He was one of the most respected and commanding Californians on the scene, and when he spoke he most often voiced deep communal aspiration. His concern for the simple life, for "life among the best and the truest of men and women," expressed the Stanford ideal, and that ideal was part of a discernible turn-of-the-century pattern, a middle class quest for the California grail. As a search for the good life, it had its restrictions, just as Jordan's thought did, but it also showed forth new possibilities for democratic living. Most Californians did not live in Palo Alto, or Berkeley or Pasadena, for that matter; but if mass culture were possible, Jordan's middle class ideal held some importance for the development of a program of California living. Although conceived as the characteristic of a saving bourgeois elite, the Stanford style, the Jordan style, was realizable on a wider scale. Its value were direct, uncomplex, and regionally appropriate. In landscaping, architecture, and commitment to upward mobility, Stanford expressed the California dream. Camping in the Yosemite, revising the college curriculum, encouraging self-supporting students, talking dreamily of Shintoism on a sunny Sunday morning, encouraging young professors to do great things, planting his garden with Luther Burbank's astonishing blooms—David Starr Jordan bore witness to the excitement and promise of California's new era.

11
Gertrude Atherton, Daughter of the Elite

In 1914, Harper and Brothers, Publishers, wishing to capitalize on interest in the forthcoming Panama-Pacific International Exposition, which was scheduled to open the next year in San Francisco, commissioned Mrs. Gertrude Atherton, novelist, to write a history of California. With her usual rapidity, Atherton dashed off *California, An Intimate History*. For twenty-four years she had been re-creating the social history of California in an elaborate story-chronicle, and the chance to attempt history in its more conventional form came as a welcome diversion. Her career as a chronicler of California, which had begun in 1890, still had time to run. In 1946, at the age of ninety, rising at 6:30 a.m. in her Pacific Heights apartment, Atherton would be finishing off her fifty-sixth volume, *My San Francisco, A Wayward Biography*. Hers was a career that began and ended in California, and in its California material made a minor, but interesting, contribution.

A writing career that commenced in the late 1880's on the Peninsula estate of her in-laws, where Spanish was the daily language and Castilian customs prevailed, and went on to include a sojourn in Hollywood as part of Samuel Goldwyn's stable of "Eminent Authors"—such a career, documenting itself all the while in careless but vivid output, expressed the edge and feel of the California experience in the years spanned by sleepy leisure and show business. Carl Van Vechten's assertion that Gertrude Atherton had done a better job chronicling California than Edith Wharton had for New York seems in retrospect farfetched, as does another critic's description of her as the George Sand of America. Yet as a novelist Atherton did attempt to fulfill her definition of that genre as "a memoir of contemporary life in the form of fiction." In a way, her effort paralleled that of other Californians in history: an attempt to structure and define the state's experience. One returns to her novels not for accomplished art, but for the record. California would have to await the fiction of John Steinbeck to receive a comparably integrated coverage.

Atherton's story-chronicle covered every decade of the state's history with the exception of the mining era, which she was content to leave to Bret Harte. Her novels did not appear in historical sequence, as she set her fiction in eras which reflected current concerns. Immediately after the desctruction of San Francisco in 1906, for instance, Atherton wrote *Rezanov* (1906), a historical novel set in the early nineteenth century, whose Russian hero dreams of building an alabaster city on the shores of San Franscisco Bay. Cumulatively, whatever the sequence of appearance, Atherton had a sustained and comprehensive story-chronicle in mind. *Rezanov*, relating the ill-fated romance between the Russian explorer and Concepción Arguello, California's first nun, covered the Spanish era, and *The Doomswoman* (1892), Mexican California during the 1830's. The short stories collected as *The Splendid Idle Forties* (1902) brought the Mexican era through the American conquest and chronicled its passing in the 1850's and 1860's. In *A Daughter of the Vine* (1899), an account of a California heiress' losing battle with alcoholism, Atherton depicted San Francisco in 1860, in the first full bloom of its provincial identity. She returned to the 1860's in *Sleeping Fires* (1922), another tale of alcoholism in what Atherton knew to have been a hard-drinking era. *The Californians* (1898) chronicled the rise of new millionaires in the 1870's and their efforts in the 1880's to come to terms with the often unpleasant lives they had created for themselves. *American Wives and English Husbands* (1898) chronicled the declining fortunes of San Francisco's Southern set in the 1870's and 1880's and the escape of one of its daughters, Lee Tarleton, from a Market Street boardinghouse to an English estate. She wrote about the 1890's in four novels: *Los Cerritos* (1890), a story of squatter conflict in Central California, *A Whirl Asunder* (1895), a tale of the San Francisco smart set, *Patience Sparhawk and Her Times* (1897), the saga of a Monterey ranch girl, and *The Travelling Thirds* (1898), which took a Southern California heroine on a European tour. In *Ancestors* (1907) Atherton told the story of the San Francisco earthquake. *The Avalanche* (1919) and *The Sisters-in-Law* (1921) chronicled San Francisco through World War I; *The Horn of Life* (1942), through the 1920's; and *The House of Lee* (1940) ended Atherton's story-chronicle in "the year of our Roosevelt, 1938."

Through cross references, interweaving and updating of plot lines, together with cameo appearances of characters from previous novels, Atherton sought to give unity and solidity to her story-chronicle, making the various novels, in effect, one ongoing saga. She eventually found it necessary to provide a brief index and description of her cumulative gallery of California portraits.

The stuff with which Atherton wove her continuing stories of California came primarily from her own long and varied experience as a would-be daughter of the California establishment. Born in 1857 in the Rincon Hill section of San Francisco, which she described as one of the "only places in those days where one could be born respectably," Atherton died in San Francisco ninety-four years later at a Pacific Heights address of corresponding exclusiveness. The conflict between New England and the South which confused so many of her heroines characterized her own ancestry. Her maternal grandfather, a New Yorker of Yankee ancestry who numbered Benjamin Franklin among his ancestors, lived in New Orleans until business failure drove him to California in the early 1850's. A Presbyterian of gloomy disposition, Stephen Franklin looked upon his continuing inability to regain his losses in California as a judgment from God. Gertrude Atherton's mother had been brought up on a Louisiana plantation and in fashionable Northern boarding schools. In California, hard economic facts forced her into a loveless marriage with a stern, dull, Connecticut-born businessman, Thomas Lodowick Horn, Gertrude's father. Gertrude's mother divorced her husband and made another disastrous marriage. "I grew up with the idea that the matrimonial condition was a succession of bickerings," Atherton remembered of that period of her life, which ended when her step-father was run out of San Francisco for forgery.[1] She moved with her mother and grandfather to a ranch near San Jose, where, like so many of her troubled, rebellious heroines, she read and read in an effort to escape the pressing monotony of rural life. William C. Ralston, president of the Bank of California and a friend of her grandfather's, had promised to sponsor Gertrude socially. His mysterious death by drowning in 1875 cut off that prospect. Devoid of opportunities, like her mother before her, Gertrude Horn drifted into a loveless marriage.

Her husband, George Atherton, took her to live in Valparaiso Park, the family's Menlo Park estate, south of San Francisco. His father, Faxon

Dean Atherton, originally of Dedham, Massachusetts, had made a fortune in Chile and had come to California with his Spanish-born wife to enjoy a life of rural leisure on the estate which he had purchased from the widow of Luis Arguello, first Mexican governor of California. The Athertons spoke Spanish at home and considered themselves Spanish Creoles rather than American bourgeoisie. Within a few years, Gertrude Atherton found herself bored with a routine of rural placidity. She hated Valparaiso Park and she hated her husband, who had inherited his mother's aristocratic pretensions but none of his father's business acumen. When a friend suggested that she write a novel of Menlo Park life, she replied that she would most likely "fall asleep over my work from sheer boredom." Fortunately for her, George died aboard a Chilean man-of-war during the course of a visit home. (His body was shipped back to California in a barrel of rum.)

Before his death the couple had been living apart, Gertrude in San Francisco trying to see her way clear to a career as a novelist. Marriage and California stood in the way. "A novelist should know the world," she complained. "What opportunity have I to study it in a hole like California? Thousands of miles from anywhere! I might as well be on Mars." Although she published a story in the *Argonaut*, Gertrude Atherton did not have a career as a local colorist in mind. In fact, she hated California. "I want to meet real men of the world, such as you read about in books," she would say. "I want to live in New York, Paris, London. I want to see beautiful things in Europe and meet all sorts and kinds of people as different from those out here as possible."[2] She and Sibyl Sanderson would walk the sandy streets of San Francisco and discuss the chances of escaping their remote, confining existence. Sibyl's departure in 1886 to enter the Paris Conservatory intensified Gertrude's desire to flee to the great world. Like herself, Sibyl had a hunger for life. The daughter of a justice of the state supreme court, when barely out of childhood Sibyl had startled a dinner party by announcing in her girlish voice that "she wanted to know life from its heights to its depths."[3] She got her wish, starring at the Grand Opera of Paris in *Thaïs*, which Massenet composed especially for her, dying tragically of pneumonia at the age of thirty-eight. With the death of George Atherton, and the death soon thereafter of her small son, Gertrude saw little keeping her in California. Leaving her daughter Muriel with her in-laws, in 1888 she entrained for New York.

Thus, in her early thirties, Gertrude Atherton left behind a California of frustration and entombment. With pleasure she shook the dust of the remote Pacific province from her feet and commenced a long residence in New York and Europe. Paradoxically, she assaulted the world of letters as a self-consciously Western writer. This Westernness did not consist in a program of regionalism. To the end of her life, in spite of her many American novels, she would prefer the international scene. But like London and Norris, her more regionally devoted contemporaries, Gertrude Atherton felt it her duty as a Californian to reject the genteel East and to turn to England and France for literary standards. In *A Whirl Asunder* Helena Belmont, a California heiress, declares that America has "gone ahead too fast to ever become great from our present beginnings; we are all brilliant shallows and no depths." Before Americans could produce a Shakespeare or a Byron, Helena asserts, "we shall have to relapse into barbarism, and emerge and develop by slow and sure stages to the condition of England when she evolved her great men."[4] For the same reason, another heroine, Hermia Suydam, prefers medieval epics to the thin stuff of American fiction. This rejection, as Gertrude Atherton saw it, had a distinctly California coloration. It dramatized the region's vigor and its European heritage. "Few American writers are popular in California, however they may be read," notes Isabel Otis in *Ancestors*, "and the reason, no doubt, lies in the mixed blood to which all Europe has contributed, and which is full of affinities little experienced by the rest of the country."[5]

Arriving in New York, Atherton saw herself not as an unknown provincial confronting the city she admitted was "the concentrated essence, the pinnacle of American civilization and achievement," but as the San Francisco champion of vital cosmopolitanism in the citadel of genteel America. This self-image helped to assuage her failure to take New York by storm. "It took me little time to discover," she recalled, "that belonging to the best Society in San Francisco cut no ice in New York." Not only society, but magazines proved unassailable. She found that "one of my candid sins was that I had not made my debut in *Century*, *Harper's*, *Scribner's*, or *The Atlantic Monthly*"—but in the San Francisco *Argonaut*. Critics ridiculed her first novel, *What Dreams May Come* (1888), pillorying her as a woman and as a Californian. "I realized even then," she wrote of this rejection, "that the only revenge worth having is success." With the refusal of publishers to accept her third novel, *Patience Sparhawk and Her Times*, she resolved to live in England. Like Joaquin Miller, Atherton learned that a favorable reception in England went a long way toward making a Californian acceptable to the East.[6]

Having achieved English acceptance and the subsequent American approval, she kept up her quarrel with the genteel. "Beside these people I feel a child of Nature," says one of her Englishwomen regarding New York society. "They have reached a pitch of correctness I never can hope to attain. They never use slang, they punctuate their sentences so beautifully, they would not drop a final g in our careless fashion for worlds; they pronounce all their syllables so distinctly!"[7] A Californian voice spoke through this English mockery. The setting was far from Frank Norris, but not the sentiment. "Has it occurred to you," Helena Belmont asks a friend, "that no American author has ever written a genuine all-round love scene? They are either thin or sensual, almost invariably the former."[8] Atherton approved of William Dean Howells' call for fiction to portray the contemporary, but she disagreed with his preference for the commonplace. "I think it a pity he ever lived," was her hardly moderate judgment, "for he was a blight on American letters. He founded the school of the commonplace, and to any young writer who hated the commonplace as I did, the Howells tradition was an almost insurmountable obstacle on his upward path."[9] She forgave Henry James his reticences for the sake of what she took to be his upper-class concerns. James's international novels, as Atherton read them, provided an anti-type to Howells' American commitment. Her attitudes betrayed her dilemma as a novelist and Californian. James provided a model of the expatriated writer on the international scene, detached from American responsibilities. He had fled Boston as she had fled San Francisco. Howells represented the challenge of remaining in, and writing of, California, the challenge of coming to terms through art with the raw California reality which had so repulsed her. Frank Norris had done so, winning Howells' praise. Gertrude Atherton rejected such a possibility. In order to escape California, she had to pose as a super-Californian, satisfied only with the aristocratic vigor of England. She arraigned Howells' democratic aesthetic as insipid because she could not bring herself to confess how much its implications frightened her. Even in her story-chronicle, she would never return to the California she had known and feared, without speaking as a superior observer. Howells might have had his reticences concerning the American girl. But Gertrude Atherton, not he, was the more fearful.

II

In the case of Spanish and Mexican California, Gertrude Atherton was torn between nostalgia and alienation. Mining the mission era for romantic ore, she felt ambivalent toward the very qualities making the period charming to an American in the first place: the padres, the pleasure-loving complacency and anti-intellectuality of its people, its remoteness from civilization—qualities, in fact, which in their American form had driven her to Europe. That the granddaughter of a would-be aristocrat who had lost the race in California, a girl brought up amid shabby genteel surroundings, should as an adult see in Old California "one of the few real aristocracies in the United States" was part of a general pattern in the 1890's, when affluent Californians turned to the mission era for images of aristocracy which mining and frontier days left unsatisfied.

In 1888, just escaped from her Pacific prison, Gertrude Atherton had little use for the missions. "To one who has been born and brought up among them," she observed, "the sentiment and the rapture which they appear to provoke in strangers is always a little amusing. . . . Looked at with the cold eye of one indifferent to material, it is doubtful if there is any structure on earth colder, barer, uglier, dirtier, less picturesque, less romantic than a California mission; so cheap are they, so tawdry, so indescribably common, so suggestive of mules harbored within, and chattering unshorn priests, and dirty Mexicans, with their unspeakable young. There is none of the mellowness, nor any of the beautiful stains of age on their glaring adobe walls; nothing but whitewash, blistered, or peeling off in patches, which makes them look as if afflicted with a species of architectural leprosy. In spite of their hundred years, there is something hopelessly modern about them, something which fatally suggests a country, the ancestors of whose population have barely passed away."[10]

Into this judgment, made from the safety of New York, Gertrude Atherton funded the bitter frustration of her girlhood and married life, her despairing of the artistic possibilities of California. She remembered the bleak, crumbling Mission San Antonio, which stood in the center of the Milpitas Ranch where she had spent a miserable year with George, who was trying ineffectually to become a rancher. Twenty-six years later, the established novelist would see the missions in another light. "That long chain of snow-white red-tiled missions," she wrote in 1914, "hedged with Castilian roses, surrounded by olive-orchards, whose leaves were silver in the sun, orange-groves heavy with golden fruit, the vast sweep of shimmering grain-fields broken by stately oaks, winding rivers set close with the tall pale cottonwoods, lakes with the long branches of willows trailing over the surface; bounded by forest and mountain and sea, and not a city to break the harmony, must have been the fairest sight in the modern world."[11]

Her attitude shifted because she had consolidated her role as the novelist of the California establishment. A real frontier, such as she had experienced with George under the shadow of Mission San Antonio, where homeless Mexicans had taken refuge, she found repulsive. The middle-aged novelist of 1914, however, could afford to indulge in pastel dreams of a nonexistent past. The anger of her alienation in 1888 had been subsumed by official acceptance into self-serving fairy tale. Californians of the more affluent classes liked to consider themselves imaginatively and even historically linked to the supposedly aristocratic order of Old California. Answering that need, Gertrude Atherton gave it a fictional history in a series of stories gathered in 1902 as *The Splendid Idle Forties*, a collection concerned with the coming of the Americans and their assumption of power after the conquest. By the late 1890's Atherton's sympathies lay with the Old Californians, tragically doomed aristocrats who represented the poetry and romance of California giving way to gringo efficiency. Ten years previously, in *The Doomswoman*, Atherton had argued that such modernization was just what Old California needed.

Instead of describing the gringo as bringing change, however, she created a Mexican protagonist of progress, Diego Estenega, a Sonoma rancher closely modeled upon General Vallejo, who already had such progressive associations in the minds of Americans. Estenega strives to make California a modern civilization, working openly for an American presence in the Mexican Department. "What have we done with it in our seventy years of possession?" he asks his fellow Californians. "Nature never works without a plan. She compounded a wonderful country, and she created a wonderful people to develop it. She has allowed us to drone on it for a little time, but it was not made for us; and I am sufficiently interested in California to see her rise from her sleep and feel and live in every part of her."[12] Estenega has a master plan that would enable California to remain Mexican in character but join the American Union. First he hopes to have Santa Ana appoint him governor, whereupon he intends to bring California into a period of enclosure and consolidation. Relations with the Mexican government will be kept to a minimum while California achieves the cohesiveness necessary to withstand the inevitable arrival of Americans. He plans a college, staffed by American professors, so that an English-speaking elite can be prepared to occupy political positions in an American state. California law will be brought into conformity with Anglo-American common law. Once American immigrations begins in earnest, Estenega intends to go to Washington and hand over a modernized Spanish-speaking province for admission into the American Union. The transformed California of which he dreams will combine the aristocratic style of a Spanish province with the economic and social dynamism of an American state. The indifference of his fellow Californians and the active opposition of the Church thwart Estenega's plans.

Twenty-five years later—in *A Daughter of the Vine*—Estenega, now in the diplomatic service of Mexico, returns to California to see his direst prophecies fulfilled: his people despised as "greasers," forbidden the mines, the upper classes losing their lands, the women marrying American men and leaving their own to Indian wives. A Santa Barbara fiesta, complete with bullfight, seems less an expression of the old gaiety than a despairing effort to forget that "they are an anachronism and will never be able to hold their own . . . against the sharp-witted American." In terms of Atherton's fable, the rejection of Estenega's plan placed the responsibility for conquest squarely upon the Old Californians. They resisted progress and now they must bow before progress' anointed ones, the North Americans. In one sense, her novel lamented that lost possibility also rued by Josiah Royce, the preservation of true, not fairy-tale, Hispanic foundations for modern California. But a woman who fled a Spanish-Yankee household could not unambivalently believe that from such structures would arise the new order. George Atherton, after all, had been the product of such a Yankee-Spanish alliance, and the Spanish California she shared with him at Menlo Park had been a hopeless backwater. For the sake of the establishment myth, and for the sake of her own role as a writer in that establishment, Gentrude Atherton did her best to sustain an illusion, but she and the Californians who read her stories were divided as to the implications of Arcadia. Behind nostalgia for a lost utopia bristled the belief that something better had taken its place. In that sense, the myth of Arcadia's passing served the imperialist fantasies of the California elite in the 1890's, as they began to envision their state as the point of embarkation for American moves in the direction of Pacific empire: the conquest of California in 1846 had been but the prologue. On the other hand, they identified with a California-in-repose, a lovely province which would be theirs in serenity. A myth of tragic displacement enabled them to have it both ways, to invoke empire—and to feel nostalgia for what would be lost. Gertrude Atherton's ambivalence served this myth. Like other Californians, she had been discontent with a backward province and had repudiated it. Suffusing the past in a haze of romance, however, she and they might struggle to return.

Her San Francisco series also chronicled a vanished aristocracy, that of an imagined California antebellum. Again came into play the personal history of a writer who was raised in a shabby-genteel boardinghouse by a mother who had the memories and the airs of a Louisiana belle. Excluded from history, Atherton returned in myth. Southerners, she argued—"suave, urbane, occasionally fire-eating and always well-dressed gentlemen from the aristocratic section of the Union"—had in the 1850's dominated San Francisco. Before the Civil War stripped them of political power, they, not the foreign element, had endowed the city with spaciousness and grace. Wives and daughters, conscious of being a minority of decent women, evolved a social code "that is still a tradition, if not a guide."[13] In the days before the railroad, a serene Southernism evolved in the mansions of Rincon Hill and South Park. It was a time possessed of "that atmosphere of happy informality peculiar to the brief honeymoon of a great city." There, in that Pacific pocket of antebellum stasis, Gertrude Atherton was born in 1857, and in retrospect South Park always stood in her mind as the perfection of upper class California life, an image of contented ascendancy among the classes, now impossible to the America of Bryan and free silver. Silver, in fact, the silver of the Nevada mines, brought about South Park's downfall. In decline since the Civil War, Southerners in the 1870's lost leadership to the new millionaires. The tasteful elegance of Rincon Hill and South Park ceded to the garish ostentation of Nob Hill. With the coming of the railroad, San Francisco changed from a maritime colony of Classic Revival mansions into "a large, flourishing, and hideous city"—"bristling with the ugliest varieties of modern architecture"—its men "burnt out with trade winds and money grubbing."[14]

In *The Californians*, one of the few of Atherton's novels that can still be read with pleasure, three families, the Yorbas, the Polks, and the Belmonts—Old Californian, Yankee, and Southern—come to terms with the California they have wrought. Colonel Jack Belmont, a fire-eating lawyer from Maryland, came to California during the Gold Rush and made a fortune. Hiram Polk, a New Englander, arrived even earlier, as a midshipman under Commodore Stockton. Resigning his commission, he went into business and by the 1870's is also a millionaire. Don Roberto Yorba, Polk's brother-in-law, proving an exception to the rule of Old California, adapted to American ways and succeeded in American business. The three build mansions atop Nob Hill, side by side: "sarcophagi," Don Roberto's daughter, Magdalena, describes them, "of the futile ambitions of three

California millionaires." For in each case financial success has precluded other possibilities. Colonel Belmont, plunging into San Francisco vice, destroys his desire to enter public life. Hiram Polk marries a beautiful Spanish-Californian, but she, unable to comprehend his Yankee obsession with business, leaves for Santa Barbara. In his empty Nob Hill mansion, Polk keeps a room ready for her return, a sort of shrine to the happiness he once glimpsed as a midshipman, enchanted with a land of sun and easy ways. He dies gazing at his wife with a look of regret and bafflement. "Poor man! I am sorry he go so soon," she says at his passing. "But all the mens die early in California now: work so hard. Live very old before the Americanos coming." Yorba, married to Polk's Boston-born sister, from whom he is estranged, is morbidly afraid that, like other native Californians, he will lose his money to the Americans. Anxious to identify himself with the Yankees, he flies an American flag from his mansion. "He felt American, every inch of him, and hated anything that might remind him of what he might become did he yield to the natural indolence and extravagance of his nature. He would have gladly drained his veins and packed them with galloping American blood." Driven insane, Don Roberto uses his American flag as a halter to hang himself. Like Eldon and Escott in Royce's *Feud of Oakfield Creek*, the characters of *The Californians* must face the burden of their experience. Each failed to achieve a harmonious way of life. Each denied basic values in the search for wealth. Magdalena Yorba, on the other hand, and Trennahan, an Eastern gentleman-scientist whom she eventually marries, achieve a *rapprochement* with California, a moderation of ambition and a realization that whoever opposes California's call to a harmonious, many-sided life, refusing at least partial surrender to its decelerating loveliness, fights against a unique life-imperative.

In the novels of the 1890's, a generation born in California but still aware of its Southern heritage moves toward a larger sense of civilization. "Born in California, nurtured on its new savage traditions, and mentally and temperamentally fitted to draw in twice her measure of its atmosphere," Helena Belmont, daughter of Colonel Belmont, symbolizes the new, headstrong generation. The pioneer and the Southern traditions confer on them an appetite for life, a fierce sense of self, "although strangely enough," a San Francisco lawyer remarks, "it has given a distincter individuality to the women than to the men."[15] The civilizing of the California girl of Southern descent is a common motif in the portions of the story-chronicle which deal with the 1890's. Before meeting an English barrister,

Helena Belmont delights in playing the temperamental heiress. Through suffering and a consequent growth of spirit, Helena learns that strutting about the California stage is not enough. A feel for the finer ranges of experience must tame this Californian savagery, not to subdue it, but to endow its vigor with civilization.

Like the myth of Arcadia, Gertrude Atherton's Southern fable blended personal and sociological needs. Herself the stepdaughter of the South, she wanted the Southern tradition put at the center of any identity decided upon by the California elite, for then she would be included among the elect, where, in their own time, her grandfather and her mother had failed to find a secure place. She exaggerated the Southern contribution because, manifested in Western women of Southern background, it stood for the elegance and vitality she aspired to. Gertrude Atherton wanted to be declared superior by verdict of history. Her search for standards, for refinement without loss of appetite, and for a usable heritage was part of a pattern. Californians, no doubt, were as susceptible to the myth of an antebellum Arcadia as they were to a Spanish one. Both projections afforded comforting assurance of romance and caste.

The question of caste had great importance. An early critic saw two themes pervading Atherton's work: the struggle of a young woman against a conventional society, and the conflict of democracy and aristocratic republicanism. A persistent type in Atherton's novels is the Hamiltonian Man, the champion of aristocratic republicanism and the foe of democracy. The hero of *Senator North* (1900) stands bravely in the Senate to argue against war with Spain. If responsible patricians like Senator North would take over the country, Atherton suggested, "the fifteen million Irish plebeians with which the country is cursed would be harmlessly raising pigs in the country." In the course of a feverish dream, North imagines that he meets Alexander Hamilton. Hamilton warns him that only a dictatorship can save America. "When the great moment comes," he tells the Senator, ". . . then you will tear the Constitution down its middle. The country is past amendments. It must begin over again. And the whole great change must come from one man. The people could never be got to vote for an aristocratic republic. They must be stunned into accepting a monarchy. After the monarchy, then the real, the great Republic."[16] *The Conqueror* (1902), Atherton's novelized biography of Alexander Hamilton, is an uninterrupted eulogy to the most Hamiltonian of Hamiltonian Men. "He is appealing to the meanest passion of mankind, vanity," says Hamilton of Thomas Jefferson, "and the United States, which we tried to make the ideal Republic, is galloping towards the most mischievous of all establishments, Democracy. Every cowherd hopes to be President. What is the meaning of civilization, pray, if the educated, enlightened, broad-minded, are not to rule?"[17]

If Atherton displayed a consistent view in *California, An Intimate History*, it was that California had been created by the strong, for the strong. Her gallery of favored protagonists tended toward the Hamiltonian: Rezanov, planning for a Russian viceroyalty; General Castro, fighting the Bear Flag rabble; William T. Coleman, head of the Vigilance Committee of 1856 and, twenty years later, defender of the establishment against the wrath of Denis Kearney and the Workingman's party; William Chapman Ralston, the great banker and entrepreneur, whose mysterious drowning off North Beach after the collapse of the Bank of California had spelled the end of her own immediate social hopes. She was devoted to James D. Phelan, forgiving him his Irishness for the sake of the patrician responsibility he brought to public life. Her view of the forces and personalities bringing California about excluded anonymous struggle and the contributions of ordinary people. She wanted men of the hour, moving with aristocratic assurance upon the California stage. This ungenerous opinion, like most of her assertions regarding her home state, was a direct measurement of what she felt lacking there in the 1880's—in this case, men capable of bold and important lives. When she returned as an historian, she found such men, for the California she chronicled had by then become part of her personal myth.

III

Herself a very vivid specimen of the species, Gertrude Atherton put the California girl at the center of the state's self-awareness. Given the contextualization of the female role, she asserted, what the women of California did, and, more importantly, what they aspired to, had the force of sociological and symbolic statement. By the time she began to write, the women of California thought of themselves as having more than held their own. The frontier had destroyed many women, but it had liberated others into new roles. Some claimed that a good climate and an outdoor life had made the California girl grow taller and had enlarged her physique, giving her, as one Englishman put it, a distinctly Amazonian dash. Outsiders praised the women of California for their spirited independence and full proportions. "San Francisco," noted Rudyard Kipling, "is a mad

Gertrude Atherton (1857–1948)

When she was a child in Sacramento, her father put her on the dinner table and encouraged her to kick the plates into the laps of his guests. He set the tone of her career. She traveled much, knew everyone, and wrote countless novels, filling them with spirited heroines who took their identity from California, yet chafed against its restrictions. She fancied herself an aristocrat. She was an outrageous snob—but one has to admire her pluck.

city—inhabited for the most part by perfectly insane people whose women are of a remarkable beauty."[18] Girl of the Golden West, and yet the daughter of something more complex than the frontier, the California woman was not Hedda Gabler, Daisy Miller—or Calamity Jane. She possessed strength and simplicity; yet she aspired to education, style, and career.

Like other things distinctly Californian, women traced their independence back to the Gold Rush. On the overland trail or bringing her children around Cape Horn, she was forced to be strong. In the ordeal of the Donner party she endured better than her men. Sarah Royce's case might stand for many such shifts of authority, when through sickness, death, desertion, the crumbling of a husband's courage, women assumed the leadership. In the mines, women were known to work alongside men, dressed in pants and red-flannel shirt. Even for those who remained in traditional roles, there occurred an upgrading of equality intrinsic to the frontier situation. Eliza Woodson Farnham, who hoped to bring a shipload of spinsters to California as brides, reported that the reverence supposedly paid women in California was a myth, that a woman had to take her chances with the rest. With only 1 per cent of the mining population female in 1850, however, women in the Mother Lode had to assume something of a symbolic role, even if not to the extent later envisioned by Harte, Belasco, and Puccini. Remembering the sentimental heroine and the whore-with-a-heart-of-gold, legend forgot the times when among ordinary people a new companionship, a befriending on mutual terms, asserted itself.

In a region which in 1850 had 92 per cent of its population male and 73 per cent between the ages of twenty and forty, sexual patterns—indeed, sexual politics—underwent drastic transformation. Scarcity of females and social instability offered new freedom to those women who wished to take advantage of it, or were forced to. Many French and South American women in Sonora, William Perkins noted in his journal, preferred to be mistresses rather than wives. Adventurers themselves, they wanted to seek the Golden Fleece on their own responsibility. Perkins disapproved ("Perfect and flawless must be the virtue of the woman that may resist the licentiousness of California!") and so did ministers, seeing a threat to the stability of the family. Even churchwomen, they pointed out, were known to show signs of recklessness once they reached California. "Ladies of California!" *The Pacific* editorialized on 31 October 1851. "It is for you to say how soon our State shall be distinguished for purity and virtue, as it has hitherto been the world over for gambling, quarrelling, intemperance, lawlessness and every excess!" Less than a year later *The Pacific* found it necessary to upbraid California women for not prosecuting their task—for taking advantage of the scarcity of women to shed unwanted mates, for falling into the California whirl "of gaieties, fashions, splendors, amusements, ambitions and selfishness." Because of the limited number of women available for social occasions, it became the custom for married women to accept admirers—that is, to attend parties, balls, and the theater in the company of young bachelors. These relationships were intended as sentimental expedients, but they stood in continual danger of developing into something more important. In a society where as late as the 1870's only one in two men could hope to marry, women had the tempting fact repeatedly dramatized to them that better husbands might be found. In 1860 San Francisco had eighty-five divorce suits and in sixty-one of these the plaintiffs were women.

When the first generation of American women in California began raising children, many tended to bring them up without much restriction. A constant theme in outside accounts of the state is how Californians spoiled their children. Since there were so few females generally, girls were particularly indulged. "It had amused my father," remembered Gertrude Atherton of herself as a young girl in Sacramento in the 1860's, "to stand me on the table when he was giving a dinner-party and encourage me to kick the plates into the laps of the guests."[19] Girls matured quickly, noted Sidney Eardly-Wilmont, an English naval lieutenant visiting California in 1870; and it was not uncommon for them to enter society at the age of fifteen, going about with men unchaperoned.

To the women of California, then, especially the spirited second generation, Gertrude Atherton turned for her central protagonists. Each stood in a vital relationship to region, whether one of acceptance or repudiation. In their ancestry, their quest for civilization, their vigor and independence, they tested and asserted the texture and pattern of California as a locale and a culture.

First of all was the question of ancestry. In the preface to her second novel *Hermia Suydam* (1889), Atherton quoted extensively from Herbert Spencer regarding the biological basis of character. So many of her novels, especially the California ones, were concerned with the interplay of biological heritage and cultural setting. In terms of the California story-chronicle, these forces converged into one question: what heritage characterized the successful Californian? Aristocratic blood laced with a touch of the exotic proved the most adaptable, as a matter of biology and metaphor. Base or unmixed descent, she implied, had little chance on the shores of the Pacific. Nina Randolph, heroine of *A Daughter of the Vine*, was born from the union of an English gentleman with a barmaid whom he married while on an alcoholic spree. Nina's own craving for grog was both a biological inheritance and the effect of early alcoholic nursing by her mother, who wished to take revenge upon her hated husband. Nina plunges into the magnificent wilds of Lake County in an effort to cure herself through a regime of healthy outdoor living, but to no avail. California cannot overcome her curse. Of unmixed Yankee descent, Patience Sparhawk of *Patience Sparhawk and Her Times* knows that she must leave California for the East, or go the way of so many "old Americans" in the state, dragging out a life of rural impoverishment as Pikers, a fate symbolized to Patience in the sight of her once-beautiful mother, broken and slatternly, frying meat on a cast-iron stove in a tumbledown Monterey ranch house.

Those with a touch of the exotic, on the other hand, survive. Magdalena Yorba of *The Californians* has difficulty harmonizing her New England and Spanish blood, a conflict of intellect and indolence. Intellect, however, saves her from the cultural defeat of her father, Don Roberto, and a taste for aesthetic leisure prevents her from missing the life-affirming possibilities of California, as had her uncle, Hiram Polk. Isabel Otis in *Ancestors*, unlike Patience Sparhawk, can remain on the land without being dragged down in defeat. A descendant of Don Jose Arguello as well as Sam Adams, she has the capacity and talent for spacious and successful ranch life. Catalina Shore of *Traveling Thirds* enjoys a dash of aboriginal Chinigchinich added to her New England ancestry, bestowing a sense of affinity with the exotic landscape of her Southern California ranch. A mixture of Southern and New England blueblood, Helena Belmont is "all Californian"—"the concentrated essence of California." Her ancestry provides spirit, health, and pride on the one hand, intellect and refinement on the other. She can act out a full range of California possibilities, combining outdoor vigor and indoor bookishness. As fantasy, this hope for a blend of the aristocratic and the exotic had parallels, say, in the concurrent search of other Californians for a Mediterranean identity, the concern for color at the Panama-Pacific International Exposition, the re-discovery of Indian culture by artists and anthropologists, or the experimentation with neo-Spanish modes of architecture. California, Atherton wanted to say, demanded color, warmth, spaciousness, cultural complexity—and those who, like herself, inherited such qualities as a matter of ancestry made the best Californians.

Yet against this aspiration ran a counter-reality. What California should be and what it was Mrs. Atherton found different things. So did her heroines. Like their creator, they detested the state's isolation. Before she resettled in California after World War I, Gertrude Atherton frankly admitted that she had fled. Even as a child, she claimed, she "knew there was a world to conquer beyond California." Her mother, an aging Southern belle, symbolized California's "stranded lives," never leaving San Francisco "save for its hated alternative the Ranch." "It was years before I could contemplate without a shudder the prospect of living again in California," Gertrude Atherton wrote of San Francisco in her autobiography, "for its memories were still heavy with the boredom of my married life, of wasted years, vain dreams, insurmountable walls. I used to walk past those long rows of houses, drab, with bow-windows, as alike as a row of lead pencils in a box, visualizing the dull eventless lives of those that lived in them, depressing my own spirits to zero. . . . I doubted if anywhere on earth could one feel so isolated, so 'blue,' so stranded, as in San Francisco."[20]

She projected this sense of isolation upon her California heroines, even those of Old California. "I am so bored in this life on the edge of the world!" exclaims Concha Arguello. Chonita Iturbi y Moncada finds herself "filled with a dull dislike" for life in Monterey in the 1830's, "a deep disgust of placid contentment, of the mere enjoyment of sunshine and air." Madeleine Talbot is so bored with San Francisco of the 1860's that she considers having children, a sure sign of desperation in one of Mrs. Atherton's heroines. In the 1880's, Magdalena Yorba hates "the monotony of Menlo, with its ceaseless calling and driving, its sameness of days and conversation." Retreating into imagination, heroines of the California story-chronicle build a counter-California within themselves, and that dream provides temptation on the path of flight. They must resist all forms of false charm, even California's. In ancestry, isolation, and restless inner life, in their search for civilization, Gertrude Atherton intended her heroines to be representative protagonists of the California experience at the turn of the century, as well as enactments of her own California story. That the parable remained muted and quasi-coherent was the result of Atherton's own intellectual and psychological confusion, not an indication that such a critique was unintended.

Love affairs provided Atherton an opportunity to say something of importance about California. Home-grown men prove inadequate for her temperamental Western females, such women embodying, as they do, the untutored vigor of a raw civilization. In each case, the man of destiny tends to be a virile and sophisticated outsider: the Russian Rezanov for Concha Arguello, English officer Dudley Thorpe for Nina Randolph, New York attorney Garan Bourke for Patience Sparhawk, Member of Parliament Cecil Maundrell for Lee Tarleton. A good deal of this, of course, is cliché—a common event in Atherton's books—yet in many cases love affairs are put into specifically cultural contexts. Living in England as Cecil Maundrell's wife, Lee Tarleton has periods of homesickness. Walking one day about her English estate, she realizes that "the great forests and terrible mountains of California may have been born in earlier throes, but they still brooded upon the mysteries of the future." In England she can have both strength and civilization. "California loomed darkly in the background, majestic but remote, and folding itself in the mist of dreams. . . . She was proud to have come out of it and glad to have known it, but it would be silent to her hereafter."[21]

Helena Belmont, quintessential Californian, undergoes, in *A Whirl Asunder*, an explicit cultural encounter; her love affair with English barrister Owin Clive is a paradigm of the civilizing of the California girl. "I never thought I should love a good man," confesses self-willed Helena, ". . . The raw material in me responds to the high developed in you. . . . I am new and crude and heterogeneous. It is the difference between the Old and the New." In spite of her California crudity, Helena tells Clive, "something English in me has survived through five generations." Her estate in the redwoods of Northern California expresses her cultural situation, externally an Old California hacienda, within an English manor house. She is haunted by a sense of failure in her life of health, wealth, and sunshine. Sitting among the redwoods, Clive is possessed of "a strong desire for the companionship of a woman who would interpret this forest to him." Helena interprets the redwoods. Clive expounds the spirit. He refuses to break his engagement with an English girl. "What are any of us but the logical results of traditions?" he soothes a crushed Helena. Clive dies in a train accident on the way back to England. With his death, Helena knows that spirit has been awakened in her previously gross California soul. She can no longer live for pleasure alone. Leaving her guest-filled hacienda, she walks broodingly in the redwood forest where she and Clive held their discussions, a Californian transformed, civilized.

Very few would disagree with the judgment that Atherton intended her work for the "stratum which has acquired enough intellectual snobbery to be contemptuous of Edgar Rice Burroughs, but cannot palate the refinements of Henry James."[22] Even to the historian willing to forgo the consolations of art, her novels prove disappointing. Atherton's lack of critical intelligence, however, provided posterity with a fund of uncompromised fantasy. Careless, confused, her response to California had an unpleasant but palpable authenticity. Its central contradiction—hatred of California's reality, unacknowledged love of its possibilities—betrayed the confusion of raw experience. A better novelist would have known better than to put such chaos on record. Gertrude Atherton was a novelist because she wrote novels, not because she had any sense of art or craft or profession. Reading her story-chronicle of California, one has an insight into the fantasy-life of a sizable section of California's aspiring elite. She was their forsaken daughter, who won her way back into their inner circles by telling them what they wanted to hear. They also had half-coherent hopes for an aristocratic heritage and an overblown sense of romance. None of Atherton's heroines came to a coherent, sustained accommodation with California. Nor did she. Nor did her elite. As a dream-construction, her story-chronicle, with its obsession with Southern aristocrats, its tacky vision of high style, represented a rejection of what California could truly be—the possibilities that were being realized even as Atherton spun out her pathetic fantasies. Only great gifts could have succeeded in so narrow a range, with so small a store of sympathies. Yet the record of her ungenerous perceptions was important. Like the last novels of Jack London and the last years of George Sterling, Gertrude Atherton's vision demonstrated that the California dream could be a route to self-delusion and unreality.

12
An American Mediterranean

The story of the attempt by Americans to identify with the Mediterranean aspects of California begins with John Charles Frémont. Although Josiah Royce later blamed him for its destruction, Frémont did his best to identify with Old California. As a further irony, Frémont was from that very Southern-Northern background which Royce considered central to California's foundations. Born in Savannah of a Virginian mother and a French émigré father, Frémont was raised in Charleston, South Carolina. Conviction and the direction of his career put him in the Northern camp, yet Frémont was no Yankee. Temperament and boyhood associations held him to the South, and there was a French Creole side to his personality, inherited from his father and brought to the level of an intellectual disposition by his mentor, the French naturalist Joseph Nicolas Nicollet. Disposed to Roman Catholicism by his French background and an Episcopalian education, Frémont had lifelong associations with Catholics. Nicollet introduced his young protégé to the educated Roman clergy of St. Louis, Baltimore, and Washington. Frémont and Jessie Benton were married in a Catholic ceremony. During the presidential campaign of 1856, when Frémont ran as the first candidate of the Republican party, he had to go out of his way to deny charges that he was secretly a papist. Suspicion that he was one cost him votes.

Although she came from Scotch-Irish Presbyterian stock, Jessie Benton Frémont, daughter of Senator Thomas Hart Benton of Missouri and one of the most colorful women of her era, had an upbringing which paralleled her husband's. "Ours," she remembered of the Benton household, "was a constant changing from an English-Protestant into a French-Catholic atmosphere."[1] The lifestyle of St. Louis combined Southern, Yankee, and Creole flavors. Jessie spoke French from infancy and was educated by French nuns at the Convent of the Sacred Heart. Among her father's clients were French planters, "generally educated in Paris," she described them; "and with the combined resources of climate, taste, and wealth, their mode of living was beautiful as well as luxurious."[2] Senator Benton and Jessie also had many Spanish friends. They spoke Spanish and admired Spanish literature.

Married to such a woman—young, beautiful, highly placed, educated in an aristocratic tradition—Frémont was no ordinary junior officer, no dutiful West Pointer, his head filled with regulations and his heart set on steady advancement to the rank of lieutenant colonel. There was much of the émigré adventurer to Frémont, and something of the headstrong Southerner. Because of his high connections, he never had to adjust to the routines of troop duty. On the exploring expeditions which brought him fame, he took along, not ordinary rankers, but French Canadians, picturesque Creoles, half-breeds, Indians, and free blacks—bound to him by personal loyalty—at whose head he rode like a *condottiere* of the Italian Renaissance.

He rode thus into California for the first time in March 1844, at the head of his column. "All armed," he described them, "four or five languages heard at once; above all a hundred horses and mules, half wild; American, Spanish, and Indian dresses and equipments intermingled."[3] He stayed only two weeks before recrossing the Sierras, but no previous American visitor to California had such an impact. Before a nation whose acquisitive instincts were at full tide, Frémont's widely read *Report of the Exploring Expedition to Oregon and North California* (1845), which Jessie helped him to write, put forth a California drenched in Mediterranean beauty. His *Report,* in fact, and his *Geographical Memoir Upon Upper California* (1848) might be considered the founding texts of the Mediterranean analogy. Frémont made extended use of the Italian comparison and was especially sensitive to the Mediterranean products in mission gardens. The soft, southern beauty of California entered her husband's heart, Jessie Frémont later wrote, and never left it.

Neither beauty nor the rights of Old Californians prevented Frémont from behaving ruthlessly when he returned in 1846. Putting himself in command of the Bear Flaggers, Frémont raised a battalion of mounted volunteers and, amidst a clattering of hooves, rode south to assist the conquest. Rossini would have loved the episode. Brigadier-General Stephen Kearny, however, felt that Captain Frémont seemed bent upon playing the Bonaparte, and when Frémont refused to acknowledge Kearny as military governor of California, even after instructions to that effect arrived from Washington, his suspicions were confirmed. Meanwhile, despite the violence of the seizure, Frémont was making friends with the Old Californians. He was a flamboyant *jefe*, and they understood and liked him better than Commodore Robert Stockton, a choleric martinet who issued insulting proclamations and showed no respect for them as a people. Frémont, on the other hand, wore their costume and made demonstrations of respect to their leaders. He remitted the death sentence against one of them for spying. Andrés Pico, who led a last-ditch attempt to resist the Americans in the South, insisted upon surrendering to Frémont because he suspected that Kearny or Stockton would have himself and others shot for violating the parole they had been given after an earlier defeat. In an agreement known as the Cahuenga Capitulation, Frémont asked only that Pico and his men lay down their arms and return home. From then on, the Old Californians revered Frémont. He was like one of them, *muy simpático*. During his quarrel with Kearny, it was even rumored that certain Old Californians had offered to take to the field in Frémont's defense. In 1856 they did what they could to back his bid for the presidency.

Allowed by President Polk to resign from the Army after being convicted of mutiny, Frémont returned to California. He had intended to settle in the Santa Clara Valley because it reminded him of South Carolina, but he acquired an estate at Mariposa, in the foothills approaching the Yosemite. There the Frémonts brought to California a spacious lifestyle which expressed their sense of themselves as linked to the Spanish and French civilizations of the Creole South. Dressed in plantation white or as an Old Californian, Colonel Frémont (he acquired his rank during the conquest) supervised the Sonorans who worked his mines and the staff of Indians, blacks, and miscellaneous Europeans who serviced the estate. Indian women of the Mariposa tribe, dressed in brightly colored calico, worked about the kitchen and the laundry like Italian peasants. When the Frémonts rode out in their carriage two mounted Delaware Indians cantered before them, dressed in the costumes of Old California, looking, Mrs. Frémont said, like supporting players in an Italian opera. Colonel Frémont wanted his estate to glory in California-as-South, California-as-Mediterranean. He employed Frederick Law Olmsted to advise

The Frémonts, John Charles (1813–1890) and
Jessie Benton (1824–1902)

The Frémonts brought to California a spacious lifestyle which expressed their sense of themselves as linked to the Creole civilizations of the South. When they took the air in an open carriage, two superbly mounted Indian retainers, dressed in the costumes of Old California, cantered before them, looking, Mrs. Frémont later said with nostalgia, like supporting players in an Italian opera.

on the landscaping. He had his home built in a villa-like style, bringing together smaller units in a way which respected the contours of the hills, and used exposed wood and decorative color decades before such a technique became the hallmark of regional architecture. For a few glorious years, the Frémonts held the stage as the first lady and gentleman of California. In San Francisco they constituted a Society above society. Mrs. Frémont relished her role as the acknowledged patroness of an emerging Pacific civilization.

Prudent or imprudent, whatever they did had style. They made many mistakes, the Colonel especially; for at bottom he was an impractical man whom history had given an exaggerated sense of his own abilities. He lost his Senate seat. He was defeated for the presidency. His mining and business ventures collapsed. He was forced to sell his Mariposa estate to pay his debts. His Civil War career proved a disappointment. When Josiah Royce interviewed him in the 1880's, he was a forgotten old man entangled in the half-lies which kept alive a few sustaining illusions. An admirer of Royce cannot be proud of Royce's delight in catching Frémont in ambiguities, in playing with him like a cat with a mouse. It would have been more appropriate had the old general turned upon his inquisitor—this young scholar with his assistant-professor anxieties, coldly married, struggling for the minor victory of departmental promotion—and admitted that, yes, he had once long ago acted ruthlessly in the face of opportunity. But Frémont was weary and distracted. He let Jessie fend off the more damaging of Royce's questions.

"I lived its earliert part," said Frémont of his life, "with the true Greek joy in existence—in the gladness of living."[4] He was not an overly intelligent man, nor, in the final sense of the term, historically important. Royce was correct in making known his faults. And yet one detects an element of resentment in Royce's obsession, the page upon page in *California* devoted to the destruction of Frémont's reputation. Although he was born in California, Santayana later remarked of Royce, he never felt at home in the sunshine. Facing each other across the interview, the Pathfinder and the assistant professor knew different Californias. Frémont knew the imperatives of style and the South. Royce knew the California of historical process, the California which had emerged into order. Frémont knew California as Mediterranean. Royce described what had been lost through the overrunning of California's Mexican civilization. Frémont won the respect and friendship of Old Californians whom he had met on the field of battle. "Tell the girls I made Frémont's acquaintance on horseback, on a trail, in the mountains," Richard Henry Dana wrote home to his wife in 1859, while visiting California after nearly a quarter-century absence. "He is a hero, every inch of him, so quiet and yet so full of will and courage and conduct!"[5]

Frémont's response to California and the quality of his preoccupations there suggest the compelling nature of the Mediterranean analogy. Arising from similarities of landscape and climate, this analogy developed into a metaphor for all that California offered as a regional civilization. Suggesting new textures and values of living, California-as-Mediterranean challenged Americans to embrace beauty and to escape the Puritan past. Depending upon the resources brought to the act of perception, the Mediterranean analogy could be as superficial as a tourist pamphlet or as profound as Mary Austin's struggle for religious contemplation. Manifesting itself as Greek to Isadora Duncan, it called to the revival of classical dance. It seemed Italian to Ernest Peixotto, who had lived in Italy, and the analogy eased his homecoming. The comparison helped P. C. Remondino organize statistics of healthfulness and longevity. For Charles Dudley Warner it graced the American table with fruit, wine, and flowers. Its guise was also French, Iberian, North African, and Near Eastern. Each refraction suggested an association which clung to the analogy as a whole. Italy called to the ordering of landscape and the enrichment of daily life. Greece connoted pageantry and art. The desert regions bespoke the mystic. Spain, the most compelling because it arose from history, asked for largeness of purpose, heroism—and romance.

The Mediterranean analogy originated in an interaction of fact and imagination. Riding horseback on the Los Angeles plain through man-high mustard abloom in vivid yellow under a Levantine sun, travelers recalled the Holy Land, and perhaps even the parable of the mustard seed. As they sailed off the coast, they thought of Morocco, Sicily, or Greece. Silhouetted at sunset, a row of cypresses outside of Fresno in the San Joaquin brought to mind a similar day's end in Lombardy or the Campagna; and, of course, the vineyards of the Bay counties suggested the south of France.

At heightened moments, California seemed a land of honey and flowers. Nature provided poppies and columbines—and in 1853 Americans brought the bees. In forest hives and canyon apiaries, they flourished on a pasturage of buckwheat, clover, sumac, sage, and wild mint. Squatting in a hunter's hut in the Coast Range, feeling himself like a wanderer of an ancient poem, Stephen Powers ate meat along with honey-comb gathered from oak trees. He remembered Virgil's prediction of the Golden Age

(*"Et durae quercus sudabunt roscida mella"*); for the hardy California oak seemed truly to sweat nectar. Living quietly in the foothills, the beekeeper seemed a figure from Hesiod or Virgil, a gatherer of honey and reflection.

The shepherd was another component of the Mediterranean analogy. In the Central Valley and Southern California, Basque and Mexican shepherds watched vast flocks made suddenly profitable by the Civil War demand for Pacific Coast wool. Armed with a staff, attired in sheepskin, his ankles bound in strips of rawhide, the shepherd appeared as wild and lonely as his preclassical Mediterranean prototype. The Basques especially seemed dropped from time. Silent, aloof, they did not come to California to blend in, but to pursue their solitary calling in the manner of the Old World. They spoke an impenetrable language of uncertain lineage. They washed down mutton and garlic in wine they carried in skins; and they came together to play games known to shepherds for thousands of years. Mary Austin wrote of them in one of the finest books ever inspired by California, *The Flock* (1906). To her way of thinking, shepherds lent immemorial dignity to the open ranges of the land of little rain. She loved the smells of their camps, sweat and leather and onions and wool. When she saw one guiding his flock across a canyon rim at twilight or heard him playing the flute to sheep settled at midday rest, she knew California to be graced by associations of Mediterranean Europe and ancient Greece.

The touchstone of the analogy, its common denominator and its most interpreted element, was the vine. Obviously symbolic of civilization, the vines planted by Spaniards suggested to those Americans who first saw them that California was not an unrelieved wilderness. Like the missions themselves, the vines of California bespoke history, solicitude, and patience. Frenchmen joined in the growing of them, and then Americans. In the early 1860's, sensing California to be on the verge of an exciting new industry, the legislature appointed Count Agoston Haraszthy as Commissioner on the Improvement and Growth of the Grape-vine. A Hungarian nobleman whose family had been connected with viticulture for centuries, Haraszthy, a Liberal, had fled to the United States for political reasons. He arrived overland in 1848 and by the late 1850's was developing the Buena Vista Vineyards in Sonoma, where he built an elegant villa and lived in the grand style. Under instructions from the legislature, Haraszthy traveled throughout Europe between 1861 and 1862, compiling information and sending back about 100,000 cuttings for experimentation. In *Grape Culture, Wines and Wine-Making* (1862) this enterprising Hungarian émigré provided California with the contours of a great dream:

hills covered by vineyards, from which went forth to the world wines which were mellow and yet, like California, had a pleasing young strength.

By the late 1860's part of the Count's dream was coming true. Vines covered the once empty hills. In the winter of 1867-68 over 400,000 were planted in Sonoma County alone. Napa County had over a million vines planted by the end of the decade. Tended by Frenchmen, Mexicans, and varieties of Southern Europeans, their ways of living easily translatable to a congenial climate, vineyards conferred upon coastal California a Mediterranean texture. "It was the pleasant vintage season at San José," wrote William Henry Bishop of a visit there in the early 1880's. "I visited, among others, the Le Franc vineyard, which dates from 1851, and is the pioneer in making wine-growing a regular industry. Here are about a hundred and seventy-five thousand vines, set out a thousand, perhaps, to the acre. The large, cheerful farm buildings are upon a gentle rise of ground above the area of vines, which is nearly level. An Alsacian foreman showed us through the wine-cellars. A servant-maid bustling about the yard was a thorough French peasant, only lacking the wooden shoes. The long tables, set for the forty hands employed in the vintage-time, were spread with viands in the French fashion. Scarcely a word of English was spoken. At other places the surroundings are as exclusively Italian or Portuguese. One feels very much abroad in such scenes on American soil."[6]

Bestowing historicity, the vine also underscored newness. The fact that Americans preferred whiskey to wine dramatized the frontier behind vineyards and villas (although temperance advocates did look to California, because of its plenitude of inexpensive light wines, to help reverse the American taste for hard liquor). It had to be admitted that much local wine was inferior. In 1865 Samuel Bowles paid no less than Count Haraszthy himself the supreme insult of finding his vintages "harsh and heady,—needing apparently both some improvement in culture and manufacture, and time for softening."[7] The wine of California, asserted Charles Loring Brace in 1869, was like California itself: full of potential, but suffering from shabby attention to detail. Robert Louis Stevenson, as usual, was more generous. "In this wild spot," he wrote of the vintage he tasted from the cellar of a small Napa winery, "I did not feel the sacredness of ancient cultivation. It was still raw; it was no Marathon, and no Johannisberg; yet the stirring sunlight, and the growing vines, and the vats and bottles in the cavern, made a pleasant music for the mind. Here, also, earth's cream was being skimmed and garnered; and the London customers can taste, such as it is, the tang of the earth in this green valley."[8]

Throughout the 1860's and 1870's phylloxera (plant lice) ravaged the vineyards of France. Californians planting vines into the millions could thus feel themselves engaged in an act of preservation and renewal, offering new life in a new soil and under another sun to the endangered vines of Europe. It was a startling, wonderful belief, one that put Californians in the service of history; and they bore witness to this new role in perhaps the most beautiful book ever produced in a city noted for its fine printing, *Grapes and Grape Vines of California*, published in San Francisco in 1877. It was the result of a three-way collaboration. Hannah Millard painted the grapes ripening on the vine. William Harring then oleographed Millard's canvases, making possible a faithful reproduction of color and detail. Edward Bosqui, dean of San Francisco printers, designed the book and set its graceful type. Published under the auspices of the State Vinicultural Association, *Grapes and Grape Vines of California* evoked the poetry and romance of the coming of the vine to California. Turning the pages of this elegant folio, one noted how beauty of medium was part of the book's central statement. Here, indeed, was a lovely harvest from the sunny hills of California: the Johannisberg Riesling, from Germany and, before that, from France and Italy, and, even more remotely, from Greece—pale, light, delicate; the Rose Chasselas, tasting faintly of musk; the White Muscat of Alexandria, of North Africa, and Sicily, and the very South of Europe, light green in color, a sturdy, unpretentious grape, for the table or for a decent everyday wine; the heavy Black Hamburgh, flourishing in the fog-cooled Coast Range; the Flame Tokay from Hungary, rank and robust, orange or ruby or rose in tint, dependent upon direct sunlight; the Zinfandel, the most planted vine in California, deep purple, obscure in its origins, perhaps even a totally new California stock (some claimed Haraszthy developed it), fragile of skin, loving the foothills and the highlands, abounding in malic acid, and in its wine, without sugary residue, recalling the raspberry and the strawberry; the seedless Sultana, opulent, from the vineyards of the Near East, running from pale green to ruby, now and then amber-tinted, needing heat for its luxuriance, and protection from fog; and of course the dark and hardy Mission Grape of ancient California lineage, the Ishmael of vines, giving a rough earthy wine, the wine of Spanish soldiers, the wine of Old California.

Grapes and Grape Vines of California celebrated the translation of the vine to America's Mediterranean shores. At the same time, some wondered if perhaps a neo-Mediterranean people might grow up there as well. Diet, climate, and converging stocks, it was speculated, might create a new race. Certainly, observers were pointing out by the 1870's, the American born and raised in California seemed an improved specimen. Only the strong, it was believed, had survived the frontier era and reproduced themselves. A healthy climate and an abundance of good food worked further modifications upon a stock already improved by elimination of the unfit. As science, this notion was at best dubious; as a self-image, it was undeserved. As a fantasy, however, it supported from the perspective of eugenics the aspiration toward regional identity. "The coast physique will, no doubt, be merely the American type improved," Charles Loring Brace predicted in 1869 of the future Californian. "The inhabitant of the Sierras and the central river bottoms will ultimately become more Asiatic or Arab-like in type—darker, sparer, and, on the whole, with less muscular vigor—for the common diet of the plains will more and more be the delicious fruits and vegetables of that region; and a fruit or vegetable-eating race is never so vigorous or energetic as a meat-eating. The south of California will tend toward an Italian or Moorish type, under the enervating influence of climate and a bountiful fruit-diet. A 'southern' aspect is already very perceptible even in the pure Anglo-Saxons of Los Angeles and its neighborhood."[9] As suggested in Brace's prediction (and the later speculations of Robert Louis Stevenson), the prevalence of Latin blood on the Coast—Mexican especially, but also Italian and Portuguese—would give the Californian of the future a Mediterranean cast. He would lose the rugged heaviness of the Northern European. He would be dark, tall, and lithe, and have soft, graceful features. "Physiologists," one observer went so far as to say, "claim that the atmosphere of California is tending to a modification of the vocal organs which will make the native sons and daughters of California, and those whose youth is spent here, a race of singers."[10]

Opinions like this reflected the fact that the ultimate drift of the Mediterranean speculation was not eugenic, but moral and aesthetic. Personalities as diverse as Bayard Taylor, the essayist and poet, Charles Wadsworth, preacher to San Francisco's Calvary Presbyterian, and Eliza Farnham, the women's rights advocate, called upon the Mediterranean analogy as a metaphorical expression of their hopes for the emerging Pacific civilization. Here, they dreamed, might be an American people possessing fire and repose, amplitude and line, a healthy naturalism and a capacity for religion. Here might the American-as-Californian, the American-as-neo-Mediterranean, reach back behind his English-speaking heritage and possess himself of the spurned gifts of the South. "Whatever Greece, Italy and Spain were in their noblest days, that we, also, hope to become . . . ," Charles H. Shinn exhorted. "A cosmopolitan people, not narrow or prejudiced, strong, earnest, truthful, original; state-builders, home-lovers, believers in education, full of nature's naturalness—this is that end to which we of a ruder, more fertile age must toil, setting our faces toward the morning."[11]

II

For many, that morning had an Italian glow. In his *Geographical Memoir upon Upper California,* Frémont made Italy the central analogue for his topographical description. California, Frémont wrote, had the same length and breadth as Italy, the same climates and products, and a similar configuration of mountains, plains, and valleys. Like Italy, it was formed for unity, "its large rivers being concentric, and its large vallies appurtenant to the great central bay of San Francisco."[12] In the course of two California sojourns, in 1849 and 1859, Bayard Taylor, the most accomplished American travel writer of his era, gave aesthetic amplitude to Frémont's topographical model. "The dry soil," Taylor wrote of the mining camp of Mokelumne Hill in the Sierras (it reminded him of similar sites in the Apennines), "with its rich tints of orange and burnt sienna—the ever green oaks, so much resembling the Italian ilex—the broad-leaved fig-trees in the gardens—the workmen with bare, sunburnt breasts—the *dolce far niente* of a few loungers in the shade—and the clear, hot, October sky, in which there was no prophecy of winter, all belonged to the lands of the Mediterranean."[13] It was a moment typical of Taylor's Italianizing response, and it continued in other writers down the century. The country north of San Francisco struck Taylor and later visitors as most noticeably Italian in texture and situation. The view eastward from the Coast Range reminded one visitor of the view from the mountaintop monastery of Camaldoli, near Naples. "The Russian River Valley," he wrote, "took the place of the Solfatara and the region towards Baiae and Cumae; a dark sombre lake supplied the place of Lake Avernus; and Naples, Pozzuoli, and the Mediterranean had their counterparts in San Francisco, Vallejo, and the Pacific."[14] When Italian-Swiss from Ticino established the Asti Colony in a wide valley on the upper Russian River, planting vines, building homes and gardens in the Northern Italian style, associations reported by earlier visitors took on a reality beyond that of metaphor. "While visiting here," Ernest Peixotto could say of Asti in the early 1900's, "I veritably passed my time in Italy, for every one I met and everything I saw was Italian."[15]

The Italian analogy could be great or small, an isolated perception or an extended metaphor. The canyons of the Coast Range might seem like the wild ravines of Italy; and the island of Santa Catalina, with its deep blue bay and wild goats, might suggest Capri. The trees of California—oak, bay, pine, and cypress—recalled Italian counterparts. "It might be Lombardy again," noted William Bishop upon seeing the cypress-lined irrigation canals outside Fresno.[16] The southern coast was made Italian through architecture and landscaping, as Ernest Peixotto discovered in the first decade of the twentieth century when he visited the terraced and villa-dotted slopes facing the Santa Barbara Channel. "The soft breeze, fanning the face like a caress," Peixotto wrote of this area, "the limpid air—the *cielo sereno* dear to every Italian heart—the scent of the orange blossoms wafted from the terraces; the shimmering olives backed by dark oaks; the suave lines of the coast reaching from the headlands of Miramar and Montecito down toward the bluffs of Ventura; the lazy blue sea sending its subdued rumble to the ear; the islands floating like a mirage upon its bosom, evoke the noble panoramas of Camaldoli, of Positano, of Nervi, of Bordighera. Even the labourers, ploughing between the lemon trees, chatter the liquid note of Italy's language, and toward evening, when nature is stilled in the hush which comes with twilight, from the cottage behind our house, come the soft notes of the romanzas of Posilippo sung by the gardeners and their families."[17]

Roman Catholicism was an integral part of the Italian comparison. In the early days of the American era, nuns in habit served on the staffs of public hospitals and orphanages; and convents at Marysville, Benicia, and San Jose provided interdenominational finishing schools for the daughters of the wealthy. Santa Clara College, Sara Lippincott discovered one drowsy summer afternoon in 1871, had a charm all its own: "The inner court, or garden, with its long piazzas, its aloes, myrtles, roses, and lemon, orange, almond, and olive trees, reminded me of the cloisters and court in the picturesque old inn of Amalfi, once a convent. The whole scene was marvelously like Italy,—the Jesuit priests, with their long black robes; the quaint old church; the older cross before it. Even the picturesque peasant figures were there, lounging about the church door, and kneeling before the shrine of the Virgin."[18]

The ecclesiastical aspect of California-as-Italy lent itself to such scene painting. It could also have a more profound effect. In conjunction with the intellectual influence of the Oxford Movement, it converted to Catholicism Peter Burnett, the first American governor of California, and Serranus Clinton Hastings of the state supreme court. In 1867, at Saint Mary's Cathedral in San Francisco, Burnett served as godfather when an Italian Jesuit baptized Charles Warren Stoddard into the Catholic Church. As part of its drama Stoddard's conversion showed a parabolic confrontation between the Calvinism of upstate New York and Catholic California. In the narrative of his path to Rome, *A Troubled Heart* (1885), Stoddard played off two milieus: the grim household of his New York grandparents, "in whose veins the blood had flowed coldly from the dark days of the Plymouth Puritans," and San Francisco, city of poetry and catholicity of temperament. Talk of hellfire and predestination filled his grandparents' house, where in early adolescence he had returned from San Francisco for a visit. Brought to a revival, Stoddard felt shamed by the shrieking, and even more degraded when he was forced to the front of the church to repent his sins. He returned to San Francisco and in time developed into a poet. Despite boyhood indoctrination against the Whore of Babylon, he found himself attracted by the Catholic liturgy. Kneeling in the congregation of Saint Mary's as Archbishop Alemany celebrated High Mass, Stoddard realized that long ago, perhaps in the course of a grim New York Sabbath, he had dreamed of an altar before which he could prostrate himself in adoration. Like San Francisco, Catholicism was an aesthetic premise. Its symbols met the needs of his imagination and the hungers of his heart. Romanism was part of a total *mise en scène*. The Latin liturgy, the Italian Jesuits of Saint Ignatius Church where he went for instructions, his developing interest in the civilizations of Southern Europe, the very Mediterranean metaphor of California itself, all massed themselves on the borders of his imagination, moving him to an assent that was an act of religion, the election of a culture—and a vision of beauty. "And it seemed to me then," wrote Stoddard of walking down the steps of Saint Mary's after his baptism, "as if my eyes were just opening upon another and a better world."[19] In Rome, shortly after, he had an audience with Pope Pius IX, who presented him with a crucifix.

As much as Stoddard's Catholicity was prompted by the Italian metaphor, California was not due to fill up with recusants, converts or crypto-Catholics, but with (and here the reference is especially to Southern California) Midwest Protestants of the middle class. California-as-Italy might not call them to Rome, but, as presented by Charles Dudley Warner in *Our Italy* (1891), it would urge Americans to pay attention to the aesthetics of living.

Radiating an Indian Summer mood of New England in search of the South, Warner was himself the paradigm of the softened Puritan into whose hands he would commend the American Italy. Born in rural Massachusetts of Mayflower descendants, raised throughout the 1830's and 1840's in the old Puritan ways, Warner spent a lifetime moving southward: to New York and Pennsylvania for an education; to the Old Southwest frontier to build up his health; to Mexico on horseback; and, most gloriously, as a traveler-essayist in North Africa, the Near East, Southern France, Sicily, Italy, Malta, and Greece. Established in Hartford, Connecticut, as co-editor of the *Courant,* Warner worked vigorously after the Civil War for the revival of the American South. Loving the South as a region, he felt Southerners had much to teach the rest of the United States, especially the Northeast of the Gilded Age. Warner hated the New England winter, and his boyhood Congregationalism gave way to Episcopalianism, but he still had something of the Puritan in his temperament. He turned to the South, American and Mediterranean, for moral values as well as for sunshine. The South, Warner asserted, called men to preindustrial values of living. There a ruthless economy did not drive men to evaluate themselves strictly in terms of financial success. Other things counted: a community remaining stable and on a human scale; orthodoxies of behavior and expectation; an afternoon in a garden: so much, in short, of what America's robber-baron civilization was casting aside.

Perhaps, Warner suggested in *Our Italy,* beauty and leisure might be regained in Southern California. Although it figured in the title, Warner did not overuse the Italian metaphor. Southern California, he wrote, was not overwhelmingly Italian in appearance, "though now and then some bay with its purple hills running to the blue sea, its surrounding mesas and cañons blooming in semitropical luxuriance, some conjunction of shore and mountain, some golden color, some white light and sharply defined shadows, some refinement of lines, some poetic tints in violet and ashy ranges, some ultramarine in the sea, or delicate blue in the sky, will remind the traveller of more than one place of beauty in Southern Italy and Sicily."[20] What was Italian about Southern California were the imperatives which arose out of its Mediterranean setting. The beauty and the climate of the region urged Americans to an Italian-like softening of the asperities of everyday life. Warner knew that Americans would continue to work in Southern California, but he hoped they could also achieve balance and integration. "It may be," he predicted of the future lifestyle of Southern California, "that engagements will not be kept with desired punctuality, under the impression that the enjoyment of life does not depend upon exact response to the second-hand of a watch; and it is not unpleasant to think that there is a corner of the Union where there will be a little more leisure, a little more of serene waiting on Providence, an abatement of the restles rush and haste of our usual life. The waves of population have been rolling westward for a long time, and now, breaking over the mountains, they flow over Pacific slopes and along the warm and inviting seas. Is it altogether an unpleasing thought that the conditions of life will be somewhat easier there, that there will be some physical repose, the race having reached the sunset of the continent, comparable to the desirable placidity of life called the sunset of old age? This may be altogether fanciful, but I have sometimes felt, in the sunny moderation of nature there, that this land might offer for thousands at least a winter of content."[21]

III

For those who saw another Greece, California called to pageantry and to art. The Greek analogy derived from the landscape in a way the Italian never could. Italy, after all, implied an ordering of landscape after long occupancy, while even in classical times there was something half-wild about Greece, something mysterious and semi-divine, mediated through myth and communicated with through outdoor rites. Hills, groves, blue seas, the islands off the the southern coast, shepherds, bees, vines, fig and olive trees served the Greek metaphor—and so did the light! "Nowhere else on earth," wrote Stephen Powers, "have I seen the light of the sun rest down on this beautiful world so tender as it streams down through this white-lilac autumn haze of California—such a light alone as could have inspired the passionate laments which Euripides puts into the mouths of Alcestis and Iphigenia, as they close their dying eyes."[22]

The Greek analogy often occurred in conjunction with predictions regarding California art. A Greek situation implied a Greek relationship to the outdoors, and an art concerned with and structured by the interaction of man with nature. At the turn of the century, mythic drama, pageant, and festival asserted themselves as popular local forms. Pasadena held its first Tournament of Roses on New Year's Day 1890, and Los Angeles its first Fiesta de Los Angeles in 1894. In the Californians' taste for garden shows, floral pageants, and civic festivals, Mary Austin saw a revival of the Greek capacity for dramaturgy, from which, she hoped, the more formalized expression of outdoor theater might emerge, as it had in Greece. In *The Triumph of Light, a California Midwinter Sun Mystery* (1904) Charles Augustus Keeler tried to fashion a theatrical experience which combined lyric drama, the allegorical masque, music, and the dance. Keeler took for his theme the ancient myth of the sun's disappearance and return, putting it into a California setting. Although it seems never to have been performed, Keeler's play was intended as a ritual celebration of California's special relationship to the sun, its proposed presentation outdoors at mid-winter being an essential part of its message.

The dedication of the Greek Theater at Berkeley in 1903 led Californians to believe that Keeler's neo-Grecian ambitions were not unwarranted. Modeled upon the theater at Epidaurus, the Greek Theater was set in a natural amphitheater on the UC campus, surrounded by eucalyptus. William Randolph Hearst put up the money for its construction. It seated over eight thousand. Like the Burnham Plan for San Francisco, the Greek Theater had its naïve side. Berkeley, after all, was not Epidaurus. And yet the impulse toward outdoor theater that the amphitheater pointed toward was genuine. Three years after its dedication, when San Francisco lay smoldering in ruins, the Greek Theater showed itself capable of supporting more than naïve hellenizing. Before a vast crowd of refugees, Sarah Bernhardt appeared in an afternoon performance of Racine's *Phèdre*. She had toured the smoking rubble that morning in an open carriage with Arnold Genthe, tears streaming down her cheeks as she saw the destruction of the city which, next to Paris, she most loved. As she stepped before her audience, Bernhardt felt overwhelmed by the drama of the occasion; the thought of the ruined city across the Bay and the sight of the brave gathering of citizens in the sunlight filled her with an unknown ardor. She afterward said that it was the greatest performance of *Phèdre* in her career. The tragic theater of the Greeks had implied just such an interaction between art and experience, and for a moment Californians felt themselves in the face of true tragedy. As if by wrath of the gods, a great city had been shaken to its foundations. Like Racine's heroine, San Francisco had met death. For a moment in the afternoon, an aging but still great actress put the Greek Theater of Berkeley to that use intended in the Grecian variation of the Mediterranean metaphor.

In the redwoods north of San Francisco, at Bohemian Grove, a truly indigenous form of outdoor theater arose from the Cremation of Care ceremony of the Bohemian Club. Although it was in the genre of American lodge rites, the Cremation of Care was a ritual of meaning and taste, taking place each August during the midsummer encampment. At night, before a bonfire beneath the redwoods, Club officiants consigned Care to the flames. The ritual began in the early 1880's, and as the years went on its pageantry increased. Those who wrote of it praised the Cremation for its impressiveness. Flickering light from the bonfire added further mystery to the redwoods overhead. Watching the robed and mitred officials go through the ceremony, one felt closer to a dawn-world of myth and ritual, in which demon Care might indeed be banished and the gifts of the gods invoked. By the early 1900's an original play was commissioned to lead into the Cremation ceremony. Presented at night against a rising incline of redwoods, the Grove Plays brought to perfection that sort of outdoor drama which the Mediterranean metaphor urged Californians to make their own. Taking subjects from history, romance, and myth (sample productions: "The Man in the Forest," "Montezuma," "Saint Patrick at Tara," "The Green Knight," and George Sterling's "The Triumph of Bohemia"), the Grove Plays used no scenery but the redwoods. Staging, costumes, and pageantry, on the other hand, were elaborate. A full orchestra played an original score. The lighting effects were nothing short of spectacular. "Such was the spell cast by the text of the play, the acting, the lighting and the cathedral forest," recalled Arnold Genthe of the 1904 production of "Hamadryads" by Will Irwin, "that it was as if a long lost dream had been given reality."[23]

Unfortunately, only the privileged few could take part in this distinctly Californian theatrical experience. The exclusiveness of the Grove Plays was both a strength and a weakness. On the one hand, membership in the assumptions and felowship of the Club was necessary to proceed psychologically from the play to the Cremation ritual, and only an association of wealthy, like-minded men could afford to mount such lavish productions in the first place. On the other hand, something so Californian, so tied up with the mystery of the redwoods and a communal response to beauty, cried out to be made available to a larger audience. Opening in 1910, the Forest Theater of Carmel was intended to make outdoor drama a little more democratic. Like the Grove Plays, the productions of the Forest Theater Society featured original plays on historical or mythological themes, acted by amateurs in an outdoor setting. A group led by George Sterling favored mythological pageants, while Mary Austin's clique wanted

Biblical and Indian verse-drama. Like the Carmel colony itself, the presentations of the Forest Theater Society were uneven. It went without saying that the Society could not match the financial and technical resources of the Bohemian Club. But it did struggle to make regional theater available to the public, and as such it represented an advance over the restricted performances of Bohemian Grove. Taken at its best—in Mary Austin's *The Arrow Maker* (1911), for instance—the Forest Theater stood for a return to a drama of myth and ritual which was part of California's Mediterranean metaphor.

The culmination of the Greek impulse came from a young girl and what she thought about the dance. Dora Angela Duncan was born in San Francisco in 1878, the fourth child of a banker and minor poet. A suave gentleman, accustomed to advise the wealthy regarding purchases of art, Joseph Duncan once wrote a poem, "Children," praising the joys of parenthood, but he abandoned his own wife and family shortly before his last child was born. Dora, or Isadora as she became known, might have grown up in the prosperous Duncan home at Geary and Taylor, having a definite place in the San Francisco scheme of things; instead, divorce and poverty threw her into a childhood of cheap flats, frequent moves, and self-sufficiency. Isadora's mother kept her children together, raising them in eccentric freedom and passionate love of intellect and art. As a daughter of the bourgeoisie, Isadora might have surrendered her intelligence to the dominating proprieties of her father. As it turned out, she developed a mind of her own. Like another neglected adolescent of the same era, Jack London, she educated herself in the Oakland Public Library under the guidance of its librarian, the poet Ina Coolbrith.

In the course of her California adolescence Isadora Duncan made a number of identifications and discoveries. Abandoned by her father, she took her status and security from her maternal grandparents. Thomas Gray, Isadora's grandfather, immigrated to the United States from Ireland at the age of sixteen. In 1849 he brought his pregnant wife, also Irish-born, across the continent in a covered wagon. Isadora's mother was born on the journey. During the Civil War, Thomas Gray fought for the Union in the East, reaching the rank of colonel. From her grandparents Isadora Duncan acquired a taste for the heroic. The influence of her divorced mother's resentment intensified her perceptions. She saw her grandparents as part of the true California epic, in contrast to the minor artiness of her absent father. An adolescent intoxication with the poetry of Walt Whitman gave cosmic, mystic sweep to this identification with a heroic West to which she was bound by birth. She felt an affinity between Whitman's mighty line, the surf-roar of the Pacific, and the soaring of the Sierras. All of this occurred in the subconscious, subeval way of adolescence. It was tied in with sexual maturation and a growing desire to do something with her life. Like Gertrude Atherton, she dreamed of the East and of Europe.

Isadora Duncan's American energies, her identification as a Californian with the heroic, was touched by Greek imperatives. As a teenager she began to experiment with a form of naturalistic dancing which she felt was both Californian and Greek. Taking its principles from nature, she claimed, her dance both recovered the dance of Greece and expressed the response of the American before the surge of the continent. Like Greece and America it was democratic, in that it did not depend upon the intricate patterns beloved by an aristocratic culture, but stressed movements accessible to ordinary people. Like Greece and like the America of Walt Whitman, it asserted the unity of spirit and flesh. "I have discovered the dance. I have discovered the art which has been lost for two thousand years," Isadora Duncan told an astonished Augustin Daly in Chicago. She had left California with her mother, brother, and sister to pursue a career, and was now rushing backstage to implore the impresario to put her, a girl of seventeen, into one of his productions. "I bring you the dance. I bring you the idea that is going to revolutionise our entire epoch. Where have I discovered it? By the Pacific Ocean, by the waving pine-forests of Sierra Nevada. I have seen the ideal figure of youthful America dancing over the top of the Rockies. The supreme poet of our country is Walt Whitman. I have discovered the dance that is worthy of the poem of Walt Whitman. I am indeed the spiritual daughter of Walt Whitman. For the children of America I will create a new dance that will express America. I bring to your theatre the vital soul that it lacks, the soul of the dancer."[24]

Though it took its origins by the Pacific, Isadora Duncan's career, like that of Sibyl Sanderson, belonged to Europe. An unconventional love life and an indifference to politics made her *persona non grata* in the United States. Returning to San Francisco after World War I, she met with hostility and contempt. And yet as a girl she had danced by the Pacific. She had dreamed of effecting an affirmation of the-body-as-art which went back to Greece and was also an imperative of California. A Californian in more than her hatred of jewelry and corsets, she brought away the Greek metaphor. "I am a pilgrim," reads a 1902 entry in her notebook; "a pilgrim and a mediante from California I came—there as a child I played in

Isadora Duncan (1878–1927)

As a child she danced by the Pacific, and she said its rhythms entered her blood. She devised a form of naturalistic dancing which she felt was both Californian and Greek. Her career as a dancer took her to Europe, where she remained. Yet she insisted that she came as a Californian, to bear witness in the dance to the soaring Sierras and the surging Pacific. She had talent and love of life. She achieved much, and she suffered. Always, in success and in defeat, she was magnificent in her devotion—and in her courage.

the meadows. California is the land of gold—not therefore the gold which is coined in money but the free glad gold of the orange and the California poppy."[25]

IV

The desert and semi-arid lands of Southern California prompted comparisons to North Africa and the Near East, a region which had given birth to prophets, mystics, and great religions. Like the vine, the desert was in itself a symbol. It bespoke asceticism and a return to vision. It also suggested death. For those who crossed it in the early years the desert was the cruel, killing barrier before the garden of the Pacific, the ordeal of Sinai before the Promised Land. By the end of the century, having settled the continental edge, Americans started to drift eastward into the desert regions. Some dreamt of conquest by irrigation, projects realized in the Owens and Imperial valleys. Others sought escape from civilization, new modes of beauty—and the reality of spirit. A desert literature arose, represented in such now-classic accounts as John Charles Van Dyke's *The Desert* (1901), Mary Austin's *The Land of Little Rain* (1903), Arthur J. Burdick's *The Mystic Mid-Region* (1904), and George Wharton James's *The Wonders of the Colorado Desert* (1906). From these accounts emerged the Californian-as-desert-dweller, just as John Muir put his Californian in the mountains and Robinson Jeffers would place his by the sea. "It is stern, harsh, and at first repellent," wrote John Charles Van Dyke of the arid regions. "But what tongue shall tell the majesty of it, the eternal strength of it, the poetry of its widespread chaos, the sublimity of its lonely desolation!"[26]

As an art critic, Van Dyke described the desert with a schooled sensitivity to color, form, and light. His book is a drama of vistas and motion. Dunes shift and color runs through the rarest combinations of the spectrum. Across an immensity of space, fantastic mountain forms are visible. Overhead, cloud formations hourly change their shape and only the flight of a hunting hawk interrupts the white light of the sun. It all seemed so eternal, so beyond the touch of time; and yet etched into rock was evidence of ancient convulsions and long-lost seas. The still heat of the day ceded to the paradox of sudden winds and the certainty of night colds. The silence was deafening, even the mighty Colorado flowing noiselessly, as through a void. Because of the scarcity of vegetation and water, the struggle for existence took on new savagery. Plant life contorted itself into weird forms, as if caught in some unexplained anguish. The scorpion, the centipede, the tarantula, and the rattlesnake gave a quality of venom to the soil itself, and the horned toad and the gila monster seemed cursed beasts from a mythic past. The heat, the thirst, the loneliness, the fragility of survival, and the pressing mysteriousness forced men in upon themselves. It was, after all, the classic landscape of mystical adventure. Figures like the desert recluse Vanamee in Norris' *The Octopus* dramatized a new possibility for the American in the West. He might walk with God. "So must have appeared the half-inspired shepherds of the Hebraic legends," wrote Norris of his desert mystic, "the younger prophets of Israel, dwellers in the wilderness, beholders of visions, having their existence in a continual dream, talkers with God, gifted with strange powers."[27]

Mary Austin wanted such communion with ultimate reality. One summer morning, as a child in Carlinville, Illinois, she came upon a walnut tree on the edge of a sloping hill as she walked through an orchard. Silhouetted against the blue sky, its branches swayed in the wind. "Quite suddenly, after a moment of quietness there," she tells us of the experience, "earth and sky and tree and wind-blown grass and the child in the midst of them came alive together with a pulsing light of consciousness. There was a wild foxglove at the child's feet and a bee dozing about it, and to this day I can recall the swift inclusive awareness of each for the whole—I in them and they in me and all of us enclosed in a warm lucent bubble of livingness. I remember the child looking everywhere for the source of this happy wonder, and at last she questioned—'God?'—because it was the only awesome word she knew. Deep inside, like the murmurous swinging of a bell, she heard the answer, 'God, God . . .' "[28]

Mary Austin grew into a natural contemplative, a woman who by force of temperament and imagination hungered for mystical experience. A Methodist background and an acutely intuitive intelligence disposed her to a probing, experimental approach. She sought God not as a theological formulation, but as "the experienceable quality in the universe." Aesthetic perception functioned as the premise of Mary Austin's mysticism, and the discernment of pattern was its method. Wedded to the materials of the Southwest, she sensed in them the elusive possibilities of mystical encounter.

It began in the semiarid regions of Southern California, in the Tejon district of the lower San Joaquin Valley. Arriving there in 1888 from Illinois, she, her widowed mother, and her brothers took up a homestead. Between 1888 and 1904, when she moved to Carmel, the important events of her life took place. She made an unsatisfactory marriage, later dissolved by divorce. She gave birth to a daughter who was retarded and was to die in early adulthood. Getting to know Mexicans, Indians, and other desert dwellers in the early 1890's, she began to write of them, and of the desert itself, for *The Land of Sunshine* and *The Overland Monthly*. She became an artist of place, an indweller. Her revolt against Methodism left her innately religious temperament restless and without context. The desert restored her sense of mystery. She encountered Something which she called the Spirit of the Arroyos, "a lurking, evasive Something, wistful, cruel, ardent; something that rustled and ran, that hung half-remotely, insistent on being noticed, fled from pursuit, and when you turned from it, leaped suddenly and fastened on your vitals. This is no mere figure of speech, but the true movement of experience. Then, and ever afterward, in the wide, dry washes and along the edge of the chaparral, Mary was beset with the need of being alone with this insistent experiential pang for which the wise Greeks had the clearest name concepts . . . fauns, satyrs, the ultimate Pan. Beauty-in-the-wild, yearning to be made human."[29]

The Spirit of the Arroyos quickened her dormant religiosity; once again, she yearned for mystical experience. And then it happened. Her spiritual drought came to an end. "It was a dry April," she wrote, "but not entirely barren; mirages multiplied on every hand, white borage came out and blue nemophila; where the run-off of the infrequent rains collected in hollows, blue lupine sprang up as though pieces of the sky had fallen. On a morning Mary was walking down one of these, leading her horse, and suddenly she was aware of poppies coming up singly through the tawny, crystal-sanded soil, thin, piercing orange-colored flames. And then the warm pervasive sweetness of ultimate reality, the reality first encountered so long ago under the walnut tree. Never to go away again; never to be completely out of call. . . . Only the Christian saints have made the right words for it, and to them it came after long discipline of renunciation. But to Mary it just happened. Ultimate, immaterial reality. You walk into it the way one does into those wisps of warm scented air in hollows after the sun goes down; there you stand motionless, acquiescing, I do not know how long. It has nothing to do with time nor circumstance; no, nor morals nor behaviors. It is the only true and absolute."[30]

She began casting about for some way of relating through prayer and asceticism to the ultimate reality she had experienced amidst the lupine and the poppies. A brief reaffiliation with the Methodist Church left her dissatisfied; and an experimental Practice of the Presence of God drew her further and further away from Christian orthodoxy. The God she encountered in her meditation was neither triune nor personal, but a principle in creation itself. The Paiute, she felt, came closest to the truth when they understood It as Wakonda or The-Friend-of-the-Soul-of-Man. As the effective principle of creation, Wakonda could be reached through prayer, not in uncertain petition as in Protestantism, but with the certainty of a chemical reaction. Addressed properly, The-Friend-of-the-Soul-of-Man always heard. Prayer as practiced by the Paiute freed Mary Austin from a Calvinist universe, with its arbitrary, personal God acting out of inscrutable purposes. To the Indian way of looking at it, men and the principle behind creation shared a relationship of necessity. Putting oneself in harmony with creation—through patterns of work, art, the dance—one prayed, knowing from the start that you were being listened to if you prayed correctly. "Prayer is the whole process of becoming," Mary Austin observed just before her death; "of complete expressiveness of which we shall never arrive at any given mark. . . . It ties and unties, patterns and unravels; the most that we can do is to take it at the flow, going with it, leaning upon it."[31]

Christ in Italy (1912) and *The Man Jesus* (1915) attest to the spiritual implications of Mary Austin's desert sojourn. In a way, the two studies represent a contrasting between California-as-Italy and California-as-Near-East. Approaching her subject through the Southwest and the Mediterranean, that is, having in mind the settings and implications of Italy, Palestine, and Southern California, Austin compared the Christ of Catholicism with the desert Jesus. She first encountered the Catholic Christ through the Mexicans of Southern California. In 1908, under mysterious circumstances, she went to Italy. She embarked upon the Italian journey convinced that she was dying of a malignancy, although she was later very unclear about the facts of the case. She hinted at a miraculous cure but would commit herself only so far as to say that in Italy, where she had come to die, her condition "dwindled into the insignificance of a mistaken diagnosis."[32] Instead of dying, she plunged herself into a study of the Roman Catholic tradition. She studied religious art. She read learned treatises in the Vatican Library. She had discussions on the theology of prayer with no less a personage than the papal secretary of state, Cardinal Rafael Merry Del Val. She lived in a convent. A Roman Jesuit instructed her in the Spiritual Exercises of Saint Ignatius. None of this made Mary Austin a Catholic, nor did she intend it to. Like the California desert, Rome and Mediterranean Catholicity helped transform a Midwest Metho-

Mary Austin (1868–1934)

In Southern California she first encountered the Spirit of the Arroyos. That, in turn, led her to The-Friend-of-the-Soul-of-Man. She went to Italy for spiritual instruction, but at odd moments, in consultation with Jesuit and cardinal, she remembered Tinnemaha, the Paiute medicine man who had first instructed her. After World War I she found that California, for her at least, no longer held the mystery of things. And yet in the land of little rain she had learned that men were not alone.

dist into a Southwesterner alive to Indian and Mexican traditions. Catholic spirituality provided her with a tradition from which she defined a private ascesis. Catholic liturgical prayer attracted her, its sacramentalism and ritual confirming what she had learned from the Indian: that prayer was a patterned movement of body and soul by which one put oneself in harmony with the rhythms of creation in order to communicate with its ultimate meaning.

Italy enriched her, but in the long run she found the weight of its history oppressive. Sitting in its cathedrals, standing before its paintings, she thought of the desert. At odd moments, in consultation with Jesuit and cardinal, she remembered Tinnemaha, the Paiute medicine man, telling her about The-Friend-of-the-Soul-of-Man. Christ in Italy, the Christ of Catholic theology and art, seemed suffocated in human accretion. She could not imagine as one and the same the Second Person of theology and the Man of Sorrows of baroque art and popular devotion. She preferred the desert Jesus, the carpenter and peasant-prophet, the village rabbi who knew his people and his tradition. After World War I, she found that California, for her at least, no longer held the mystery of things. The Spirit of the Arroyos seemed to depart to New Mexico and she followed it there, to Santa Fe where the life of the Southwest, first encountered in Southern California, still lingered on. Southern California's land of little rain had revitalized her spirit. In the desert she had learned that men were not alone. They were linked to each other; and through The-Friend-of-the-Soul-of-Man they were linked to ultimate reality itself. "At the core of our Amerindian life," Mary Austin wrote, "we are consummated in the dash and color of collectivity. It is not that we work upon the Cosmos, but it works in us."[33] It was a good lesson for a lonely woman to learn, helped, as she was, by the arid regions of Southern California, which like the deserts of North Africa and the Near East drove men to dream of God.

V

The Spanish analogy had behind it the force of history, in that California began as part of the Spanish Empire. Travelers also discerned similarities of landscape between Old Spain and its New World outpost, especially the region along El Camino Real between Monterey and San Francisco, which prompted comparison to the plateaus of Castile and the northern coast of Asturias. For Forty-niners coming by sea, the encounter with Hispanic civilizations began on the voyage out. While anchored in the bay of Rio de Janeiro, they visited the city's magnificent Public Gardens, saw the Emperor in his box at the opera, and—invariably—made much of the racial mixture of the population. Valparaiso was the next port of call. "I fear the morals of Valparaiso are not of the highest order," observed one American; "yet a more social, hospitable and polite people I have never met."[34] Other responses, especially in matters of race and religion, were more hostile. Bayard Taylor reported seeing Americans light their cigars from the devotional tapers before the alter of the cathedral at Panama City. The democracy of Latin American worship, however, managed to impress some Yankees. "No pews invited the worshiper," said a Californian of his visit to the cathedral of Rio de Janeiro in 1849, "but princess and beggar knelt side by side under the swelling dome and worshiped at a common altar without distinction of person or purpose."[35]

Once in California, the American could not remain aloof from Mexican culture. Spanish phrases filled his conversation. Many Americans dressed Mexican style—sombrero, short jacket, serape, sash, bell-bottomed pants—and used the Mexican saddle. Most women in the state were Spanish-speaking. In Southern California, where the Mexican culture of Old California lasted until the 1870's, its influence upon Americans became even more noticeable. Throughout the 1850's and 1860's, Los Angeles remained a cluster of low-lying adobes grouped around a plaza, its American population (the better sort) locally married; speaking Spanish, using Mexican money, drinking mescal and aguardiente, and eating Mexican food. On the great ranchos of Central and Southern California, life went on as before the conquest, save that rancheros now bore non-Spanish names.

Frémont's cordial relations with Old Californians suggested that dialogue with Hispanic California was the fundamental imperative of the Iberian analogy. Ironically, dialogue began as an intention to despoil Mexicans of their claim to the land. Litigation drove Americans to the archives, and out of this early legal research originated the first understanding of the structure and aims of Old California. William Carey Jones, a lawyer and the brother-in-law of Frémont, was sent in 1849 to California as confidential agent of the Secretary of the Interior, to investigate the status of Mexican land titles. Jones researched the archives of San Diego, Los Angeles, Monterey, San Jose, and San Francisco. He was probably the first American to use such sources for historical enquiry. Jones' *Report on the Subject of Land Titles in California* (1850), published upon his return to Washington, provided a broad social survey of Hispanic California, and as such it must be considered the founding text of post-conquest dialogue between American and Old Californian. When John W. Dwinelle took to court San Francisco's claim of land owed the city under Mexican law, he backed his argument with an extensive investigation into the ancient, colonial, and modern laws of Spain and Mexico, and San Francisco's development in that context. Dwinelle's *The Colonial History of the City of San Francisco* (1863) set forth an elegant legal brief—and anchored San Francisco's conception of itself deeply, irretrievably, onto the Hispanic past. In later years, imagination built upon legal continuity. Much of California's history was written by lawyers directly concerned with problems of land title, the subject providing ready-made training in historiography. Frederic Hall, for example, grew wealthy as a land law specialist in Santa Clara County. He briefly acted as legal advisor to Emperor Maximilian I. Hall's *History of San Jose and Surroundings* reflected his knowledge of, and sympathy for, Mexican society, plus the disciplining effect of a large collection of Spanish and Mexican documents.

Land titles implied a continuity, whereas the basic situation was violent and disruptive. John Rollin Ridge, a San Francisco journalist and poet, himself a Georgian Cherokee who knew what it was to lose ancestral lands, put forth the Mexican case in *The Life and Adventures of Joaquin Murieta, the Celebrated California Bandit* (1854). The fact that Ridge's hero had little in common with various Mexican desperadoes plaguing California under the name Joaquin did not imply that Ridge was uninterested in history. Ridge claimed that he was setting down Murieta's murderous career not to minister to depraved taste, but "to contribute my mite to those materials out of which the early history of California shall one day be composed." A burden of injustice was California's because of the American treatment of Mexicans, and Ridge intended to see that it was not lost to memory. Joaquin was an upper-class Mexican youth, driven into banditry by Americans after they had raped his fiancée, lynched his half-brother, and given him a humiliating public whipping. He represented the displaced and violently abused Mexican Californians of the 1850's, many of whom, like Murieta, took to the hills as outlaws. Murieta, Ridge insisted, was no criminal, but the Rinaldo Rinaldini of California—"a hero who has revenged his country's wrongs and washed out her disgrace in the blood of her enemies." Backed by prominent Mexican Californians, Joaquin organizes a brigade to sweep Southern California free of Americans. The lesson of Murieta's career, Ridge insisted, was "that there is nothing so dangerous in its consequences as injustice to individuals—whether it arise from prejudice of color or from any other source; that a wrong done to one man is a wrong to society and to the world."[36]

General Mariano Guadalupe Vallejo offered Americans a figure of reconciliation. Born in Monterey in 1808, the son of a soldier who broke off studies for the priesthood to join the army, Vallejo received a Californian upbringing and at sixteen was made a cadet. Commissioned ensign in 1827, he filled out the idleness of garrison life with enough reading to make him an anomaly in Old California, a native-born citizen with an education. In 1830 he was elected to the legislature, and in 1836, when Alvarado declared California independent, he named Vallejo commandant general, an office which Mexico confirmed in 1838, when Alta California returned to Federal jurisdiction. Vallejo adjusted easily to the American occupation; for the Yankee way of doing things appealed to his secular, progressive instincts. He sent his son Platon to New York to attend Columbia's College of Physicians and Surgeons. Graduating at the head of his class, Platon Vallejo was the first Spanish-speaking Californian to win the M.D. degree. He later served in the medical corps of the Union Army. Vallejo himself assured Lincoln of the loyalty of California's Spanish-speaking population. Visiting various Army headquarters, he renewed acquaintanceships with high-ranking officers he had known as captains and lieutenants when the Army occupied California. He scandalized Platon by addressing General Grant as "Grant," and being addressed in return as "Vallejo." "Why not?" Vallejo asked his son. "Aren't we both generals?"[37]

From the 1860's onward General Vallejo assumed a place of importance in the imagination of American California. He symbolized the hope that all of Old California had not been lost. *The Annals of San Francisco*, which had nothing but contempt for the majority of Mexicans, cited General Vallejo as the very model of the Old California gentleman. Five years later, in 1860, Vallejo occupied with Frémont the stage of the New Music Hall in San Francisco as Edmund Randolph orated for three hours concerning California's days of Spanish glory. During the conquest, Frémont had thrown Vallejo into the calaboose. Their appearance side by side signified the *rapprochement* of Latin and American Californians. "In him we recognize a noble type of the generous, hospitable Native Californian," said an orator of the General in 1870, before the Society of California Pioneers, "a type of that race among us that is fast passing away. No! not passing away, but mingling its blood with the Anglo-Saxon hordes, contributing an element of Latin fire and dash to Scandinavian descendants, which is, and is to be, the perfection of the human family."[38] After the conquest, Vallejo served as a delegate to the Constitutional Convention at Monterey, and later as state senator and mayor of Sonoma. His presence

Mariano Guadalupe Vallejo (1808–1890)

Intelligent, widely read, secular by temperament and progressive by inclination, General Vallejo was believed to have favored annexation to the United States, a belief flattering to Americans in that Vallejo was perhaps the most powerful man in the Mexican territory of Alta California. Americans liked to think that, as a hidalgo of Old California thriving in the new order, Vallejo symbolized the continuity of the two cultures.

brought an aura of Old California to official gatherings. As Bancroft put it: "He was the noblest Californian of them all!"[39]

As complexities multiplied, the image of Old California grew more appealing. "Without disturbance, without bloodshed, with scarcely a ripple on the calm surface of their simple society," wrote Franklin Tuthill in the mid-1860's, "these occupants of a wild and unknown portion of the continent drifted through two generations."[40] In the opinion of Judge Elisha W. McKinstry, addressing the Society of California Pioneers in 1871, something precious had been lost in the passing of Old California. By contrast, American California seemed opulent, pretentious, and vulgar. "Such a generation," Judge McKinstry upbraided silver-rich San Franciscans, "can hardly comprehend that elegance and beauty may as well be nourished by a diet of *tortillas* and *olla podrida* as by *pâté de foie gras* and *bourgogne*."[41] Attorney William J. Shaw, himself on the verge of leaving legal practice to enjoy a life of learned leisure, made a similar point five years later, telling the Pioneers "that our predecessors here enjoyed more genuine human happiness with their wooden carts and plows of sticks than has ever been seen in our societies."[42]

One of the most interesting examples of the tendency to endow Spanish California with the attributes of a lost utopia appears in *The California of the Padres; or, Footprints of Ancient Communism* (1875), by Elizabeth Hughes. California's current social troubles, Mrs. Hughes wrote, were but one instance of the breakdown of human community brought on by nineteenth-century industrialism. What had the American transplanted to California but "a life of fevered ambition for the attainment of an uncertain end"? Look at the vulgarity and materialism of American architecture, Mrs. Hughes urged; then contrast Nob Hill ostentatiousness with the spiritual dignity of mission buildings and the simple grace of the adobe. In each case, the soul of the society shone through its dwellings. She was no advocate of Romanism, Mrs. Hughes cautioned, but modern California, if it ever were to fulfill its promise, had to take the mission system for its model of industrial organization and social reform. "Nature has prepared the place," she said of California, "for a laboratory of new ideas, and a new social order." Let the state get busy with its destiny. As an imaginative ideal, the vision of an appropriately Californian organization of community life lingered on through the turn of the century. Amidst the American clamor, the myth of pre-conquest contentment remained a haunting alternative.

In many cases, romanticization of the mission era had a hollow ring.

Bancroft's *California Pastoral, 1769-1848* (1888) dramatized the ambivalence behind the myth. Packed with colorful anecdotes of Spanish and Mexican days, *California Pastoral* supposedly celebrated the Latin past. Yet undertones of contempt pervaded the book, undertones which broke out into expressions of hatred for all that was supposed to be so glorious. There had been so much anti-Catholicism in the first volume of Bancroft's *History of Central America* that a committee of irate Roman churchmen demanded that it be rewritten. Henry L. Oak, a disciplined historian, kept anti-Catholic attitudes out of the *History of California*. In *California Pastoral*, however, which Bancroft wrote personally, anti-Catholic tirades reached heights of intemperate and inarticulate fury. Hatred was hardly the basis for romantic appropriation. Like the starch-collared fundamentalists who, to the amusement of Frank Lloyd Wright, later sat so uncomfortably in neo-mission bungalows, Bancroft never felt at home in his Hispanic edifice. At its most harmless, the myth he advanced resulted in dishonest architecture. At its worst, its pastel nostalgia contrasted mockingly with the lot of California's Spanish-speaking people, a despised minority, deprived of their lands, given their only dignity in the realms of gringo fantasy.

Idealization of the mission era received its biggest boost from *Ramona* (1884), a best-selling novel by Helen Hunt Jackson. A Massachusetts-born widow, Mrs. Jackson dedicated the last six years of her life to Indian philanthropy. So widespread was her reputation as an expert in Indian affairs that in 1883 the Department of the Interior, in a move unusual for the times, appointed her and Abbot Kinney to investigate the condition of Mission Indians in the southern counties of California, especially in regard to contested land rights. In their *Report on the Condition and Needs of the Mission Indians* (1883) Jackson and Kinney protested the systematic removal of the Indians from lands they had occupied since the days of the Spanish. They called for a survey of Indian-held lands, the removal of white squatters, and free legal counsel for Indian litigants in land disputes, together with medical and educational assistance. Despairing that her *Report* would have any effect in Washington, Mrs. Jackson sat down in her room in the Berkeley Hotel in New York City to write an Indian *Uncle Tom's Cabin*. *Ramona* described how an Indian sheepherder, Alessandro Assis, and his half-breed wife, Ramona Ortega, had their lives destroyed by white greed. A mood of nostalgia and romance, however, warred against social protest. During visits to Southern California, Mrs. Jackson had been incensed at the treatment of the Indians, but she had also fallen in love with the romance of the mission era. As she wrote, sentiment overcame outrage. Her novel moved in the direction of a glorification of a Southern California suffused with the golden memory of pastoral days, rather than an indictment of present injustices. Aunt Ri, a white woman won over to the cause of the Indian because of her friendship with Alessandro and Ramona, makes a number of trenchant observations; but it is the ancient Franciscan Padre Salvierderra, with his memories of old mission days, who has really captured Mrs. Jackson's imagination.

Charles Fletcher Lummis made a more informed identification with the Spanish associations of Southern California. In various ways—as historian, poet, ethnologist, journalist, and librarian—Lummis spent a lifetime encouraging Southern Californians to reappropriate their Hispanic heritage. He was a Massachusetts Yankee and a Harvard man, and his identification with the frontier, in his case the frontier of the Spanish Southwest, should be seen in the context of similar turn-of-the-century alignments on the part of two other Harvard men, Owen Wister and Theodore Roosevelt, for whom the vanishing West served as the corrective symbol for personal and social values under assault. In 1884 Lummis walked from Ohio to California, as on a pilgrimage. It took him 112 days, and the eccentricity of it attested to the fact that his would be no routine relationship to Southern California. As a locale and as an imaginative ideal, the Spanish Southwest provided Lummis with a counter-force to some very destructive urges.

In the drama of Southern California's self-discovery, Charles Fletcher Lummis played a leading role. From 1895 to 1903 he served as editor of *Land of Sunshine* (changed in 1902 to *Out West*), which he struggled to make as influential in the South as *The Overland Monthly* had been during the coming-of-age of the North a generation previously. Through the vehicle of his column, "The Lion's Den," Lummis did what he could to guide Southern California in the right direction. He wanted more than a stage-set of bungalows and orange groves. He wanted a real alternative in the matter of American lifestyles, a hitherto unachieved blend of physical, moral, and intellectual culture. As librarian of the City of Los Angeles from 1905 to 1911, Lummis made the public library function in its best American manner: the people's free university, active agent in the American quest for self-improvement and expanded horizons, not just the passive repository of books. As founder of the Landmarks Club he led in the fight to restore the missions before they crumbled away completely and to preserve other places of historical interest. Defender of Indian rights as a journalist, Lummis studied Indian cultures as a devoted amateur ethnologist. He helped found the Southwest Museum to accord preservation and tribute to the relics and artifacts of the great Indian cultures of the Southwest.

But it was as a scholar and defender of the Spanish heritage that Lummis made his most lasting contribution. In his literary work of the 1890's —most significantly represented in *The Spanish Pioneers* (1893)—and throughout thousands of pages of journalism, Lummis struggled to bring Americans first to acknowledge the Spanish heritage, next to respect it, and then to make a deeper act of appropriation. Above all, it was the austerity of Spanish frontier civilization, its internalization of complex ideals and its sparseness of external detail, which most attracted Lummis. Personally, he could never keep his house in order. Until his fires banked in later years, a compulsive love life made him notorious. Moderation—in anything—never came easily. As city editor of the Los Angeles *Times* he worked, drank, and dissipated himself into a paralytic stroke. Like Roosevelt, Lummis plunged himself into the frontier to restore a shattered system. From 1888 to 1892 he lived in San Mateo, New Mexico, bringing himself to health through a regime of enforced outdoor activity. It was not an uninterrupted recuperation. While in New Mexico he suffered two more strokes, the last of which left him a speechless invalid. He had to be lifted onto his horse and he could manage to fish only by lying at the side of the river in the prone position. By 1892, however, when he left on an archeological expedition to Bolivia and Peru, Lummis had regained his health.

The Spanish Southwest served him as the locale and the objective correlative of a desired restoration. For the rest of his life he tried to counter his disorderly impulses with what he took to be the Spanish imperatives of restraint and purpose. Out of the confusion of his personal life he had fled to work as to a narcotic, and it had left him a bedridden invalid. Now he returned to Los Angeles to preach the pace of the land of *poco tiempo*, where things occurred in stride and where there was a time and a place for everything. He had suffered a confusion of instincts and goals; now he would organize his life around the all-compelling task of coaxing the emerging American Southwest and Southern California toward an organic integration of Latin values into its way of living. On the historical front, he wanted the epic of the Spanish frontier made part of the colonial heritage of those states and territories stretching from Texas to the Pacific. The American of this region, Lummis insisted, was the cultural descendant

Charles Fletcher Lummis (1859–1928)

He belonged to a generation of college-trained Easterners who sought renewal through an imaginative relationship to region and to the ideals of the frontier. In his case the locale was Southern California and the Spanish Southwest. Lummis wanted the region to be more than a stage-set of orange groves and bungalows. He wanted Southern Californians to see themselves as the moral heirs of Spain. He encouraged them to internalize in an American way the aesthetic austerity of the civilization which had prepared the way for their own.

of both Puritan and conquistador. As such, he should live differently, that is, in ways that showed his Spanish heritage. Lummis himself, known to his friends as Don Carlos, dressed in a corduroy suit, vaguely Spanish in cut, and wore a sash and Spanish hat. Making himself an expert in the language, he collected the folklore and songs of the Spanish borderlands and of Old California. With the help of Indian artisans he built a stone-and-adobe hacienda, called El Alisal, the Sycamore, from the grove which surrounded it. It took him about fifteen years to finish, and, once complete, El Alisal stood, as Lummis intended it to, as an architectural enactment of Southern California's inner metaphor. Built around a patio, its walls hung with Indian rugs and California paintings, its ceilings crossed by beams showing the rough cut of an ancient adze, El Alisal dramatized perhaps better than anything he had written Lummis' feeling for the rugged romance of Southern California as daughter of New Spain. There, gathering the talent and literati of the day, Lummis would urge them along toward that shimmering Southern California which ever held his imagination.

He did not intend the theatricality of his own witness as a literal paradigm. Southern Californians, after all, might well balk at corduroy suits and sombreros and find themselves unable to build spacious haciendas. They could, however, respond to the Spanish metaphor, making it a part of their self-image as Californians. Proud of the large numbers of educated middle-class Easterners and Midwesterners filling up Southern California, Lummis wanted them imaginatively integrated into the historical imperatives of their new environment. Southern California was not a *tabula rasa*, Lummis asserted, despite its vast unsettled spaces. If the new Californian would only listen, he might catch echoes of an experience which went back farther than his own colonial legacy. Hearing this, responding to a new nexus of landscape, climate, and history, the American in Southern California might set about the realization of a truly authentic American alternative.

Lummis, like Mary Austin, whom he sponsored, despised the sort of fake mission romance engendered by *Ramona*. As a journalist, he campaigned for both the preservation and proper interpretation of the missions. Contrary to what the mission myth would have Americans believe, Lummis roared from the pages of "The Lion's Den," Southern California had never supported such a pastel, pseudo-Castilian *mise en scène*. It had been a rugged frontier, true, but one touched by beauty. The Californian need not turn the mission into something resembling a La Scala production of *La Forza del Destino* in order to feel its ideality and charm. These frontier churches strung up the California coast like so many beads in a rosary stood for spiritual foundations as impressive as the spires of Massachusetts. One need not be a Catholic, Lummis asserted, to feel their power as historical monuments or to internalize them as symbolic elements in a cultural landscape. If Americans were willing to respond to Mediterranean analogies as diverse and tenuously related as Italy, Greece, and the Near East, then how much more important should be the historical presence of Spain as represented in the Franciscan cloisters?

Whatever the unevenness of his talents or the egocentricity of his methods, Charles Fletcher Lummis, fifty years or so after the conquest, embarked singlehandedly upon a work of reconciliation between Spain and the United States. The War of 1898, when once again the Yankee rose up in anti-Spanish jingoism, set back his efforts, but he persevered. A Latin-Yankee California had existed briefly before the conquest. Lummis envisioned its return as an American Southern California alert to the implications of the Spanish metaphor. Whatever it decided it was, California could not ignore its Spanish-speaking past.

VI

The Mediterranean analogy was noticeable in Californian architecture and city planning. In 1908, John Nolen, city planner and landscape architect of Cambridge, Massachusetts, came to San Diego at the request of the Civic Improvement Committee to prepare a comprehensive plan of urban development. Like Burnham in San Francisco, Nolen found that San Diego had mismanaged its opportunities. Instead of being a spacious expression of Southern California, San Diego was just another shabby provincial town. Taking into account factors of population, topography, climate, and cultural expectations, Nolen fashioned an ideal San Diego.

It was an open Mediterranean city. Nolen widened San Diego's streets, arranging them in harmony with landscape. He removed overhead wires and planted trees along sidewalks. He advocated replacing such dull designations as D Street and Fifth Street with names taken from California history and literature or from Spanish topographical terms. He scattered squares and open places throughout the city, including a magnificent downtown plaza. He suggested that an esplanade, part rialto, part recreational center, be built along the harbor. "The vision of this new San Diego from the Bay," wrote Nolen, "with the mountains of Southern California and Mexico, noble in outline and rich in color, in the background, is enough to move the most sluggish to action."[43] The idle 1400-acre area in the heart of the city, set aside for public purposes but never utilized, Nolen wanted developed as the matrix of a park network which would include the Bay Front, Point Loma, La Jolla, Soledad Mountain, Fort Stockton, and Torry Pines. As part of the development of Mission Cliff, San Diego De Alcala, first of the California missions, would be restored. A *paseo* (a promenade uninterrupted by crossings) swept through the city to the Bay Front, where it dramatically opened into a width of 1200 feet. Flower beds, pergolas, terraces, splashing fountains, basins, and cascades lined its path.

The cities of Southern Europe and Latin America provided Nolen with his inspiration. Naples suggested how San Diego—which called itself the Naples of America—should develop its waterfront. Nice and the resort cities on the Italian lakes suggested how San Diego might handle its public gardens. Rio de Janeiro taught how to sweep the harbor with construction, and Buenos Aires how to harmonize boulevards and open spaces. Nolen was impressed with the way sky, sea, mesa, canyon, mountain, and beach played off one another with Mediterranean clarity. His sketches for San Diego's proposed civic center demonstrated the ideality of his response: an orchestration of Italian and Spanish buildings, palm-lined avenues and sunny plazas, all in counterpoint to land, sea, and sky. He wanted his proposals to evoke "the peculiar opportunity for joy, for health, for prosperity, that life in Southern California, more especially in San Diego, offers to all."[44] The Burnham Plan set forth San Francisco as a neo-baroque imperial city, mistress of Pacific empire. The Nolen plan set forth another California alternative, that of a seaside celebration of sun and sky, an urban arena for the Mediterranean encounter of line, color, warmth, and spaciousness.

As was the case in San Francisco, San Diego's Panama-California Exposition proceeded from the same developmental impulse as its city plan. And as in San Francisco, the Exposition alone achieved concrete expression. Fairs were better business than urban renewal. From a sleepy town of 39,750 in 1909, when planning for the Panama-California Exposition commenced, San Diego grew to a population of more than 100,000 in 1915, when the Fair opened. In that growth, the Nolen Plan had only mild victories, and these were achieved through the agency of the Exposition. Most importantly, San Diego developed, as Nolen had suggested, the 1400-acre tract in the city's center. Its very barrenness had stood as a symbol of unfulfilled expectations since that day in 1868 when the frontier community had set it aside for use as a public park. Choosing these barren canyons as site for the Exposition, San Diego voted $1,850,000 in bonds for park improvement and named the area after the discoverer of the Pacific, Vasco Nuñez de Balboa. There, on hills overlooking American reality, San Diego built its dream-city.

To interpret the Mediterranean ideal of San Diego in the language of exposition architecture, the city fathers selected an Easterner, Bertram Grosvenor Goodhue of New York City. Then at the peak of his career, Goodhue had been working in Spanish Colonial for the decade prior to the Panama-California Exposition. Its romance appealed to his dreamy imagination, always in search of aesthetic escape. Goodhue loved the remote, the forgotten in time. The anti-modernism of Goodhue's aesthetic dated back to the 1890's, when he was associated with a short-lived pre-Raphaelite journal, *The Knight Errant*. His nostalgia sustained itself through a variety of architectural styles. To Goodhue Spanish Colonial stood for a revisionist, anti-industrial aesthetic. As a Mexican tradition, it had emerged from a society which was organized around religion and a peasantry, both of which Goodhue saw as essential to a thriving art-sense and which he found lacking in the civilization north of the Rio Grande. He became a leading exponent of Spanish Colonial in the United States, a revival especially appropriate, he thought, in the American Southwest, where Mexican civilization had once held sway.

There was another movement in Goodhue's thought and taste, however, a thrust toward modernity. As steel frames and reinforced concrete entered American building, Goodhue envisioned a new American architectural idiom. What Goodhue was probing is evident in two designs completed just before his early death in 1924, those for the Nebraska State Capitol and the Los Angeles Public Library. In both buildings, concrete masses were brought into calm and ordered harmony with a minimum of surface ornament, arrangements which recalled traditional relationships but were also startlingly new. Believing that "nothing that apes the past is genuine art," Goodhue attempted to pass through traditional modes on the way to the modern.

In that journey Spanish Colonial proved an important stage. It satisfied two needs in Goodhue: a need for history and a need for suggestions on how to handle form, mass, texture, and color in that way of the future haunting his imagination. Spanish Colonial, not Mission, seemed to Goodhue the best basis for Southern Californian architecture. Its simplicity, blank spaces, tile, and masonry possessed more utility and beauty, more modern resonances, than tortuously derivative adaptations of Mission. A Spanish Colonial revival could be both romantic and modern. Goodhue had first been in Southern California in the late 1890's as a consultant to J. M. Gillespie in the designing of El Fureides, a Mediterranean villa in Montecito, a home judged by contemporaries to be one of California's great regional expressions. That Goodhue was in sympathy with California's search for a Mediterranean identity was evident in the designs he submitted in 1910 to the Roman Catholic Archdiocese of Los Angeles for a cathedral and hospital complex. Over tile-roofed villas, Spanish or Italian in style, Goodhue's cathedral dominates a Mediterranean city of pastel ideality. Cypresses line boulevards where neither streetcars, automobiles, nor signs attest to American occupation. It was no surprise that in 1910 Goodhue was chosen Chief Architect for the Panama-California Exposition. The New York architect and San Diego boosters found their interests mutual. Each had an ideal city secreted within themselves. Each wanted the romance of the past and the promise of modernity.

With great relish, Goodhue set out to interpret San Diego and Southern California. He wanted the Panama-California Exposition to express the ideal-mind of the American Southwest. This region had a history older than the East Coast, asserted Goodhue. San Diego should give that heritage spatial expression in intimate harmony with "the tenderest of skies, the bluest of seas, mountains of perfect outline, the richest of sub-tropical foliage, the soft speech and unfailing courtesy of the half-Spanish, half-Indian peasantry." Goodhue admitted that "exposition architecture differs from that of our everyday world in being essentially the fabric of a dream —not to endure but to provide, after the fashion that stage scenery provides—illusion rather than reality." He would create "such a city as would have fulfilled the visions of Fray Junipero Serra as he toiled and dreamed while he planted missions from San Diego to Monterey."[45]

In a setting of semi-tropical vegetation, atop a mesa triangulated by deep arroyos, Goodhue built a fantastic Spanish city, its white walls and multicolored tiles glistening in the blue California sky. An arched bridge of reinforced concrete swept breathtakingly across a deep canyon to join the Exposition with San Diego proper. Critics praised the dramatic cohesiveness of the arrangement, comparing it to El Greco's painting of Toledo before a storm. Christian Brinton found the whole affair "a visible expression of the collective soul of the Southwest," seeming "to have sprung spontaneously from the soil and the vivid race consciousness of those who inhabit this vast and fecund hinterland."[46] It seemed as if San Diego's consciousness had been probed, its inner fantasies revealed. Critics praised the fact that the Exposition was intended as a metaphor for future growth. No fences or hedges marked off the fairgrounds from the city. Landscaping was continuous, weaving its motifs into parts of San Diego proper. Buildings in the California Quadrangle were permanent, intended as the nucleus of a recreational center which would include a museum, library, art gallery, and zoological garden. "It is a very pleasing thought of the San Diego of the future," noted Eugen Neuhaus, "with its ever-growing development entirely encircling this great garden spot we now admire as an Exposition."[47]

Like Maybeck's Palace of Fine Arts, Goodhue's California Quadrangle, especially the cathedral-like California State Building, conferred romantic historicity upon a rather raw American city. It was variously compared to the Giralda Tower of Seville, the cathedral of Cordova, the Balvanera Chapel of the Church of San Francisco in Mexico City, the cathedral at Oaxaca, Mexico, or the church of Montepulciano in Italy. The very roll call of these names gave satisfaction. Such were the associations San Diegans had sought to evoke. Goodhue planned that the Panama-California Exposition should recapitulate the architectural history of Spain in America. With rare scholarship, Exposition buildings set forth the epic of Spanish Colonial, beginning in Renaissance Europe, continuing through the great monuments of Mexico, spanning the Indian simplicity of pueblo-like desert chapels and the Franciscan romance of the California missions.

Thus Goodhue built a dream-city, for himself and for San Diego. Significantly, he had been chosen over local architect Irving Gill for the commission. Aside from political considerations (that is, aside from Goodhue's more successful lobbying), Gill's geometric use of poured concrete symbolized a California of full modernity. He and Goodhue both reverenced the canon of Spanish Southwestern architecture, but while Goodhue was content to move toward its imperatives of clean, bold line through historicism, Gill went there directly, ignoring scholarship in favor of a daring, ahistorical idiom. Only Goodhue's post-Exposition work, homes of white-walled, adobe-like simplicity, showed him catching up to what Gill was practicing in the early 1900's. In 1910 Goodhue was just at that stage where he could remarkably fulfill San Diego's needs: poised between past and present, glimpsing the modern but filled with nostalgia for an imagined past.

The theory and practice of gardening and domestic architecture showed the effect of the canonization by the Panama-California Exposition of Spanish Revival as the official California style. The quest for the perfect California garden had always been an important factor in local design. In San Diego itself, Irving Gill invented a new form of housing, the garden apartment. City plans commissioned during this period for San Jose, Oakland, and Santa Barbara stressed the necessity for a distinctly Californian answer to the problem of landscaping. Planner C. M. Robinson suggested that San Jose tear down every fence within the city limits and landscape the city as a whole, integrating itself with surrounding orchards and flowering fields. Cities and towns rarely achieved such ideals, but private builders found the goal of garden living more attainable. The California bungalow featured lovely garden effects. In Southern California, a critic observed, "house and garden are often designed together so that the garden will conform to the lines of the house and the planting control the view, with the result that from within doors interesting perspectives open, leading perhaps from room to room and finally through glass doors down a brick-paved pergola overgrown with luxuriant vines, or into a sunny courtyard, or broad shady veranda, furnished and used as a living-room."[48]

In 1904 the Berkeley poet Charles Augustus Keeler provided California with a garden ideology. He saw the garden as the enactment of the poetry and romance of California life. In Keeler's mind, California offered a chance for aesthetic moderation, privacy, health, learning, and domestic leisure. The Californian pruned, subdued, and harmonized his garden in order to invoke on a manageable and symbolic scale values of reforming refinement. "Let us have gardens," Keeler urged Californians, "wherein we can assemble for play or where we may sit in seclusion at work; gardens that will exhilarate our souls by the harmony and glory of pure and brilliant color, that will nourish our fancy with suggestions of romance as we sit in the shadow of the palm and listen to the whisper of rustling bamboo; gardens that will bring nature to our homes and chasten our lives with the purity of the great Earth Mother."[49]

Palm and bamboo—Mediterranean and Oriental images: there was the usual California problem of appropriation. Keeler's aesthetic emphasized ordered luxuriance. Gardens grew easily in California—"like rank weeds," he noted ambiguously. The problem was to cut back, to guide certain growth, to have richness within limits. Bruce Porter felt that there was a quality of too-muchness to California gardens. Human care seemed immaterial in the face of such fertility. Porter missed "the quality of appeal, of tenderness, of the hint of a delicate care bestowed, that gardens speak of in more difficult climates, where lavish growth and bloom is a definite attainment on the part of everybody and everything concerned." Rampant abundance did not express the balance and serenity of the California ideal. In Southern California everything seemed to grow; hence the exotic offered a special temptation. Frank Lloyd Wright shuddered at the phantasmagoric carnival of Southern California planting. He condemned the failure to select, to refuse indulgence in the exotic for its own sake, and he saw this as but one indication of the overly eclectic quality of Southern California life.

The appropriation of Oriental and Mediterranean garden aesthetics offered an ideological solution. California had historical links with both traditions, with the Oriental garden through its Chinese and Japanese citizens and its position facing the Far East, with the Mediterranean garden through Mission planting, which had been in the tradition of Southern Europe. Both were highly formal traditions, emphasizing control over nature. The Mission garden was considered especially appropriate. It had been exuberant enough, but at the same time it had never lost its links with Mediterranean design. As a formal tradition, the Mission or neo-Mediterranean garden ordered vigor and conferred historicity; as a frontier tradition, it justified a taste for experiment, for the hybrid and near chaotic. Keeler wanted the California garden to be "a compromise between the natural and formal types"—"one that simulates, as nearly as may be, the charm of the wilderness, tamed and diversified for convenience and accessibility."[50]

It was the persistent California quest, defined this time in garden terms: how to maintain both vigor and refinement, a sense of fresh beginnings and fertile possibilities, as well as a sense of order, design, historicity. On the one hand, Keeler advocated the planting of bamboo, palm, dracaenas, magnolias, orange, banana, eucalypti, acacias, pittosporums, grevillias, and araucarias. On the other, he wanted this diverse flora brought into comforting harmony. Such was the thrust of turn-of-the-century garden theory in California: a desire to strike a balance between variety and design, indulgence and restraint. The Mediterranean analogy helped in the attempt.

Even more than garden theory, architecture turned to the Mediterranean. Goodhue's Iberian extravaganza climaxed and consolidated California's appropriation of Mediterranean models as the basis of its regional architecture. When the Colonial Revival, set off by the New England

Exhibit at the Philadelphia Centennial of 1876, reached California in the 1880's, architects turned to the mission era as California's equivalent colonial period. The arcades of Stanford University and Arthur Benton's Mission Inn at Riverside attested to the vitality of Mission Revival in the late 1880's and early 1890's. A. Page Brown's California State Building at the Chicago Exposition of 1893 put Mission before the world as California's official style. Edward R. Swain's 1896 Golden Gate Park Lodge raised the Mission Revival to its highest level of suitability and taste. It was first thought that the Panama-California Exposition should be in Mission, but Goodhue objected. It was obvious to him that the Mission Revival had passed its peak. Goodhue pushed the architecture of the Fair back in time, to the style of which Mission had been but a faint recollection, Spanish Colonial. In a sense, he forced the Mission Revival to its logical conculsion. If California were to return to history, argued the scholarship of Goodhue's buildings, then let that history be accurate and pure.

In another sense, Goodhue consolidated under the banner of Spanish Colonial the entire Mediterranean advance of California architecture. If one includes Classical and Beaux Arts Imperial, most turn-of-the-century architecture in California was Mediterranean in inspiration. Public buildings tended to be Classical in the north and Romanesque in the south. Most of the representative homes discussed by Porter Garnett in *Stately Homes of California* (1915) were in the Italian style. Spanish architecture existed on a wide variety of fronts: from Charles Fletcher Lummis' El Alisal to James D. Phelan's Montalvo, an elegant Renaissance mansion overlooking the Santa Clara Valley. Lummis' home looked to the Spain of the American Southwest; Mrs. Phoebe A. Hearst's Hacienda Del Pozo de Verona near Pleasanton looked to the Spain of the Moor. The San Francisco Ferry Building reproduced the Giralda Tower of the cathedral of Seville. Rebuilt San Francisco featured a rich variety of Spanish Renaissance homes, a mode which, on a much more elaborate scale, William Randolph Hearst chose for San Simeon. A subdued, intimate Spanish Colonial style characterized Santa Barbara.

In all these variations flourished the dream of California as a Mediterranean littoral. Aside from its romantic implications, Mediterranean architecture made a point about constraint, simplicity, and order, paralleling what was being said in garden theory. Even in its diffuse and derivative California representations, the Mediterranean style had within itself a strong urge toward the control of lushness through design. At its best, neo-Mediterranean did not lose elegant simplicity. Whatever the abuses of neo-Mediterranean as practiced on the Pacific Slope, all was simplicity and order in comparison to the machine-cut elaboration of the San Francisco Style. Goodhue saw the Panama-California Exposition as moving California further along the path upon which it had already set out through its revival of Mediterranean, toward simplicity of line, drama of mass, and harmony with landscape. Such to him constituted the usable California tradition.

Not every California architect wanting these things turned to historical models. The geometric concrete structures of Irving Gill in San Diego, the spreading wooden bungalows of Henry Mather Greene and Charles Sumner Greene in Pasadena, and the shingled homes of Bernard R. Maybeck in Berkeley represented an innovative, non-historical attempt at regional expression. The name "Bay Region" was first applied by Lewis Mumford to a semi-unified style of architecture that flourished in the San Francisco Bay Area at the turn of the century, a style characterized by simple lines, integration of outdoors and indoors, concern for view, a free flow of space, and the use of wood and stone and textured materials. Many Bay Region architects had served an apprenticeship in Chicago during the 1890's, when a new American architecture was in the making; and in one sense, Bay Region represented Louis Sullivan's taste for the organic and the functional translated into Bay Area terms. As such, there was no sustained ideology, but rather a like response to materials and locale by a group of architects sharing similar aesthetic assumptions.

In *The Simple Home* (1904), Charles Augustus Keeler provided something of an ideological statement for Bay Region, from the point of view of the type of person who commissioned and lived in such homes. For Keeler the Bay Region home was a vital and artistic expression of the ideal California way of life. It emphasized localism, naturalism, and simplicity. Wood was the true California material, insisted Keeler, and should be used extensively in the California home: unpainted shingles on the exterior; exposed structural work on ceilings; redwood paneling; hardwood floors. Wood should be used honestly and not as a substitute for other materials. Ornament should express construction and not be merely decorative, like the machine-cut moldings of the San Francisco Style. If there must be decoration, it should imitate animal or vegetable forms and avoid the historical or the representational. Within, there should be no wallpaper, but solid colors, mixed in with the plaster. Curtaining should consist of textured fabrics like leather or burlap. Art hung on the wall should be by Californians, simply framed to harmonize with the home itself. The simple home manifested and reinforced an anti-industrial view of life and society. Machinery, Keeler wrote, enabled bad taste to be implemented wholesale, and an industrial economy fostered unselective consumption. Men worked hard so that they could live in over-furnished, vulgarly ornamentative houses. The simple home defied the consumer economy and its lack of taste. "Let those who would see a higher culture in California," Keeler urged, "a deeper life, a nobler humanity, work for the adoption of the simple home among all classes of people, trusting that the inspiration of its mute walls will be a ceaseless challenge to all who dwell within their shadow, for beauty and character."[51]

In Southern California the simple home was being realized as the bungalow. Characterized by low horizontal lines, wide eaves, and a veranda roof, the bungalow was an achieved architectural genre by the turn of the century. Within this genre, the Greene Brothers of Pasadena created masterpieces, bringing the use of wood—Keeler's California material—to perfection. Although possessing no one ideologue like Keeler, the bungalow had enormous social implications. It was the architecture of middle class California. "The comfort betokened," wrote Montgomery Schuyler of the bungalows he saw in Los Angeles in 1906, "is that moderate degree to which any American of ordinary education and ordinary aptitudes may reasonably aspire, when it does not imply that anybody has been depressed that a favored few may be exalted, when, in a word, it is a triumph of democracy." As a social symptom, Schuyler felt, the bungalow bore witness to the fact that an increasing number of Americans of moderate means were able "in their abodes and their surroundings to give evidence of culture and refinement, to avoid the vulgarity of crudity on the one hand and the vulgarity of ostentation on the other."[52]

Californians thus advanced their search for a regional architecture on two fronts, the historical or neo-Mediterranean, and the non-historical or progressive. The wealthy favored neo-Mediterranean modes: in the peninsula south of San Francisco, in Santa Barbara, and in Montecito. Progressive architecture received support from middle class professionals, the bungalow, of course, reaching downward into mass housing. Both styles shared common assumptions about California: its architecture should be orderly, simple, and possessed of a strong spirit of place. The Panama-California Exposition turned popular support in favor of historicism as represented by Spanish Colonial. By the early 1920's most significant domestic construction was in neo-Spanish. The whole thing sickened Frank Lloyd Wright. "The eclectic procession of to and fro in the ragtime and cast-off of all the ages was never going to stop—so it seemed to me," he said of Southern California in the late teens of the century. "Another fair, in San Diego this time, had set up Mexico-Spanish for another run for another cycle of thirty years."[53] Yankees could never get used to the California sunshine, Wright believed, and the Spanish Revival was merely a pathetic attempt to overcome their discomfort with Southern California's luxuriance. Sitting in his neo-Spanish home, the Californian looked as incongruous as a Spanish friar in a Medwestern parlor.

In so many ways, Wright's judgment was correct. At its least attractive level, the Spanish Revival represented an insincere, sales-oriented pastoralism, a way of dressing up tract housing with pseudo-romance. Even an ardent advocate of the Spanish Revival had to admit a critic's judgment, made in the late 1920's, that "much of the work, especially that to be found in some of the 'developments' and 'sub-divisions,' is little less than theatrical stage-sets."[54] Wright could never get over the humor of such tract homes: picturesque Spanish romance on the outside, tile bathrooms, kitchenettes, and sincere Midwest parlors within. Had the battle for a tasteful and appropriate California architecture been lost? Had the Mediterranean analogy condemned the state to confusion in the matter of its design?

Those who saw only the debased instances of Spanish Revival—and there was enough debasement to see—would unhesitatingly say yes. But the neo-Spanish homes created by Goodhue, George Washington Smith, Myron Hunt, Elmer Grey, and Reginald Johnson could not be dismissed in the same category as their mass-produced stucco counterparts. The battle for democratic taste, which Schuyler saw the bungalow winning, was lost in the Spanish Revival. Its romanticism, successful when disciplined by scholarship, became vulgar theatricality when reproduced on a mass scale. But other aspects of the Californian architectural ideology continued to be developed under the temporarily exclusive banner of neo-Spanish. Critics of the Revival discerned perennial California concerns at work. I. F. Morrow felt the movement "progress without pedantry"—"not archeology but a living architecture." When, in 1922, Morrow surveyed the work of James Osborne Craig in Santa Barbara, the distance from Keeler's hopes of twenty years past was not that great, although the preferred architectural idiom had shifted. Very few great styles developed unconsciously, Morrow asserted, and so Southern California had the right to appropriate neo-Spanish as its regional expression because neo-Spanish dramatized distinct California beliefs: "that motion is not necessarily progress, that not all systems are efficient ones, and that, after all, the most efficient life is hardly worth while if not enjoyed." "Our Spanish predecessors enjoyed life. The reversion to a Spanish attitude or point of view is in the nature of a return to first principles."[55]

Thus Morrow repeated Keeler's brief for Bay Region: a California architecture must be life-serving, must make some sort of an anti-industrial gesture, and must conserve values of intimacy, harmony, and health. Such, of course, had been the ambitions of pre-Exposition progressive architecture, now in eclipse. Today it appears shameful that those like Gill and the Greene Brothers, better prepared to advance the Californian cause, should have been shunted aside. Ideologically, at least, California's search for regional values in architecture continued along lines that did a minimum of violence to progressive hopes.

Like Bungalow and Bay Region, the best of Spanish Revival sought intimacy, outdoor-indoor living, and harmony with landscape. A passion for simplicity remained a fundamental California concern. What Keeler sought in unpainted shingled exteriors, projecting eaves and exposed beams, Spanish Revival made available in massy textured walls, unornamented and geometric, low silhouettes, and patio-centered construction. Much of what Irving Gill pioneered found expression in the neo-Spanish preference for bold unrelieved surfaces, for concrete expressed in terms of itself. In the early part of the century, Montgomery Schulyer predicted that the lesson of the missions—simplicity—would be of vital importance to California in the coming age of poured-concrete construction. Bearing out the truth of Schuyler's observation, the Spanish Revival purified the mission tradition of its histrionic vocabulary and showed itself amenable to the latest building techniques. "Here in California we are tired, very tired," said John Galen Howard in 1916, "not of the Missions, but of the sort of thing which has so long masqueraded in their name." California had purified its appropriation of an Iberian past. "The new spirit is to do without non-essentials," noted Howard of Spanish Revival, "and give thought solely to making the facts themselves beautiful." In this way only, and not through the providing of literal models, "the work of the padres has set its stamp for good and all upon the architecture of the Pacific Coast."[56]

Goodhue's own career dramatized the process. After the California Quadrangle, his work moved remorselessly in the direction of simplicity, as if he wished himself to become the prime exponent of the implications underlying Spanish Colonial. He pushed himself back to the adobe tradition, which is where American California architecture first began—in 1837 when Thomas O. Larkin of Monterey upgraded adobe with American frame-construction. Irving Gill had also begun with the adobe, and the distance between Goodhue's La Cabana, built in Montecito in 1920, and much of Gill's work is not that great. At the converging point of the adobe, the historical and the modern stood reconciled. That an ahistorical architecture anticipated and surpassed the historicist's conclusions only reinforced the significance of the whole process: in California, no matter what the source, authentic and honest modes converged in the demands of the region. Perhaps, then, the victory of the Mediterranean analogy which the Panama-California Exposition brought about had not proved such an architectural disaster after all. Perhaps Californians needed to purify one of their central myths before moving into an era that would see it the most exciting architectural region in the United States. Certainly that which emerged from the Spanish Revival—a reconfirmation of the Californian necessity for design to contain and to order luxuriance and to serve values of better everyday living —proved a useful heritage.

As evident from its scattered manifestations, Mediterraneanism was neither a process nor a program, although the Spanish Revival did mass under the banner of architecture a variety of South-seeking impulses. Yet as an analogy and as a metaphor, Mediterraneanism arose from a cluster of stable influences—landscape, climate, and the Hispanic past being among the most convincing. Surfacing early, the spell of California-as-South remained a point of reference down through the years of frontier and transition. By the turn of the century it was a key factor in the regional equation. It challenged Californians to achieve something better in the manner of American living: to design their cities and homes with reference to the poetry of the past and in harmony with the land and the smiling sun. It asked them to bring their gardens to ordered luxuriance. It celebrated the vine as a symbol of maturity and it introduced to agriculture sun-loving trees which coaxed forth the Mediterranean implications of the landscape and filled American marketplaces with dates and figs and olives.

Above all, California-as-South encouraged new attitudes toward work and leisure and what was important to live for. As a metaphor, it stood for a culture anxious to foster an alternative to the industrial ethic. Here in California, Mediterraneanism suggested, might emerge a people living amidst beauty—from household artifact to city scheme—a people animated by a full play of sense and spirit. In and through the Mediterranean metaphor was felt the strength of a persistent American longing. At the forward edge of a history that demanded to be gotten on with, the American dreamed of repose. In a civilization whose premises were so uncertain and whose structures collapsed and combined without warning, the American—not always, but now and then—yearned for stability and a time of savoring. On Pacific shores, might he not broaden the myth of his identity? At the nexus of a California of fact and a California of imagination, might there not occur a meeting of North and South, Europe and America? Might not the Latin past enrich the American present? These questions gave unity to the California quest. What else but they brought together such disparate figures in the same symbolic landscape? All of them—soldier, traveler, dancer, mystic, poet, vineyardist, historian, city planner, and architect—found a measure of liberation in the contemplation of California as America's Mediterranean littoral. It released energy and gave them courage to struggle against that restriction of spirit, that harsh materialism, which continually threatened to make a further mockery of an already embattled American dream.

13
Americans and the California Dream

In the years of its emergence as a regional civilization, what California meant, and what it would continue to mean, was never resolvable into a clear formula. The experience had been so haphazard, so bewildering in variety, that even its most devoted protagonists could not agree on one single interpretation.

Unlike New Englanders or the citizens of Oregon and Utah, Californians could not justify themselves on the basis of founding ideals. High and serious ambitions had animated many during the frontier, especially men of the cloth, and later (in Royce above all) there had been great moments of retrospective idealization; but even the most convinced Californians had to admit that those who pursued ideals, those who reflected upon experience from the vantage point of an ennobling ideology, did not set the tone of society, or, indeed, have much to say about its direction. They were the prophets and preservers of a better California, and it took decades for their work to take effect. Only Thomas Starr King (and he in special circumstances and for a passing moment) wielded real influence. Educators and reforming journalists fared better; but theirs, too, was a struggle with visible results few and far between.

Unlike the Confederate South, California could not take its identity from a tragic past culminating in an ordeal in which it romantically defended a deeply mythic conception of itself. Although just as violent, California's sins were less institutionalized. The Indian was not kept in formal slavery, but he was exterminated at the wish and at the expense of the legislature; and for years in the southern part of the state, under the guise of penal labor, Indians were hawked from the auction-block. The American South paid its price and continued to pay it. Complicity and atonement lay at the core of its experience, darkly tangled and then flowering forth in a literature great because it was earned in guilt and pain. But California concealed its sins and all but banished the tragic sense. Crimes remained unacknowledged or were sentimentalized, and, as if by common consent, responsibility was forgotten in the sunshine. A discernible thinness crept into California literature because of this refusal to come to terms with the darker elements of identity. There were exceptions, of course, but local writers too often ignored the enduring dilemmas of human life in favor of a sentimentally affirmative humor or an optimism which took an ever-smiling nature as its too easy correlative. Most of California lay in the same latitudes as the Confederate South; many Southerners migrated there; the state articulated itself through a myth of fertility and sunny luxuriance similar to that of the Confederacy. But in the deeper reaches of cultural consciousness California did not resemble the South.

It resembled the Midwest, in that the Central Valley supported vast plains of wheat. Elsewhere, however, in the mountain orchards of the north, in the vineyards of the Coast Range, in the irrigated groves south of the Tehachapis, climate and produce showed a diversity unknown in America's heartland. The texture of California ranch life differed from that of life on a Midwest farm. In the central regions it tended to be less developed domestically, more on the way toward the impersonal agribusiness of later decades, vast acres being owned by corporations and run through employees. In the citrus-, date-, and olive-growing south, intensive farming took hold in a way impossible in the wheat-and-corn-growing Midwest. In Southern California rural life showed a pattern approaching the bourgeois suburbanism of later days, while the coastal regions resembled the East with its diversity of one-family holdings. There was not, in short, the monotony of the Midwest; nor was there the anxiety brought about by endless empty space. Psychologically, Sierra and seacoast were never that far away.

There were aspects of Louisiana and the Old Southwest in California, in that it blended the American frontier (largely Scots-Irish) with the Franco-Spanish Creole. San Francisco was not New Orleans, but it sometimes tried to be; and certainly the Latin element did much to soften raw Americanness. In Louisiana, however, the European past was much more authentically present than in California, where it had its main vitality as an aesthetic hope on the part of an intelligentsia. As time went on, of course, the mellowing of the landscape through cultivation by immigrant Europeans tended to make it look more European. But California's European heritage lacked the density of Louisiana's. Based on fragile premises, surviving at one point in little more than the rain-washed, owl-haunted ruins of a few adobe missions, it functioned more as a suggestion than a fact; confronted with the American present, it continually threatened to reveal itself as an illusion.

By the years which close this narrative, however, the Hispanic past had been subsumed into a totality with which Californians identified themselves. The totality included several other factors: the Gold Rush, most obviously, and its continuing legacy of easy money and broken hopes; the sense of autonomy which came from an overnight development, years ahead of the advancing frontier; the varieties of peoples who arrived, and what they brought along; how cultures remained intact and how they altered the larger texture of life; the cities built, the harvests gathered; in short, all that Walt Whitman described in "Song of the Redwood-Tree" (1874) as:

The flashing and golden pageant of California,
The sudden and gorgeous drama, the sunny and ample lands,
The long and varied stretch from Puget sound to Colorado south,
Lands bathed in sweeter, rarer, healthier air, valleys and mountain cliffs,
The fields of Nature long prepared and fallow, the silent, cyclic chemistry,
The slow and steady ages plodding, the unoccupied surface ripening, the rich ores forming beneath;
At last the New arriving, assuming, taking possession,
A swarming and busy race settling and organizing everywhere,
Ships coming in from the whole round world, and going out to the whole world,
To India and China and Australia and the thousand island paradises of the Pacific,
Populous cities, the latest inventions, the steamers on the rivers, the railroads, with many a thrifty farm, with machinery,
And wood and wheat and the grape, and diggings of yellow gold.

This was the epic of California. These were the public contours of the California dream.

II

At the core of the dream was the hope for a special relationship to nature. A passion for beautiful California filled the souls of the artists and intellectuals of the 1850-1915 period. Regardless of calling or capabilities, those who achieved a significant mode of local living invariably put forward their love of the outdoors as the key component in the structure of their regionalism. King, Muir, Jordan, London, Norris, Sterling, Austin, Lummis: relationships to environment varied, but they were always important.

Nature, that awesome setting for the California dream! Heroic, eternal, overwhelming, it proved a glory, and a problem. It promised a profusion of gifts: beauty, life, health, abundance, and, perhaps most important of all, a challenging correlative to inner aspiration. But it could also intimidate; the challenge could become a mocking measurement of failure. In such a grand setting, the civilization of provincial California seemed trivial. This contrast was the theme of California's earliest county history, the *Annals of Trinity County* (1858) by Isaac Cox; and the anxiety continued down the century. Thoreau claimed that anger over their diminution led Californians to deface their environment in envy and revenge. There was evidence that he was right. Even for those who revered their setting it was discouraging to be measured against what one most cherished—and always to be found wanting. The example of Muir, admirable as it was, did not solve the problem. Muir's was essentially an eremitical relationship, working toward mystic communion at a point of utterly private transcendence. The Sierra Club incorporated this into its quasi-social ideal, bringing the community into the wilderness. Yet it left unanswered the problem of day-to-day living, the problem of giving social extension to the desire (all-compelling in the most devoted) to internalize the grandeur of geography. On holiday, the Californian might feel himself alive to the fingertips with physical and spiritual energy. He was the heir of creation, the destined lover of mountain and seacoast. But what was he in his cities and towns?

Not much, thought Henry James, who visited the Pacific Coast in March and April of 1905, and whose observations showed how sharply California could be judged. Finding the region breathtakingly beautiful, James compared it to "a sort of prepared but unconscious and inexperienced Italy, the primitive *plate*, in perfect condition, but with the impression of History all yet to be made."[1] From the gracious repose of the Hotel del Coronado at Coronado Beach, he wrote to his sister-in-law of his delight in "the charming sweetness and comfort of this spot." Southern California, James asserted, "has completely bowled me over—such a delicious difference from the rest of the U.S. do I find in it. (I speak of course all of nature and climate, fruits and flowers; for there is absolutely nothing else, and the sense of the shining social and human inane is utter.) The days have been mostly here of heavenly beauty, and the flowers, the wild flowers just now in particular, which fairly *rage*, with radiance, over the land, are worthy of some purer planet than this. I live on oranges and olives, fresh from the tree, and I lie awake nights to listen, on purpose, to the languid list of the Pacific, which my windows overhang."[2]

Flowers raging with radiance, the languid list of the Pacific, oranges and olives—and absolutely nothing else. Here was the devastating opinion of the sophisticated, the irony of regional aspiration! James expanded upon it in *The American Scene* (1907). California, he wrote, was not so bad as Florida, which was completely trivial as a civilization; yet California as a culture was a long way from living up to its setting. "I was to find her," James wrote, "especially at the first flush, unlike sweet frustrated Florida, ever so amiably strong: which came from the art with which she makes the stoutnesses, as I have called them, of natural beauty stand you in temporary stead of the leannesses of everything else (everything that might be of an order equally interesting). This she is on a short acquaintance quite insolently able to do, thanks to her belonging so completely to the 'handsome' side of the continent, of which she is the finest expression. The aspect of natural objects, up and down the Pacific coast, is as 'aristocratic' as the comprehensive American condition permits anything to be: it indeed appears to the ingenious mind to represent an instinct on the part of Nature, a sort of shuddering, bristling need, to brace herself in advance against the assault of a society so much less marked with distinction than herself."[3]

In the annals of tourist opinion rarely had there been such a crushing judgment. With a shrug of his shoulders the Master dismissed over fifty years of American effort. In its human dimension, California had come to little.

George Santayana was more encouraging. Coming to California in August 1911 to address the Philosophical Union at Berkeley, Santayana liked what he saw. He liked the scenery and he liked the people. He found them brave, eager, and full of hope. Berkeley might not have the historical resonances of Cambridge, Massachusetts; but it struck Santayana as an alert, progressive university town, robust with the energies of student life and mellowed in scholarship. On 25 August 1911 Berkeleyans flocked to his lecture; and—significantly for the time and the place—Santayana used the occasion to announce the passing of the genteel.

American thought and culture had long labored under the restrictions of the genteel tradition, Santayana told the Union. An offshoot of an older civilization, intellectual America tended to take refuge in what it considered in its intimidation to be the orthodoxies of the mother-culture, but which, ironically and more than a little sadly, often turned out to be the abandoned assumptions of a previous era. Proper culture in America tended to have a maiden-aunt atmosphere, or, more accurately, to resemble a prematurely aged child. When Calvinism declined, it left certain needs ingrained in the American psyche: a taste for self-scrutiny and a relish for the pleasures of an agonized conscience, an obsession with election and damnation, a sense of code and final purpose. The genteel fulfilled these hungers. It made possible a universe of stable value, a set of norms by which thinking Americans might take their own measure and judge the worth of others. Like grace, you had culture or you did not. You were genteel, or you were not. It was all very simple.

A further characteristic, according to Santayana, was a peculiar way of relating to landscape, arising out of an enervated transcendentalism. Subconsciously aware that its vigor was on the wane, genteel America tried to restore itself through a devotion to scenery. The luminous heat of the Romantic response to the wild and the sublime, however, was far beyond its strength. Genteel Americans thought themselves in the throes of some rapturous interpenetration of mind and nature—when they were doing little else than taking the air. Like great music (and with little effort on their part), scenery filled them with a sense of their own worth. Surely they were as eloquent and enduring as the mountains and the sea toward which their sympathies surged in yearning benevolence! Certainly America's scenic grandeur was in some sense theirs by right of transcendental possession!

Meanwhile, a continent was being explored, cities settled, governments established; and countless inventions were registered in the Patent Office. The American sensibility seemed divided down the middle, venturesome and capable in action, timid and pedantic in reflection. "The American Will inhabits the sky-scraper," Santayana told his Berkeley audience; "the American Intellect inhabits the colonial mansion. The one is the sphere of the American man; the other, at least predominantly, of the American woman. The one is all aggressive enterprise; the other is all genteel tradition."[4]

Santayana saw signs that this gap was narrowing. The philosophical thought of Santayana's Harvard colleague William James (Henry's brother, dead now just a year) had dealt the genteel a stunning blow.

James's Pragmatism (a term James himself first used when addressing this same Union in 1898), was described by Santayana as "an impassioned empiricism, welcoming popular religious witnesses to the unseen, reducing science to an instrument of success in action, and declaring the universe to be wild and young, and not to be harnessed by the logic of any school."[5] Pragmatism, in other words, articulated what had always been the most creative American attitude: that, after all, one knew very little, that the true and good also seemed to be useful, that experience generated categories more compelling than received doctrines, and that certainties lasted only as long as they worked, as long, that is, as they aided the business of living.

What had all this to do with California? Quite a bit, Santayana thought. Turning to his audience in the last moments of his lecture, he addressed them precisely as Californians. Limitations of time had necessitated an elliptical development of his ideas, but consider the scenario which Santayana had just sketched out, and which he now brought to eloquent conclusion. Most profoundly, he had been talking about an America on the verge of laying claim to its own best self. At America's contemplative core a revolution was stirring. For years the best moral, intellectual, and aesthetic possibilities of America had lain enchained by the intimidations of the genteel. That creative experimentalism, temperamental and philosophic; that abiding openness to experience, which had pulsated through Jonathan Edwards, Benjamin Franklin, Abraham Lincoln, and Walt Whitman, but which somehow had been exchanged for the Jacob's pottage of tepid conformity and snobbish security—would now assert itself as America's major premise. Too long had it been sustained solely as a capacity for practical ends. It was a deeply philosophic relationship, as William James had shown. America should mean a massive liberation into experience, not the restriction of experience through warmed-over assumptions. Fear was at the core of the genteel: fear of experience, fear of the idea of America, fear of her diverse lineage; fear, indeed, of the rivers, mountains, and ceaseless skies of the continent itself. That fear, Santayana suggested, helped lead to the trivial, quasi-transcendental appropriation of nature as a reinforcement for threatened psyches. That fear led to a self-authenticating relationship to nature which was unworthy of America's better instincts—and unworthy of the land itself.

But here in California things should be different, and perhaps they were. In a peroration so tightly knit that it must be quoted at some length, Santayana told Californians that they especially should sympathize with the repudiation of the genteel. "This revolution, I should think," he told Californians, "might well find an echo among you, who live in a thriving society, and in the presence of a virgin and prodigious world. When you transform nature to your uses, when you experiment with her forces, and reduce them to industrial agents, you cannot feel that nature was made by you or for you, for then these adjustments would have been preëstablished. You must feel, rather, that you are an offshoot of her life; one brave little force among her immense forces. When you escape, as you love to do, to your forests and your Sierras, I am sure again that you do not feel you made them, or that they were made for you. They have grown, as you have grown, only more massively and more slowly. In their non-human beauty and peace they stir the sub-human depths and the superhuman possibilities of your own spirit. It is no transcendental logic that they teach; and they give no sign of any deliberate morality seated in the world. It is rather the vanity and superficiality of all logic, the needlessness of argument, the finitude of morals, the strength of time, the fertility of matter, the variety, the unspeakable variety, of possible life. Everything is measurable and conditioned, indefinitely repeated, yet, in repetition, twisted somewhat from its old form. Everywhere is beauty and nowhere permanence, everywhere an incipient harmony, nowhere an intention, nor a responsibility, nor a plan. It is the irresistible suasion of this daily spectacle, it is the daily discipline of contact with things, so different from the verbal discipline of the schools, that will, I trust, inspire the philosophy of your children. A Californian whom I had recently the pleasure of meeting observed that, if the philosophers had lived among your mountains their systems would have been different from what they are. Certainly, I should say, very different from what those systems are from which the European genteel tradition has handed down since Socrates; for these systems are egotistical; directly or indirectly they are anthropocentric, and inspired by the conceited notion that man, or human reason, or the human distinction between good and evil, is the center and pivot of the universe. That is what the mountains and the woods should make you at last ashamed to assert. From what, indeed, does the society of nature liberate you, that you find it so sweet? It is hardly (is it?) that you wish to forget your past, or your friends, or that you have any secret contempt for your present ambitions. You respect these, you respect them perhaps too much; you are not suffered by the genteel tradition to criticize or to reform them at all radically. No; it is the yoke of this genteel tradition itself, your tyrant from the cradle to the grave, that these primeval solitudes lift from your shoulders. They suspend your forced sense of your own importance not merely as individuals, but even as men. They allow you, in one happy moment, at once to play and to worship, to take yourselves simply, humbly, for what you are, and to salute the wild, indifferent, non-censorious infinity of nature. You are admonished that what you can do avails little materially, and in the end nothing. At the same time, through wonder and pleasure, you are taught speculation. You learn what you are really fitted to do, and where lie your natural dignity and joy, namely, in representing many things, without being them, and in letting your imagination, through sympathy, celebrate and echo their life."[6]

Behind Santayana's exhortation lay assumptions decipherable only to the philosphically instructed: especially propositions regarding the relationship of mind to external event, to the understanding of which he brought his own synthesis of Skeptical and Platonic insights. The cultural and psychological implications of what he was saying, however, were apparent—and deeply welcomed. In the matter of nature and civilization, Santayana was offering Californians a way out of their dilemma. He was, in fact, suggesting that they were making their own escape even before he arrived on the scene to formulate the problem.

What was needed to break through the genteel (and what the best of Californians were trying to achieve) was respect for the non-human world on its non-human terms. This demanded proper distinctions between men and nature, and proper conjunctions. As geography, California was not a psychic projection, nor was it available as an easy metaphor of human intention. Nor should it be used as a crushing judgment against those who dwelt amidst its grandeur. In that men were part of nature, they shared in the totality of its mighty process by the mere fact of their existence. In that men were separated from nature by mind, they stood in a different relationship, an interior one of reflection and imaginative response. The two relationships were distinct and should not be used one against the other. It was wrong to say that Californians were not as imposing as the Sierras, if one judged merely by external circumstances; for one would be mismatching norms of judgment. The true key to the success of California as a civilization, Santayana suggested, would be its interior life in relationship to its environment; and although he had been there but a short time, he found much to compliment Californians about in this regard. Taken for a moment at his best, the Californian had disciplined himself to the objectivity—the otherness—of his superb surroundings, and so had received back into interior possession those very gifts of nature he had refused to appropriate gratuitously.

Even in cultural terms, much less in its philosophical significance, it was a severe scheme, one that anticipated the philosophy of inhumanism advocated by California's great poet Robinson Jeffers. It demanded the surrender of easy myths of historical destiny, or at least the instant corroboration of those myths through reference to landscape. On the other hand, it warred against such harsh judgments as that made by Henry James. Few Californians might find their way through to Santayana's philosophical premises, but many could appreciate the more immediate resonances of what he was telling them. An outsider had chosen to judge them against their setting, and he had called them failures. But he was not necessarily right. They knew their region better than any tourist who appropriated it as a tool of snobbery and who was himself most likely in the grips of intimidation before the landscape. They, the Californians, the best of them, were struggling as well perhaps as Americans could with an interior landscape (the gift of their environment) which because of its grandeur might have driven the less courageous into permanent self-hatred. If Californians seemed awkward and silent, it was partly because they lived day by day in the presence of a mighty, non-human music. Outsiders, hearing that music for the first time, were liable to make defensive judgments.

And besides—during the Pullman pilgrimage of Henry James, as he moved up the Coast from the Del Coronado in San Diego to the Del Monte in Monterey, lecturing on the way to literary ladies in Los Angeles, entertained at the Bohemian Club in San Francisco, staying at the St. Dunstan's—did he really have ample exposure to the human factor? Could even the Master justify his judgments, capable as he was, in another landscape, of using the slightest detail to guide his explorations? He was tired, bored, preoccupied, and sixty-one when he came, his imagination (even by the blue Pacific) riveted to the New England scenes of his youth, to which he had just returned. He seemed to meet only those whom he could judge by his own standards, Society and the intelligentsia; and, of course, in comparison to London and Newport, these were bound to prove, at first glance, disappointing. He did not encounter the sort of Californian who was trying to achieve something better than an imitation of the East, something appropriate to the environment he so praised. But then again, if he had met them, would he have understood? (A few years later, in London, he met Mary Austin and was bored.) As far as we can tell, only once, in San Francisco—which he described as having "a poverty of aspect and quality"—did he feel anything resembling a surge of sympathy. The owner of the St. Dunstan's, Leon Edel tells us, insisted that James pay no charge when he checked out; for the Master had honored his establishment by staying there. The generous gesture prompted from James a compliment which was ruined by its oblique facetiousness: "Brave golden California, more brave and golden for *such* possibilities surely, than any other country under the sun!"[7]

Unfortunately, James seemed to miss that which Santayana described as crucial: the interior life of a community in contemplative exchange with its environment. Far from being absent, such a dialogue characterized the core of California as a regional culture. Many had devoted their best efforts to see that this would be the case, and none more prominently than California's single most influential teacher, Joseph Le Conte, professor of geology and natural history at Berkeley.

In an old-fashioned Victorian way, Le Conte's scientific learning encompassed geology, physics, biology, botany, optics, and anatomy. Born in Georgia in 1823, he had studied medicine in his youth, and later spent time doing research in natural history under Louis Agassiz at Harvard. Arriving on the Pacific Coast in 1869, Le Conte was perhaps the most eminent representative of that class of displaced Southerners who made new starts in California after the war. He claimed that his move West had liberated his best energies, and he, in turn, brought a welcomed prestige to Berkeley as its only faculty member with an international reputation. Before the arrival of David Starr Jordan, it was Le Conte who was most instrumental in defining the California academic style as a blend of serious thinking and passionate outdoorsmanship. When, as a freshman, Josiah Royce discovered that he was ineligible to take Le Conte's geology course, he would sit outside the classroom door to overhear the lectures. He later compared his three years of study under Le Conte as "something like the escape of the men of the cave, in the story in Plato's *Republic*, from their world of shadows."[8] Even Frank Norris, who felt a gentlemanly obligation to neglect his studies, fell under the spell of the great professor.

"The domains of science and philosophy are not separated by hard and fast lines," Le Conte firmly believed; "they largely overlap; and it is in this border land that I love to dwell." In that mid-region he hoped to find a synthesis of science, religion, and evolutionary thought. He was convinced that the mission of his generation of American scientists was to

Joseph Le Conte (1823–1901)

He came to California after the Civil War, one of many Southerners to do so. As professor of geology and natural history at the University of California at Berkeley, he encouraged students to take a broad, philosophical view of science, and most especially to see the compatibility between theism and evolution. Josiah Royce and Frank Norris dated their intellectual awakening to his tutelage. On the Californian scene, he stood for Victorian ideals of high thinking, rigorous living, and devotion to locale.

prove to the world "that a materialistic implication is wholly unwarranted, that evolution is entirely consistent with a rational theism and with other fundamental religious beliefs."[9]

In *Evolution and Its Relation to Religious Thought* (1888) Le Conte expounded his position with learning and a masterful architecture of argument. God was immanent in nature, claimed Le Conte, and evolution was the differentiation and upward movement of divinity working through matter. "I believe," he wrote," "that the spirit of man *was* developed out of the *anima* or conscious principle of animals, and that this, again, was developed out of the lower forms of life-force, and this in its turn out of the chemical and physical forces of Nature; and that at a certain stage in this gradual development, viz., with man, it *acquired* the property of immortality precisely as it now, in the individual history of each man at a certain stage, acquires the capacity of abstract thought." Right action, then, consisted in the attempt on the part of men to effect in themselves that upward harmony of the material, the biological, the intellectual, and the spiritual which characterized the evolutionary process itself. "True virtue," Le Conte warned, "consists, not in the extirpation of the lower, but in its subjection to the higher. The stronger the lower is, the better, *if only* it be held in subjection. For the higher is nourished and strengthened by its connection with the more robust lower, and the lower is purified, refined, and glorified by its connection with the diviner higher, and by this mutual action the whole plane of being is elevated."[10]

No wonder Joseph Le Conte had such influence! The essence of his thought—physicality seeking a return to the spirit, without pseudo-transcendence, without repudiation of physicality's best gifts—was at the inner nexus of Californian aspiration. It accounted, in fact, for the region's finest moments. Even George Sterling tried to bear witness to this ideal. Josiah Royce asserted at sixty that boyhood wonder at the magnificence of his environment had been an important element in his development. Studying under Le Conte had helped him achieve some perspective on that wonder. Charged with the tension of evolutionary struggle and the horror of evolutionary retrogression, Frank Norris' novels were soaked through with the influence of Le Conte. And certainly Jack London, although he spent but a semester at Berkeley and owed more to Jordan than to anyone else, wrote his most powerful fiction when he documented the interaction in human beings of the animal, the spiritual, and the environmental: how delicate was the evolutionary balance, how quick to regress in an extreme situation. Jordan, in fact, might be seen as carrying on the Berkeley professor's work (Le Conte retired in 1896), giving it more social extension, since Jordan was more involved in day-to-day problems, yet carrying on Le Conte's central message: that the challenge before California as a civilization was to attain the best possible ethical and aesthetic relationship to its ecology.

Le Conte died in 1901, while on a trip to the Yosemite with the Sierra Club; he was not on the scene when Henry James arrived. Perhaps had they met and talked, or had James met and talked at length with any serious Californian, his reaction might have been more positive. As it was, the Master's judgments arose out of intuitions garnered from a passing train, society hotels, literary lectures, and an evening at the Bohemian Club. What else, if anything, characterized Le Conte and Californians like him, if not the solidity and seriousness James claimed was lacking—and even something of that aristocratic attitude he suggested was called for by the handsomeness of the setting? To his credit, Santayana understood this, although he also was—by birth as well as by acquisition—the heir of a mellow and complex tradition.

Le Conte embarked upon one of the important California quests, and it is best to see him and it in retrospect. Le Conte gave guidance and inspiration to so much of what was achieved culturally throughout the period 1870-1900. He helped bring into focus a cluster of issues regarding thought, value, and style whose clarification was crucial to California's maturity. His *A Journal of Ramblings Through the High Sierras of California by the University Excursion Party* (1875) reveals his most attractive side: the good-humored companion of undergraduates, competent in the details of the trail, halting the horses to give an impromptu lecture on flora or topography, sharing the bantering conversation around the evening fire. Students remembered these fine mountain times and they remembered Le Conte's superbly structured lectures, the organized detail of which still shines through Royce's undergraduate notebooks in the Harvard Archives. Le Conte taught the young men and women of California to engage their environment in that manner later praised by Santayana, with intensity and intelligence, refusing sentimental solace, but sparing no effort of mind or body to attain those communions born of deep understanding which were among the glories of the California dream.

In retrospect one also turns briefly to Luther Burbank of Santa Rosa for confirmation of a better California than that encountered by the Master—although it boggles the mind to imagine Henry James in Santa Rosa!

Born and raised in rural Massachusetts, and, like so many Americans of inventive genius, largely self-educated, Burbank followed three older brothers to California in 1875. He had already shown signs of extraordinary talent as a nurseryman. In 1868, when he was nineteen, he obtained from the Lancaster Public Library the two newly published volumes of Charles Darwin's *The Variations of Animals and Plants Under Domestication.* Under the influence of Darwin's work, Burbank conducted a series of experiments in hybridization of the seventeen-acre farm he ran outside Lunenburg. At the time he left for California, he had already contributed to the world the improved potato which now bears his name.

He later claimed that some obscure evolutionary force had impelled him to California, convincing him subconsciously that his experimental, self-instructed talent required more psychological freedom and sunny luxuriance than was available in wintry New England, where sunlight was uncertain and botany belonged to the professors. "I had no choice in the matter," he said, "I was bound to go!" Arrived in the town of Santa Rosa, in the Sonoma Valley north of the Bay Area, he experienced a conviction of liberation and opportunity. Like Muir entering the Yosemite a few years earlier, Burbank found a setting that was also a life's work and a consecration. "I firmly believe from what I have seen," he wrote home, "that it is the *chosen* spot of *all this earth* as far as *nature* is concerned, and the people are far better than the average. The air is so sweet it is a pleasure to drink it in. The sunshine is pure and soft, the mountains which gird the valley are very lovely. The valley is covered with majestic oaks placed as no human hand could arrange them for beauty. I cannot describe it. I almost have to cry for joy when I look upon the lovely valley from the hillsides. The gardens are filled with tropical plants, palms, figs, oranges, vines, etc. Great rose trees climb over the houses loaded with every color of blossoms. Do you suppose I am not pleased to see the fuchsias in the ground 12 ft. high, the trunk 10 inches in circumference, and loaded with color?"[11]

For the next fifty years, Burbank busied himself in the creation and improvement of innumerable stocks of vegetables, fruits, and flowers. Not a scientist in the speculative sense of the term, he kept but fragmentary notes regarding his countless experiments. His aim was not systematized knowledge, but better plums, better apricots, better raspberries, a spineless cactus to feed cattle in arid areas. He turned his talent to making life more beautiful as well, an anyone knew who thrilled to the subtle colors and fragrances of his lilies, poppies, roses, callas, and daisies.

If ever there was a Californian liberated from the genteel, it was Burbank. He hated dogmatism of any kind. Having thrown off New England Calvinism in his youth, he put his adult faith in the variety and pliability of life, to which he sustained something resembling an artist's loving knowledge. Jordan appointed him a Lecturer on Plant Evolution, sharing with the Santa Rosa savant his own course in Bionomics. Hybrids from Burbank's nurseries garnished the garden of Xasmin House, Jordan's official Stanford residence. "In his own way," wrote Jordan, "Burbank belongs in the class of Faraday and the long array of self-taught great men who lived while the universities were spending their strength on fine points of grammar and hazy conceptions of philosophy." As a cultural symbol, Burbank bespoke to Californians the value of individual effort outside the context of complex, mediating civilizations. Jordan deplored the term "wizard" so often applied to Burbank. He was not a magician, argued Jordan, but an ascetic, a man who brought himself in harmony with nature and, in the true spirit of science, learned nature's lessons with a minimum of fanfare. Burbank's simple lifestyle, with its blend of physical and intellectual work, the serenity of his personality, "as sweet, straightforward, and as unspoiled as a child, always interested in the phenomena of Nature, and never seeking fame or money or anything for himself," dramatized one of California's highest forms of fulfillment.[12]

One of the most prominent Californians of his generation, the subject of countless newspaper articles (most misleading; some even suggesting he was a faker), Burbank was not without aspirations arising out of the California dream. His *The Training of the Human Plant* (1907) resonated with the California hope that spirit and flesh might know new life. Just as Isadora Duncan dreamt of children in joyous dance, Burbank, as he bent over his plants, dreamed of children removed from fear, growing strong in freedom and sunlight. Contemporary education, he believed, stifled children. They were herded at a tender age into cramped, unventilated classrooms, where their bodies were damaged by confinement and their imaginations intimidated by the rote learning of inanimate information. Children, he thought, should be kept out of school until the age of ten. They should be raised as much as possible in the country, their early influences (aside from love and trust) being outdoor play and association with nature. When finally sent to school, they should not be regimented, but allowed to develop at their own pace. Their years in the outdoors, balanced off by the restraints of a good family life, would constitute a superb preparation for academic study; from their time of outdoor free-

Luther Burbank (1849–1926)

Coming from Massachusetts in 1875, he settled in Santa Rosa, which he described as "the chosen spot of all this earth as far as Nature is concerned." Over the next fifty years he developed a prodigious number of new fruits and flowers and improved countless other stocks. He was not exactly a scientist; he was a self-taught nurseryman of genius, a patient artist of hybridization. As he bent over his flourishing plants, he dreamed that one day the children of America might also know such gifts of growth and strength and sunlight.

dom children would have acquired independence, inquisitiveness, and—most importantly—wonder before the mystery of things.

Burbank's American utopia (for *The Training of the Human Plant* is a utopian tract) welcomed immigrants. As in botany, grafting improved the human stock. Concerned about human health, Burbank avoided the racist overtones which pervaded so much discussion of eugenics during the period. His was an emphasis, an urge to awareness, not an authoritarian program. He hoped in all humility that in these delicate matters the collective common sense might find a way to improve the race while not forgetting the sacredness of human life or the preciousness of human freedom. What moved Burbank was the vision, not the details of implementation. He saw a long struggle ahead, and he did not presume to know all the answers.

Santa Rosa functioned as the environment and premise of what he had to say. There, for half a century, Burbank saw plants and children flourish in the sunlight. Childless himself, he adopted the children of the lovely California town where he passed his serene life doing such useful things with plants. The rhythms and possibilities of Santa Rosa were also his. Burbank loved the quiet days and drowsy afternoons; the great oak trees that gave shade; the farmers from the countryside who would drop by to ask advice, as from one grower to another (Jack London among them, riding over from the Valley of the Moon); the cottages smothered in vines and roses, banked by fine lawns, watched over by eucalyptus, palm trees, and Cedars of Lebanon like the one protecting his own simple home, under which he would eventually rest.

Only in small towns did Burbank's educational ideas stand the remotest chance of being put into practice; for they had been inspired by a small-town New England boyhood and the longer idyll of Santa Rosa. The life and thought of Luther Burbank, however, needed no qualifications as a California testimony. He believed in new beginnings. He believed in freedom from the oppression that came from deliberately difficult doctrines. He thirsted for results, for present happiness. He had a near-religiosity regarding the pliability and inexhaustibility of life. With an artist's insight he attuned himself to living things, and like an artist he coaxed life to better expressions. He wanted American children to thrive in as many ways as possible, to have good food, to move in the open air, to grow in joy and confidence. Like Le Conte, he felt that men learned best when they learned from nature. Like Le Conte, he dedicated his talents to the upgrading of human life. The lives of both men, like the lives of so many other Californians, asserted that a number of Americans were struggling to achieve something worthy of their surroundings.

III

But what about more searching judgments, those made after investigation and long residence? Commitment to California did not preclude scrutiny, nor did admiration always blind one to her faults.

In 1913 two books appeared, both written by Englishmen: *California Coast Trails, A Horseback Ride From Mexico to Oregon*, by J. Smeaton Chase, and *California, An Englishman's Impressions of the Golden State*, by Arthur T. Johnson. Chase belonged to the genre of Anglo-Californian which had provided the state with some of its most appreciative and perceptive citizens, outdoorsmen for the most part, whose love of the land went hand in hand with a ready pen and a trenchant attitude toward the less edifying aspects of American possession. London-born, settling in Southern California in 1890 at the age of twenty-six, Chase worked variously as a teacher, a social worker, and a retailer; but his real life took place in the outdoors, the Sierras and the Yosemite especially, about which he wrote with such feeling and lucidity that Lawrence Clark Powell ranks him among the best interpreters of the California landscape. Johnson, on the other hand, represented, not the Anglo-Californian, but the skeptical British tourist, a sort who had produced some of the best literature of pre-statehood days and the Gold Rush, and who in a later era (represented, say, by Aldous Huxley and Evelyn Waugh) would turn Southern California to purposes of superb satire.

The two Englishmen were reporting upon a similar journey north, which Chase made by horseback and Johnson by buckboard. Above San Francisco, Chase continued up the coast to the Oregon line, while north of Healdsburg Johnson veered eastward, moving up the Sacramento Valley through Chico, Red Bluff, and Redding, ending his journey under the shadow of Mount Shasta. Both writers, in very different ways, were anxious about California: what had been achieved, what was passing—and what seemed on the horizon.

Past, present and future converge in Chase's *California Coast Trails*. Written with an elegance born of restraint, Chase's narrative of his progress up the coast has to it a quality of elegy, of half-acknowledged lament. Fearful of California-to-come, Chase, haunted by history, takes one last lyric ride up the shores of memory, in search of California-passing. Not much longer, he felt, would such a journey be possible. On such an excursion one rode with Spanish soldiers and priests. One saw the southern coast remembering Richard Henry Dana and entered Monterey in the company of Robert Louis Stevenson. Padre, ranchero, trapper, trader: one might yet catch glimpses of what they saw. One might still see California through the eyes of Lapérouse and Alfred Robinson—but not for long.

And so J. Smeaton Chase chose carefully what he would visit and write about. On this last ramble he would savor nature and what remained of the old civilization. Images of modernization mock him as he rides. A touring car sputters by, causing his horse to shy in fright. He is aware that air travel up the coast will someday be possible. Paved roads and subdivisions will soon destroy much of the landscape through which he is now riding at a leisurely pace. Traveling through San Francisco, Chase, defiant in camp clothes, rode his horse down Market Street, past the concrete skyscrapers of the rebuilt city, to the Ferry Building. On the whole he avoided settled areas, preferring to sleep under canvas or to bunk in a ranch house.

What was he after, this Anglo-Californian riding so regretfully ahead of the twentieth century? Landscape, first of all: classic, unspoiled California landscape, like the valley near El Toro in the south, through which Chase rode one afternoon along with the artist Carl Eytel, who accompanied him on the first portion of the journey.

"As soon as we passed the gates of the ranch," Chase wrote, "we entered a league-long valley from which rose smooth slopes of pale-golden grass. The rounded swells and folds of the land took the light as richly as a cloth of velvet. In the bottom lay the creek, in isolated pools and reaches, its course marked sharply by a border of green grass and rushes. Red cattle grazed everywhere or stood for coolness in the weed-covered pools. The hillsides were terraced by their interlacing trails. Elders and willows grew at wide intervals, a blot of shadow reaching from each. Under them the rings of bare gray earth were tramped hard as brick where generations of cattle had gathered for shade. In one side reach of the valley was a little bee-ranch of a score or two of hives, with the typical shanty of the bee-man closed and apparently deserted. It was an 'off-year' for bees near the coast: excess of fog had spoiled the honey-flow. . . . As we rode, blue mountains rose on the northern horizon. They were the Santa Ana Mountains, fifteen miles away. That was the only ingredient in the view that could come under the term 'picturesque': the rest was open, bald, commonplace. European painters—Americans, too, all but a few—would have declared it crude and impossible. The yellow horizon was cut on the blue of the sky in a clean, hard line. At one spot, where the creek in winter flood had cut out a fifteen-foot bluff, the shadow was a slash of inky blackness on the glaring expanse of sun-bleached grass. There was always a buzzard or two swinging slowly in the sky, and once one rose near by with a heavy, shambling flight from his surfeit on the carcass of a dead steer. That was all: but to Eytel, and indeed to me, though I am no artist, it was complete and perfect. If beauty consists, as theorists, I understand, declare, in the true expression of spirit, then certainly this landscape complied with the terms. It was a very summary of the native and original California del Sur, California of the South, as Nature designed it. And even the sophisticated mind, trained to weigh tone values and balance of line, found the composition ideal in its magnificent Western simplicity. Pretty? a thousand miles from it. Picturesque? the very word sounds puerile. But simple, strong, dignified (which I take to be the primaries of art, after all), these were the very facts of the case, the materials of the landscape."[13]

A ride through such landscape restored one's sense of the special texture of geographical California, and one's sense of the past. Through cañons such as this—solitary, elemental, in sight of mountains, buzzards circling overhead—Portolá and Serra pushed the Spanish frontier northward. In the decades following, such places knew but little disturbance. Half-wild cattle grazed there in the years of Hispanic possession. Now and then a party of American trappers filed through, making camp for the night under a great oak. Later, much later, a few squatters here and there threw up an unpainted shack or two; and a hermit bee-keeper set out a row of hives. Sensitive to what was happening in Southern California, Chase knew that many of these cañons would not remain untouched for long. Bungalows and roadways would spread out to engulf them. It was necessary and it was tragic. The passing of such landscape deserved at least one journey of elegiac farewell.

Chase was trying to reach as far back behind the American present (and the American future) as he could. When weather drove him indoors, he stayed as much as possible with Mexicans, preferring their gracious hospitality to that of American hotels. The southern portion of his journey is literally a pilgrimage from mission to mission, up *El Camino Real*. Tourists came by streetcar to see Mission San Gabriel Arcángel in the village of El Monte (not yet swallowed by Los Angeles); elsewhere, however, at San Luis Obispo and Santa Ines for instance, Indians still gathered for Sunday Mass as they had in the eighteenth century. Other missions were in ruins, as were La Purisíma Concepción and San Antonio De Padua, where Chase slept beneath some ancient olive trees. Perhaps his most nostalgic stay was at San Juan Capistrano, approached across "wide levels of yellow grass that shone like silk in the sunlight," where Chase passed some very pleasant days in the mission library browsing amidst "slender tomes in rough sheepskin, like tall, pale old gentlemen, written closely in Spanish with records of christenings and burials, each volume devoutly rounded off with its 'Laus Deo,' a triumph of flamboyant calligraphy; ancient sets of Bossuet and Massillon; breviaries, missals, what-not; —all endued with that odor of sanctity which is neither Catholic nor Protestant, the sanctity of age and bygone human usage."[14]

At Mission Santa Ines the priest in charge, after putting Chase up for three days, sent him off the morning of his departure with a thunderous piano rendition of Wagner's "Pilgrim's Chorus." Chase, of course, was truly on pilgrimage, the age and threatened romance of California his reverent preoccupation. He was thrilled to discover that a few trees planted by the padres still bore pears and apples. A few altars still smelled of incense; and long after Stevenson thought that he would perhaps be the last to hear such music, a few adobe missions yet echoed with Gregorian chant. A handful of Spaniards, children at the time of the conquest, had managed to hold on to their lands in the area above Point Conception. Calling on them, Chase encouraged them to talk about Old California. In the Nipomo Valley he called upon John Dana, the son of Richard Henry Dana's cousin William Goodwin Dana, who had settled in California before the conquest, marrying a Carrillo. That evening even more Danas gathered for dinner. Seeing three generations of Yankee-Latins gathered around the huge table, hearing the laughter, the talk in Spanish and English, Chase felt in the presence of bygone Yankee-California, the civilization that Thomas Oliver Larkin and others had long ago hoped would be the pattern of the future. It had not been the future, but somehow it had held on, and Chase enjoyed an evening in its company.

Symbolic statement in *California Coast Trails* is not rigidly structured, but always present. Chase finds the hacienda of the Alvarado Rancho, for instance, inhabited by a desperately overworked American ranch-wife and her two unkempt, unruly sons. Their ramshackle seediness seemed symbol enough (Chase was, after all, a Los Angeles social worker) that time and Americans had brought their own range of pressing problems. He is deliberately sardonic in the matter of collapsed boom towns. He notes them all, delighting in their atmosphere of American bravado brought to nought, their railroad stations taken off the timetables, their hotels standing empty—like the town of Fallbrook, California, where "the only signs of life revealed by a careful survey of the main street at midday were two urchins eating ice cream and an elderly man with a faded valise who stood gazing up and down the street, evidently looking for means of escape."[15]

Chase himself has a kind of escape in mind, a deliverance into nature and the past. One of the charms of his recessional journey is its litany of Spanish place-names which weave together strands of ecology and bygone human usage. He keeps us continually aware of weather: the sudden rains of late autumn, the sea-fogs burned off by the morning sun. And always we hear the surf breaking on the coast; for this—as well as Wagner's "Pilgrim's Chorus"—is the music Chase travels to. He hears the Pacific at dawn as he warms coffee over last night's embers. He hears it as he rides through the day. It keeps him company at night as he lies rolled in blankets beneath the California stars: it is the western sea of nineteenth-century American attainment, beside which the energies of the twentieth century are now reaching a point of critical mass.

Past and present, nature and civilization, receive a partial reconciliation in the area of Monterey, capital of Old California, mid-point of Chase's travels, and symbolic center of his narrative. Just below Point Lobos Chase catches an especially lovely view of the Pacific. "The sea was a splendor of deep Mediterranean blue," he writes, "and broke in such dazzling freshness of white that one might have thought it had been that day created. How amazing it is, that the ancient ocean, with its age-long stain of cities and traffic, toil and blood, can still be so bright, so uncontaminated, so heavenly pure! It seems an intentional parable of Divinity, knowing and receiving all, evil as well as good, yet through some deathless principle itself remaining forever right, strong, and pure, the Unchanging Good."[16]

In Monterey that evening, Chase strolled the cypress-lined streets, past adobes giving forth the mingled odors of roses and Spanish cooking. "On a side street," he writes, "a modern wooden church with a painful spire was lighted up, probably for choir practice. Protestant as I am, I turned away and walked again past the old Catholic Mission. The last swallows were wheeling home, and the sparrows in the ivy were sleepily querulous. The fading light lingered on the crumbling cornices, and the tile-capped belfry rose peacefully into the clear dusk of the sky. After all, age is a kind of sacrament."[17]

Chase is here confronting time and the meaning of history. Perceived as a burden of sin, history is washed clean in the sea. Lending itself to men as a symbol of a force subsuming both good and evil, the unchanging Pacific prompts in Chase a leap of faith that human difficulties might be resolved as well, that the future need not be totally feared. Nature yet renewed herself in the face of human error. In 1913 California-as-nature yet seemed capable of coping with California-as-history. Whatever was occurring, whatever mistakes men were making, Chase wanted to have hope. He wanted to believe that in the years ahead creation would continue to heal.

That, paradoxically, is why he revered the past, why on that evening in Monterey he strolled back to Mission San Carlos Borromeo for the second time, passing up the American church. Age, he claimed, was a kind of sacrament. In this, age resembled nature. Both offered atonement. Throughout *California Coast Trails* Chase was giving portraits of those who lived well because they lived simply. This is what Chase experienced most deeply as he strolled at dusk near the mission, hearing the sleep-song of sparrows: the simplicity and the peace of the past. Admittedly, this message was embedded in myth and romance. How else could it survive the assaults of the present? California had once known simpler ways, which was important to remember. In the second decade of the twentieth century, some still considered simplicity and peace the precious meaning of the California dream. J. Smeaton Chase was among their number. Undertaken as a pilgrimage of farewell, his journey up the coast now and then disclosed vistas of the old hope.

Arthur T. Johnson, on the other hand, saw much that discouraged him. *California, An Englishman's Impressions of the Golden State* documented some stresses the dream had come under. As an Englishman, he admired the beauty of California-as-garden. Southern California, in fact, impressed him as a vast conservatory, bungalows smothered in flowers, avenues lined with exotic trees. Not an outdoorsman by temperament the way Chase was, Johnson nevertheless managed some fine depictions of the ecologies through which he drove his wagon-camper. He was primarily interested, however, in the sociology and the psychology of California; and there he found a lot that worried him.

First of all, Californians seemed tormented by discontent. North and south, nobody seemed satisfied. "On the ranch and in the store," Johnson claimed, "on the road, in the streetcar, everywhere, one hears the same tale of discontent, sees the same shrug of the shoulders when any question relating to prosperity is mentioned. There are prevailing symptoms of uncertainty, instability, unrest on all sides."[18] For all their talk of creating a commonwealth of homes, Californians were quick to drive a For Sale sign into their front lawns when down the block, in the next town, 500 miles away, something better seemed in the offing. For all the talk of life on the land, the turn-over rate of farms was astonishing. Promotional rhetoric promised happiness to those flocking to the Golden State, but Johnson found strong evidence of broken dreams. Considered as a culture, Southern California often seemed little more than a compulsive scratching of appetites.

Los Angeles epitomized the situation. It impressed Johnson as a city of bizarre eccentricity, on the verge of erupting into a full-scale sideshow. His encounter with the city resembled that of Bob Orde in Stewart Edward White's novel *The Rules of the Game* (1910). Strolling after dark through downtown Los Angeles, Orde, just arrived from the East, is amazed to find attire running from straw hats to fur coats. "Each extreme of costume seemed justified, either by the balmy summer-night effect of the California open air, or by the hint of chill that crept from the distant mountains. Either aspect could be welcomed or ignored by a very slight effort of the will. Electric signs blazed everywhere. Bob was struck by the numbers of clairvoyants, palm readers, Hindu frauds, crazy cults, fake healers, Chinese doctors, and the like thus lavishly advertised. The class that elsewhere is pressed by necessity to the inexpensive dinginess of back streets, here blossomed forth in truly tropical luxuriance. Street vendors with all sorts of things, from mechanical toys to spot eradicators, spread their portable lay-outs at every corner. Vacant lots were crowded with spielers of all sorts—religious or political fanatics, vendors of cure-alls, of universal tools, of marvellous axle grease, of anything and everything to catch the idle dollar. Brilliantly lighted shops called the passer-by to contemplate the latest wave-motor, flying machine, door check, or what-not. Stock in these enterprises was for sale—and was being sold! Other sidewalk booths, like those ordinarily used as dispensaries of hot doughnuts and coffee, offered wild-cat mining shares, oil stock and real estate in some highly speculative suburb."[19]

Yellow journalism, Orde discovers, is nowhere more yellow than Los Angeles. Headlines blatantly distorted the truth; stories were outrageously slanted; and editorials indulged in blatant character-assassination. Advertising ran the gamut from abortions and VD cures to Oriental faith-healing. At a dinner party in one of the more elegant districts, costumes ranged from Greek gowns to peasant blouses. Men in evening attire spiced convention with Left Bank cravats or scarlet sashes which made them look like operetta banditti at a diplomatic reception. At the party, Orde meets a painter of undersea-scapes who insists upon doing his work while standing half-submerged in a tank of water. There is also Painless Parker, a dentist who extracts teeth as part of a vaudeville act, assisted by chorus-girls in nurses' outfits; Sonny Larue, a guru at the Colony of Unlimited Life ("At three we arise and break our fast, quite simply, with three or four dry prunes, and then, going forth to the high places for one hour, we hold steadfast the thought of Love"); and an unnamed reformer who refuses to sit in chairs ("When humanity shall come into its own we shall assume the graceful and hygienic postures of the oriental peoples"). "They do it all here," a real estate developer tells Orde, "from going barefoot, eating nuts, swilling olive oil, rolling down hill, adoring the Limitless Whichness, . . . the works."[20]

As an English visitor, Arthur T. Johnson was amused at the merely eccentric side of all this: the lady-barbers in evening gowns, the performing saurian at Alligator Ranch, the continuous performances of a review entitled "The Garden of Eden," directed by Darwin, Jr., in which the snake gobbled down the apple for comic relief. With droll satisfaction he clipped the following item from a newspaper. It appeared under the headline DEAD MAN SINGS ANTHEM WHILE HIS DEATH IS BEING MOURNED: "Wm. Faxon's voice was heard yesterday at his own funeral here. While his body lay in a casket, those gathered to pay final tribute heard two hymns by him, and also heard him as one of a trio, including his son and daughter, in sacred song. When the mourners had gathered in the parlor of the Faxon home, in which his open coffin lay, they were surprised to hear his voice pealing an anthem from behind a screen of flowers and palms. Three years ago, believing his life was nearing its close, Faxon conceived the idea of preserving his voice to be a part of the service when he died. He used a phonograph, and the records were reproduced before he was buried. Faxon was ninety years old, and was one of the wealthiest men in the county. He was the first Methodist convert in this district, and built a church for that faith. Almost until the time of his death he participated regularly in the song service."[21]

Behind the eccentricity, however, behind the strained flamboyance, Johnson detected something elusively evil, as if freedom, becoming license, were about to writhe back and gorge upon itself. Beneath the sense that all was possible, that anything went, lurked a baffled yearning for limits, which in its frustration threatened to turn at any minute into a repressive counter-force that denied the dream of liberation through which Californians mythically defined themselves. Johnson laughed at the naïve fundamentalism of the funeral parlor, but he bristled in anger before the rather successful attempts of church-groups to throw a veneer of rectitude over Southern California. Put into the same context as all the unrestraint—the acting-out through costume and architecture, the theosophy, the neo-paganism, the free love—the blue laws of towns like Pasadena tended to confer a quality of schizophrenia, indeed, Manicheanism, upon this civilization of the South.

What sort of social polity could keep such contradictions together, Johnson asked, caught, as he was, between thinking Southern California funny—and fearing it. Had it been pushed too far, this American lust for something better? Was the eccentricity the fruit of some dangerous inner confusion? Was some final, inevitable misery lurking at the core of the California dream?

In terms of the future Johnson was not optimistic. Far from being naïve about California-as-nature (north of Gaviota he almost lost his life in quicksand), J. Smeaton Chase hoped that in the long run it would still prove an enduring and redemptive metaphor to California-as-society. Johnson had little such hope. He was intensely more sensitive to the nether side of California-as-nature than Chase. His itinerary took him away from the lovely redwood coastal route, which Chase followed up to Oregon, and into the sirocco-scorched Sacramento Valley, which the Englishman described as the Plains of Desolation. There he seemed more aware of the inhuman heat, the lack of softening associations, and the malaria carried by mosquitoes breeding in stagnant irrigation ditches than he was of any special Californian dialogue with nature. The only fellow camper Johnson seems interested in is one who a week earlier had committed suicide near his own campsite.

IV

The assessments of Chase and Johnson underscored the ambiguities of California. In retrospect, the elements of hope were discernible, and so were the social sources of distress. Because this narrative concerns itself primarily with imaginative experience, political and socio-economic factors have been merely suggested. They have not, however, been forgotten. Monopolies of land and transportation, the control of politics by corporations (especially the Southern Pacific), predatory banking practices, an unjust tax structure—these and other abuses were the odds against which Californians struggled in pursuit of their dream. Indeed, the story of California setting its house in order constitutes the bulk of state history as it now stands written. It needs no repetition in these pages. Suffice it to say that, as is usual in human affairs, matters of getting, spending, and governance—and certainly not matters of aesthetics—consumed the most time and energy. Mention might be made also of the thousand natural shocks flesh was heir to, together with the misery men created for themselves, except that such documentation would belabor the obvious. To say that men and women passed their lives in California 1850-1915 is to say that disease struck, children died, and human beings suffered. There was the usual harvest of rape, murder, and mayhem. The California dream did not keep prisons, hospitals, or cemeteries empty; many claimed, in fact, that it kept them more occupied than was necessary, that symptoms of social stress—alcoholism, insanity, crime—were everywhere.

Be that as it may, what concerns us here is a more subtle stress, arising from the California dream itself, with its constant dialectic of hope against hope. Even at a continent's distance Walt Whitman could sense it. In "Facing West From California's Shores" (1860), Whitman put his universalized protagonist on the edge of the Pacific, looking across to Asia from which the great westward migrations of peoples had begun ages previously. It is a triumphant, mythic moment. With the settlement of California, the encirclement of the globe is virtually complete. The lyric ends, however, on a note of sadness and loss. "But where is what I started for so long ago?" Whitman's figure asks himself. "And why is it yet unfound?"

Why indeed? Such was perhaps the central question of the California experience: what, after all, was human happiness, and—whatever it was—why did it prove so elusive? There were few answers and more than enough paradox. By the early 1870's, when California had witnessed a quarter-century of American ambition, a sympathetic visitor found it necessary to say: "Ah! heavy is my heart with sorrow and with pity, when I look back and remember the sad, fallen humanity I have encountered in this sunny clime, and with whom I have sat or wandered, listening to their broken stories, and beholding the bitter tears they wept in the anguish of a wasted and ruined life. O California, the peerless, so young, so beautiful, yet so old in sorrow and remorse!"[22] Descriptions of the insane asylums at Napa and Stockton frequently appeared in tourist literature, accompanied, of course, by moralizings as to how many wretches had been brought to their present plight by the failure to make immoderate dreams come true.

An obsession with self-fulfillment proved one of the dangers of the California dream. Local apologists had a special relish for Social Darwinism as a public philosophy, feeling that the history of California above anything else proved that when the strong survived society flourished. At the Panama-Pacific International Exposition of 1915, Louis Christian Mullgardt's Court of Ages gave that cherished belief the testimony of narrative architecture. This self-image, structured by Social Darwinism, stressed California as the scene of extraordinary opportunity. Here, Gertrude Atherton was fond of saying, young America had its day, seizing and settling an empire, pushing rails across the Sierras, all before reaching forty. Left undescribed, however, were the residual effects this orgy of self-assertiveness had upon the California psyche in both its private and public modes. A restless selfishness, a preoccupation with untutored private ends which sometimes amounted to a mania, conferred a quality of instability and cranky self-absorption upon many figures of the pre-1890 period, especially upon those who, having made money, did not know what to do with it, and upon those who, having failed to make a bonanza (or worse, having made and lost it), considered their lives wasted.

In Southern California from the mid-1880's onward the health factor contributed to the possibilities of self-contemplating discontent. Promotional books such as *California of the South* (1888), written by two physicians, Walter Lindley and J. P. Widney, helped to create a myth of healthfulness and longevity which, like that of easy riches during the Gold Rush, was bound to prove disappointing. "Here disease and death may be kept at bay," Doctor P. C. Remondino wrote in the preface to *The Mediterranean Shores of America* (1892), "and life enjoyed to the end of the term of man's natural existence." Southern California filled up with the dying and the sick who, fleeing death, were yet uncertain of the outcome. At one time it seemed as if the region would become one vast sanitarium. This Southern Californian infirmary culture contradicted Social Darwinism in everything except self-preoccupation. It laid the foundations for a later obsession with death, the cemetery culture arising after World War I, and in the meanwhile it gave a murky cast to the California dream.

There were problems which California took into the twentieth century from the nineteenth; and there were new problems. Stated baldly, they do not differ from the problems faced by America as a whole in the period after 1915: population growth; the rise of an urban industrial socity; race relations; labor-management relations; questions of conservation and ecology; questions of health, education, and welfare. These were national problems—with a local texture; and that conjunction said much about the California experience as a whole. It was American and it was regional. In a very real sense, the California dream was the American dream undergoing one of its most significant variations. The hope raised by promotional writers, such as Charles Nordhoff in *California, For Health, Pleasure, and Residence* (1872), was the simple yet subtle hope for a better life animating America since its foundation. California provided a special context for the working-out of this aspiration, intensified it, indeed, gave it a probing, prophetic edge in which the good and evil of the American dream was sorted out and dramatized. In 1915, after sixty-five years of statehood, as, north and south, great expositions opened their gates, California, like America herself, remained an intriguing, unanswered question.

This narrative has gathered selected acts of definition, moments when vision and event betrayed their interchange, and the aesthetic pattern and moral meaning of social experience became clear. History grants few such occasions. An even smaller number go on record. In the flux and complexity of its inner life, California 1850-1915 defies our full understanding because the past (even the recent past) has a way of reserving its most precious meaning to itself. Unintimidated by this resistance, memory keeps the past alive, lest the identities of the present crumble away. The work of memory is only partially that of retrospective analysis.

Analysis, whose goal is conceptual control, defines its terms, focuses its scrutiny, and seeks the consolations of argument. Memory covets the present possession of past experience, the recovery of time's burden in all its fullness and baffling impenetrability. Abiding in the total self, and not just in the intellect, it musters conscious and subconscious perceptions into one knowing moment. Unafraid of mystery and unembarrassed by the poetry of the past, memory (named Mother of the Muses by the Ancients) is alert to the echoes of history, its lost gestures and hidden music. Memory passes judgment. It also preserves and commemorates.

This narrative is an act of memory, a gathering from the California past of some inner strands, understood and obscure. California 1850-1915 mocks the blunders of the present and is partially responsible for them. The dream lives on, promising so much in the matter of American living. It also threatens to become an anti-dream, an American nightmare. Memory, then, must come to our aid; for while the recovery of the past can traumatize, it can also heal. A culture failing to internalize some understanding of its past tragedies and past ideals has no focus upon the promise and dangers of the present.

In this regard, the elusiveness (the failure, if you will) of the California dream proves a blessing. Bringing the protagonists of this narrative forward in memory, we judge what they stood for—and such judgments, fixed in the consciousness of the present, can perhaps further today's struggle for value and corrective action. Old in error, California remains an American hope.

Notes

1

1. "Duhaut-Cilly's Account of California in the Years 1827-28," *California Historical Society Quarterly*, 8 (1929), 317 [hereafter cited as *CHSQ*].
2. *Voyage of the Venus: Sojourn in California* (Los Angeles, 1956), p. 14.
3. *Narrative of a Journey Round the World, During the Years 1841 and 1842* (2 vols., London, 1847), I, 274, 308-9, 408.
4. Abraham Nasatir, "The French Consulate in California, 1845-1856," *CHSQ*, 11 (1932), 340.
5. *Narrative*, I, 327.
6. George P. Hammond (ed.), *The Larkin Papers: Personal, Business, and Official Correspondence of Thomas Oliver Larkin, Merchant and United States Consul in California* (10 vols., Berkeley and Los Angeles, 1951-64), IV, 307.
7. *A Journey to California, 1841* (Berkeley, 1964), p. 51.
8. *Los Gringos: An Inside View of Mexico and California* (New York, 1849), pp. 112-13.
9. [William Robert Garner], "Letters From California, 1846, to the Editors of *The North American*," *The Magazine of History*, 26 (Extra No. 103), 221.
10. *The Emigrants' Guide to Oregon and California* [1845], Reproduced in facsimile (Princeton, 1932), p. 151.
11. *Journal of a Voyage Between China and the North-Western Coast of America, Made in 1804* (Claremont, 1935), p. 78.
12. David H. Coyner, *The Lost Trappers: A Collection of Interesting Scenes and Events in the Rocky Mountains Together With a Short Description of California* (New York, 1847), p. 196.
13. *Four Years in a Government Exploring Expedition* (New York, 1852), pp. 319-21.
14. *Travels in California and Scenes in the Pacific Ocean* [1844] (Oakland, 1947), pp. 67, 138, 148, 127-28, 161-62.
15. *What I Saw in California* [1848] (Palo Alto, 1967), p. 430.

16. *Narrative of the Adventures of Zenas Leonard* (Clearfield, Pa., 1839), ed. by John C. Ewers as *Adventures of Zenas Leonard, Fur Trader* (Norman, 1959), p. 89.
17. *Life in California During a Residence of Several Years in That Territory* [1846] (San Francisco, 1891), p. 91.
18. *Two Years Before the Mast, a Personal Narrative of Life at Sea, Edited From the Original Manuscripts and From the First Edition, With Journals and Letters of 1834-1836 and 1859-1860*, ed. by John Haskell Kemble (2 vols., continuously paged, Los Angeles, 1964), pp. 81, 84-85.
19. *Edward Vischer's First Visit to California* (San Francisco, 1940), p. 9.
20. *What I Saw in California*, p. 319; William Health Davis, *Sixty Years in California* (San Francisco, 1889), p. 131.
21. Joseph Warren Revere, *A Tour of Duty in California* (Boston and New York, 1849), pp. 42-43; Bidwell, *Journal*, p. 48.
22. *What I Saw in California*, p. 419.
23. Colton, *Three Years in California* (New York, 1852), pp. 223, 342, 345, 353, 355, 360, 390.
24. Maurice S. Sullivan, *The Travels of Jedediah Smith, a Documentary Outline Including the Journal of the Great American Pathfinder* (Santa Ana, 1934), p. 63.
25. "Captain Jedediah Strong Smith, A Eulogy of That Most Romantic and Pious of Mountainmen, First American By Land Into California," *Illinois Monthly Magazine* (June 1832), reprinted in Edwin L. Sabin, *Kit Carson Days* (2 vols., New York, 1935), I, 821-26.
26. Harrison Clifford Dale, *The Ashley-Smith Explorations And The Discovery of a Central Route to the Pacific, 1822-1829, With the Original Journals* (Gendale, 1941), pp. 249-50.
27. Robert F. Lucid (ed.), *The Journal of Richard Henry Dana, Jr.* (3 vols., Cambridge, 1968), I, 25.
28. Letter of 13 March 1835, *Two Years Before the Mast*, p. 387.
29. *Two Years Before the Mast*, p. 251.
30. Ibid. pp. 96, 107-8, 250.
31. *Journal*, I, xxxviii; *The Education of Henry Adams* (Boston, 1961), p. 29.
32. Lawrence, *Studies in Classic American Literature* (New York, 1964), p. 129; *Two Years Before the Mast*, p. 423; *Journal*, I, xxxii.

2

1. *Alonzo Delano's California Correspondence* (Sacramento, 1952), p. 22.
2. George Payson, *Golden Dreams and Leaden Realities* [1853] (Upper Saddle River, N.J., 1970), p. 187.
3. *One Man's Gold, The Letters and Journal of a Forty Niner* (New York, 1930), p. 110.
4. *From the Journal of Garrett W. Low, Gold Rush by Sea* (Philadelphia, 1941), p. 174.
5. *Seeking the Golden Fleece* (San Francisco, 1876), p. 145.
6. *One Man's Gold*, p. 178.
7. *Three Years in California, William Perkins' Journal of Life at Sonora, 1849-1852* (Berkeley and Los Angeles, 1964), pp. 159-60.

8. *An Excursion to California, With a Stroll Through the Diggings and Ranches of That Country* (2 vols., London, 1851), II, 25.
9. *Seeking the Golden Fleece,* p. 143.
10. *California Emigrant Letters,* ed. by Walker D. Wyman (New York, 1952), p. 85.
11. *One Man's Gold,* p. 106.
12. *The Letters of a Young Miner,* 1849-1852 (San Francisco, 1964), p. 23.
13. *California As It Is* [1851] (San Francisco, 1954), p. 35.
14. *Scenery of the Plains, Mountains and Mines* [1855] (Princeton, 1932), p. 192.
15. *California Correspondence,* p. 95.
16. Linville J. Hall, *Around the Horn in '49. Journal of the Hartford Union Mining and Trading Company* (Wethersfield, Conn., 1898), p. 131.
17. John Pomfret (ed.), *California Gold Rush Voyages, 1848-1849: Three Original Narratives* (San Marino, 1954), pp. 124, 130.
18. Richard Lunt Hale, *The Log of a Forty-Niner. Journal of a Voyage from Newbury-port to San Francisco* (Boston, 1923), p. 31.
19. Dale Morgan (ed.), *Overland in 1846, Diaries and Letters of the California-Oregon Trail* (2 vols., Georgetown, Calif., 1963), II, 526.
20. *Way Sketches* (New York, 1926), pp. 123-24.
21. *Eldorado, or, Adventures in the Path of Empire* [1850] (2 vols., New York, 1854), I, 114.
22. *Seeking the Golden Fleece,* p. 164.
23. *Three Years in California,* pp. 89-90.
24. *A Quaker Forty-Niner, the Adventures of Charles Edward Pancoast on the American Frontier* (Philadelphia, 1930), p. 326.
25. *Sixteen Months at the Gold Diggings* (New York, 1851), p. 63.
26. *One Man's Gold,* p. 162.
27. *Eldorado,* I, 116.
28. John Woodhouse Audubon, *Audubon's Western Journal: 1849-1850* (Cleveland, 1906), p. 206.
29. *A Yankee Trader in the Gold Rush, the Letters of Franklin A. Buck* (Boston and New York, 1930), p. 105.
30. *Prentice Mulford's Story, Life By Land and Sea* (New York, 1889), p. 7.
31. *California Emigrant Letters,* p. 24.
32. *California Letters, 1849-1855* (Madison, 1931), p. 68.
33. Samuel D. Woods, *Lights and Shadows of Life on the Pacific Coast* (New York and London, 1910), p. 9.
34. *In Pursuit of the Golden Dream, Reminiscences of San Francisco and the Northern and Southern Mines, 1849-1857* (Stoughton, Mass., 1970), p. 281.
35. "Early Recollections of the Mines," *The Magazine of History,* 42 (Extra No. 165) 38.
36. Anna Lee Marston, (ed.), *Records of a California Family; Journals and Letters of Lewis C. Gunn and Elizabeth Le Breton Gunn* (San Diego, 1928), pp. 66-67, 163, 205, 251.
37. *The Complete Works of Ralph Waldo Emerson* (12 vols., Boston, 1903-4), VI, 255-56.
38. *The Journal of Henry D. Thoreau* (14 vols., Boston, 1949), III, 266.

3

1. *Hasting to be Rich* (New Haven, 1849), p. 17.
2. *The Price of Gold* (Boston, 1852), pp. 15-16.
3. *California As She Was: As She Is: As She Is To Be* (Sacramento, 1850), p. 13.
4. *Farewell Discourse* (San Francisco, 1854), p. 11.
5. Frank Soule, John H. Gihon, and James Nisbet, *The Annals of San Francisco* (Palo Alto, 1966), p. 687.
6. *The AHMS Thirty-First Report* (New York, 1857), p. 105.
7. *Decade Sermons* (San Francisco, 1859), p. 45.
8. *The Wedge of Gold; or, Achan in El Dorado* (San Francisco, 1855), p. 171.
9. *A Call To Praise* (San Francisco, 1868), p. 15.
10. "Address," *Proceedings of the First State Convention of the Colored Citizens of California* (Sacramento, 1855), pp. 4-5.
11. *Autobiography* (San Francisco, 1888), pp. 174-76.
12. *William Taylor of California, Bishop of Africa, An Autobiography* (London, 1897), p. 115.
13. Isaac Brayton, *The Home Missionary*, 23 (1851), 279.
14. *California Life Illustrated* (New York, 1858), pp. 97-98.
15. G. B. Cheever, "The Missionary Aspect of California," *The Home Missionary*, 21 (1849), 237.
16. *Address Before the New England Society of San Francisco* (San Francisco, 1853), p. 20.
17. Linville J. Hall, *Around the Horn in '49*, pp. 62-63.
18. MS letter headed "Falcon. 26 Dec. 1848. Within a days sail of the Isthmus" (California Historical Society Library, San Francisco).
19. *Sermon Suggested by the Execution of Jenkins on the Plaza* (San Francisco, 1851), pp. 13, 19.
20. *The Home Missionary*, 29 (1856), 114.
21. Quoted in Howard Allen Bridgman, *New England in the Life of the World* (Boston and Chicago, 1920), p. 182.
22. Edwin Whipple, "Memoir," in Thomas Starr King, *Christianity and Humanity, a Series of Sermons* (Boston, 1878), xlvi.
23. Quoted in Richard Frothingham, *A Tribute to Thomas Starr King* (Boston, 1865), pp. 174, 243-47.
24. King to Randolph Ryers, 10 Sept. 1860, 10 March 1862, *Letters and Papers of Thomas Starr King*, 1839-1863 (The Bancroft Library, Berkeley).
25. *The White Hills, Their Legends, Landscape and Poetry* (Boston, 1887), p. 394.
26. "Selections From a Lecture-Sermon After Visiting Yosemite Valley," *The California Scrap-Book*, comp. by Oscar T. Shuck (San Francisco, 1869), p. 457; "Lessons From the Sierra Nevada," *Christianity and Humanity*, p. 293.

4

1. *The Annals of San Francisco*, pp. 283, 362.
2. *History of California* (Boston, 1854), pp. 77, 129.
3. *The Annals of Trinity County* (Eugene, 1940), xxviii.

4. Bancroft, *Essays and Miscellany* (San Francisco, 1890), p. 165.
5. *History of California* (San Francisco, 1866), vii-viii.
6. Citations in the following discussion are from Bancroft's *Literary Industries* (San Francisco, 1890), pp. 15, 95, 102, 116, 144, 228-29, 654.
7. John Walton Caughey, *Hubert Howe Bancroft: Historian of the West* (Berkeley and Los Angeles, 1946), p. 384.
8. *History of California* (7 vols., San Francisco, 1884-90), I, x.
9. *Literary Industries,* pp. 286, 336, 342.
10. *An Outline of the History of California From the Discovery of the Country to the Year 1849* (San Francisco, 1860), p. 67.
11. Ide, *The Conquest of California* (Oakland, 1944), p. 92.
12. *Popular Tribunals* (2 vols., San Francisco, 1887), I, 577.
13. *Mining Camps, A Study in Frontier Government* (New York, 1885), pp. 3, 125, 135, 177, 224, 287.
14. *The Resources of California* (San Francisco, 1863), p. 362.
15. *The Californians* (London, 1876), p. 128.
16. *The Lights and Shades in San Francisco* (San Francisco, 1876), pp. 31, 145.
17. *The Californians,* p. 108.
18. *A History of the City of San Francisco and Incidentally of the State of California* (San Francisco, 1878), pp. 448, 454-55, 461.
19. *Lights and Shades,* p. 470.
20. *The Annals of San Francisco,* p. 368.
21. *A History of the City of San Francisco,* p. 448.
22. *The Native Races of the Pacific States of North America* (5 vols., San Francisco, 1874-75), II, 1, 20, 34.
23. *Literary Industries,* pp. 2, 4-5.
24. C. F. McGlashan, *History of the Donner Party* (Sacramento, 1907), pp. 221-22.
25. *The History of San Jose* (San Francisco, 1871), p. 288.
26. *History of California,* p. 123.
27. *The Californians,* pp. 72-73.
28. *Afoot and Alone* (Hartford, 1872), p. 324.
29. Frost, *History of California,* p. 260; Capron, *History of California,* p. 170; Fisher, *The Californians,* pp. 71-72, 109, 126, 200; Hittell, *History of the City of San Francisco,* pp. 458-59; *The Resources of California,* pp. 442, 452-53.
30. *Roughing It,* ed. by Henry Nash Smith (New York, 1959), Part II, p. 132.
31. *The Life and Adventures of James W. Marshall* (Sacramento, 1870), pp. 173-74.
32. *Three Years in California,* p. 70.
33. *The Overland Monthly,* 1 (1868), 304-6 [hereafter cited as *OvM*].
34. *The Resources of California,* pp. 459-60.
35. *Literary Industries,* p. 103.
36. *OvM,* I, 301.
37. *Our Land and Land Policy* (San Francisco, 1871), pp. 14, 17, 25, 27.
38. *Progress and Poverty* (San Francisco, 1879), pp. 201, 228, 266, 310.
39. *Oration on the Thirty-Second Anniversary of the Society of California Pioneers* (San Francisco, 1882), p. 15.
40. *Progress and Poverty,* p. 457.

5

1. Sarah Royce, *A Frontier Lady: Recollections of the Gold Rush and Early California*, ed. by Ralph Gabriel (New Haven, 1932), p. 109.
2. Ibid. p. 50.
3. *California*, p. 246.
4. *A Frontier Lady*, p. 109.
5. *The Religious Aspect of Philosophy* (Boston, 1885), p. 55.
6. "Words of Professor Royce at the Walton Hotel at Philadelphia, December 29, 1915," *Papers in Honor of Josiah Royce on His Sixtieth Birthday*, p. 279.
7. *Lincoln Observer* for June 1869, Josiah Royce Papers, Archives of Harvard University.
8. "The Old and the New–a Lesson," *The University of California Chronicle*, 5 (1902), 94-95.
9. "The Problem of Class Feeling," *The Berkeleyan*, I (Feb. 1874), Royce Papers.
10. "Comments Suggested by a Principle in the Science of History," *The Berkeleyan*, I (Aug. 1874), Royce Papers.
11. "The Holy Grail of Tennyson," *The Berkeleyan*, II (June 1875), Royce Papers.
12. Royce to Gilman, 16 Sept. 1878, *The Letters of Josiah Royce*, ed. by John Clendenning (Chicago, 1970), p. 61.
13. Royce to George B. Coale, 16 Sept. 1878, *Letters*, pp. 62-63.
14. "Meditation Before the Gate," *Fugitive Essays*, ed. by J. Loewenberg (Cambridge, 1920), p. 7.
15. Sill to Daniel Coit Gilman, 4 Sept. 1878, in William Belmont Parker, *Edward Rowland Sill, His Life and Work* (Boston and New York, 1915), p. 173.
16. The Berkeley Club, *A Memorial of Edward Rowland Sill* (Oakland, 1887), pp. 21-22.
17. Royce to William James, 14 Jan. 1879, 8 Jan. 1880, Ralph Barton Perry, *The Thought and Character of William James* (2 vols., Boston, 1935), I, 781, 785.
18. *The Letters of William James*, ed. by Henry James (2 vols., Boston, 1920), I, 205.
19. See "The Nature of Voluntary Progress" [1880] in *Fugitive Essays*.
20. *The Religious Aspect of Philosophy*, pp. 83, 175.
21. Ibid. pp. 435, 441, 464-68; *The Spirit of Modern Philosophy* (Boston, 1892), viii.
22. Royce to Oak, 17 September 1885, *Letters*, p. 178.
23. *California*, viii; *Fugitive Essays*, p. 126.
24. *California*, pp. 276, 501.
25. *The History of San Jose*, pp. iv, 249-50, 331-32.
26. *The Annals of San Francisco*, pp. 697, 699-700.
27. *California*, pp. 393-96, 397-98.
28. Royce to Shinn, 7 Aug. 1886, *Letters*, p. 199.
29. "Two Recent Books Upon California History," *The Nation*, 42 (1886), 220; *California*, pp. 30-36, 40-41, 51, 111-12, 490.
30. *California*, pp. 32, 156.
31. Ibid. p. 307.
32. Ibid. pp. 259, 465.

33. "An Episode of Early California Life: The Squatter Riot of 1850 in Sacramento," *Studies in Good and Evil* (New York, 1898), pp. 304, 325.
34. *Popular Tribunals*, I, 584.
35. Royce to Milicent Shinn, 16 July 1886, *Letters*, p. 192.
36. "Royce's California," *OvM*, ns, 8 (1886), 222-23.
37. *California*, p. 499.
38. *Race Questions, Provincialism, and Other American Problems* (New York, 1908), p. 61.
39. Ibid. pp. 73-74, 96, 98.
40. "Provincialism Based Upon a Study of Early Conditions in California," *Putnam's Magazine*, 7 (1909), 233-35, 237.
41. "Some Characteristic Tendencies of American Civilization," unpublished MS, Royce Papers.
42. "Provincialism," *Putnam's Magazine, loc. cit.*, 236.
43. Ibid. p. 234.
44. "Words of Professor Royce," *Papers in Honor of Josiah Royce*, p. 283.
45. Ralph Barton Perry, *In the Spirit of William James* (New Haven, 1938), p. 36.
46. "The Opening of the Great West: Oregon and California" [1893], unpublished MS, Royce Papers.

6

1. "The Pacific Coast, A Psychological Study of the Relations of Climate and Civilization" (1898), *Race Questions*, pp. 203, 208.
2. *At Home and Abroad, Second Series* (New York, 1862), p. 155.
3. *Journal*, X, 89-90.
4. *À La California* (San Francisco, 1873), p. 221.
5. *The Rules of the Game* (New York, 1910), p. 241.
6. *Adventures*, p. 13.
7. William H. Brewer, *Up and Down California in 1860-1864*, ed. by Francis P. Farquhar (New Haven, 1930), p. 318.
8. *À La California*, p. 183.
9. James Bradley Thayer, *A Western Journey With Mr. Emerson* (Boston, 1884), pp. 67, 76.
10. John Muir, *The Story of My Boyhood and Youth* (Boston and New York, 1913), pp. 63-64.
11. Ibid. pp. 76-77.
12. Ibid. p. 77.
13. *The Yosemite* (New York, 1912), p. 4.
14. Linnie Marsh Wolfe, *Son of the Wilderness: The Life of John Muir* (New York, 1945), p. 163.
15. *The Story of My Boyhood and Youth*, pp. 180-81.
16. *My First Summer in the Sierras* (Boston and New York, 1917), pp. 15-16.
17. Wolfe, *Son of the Wilderness*, p. 163.
18. *The Story of My Boyhood and Youth*, p. 1.
19. *Overland in 1846*, I, 304.
20. *The Irish Race in California* (San Francisco, 1878), p. 135.

21. "Early Recollections of the Mines," *loc. cit.*, p. 22.
22. *At Home and Abroad*, p. 51.
23. *Mountaineering in the Sierra Nevada* (Boston, 1872), pp. 110-11.
24. *An Overland Journey, From New York to San Francisco in the Summer of 1859* (New York, 1860), p. 357.
25. *Afoot and Alone*, p. 304.
26. Ibid. p. 315.
27. *Distant Fields, A Writer's Autobiography* (London, 1937), p. 69.
28. *The Procession of Life* (New York, 1899), p. 34.
29. Ibid. pp. 182, 318.
30. *Life and Sport on the Pacific Slope* (New York, 1901), pp. 124-25, 128.
31. James Fowler Rusling, *The Great West and Pacific Coast* (New York, 1877), p. 341.
32. *Homes and Happiness in the Golden State of California* (San Francisco, 1884), p. 12.
33. John Codman, *The Round Trip* (New York, 1879), p. 56.
34. "Social Change in California," *The Popular Science Monthly*, 26 (1891), 798.
35. *Living the Radiant Life, a Personal Narrative* (Pasadena, 1916), p. 15, also pp. 70, 73.
36. *The Indians' Secrets of Health, or What the White Race May Learn From the Indian* (Pasadena, 1917), p. 38.
37. *The Cabin* (New York, 1911), p. 37.

7

1. To Alice Lyndon, 29 July 1909, *Letters From Jack London*, ed. by King Hendricks and Irving Shepard (New York, 1965), p. 282.
2. *John Barleycorn* (New York, 1913), p. 102.
3. *Letters*, p. 14, p. 86.
4. Charmian London, *The Book of Jack London* (2 vols., New York, 1921), II, 200-201.
5. Joseph Noel, *Footloose in Arcadia* (New York, 1940), p. 125.
6. Ibid. p. 168.
7. *The Book of Jack London*, I, 29.
8. Frederick L. Pattee, *Side-lights on American Literature* (New York, 1922), p. 47.
9. To William T. Hoyt, 17 June 1913, *Letters*, p. 387.
10. To Frank Lydston, 26 March 1914, *Letters*, p. 419.
11. *The Book of Jack London*, II, 224.
12. Louis J. Stellman, "Jack London—the Man," *OvM*, ns. 70 (1917), 386.
13. Joan London, *Jack London and His Times* (New York, 1939) p. 284.
14. To Cloudesley Johns, 24 Oct. 1899, *Letters*, p. 61.
15. To Cloudesley Johns, 2 May 1900, *Letters*, p. 104.
16. To Alice Lyndon, 29 July 1909, *Letters*, p. 282.
17. *The Book of Jack London*, II, 255.
18. To Walter S. Kerr, 26 Jan. 1915, *Letters*, p. 443.
19. To George P. Brett, 21 Sept. 1914, *Letters*, p. 429.

20. *Footloose in Arcadia*, p. 266.
21. To Roland Phillips, 14 May 1913, *Letters*, p. 374.
22. *The Book of Jack London*, II, 266, 268, 276.
23. "The House Beautiful," *Revolution and Other Essays* (New York, 1910).
24. To Roland Phillips, 14 March 1913, *Letters*, p. 374.
25. *Footloose in Arcadia*, p. 201.
26. *The Book of Jack London*, II, 271-72.
27. To Roland Phillips, 14 March 1913, *Letters*, p. 374.
28. *Footloose in Arcadia*, p. 179.
29. To Eileen Moretta, 18 Oct. 1911, *Letters*, p. 353.
30. Irving Stone, *Sailor on Horseback* (Boston, 1938), p. 309.
31. *The Book of Jack London*, I, 35.
32. To Mabel Applegarth, 30 Nov. 1898, *Letters*, pp. 6-7.
33. *The Book of Jack London*, I, 62; II, 42-47, 82-83, 244, 344.
34. *Footloose in Arcadia*, p. 94.
35. To Hugh Erichsen, 16 Oct. 1916, *Letters*, p. 476.

8

1. *The American Commonwealth* (2 vols., New York and London, 1895), II, 428.
2. *California, a Pleasure Trip From Gotham to the Golden Gate* (New York, 1877), p. 121.
3. William Henry Irwin, *The Readjustment* (New York, 1910), pp. 44-45.
4. Quoted in Lois Rodecape, "Gilding the Sunflower, a Study of Oscar Wilde's Visit to San Francisco," *CHSQ*, 19 (1940), 97.
5. "George Sterling at Carmel," *The American Mercury*, 11 (1927), 65.
6. *As I Remember* (New York, 1936), p. 69.
7. Quoted in Warren Unna, *The Coppa Murals, A Pageant of Bohemian Life in San Francisco at the Turn of the Century* (San Francisco, 1952), p. 51.
8. *Bayside Bohemia, Fin de siècle San Francisco and Its Little Magazines* (San Francisco, 1954), pp. 20-21.
9. "An Opening For Novelists: Great Opportunities For Fiction Writers in San Francisco" [*The Wave*, 22 May 1897], in Donald Pizer (ed.), *The Literary Criticism of Frank Norris* (Austin, 1964), p. 29.
10. *Ancestors* (New York, 1907), p. 369.
11. To Charmian London, 29 Jan. 1914, *Letters*, p. 413; to Eliza Shepard, 18 Jan. 1912, *Letters*, p. 358; *The Book of Jack London*, II, 236.
12. *Blix*, in James D. Hart (ed.), *A Novelist in the Making* (Cambridge, 1970), pp. 277-78.
13. Rusling, *The Great West*, p. 310.
14. *Bayside Bohemia*, x.
15. "George Sterling at Carmel," pp. 66-67.
16. Ibid. p. 66.
17. *As I Remember*, p. 73.
18. *Carmel-by-the-Sea, A Summer and Winter Resort That Appeals to the Artistically Inclined* (Carmel-by-the-Sea, n.d.), The Bancroft Library.

19. *An Autobiography* (New York, 1965), pp. 195-96.
20. "California Art," *The Wasp*, 9 June 1883, The Bancroft Library.
21. "The Ideal Bohemian, By One Who Does Not Love Him," *The Wasp*, 16 June 1883, The Bancroft Library.
22. To George Sterling, 11 Feb. 1911, *The Letters of Ambrose Bierce*, ed. by Bertha Clark Pope (San Francisco, 1922), pp. 170-71.
23. To George Sterling, 15 March 1902, Ibid. p. 52.
24. "The Shadow Maker," *The American Mercury*, 6 (1925), 18.
25. *The Book of Jack London*, I, 365.
26. Kipling, *Letters From San Francisco* (San Francisco, 1949), p. 23; Rodecope, *CHSQ*, 19 (1940), 105.

9

1. Quoted in Daniel Hudson Burnham, *Report on a Plan for San Francisco*, ed. by Edward F. O'Day (San Francisco, 1905), p. 7 [hereafter cited as *Burnham Report*].
2. "Extract From a Paper on the Commercial Value of Beauty," *Park Improvement Papers*, ed. by Charles Moore (Washington, D.C., 1903), p. 176.
3. Charles Moore, *Daniel Hudson Burnham, Architect, Planner of Cities* (2 vols., Boston and New York, 1921), II, 170.
4. "The Promised City of San Francisco," *The Architectural Record*, 19 (1906), 425-26, 430-31, 435.
5. Quoted in Mel Scott, *The San Francisco Bay Area, A Metropolis In Perspective* (Berkeley, 1959), p. 115.
6. All newspaper citations are from Russell Quinn, "The San Francisco Press and the Fire of 1906," Monograph Number Five of *The History of San Francisco Journalism* (San Francisco, Works Project Administration of Northern California, 1940).
7. *Some Cities and San Francisco/Resurgam* (New York, 1907), pp. 54-60.
8. Ibid. pp. 26, 61-62.
9. A. C. David, "The New San Francisco: Architectural and Social Changes Wrought by the Reconstruction," *The Architectural Record*, 31 (1912), 9.
10. *The City That Was* (New York, 1906), pp. 7-8.
11. John D. Barry, *The Meaning of the Exposition* (San Francisco, 1915), p. 18.
12. *The Art of the Exposition* (San Francisco, 1915), pp. 3-4.
13. Quoted in Elmer Grey, "The Panama-Pacific International Exposition of 1915," *Scribner's Magazine*, 54 (1913), 48.
14. "Color Scheme of the Panama-Pacific International Exposition," *The American Architect*, 105 (1914), 28.
15. "Art Influence in the West," *The Century*, 67 (1915), 829-833.
16. "The Pageant of California Art," *Art in California* (San Francisco, 1916), pp. 51-52.
17. Ibid. p. 60.
18. "Six Landscape Painters of Southern California," *Art in California*, p. 65.
19. "The Beginnings of Art in California," Ibid. p. 32.
20. Stella George Perry, *The Sculpture and Mural Decorations of the Exposition* (San Francisco, 1915), pp. 10, 34.

21. Franklin Morton Todd, *The Story of the Panama-Pacific International Exposition* (5 vols., New York and London, 1921), II, 270.
22. Rose Berry, *The Dream City, Its Art in Story and Symbolism* (San Francisco, 1915), p. 57.
23. "The Panama-Pacific International Exposition," *The World's Work*, 730 (1915), 361.
24. Louis Christian Mullgardt, *The Architecture and Landscape Gardening of the Exposition* (San Francisco, 1915), p. 50.

10

1. *The Blood of the Nation* (Boston, 1902), p. 28.
2. *The Human Harvest* (Boston, 1907), pp. 115-16.
3. *The Heredity of Richard Roe* (Boston, 1911), pp. 120-21.
4. *The Care and Culture of Men* (San Francisco, 1896), p. 9.
5. *California and the Californians* (San Francisco, 1899), pp. 9-10.
6. *The Stability of Truth* (New York, 1911), pp. 4, 51.
7. *California and the Californians*, pp. 13, 17-29, 46.
8. Ibid. pp. 10, 23-24, 30-33, 36-38, 42-43, 48.
9. Ibid. pp. 39, 47-48; "The College of the West," *Popular Science Monthly*, 65 (1904), 34; *The Care and Culture of Men*, pp. 81, 142, 170.
10. *Across the Busy Years* (2 vols., New York, 1939), I, 149-52.
11. Andrew D. White, *Autobiography* (2 vols., New York, 1905), II, 448; *The Memoirs of Ray Lyman Wilbur* (Stanford, 1960), p. 37; *The Letters of William James*, II, 82; Edwin E. Slosson, "Leland Stanford Junior University," *The Independent* (1 April 1909), 662.
12. Orrin Elliott, *Stanford University, the First Twenty-Five Years* (Palo Alto, 1937), pp. 26-27, 596-99, 607.
13. "The Leland Stanford Junior University," *OvM*, ns, 18 (1891), 342.
14. The English Club of Stanford, *The First Year at Stanford* (Stanford, 1905), p. 46.
15. "The California of the Padre," in *The Story of the Innumerable Company and Other Sketches* (San Francisco, 1896), pp. 89-90, 113-14, 118.
16. George Thomas Clark, *Leland Stanford* (Palo Alto, 1931), p. 421.
17. *Souvenir of the Leland Stanford Junior University And a Description of Palo Alto, the University Town* (San Francisco, 1888), pp. 11-12; Orrin Elliott, *Stanford University and Thereabouts* (San Francisco, 1896), p. 62.
18. *America's Conquest of Europe* (Boston, 1913), p. 42; *The Care and Culture of Men*, pp. 266-67; *The Voice of the Scholar* (San Francisco, 1903), p. 266.
19. Van Wyck Brooks, *An Autobiography*, p. 204; *Mitchell of California: The Memoirs of Sydney B. Mitchell* (Berkeley, 1960), pp. 173-74; Hans Zinsser, *As I Remember Him* (Boston, 1940), pp. 188-89, 193-194; Charles Kellogg Field, *The Story of Cheerio* (Garden City, 1936), p. 114.
20. Vernon Lyman Kellogg, *Herbert Hoover, The Man and His Work* (New York, 1920), p. 56; Edward Alsworth Ross, *Seventy Years of It* (New York, 1936), pp. 53-55.

21. Henry Rushton Fairclough, *Warming Both Hands* (Stanford, 1941), p. 120.
22. Ross, *Seventy Years of It*, pp. 54-55; *The Letters of William James*, II, 243; James, "Stanford's Ideal Destiny," in *Memories and Studies* (London and New York, 1911), p. 360.
23. Mrs. Jane Lathrop Stanford, "Address to the Board of Trustees, 3 October 1902," *Trustees' Series* (No. 5), p. 11.
24. "Address to the Board of Trustees, 11 February 1897," *Trustees' Series* (No. 2), pp. 7-8.
25. *The First Year at Stanford*, p. 47.
26. *Letters of William James*, II, 240-44; James, *Memories and Studies*, pp. 365-67.
27. Robert L. Duffus, *The Innocents at Cedro* (New York, 1944), p. 110; *Stanford Stories, Tales of a Young University* (New York, 1900) pp. 268-69.
28. Quoted in Franklin Walker, "Frank Norris at the University of California," *The University of California Chronicle*, 33 (1931), 331.
29. Jordan, *The Voice of the Scholar*, p. 232; Jack F. Sheehan and Louis Honig, *The Games of California and Stanford* (San Francisco, 1900), pp. 6-7, 11-12, 14, 16-17, 20.
30. *The Call of the Twentieth Century* (Boston, 1903), pp. 37-38; *The Care and Culture of Men*, p. 43; *The Voice of the Scholar*, p. 19.
31. *The Memoirs of Herbert Hoover, Years of Adventure 1874-1920* (New York, 1951), pp. 17, 21-22.
32. Will Irwin, *Herbert Hoover, a Reminiscent Biography* (New York, 1928), pp. 64-65; Rose Wilder Lane, *The Making of Herbert Hoover* (New York, 1920), pp. 154, 156, 239; *Memoirs of Ray Lyman Wilbur*, p. 66.
33. *Seventy Years of It*, p. 55.
34. *The Voice of the Scholar*, p. 138.
35. *Principles of Mining* (New York, 1909), pp. 186, 192-93.
36. *The Call of the Twentieth Century*, pp. 14-15.
37. *Hoover*, p. 60.
38. *The Care and Culture of Men*, p. 17.

11

1. *Adventures of a Novelist* (New York, 1932), pp. 24-25.
2. Ibid. p. 103, p. 105.
3. Amelia Ransome Neville, *The Fantastic City, Memoirs of Social and Romantic Life of Old San Francisco* (Boston and New York, 1932), pp. 102-4.
4. *A Whirl Asunder* (New York, 1895), p. 89.
5. *Ancestors*, p. 528.
6. *Adventures of a Novelist*, pp. 142, 144-45, 227.
7. *The Aristocrats* (London, 1901), p. 112.
8. *A Whirl Asunder*, p. 87.
9. *Adventures of a Novelist*, p. 102.
10. "A Native on the California Missions," *The Critic*, ns, 9 (1888), 271.
11. *California, An Intimate History* (New York, 1914), p. 31.
12. *The Doomswoman* (New York, 1892), p. 222.

13. *California*, pp. 202-4.
14. *A Daughter of the Vine* (London, 1899), pp. 273-76.
15. *A Whirl Asunder*, p. 54.
16. *Senator North* (London, 1900), pp. 331, 349.
17. *The Conqueror* (New York, 1902), p. 507.
18. *Letters From San Francisco*, p. 4.
19. *Adventures of a Novelist*, pp. 9-10.
20. Ibid. pp. 218-20.
21. *American Wives and English Husbands* (New York, 1898), p. 333.
22. Lionel Stevenson, "Atherton versus Grundy: the Forty Years' War," *Bookman*, 69 (1929), 472.

12

1. *A Year of American Travel* [1878], Introduction by Patrice Manahan (San Francisco, 1960), p. 16.
2. Ibid. p. 18.
3. *Report of the Exploring Expedition to the Rocky Mountains in the Year 1842 and to Oregon and North California in the Years 1843-44* (Washington, D.C., 1845), p. 257.
4. *Memoirs of My Life* (Chicago and New York, 1887), p. 55.
5. *Two Years Before the Mast*, p. 426.
6. *Old Mexico and Her Lost Provinces* (New York, 1883), p. 359.
7. *Across the Continent* (Springfield and New York, 1869), p. 284.
8. *From Scotland to Silverado*, ed. by James D. Hart (Cambridge, 1966), pp. 208-9.
9. *The New West; or, California in 1867-1868* (New York, 1869), pp. 370-71.
10. George Ward Burton, *Burton's Book on California and Its Sunlit Skies of Glory* (3 vols., Los Angeles, 1909), I, 70-71.
11. Quoted in Oscar T. Shuck (ed.), *The California Anthology* (San Francisco, 1880), pp. 380-81.
12. *Geographical Memoir Upon Upper California*, Introductions by Allan Nevins and Dale L. Morgan (San Francisco, 1964), p. 39.
13. "New Pictures From California," in *At Home and Abroad, Second Series* (New York, 1862), p. 166.
14. J. W. Boddam-Whetham, *Western Wanderings* (London, 1874), p. 344.
15. *Romantic California* (New York, 1910), p. 9.
16. *Old Mexico and Her Lost Provinces*, p. 394.
17. *Romantic California*, pp. 3-4.
18. *New Life in New Lands* (New York, 1873), p. 214.
19. *A Troubled Heart and How It Was Comforted At Last* (Notre Dame, 1885), p. 113.
20. *Our Italy* (New York, 1891), p. 18.
21. Ibid. p. 89.
22. *Afoot and Alone*, p. 322.
23. *As I Remember*, p. 61.
24. Isadora Duncan, *My Life* (New York, 1927), pp. 30-31.

25. Quoted in Walter Terry, *Isadora Duncan* (New York, 1964), p. 4.
26. *The Desert* (New York, 1901), p. 26.
27. *The Octopus* (New York, 1964), pp. 29-30.
28. Mary Austin, *Experiences Facing Death* (Indianapolis, 1931), p. 25.
29. *Earth Horizon* (Boston and New York, 1932), p. 187.
30. Ibid. p. 198.
31. *Can Prayer Be Answered?* (New York, 1934), p. 48.
32. *Experiences Facing Death,* p. 18.
33. *Earth Horizon,* p. 368.
34. Luther Melancthon Schaeffer, *Sketches of Travels in South America, Mexico and California* (New York, 1860), p. 24.
35. Samuel D. Woods, *Lights and Shadows of Life on the Pacific Coast* (New York and London, 1910), p. 4.
36. *The Life and Adventures of Joaquin Murieta, The Celebrated California Bandit* [1854], Introduction by Joseph Henry Jackson (Norman, 1955), pp. 7, 80, 158.
37. George D. Lyman, "The First Native-Born Californian Physician," *CHSQ,* 4 (1925), 287-88.
38. Lansing B. Mizner, *Oration on the Twentieth Anniversary of the Society of California Pioneers* (San Francisco, 1870), p. 17.
39. *Literary Industries,* p. 382.
40. *History of California,* p. 112.
41. *Oration on the Twenty-First Anniversary of the Society of California Pioneers* (San Francisco, 1871), p. 12.
42. *Oration on the Twenty-Sixth Anniversary of the Society of California Pioneers* (San Francisco, 1876), p. 13.
43. *San Diego, A Comprehensive Plan For Its Improvement* (Boston, 1908), p. 46.
44. Ibid. pp. 2-3, 5, 10.
45. "Introduction" to Carleton Monroe Winslow, *The Architecture and the Gardens of the San Diego Exposition* (San Francisco, 1916), pp. 3-9.
46. *Impressions of the Art at the Panama-Pacific Exposition* (New York, 1916), pp. 31, 35, 40.
47. *The San Diego Garden Fair* (San Francisco, 1916), xii-xiii.
48. Florence Williams, "Bungalows of Southern California," *House Beautiful,* 36 (1914), 16.
49. *The Simple Home* (San Francisco, 1904), pp. 7-9, 16.
50. Ibid. pp. 11-15.
51. Ibid. p. 55.
52. "Round About Los Angeles," *The Architectural Record,* 24 (1908), 431, 437-40.
53. *Autobiography* (New York, 1943), pp. 225-26, 231-34, 246, 251.
54. Rexford Newcomb, "Preface" to *Mediterranean Domestic Architecture in the United States* (Cleveland, 1928).
55. "A New Addition to California's Spanish Tradition," *Architect and Engineer,* 67 (1921), 47-48; "A Step in California's Architecture," *Architect and Engineer,* 70 (1922), 48-57.
56. "Country House Architecture on the Pacific Coast," *The Architectural Record,* 40 (1916), 323-24, 327, 354.

13

1. *The American Scene,* Introduction and Notes by Leon Edel (Bloomington, 1968), p. 462.
2. To Mrs. William James, 5 April 1905, *The Letters of Henry James,* sel. and ed. by Percy Lubbock (2 vols., New York, 1920), II, 33.
3. *The American Scene,* pp. 411-12.
4. *The Genteel Tradition in American Philosophy* (Berkeley, 1911), p. 5.
5. Ibid. p. 24.
6. Ibid. pp. 25-26.
7. Leon Edel, *Henry James, The Master,* 1901-1916 (Philadelphia and New York, 1972), p. 286. See pp. 284-87 for Edel's account of James' California visit.
8. Royce, *The University of California Chronicle,* 5 (1902), 94.
9. *The Autobiography of Joseph Le Conte* (New York, 1902), pp. 288, 335.
10. *Evolution And Its Relation to Religious Thought* (New York, 1888), pp. 295, 338.
11. Luther Burbank with Wilbur Hall, *The Harvest of the Years* (Boston and New York, 1927), p. 32.
12. *The Scientific Aspects of Luther Burbank's Work* (San Francisco, 1909), pp. 78-81.
13. *California Coast Trails, A Horseback Ride From Mexico to Oregon* (Boston and New York, 1913), pp. 23-24.
14. Ibid. p. 30.
15. Ibid. p. 33.
16. Ibid. pp. 213-14.
17. Ibid. p. 223.
18. *California, An Englishman's Impressions of the Golden State* (London, 1913), p. 58.
19. White, *The Rules of the Game,* p. 137.
20. Ibid. pp. 143, 146.
21. *California, An Englishman's Impressions of the Golden State,* p. 87.
22. Stephen Powers, *Afoot and Alone,* p. 325.

Further Sources

Aside from materials cited in the text or in footnotes, the following items have also shaped my interpretation. Abbreviated titles are sometimes used in the full confidence that anyone interested might find the full listing in the magisterial *California, Local History, A Bibliography and Union List of Library Holdings*, 2nd Ed. Revised and Enlarged, ed. by Margaret Miller Rocq for the California Library Association (Stanford University Press, 1970).

1

Regarding Old California, see Irving Berdine Richman, *California Under Spain and Mexico, 1535-1847* (Boston and New York, 1911); Margaret Mackey and Louise Sooy, *Early California Costumes, 1769-1847* (Stanford, 1932); and Manuel P. Servín, "The Secularization of the California Missions: a Reappraisal," *Southern California Quarterly*, 47 (1967), 133-49.

For the French view, consult Abraham P. Nasatir, *French Activities in California* (Stanford, 1945); Rufus Kay Willys, "French Imperialists in California," *CHSQ*, 8 (1929), 116-29, and the following reports: Jean François Galaup de Lapérouse, *Voyage Autour Du Monde*, trans. by Charles N. Rudkin as *The First French Expedition to California* (Los Angeles, 1959); Edmond Le Netrel, *Voyage of the "Heroes" Around the World With Duhaut-Cilly*, trans. by Blanche Wagner (Los Angeles, 1951); Charles N. Rudkin, *Camille de Roquefeuil in San Francisco, 1817-1818* (Los Angeles, 1954); "The Report of Captain La Place," *CHSQ*, 18 (1939), 315-28; "The Report of Captain De Rosamel," *CHSQ*, 37 (1958), 63-77.

Regarding Drake, see *The Plate of Brass, Evidence of the Visit of Francis Drake to California in the Year 1579* (San Francisco, 1953). The British sense of California unfolds through George Vancouver, *The Voyage of Discovery to the Pacific Ocean and Round the World* (2 vols., London, 1798); Frederick William Beechey, *A Narrative of a Voyage to the Pacific and Beering's Strait In 1825, '26, '27, '28* (2 vols.,

London, 1831); William Ruschenberger, *Narrative of a Voyage Around the World During the Years 1835, '36, '37* (2 vols., London, 1838); Edward Belcher, *Narrative of a Voyage Round the World During the Years 1836-1842* (2 vols., London, 1843); and John Coulter, *Adventures on the Western Coast of South America and in the Interior of California* (London, 1847). See also "Archibald Menzies' Journal of the Vancouver Expedition," *CHSQ*, 2 (1924), 265-340; and Thomas Coulter, "Notes on Upper California," *The Journal of the Royal Geographical Society of London*, 5 (1835), 59-70. The stories of two Anglo-Californians are told by Susanna Bryant Dakin in *A Scotch Paisano: Hugo Reid's Life in California, 1832-1852, Derived From His Correspondence* (Berkeley, 1939) and *The Lives of William Hartnell* (Stanford, 1949).

A translation of Rezanov's report was edited by Thomas C. Russell as *The Rezanov Voyage to Nueva California in 1806* (San Francisco, 1926). Russell also issued *Langsdorff's Narrative of the Rezanov Voyage* (San Francisco, 1927). Regarding the Russian experience in California, see also August C. Mahr, *The Visit of the "Rurik" to San Francisco in 1816* (Stanford, 1932); Vassilli Petrovitch Tarakanoff, *Statement of My Captivity Among the Californians* [1814-16], trans. by Ivan Petroff (Los Angeles, 1953); K. T. Khlebnikov, "Memoirs of California" [1829], *The Pacific Historical Review*, 9 (1940), 307-36; and Alexander Markoff, *The Russians on the Pacific Ocean* [1856], trans. by Ivan Petroff (Los Angeles, 1955).

Also helpful were Paolo Emilio Botta, *Observations on the Inhabitants of California, 1827-1828*, trans. by John Bricca (Los Angeles, 1952); and G. M. Waseurtz af Sandels, *A Sojourn in California, 1842-1843* (San Francisco, 1945).

Robert Glass Cleland, *The Early Sentiment for the Annexation of California* (Austin, 1915), Henry Nash Smith, *Virgin Land: The American West as Symbol and Myth* (Cambridge, 1950), and James D. Hart, *American Images of Spanish California* (Berkeley, 1960) are crucial to an understanding of the impact of California upon the American imagination.

Regarding Smith and other trappers, see Dale L. Morgan, *Jedediah Smith and the Opening of the West* (Indianapolis and New York, 1953); and Robert Glass Cleland, *This Reckless Breed of Men. The Trappers and Fur Traders of the Southwest* (New York, 1950). Washington Irving wrote charmingly of the Walker party in *The Adventures of Captain Bonneville, U.S.A., in the Rocky Mountains and the Far West* (New York, 1868). Charles Wilkes, *Narrative of the United States Exploring Expedition During the Years 1838, 1839, 1840, 1841, 1842* (5 vols., and atlas, London, 1845) is a mine of information. See also Titian Ramsey Peale, *Diary, Oregon to California, September and October 1841*, ed. by Clifford M. Drury (Los Angeles, 1957).

Regarding Dana's voyage and subsequent career, see Charles Francis Adams, *Richard Henry Dana* (2 vols., Boston and New York, 1890); Samuel Shapiro, *Richard Henry Dana, Junior, 1815-1882* (East Lansing, 1961); and James D. Hart, "The Education of Richard Henry Dana, Jr.," *New England Quarterly*, 9 (1936), 3-25. Further maritime visits of interest are Richard J. Cleveland, *A Narrative of Voyages and Commercial Enterprises* (2 vols., Cambridge, 1842); Philo White, *Narrative of a Cruize in the Pacific to South America and California*, ed. by Charles L. Camp (Denver, 1965); "Commodore Thomas ap Catesby Jones' Narrative of His Visit to Governor Micheltorena," *Southern California Quarterly*, 17 (1935), 123-34; William

Maxwell Wood, *Wandering Sketches of People and Things in South America, Polynesia, California and Other Places* (Philadelphia, 1849); and Chester S. Lyman, *Around the Horn to the Sandwich Islands and California, 1845-1850*, ed. by Frederick J. Teggart (New Haven, 1924).

Regarding American merchants in Old California, see Samuel Eliot Morison, *The Maritime History of Massachusetts, 1783-1860* (Boston, 1921); "The Life and Letters of William Goodwin Dana," *Southern California Quarterly*, 19 (1937), 49-62; Adele Ogden, *The California Sea Otter Trade, 1784-1848* (Berkeley and Los Angeles, 1941); Adele Ogden, "Alfred Robinson, New England Merchant in Mexican California," *CHSQ*, 23 (1944), 193-218; Donald Mackenzie Brown (ed.), *China Trade Days in California: Selected Letters From the Thompson Papers, 1832-1863* (Berkeley and Los Angeles, 1947); Andrew F. Rolle, *An American in California, the Biography of William Heath Davis, 1822-1909* (San Marino, 1956); John A. Hawgood, "The Pattern of Yankee Infiltration in Mexican Alta California, 1821-1846," *The Pacific Historical Review*, 27 (1958), 27-37; and Doyce B. Nunis, Jr. (ed.), *The California Diary of Faxon Dean Atherton, 1836-1839* (San Francisco and Los Angeles, 1964).

Regarding those arriving overland, see George Lyman, *Dr. John Marsh, Pioneer* (New York, 1930); *The Life and Adventures of George Nidever, 1802-1883*, ed. by William Henry Ellison (Berkeley, 1937); Iris Higbie Wilson, *William Wolfskill, 1798-1866: Frontier Trapper to California Ranchero* (Glendale, 1965); and *George C. Yount and His Chronicles of the West*, ed. by Charles L. Camp (Denver, 1966).

Regarding the conquest of California by land, see W. H. Emory, *Notes of a Military Reconnoissance from Fort Leavenworth to San Diego* (New York, 1948); Philip St. George Cooke, *The Conquest of New Mexico and California* [1878] (Albuquerque, 1964); and "The Diary of John S. Griffin, Assistant Surgeon with Kearny's Dragoons, 1846-47," ed. by George Walcott Ames, Jr., *CHSQ*, 21 (1942), 193-224, 333-57; 22 (1943), 41-66. Regarding the Mexican-Californian resistance, see Arthur Woodward, *Lances at San Pascual* (San Francisco, 1948). For the Naval side of the take-over, see "The Journal of Lieutenant Tunis Augustus Macdonough Craven, U.S.N.," ed. by John Haskell Kemble, *CHSQ*, 20 (1941), 193-234; Joseph T. Downey, *The Cruise of the Portsmouth, 1845-1847: a Sailor's View of the Naval Conquest of California*, ed. by Howard Lamar (New Haven, 1963); and *A Navy Surgeon in California, 1846-1847: the Journal of Marius Duvall*, ed. by Fred Blackburn Rogers (San Francisco, 1962).

For the years of military occupation, see Samuel Hopkins Willey, *The Transition Period of California From a Province of Mexico in 1846 to a State of the American Union in 1850* (San Francisco, 1901); and Clifford M. Drury, "Walter Colton, Chaplain and Alcalde," *CHSQ*, 35 (1956), 97-117. Regarding statehood, see J. Ross Browne, *Report of the Debates in the Convention of California on the Formation of the State Constitution in September and October, 1849* (Washington, D.C., 1850).

Remarks regarding architecture, here and in later chapters, are guided by Harold Kirker, *California's Architectural Frontier, Style and Tradition in the Nineteenth Century* (San Marino, 1960). Although it appeared after I completed the bulk of my research, I found Lawrence Clark Powell, *California Classics: The Creative Literature of the Golden State* (Los Angeles, 1971) both a stimulus to my imagination and a challenge to my thinking.

2

Generalizations regarding the Gold Rush have been guided by John Walton Caughey, *Gold Is the Cornerstone* (Berkeley and Los Angeles, 1948); Rose Eyring, "The Portrayal of the California Gold-Rush Period in Imaginative Literature From 1848 to 1875" (unpublished Ph.D. dissertation, Dept. of English, The University of California at Berkeley, 1944); and Jaquelin Smith Holliday, "The California Gold Rush in Myth and Reality" (unpublished Ph.D. dissertation, Dept. of History, The University of California at Berkeley, 1959).

Sea voyages of interest are Samuel C. Upham, *Notes of a Voyage to California* (Philadelphia, 1878); Joseph Lamson, *Round Cape Horn* (Bangor, 1878); *The Wanderings of Edward Ely, a Mid-19th Century Seafarer's Diary*, ed. by Anthony and Allison Sima (New York, 1954); and Robert Samuel Fletcher, *Eureka, From Cleveland By Ship to California, 1849-1850* (Durham, 1959). See also Oscar Lewis, *Sea Routes to the Gold Fields* (New York, 1949).

Gold Rush: The Journals, Drawings, and Other Papers of J. Goldsborough Bruff, Captain, Washington City and California Mining Association, April 2, 1849-July 20, 1851, ed. by Georgia Willis Read and Ruth Gaines (2 vols., New York, 1944) is capacious and fascinating. See also Alonzo Delano, *Across the Plains and Among the Diggings* [1853] (New York, 1936); William L. Manly, *Death Valley in '49* [1894] (Chicago, 1927); George W. B. Evans, *Mexican Gold Trail, The Journal of a Forty-Niner*, ed. by Glenn S. Dumke (San Marino, 1945); *Letters of Lewis Granger*, ed. by LeRoy R. Hafen (Los Angeles, 1959).

Louise Amelia Knapp Smith Clappe, *The Shirley Letters From the California Mines, 1851-1852*, ed. by Carl I. Wheat (New York, 1949) is a classic account. Also superb is *Apron Full of Gold, The Letters of Mary Jane Megquier from San Francisco, 1849-1856*, ed. by Robert Glass Cleland (San Marino, 1949). In addition, see Edward Gould Buffum, *Six Months in the Gold Mines* [1850], ed. by John W. Caughey (Los Angeles, 1959); *California, Report of Hon. T. Butler King* (Washington, D.C., 1850); Leonard Kip, *California Sketches* [1850] (Los Angeles, 1946); Hinton Rowan Helper, *The Land of Gold, Reality Versus Fiction* (Baltimore, 1855); and *Twenty Years on the Pacific Slope, Letters of Henry Eno From California and Nevada, 1848-1871*, ed. by W. Turrentine Jackson (New Haven, 1965). Of special significance is Sylvan J. Muldoon, *Alexander Hamilton's Pioneer Son* (Harrisburg, 1930).

The British made fine reporters of the Gold Rush. See, for instance, Frank Marryat, *Mountains and Molehills* (New York, 1855); and J. Douglas Borthwick, *Three Years in California* (Edinburgh and London, 1857).

The humorous side of the Gold Rush found expression in Alonzo Delano, *Pen Knife Sketches; or, Chips of the Old Block* (Sacramento, 1853); and Delano's *Old Block's Sketch-Book; or, Tales of California Life* (Sacramento, 1856); George Horatio Derby, *Phoenixiana; or, Sketches and Burlesques by John Phoenix* (New York, 1856); Prentice Mulford, *California Sketches*, ed. by Franklin Walker (San Francisco, 1935); *Sam Ward in the Gold Rush*, ed. by Carvel Collins (Stanford, 1949); and Joseph G. Baldwin, *The Flush Times of California*, ed. by Richard E. Amacher and George W. Polhemus (Athens, Ga., 1966).

Further Gold Rush reminiscences that proved to be of value were G. W. Sullivan, *Early Days in California* (San Francisco, 1888); James W. Steele, *Old California Days* (Chicago, 1889); C. W. Haskins, *The Argonauts of California* (New York, 1890); W. F. Swasey, *The Early Days and Men of California* (Oakland, 1891); Stephen J. Field, *Personal Reminiscences of Early Days in California* [1877] (n.p., 1893); John Steele, *In Camp and Cabin* [1901], ed. by Milo M. Quaife (Chicago, 1928); Hiram Dwight Pierce, *A Forty-Niner Speaks* (Oakland, 1930); and Elisha Oscar Crosby, *Memoirs, Reminiscences of California and Guatemala from 1849 to 1864*, ed. by Charles Albro Barker (San Marino, 1945).

3

Of invaluable use in this chapter were two guides prepared by Clifford M. Drury: *California Imprints, 1846-1876, Pertaining to Social, Educational, and Religious Subjects* (Glendale, 1970); and "Index to References to Churches, Clergymen, and Religious Subjects Mainly on the Pacific Coast, in *The Pacific*, Organ of the Northern California Congregational Conference, 1851-1868, Made at the San Francisco Theological Seminary, San Anselmo, California, Under the Direction of the Reverend Clifford M. Drury, 1950-1958" (microfilm, Library of the San Francisco Theological Seminary).

A number of collections were consulted. At the San Francisco Theological Seminary: Timothy Dwight Hunt, "Diaries, Letters, and Papers"; William C. Anderson, "Journal for 1856"; Samuel Hopkins Willey, "Records and Papers." At the Bancroft Library: The American Home Missionary Society, "California Correspondence, 1848-1856" (microfilm); Samuel Hopkins Willey, "Personal Memoranda on California." At the Library of the California Historical Society: Ferdinand C. Ewer, "Diary, 1826-1860." Also reviewed were the files of *The Home Missionary, The Pacific*, the *Minutes* of the General Association, and the *Proceedings* of the Protestant Episcopal Church. In addition, see "Los Angeles in 1854-5, the Diary of Rev. James Woods," *Southern California Quarterly*, 23 (1941), 65-86; and Osgood Church Wheeler, "Selected Letters," ed. by Sandford Fleming, *CHSQ*, 27 (1948), 9-18ff.

Clerical autobiographies proved to be of special value: William Taylor, *Seven Years' Street Preaching in San Francisco* (New York, 1856); Jean Leonhard Ver Mehr, *Checkered Life: In the New and Old World* (San Francisco, 1877); James Woods, *Recollections of Pioneer Work in California* (San Francisco, 1878); Samuel Hopkins Willey, *Thirty Years in California* (San Francisco, 1879); Albert Williams, *A Pioneer Pastorate and Times* (San Francisco, 1882); Andrew Leete Stone, *Leaves From a Finished Pastorate* (New York and San Francisco, 1882); Osgood Church Wheeler, *The Story of Early Baptist History in California* (Sacramento, 1889); William Ingraham Kip, *The Early Days of My Episcopate* (New York, 1892); Samuel Hopkins Willey, *The History of the First Pastorate of the Howard Presbyterian Church, San Francisco, California, 1850-1862* (San Francisco, 1900); Oscar P. Fitzgerald, *Fifty Years: Observations, Opinions, Experiences* (Nashville, 1903); William C. Pond, *Gospel Pioneering* (Oberlin, 1921). See also William Ingraham Kip, *A California Pilgrimage* [1856] (Fresno, 1921) and "Historical Discourse by the Bishop," *Celebration of the Twenty-Fifth Anniversary of the Consecration of the Bishop of California* (San Francisco, 1878); William Anderson Scott, *My Residence In and Departure*

From California (Paris, 1861); Miflin Harker, *The Churches of San Francisco: Their Church Polity, and a Short Treatise on Church Government* (San Francisco, 1866); Joseph Augustine Benton, "Early Congregationalism in California," *OvM*, ns, 5 (1885), 87-98; Osgood Church Wheeler, "Early Baptists," *OvM*, ns, 5 (1885), 231-38; Oscar P. Fitzgerald, *California Sketches, New and Old* (Nashville, 1895).

Some useful denominational histories are J. C. Simmons, *The History of Southern Methodism on the Pacific Coast* (Nashville, 1886); C. V. Anthony, *Fifty Years of Methodism* (San Francisco, 1901); Douglas Ottinger Kelley, *History of the Diocese of California, 1849-1914* (San Francisco, 1915); Edward Arthur Wicher, *The Presbyterian Church in California, 1849-1927* (New York, 1927); Sandford Fleming, *God's Gold: The Story of Baptist Beginnings in California, 1849-1860* (Philadelphia, 1949); and Arnold Crompton, *Unitarianism on the Pacific Coast, the First Sixty Years* (Boston, 1957). Of particular help were Clifford M. Drury, "A Chronology of Protestant Beginnings in California," *CHSQ*, 26 (1947), 163-74; and Drury's *William Anderson Scott* (Glendale, 1967).

Sermons provided welcomed insights. Sermons of departure: Charles Henry Brigham, *An Address to the Companies of California Adventurers* (Taunton, 1849); George Shepard and S. Luther Caldwell, *Address to the California Pilgrims* (Bangor, 1849); Samuel Roosevelt Johnson, *California* (New York, 1849); George William Perkins, *An Address to the Pacific Pioneers* (West Meriden, 1849); Samuel Melanchton Worcester, *California* (n.p., 1849); J. H. Avery, *The Land of Ophir, Ideal and Real* (New York, 1853); George Burgess, *The Gospel in Its Progress Westward* (Albany, 1853); and William W. Newell, *The Glories of a Dawning Age* (Syracuse, 1853). Sermons praising California as a moral challenge: Charles A. Farley, *The Moral Aspect of California* (New York, 1851); and Horace Bushnell, *Society and Religion* (San Francisco, 1856). Sermons which were a little less enthusiastic: Joseph C. Foster, *The Uncertainty of Life* (Brattleboro, 1849); Nathaniel Langdon Frothingham, *Gold* (Boston, 1849); William P. Lunt, *The Net That Gathered of Every Kind* (Boston, 1849); Timothy Dwight Hunt, "Haste To Be Rich," *The Pacific*, 1 Aug. 1851, and "Fast Living," *The Pacific*, 14 Nov. 1851; and A. Boutelle, *Sermon Occasioned by the Death of Newell Marsh* (Concord, N.H., 1853). Sermon given on Thanksgiving: Rufus Putnam Cutler, A *Thanksgiving Sermon* (San Francisco, 1856). At the dedication of a church: Flavel S. Mines, *Sermon at the Opening of Trinity Church* (San Francisco, 1852). On the removal from one building to another: Samuel Hopkins Willey, *Discourse at the Closing Exercises of the Howard Street Presbyterian Church* (San Francisco, 1867). On special occasions: William Anderson Scott, *The Pavillion Palace of Industry* (San Francisco, 1857); William C. Anderson, *The Ocean Telegraph* (San Francisco, 1858); William Ingraham Kip, *Lessons of the Faith in Europe* (San Francisco, 1865); Andrew Leete Stone, *The Finger of God, a Sermon Preached After the Great Earthquake* (San Francisco, 1868); and Israel Edson Dwinell, *The Higher Reaches of the Great Continental Railway, a Sermon Preached on the Completion of the Overland Railway* (Sacramento, 1869). There were collections of sermons, such as *Sermons by Charles Wadsworth, Minister of Calvary Church, San Francisco* (New York and San Francisco, 1869). And even scholarship: William Ingraham Kip, *The Unnoticed Things of Scripture* (New York and San Francisco, 1868).

Regarding Roman Catholicism, see William Gleeson, *History of the Catholic Church in California* (2 vols., 1871-72); Francis J. Weber, *California's Reluctant Prelate, the Life and Times of Right Reverend Thaddeus Amat, C.M.* (Los Angeles, 1964); John Bernard McGloin, S.J., *California's First Archbishop, the Life of Joseph Sadoc Alemany, O.P.* (New York, 1966); and William E. Franklin, "The Religious Ardor of Peter H. Burnett," *CHSQ*, 45 (1966), 125-31.

Regarding the black experience, see Darius Stokes, *A Lecture Upon the Moral and Religious Elevation of the People of California* (San Francisco, 1853); *Proceedings of the Second Annual Convention of Colored Citizens of California* (San Francisco, 1856); Peter Cole, *Cole's War With Ignorance and Deceit* (San Francisco, 1857); I. Garland Penn, *The Afro-American Press and Its Editors* [1891] (New York, 1969); Mifflin Wistar Gibbs, *Shadow and Light, An Autobiography* (Washington, D.C., 1902); Rudolph M. Lapp, "The Negro in Gold Rush California," *Journal of Negro History*, 49 (1964), 81-98; "Negro Rights Activities in Gold Rush California," *CHSQ*, 45 (1966), 3-20; and Rudolph M. Lapp, "Jeremiah B. Sanderson: Early California Negro Leader," *Journal of Negro History*, 53 (1968), 321-33.

In *Oration Delivered in the Congregational Church, Sacramento, July 4, 1857* (San Francisco, 1857), Charles Edward Pickett called for a Pacific Republic.

Kenneth L. Janzen's "The Transformation of the New England Religious Tradition in California, 1849-1869" (unpublished Ph.D. dissertation, Claremont Graduate School, 1964) is crucial to an understanding of New Englandism in California. Also important are "The Evangelization of the West. How Shall It Be Effected? And By Whom?" *The New Englander*, 4 (1846), 29-39; Horace Bushnell, "California, Its Characteristics and Prospects," *The New Englander*, 16 (1858), 142-82; Samuel Hopkins Willey, *Decade Sermons* (San Francisco, 1859); and Willey, *Farewell Discourse* (San Francisco, 1862); John E. Bennett, "New England Influences in California," *New England Magazine*, 17 (1898), 688-708; Octavius Thorndike Howe, *Argonauts of '49, History and Adventures of the Emigrant Companies from Massachusetts, 1849-1850* (Cambridge, 1923); Colin Brummitt Goodykoontz, *Home Missions on the American Frontier, With Particular Reference to the American Home Missionary Society* (Caldwell, 1939); Richard Lyle Power, "A Crusade to Extend Yankee Culture," *New England Quarterly*, 13 (1940), 638-53; and Stewart H. Holbrook, *The Yankee Exodus, An Account of Migration from New England* (New York, 1950). For a critical view, see William Hanchett, "The Question of Religion and the Taming of California, 1849-1854," *CHSQ*, 32 (1953), 49-56, 114-19; and Hanchett, "The Blue Law Gospel in Gold Rush California," *The Pacific Historical Review*, 24 (1955), 361-68.

Philip Thaxter (New York, 1861), a novel by Charles Ames Washburn, is the detailed story of the degradation and redemption of a New Englander in California.

During the rule of the Vigilance Committees of 1851 and 1856, *The Pacific* ran a number of pertinent editorials. See esp. "The Irish and the Committee" (29 May 1856) and "Virtue Necessary for Revolutions" (10 July 1856). Among key sermons dealing with the crisis are Samuel Hopkins Willey, "The People Responsible for the Character of Their Rulers," *The Pacific* (29 Aug. 1851); Benjamin Brierly, *Thoughts for the Crisis* (San Francisco, 1856); and William Anderson Scott, *A Discourse for the Times: Education and Not Punishment, the True Remedy for the Wrong-doings and Disorders of Society* (San Francisco, 1856). Regarding the impact of the assassination of James King of William, see the funeral sermons gathered in *A True and Minute History of the Assassination of James King of Wm.*, comp. by Frank F. Fargo (San Francisco, 1856); M. Evans, *Discourse at the Funeral Obsequies in Grass Valley* (Grass Valley, 1856); Walter Frear, *A Sermon Preached at Iowa Hill* (Iowa Hill, 1856). Regarding King of William himself, see "The Vigilance Editorials of the San Francisco Journalist James King of William," sel. and ed. by Richard H. Dillon, *CHSQ*, 37 (1958), 137-69. See also Peyton Hunt, "The Rise and Fall of the 'Know Nothings' in California," *CHSQ*, 9 (1930), 16-49, 99-128; and Raymond Billington, "Anti-Catholic Propaganda and the Home Missionary Movement, 1800-1860," *Mississippi Valley Historical Review*, 22 (1935), 361-84.

Regarding higher education, see Samuel Hopkins Willey, *Statement in Regard to the College of California* (New York, 1855); William Anderson Scott, *Oration on the Occasion of the First Anniversary of the College of California* (San Francisco, 1856); Edward Bannister, *True Greatness, an Address Delivered at the University of the Pacific* (San Francisco, 1857); Horace Bushnell, *Movement for a University in California* (San Francisco, 1857); Samuel Hopkins Willey, *A History of the College of California* (San Francisco, 1887); and Rockwell D. Hunt, *History of the College of the Pacific, 1851-1951* (Stockton, 1951). Regarding the common schools, see Frederick Billings, *An Address at the Dedication of the School House in the Fifth District* (San Francisco, 1854); and Edward Silas Lacy, *The Schools Demanded by the Present Age* (San Francisco, 1856). See also John Cotter Pelton, *Life's Sunbeams and Shadows* (San Francisco, 1893); and William Warren Ferrier, *Ninety Years of Education in California, 1846-1936* (Berkeley, 1937). Of great importance are John Swett, *History of the Public School System of California* (San Francisco, 1876) and *Public Education in California* (New York, 1911). See also William G. Carr, *John Swett, the Biography of an Educational Pioneer* (Santa Ana, 1933); and Nicholas C. Poios, "A Yankee Patriot: John Swett, the Horace Mann of the Pacific," *History of Education Quarterly*, 4 (1964), 17-32.

For libraries, see William Anderson Scott, *Trade and Letters, Three Discourses Before the Mercantile Library Association of San Francisco* (New York, 1856); and Ray S. Held, *Public Libraries in California, 1849-1878* (Berkeley and Los Angeles, 1963). See also Louis B. Wright, *Culture on the Moving Frontier* (Bloomington, 1955), Chapter Four, "Culture and Anarchy on the Pacific Coast: the Age of Gold."

California's mission to the Orient is suggested by Timothy Dwight Hunt's *The Past and Present of the Sandwich Islands* (San Francisco, 1853) and many items by William Speer, among which are: "Influence of Christian Commerce on the East," *The Pacific* (4 Feb. 1853); *China and California* (San Francisco, 1853); *An Humble Plea in Behalf of the Immigrants from China* (San Francisco, 1856); and *An Answer to the Objections to Chinese Testimony* (San Francisco, 1857).

For the role of women, see "Influence of Women in California," *The Pacific* (31 Oct. 1851); "Our Ladies," ibid. (4 June 1852); and Eliza Woodson Farnham, *California Indoors and Out; or, How We Farm, Mine, and Generally Live in the Golden State* (New York, 1856).

Biographical studies of Thomas Starr King include William Day Simonds, *Starr King in California* (San Francisco, 1917); Charles W. Wendte, *Thomas Starr King,*

Patriot and Preacher (Boston, 1921); and Arnold Crompton, *Apostle of Liberty, Starr King in California* (Boston, 1950). Regarding King's eloquence, see J. A. Wagner, "The Oratory of Thomas Starr King," *CHSQ*, 33 (1954), 219-27, and King's own "Daniel Webster," in *Substance and Show, and Other Lectures*, ed. by Edwin P. Whipple (Boston, 1877). King's Yosemite reportage has been gathered by John A. Hussey as *A Vacation Among the Sierras: Yosemite in 1860* (San Francisco, 1962). For examples of King's Civil War preaching, see "Address Delivered at the Grave in Lone Mountain Cemetery, San Francisco, Previous to the Interment of Col. Baker's Body," in *Representative and Leading Men of the Pacific*, ed. by Oscar Tully Shuck (San Francisco, 1870), pp. 80-83; *Peace, What It Would Cost Us* [1861] (San Francisco, 1891); *Fourth of July Oration* (San Francisco, 1862); "The Privileges and Duties of Patriotism," in *Substance and Show*, pp. 389-412; and *American Nationality* (San Francisco, 1863). See also Russel M. Posner, "Thomas Starr King and the Mercy Million," *CHSQ*, 43 (1964), 291-308. The growth of King's reputation can be traced through C. A. Bartol, *The Unspotted Life* (Boston, 1864); Robert Bunker Swain, *Address Before the First Unitarian Society* (San Francisco, 1864); Henry W. Bellows, *In Memory of Thomas Starr King* (San Francisco, 1864); and Irving M. Scott, *Thomas Starr King as a Patriot* (San Francisco, 1892).

4

Crucial to an understanding of this era are Joseph Ellison, *California and the Nation, 1850-1869* (Berkeley, 1927); William Henry Ellison, *A Self-governing Dominion, California, 1849-1860* (Berkeley and Los Angeles, 1950); and W. W. Robinson, *Land in California* (Berkeley and Los Angeles, 1948).

George R. Stewart's *Ordeal by Hunger, The Story of the Donner Party*, new edition with a supplement and three accounts by survivors (Boston, 1960), is in itself a classic of California literature. Also consulted were Eliza P. Donner Houghton, *The Expedition of the Donner Party and Its Tragic Fate* (Glendale, 1920); and *Donner Miscellany, 41 Diaries and Documents*, ed. by Carroll D. Hall (San Francisco, 1947).

Consulted for background regarding the writing of California history were Oscar T. Shuck, *Bench and Bar in California* (San Francisco, 1888); Henry Lebbeus Oak, *Literary Industries in a New Light* (San Francisco, 1893); Alice Bay Maloney, "The Distressingly Virtuous Isaac [Cox]," *CHSQ*, 21 (1942), 127-40; Richard A. Dillon, "Introduction" to *Annals of San Francisco* (Palo Alto, 1966); Kenneth M. Johnson, "Frederic Hall," *CHSQ*, 38 (1958), 47-59; Charles Albro Barker, "Henry George and the California Background of Progress and Poverty," *CHSQ*, 24 (1945), 97-115; and Robert W. Righter, "Theodore Henry Hittell: California Historian," *Southern California Quarterly*, 48 (1966), 289-306.

See also *Masterpieces of E. D. Baker*, ed. by Oscar T. Shuck (San Francisco, 1899); James O'Meara, *Broderick and Gwin* (San Francisco, 1881); David A. Williams, *David C. Broderick, a Political Portrait* (San Marino, 1969); and Allen Stanley Lane, *Emperor Norton* (Caldwell, 1939).

Promotional writing of importance is Felix Paul Wierzbicki, *California As It Is And As It May Be* [1849], Introduction by George D. Lyman (San Francisco, 1933); Ernest Seyd, *California and Its Resources* (London, 1858); J. Ross Browne, *Resources of the Pacific Slope* (New York, 1869); and John S. Hittell, *The Commerce and Industries of the Pacific Coast* (San Francisco, 1882). See also Claude R. Petty, "John S. Hittell and the Gospel of California," *The Pacific Historical Review*, 24 (1955), 1-16.

On the turmoil of the 1870's, see Henry George, "The Kearney Agitation in California," *Popular Science Monthly*, 17 (1880), 433-53; Pierton W. Dooner, *Last Days of the Republic* (San Francisco, 1880); Robert Glass Cleland, "The Discontented Seventies," *A History of California* (New York, 1922), pp. 402-23; and Ralph Kauer, "The Workingmen's Party of California," *The Pacific Historical Review*, 13 (1944), 278-91.

5

Biographical studies of Josiah Royce are few. Consulted were George Herbert Palmer, "Josiah Royce," *The Harvard Graduates' Magazine*, 25 (1916), 165-70; George Santayana, *Character and Opinion in the United States* [1920] (New York, 1967); and Ronald Albert Wells, "A Portrait of Josiah Royce" (unpublished Ph.D. dissertation, Dept. of History, Boston University, 1967). Regarding Royce and California, see Frank M. Oppenheim, S.J., "Some New Documents on Royce's Early Experiences of Communities," *Journal of the History of Philosophy*, 6 (1968), 381-85; Robert Glass Cleland, "Introduction," Royce's *California* (New York, 1948); and Earl Pomeroy, "Josiah Royce, Historian in Quest of Community," *The Pacific Historical Review*, 40 (1971), 1-20.

For the background and feel of the University of California at Berkeley during Royce's stay there, see Frederick Law Olmsted, *Report Upon a Projected Improvement of the Estate of the College of California at Berkeley* (New York, 1866); Daniel Coit Gilman, *Statement of the Progress and Condition of the University of California* (Berkeley, 1875); William Carey Jones, Jr., *Illustrated History of the University of California* (Berkeley, 1901); William Warren Ferrier, *Origin and Development of the University of California* (Berkeley, 1930); and Ferrier, *Berkeley, California: the Story of the Evolution of a Hamlet into a City of Culture and Commerce* (Berkeley, 1933). For the feel of student life of a slightly later era, see Joy Lichtenstein, *For the Blue and Gold, a Tale of Life at the University of California* (San Francisco, 1901).

Volume 53 of the Royce Papers in the Harvard University Archives ("Records of Student Days—the University of California") contains many items suggesting Royce's development as an undergraduate. See also Royce's early essay "The Life Harmony," *OvM*, 15 (1875), 157-64. "Thought Diary—24 September 1878 to 3 February 1881," Royce Papers, gives some hint of Royce's inner life as a Berkeley faculty member. See also "Two Days in Life's Woods," *OvM*, ns, 1 (1883), 594-95.

Royce's response to Frémont might be followed out in *The Nation*, 43:99-101, 44: 39-40; 48:140-42, 164-65; 52:423-25; and (as if this were not enough!) in "Light on the Seizure of California," *Century Magazine*, 40 (1890), 792-97; "Frémont," *The Atlantic Monthly*, 66 (1890), 548-57; and "Montgomery and Frémont, New Documents on the Bear Flag Affair," *Century Magazine*, 41 (1891), 780-83. For other views, see William Carey Jones, Jr., "The First Phase of the Conquest of California," *Papers* of the California Historical Society, 1 (1887), 61-94; Milicent W. Shinn, "The 'Bears' and the Historians," *OvM*, ns, 16 (1890), 300-311, 531-43; Willard B. Farwell, "Frémont's Place in California History," *OvM*, *ns*, 16 (1890), 519-30, 575-93. For Henry L. Oak's review, see "Dr. Royce's California," *OvM*, ns, 8 (1886), 329-30.

Also important to this chapter are Josiah Royce, "Is There a Philosophy of Evolution" *Unitarian Review*, 32 (1889), 1-29, 97-113; and Royce, *The Philosophy of Loyalty* (New York, 1908).

6

Earl Pomeroy, *In Search of the Golden West: the Tourist in Western America* (New York, 1957) is invaluable. In addition to items cited in text and notes, see Albert D. Richardson, *Beyond the Mississippi* (New York, 1867); Samuel Bowles, *Our New West* (Hartford, 1869); John Todd, *The Sunset Land* (Boston, 1870); J. G. Player-Frowd, *Six Months in California* (London, 1872); John Hanson Beadle, *The Undeveloped West* (Philadelphia, 1873); Sidney Eardley-Wilmot, *Our Journal in the Pacific* (London, 1873); Benjamin F. Taylor, *Between the Gates* (Chicago, 1878); Amelia Woodward Truesdell, A *California Pilgrimage* (San Francisco, 1884); Susie C. Clark, *The Round Trip From the Hub to the Golden Gate* (Boston, 1890); Charles Augustus Stoddard, *Beyond the Rockies, a Spring Journey in California* (New York, 1894); and Montgomery Schuyler, *Westward the Course of Empire* (New York, 1906).

Robert L. Kelley, *Gold vs. Grain, The Hydraulic Mining Controversy in California's Sacramento Valley* (Glendale, 1959) is central to any considerations of ecology.

Regarding Charles Frederick Holder, see his *Southern California* (Los Angeles, 1888); *All About California and Its Vicinity* (Boston, 1889); *An Isle of Summer, Santa Catalina Island* (Los Angeles, 1892); *Life in the Open; Sport With Rod, Gun, Horse and Hound in Southern California* (New York, 1906); *The Channel Islands of California* (Chicago, 1910); and *Recreations of a Sportsman on the Pacific Coast* (New York, 1910). For Stewart Edward White, see also *The Forest* (New York, 1904); *The Mountains* (New York, 1904); *The Pass* (New York, 1906). And regarding George Wharton James, see *Travelers' Handbook to Southern California* (Pasadena, 1904) and *Singing Through Life With God* (Pasadena, 1920).

The growing appreciation of sport and outdoor life is seen in Isaac Mast, *The Gun, Rod and Saddle; or, Nine Months in California* (Philadelphia, 1875); Theodore S. Van Dyke, *Flirtation Camp; or, The Rifle, Rod, and Gun in California* (New York, 1881); and Van Dyke, *Southern California* (New York, 1886); Dio Lewis, *Gypsies, or Why We Went Gypsying in the Sierras* (Boston, 1881); Lucius Harwood Foote, A *Red-Letter Day and Other Poems* (Boston, 1882); Thaddeus S. Kenderine, A *California Tramp* (Philadelphia, 1888); and Mrs. Jacob Barzilla Rideout, *Camping Out in California* (San Francisco, 1889). Consulted also was The Southern Pacific Passenger Department, *Pacific Slope Reference Library* (13 vols., San Francisco, 1907-8).

Regarding the State Geological Survey, see Josiah Dwight Whitney's three works: *The Geological Survey of California* (San Francisco, 1861); *An Address on the Propriety of Continuing the State Geological Survey of California* (San Francisco, 1868); and "State Geological Survey," *OvM*, 8 (1872), 80-87. Regarding Clarence King, see Thurman Wilkins, *Clarence King, a Biography* (New York, 1958); and King's fascinating essay "Catastrophism and Evolution," *The American Naturalist*, 11 (1877),

449-70. See also A. C. Isaacs, *An Ascent of Mount Shasta: 1856* (Los Angeles, 1952); Richard G. Stanwood, "An Ascent of Mount Shasta in 1861," *CHSQ*, 6 (1927), 69-76; and A. Phimister Proctor, *An Ascent of Half Dome in 1884* (San Francisco, 1945).

Relevant Yosemite literature is Geological Survey of California, *The Yosemite Guide-Book* (Cambridge, 1869); James M. Hutchings, *In the Heart of the Sierras* (Oakland, 1888); Lafayette Houghton Bunnell, *Discovery of the Yosemite and the Indian War of 1851* (Los Angeles, 1911); Hans Huth, "Yosemite: the Story of an Idea," *Sierra Club Bulletin*, 33 (1948), 47-78; and Shirley Sargent, *Galen Clark, Yosemite Guardian* (San Francisco, 1964). See also Mary V. Jessup Hood and Robert Bartlett Haas, "Eadweard Muybridge's Yosemite Valley Photographs, 1867-1872," *CHSQ*, 42 (1963), 5-26; William Hawley Davis, "Emerson the Lecturer in California," *CHSQ*, 20 (1941), 1-11; John Q. Anderson, "Emerson and California," *CHSQ*, 33 (1954), 241-248; and Francis P. Farquhar, *History of the Sierra Nevada* (Berkeley and Los Angeles, 1965). Of interest is a strange novel by Therèse Yelverton, *Zanita, a Tale of the Yo-semite* (New York, 1872), in which Muir appears. Also important are The Sierra Club, *Articles of Association, Articles of Incorporation, By-Laws, and List of Charter Members* (San Francisco, 1892); and Holway R. Jones, *John Muir and the Sierra Club* (San Francisco, 1965).

Regarding Frank Norris, see Franklin Walker's excellent biography (New York, 1932). See also Irving McKee, "Notable Memorials to Mussel Slough," *The Pacific Historical Review*, 17 (1948), 19-27.

For further impressions of California rural life, see Titus Fey Cronise, *The Natural Wealth of California* (San Francisco, 1868); Ezra S. Carr, *The Patrons of Husbandry on the Pacific Coast* (San Francisco, 1875); Joseph J. Perkins, *A Business Man's Estimate of Santa Barbara County* (Santa Barbara, 1881); Thomas A. Garey, *Orange Culture in California* (San Francisco, 1882); *Ventura County, California, Its Resources* (San Buenaventura, 1885); and H. S. Foote (ed.), *Pen Pictures From the Garden of the World; or, Santa Clara County, California* (Chicago, 1888). Robert Glass Cleland's *The Place Called Sespe, the History of a California Ranch* (San Marino, 1940) is a classic of California literature. See also his superb *The Cattle on a Thousand Hills, Southern California, 1850-1870* (San Marino, 1941). Other investigations of importance are Walton Bean, "James Warren and the Beginnings of Agricultural Institutions in California," *The Pacific Historical Review*, 13 (1944), 361-75; Paul S. Taylor, "Foundations of California Rural Society," *CHSQ*, 24 (1945), 193-228; H. E. Erdman, "The Development and Significance of California Cooperatives, 1900-1915," *Agricultural History*, 32 (1958), 179-84; and Paul W. Gates, *California Ranchos and Farms, 1846-1862* (Madison, 1967). Regarding San Bernardino, Anaheim, and Pasadena, see *History of San Bernardino and San Diego Counties* [1883] (Riverside, 1965); Mildred Yorba MacArthur, *Anaheim, the Mother Colony* (Los Angeles, 1959); and J. W. Wood, *Pasadena, California, Historical and Personal* (Pasadena, 1917).

For the role of women in rural life, see "Agriculture as an Occupation for Women in California," *OvM*, ns, 9 (1889), 652-58. Margaret Collier Graham's sensitive portraits of rural women in Southern California were collected in *Stories of the Foothills* (Boston, 1895) and *The Wizard's Daughter and Other Stories* (Boston and New

York, 1905). For further fiction by women about women on the land, see Eliza Woodson Farnham, *The Ideal Attained* (New York, 1865); Maud Howe Elliott, *The San Rosario Ranch* (Boston, 1884); Tryphena Margaret Browne, *The Musgrove Ranch, a Tale of Southern California* (New York, 1888); Leela B. Davis, *A Modern Argonaut* (San Francisco, 1896); and Beatrice Harraden, *Hilda Strafford, a California Story* (New York, 1897). Memoirs of importance are *Pioneer Notes From the Diaries of Judge Benjamin Hayes, 1849-1875* (Los Angeles, 1929); E. M. H., *Ranch Life in California* (London, 1886); Helena Modjeska, *Memories and Impressions* (New York, 1910); Horace Annesley Vachell, *Bunch Grass, a Chronicle of Life on a Cattle Ranch* (London, 1912); and Sarah Bixby-Smith's hauntingly beautiful *Adobe Days, a Book of California Memories* (Cedar Rapids, 1925).

7

Lewis Mumford's "Jack London," *New Republic*, 30 (1922), 145-47, is an early, brief, but unsurpassed assessment. See also Maxwell Geismar, *Rebels and Ancestors: the American Novel, 1890-1915* (Boston, 1953); Kenneth S. Lynn, *The Dream of Success* (Boston, 1955); Earle Labor, "Jack London's Symbolic Wilderness: Four Versions," *Nineteenth-Century Fiction*, 17 (1962), 149-61; and Richard O'Connor, *Jack London, a Biography* (Boston, 1964). The files of the *Santa Rosa Press Democrat* (1909-16) contain numerous articles on London and his ranch. See also Millard Bailey, "Jack London, Farmer," *Bookman*, 44 (1916), 151-56, and "Valley of the Moon Ranch," *OvM*, ns, 69 (1917), 411-15; John D. Barry, "Personal Qualities of Jack London," *OvM*, ns, 69 (1917), 431-32; George Wharton James, "A Study of Jack London in His Prime," *OvM*, ns (May 1917), 361-99; Wilfrid Lay, "John Barleycorn Under Psychoanalysis," *Bookman*, 45 (1917), 47-54. Of great importance is Alfred S. Shivers, "Jack London: Not a Suicide," *Dalhousie Review*, 49 (1969), 43-57.

8

Aside from titles mentioned in the text and notes, generalizations regarding poetry in California are also based upon Bret Harte (comp.), *Outcroppings: Being Selections of California Verse* (San Francisco, 1860); John R. Ridge, *Poems* (San Francisco, 1868); May Wentworth Newman, *Poetry of the Pacific* (San Francisco, 1867); Daniel O'Connell, *Lyrics* (San Francisco, 1881); Charles H. Phelps, *Californian Verses* (San Francisco, 1882); Denis Oliver Crowley and Charles Anthony Doyle (eds.), *A Chaplet of Verse by California Catholic Writers* (San Francisco, 1889); and Augustin S. MacDonald (comp.), *A Collection of Verse By California Poets From 1849 to 1915* (San Francisco, 1914).

As an example of San Francisco's self-consciousness, see Theodore Augustus Barry and B. A. Patten, *Men and Memories of San Francisco in the Spring of '50* (San Francisco, 1873). For the feel of the turn of the century, see Charles Augustus Keeler, *San Francisco and Thereabout* (San Francisco, 1902); Allan Dunn, *Care-free San Francisco* (San Francisco, 1913); Clarence E. Edwords, *Bohemian San Francisco* (San Francisco, 1914). See also Herbert Asbury, *The Barbary Coast* (New York,

1933); and Robert Ernest Cowan, 1850-1870, *Forgotten Characters of Old San Francisco* (Los Angeles, 1938). For fiction with a developed San Francisco locale, see George Henry Jessop, *Gerald Ffrench's Friends* (New York, 1889); Robert Louis Stevenson, *The Wrecker* (London, 1892); Gelett Burgess and Will Irwin, *The Picaroons* (New York, 1904); and Charles Tenny Jackson, *The Day of Souls* (Indianapolis, 1910).

The *Annals of the Bohemian Club, 1872-1906*, ed. by Robert H. Fletcher (4 vols., San Francisco, 1898-1909, 1930) are filled with anecdote and information. See also Porter Garnett, *The Bohemian Jinks, a Treatise* (San Francisco, 1908); and Agnes Foster Buchanan, "The Story of a Famous Fraternity of Writers and Artists," *The Pacific Monthly*, 17 (1907), 65-83. Oscar Lewis' *Bay Window Bohemia* (New York, 1956) and Albert Parry's *Garrets and Pretenders, a History of Bohemianism in America* (New York, 1960) are essential to this chapter. See also James Anthony Froude, *Oceana* (New York, 1888); Daniel O'Connell, *Songs From Bohemia* (San Francisco, 1900); Jerome A. Hart, *In Our Second Century* (San Francisco, 1931); Will Irwin, *The Making of a Reporter* (New York, 1942).

Regarding Bierce, see Franklin Walker, *Ambrose Bierce, the Wickedest Man in San Francisco* (San Francisco, 1941).

Regarding Stoddard, see his own three works: "In Old Bohemia, Memories of San Francisco in the Sixties," *The Pacific Monthly*, 3 (1900), 639-50; *In the Footprints of the Padres* (San Francisco, 1902); and *Exits and Entrances* (Boston, 1903). See also Barnett Franklin, "The Passing of Charles Warren Stoddard," *OvM*, ns, 6 (1909), 527-31; and Nellie Van De Grift Sanchez, "Charles Warren Stoddard and the Artist Colony," *The Oakland Tribune* (26 Dec. 1920).

James Duval Phelan's *Correspondence and Papers* are in the Bancroft Library. See also Phelan's *The New San Francisco* (San Francisco, 1896); *Adresses by Mayor James D. Phelan* (San Francisco, 1901); and *Travel and Comment* (San Francisco, 1923). Consulted also were George J. Duraind, "James Duval Phelan, Statesman, An Epic of Public Service" (4 vols., typescript, 1927), *Correspondence and Papers;* and Dorothy Kaucher, *James Duval Phelan, a Portrait, 1861-1930* (Saratoga, 1965).

Regarding Norris the reporter, see *Frank Norris of "The Wave," Stories and Sketches From the San Francisco Weekly, 1893 to 1897*, Foreword by Charles G. Norris and Introduction by Oscar Lewis (San Francisco, 1931); and *The Letters of Frank Norris*, ed. by Franklin Walker (San Francisco, 1956).

The George Sterling Collection is in the Bancroft Library. See esp. the six volumes of "The Carmel Diaries." Of invaluable aid was Michael Paul Orth, "A Biography of George Sterling" (unpublished M.A. dissertation, San Francisco State College, 1963). See also "The George Sterling Memorial Issue," *OvM*, ns, 85 (Dec. 1927); Miriam Allen De Ford, "Laureate of Bohemia: George Sterling," in *They Were San Franciscans* (Caldwell, 1941), pp. 295-321; and William McDevitt, *My Father, Father Tabb* (San Francisco, 1945). Generalizations regarding Sterling's poetry are based primarily upon a study of *The Testimony of the Suns and Other Poems* (San Francisco, 1903), *A Wine of Wizardry and Other Poems* (San Francisco, 1909), and *The House of Orchids and Other Poems* (San Francisco, 1911). Sterling's bitterness and confusion are evident in his column for *The Overland Monthly*, "Rhymes and Reactions," ns, 83-84 (Nov. 1925 to Dec. 1926). See also "Joaquin Miller," *The*

American Mercury, 7 (1926), 220-29. In 1910 he edited the *Poems* of Nora May French.

Regarding the Carmel colony, Franklin Walker's *The Seacoast of Bohemia, An Account of Early Carmel* (San Francisco, 1966) is informative and complete. See also Michael Orth, "Ideality to Reality: The Founding of Carmel," *CHSQ*, 48 (1969), 195-210; and Mary Austin's allegorical novel *Outland* (New York, 1919). Daisy F. Bostick and Dorothea Castelhun, *Carmel—at Work and Play* (Carmel, 1925) documents Carmel's later artiness.

A fine example of San Francisco printing is Timothy H. Rearden, *Petrarch and Other Essays* (1897). Studies of the art include Charles H. Shinn, "Early Books, Magazines, and Book-Making," *OvM*, ns, 12 (1888), 337-52; Harry R. Wagner, "Edward Bosqui, Printer and Man of Affairs," *CHSQ*, 21 (1942), 321-31; James D. Hart, *Fine Printing in California* (Berkeley, 1960); Frances Case Theiss, "The Development of Fine Printing in San Francisco, a Historical Survey," (unpublished M.A. dissertation, Dept. of Librarianship, San Jose State College, 1969); George L. Harding, "Charles A. Murdock, Printer and Citizen of San Francisco" (corrected page proofs, courtesy of the author).

9

David Starr Jordan (ed.), *The California Earthquake of 1906* (San Francisco, 1907) brings together the best eyewitness accounts. Regarding the determination to rebuild, see Charles Augustus Keeler, *San Francisco Through Earthquake and Fire* (San Francisco, 1906); Pierre N. Beringer, "The Destruction of San Francisco," *OvM*, ns, 47 (1906), 391-406; Arthur Inkersley, "What San Francisco Has to Start With," *OvM*, ns, 47 (1906), 466-83; James D. Phelan, 'The Builders," *OvM*, ns, 48 (1906), 3-7; Edwin Duryea, "A Better City," *OvM*, ns, 48 (1906), 109-21; and Arthur J. Ryan, "San Francisco as a Cynosure of the Eyes of America and the World," *OvM*, ns, 48 (1906), 413-26. Regarding the rebuilt city, see Rufus Steele, *The City That Is, the Story of the Rebuilding of San Francisco in Three Years* (San Francisco, 1909); and William Winthrop Kent, "The New San Francisco," *The Architectural Review* (US), 7 (1918), 87-91; 8 (1919), 99-101, 127-28.

As background to the Panama-Pacific International Exposition, see Hubert Howe Bancroft, *The New Pacific*; and H. Morse Stephens and Herbert E. Bolton (eds.), *The Pacific Ocean in History* (New York, 1917). See also *The Legacy of the Exposition* (San Francisco, 1916).

Regarding the Palace of Fine Arts, see Louis J. Stellman, *The Vanished Ruin Era, San Francisco's Classic Artistry of Ruin Depicted in Picture and Song* (San Francisco, 1910); and, of course, Bernard R. Maybeck's own *The Palace of Fine Arts and Lagoon* (San Francisco, 1915). Regarding the Court of the Ages, see Louis Christian Mullgardt, "The Panama-Pacific Exposition," *The Architectural Record*, 37 (1915), 193-228; and Robert J. Clark, "Louis Christian Mullgardt and the Court of the Ages," *Journal of the Society of Architectural Historians*, 21 (1962), 171-78. Regarding the color-scheme, see William Lee Woollet, "Color in Architecture at the Panama-Pacific International Exposition," *The Architectural Record*, 37 (1915), 437-44; Woollet, "Scene Painting in Architecture," *The Architectural Record*, 38 (1915), 571-74; and

Paul E. Denivelle, "Texture and Color at the Panama-Pacific International Exposition," *The Architectural Record*, 38 (1915), 562-70. Regarding the art of the Exposition, see Eugen Neuhaus, *The Galleries of the Exposition* (San Francisco, 1915); *Catalogue De Luxe of the Department of Fine Arts, Panama-Pacific International Exposition*, ed. by John E. D. Trask and J. Nilsen Laurvik (2 vols., San Francisco, 1915); and The Department of Art of the University of California at Davis, *Fifteen and Fifty: California Painting at the 1915 Panama-Pacific International Exposition* (Davis, 1965).

Other material of importance is North American Press Association, *Standard Guide to San Francisco and the Panama-Pacific International Exposition* (San Francisco, 1913); *Official Guide of the Panama-Pacific International Exposition* (San Francisco, 1915); John D. Barry, *The City of Domes* (San Francisco, 1915); Katherine Delmar Burke, *Storied Walls of the Exposition* (San Francisco, 1915); Porter Garnett, *The Inscriptions at the Panama-Pacific International Exposition* (San Francisco, 1915); Juliet James, *Palaces and Courts of the Panama-Pacific International Exposition* (San Francisco, 1915); Benjamin Macomber, *The Jewel City* (San Francisco, 1915); Anna Simpson Pratt, *Problems Women Solved, the Woman's Board of the Exposition;* and Louis J. Stellman, *That Was a Dream Worth Building* (San Francisco, 1916).

Of great importance is George E. Mowry, *The California Progressives* (Berkeley and Los Angeles, 1951), Chapter Four, "What Manner of Men: the Progressive Mind."

10

Jordan's autobiography, *The Days of a Man* (2 vols., Yonkers-on-Hudson, 1922), and Edward McNall Burns's *David Starr Jordan: Prophet of Freedom* (Stanford, 1953) are depended upon continually. Also consulted were Jordan's yearly *Reports to the Trustees*, 1903-13. Other books and articles by Jordan pertinent to the discussion are *The Strength of Being Clean* (Boston, 1900); *The Philosophy of Despair* (San Francisco, 1902); *The Alps of King-Kern Divide* (San Francisco, 1907); *Life's Enthusiasms* (Boston, 1908); and *The Religion of a Sensible American* (Boston, 1909); *War and Waste* (Garden City, 1913); *War's Aftermath* (Boston and New York, 1914); *War and the Breed* (Boston, 1915); "The Policy of the Stanford University," *Educational Review*, 4 (1892), 1-5; "College Discipline," *North American Review*, 165 (1897), 403-8; "The Ideals of Stanford," *Land of Sunshine*, 9 (1898), 3-12; "What California Has Done for Civilization," *For California*, 1 (1904), 3-4ff; and, with Vernon L. Kellogg, *The Scientific Aspects of Luther Burbank's Work* (San Francisco, 1909).

Regarding Senator and Mrs. Stanford, see Hubert Howe Bancroft, *History of the Life of Leland Stanford, a Character Study* [1889] (Oakland, 1952); Oscar Lewis, *The Big Four* (New York, 1938); David Starr Jordan, *The Story of a Good Woman, Jane Lathrop Stanford* (Boston, 1912); Bertha Berner, *Mrs. Leland Stanford, an Intimate Account* (Palo Alto, 1935). See also Mrs. Stanford's *Address Upon Her Inauguration as President of the Board of Trustees* (San Francisco, 1903); and *Address on the Right of Free Speech* (San Francisco, 1903).

The student newspaper *The Palo Alto* ran from 1891 to 1892. Also consulted was

The Sequoia, published bi-weekly by the Associated Students, 9 Dec. 1891 and following. See also W. H. Thomson, "Student Life at Stanford University," *Out West*, 21 (1904), 425-38; Davida French, Esther Stevens, and Laura Wells, *Not Included in a Sheepskin, Stanford Stories* (Stanford, 1907).

Histories, biographies, and autobiographies also of importance are George E. Crothers, *Founding of the Leland Stanford Junior University* (San Francisco, 1932); Edward Howard Griggs, *The Story of an Itinerant Teacher* (Indianapolis and New York, 1934); Joseph Dorfman, *Thorstein Veblen and His America* (New York, 1935); Norris E. James, *Fifty Years on the Quad* (Stanford, 1938); Dallas E. Wood and Norris E. James, *History of Palo Alto* (Palo Alto, 1939); Ellen Coit Elliott, *It Happened This Way* (Stanford, 1940); John Pearce Mitchell, *Stanford University, 1916-1941* (Palo Alto, 1958); Edith R. Mirrielees, *Stanford, the Story of a University* (New York, 1959); and *Stanford Mosaic, Reminiscences of the First Seventy Years*, ed. by Edith R. Mirrielees (Palo Alto, 1962). Of special importance is Diane Kostial McGuire, "Early Site Planning on the West Coast: Frederick Law Olmsted's Plan for Stanford University," *Landscape Architecture*, 47 (1957), 344-49.

For Jordan on Hoover, see "The Americans of the Hour in Europe," *Sunset*, 34 (1915), 1175-79; and "Herbert Hoover," *The Landmark*, 4 (1922), 792-96. For Hoover on America, see *American Individualism* (Garden City, 1922); and *A Boyhood in Iowa* (New York, 1931).

11

There is not much written about Gertrude Atherton. Consulted were Frederic Cooper, "Gertrude Atherton," *Bookman*, 30 (1909), 357-63; Pendennis, "My Types: Gertrude Atherton," *Forum*, 58 (1917), 585-94; Carl Van Vechten, "A Lady Who Defies Time," *Nation*, 126 (1923), 194, 196; Isabel Paterson, "Gertrude Atherton, a Personality," *Bookman*, 59 (1924), 632-37; A. B. Maurice, "Gertrude Atherton," *Bookman*, 72 (1930), 62-64; Henry James Forman, "A Brilliant California Novelist: Gertrude Atherton," *CHSQ*, 40 (1961), 1-10; Joseph Henry Jackson, *Gerutrude Atherton* (New York, 1940); and "Gertrude Atherton Writes Her Fifty-sixth Book," *Life*, 21 (1946), 95-98.

12

Franklin Walker's *A Literary History of Southern California* (Berkeley and Los Angeles, 1950) was the occasion and the guide for this chapter.

Regarding its cast of characters, see also Jessie Benton Frémont, *Souvenirs of My Time* (Boston, 1889) and *Far-West Sketches* (Boston, 1890); and Mrytle M. McKittrick, *Vallejo, Son of California* (Portland, 1944); Charles Dudley Warner, *On Horseback* (Boston and New York, 1888), *As We Were Saying* (New York, 1891); *As We Go* (New York, 1894), and *Fashions in Literature* (New York, 1902); Edwin R. Bingham, *Charles F. Lummis, Editor of the Southwest* (San Marino, 1955); Mary Austin, *Lost Borders* (New York and London, 1909), *Love and the Soul Maker* (New York and London, 1914), *Mother of Felipe and Other Early Stories*, col. and ed. by Franklin Walker (San Francisco, 1950); Donald P. Ringler, "Mary Austin:

Kern County Days, 1888-1892," *Southern California Quarterly,* 65 (1963), 25-63; and Peter Robertson, "Peixotto and His Work," *Out West,* 19 (1903), 133-45.

Regarding viticulture, see T. Hart Hyatt, *Handbook of Grape Culture* (San Francisco, 1876); Vincent P. Carosso, *The California Wine Industry, a Study of the Formative Years,* 1830-1895 (Berkeley and Los Angeles, 1951); and Joan Donohoe, "Agostin Haraszthy," *CHSQ,* 48 (1969), 153-163.

Of great charm are John S. Harbison, *The Bee-Keeper's Directory; or, The Theory and Practice of Bee Culture* (San Francisco, 1861); and Louis Prevost, *California Silk Grower's Manual* (San Francisco, 1867). See also John E. Baur "California Crops That Failed," *CHSQ,* 45 (1966), 41-68.

Regarding the population of California, see Doris Marion Wright, "The Making of Cosmopolitan California, An Analysis of Immigration, 1848-1870," *CHSQ,* 19 (1940), 323-43; 20 (1941), 65-79. See also H. F. Raup, 'The Italian-Swiss in California," *CHSQ,* 30 (1951), 305-14; Frederick G. Bohme, "The Fortuguese in California," *CHSQ,* 35 (1956), 233-52.

For examples of outdoor drama, see Mary Austin, *The Basket Woman* (Boston and New York, 1904); Jack London, *The Acorn Planter, a California Forest Play* (New York, 1916); and, most importantly, *The Gorve Plays of the Bohemian Club,* ed. by Porter Garnett (3 vols., San Francisco, 1918).

For further examples of the Mediterraneanization of Southern California, see Benjamin Cummings Truman, *Semi-Tropical California* (San Francisco, 1874); Ludwig Louis Salvator, *Los Angeles in the Sunny Seventies* [1878], trans. by Marguerite Eyer Wilbur (Los Angeles, 1929); Helen Hunt Jackson, *Glimpses of Three Coasts* (Boston, 1886); Edward Roberts, *Santa Barbara and Around There* (Boston, 1886); John Wesley Hanson, *The American Italy* (Chicago, 1896); and Charles Augustus Keeler, *Southern California* (Los Angeles, 1899).

Charles Mulford Robinson's intentions are evident in *A Plan of Civic Improvement for the City of Oakland* (Oakland, 1906), *Report Regarding the Civic Affairs of Santa Barbara* (Santa Barbara, 1909), and *The Beautifying of San Jose* (San Jose, 1909). See also Grace Ellery Channing, "What We Can Learn From Rome," *Out West,* 19 (1903), 239-49, 357-68, 473-83. Victoria Padilla, *Southern California Gardens, An Illustrated History* (Berkeley and Los Angeles, 1961), is a magnificent guide to the subject. Regarding the gardens of early California, see Charles Gibbs Adams, "Gardens of the Spanish Days of California," *Annual Publications, Historical Society of Southern California,* 15 (1932), 347-55; Florence Atherton Eyre, *Reminiscences of Peninsula Gardens From 1860 to 1890* (San Francisco, 1933); and Bell M. Magee, *Reminiscences of East Bay Gardens From 1860 to 1890* (San Francisco, 1933). See also Belle Sumner Angier, *The Garden Book of California* (San Francisco and New York, 1906); John McLaren, *Gardening in California, Landscape and Flower* (San Francisco, 1909); Edward J. Wickson, *California Garden—Flowers, Shrubs, Trees and Vines* (San Francisco, 1915); and Winifred Starr Dobyns, *California Gardens* (New York, 1931).

Leonard Pitt, *The Decline of the Californios, a Social History of the Spanish-Speaking Californians,* 1846-1890 (Berkeley and Los Angeles, 1966), is a first-rate contribution to the writing of California history. See also two novels: *The Amulet, a Tale of Spanish California* (London, 1865); and Maria Amparo Ruiz Burton, *The*

Squatter and the Don (San Francisco, 1885). The mission-myth can be traced through Edward Vischer, *Missions of Upper California* (San Francisco, 1872); Laura Bride Powers, *The Story of the Old Missions of California* (San Francisco, 1893); and George Wharton James, *Old Missions and Mission Indians of California* (Los Angeles, 1895). See also Zona Gale, *Frank Miller of Mission Inn* (New York, 1938). Mission fiction includes Horace Annesley Vachell, *John Charity* (New York, 1901); Mary Austin, *Isidro* (Boston and New York, 1905); and Owen Wister, *Padre Ignacio* (New York, 1911). See also Chester Gore Miller, *Father Junipero Serra, a Drama in Four Acts* (Chicago, 1894).

Impressions of San Diego were gathered from Theodore S. Van Dyke's *The Advantages of San Diego for Residence or Business* (San Francisco, 1883); and Van Dyke, *County of San Diego, the Italy of Southern California* (National City, 1887). See also Clarence Alan McGrew, *City of San Diego and San Diego County* (2 vols., Chicago and New York, 1922).

Regarding Bertram Grosvenor Goodhue, see his *A Book of Architectural and Decorative Drawings* (New York, 1914) and his "The Home of the Future," *The Craftsman*, 29 (1916), 449-55, 543-44. For Goodhue's attraction to Spanish Colonial, see his *Mexican Memories* (New York, 1892); his "Plans" in Sylvester Baxter, *Spanish-Colonial Architecture in Mexico* (12 vols., Boston, 1901); and his "Introduction" to Austin Whittlesey, *The Minor Ecclesiastical, Domestic, and Garden Architecture of Southern Spain* (New York, 1917). See also Montgomery Schuyler, "The Works of Cram, Goodhue and Ferguson," *The Architectural Record*, 29 (1911), 1-112; Charles Harris Whitaker (ed.), *Bertram Grosvenor Goodhue, Architect and Master of Many Arts* (New York, 1925); Fiske Kimball, "Goodhue's Architecture: a Critical Estimate," *The Architectural Record*, 62 (1927), 537-39; H. F. Cunningham, "Mr. Goodhue, the First True Modern," *Journal, American Institute of Architects*, 16 (1928), 246-48; and John F. Castagna, "Bertram G. Goodhue and Frank Lloyd Wright, Their Ideals and Their Influence in 'The Arts,'" *Bulletin*, New York University School of Architecture and Applied Arts, 2 (1939), 35-44.

Esther McCoy's *Five California Architects* (New York, 1960) is, along with Kirker's *California's Architectural Frontier*, a book of great significance to this study. Other items of importance are Elmer Grey, "Architecture in Southern California," *The Architectural Record*, 17 (1905), 1-17; Herbert D. Croly, "The Country House in California," *The Architectural Record*, 34 (1913), 483-512; E. M. Roorbach, "The Garden Apartments in California," *The Architectural Record*, 34 (1913), 521-30; Josephine Clifford McCrackin, "Villa Montalvo," *OvM*, ns, 65 (1915), 301-11; Dwight James Baum, "An Eastern Architect's Impression of Recent Work in Southern California," *Architecture*, 38 (1918), 177-80, 217-21; Baum, "Architectural Impressions of Southern California," *American Architect*, 133 (1928), 71-80; Elmer Grey, "Southern California's New Architecture," *Architecture*, 39 (1919), 57-61, 103-7; William Winthrop Kent, "Domestic Architecture of California," *The Architectural Forum*, 32 (1920), 95-100, 151-56; and Kent, "The Modern Country House in California," *Country Life in America*, 37 (1920), 122, 124, 126.

Regarding the Panama-California Exposition, see Bertram Grosvenor Goodhue, "The Panama-California Exposition, San Diego," *Construction Details*, 6 (1914), 142-59; North American Press Association, *Standard Guide to Los Angeles, San*

Diego, and the Panama-California Exposition (San Francisco, 1914); Walter V. Woehlke, "Nueva Espana by the Silver Gate," *Sunset*, 33 (1914), 1119-32; Woehlke, "Magic Spanish City at San Diego," *Out West*, 8 (1914), 291-306; Mark S. Watson, "Fine Arts at the San Diego Exposition," *Art and Progress*, 6 (1915), 446-55; George Wharton James, *Exposition Memories* (Pasadena, 1917). Some idea of the influence of the San Diego Exposition upon California's architecture can be gathered from Henry F. Withey, "A Revival of True Andalusian Spanish Architecture," *Architect and Engineer*, 55 (1918), 65-79; I. F. Morrow, "A Revival of Adobe Buildings," *Architect and Engineer*, 69 (1922), 47-57; Morrow, "A Step in California's Architecture," *Architect and Engineer*, 70 (1922), 47-103; Rexford Newcomb, "Some Spanish Residences in Southern California by George Washington Smith, Architect," *Western Architect*, 31 (1922), 58-61; and Newcomb, *The Spanish House for America* (Philadelphia and London, 1927). See esp. H. Phillip Staats, *California Architecture in Santa Barbara* (New York, 1929).

13

Regarding Royce's assessment of Le Conte, see Royce's "Joseph Le Conte," *International Monthly*, 4 (1901), 324-34. In *The Novels of Frank Norris* (Bloomington, 1966), pp. 3-22, Donald Pizer gives the issues and details of Le Conte's influence on Norris.

Consulted also regarding Burbank were *New Creations in Fruits and Flowers* (Santa Rosa, 1893-1894, 1898, 1899, 1901) and *My Beliefs* (New York, 1927).

For an account of J. Smeaton Chase, see Lawrence Clark Powell, *California Classics*, pp. 197-207. See also Chase's *Yosemite Trails* (Boston, 1911) and *Cone-Bearing Trees of the California Mountains* (Chicago, 1911).

Regarding the health factor, see John E. Baur's extremely illuminating *The Health-Seekers of Southern California, 1870-1900* (San Marino, 1959).

Index